DICTIONARY
of
ADMIRALS
of the
U.S. NAVY

DICTIONARY
of
ADMIRALS
of the
U.S. NAVY

VOLUME 2
1901–1918

E PLURIBUS UNUM

William B. Cogar

NAVAL INSTITUTE PRESS • ANNAPOLIS, MARYLAND

Library of Congress Cataloging-in-Publication Data
(Revised for vol. 2)

Cogar, William B., 1949–
   Dictionary of admirals of the U.S. Navy.

   Bibliography: v. 1, p. 215–217.
   Bibliography: v. 2, p.
   Contents: v. 1. 1862–1900—v. 2. 1901–1918.
   1. Admirals—United States—Biography—Dictionaries.
2. United States. Navy—Biography—Dictionaries.
I. Title.
V62.U64   1989   359.3′31′092273   89-3339
   ISBN 0-87021-431-4 (v. 1)
   ISBN 0-87021-195-1 (v. 2)

Printed in the United States of America on acid-free paper ∞

2   4   6   8   9   7   6   5

First printing

Photo Credits:

Department of the Navy, Bureau of Medicine and Surgery: p. 9 top, p. 60 bottom.
   Naval Historical Center: p. 3 top, p. 4, p. 6 top and bottom, p. 10, p. 13, p. 15, p. 17 top and bottom, p. 18, p. 21, p. 22 top, p. 24, p. 28, p. 33, p. 34, p. 35, p. 36 top and bottom, p. 38, p. 39 bottom, p. 41 top, p. 43, p. 47, p. 48, p. 51, p. 54 bottom, p. 55, p. 58, p. 59, p. 60 top, p. 62, p. 65, p. 69 top, p. 70, p. 72, p. 74, p. 75, p. 76 top and bottom, p. 78, p. 82, p. 85, p. 88 top and bottom, p. 93, p. 94, p. 96, p. 98, p. 99, p. 100, p. 105 top bottom, p. 106, p. 107, p. 108, p. 110, p. 113, p. 114, p. 115, p. 116, p. 117, p. 119, p. 121, p. 124, p. 125 top and bottom, p. 127, p. 128, p. 131, p. 132 bottom, p. 134, p. 135, p. 136 top and bottom, p. 139 top, p. 141, p. 142, p. 143, p. 144, p. 145, p. 146, p. 149, p. 151 bottom, p. 153 bottom, p. 155, p. 156 bottom, p. 157, p. 159, p. 160, p. 163, p. 164, p. 166 top, p. 168, p. 169 top and bottom, p. 170, p. 171, p. 172, p. 176 bottom, p. 177, p. 178, p. 180, p. 182, p. 183, p. 184, p. 185 top and bottom, p. 187, p. 190, p. 192, p. 193, p. 196 top and bottom, p. 197, p. 198, p. 199, p. 204, p. 205, p. 206 top, p. 207, p. 208, p. 209, p. 210, p. 211, p. 214, p. 215, p. 216 top and bottom, p. 217, p. 219, p. 222 bottom, p. 223, p. 224 bottom, p. 226, p. 228, p. 229, p. 230 top, p. 231, p. 232, p. 233, p. 234, p. 235, p. 237 bottom, p. 239, p. 242 top and bottom, p. 243, p. 244, p. 245, p. 246 bottom, p. 250 bottom, p. 251, p. 252, p. 257 top, p. 259, p. 260, p. 262, p. 264, p. 265, p. 266 bottom, p. 267, p. 269, p. 271, p. 273 top, p. 278, p. 283, p. 284, p. 285, p. 288, p. 289, p. 295 top and bottom, p. 297, p. 298, p. 303, p. 304, p. 306, p. 307, p. 308.
   National Cyclopedia of American Biography (New York: James T. White & Co., 1906): p. 7, p. 25, p. 30, p. 81, p. 225, p. 235, p. 273 bottom, p. 274.
   Nimitz Library, U.S. Naval Academy: p. 2, p. 16, p. 20, p. 26, p. 32, p. 45, p. 49, p. 50, p. 61, p. 63 top and bottom, p. 80 bottom, p. 101, p. 102, p. 104, p. 118, p. 123, p. 126, p. 129, p. 132 top, p. 138, p. 166 bottom, p. 175, p. 176 top, p. 186, p. 189, p. 191 bottom, p. 195, p. 206 bottom, p. 220, p. 230 bottom, p. 237 top, p. 246 top, p. 248, p. 257 bottom, p. 258, p. 263, p. 272, p. 279, p. 280, p. 290, p. 293 bottom, p. 313, p. 314.
   U.S. Naval Academy Museum: p. 69 bottom, p. 111, p. 161, p. 309.
   U.S. Naval Institute: p. 12, p. 22 bottom, p. 41 bottom, p. 44, p. 46, p. 53, p. 54 top, p. 57, p. 64, p. 66, p. 71, p. 83, p. 84, p. 86, p. 90, p. 95, p. 103, p. 122, p. 130 bottom, p. 139 bottom, p. 147, p. 162 top, p. 173, p. 179, p. 181, p. 191 top, p. 201, p. 213, p. 218, p. 240, p. 247, p. 249, p. 250 top, p. 253, p. 255, p. 262, p. 275, p. 277, p. 286, p. 291, p. 293 top, p. 299 top and bottom, p. 300, p. 305, p. 310, p. 311, p. 312.
   U.S. Naval Observatory: p. 80 top, p. 200.

Contents

Preface

The opening decades of the twentieth century were of great importance for the United States and its naval service. The "New Navy" emerged in 1898 from the overwhelming victory over Spain with confidence, energy, and a larger and more international mission. The navy was a source of tremendous pride to the American public and, under the aggressive leadership of Theodore Roosevelt and others, it was expanded and modernized. By 1917 and America's entry into World War I the navy was a force second only to the Royal Navy and with a building program to make it "second to none." The men who reached flag rank during those years, men like A. T. Mahan, William S. Sims, Bradley Fiske, and "Fighting Bob" Evans, to mention only a few, represented in large part the spirit, energy, hope, and aspiration that the navy and the nation at large held.

Between 1 January 1901 and 31 December 1918, 330 men reached the rank of rear admiral on either the active or retired list. This was a dramatic increase over the 211 officers who achieved flag rank during the previous thirty-eight years since 1862, when the navy first used the rank of rear admiral. This increase reflected the overall and rapid increase in the entire service. While the navy's personnel grew in number, while vessels and weapons increased in size and technological complexity, and while the scope of the navy's operations expanded worldwide, the overall organization and the rank system of the service remained much the way it was immediately following the Spanish-American War. With only a few changes, the service continued to be headed by a civilian secretary who administered the navy through separate bureaus, although there were persistent and determined demands for major reforms. Similarly, officer ranks and the system of promotion and retirement saw relatively few changes during the period. And, like the navy's administrative hierarchy, there were cries for reform and improvement in these areas.

The following introductory pages describe those changes in naval ranks and the navy's organizational structure from 1901 through 1918. For a description of the origins and development of naval ranks to 1901, I refer the reader to Volume I of this series. The format of this volume is the same as the previous one, whereby each entry begins with personal information followed by the ranks that the officer achieved and the dates of each promotion. Next follows a chronological summary of the man's career, beginning with his first entry into the service and ending with either his retirement, resignation, or death. After the career summary for most of the entries is a paragraph or two covering the highlights of the man's career. Finally, there is a bibliographical section that includes whatever personal papers exist and their location, as well as any writings by or about him.

As with the first volume, I owe a great amount of gratitude to many people who have helped me in a variety of ways in putting this series together. Most are listed in the first volume. However, I wish to add the names of Ms. Karen White and Ms. Mary Lou Kenney, of the Naval Institute Press, Ms. Bea Jackson, formerly of the Institute Press, and Ms. Therese D. Boyd for their tireless assistance and patience. Again, the greatest thanks go to my wife and family who not only understand but who consistently encourage.

Ranks in the United States Navy

Although there were great changes in the navy in terms of its size, strength, and operations between 1900 and 1919, there were relatively few changes in the service's ranks. By the 1899 Personnel Act, the rank of commodore was abolished (temporarily), and those men on active duty who held the rank of commodore were advanced to rear admiral. Commodores on the retired list remained at that grade. The 1899 act divided the rank of rear admiral into two levels or "halves," upper and lower. These two grades corresponded to the army's ranks of brigadier general and major general, respectively. The act also restored the rank of admiral and awarded it to Rear Admiral George Dewey, who became known officially as Admiral of the Navy. Exempt from mandatory retirement, Dewey held this title and rank until his death in 1917 when, according to the 1899 act, the rank of admiral was to cease. However, Congress bestowed in 1916 the temporary rank of admiral upon the recently created chief of naval operations.

On 3 March 1915, Congress raised the commanders of the Atlantic, Pacific, and Asiatic Fleets, all rear admirals, to the temporary rank of admiral, while the officers next in command were elevated to the temporary rank of vice admiral. The reason for these changes was that American flag officers on foreign station normally found themselves outranked by commanders in other, often smaller, navies. Similarly, in 1922 when the Atlantic and Pacific Fleets were renamed the United States Fleet, the commander-in-chief was promoted to the temporary rank of admiral. All flag officers reverted to the rank of rear admiral when they went on the retired list.

While the 1899 Personnel Act settled the thorny issue of relative ranks and made the engineering officers a part of the line, there was nothing in the act that changed the titles of officers in the staff corps. As a result, staff officers continued to be addressed by functional title and line officers by rank. In his campaign to make the service more democratic, Navy Secretary Josephus Daniels ordered on 12 September 1918 that "every officer in the Navy shall be designated and addressed by the title of his rank without any discrimination whatever. In written communication the name of the corps to which a staff officer belongs shall be stated immediately after his name." With the exception of the Chaplain Corps, where officers of all ranks are addressed as "chaplain," this is the present practice.

By far and away the most important act on ranks between the Spanish-American War and the end of World War I was the 29 August 1916 act that fixed the authorized number of officers in each staff corps at a percentage of the number of line officers, the latter being fixed at a percentage of the authorized number of enlisted men. This act also authorized the rank of rear admiral for staff officers, there having been no such rank previously for such officers except as a chief of one of the bureaus.

The 1916 act determined the numbers in the various ranks as percentages of the total number in the corps. The percentages in each rank were fixed according to what were considered the needs for the services performed by these officers. This new method had one detrimental effect on many line officers. Since the increases in the ranks of captain and commander were not distributed over a period of years but instead came rather suddenly, some staff officers were promoted ahead of their line classmates. Similar to the nineteenth century when the staff officers campaigned for recognition, the line officers now said that staff officers received favoritism. The issue was discussed and debated, but nothing was done about it until the passage in 1926 of the so-called equalization bill.

The years from the Spanish-American War through World War I saw significant changes at the Naval Academy in Annapolis. The budget, physical plant, and size of the brigade all increased tremendously. Beginning on 1 July 1902, the older and more traditional rank of midshipman was restored, replacing the rank of cadet, which had been in use there since 1882. Furthermore, in 1912, Congress lowered the course of study from six to four years and allowed the immediate commissioning of graduates. Under Secretary Daniels, the enrollment continued to expand, and the four-year course was temporarily reduced to three with America's entry in war, the class of 1917 graduating in February of that year. The regular four-year course of study was resumed after World War I.

The 1899 Personnel Act ended relative ranks for the Chaplain Corps as it did for all other staff corps. However, the act neither established rank for the newly commissioned chaplains nor increased the number of chaplains, authorized at twenty-four by the 3 March 1871 act. After persistent lobbying by navy chaplains and others, Congress authorized on 28 June 1906 the commissioning of chaplains at the rank of lieutenant (junior grade). In addition, the 30 June 1914 Naval Appropriations Act not only increased the number of navy chaplains by establishing the desired ratio of one chaplain for every 1,250 naval personnel, but also established the ratio of chaplains to ranks. Ten percent of the corps held the grade of captain, 20 percent were commanders, and another 20 percent were lieutenant commanders. The remainder of the corps were lieutenants or lieutenants (junior grade), and as such, the Chaplain Corps enjoyed the highest percentages in the upper grades ever bestowed by Congress to any corps, line or staff.

While other corps enjoyed a chief, no such officer existed for chaplains and from 1871 chaplains campaigned to have one of their own as chief and thus better represent the corps' interest in Washington. It was not, however, until 5 November 1917 and the demands of war that the navy appointed the first chief of chaplains for a four-year billet. While appointing a chief, the office of Chief of Naval Chaplains was not officially created until December 1944, at which time the rank of rear admiral was attached to the position, although the title "Chief of Chaplains" was used before that date. The increase in navy personnel saw an increase in the number of chaplains on sea duty and thus the need for experienced chaplains to oversee the activities of all shipboard chaplains, much like a bishop. As such, the office of Fleet Chaplain was created on 8 June 1918.

Two more corps saw significant changes in the early twentieth century, the Naval Construction Corps and the Civil Engineering Corps. The 1899 Personnel Act increased and fixed at forty the number of naval and assistant naval constructors. This number proved to be too few as construction of new vessels accelerated. By the Naval Appropriation Act of 1 July 1902, the corps' number rose to forty-six, and in the next year, to seventy-five. The numbers in the ranks of captain and commander, set at two and three respectively, were not, however, changed. The size of the Naval Construction Corps remained at this level until 29 August 1916, when it was again increased.

Not surprisingly, given the extension of the navy in ship sizes and types, the need for more civil engineers became evident. On 3 March 1903, the Civil Engineering Corps was increased from ten, established in February 1881, to forty. This corps, like all corps in the navy, was increased by the 29 August 1916 act.

PROMOTIONS AND RETIREMENTS

By the end of the nineteenth century, promotion in the navy was guided principally by seniority rather than by a selection system based on merit. As a result, there existed during the 1890s a severe logjam or "hump" in promotions. The periods during and immediately after the Civil War witnessed rapid promotions. This was followed by a period of few promotions. Consequently, there was a disproportionately high number of officers in the lower grades, where it was not uncommon for lieutenants to remain in that rank for twenty years with some men in that grade being fifty years old. Similarly, there was a disproportionately few number of senior-ranking officers who reached command rank at a relatively young age, stayed in the service until retirement, and thus acted as a block to the promotion of younger officers.

For those who did reach command rank, they did so at an advanced age and close to the end of their career. By 1900, the average age at which one reached the rank of rear admiral was sixty-one, and the age of retirement was sixty-two. Captains averaged fifty-eight years of age. Few officers gained any fleet or squadron command experience until they reached these advanced ages and were ready to retire. The entire system of promotion by seniority had a generally demoralizing effect.

The 1899 Personnel Act slightly improved the system and increased promotions by allowing the secretary of the navy to keep a list of "applicants for voluntary retirement." If the number of vacancies for each year in each rank did not equal certain numbers, the president could select from the list the needed number of officers and retire them. If this procedure failed to meet the specified number of vacancies, the secretary could convene a board to select the needed number of officers for retirement. Despite the 1899 Act and its action on retirement, however, officers still reached flag rank late in their career.

Many, including Theodore Roosevelt, believed that officers who commanded fleets were far too old for the rigors of that duty and that they reached flag rank so late that they could not receive proper training before assuming command. Roosevelt favored selecting fit officers of the lower grades for advancement, removing unfit officers from the service, and thus allowing qualified officers to reach command and flag rank at an earlier age. Many remedies were proposed to end the congestion, which included, for example, reviving the ranks of admiral, vice admiral, and commodore to provide a slight measure of relief. Some reform was provided in 1900 by the creation of a personnel board that examined the records of officers and retired those it believed to be undesirable or unneeded. While some officers were removed and thus prevented from achieving high rank, this "plucking board" did not alleviate the problem. In 1904, there was a suggestion of an earlier retirement for admirals at the age of fifty-five or sixty.

Several changes were made in 1906. On 29 June, Congress advanced one additional grade all naval officers on the retired list who had credible service during the Civil War. While this rewarded a good number of retired officers, it did not remove the problem of the hump in the promotion system. Every indication still suggested that midshipmen would normally reach the rank of lieutenant at the age of forty-five or fifty. In August 1906, Navy Secretary Charles J. Bonaparte appointed a personnel board, which recommended a long list of changes, including fixing the time an officer should spend in each grade, removing officers in excess of needed numbers for each grade, creating a reserve list of officers for shore duty to which those of various ranks might be retired, and the retirement of all officers physically disabled. All of these remedies, however, had seniority as the basis for promotion.

In June 1909, Navy Secretary George von Lengerke Meyer began to "withdraw" retired officers from active duty and replace them with younger men. On 25 February 1910, he asked Congress that the number of officers to reach flag rank be limited but that their promotions be made earlier, whereby there would be one admiral and one vice admiral, and all other officers, line and staff, would be spread through the grades in percentages and thereby remove the promotion hump. Congress failed, however, to respond to any of these requests.

It was only during the Wilson administration that the promotion system was substantially improved. Beginning in March 1913, Navy Secretary Daniels first refused to promote any officer who had not performed the normal and required sea duty that went with his rank. He then directed promotion boards to consider carefully an officer's attendance at the Naval War College as a factor for promotion, and required attendance at Newport for the promotion of more senior officers. He also stipulated that the four years that midshipmen spent at Annapolis would not count either for promotion or retirement.

The Secretary also persuaded Congress on 3 March 1915 to abolish the "plucking board," and thereby base promotion on merit rather than on simply making room for younger officers by "selecting out" senior officers. Similarly, Congress repealed a part of the 1899 Personnel Act that forced the retirement of a specified number of officers a year, although implementation of this act was not made until the middle of 1916.

The 29 August 1916 Act was an important milestone in the promotion system. It established the number of line and staff officers by fixing the number of officers at 4 percent of the number of enlisted personnel and, in hopes of leveling out the disproportionate number of officers in the grades, the number in each rank would increase automatically as the number of enlisted men increased. In order to implement the promotion of senior line officers on selection rather than on merit, a board of nine rear admirals would recommend to the secretary those selected to fill vacancies for the following year. A similar board dealt with promotion for the lower officers. The act also raised the retirement age from sixty-two to sixty-four. As this act applied only to line officers, it was followed by legislation pertaining to staff officers. On 22 May 1917, examinations for promotions in all staff corps were abolished, and on 1 July 1918, promotion by selection was extended to the staff. Finally, after 30 June 1920, an "age-in-grade limit" was placed upon promotion in the grades from lieutenant commander through captain. If not promoted, a captain reaching fifty-six, a commander reaching fifty, and a lieutenant commander reaching forty-five years old would be retired.

Administration and Management

The idea of creating a panel or committee to assist the secretary of the navy in coordinating the work of the eight bureaus began as early as the Civil War, and several attempts were made to centralize the system in the name of efficiency. However, owing to opposition in Congress and from many of the bureau chiefs themselves, nothing of significance came of these reform attempts. With the exigencies of war in 1898, the Naval War (or Naval Strategy) Board was established as a temporary body to help the secretary of the navy in planning and implementing strategy. Once the war ended in the autumn of that year, so did the Naval War Board.

The desire to increase naval efficiency in general and the administrative difficulties made evident by the war in particular produced a movement to establish a permanent board along similar lines as that of the Naval War Board. Proponents of the movement claimed that such a board would handle more efficiently those important naval functions and duties that did not specifically fall within the parameters of particular bureaus. These included, said the proponents, the preparation of war plans, the examination and study of strategic issues and problems, the gathering of military information, coordinating the bureaus, and advising the secretary of the navy on many subjects.

While not going as far as some wanted and creating more of a general staff, something that the U.S. Army would create in 1903, Navy Secretary John D. Long established the General Board on 13 March 1900. Designed to improve the Navy Department's management and to help coordinate the growing size and complexity of the navy, the General Board was headed by Admiral George Dewey and consisted of the chief of the Bureau of Navigation and his assistant, and three other officers of at least the rank of lieutenant commander. Membership on the board changed several times until 1905 when it consisted of Admiral Dewey, the chief of the bureau of navigation, the navy's chief intelligence officer, the president of the Naval War College, and such additional officers above the rank of commander in order to maintain the board's total membership at seven.

While very influential, the General Board acted merely in an advisory capacity, possessing no legislative authority to perform administrative or operational functions or duties. To many, the board was not what was needed to make the navy's administration as efficient as it needed to be for the navy's increasingly active global role. There thus emerged a campaign by successive secretaries of the navy, by President Roosevelt, and by many within the navy to replace the General Board with a naval general staff that had greater powers and that could issue orders and exercise control over the navy's bureaus. But in each of these attempts, Congress failed to respond favorably, opposition coming from many within the navy as well as from within Congress.

Aware of his predecessors' unsuccessful attempts to change the Navy Department's organization and to coordinate the work of the bureaus, Secretary Meyer decided in December 1909 to divide the Department into four general areas: operations of the fleet, personnel, material, and inspections. The eight existing bureaus were placed under one of these divisions, depending on their function, and a senior line officer, designated an "aide," headed each division. Each aide advised the secretary on his particular area, and the four aides collectively coordinated the work of the bureaus and advised the secretary on overall department matters and administration. Secretary Meyer tried unsuccessfully to get Congressional sanction for his aides and, thus lacking legislative authority, they could not issue any orders to the bureaus. This system of naval aides continued for four years until abandoned by President Woodrow Wilson's secretary of the navy, Josephus Daniels.

Another major change in the Navy Department's organization during the secretaryship of Meyer came on 19 January 1910 when the House Naval Affairs Committee agreed to abolish the Bureau of Equipment. The Bureau's remaining functions were taken by other bureaus and by an act of 30 June 1914, the Bureau of Equipment was formally abolished. In addition, Meyer ruled that bureau chiefs could not serve longer than eight years.

The possibility that the United States might be drawn into the European war finally persuaded Congress that the bureau system of management needed some form of coordinating authority for assisting the secretary. On 3 March 1915, Congress created the Office of Chief of Naval Operations who, appointed by the President, would be "charged with the operations of the fleet and the preparation and readiness of plans for its use in war." In January of the following year, the chief of naval operations was given a four-year term. Originally designated an active duty officer at the rank of captain plus four years, Congress authorized in August 1916 the grade of admiral for the man holding the office and directed that "all orders issued by [him] in performing the duties assigned to him shall be performed under the authority of the Secretary of the Navy, and his orders shall be considered as emanating from the Secretary and shall have the full force and effect as such."

While Secretary Daniels effectively used the office of chief of naval operations to prevent any further attempt to create for the navy a general staff, he relied primarily in the growing anticipation of war on an advisory board composed of himself, Assistant Secretary Franklin D. Roosevelt, the chief of naval operations, the seven bureau chiefs, the judge advocate general, and the commandant of the Marine Corps.

The airplane and its increasing use in the navy resulted in some changes within the Navy Department's organization. In September 1910 the department created an assistant for aeronautics to the Aide for Material, and on 14 April 1911, naval aeronautics was placed under the Bureau of Navigation. On 1 July 1914, the Office of Naval Aeronautics was established, and in the following year it was transferred to the newly created office of chief of naval operations where it remained until after World War I. By 1919 the airplane had become such an important part of the navy's arsenal that it could not be handled under the prewar management system. As such, the first expansion of the bureau system since 1862 took place on 12 July 1921 when Congress established the Bureau of Aeronautics.

Not until 1898 was there a definite branch of the service created to train men employed in sick bays on ships and at hospitals on shore. The war with Spain pointed out clearly the need for a better organization and for training personnel in these areas. An act of 17 June 1898 established the Hospital Corps to provide trained assistants to medical officers and male nurses to care for the sick and wounded, the new corps coming under the Medical Department of the Bureau of Medicine and Surgery. On 13 May 1908, Congress established the female Nurse Corps as a part of the navy's Medical Department. The head of this corps was the superintendent of nurses, appointed by the secretary of the navy. Under the superintendent, there were to be as many chief nurses, nurses, and reserve nurses as required, all to be appointed by the surgeon general of the navy with the navy secretary's approval.

The navy originally had made no provision for dentists, but legislation of 22 August 1912 authorized the appointment of not more than thirty assistant dental surgeons to be part of the navy's Medical Department and to receive the same pay and allowances and to take rank in the same manner as the Medical Corps. From this start grew the Dental Corps. A portion of the act establishing the Dental Corps also made provision for a Medical Reserve Corps in order to supply additional doctors in the event of a national emergency. It provided a large proportion of the doctors needed in World War I. In 1913, a Dental Reserve Corps was established.

Finally, with the increase in the overall size and administrative complexity of the navy between 1900 and 1919, the number of personnel employed in the Navy Department increased. In 1897, there were fewer than three hundred civilians, and this number more than doubled by 1905 alone. The Navy Department building proved too small for the increase and in 1903 the Naval Annex was established in buildings located near the Navy Department building. This provided quarters for the Naval Intelligence Office, Hydrographic Office, General Board, office of the admiral, office of the Marine Corps, Naval Pay Office, the boards of inspection and survey, examining, retiring, and medical examiners, and the Medical Dispensary.

NAVAL MILITIA AND NAVAL RESERVE

From the latter part of the nineteenth century, the cost of maintaining regular navies was rapidly rising. To provide a means of augmenting the regular establishment in time of war, major maritime powers established the policy of training civilian volunteers. Such a move began in the United States in the 1880s.

Militia units, by the Constitution, were under state control. Several states added naval branches to their existing militia forces and by 1894 twenty-five such branches had been created. Congress supported this nonregular auxiliary on 2 March 1891 by providing money for arms and munitions as authorized by the secretary of the navy. This was followed on 3 August 1894 by an act that allowed the navy to loan vessels to state naval militia. Finally, the U.S. Auxiliary Navy Force was created on 26 May 1898 during the Spanish-American War. Officers and men of the state naval militia, with the consent of their governors, could be mustered into the new force for active service with the U.S. Navy. Those of the naval militia who did not transfer to the Auxiliary Naval

Force manned older vessels for coast and harbor protection within the boundaries of their respective states. After the war, members of the auxiliary force were released from federal service.

The events of 1898 clearly pointed to the need for some form of naval reserve force under federal control. On 21 January 1903, Congress placed the land militia under control of the War Department, whereby one part of the militia would be a ready reserve, called the National Guard, and the other part would be a "reserve militia." The National Guard received financial assistance from the federal government, was organized, armed, and disciplined like the regular army, and could be called into federal service for a nine-month period by the president. The way was thus paved for federal control of the states' naval militia. Those in charge of the naval militia units, however, were reluctant to lose control of them, and it was not until 16 February 1914 that Congress gave the Navy Department the same powers and responsibilities for the state naval militia as the War Department had for the National Guard units. In an emergency, the naval militia were to be called into federal service before any volunteer force.

With war in Europe, Congress created on 3 March 1915 the naval reserve, consisting of "citizens of the United States who have been or may be entitled to be honorably discharged from the Navy." The Reserve was to consist of two classes: those who enlisted in the naval reserve within four months after discharge, called the Naval Militia, and those who enlisted more than four months after discharge, known as the Fleet Reserve. For a little more than a year, these two naval reserve organizations, one under state control and the other under federal, existed side by side. Then, by act of Congress of 29 August 1916, the Naval Militia and the Fleet Reserve were merged into the National Naval Volunteers, and the expanded reserve force was divided into six classes.

In effect, naval militiamen served two masters: the state and the federal governments. The obligation to the federal government was paramount, for under it a member could be called into active service with the navy without the consent of the governor of his state. The authority of the state naval militia was further reduced and the naval reserve strengthened by legislation of 1 July 1918 empowering the president to transfer personnel of the National Naval Volunteers to appropriate classes of the naval reserve force. Subsequent legislation of 4 and 20 June 1920 and of 28 February 1925 modified the naval reserve and militia setups. The Naval Reserve Act of 28 February 1925 replaced the 29 August 1916 one and provided for a fleet naval reserve, a merchant marine reserve, and a voluntary naval reserve.

BUREAU CHIEFS (1901–1919)

Bureau of Yards and Docks

Mordecai T. Endicott	4 Apr 1898–8 Jan 1907
Richard C. Hollyday	26 Mar 1907–12 Jan 1912
Homer R. Stanford	14 Jan 1912–21 Jan 1916
Frederic R. Harris	21 Jan 1916–26 Dec 1917
Charles W. Parks	11 Jan 1918–15 Dec 1921

Bureau of Equipment (deactivated 1910; abolished 1914)

Royal B. Bradford	7 Sep 1897–27 Oct 1903
George A. Converse	27 Oct 1903–15 Mar 1904
Henry N. Manney	15 Mar 1904–22 Jan 1906
William S. Cowles	23 Jan 1906–19 Jan 1910

Bureau of Navigation

Arent S. Crowinshield	8 Apr 1897–30 Apr 1902
Henry C. Taylor	30 Apr 1902–26 Jul 1904
George A. Converse	1 Aug 1904–18 May 1907
William H. Brownson	19 May 1907–24 Dec 1907
John E. Pillsbury	14 Jan 1908–30 Jun 1909
William Potter	1 Jul 1909–1 Dec 1909
Reginald F. Nicholson	1 Dec 1909–31 Dec 1911
Philip Andrews	1 Jan 1912–26 Mar 1913
Victor Blue	26 Mar 1913–7 Aug 1916
Leigh C. Palmer	7 Aug 1916–12 Nov 1918
Victor Blue	19 Dec 1918–5 Aug 1919

Bureau of Ordnance

Charles O'Neil	1 Jun 1897–15 Mar 1904
George A. Converse	15 Mar 1904–31 Jul 1904
Newton E. Mason	1 Aug 1904–25 May 1911
Nathan C. Twining	25 May 1911–9 Oct 1913
Joseph Strauss	21 Oct 1913–23 Dec 1916
Ralph Earle	23 Dec 1916–5 May 1920

Bureau of Construction and Repair

Philip Hichborn	23 Jul 1893–4 Mar 1901
Francis T. Bowles	4 Mar 1901–31 Oct 1903
Washington L. Capps	31 Oct 1903–2 Oct 1910
Richard M. Watt	2 Oct 1910–13 Dec 1914
David W. Taylor	13 Dec 1914–1 Jul 1922

Bureau of Steam Engineering

George W. Melville	9 Aug 1887–8 Aug 1903
Charles W. Rae	9 Aug 1903–13 May 1908
Washington L. Capps (acting Chief)	13 May 1908–9 Jun 1908
John K. Barton	9 Jun 1908–21 May 1909
Hutch I. Cone	21 May 1909–18 May 1913
Robert S. Griffin	18 May 1913–27 Sep 1921

Bureau of Supplies and Accounts

Albert S. Kenny	5 May 1899–1 Jul 1903
Henry T. B. Harris	1 Jul 1903–1 Nov 1906
Eustace B. Rogers	1 Nov 1906–30 Jun 1910
Thomas J. Cowie	1 Jul 1910–1 Jul 1914
Samuel McGowan	1 Jul 1914–31 Dec 1920

Bureau of Medicine and Surgery

William K. Van Reypen	22 Oct 1897–25 Jan 1902
Presley M. Rixey	10 Feb 1902–4 Feb 1910
Charles F. Stokes	7 Feb 1910–11 Feb 1914
William C. Braisted	11 Feb 1914–29 Nov 1920

Abbreviations

act.	acting	dir.	director
Adm, adm	admiral	dist.	district
Afr.	African	div.	division
AK	Alaska	E.	East
AL	Alabama	engr.	engineer
Am.	American	Ens	ensign
Apr	April	Ensjg	ensign (junior grade)
AR	Arkansas	equip.	equipment
Asia.	Asiatic	Eur.	European
asst.	assistant	evol.	evolution
Atl.	Atlantic	exam.	examining/examination
Aug	August	exec.	executive
AZ	Arizona	expd.	expedition
bd.	board	expl.	exploring
BGen	brigadier general	Feb	February
Blk.	Blockading	FL	Florida
Braz.	Brazil	flgs.	flagship
bur.	bureau	flot.	flotilla
bvt.	brevet	flt.	fleet
c.	circa	ft.	feet/fort
CA	California	GA	Georgia
Capt, capt	captain	Gen, gen	general
capt.yd.	captain of yard	gov.	governor
Cdr, cdr	commander	HI	Hawaii
CO	Colorado	hosp.	hospital
Col	colonel	HQ	headquarters
Commo	commodore	IA	Iowa
comdt.	commandant	ID	Idaho
const.	constructor	IL	Illinois
cst.	coast	IN	Indiana
CT	Connecticut	Ind.	India
DC	District of Columbia	insp.	inspector
DE	Delaware	inst.	instructor
Dec	December	Jan	January
dept.	department	Jul	July

Jun	June		PAsst.	passed assistant
KS	Kansas		Paymstr.	paymaster
KY	Kentucky		P.I.	Philippine Islands
LA	Louisiana		PMidn	passed midshipman
LCdr	lieutenant commander		prac.	practice
LtCol	lieutenant colonel		pres.	president
LtGen	lieutenant general		prof.	professor
L.h.	lighthouse		q.v.	*quod vide* [which see]: see also
lib.	library		RAdm	rear admiral
Lt, lt	lieutenant		rec.	receiving
Ltjg	lieutenant (junior grade)		rel.	relative
lv.	leave		ret.	retirement
l.o.a.	leave of absence		Ret.Lst.	Retired List
MA	Massachusetts		RI	Rhode Island
Mar	March		Rndv.	Rendezvous
Maj	major		S.	South
math.	mathematics		s.a.	settle accounts
MB	Marine Barracks		SC	South Carolina
MD	Maryland		SD	South Dakota
ME	Maine		sec.	secretary
Med.	Mediterranean		Sep	September
medl.	medical		serv.	service
MGen	major general		spec.	special
MI	Michigan		sqdn.	squadron
Midn, midn	midshipman/midshipmen		sta.	station
MN	Minnesota		supt.	superintendent
MO	Missouri		surg.	surgeon
MS	Mississippi		surv.	surveying
Mstr, mstr	master		temp.	temporary
MT	Montana		TN	Tennessee
N.	North		torp.	torpedo
nav.	navigation		TX	Texas
NB	Nebraska		univ.	university
NC	North Carolina		U.S.	United States
ND	North Dakota		USA	United States Army
NH	New Hampshire		USMA	United States Military Academy
NJ	New Jersey			
NM	New Mexico		USMC	United States Marine Corps
n.d.	no date		USN	United States Navy
Nov	November		USNA	United States Naval Academy
NV	Nevada		UT	Utah
NWC	Naval War College		VA	Virginia
NY	New York		VAdm	vice admiral
Oct	October		VT	Vermont
off.	officer		W.	West
OH	Ohio		WA	Washington
OK	Oklahoma		WI	Wisconsin
OR	Oregon		w.o.	waiting orders
ord.	ordnance		WV	West Virginia
PA	Pennsylvania		WY	Wyoming
Pac.	Pacific			

Collections and Libraries

ALP	Abraham Lincoln Papers, IL State Historical Society
ASHF	American Swedish Historical Foundation, Philadelphia, PA
ASAL	Archibald Stevens Alexander Lib., Rutgers Univ.
BAKL	Baker Lib., Harvard Univ.
BL	Bancroft Lib., Univ. of CA, Berkeley
BLYU	Beinecke Lib., Yale Univ.
EFMC	Eric F. Menke Collection, Georgetown Univ.
EMHL	Eleutherian Mills Historical Lib., Greenville, DE
FDRL	Franklin D. Roosevelt Lib., Hyde Park, NY
GARL	George Arents Research Lib., Syracuse Univ.
HHL	Henry Huntington Lib., San Marino, CA
ISHS	Illinois State Historical Society, Springfield, IL
LC	Lib. of Congress, Washington, DC
LSUL	Louisiana State Univ. Lib.
MCHC	Marine Corps Historical Center, Washington Navy Yard
NHF,LC	Naval Historical Foundation, Lib. of Congress
NHF,WNY	Naval Historical Foundation, Washington Navy Yard
NL	Nimitz Lib., U.S. Naval Academy, Annapolis, MD
NYHS	New York Historical Society
NYPL	New York Public Lib.
RHTRL	Robert Hudson Tannahill Research Lib., Dearborn, MI
SCL	South Caroliniana Lib., Columbia, SC
SHC	Southern Historical Collection, Univ. of NC
SML	Sterling Memorial Lib., Yale Univ.
USMA	U.S. Military Academy, West Point, NY
USNAM	U.S. Naval Academy Museum, Annapolis, MD
WLCL	William L. Clements Lib., Ann Arbor, MI
WPL	William Perkins Lib., Duke Univ.

DICTIONARY
of
ADMIRALS
of the
U.S. NAVY

SETH MITCHELL ACKLEY Born in Nantucket, MA, on 13 Oct 1845, the son of Mrs. C. C. Colby, his father having died during his youth. Died in Washington, DC, in 1908.

Ranks Midn (4 Oct 1862); Ens (12 Mar 1868); Mstr (26 Mar 1869); Lt (21 Mar 1870); LCdr (30 Jun 1887); Cdr (4 May 1896); retired as Capt (25 Oct 1901); restored to Active List (8 Apr 1904); RAdm (24 Feb 1907); placed on Ret.Lst. (13 Oct 1907).

Career Summary Received appointment from MA (4 Oct 1862); USNA (Oct 1862-Jun 1866); l.o.a. and w.o. (Jun-Oct 1866); *Yantic*, Navy Yard, Norfolk, VA (Oct-Nov 1866); flgs., *Rhode Island*, N.Atl.Sqdn. (Nov 1866-Jan 1867); flgs., *Susquehanna*, N.Atl.Sqdn. (Jan-Jun 1867); *Guerriere*, then *Huron*, S.Atl.Sta. (Jun-Dec 1867); sick lv. (Dec 1867-Mar 1868); *Contoocook* and *Gettysburg*, N.Atl.Sqdn. (Mar 1868-Oct 1869); *Yantic*, N. Atl. Sqdn. (Feb 1870-Jul 1871); w.o. (Jul-Oct 1871); Naval Observatory, Washington, DC (Nov 1871-Jun 1872); w.o. (Jun-Jul 1872); *Omaha* and *Onward*, S.Pac.Sta. (Aug 1872-Apr 1875); *Richmond*, S.Pac.Sta. (Apr-Aug 1875); w.o. (Aug-Nov 1875); ord. duty, Navy Yard, Washington, DC (Nov 1875-Apr 1876); *Michigan*, on Great Lakes (Apr-Dec 1876); rec. ship, *Wyoming*, Washington, DC (Jan-Feb 1877); cst.surv. duty (Feb 1877-Feb 1881); w.o. (Feb-Mar 1881); *Palos*, spec. assignment, Far East (May 1881-May 1883); *Richmond*, Asia.Sta. (May-Jul 1883); *Palos*, Asia.Sta. (Jul-Nov 1883); l.o.a. (Nov 1883-Sep 1884); Hydrographic Office, Washington, DC (Oct 1884-May 1886); torp. instruction, Newport, RI (Jun-Sep 1886); NWC (Sep-Nov 1886); w.o. (Nov 1886-May 1887); *Quinnebaug*, Eur.Sta. (May 1887-Jun 1889); w.o. (Jun-Aug 1889); member, court-martial board (Aug-Sep 1889); Hydrographic Insp., Cst.Surv. Office (Oct 1889-Oct 1893); cdr, *Yantic*, S.Atl.Sta. (Dec 1893-Oct 1895); l.o.a. (Oct 1895-Mar 1896); ord. instruction, Navy Yard, Washington, DC (Mar-May 1896); insp., 6th L.h. Dist., Charleston, SC (May 1896-Mar 1898); sec., L.h. Bd., Washington, DC (Mar 1898-Apr 1899); Naval Hosp., Yokohama, Japan (Jun-Sep 1899); cdr, *Concord*, Asia.Sqdn. (Sep 1899-Jun 1900); return and sick lv. (Jun 1900-Jan 1901); Navy Yard, Washington, DC (Jan 1901-Mar 1901); cdr, training ship, *Dixie* (Mar-Jul 1901); home and sick lv. (Jul-Oct 1901); placed on Ret.Lst. (25 Oct 1901); restored to Active List (8 Apr 1904); temp. duty, Gen Bd., Washington, DC (May-Jun 1904); comdt., Subic Bay Naval Reserve and Cavite Naval Sta., and cdr, sta. ship, *Mohican*, P.I. (Aug 1904-Jan 1906); Naval Hosp., Mare Island, CA (Mar 1906); w.o. (Mar-Apr 1906): spec. duty, Bur. of Nav., Washington, DC (Apr-May 1906); NWC (Jun-Oct 1906); w.o. (Oct 1906-Oct 1907); placed on Ret.Lst. (13 Oct 1907).

JAMES DEXTER ADAMS
1848-1922

JAMES DEXTER ADAMS Born on 4 May 1848 in Catskill, NY, son of Frederick Chollet and Mary Dexter (Reynolds) Adams. Married Margaret J. Phelps on 6 May 1873. One son, Capt. L. F. Adams, USN, and two daughters. Died at his home in Washington, DC, on 19 Feb 1922. Buried in Arlington National Cemetery.

Ranks Midn (27 Sep 1864); Ens (19 Apr 1869); Mstr (12 Jul 1870); Lt (15 Sep 1873); LCdr (7 Sep 1894); Cdr (3 Mar 1899); Capt (31 Dec 1903); RAdm (25 Oct 1908); placed on Ret.Lst. (4 May 1910).

Career Summary Received appointment from MS (27 Sep 1864); USNA (Sep 1864-Jun 1868); w.o. (Jun-Sep 1868); flgs., *Contoocook*, N.Atl.Sqdn. (Sep 1868-Jun 1869); *Gettysburg*, N.Atl.Sqdn. (Jul-Aug 1869); *Frolic*, NY (Sep-Nov 1869); w.o. (Nov 1869-Feb 1870); *St. Mary's*, Pac.Sqdn. (Mar 1870-Oct 1871); *Mohican*, Pac.Sqdn. (Oct 1871-Jun 1872); rec. ship, *Independence*, Mare Island, CA (Jun 1872-Apr 1873); w.o. (Apr-Jun 1873); cst.surv. duty (Jul 1873-May 1876); torp. instruction, Newport, RI (Jun-Aug 1876); Navy Yard, Mare Island, CA (Aug 1876-Jul 1877); rec. ship, *Independence*, Mare Island, CA (Jul-Aug 1877); flgs., *Pensacola*, Pac.Sqdn. (Aug 1877-Aug 1880); w.o. (Aug-Dec 1880); Navy Yard, Mare Island, CA (Jan 1881-Mar 1883); w.o. (Mar-Apr 1883); torp. instruction, Newport, RI (Apr-Aug 1883); *Powhatan*, spec.serv. (Aug 1883-Jun 1884); flgs., *Lancaster*, Eur.Sta. (Jul-Aug 1884); *Kearsarge*, Eur.Sta. (Aug 1884-Nov 1886); w.o. (Nov 1886-Mar 1887); rec. ship, *Vermont*, NY (Mar 1887-Dec 1888); ord. instruction and duty, Navy Yard, Washington, DC (Dec 1888-Nov 1889); *Dolphin*, N.Atl.Sta. (Nov 1889-Apr 1891); l.o.a. (Apr-May 1891); Compass Office, Bur. of Equip. and Recruiting, Washington, DC (May-Aug 1891); w.o. (Aug-Oct 1891); Hydrographic Office, Washington, DC (Oct 1891-Mar 1892); USNA (Mar 1892-Apr 1895); exec.off., *Amphitrite*, N.Atl.Sqdn. (Apr 1895-Jul 1897); home and l.o.a. (Jul-Sep 1897); Hydrographic Office, Washington, DC (Sep 1897-Jul 1900); cdr, *Machias*, Boston (Jul-Aug 1900); cdr, *Bancroft*, surv. duty (Aug 1900-Apr 1901); cdr, *Mayflower*, San Juan, Puerto Rico (Apr-Aug

1901); cdr, training vessel, *Alert*, Pac.cst. (Aug 1901-Sep 1902); home, w.o., and l.o.a. (Sep-Nov 1902); Navy Yard, NY (Dec 1902-Sep 1903); member, bd. of inspection and other bd. duties (Sep 1903-May 1905); cdr, *Olympia*, N.Atl.Sqdn. (Jun 1905-Apr 1906); gen insp., *Washington*, Philadelphia (Apr-Aug 1906); cdr, *Washington*, spec.serv. (Aug 1906-Jun 1907); capt.yd., Navy Yard, NY (Jun 1907-Nov 1908); comdt., Navy Yard, and cdr, 6th Naval Dist., Charleston, SC (Jan 1909-Jun 1910); placed on Ret.Lst. (4 May 1910).

ALFRED ADAMSON Born in Brownsville, NY, on 19 Sep 1836. Married with at least one son. Died at his home in Brookline, MA, on 22 Feb 1915. Buried in West Laurel Hill Cemetery, Philadelphia.

Ranks 3rd Asst.Engr. (13 May 1861); 2nd Asst.Engr. (17 Dec 1862); 1st Asst.Engr. (1 Jan 1865); Chief Engr. (19 May 1879); Chief Engr. with rel. rank of Cdr (25 May 1894); Chief Engr. with rel. rank of Capt (29 Jul 1897); placed on Ret.Lst. (19 Sep 1898); Chief Engr. with rank of RAdm. on Ret.Lst. (29 Jun 1906).

Career Summary Received appointment from WI (13 May 1861); *Pawnee*, S.Atl.Blk.Sqdn. (Jun 1861-Aug 1864); *Montauk*, S.Atl.Blk.Sqdn. (Aug 1864-Mar 1865); w.o. (Mar-Aug 1865); *Ticonderoga*, Eur.Sqdn. (Sep 1865-Dec 1868); w.o. (Dec 1868); Navy Yard, Philadelphia (Jan 1869-Feb 1871); on furlough (Feb 1871-May 1872); *Tuscarora*, Pac.Sqdn. (May 1872-Sep 1873); *Monocacy*, Asia.Sqdn. (Sep 1873-May 1875); w.o. (May-Oct 1875); Navy Yard, League Island, PA (Oct 1875-Oct 1878); temp. duty, asst. to coal insp., Philadelphia (Nov 1878-Jul 1879); w.o. (Jul-Dec 1879); *Swatara*, Asia.Sqdn. (Dec 1879-Dec 1882); w.o. (Dec 1882-Sep 1883); l.o.a. and w.o. (Sep 1883-Oct 1885); *Iroquois*, Pac.Sta. (Nov 1885-Mar 1888); w.o. (Mar-Jun 1888); rec. ship, *Wabash*, Boston (Jun 1888-Sep 1891); *Yorktown*, Pac.Sta. (Sep 1891-Oct 1892); w.o. (Oct 1892-Jan 1893); Philadelphia, Atl.Sqdn. and Naval Review Flt. (Jan-Jun 1893); member, experiment bd., NY (Jun-Aug 1893); *Miantonomoh*, N.Atl.Sta. (Aug 1893-Nov 1894); home and l.o.a. (Nov 1894-Feb 1895); rec. ship, *Wabash*, Boston (Feb 1895-May 1897); Navy Yard, Boston (May 1897-Sep 1898); placed on Ret.Lst. (19 Sep 1898).

ALFRED ADAMSON
1836-1915

LOUIS JOSEPH ALLEN Born on 23 Feb 1840 in Baltimore. Married Mary E. Allen. Two daughters. Died in NY City on 29 Jun 1905. Buried in Arlington National Cemetery.

Ranks 3rd Asst.Engr. (3 May 1859); 2nd Asst.Engr. (13 May 1861); 1st Asst.Engr. (20 May 1863); Chief Engr. (4 Mar 1871); Chief Engr. with rel. rank of Capt (21 Mar 1895); Capt (3 Mar 1899); retired with rank of RAdm. (14 Jan 1902).

Career Summary Received appointment from MD (3 May 1859); spec. duty, Baltimore (May 1859-Feb 1860); *Dacotah*, E.Ind.Sqdn. (Feb 1860-Dec 1861); spec. duty, Novelty and Morgan Iron Works, NY (Jan-Apr 1862); *Adirondack*, S.Atl.Blk.

Sqdn. (Apr-Aug 1862); home and w.o. (Aug-Sep 1862); *Conemaugh*, S.Atl.Blk.Sqdn. (Sep 1862-Sep 1863); w.o. (Sep-Oct 1863); spec. duty, NY (Oct 1863-May 1864); spec. duty, Baltimore (Jun 1864-Jan 1865); *Monocacy*, Baltimore (Jan 1865-Sep 1866); sick lv. (Sep-Dec 1866); Naval Rndv., Philadelphia (Dec 1866-Sep 1867); temp. duty, *Chattanooga*, Navy Yard, Philadelphia (May-Jun 1867); USNA (Sep 1867-Jun 1869); *Dictator*, N.Atl.Sqdn. (Jun 1869-Nov 1870); w.o. (Nov 1870-Jan 1871); w.o. (Jan-May 1871); *Resaca*, Pac.Sqdn. (May 1871-Nov 1872); insp. of machinery, Navy Yard, Mare Island, CA (Dec 1872-Mar 1873); *Tuscarora*, surv. duty, Pac. Ocean (Apr 1873-Sep 1874); home and w.o. (Sep-Dec 1874); Navy Yard, Pensacola, FL (Jan 1875-Jul 1877); *Marion*, Eur., N., and S.Atl.Sqdns. (Aug 1877-Nov 1880); spec. duty, Baltimore (Nov 1880-Feb 1881); member, bd. of examiners, Philadelphia and NY (Feb-Dec 1881); spec. duty (Dec 1881-Oct 1882); w.o. (Oct 1882-Apr 1883); spec. duty, NY (Apr 1883-Jan 1884); rec. ship, *Vermont*, NY (Jan-Jun 1884); *Quinnebaug*, Eur.Sta. (Jul 1884-Oct 1887); w.o. (Oct 1887-Jan 1888); Navy Yard, NY (Jan 1888-May 1889); w.o. (May-Jun 1889); Navy Yard, League Island, PA (Jun 1889-Dec 1890); w.o. (Dec 1890-Jan 1891); insp. of boilers, Lake Erie Boiler Works, Erie, PA (Jan-Nov 1891); *Chicago*, S.Atl. and Eur.Stas. (Nov 1891-May 1895); flt.engr., Naval Review Flt., *Chicago* (May-Jun 1893); flt.engr., Eur.Sta., *Chicago* (Jun 1893-May 1895); member, experimenting bd., Navy Yard, NY (May 1895-Aug 1897); Continental Iron Works, NY (Aug 1897-Jan 1898); Union Iron Works, San Francisco (Jan 1898-Sep 1899); Navy Yard, Mare Island, CA (Sep 1899-Aug 1901); home, l.o.a., and w.o. (Aug 1901-Jan 1902); retired (14 Jan 1902).

EDWIN ALEXANDER ANDERSON Born in Wilmington, NC, on 16 Jul 1860, son of Confederate BGen George B. Anderson, who died at Antietam. Married Mertie Lorain. One son. Died at his home in Wilmington on 23 Sep 1933. Buried at Arlington National Cemetery.

Ranks Cadet Midn (28 Jun 1878); Ens (1 Jul 1884); Ltjg (30 Sep 1894); Lt (28 Mar 1898); LCdr (11 Sep 1903); Cdr (6 Dec 1907); Capt (14 Jun 1911); temp. RAdm (31 Aug 1917); RAdm (28 Nov 1918); VAdm (26 Apr 1922); Adm (28 Aug 1922); retired (23 Mar 1924).

Career Summary Received appointment from NC (28 Jun 1878); USNA (Jun 1878-Jun 1882); *Kearsarge*, N.Atl.Sta. (Jun 1882-Jun 1883); *Alliance*, N.Atl.Sta. (Jun 1883-Jan 1884); sick lv. (Jan-May 1884); USNA (May-Jun 1884); w.o. (Jun-Jul 1884); *Passaic*, USNA (Jul-Oct 1884); w.o. (Oct 1884-Mar 1885); flgs., *Pensacola*, Eur.Sta. (Mar-Jun 1885); *Kearsarge*, Eur.Sta. (Jun 1885); *Quinnebaug*, Eur.Sta. (Jun 1885-Oct 1887); Naval Hosp., NY (Oct-Nov 1887); sick lv. (Nov 1887-Jan 1888); *Quinnebaug*, Eur.Sta. (Jan 1888); l.o.a. (Jan-Apr 1888); cst.surv. duty (Apr 1888-Sep 1890); *Alert*, Bering Sea (Oct 1890-Jan 1891); Fish Commission steamer, *Albatross* (Jan 1891-Oct 1893); l.o.a. (Oct 1893-Jan 1894); in charge, branch hydrographic office, New Or-

EDWIN ALEXANDER ANDERSON
1860-1933

leans (Feb 1894-May 1895); spec.serv., *Michigan*, on Great Lakes (May-Nov 1895); Hydrographic Office, Washington, DC (Nov 1895-Mar 1896); ord. instruction, Navy Yard, Washington, DC (Mar-Apr 1896); *Columbia*, N.Atl.Sta. (Apr 1896-Jan 1897); *Marblehead*, N.Atl.Sta. (Jan 1897-Sep 1898); cdr, *Sandoval*, N.Atl.Flt. (Sep 1898-May 1899); additional duty, cdr, *Alvarado*, N.Atl.Flt. (Feb-May 1899); Torp.Sta., Newport, RI (May-Jun 1899); insp. of ord., Bridgeport, CT (Jul 1899-Apr 1901); *Solace*, Pac.Sqdn. (Apr-May 1901); cdr, *Nanshin*, Asia.Flt. (May 1901-Feb 1902); *Manila*, Asia.Sta. (Feb-Mar 1902); Naval Sta., Cavite, P.I. (Mar-Apr 1902); cdr, *General Alava*, Asia.Sta. (Apr-Jun 1902); exec.off., *Vicksburg*, Asia.Sta. (Jun-Dec 1902); cdr, *Callao*, Asia.Sta. (Dec 1902-Nov 1903); cdr, *Don Juan de Austria*, Asia.Sta. (Nov-Dec 1903); cdr, *Isla de Cuba*, Asia.Sta. (Dec 1903); home and w.o. (Dec 1903-Feb 1904); Naval Gun Factory, Navy Yard, Washington, DC (Feb 1904-Feb 1905); *Pennsylvania*, Philadelphia (Mar 1905-Jun 1906); cdr, 2nd Torp.Flot. (Jun 1906-Oct 1907); in charge, Naval Recruiting Sta., Cincinnati, OH (Dec 1907-Apr 1908); ord.off., Navy Yard, Mare Island, CA (May 1908-Sep 1910); additional duty, insp. of ord., Union Iron Works, San Francisco (Oct 1909-Sep 1910); cdr, *Yorktown*, Pac.Flt. (Nov 1910-Aug 1911); home, w.o., and l.o.a.(Aug-Oct 1911); cdr, training ship, *Iowa* (Oct-Nov 1911); capt.yd., Navy Yard, Philadelphia (Nov 1911-Dec 1913); cdr, *New Hampshire*, Atl.Flt. (Dec 1913-Dec 1915); NWC (Jan-Dec 1916); supervisor of naval auxiliaries, Norfolk, VA (Jan-Apr 1917); cdr, Sqdn. 3, Patrol Force, Atl.Flt., *Dolphin* (Apr-Jul 1917); cdr, Sqdn. 1, Patrol Force, Atl.Flt., *Dolphin* (Jul-Aug 1917), then *Tallapoosa* (Aug 1917-Nov 1919); comdt., Navy Yard, and 6th Naval Dist., Charleston, SC (Nov 1919-May 1922); cdr, Naval Forces, Eur. waters, *Utah* (May-Jun 1922); cdr, Asia.Flt., *Huron* (Jun 1922-Nov 1923); Office of Naval Operations, Navy Dept., Washington, DC (Dec 1923-Mar 1924); retired (23 Mar 1924).

Career Highlights Advanced five grades for heroism during actions off Cienfuegos and at Camp McCalla, Guantanamo Bay, Cuba during Spanish-American War. In Apr 1914, commanded the *New Hampshire* at Vera Cruz, Mexico, leading the 2nd Seaman Regiment of Marines and Bluejackets against entrenched Mexican forces, subsequently receiving Medal of Honor for his action. Awarded Distinguished Service Medal for efforts in organizing, administering, and operating the American Patrol during World War I. Served as gov. of Puerto Rico. While commanding Asia.Flt., decorated by Japanese government for his humanitarian efforts during that country's earthquake and tidal wave in 1923.

References

Personal Papers: a) c. 800 items (1878-1939) in SHC. b) 13 items (1915-18) in WPL.

Other Sources: Calvin D. Jarrett, "A Fighting Admiral Who 'Should Have Been a Marine,'" *Our Navy* (Mar 1967): 10-12.

CIPRIANO ANDRADE
1840-1911

CIPRIANO ANDRADE Born in Tampico, Mexico on 1 Sep 1840, son of Cipriano and Elizabeth (Edwards) Andrade. Early education in public and private schools in Philadelphia. Studied engineering at the Franklin Institute in Philadelphia. Connected with a practical course at Southwark Foundry in Philadelphia from 1858 to 1861. Married Annie A. Berry on 1 Jun 1870. At least one son. Died on 18 Jun 1911 in South Norwalk, CT. Buried in Arlington National Cemetery.

Ranks 3rd Asst.Engr. (1 Jul 1861); 2nd Asst.Engr. (18 Dec 1862); 1st Asst.Engr. (30 Jan 1865); title changed to PAsst.Engr. (24 Feb 1874); PAsst.Engr. with rel. rank of Lt (16 Dec 1876); Chief Engr. (11 Sep 1881); Chief Engr. with rel. rank of Cdr (12 Sep 1894); Chief Engr. with rel. rank of Capt (7 Feb 1898); Capt (3 Mar 1899); placed on Ret.Lst. as Chief Engr. with rank of RAdm (1 Jul 1901).

Career Summary Received appointment from PA (1 Jul 1861); flgs., *Lancaster*, Pac.Sqdn. (Aug 1861-Oct 1863); w.o. (Oct 1863-May 1864); *Pontiac*, S.Atl.Blk.Sqdn. (May 1864-Jun 1865); *Tuscarora*, Pac.Sta. (Aug 1865-Dec 1867); home and w.o. (Dec 1867-Mar 1868); spec. duty, machinery trials (Mar-Jun 1868); w.o. (Jun-Oct 1868); trial duty, *Neshaminy*, NY (Oct-Nov 1868); w.o. (Nov 1868-Apr 1869); *Saugus*, N.Atl.Flt. (Apr 1869-May 1870); w.o. (May-Sep 1870); Navy Yard, League Island, PA (Oct 1870-Aug 1872); *Benicia*, Pac.Sqdn. (Sep 1872-Apr 1873); Navy Yard, Mare Island, CA (May-Dec 1873); recruiting duty, San Francisco (Dec 1873-Jan 1874); Navy Yard, Mare Island, CA (Jan-Sep 1874); *Tuscarora*, N.Pac.Sta. (Sep 1874-Aug 1876); w.o. (Aug-Dec 1876); spec. duty, *Trenton*, Apia, Samoa (Dec 1876-Feb 1877); spec. duty, Providence, RI (Mar 1877-May 1878); experimental duty, NY (Jun-Aug 1878); senior asst.engr., Navy Yard, NY (Sep 1878-Dec 1879); *Benicia*, Asia.Sqdn. (Jan-May 1880); *Ashuelot*, Asia.Sqdn. (May 1880-Oct 1881); home, w.o., and l.o.a. (Oct 1881-Feb 1882); Navy Yard, NY (Feb-Jul 1882); insp. of coal, Philadelphia (Jul 1882-Feb 1884); *Yantic*, N.Atl.Sta. (Mar 1884-Oct 1885); *Swatara*, N.Atl.Sta. (Oct 1885-Oct 1886); w.o. (Oct 1886-Aug 1887); spec. duty, Philadelphia (Aug 1887-Apr 1889); Sqdn. of Evol., *Yorktown* (Apr 1889-Sep 1891); insp., *Columbia*, Philadelphia (Sep 1891-Apr 1894); *Columbia*, N.Atl.Sta. (Apr 1894-Jan 1895); flt.engr., N.Atl.Sta., *New York* (Jan 1895-Apr 1897); home and l.o.a. (Apr-May 1879); member, engr.exam.bd., Philadelphia (May 1897-May 1898); temp. duty, Interior Cst. Defense and the U.S. Auxiliary Naval Force (May-Aug 1898); member, bd. of inspection and surv. (Aug-Sep 1898); member, then pres., engr.exam.bd., Philadelphia (Oct 1898-Apr 1899); member, bd. of examiners, Washington, DC (Jun 1899-Jan 1900); inspection duty, Bur. of Steam Engineering, Washington, DC (Sep 1899-Jul 1901); placed on Ret.Lst. (1 Jul 1901).

CONWAY HILLYER ARNOLD Born in NY City on 14 Nov 1848, son of navy Cdr Henry Nathan Tewkesbury and Cornelia Van Vleck (Sleight) Arnold. On 17 Nov 1870, married Fanny

CONWAY HILLYER ARNOLD
1848-1917

Wood, daughter of navy's Engr.-in- Chief, William W. W. Wood. Died at his home in NY City on 16 Jul 1917. Buried at Oak Hill Cemetery in Washington, D.C.

Ranks Midn (30 Sep 1863); Ens (18 Dec 1868); Mstr (21 Mar 1870); Lt (22 Jun 1871); LCdr (10 Jan 1892); Cdr (11 May 1898); Capt (17 Sep 1902); RAdm (30 Jun 1908); placed on Ret.Lst. (14 Nov 1910).

Career Summary Received appointment by virtue of being the son of an officer (30 Sep 1863); USNA (Sep 1863-Jun 1867); training vessel, *Minnesota* (Jul 1867-Jan 1868); flgs., *Severn*, N.Atl.Sqdn. (Jan 1868-Aug 1870); l.o.a. and w.o. (Aug 1870-Jan 1871); rec. ship, *Vermont*, NY (Jan-May 1871); spec. duty, NY (May 1871-Jan 1872); *Wasp*, S.Atl.Sta. (Jan 1872-Nov 1873); home and w.o. (Nov 1873-Apr 1874); Naval Observatory, Washington, DC (Apr 1874-Nov 1875); flgs., *Hartford*, N.Atl.Sta. (Nov 1875-Aug 1877); flag lt, N.Atl.Sta., *Powhatan* (Sep 1877-Nov 1878); w.o. (Nov 1878-Jan 1879); cdr, *Wyandotte*, N.Atl.Sta. and spec. cruises (Jan 1879-Sep 1881); flgs., *Lancaster*, Eur.Sta. (Sep 1881-Jul 1882); sick lv. and w.o. (Jul-Sep 1882); *Miantonomoh*, Washington, DC (Oct 1882-Mar 1883); *Nipsic*, S.Atl.Sta. (Mar 1883-Jun 1886); w.o. (Jun-Aug 1886);Nav. Dept., Navy Yard, NY (Aug 1886-Feb 1889); flgs., *Philadelphia*, N.Atl.Sta. (Feb 1889-Jul 1892); member, bd. for inspectionof merchant vessels, Navy Yard, NY (Jul 1892-May 1894); in charge, branch hydrographic office, NY (Jun 1894-Jun 1896); exec.off., *Massachusetts*, on trials (Jun-Dec 1896); cdr, *Bancroft*, Eur.Sta. (Jan-Dec 1897); l.o.a. (Dec 1897-Mar 1898); insp., 6th L.h. Dist., Charleston, SC (Mar 1898-Mar 1899); cdr, 5th, then 6th, Dist., Cst. Defense System, Norfolk, VA (Apr-Aug 1898); cdr, *Glacier*, Asia.Sta. (Sep 1898-Apr 1899); cdr, *Bennington*, Asia.Sqdn. (Apr 1899-Apr 1901); home and w.o. (Apr-Aug 1901); Navy Yard, NY (Sep-Nov 1901); cdr, schoolship *Enterprise* (Nov 1901-May 1902); home and sick lv. (May-Aug 1902); member, then pres., naval wireless telegraph bd. (Aug 1902-Aug 1903); cdr, rec. ship, *Puritan*, Philadelphia (Aug-Nov 1903); cdr, rec. ship, *Lancaster*, Philadelphia (Nov 1903-Oct 1904); gen insp., *West Virginia*, Newport News, VA (Oct 1904-Feb 1905); cdr, *West Virginia*, Atl.Flt. (Feb 1905-Mar 1907); home and w.o. (Mar-May 1907); Navy Yard, NY (May-Nov 1907); NWC (Nov 1907-Apr 1908); naval exam. and ret. bds., Washington, DC (Apr-Sep 1908); cdr, 3rd Sqdn., Atl.Flt., *Dolphin* (Sep-Nov 1908), then *Maine* (Nov 1908-May 1909); home and w.o. (May-Jun 1909); pres., naval exam. and ret. bds., Washington, DC (Jun 1909-Nov 1910); placed on Ret.Lst. (14 Nov 1910).

PETER CHRISTIAN ASSERSON Born on Egersund Island, Norway, on 5 Jan 1837, son of Asser Johannsen and Malen (Midbrod) Asserson. Served in merchant ships from 1853-59, when he emigrated to the U.S. Served in cst.surv. from 1859-60. Studied engineering at Cooper Union and by private tutors. Became naturalized citizen in Jun 1871. Married Mary Ann Wilson on 30 Aug 1864. Eight children, including Capt William

PETER CHRISTIAN ASSERSON
1837-1906

Christian Asserson, USN, and Dr. Frederick Asser Asserson, USN. One daughter, Malena, married RAdm William Bartlett Fletcher, USN (1862-1957), and another, Ane Gertrude, married LtCol William Francis Spicer, USMC. Died at his home in Brooklyn, NY, on 6 Dec 1906. Buried at the USNA Cemetery.

Ranks Master's Mate (27 May 1862); Act.Ens (26 Nov 1862); discharged (28 Feb 1869); Civil Engr. (6 Mar 1874); Civil Engr. with rel. rank of Capt (16 Feb 1882); placed on Ret.Lst. as Civil Engr. with rank of RAdm (5 Jan 1901).

Career Summary Enlisted in volunteer navy (27 May 1862); Navy Yard, NY (May-Aug 1862); *Vixen*, S.Atl.Blk.Sqdn. (Aug-Nov 1862); *Patroon*, S.Atl.Blk.Sqdn. (Nov 1862); *Wamsutta*, S.Atl.Blk.Sqdn. (Nov 1862-Sep 1863); cdr, *Zouave*, N.Atl.Blk.Sqdn. (Sep 1863-Jun 1865); *Florida*, Gulf Sqdn. (Jun 1865-Jan 1866); l.o.a. (Jan-Mar 1866); Navy Yard, Norfolk, VA (Mar 1866-Aug 1868); cst.surv. duty (Aug 1868-Feb 1869); discharged (28 Feb 1869); received appointment from VA as civil engr. (6 Mar 1874); Navy Yard, Norfolk, VA (Mar 1874-Feb 1885); Bur. of Yards and Docks, Washington, DC (Feb-Apr 1885); Navy Yard, Norfolk, VA (Apr-May 1885); Navy Yard, NY (May 1885-Jul 1895); Navy Yard, Norfolk, VA (Aug 1895-Jun 1898); Navy Yard, NY (Jul 1898-Jan 1901); placed on Ret.Lst. (5 Jan 1901).

RALPH ASTON Born in Middletown, CT, on 31 Jan 1841, son of Henry Hungerford and Ann (Sheppard) Aston. Educated at the Chase Seminary and by private tutors. Married Jennie R. Prestwich in Oct 1869. She died in 1876. Married Salena Hinman on 26 Oct 1882. Two sons and a daughter. Resided in Brooklyn, NY, where he died on 12 Dec 1904 and where he was buried.

Ranks 3rd Asst.Engr. (9 Dec 1861); 2nd Asst.Engr. (8 Sep 1863); 1st Asst.Engr. (1 Jan 1868); title changed to PAsst.Engr. (24 Feb 1874); Chief Engr. (28 Jul 1888); Chief Engr. with rel. rank of Cdr (14 Dec 1896); Chief Engr. with rel. rank of Capt (28 Feb 1899); Capt (3 Mar 1899); retired with rank of RAdm (20 Jan 1902).

Career Summary Received appointment from CT (9 Dec 1861); *Cayuga*, W.Gulf Blk.Sqdn. (Dec 1861-Oct 1864); sick lv. and w.o. (Oct 1864-Jan 1866); *Ashuelot*, Asia.Sqdn. (Jan 1866-Aug 1869); home and w.o. (Aug 1869-Nov 1870); *Terror*, N.Atl.Sqdn. (Nov 1870-Aug 1872); *Omaha*, S.Pac.Sta. (Aug 1872-Jul 1875); w.o. (Jul-Sep 1875); Naval Rndv., NY (Sep 1875-Jul 1876); w.o. (Jun 1876-Sep 1877); temp. duty, NY (Sep 1877-Dec 1878); cst.surv. duty (Dec 1878-Mar 1882); w.o. (Mar-Jun 1882); in charge of machinery, *Intrepid*, NY (Jun-Sep 1882); w.o. (Sep-Oct 1882); l.o.a. (Oct 1882-Oct 1883); w.o. (Oct 1883-May 1884); spec. duty, Bristol, RI (May 1884-Apr 1885); *Kearsarge*, Eur.Sta. (Jun 1885-Nov 1886); w.o. (Nov 1886-Mar 1887); *Ossipee*, N.Atl.Sta. (Mar 1887-Jun 1888); w.o. (Jun-Jul 1888); *Terror*, NY (Aug 1888); w.o. (Aug-Nov 1888); insp. of machinery, *Bennington*, Chester, PA (Nov 1888-Jun 1889); Delaware River Shipbuilding and Iron Works, Chester, PA

(Jun 1889-Jan 1891); *Bennington*, S.Atl. and Eur.Stas. (Jan 1891-Aug 1894); home and w.o. (Aug-Nov 1894); inspection duty, Continental Iron Works, Brooklyn, NY (Nov 1894-Aug 1897); *Cincinnati*, S. and N.Atl.Stas. (Aug 1897-Nov 1898); *Brooklyn*, N.Atl.Sta. (Dec 1898-Apr 1899); home and w.o. (Apr-May 1899); insp. of machinery, Brooklyn, NY (Jun 1899-Jan 1902); retired (20 Jan 1902).

JOSEPH GERRISH AYRES Born in Canterbury, NH, on 3 Nov 1839, son of Charles H. and Almira S. (Gerrish) Ayres. Educated at Univ. of VT and at Columbia Univ. Married Olinda A. Austin on 11 Jul 1884. Two sons. Died in Montclair, NJ, on 21 Mar 1922. Buried in Canterbury, NH.

Ranks Act.Asst.Surg. (17 Dec 1864); Asst.Surg. (8 Oct 1866); PAsst. Surg. (12 Oct 1869); Surg. (7 Jan 1878); Medl.Insp. (25 Feb 1895); Medl.Dir. (12 Dec 1898); placed on Ret.Lst. with rank of RAdm. (3 Nov 1901).

Career Summary 2nd, then 1st Lt., 15th NH Volunteers (11 Oct 1862-13 Aug 1863); act.asst.surg., USA (Jun-Oct 1864); received appointment from NH as act.asst.surg. (17 Dec 1864); rec. ship, *Ohio*, Boston (Dec 1864); *Kennebec* and *Port Royal*, W.Gulf Blk.Sqdn. and Gulf Sqdn. (Jan 1865-May 1866); w.o. (May-Jul 1866); l.o.a. (Jul-Sep 1866); discharged from volunteer serv. (24 Sep 1866); received appointment from NH as asst.surg. (8 Oct 1866); w.o. (Oct-Nov 1866); USNA (Nov 1866-Feb 1868); flgs., *Wampanoag*, N.Atl.Sqdn. (Feb-Mar 1868); flgs., *Contoocook*, and *Penobscot*, N.Atl.Sqdn. (Mar 1868-Jun 1869); w.o. (Jun-Jul 1869); Navy Yard, Washington, DC (Jul-Sep 1869); Naval Hosp., Washington, DC (Oct 1869-Sep 1870); *Resaca*, Pac.Sqdn. (Oct 1870-Nov 1872); spec. duty, Washington, DC (Dec 1872-Jun 1873); *Saco*, Asia.Sqdn. (Jul 1873-Apr 1876); Naval Hosp., Yokohama, Japan (Apr-Nov 1876); flgs., *Tennessee*, Asia.Sqdn. (Nov 1876-Jan 1877); *Ashuelot*, Pac.Sta. (Jan 1877-Jan 1878); return and w.o. (Jan-Mar 1878); rec. ship, *Colorado*, NY (Apr-Nov 1878); Naval Laboratory, NY (Nov 1878-Feb 1881); rec. ship, *Franklin*, Norfolk, VA (Feb-May 1881); prac. ship, *Constellation* (May-Aug 1881); l.o.a. and w.o. (Sep 1881-Jan 1882); *Adams*, Pac.Sta. (Mar 1882-Sep 1884); l.o.a. and w.o. (Sep 1884-Mar 1885); Naval Laboratory, NY (Mar-Apr 1885); Torp.Sta., Newport, RI (Apr 1885-Oct 1887); w.o. (Oct-Nov 1887); flgs., *Galena*, N.Atl.Sta. (Nov 1887-Nov 1890); rec. ship, *Wabash*, Boston (Nov 1890-Sep 1891); Navy Yard, Portsmouth, NH (Sep 1891-Nov 1894); w.o. (Nov 1894-Feb 1895); *Olympia*, Asia.Sqdn. (Feb 1895-Sep 1897); flt.surg., Asia.Sqdn., *Olympia* (Dec 1895-Sep 1897); home and l.o.a. (Sep 1897-Jan 1898); Navy Yard and Hosp., Portsmouth, NH (Jan-May 1898); in charge, Naval Hosp., Boston (May 1898-Oct 1901); w.o. (Oct-Nov 1901); placed on Ret.Lst. (3 Nov 1901).

SAMUEL LORING PERCIVAL AYRES Born on 29 Jul 1835 in Stamford, CT, son of Dr. Chauncey and Deborah Ann (Percival) Ayres. Married Almira J. Stonaker on 17 Aug 1867.

JOSEPH GERRISH AYRES
1839-1922

Later married to Mrs. Ellis Jackson Ayres. Two sons. Died in Philadelphia on 29 Apr 1917 and buried in West Laurel Hill Cemetery.

Ranks 3rd Asst.Engr. (21 Jul 1858); 2nd Asst.Engr. (17 Jan 1861); 1st Asst.Engr. (21 Apr 1863); Chief Engr. (21 Mar 1870); Chief Engr. with rel. rank of Cdr (30 Jun 1887); Chief Engr. with rel. rank of Capt (13 Jul 1894); Placed on Ret.Lst. (29 Jul 1897); Chief Engr. with rank of RAdm on Ret.Lst. (29 Jun 1906).

Career Summary Received appointment from CT (21 Jul 1858); flgs., *Roanoke,* Home Sqdn. (Aug 1858-Sep 1860); spec. duty, Navy Yard, NY (Sep 1860-Feb 1861); *Michigan,* on Great Lakes (Mar-Aug 1861); *Pensacola,* W.Gulf Blk.Sqdn. (Aug 1861-Jun 1863); w.o. (Jun-Aug 1863); *Nipsic* and *Juniata,* S.Atl.Blk. and S.Atl.Sqdns. (Aug 1863-Jun 1867); w.o. (Jun-Aug 1867); spec. duty, Navy Yard, Portsmouth, NH (Aug 1867-Oct 1869); *Benicia,* on trials (Oct 1869); Navy Yard, Portsmouth, NH (Oct 1869-Jun 1870); w.o. (Jun-Jul 1870); *Shenandoah,* Eur.Sqdn. (Aug 1870-Aug 1873); home and w.o. (Aug-Oct 1873); in charge of stores and insp. of machinery, Navy Yard, Norfolk, VA (Oct 1873-Oct 1874); member, engr.exam.bd., Philadelphia and NY (Oct 1874-Feb 1876); *Brooklyn,* N.Atl.Sta. (Feb-Jul 1876); w.o. (Jul-Dec 1876); *Alliance,* Eur.Sta. (Dec 1876-Jan 1880); w.o. (Jan-Feb 1880); member, engr.exam.bd., Philadelphia (Feb 1880-Dec 1884); spec. duty, insp. of machinery, Chester, PA (Jan-Oct 1885); *Brooklyn,* Asia.Sqdn. (Oct 1885-Jun 1887); flt. engr., Asia. Sta., *Brooklyn* (Jun 1887-May 1889); insp., Columbia Iron Works, Baltimore, and William Cramp and Sons Iron Works, Philadelphia (Jun-Oct 1889); member, engr.exam.bd., Philadelphia (Oct 1889-Jun 1891); Navy Yard, NY (Jun 1891-Aug 1895); member, then pres., engr.exam.bd., Philadelphia (Aug 1895-Jul 1897); placed on Ret.Lst. (29 Jul 1897); duty with Interior Cst. Defense System (Jun 1898); inspection duty, Bur. of Steam Engineering, Nicetown, PA (Jun 1898-Jan 1899).

JOHN HOSEA BABIN
1842-1907

JOHN HOSEA BABIN Born in Canada on 15 Dec 1842. Emigrated to MA. Married. Died on 25 Oct 1907 in Brooklyn, NY. Buried at Jersey City, NJ.

Ranks Act.Asst.Surg. (10 Feb 1865); Asst.Surg. (13 May 1865); PAsst.Surg. (23 Jun 1869); Surg. (17 Mar 1876); Medl. Insp. (22 Jun 1894); Medl.Dir. (7 May 1898); transferred to Ret.Lst. with rank of RAdm (15 Dec 1904).

Career Summary Received appointment from MA (10 Feb 1865); rec. ship, *Ohio,* Boston (Feb-Mar 1865); *Mercedita,* W.Gulf Blk.Sqdn. (Mar-May 1865); received appointment from MA as asst.surg. (13 May 1865); Navy Yard, Washington (May 1865); prac. ship, *Marblehead* (Jun-Sep 1865); w.o. (Sep-Oct 1865); spec.serv., *Stonewall* (Oct-Dec 1865); w.o. (Dec 1865-Feb 1866); rec. ship, *Vermont,* NY (Feb-Mar 1866); *Paul Jones,* Gulf Sqdn. (Mar 1866-May 1867); w.o. (May-Jun 1867); prac. ship, *Sabine* (Jun 1867-May 1868); w.o. (May 1868-Feb 1869); rec. ship, *Potomac,* League Island, PA (Feb-Aug 1869); flgs., *Severn,* N.Atl.Sqdn. (Aug 1869-Aug 1871); w.o. (Aug-Oct 1871); Navy

Yard, Boston (Oct 1871-Jun 1872); spec. recruiting duty, NY (Jun-Sep 1872); flgs., *Hartford*, Asia.Sqdn. (Oct 1872-Oct 1875); w.o. (Oct-Dec 1875); rec. ship, *Colorado*, NY (Dec 1875-May 1876); w.o. (May-Sep 1876); MB, Brooklyn, NY (Sep 1876-Dec 1879); *Marion*, S.Atl.Sta. (Dec 1879-Dec 1882); w.o. (Dec 1882-Apr 1883); Marine Rndv., NY (Apr 1883-Jun 1884); training ship, *Minnesota* (Jun-Aug 1884); Marine Rndv., NY (Aug 1884-Feb 1886); flgs., *Vandalia* and *Mohican*, Pac.Sta. (Feb 1886-Mar 1889); return and w.o. (Mar-Sep 1889); rec. ship, *Vermont*, NY (Sep 1889-Apr 1893); w.o. (Apr-May 1893); spec. duty, USNA (May 1893); w.o. (May-Jul 1893); Naval Sta., Port Royal, SC (Aug-Sep 1893); w.o. (Sep 1893-Jan 1894); spec. duty, and member, bd. of inspection and surv. (Jan-Jul 1894); *San Francisco*, Eur.Sta. (Jul 1894-Jun 1897); flt.surg., Eur.Sta., *San Francisco* (Feb 1895-Jun 1897); home and l.o.a. (Jun-Aug 1897); bd. duties (Sep 1897-Jul 1900); in charge, Naval Hosp., NY (Aug 1900-Dec 1904); transferred to Ret.Lst. (15 Dec 1904).

ALBERT WILLIAMSON BACON Born in Philadelphia on 5 Jan 1841, son of James Ware and Alice Ann (Riggs) Bacon. Educated in private and public schools in Frankfort, KY, and in Philadelphia. Married Kate S. Stoughton on 23 Jan 1873. Died on 23 Sep 1922 at Santa Barbara, CA.

Ranks Captain's Clerk (10 Dec 1861); discharged (30 Oct 1862); Act.Asst.Paymstr. (7 Nov 1863); Asst.Paymstr. (23 Jul 1866); PAsst.Paymstr. (1 Aug 1866); Paymstr. (25 Oct 1874); Paymstr. with rel. rank of Cdr (12 Feb 1898); Pay Dir. with rank of Capt (10 Jul 1900); placed on Ret.Lst. with rank of RAdm (5 Jan 1903).

Career Summary Captain's clerk, *Horace Beals*, Gulf Blk.Sqdn. (Dec 1861-Oct 1862); discharged (30 Oct 1862); received appointment from PA (7 Nov 1863); *Galatea*, W.Ind.Sqdn. (Nov 1863-Jul 1865); s.a. and w.o. (Jul-Dec 1865); *Yantic*, Atl.Sqdn. (Dec 1865-Sep 1866); s.a. and w.o. (Sep-Dec 1866); *Aroostook*, Philadelphia (Dec 1866); *Marblehead*, N.Atl.Sqdn. (Dec 1866-Aug 1867); s.a. and w.o. (Aug 1867-Mar 1868); Bur. of Provisions and Clothing, Washington, DC (Mar-Dec 1868); *Portsmouth*, S.Atl.Sqdn. (Dec 1868-Nov 1871); s.a. and w.o. (Nov 1871-Jan 1872); Bur. of Provisions and Clothing, Washington, DC (Jan 1872-Jan 1873); temp. duty, purchasing paymstr., Washington, DC (Jun-Sep 1872); naval storekeeper, Rio de Janeiro, Brazil (Apr 1873-Mar 1876); s.a. and w.o. (Mar-May 1876); Bur. of Provisions and Clothing, Washington, DC (Jun 1876-Oct 1877); w.o. (Oct 1877-Jan 1878); Navy Yard, Washington, DC (Feb 1878-May 1879); naval storekeeper, Rio de Janeiro, Brazil (Aug 1879-May 1880); return, s.a., and w.o. (May-Nov 1880); spec. duty, Washington, DC (Nov 1880-May 1881); l.o.a. (May-Oct 1881); in charge of stores, Villefranche, France (Jan 1882-Oct 1883); return, s.a., and w.o. (Oct 1883-Mar 1885); *Omaha*, Philadelphia (Mar 1885); w.o. (Mar 1885-May 1886); *Atlanta*, N.Atl.Sqdn. (Jul 1886-Nov 1888); s.a. and w.o. (Dec 1888-Mar 1889); member, naval exam. bd., Washington, DC (Mar-Apr

1889); paymstr., Navy Yard, Washington, DC (May 1889-Jan 1893); general storekeeper, Navy Yard, Mare Island, CA (Jan 1893-Apr 1895); *Olympia*, Asia.Sqdn. (Feb-Nov 1895); flt.paymstr., Asia.Flt., *Olympia* (Nov 1895-Jan 1897); general storekeeper, Navy Yard, Mare Island, CA (Feb 1897-Dec 1902); s.a. and w.o. (Dec 1902-Jan 1903); placed on Ret.Lst. (5 Jan 1903).

CHARLES JOHNSTON BADGER
1853-1932

CHARLES JOHNSTON BADGER Born in Rockville, MD, on 6 Aug 1853, son of navy Commo Oscar Charles and Margaret M. (Johnston) Badger. Married Sophia Jane Champlin on 4 Oct 1882. One son, VAdm Oscar Charles Badger, USN (1890-1958), and one daughter, Mrs. Henry F. Bryant, wife of RAdm Henry F. Bryant, USN. Died at Blue Ridge Summit, PA, on 8 Sep 1932. Buried at Arlington National Cemetery.

Ranks Midn (24 Jun 1869); title changed to Cadet Midn (15 Jul 1870); Midn (31 May 1873); Ens (16 Jul 1874); Mstr (1 Nov 1879); title changed to Ltjg (3 Mar 1883); Lt (5 Jan 1886); LCdr (3 Mar 1899); Cdr (18 Jun 1902); Capt (1 Jul 1907); RAdm (8 Mar 1911); placed on Ret.Lst. (6 Aug 1915).

Career Summary Received appointment at large (24 Jun 1869); USNA (Jun 1869-May 1873); w.o. (May-Aug 1873); *Narragansett*, spec.serv. (Sep 1873-Jul 1875); w.o. (Jul-Oct 1875); Navy Yard, Washington, DC (Oct 1875-Jan 1876); *Alarm*, spec.serv. (Jan-Jul 1876); w.o. (Jul-Aug 1876); *Ashuelot*, *Alert*, *Monocacy*, and *Monongahela*, Asia.Sta. (Sep 1876-Nov 1879); w.o. (Nov-Dec 1879); Bur. of Nav., Washington, DC (Dec 1879-Apr 1880); cst.surv. duty (Apr 1880-Aug 1881); w.o. (Aug-Sep 1881); *Yantic*, N.Atl.Sta. (Sep 1881-Sep 1882); w.o. (Sep-Oct 1882); Navy Yard, Boston (Oct 1882-Jan 1884); Fish Commission steamer *Fish Hawk* (Jan-Mar 1884); Hydrographic Office, Washington, DC (Mar 1884); w.o. (Mar-Apr 1884); exec.off., *Alert*, Greely Relief Expd. (Apr-Nov 1884); ord. instruction, Navy Yard, Washington, DC (Nov 1884-Apr 1885); *Tennessee*, Isthmus of Panama (Apr-May 1885); Navy Yard, Washington, DC (May 1885); l.o.a. (May-Oct 1885); *Brooklyn*, Asia.Sta. (Oct 1885-May 1889); w.o. (May-Aug 1889); ord. duty, Navy Yard, Washington, DC (Aug 1889-Nov 1892); flgs., *Chicago*, Sqdn. of Evol. (Nov 1892-Feb 1893); *Dolphin*, Sqdn. of Evol. (Mar 1893-Oct 1895); Navy Yard, Washington, DC (Oct 1895-June 1897); NWC (Jun-Aug 1897); *Cincinnati*, S.Atl.Sta. (Aug 1897-Feb 1899); insp. of equip., *Kentucky*, NY (Feb 1899-Sep 1899); *Alabama*, on trials (Sep 1899-Oct 1900); exec.off., *Alabama*, N.Atl.Sta. (Oct 1900-Jun 1902); Bur. of Equip. and Recruiting, Washington, DC (Jun 1902-Apr 1903); comdt. of midshipmen, USNA (Apr 1903-May 1905); cdr, training ship, *Newark* (May-Sep 1905); cdr, flgs., *Chicago*, Pac.Flt. (Oct 1905-Dec 1906); home and w.o. (Dec 1906-Jan 1907); Bur. of Equip. and Recruiting, Washington, DC (Feb-Apr 1907); Bur. of Nav., Washington, DC (Apr-May 1907); asst. to chief, Bur. of Nav., Washington, DC (May-Jul 1907); supt., USNA (Jul 1907-Jun 1909); cdr, *Kansas*, 2nd Battleship Div., Atl.Flt. (Jun 1909-Apr 1911); temp. duty, Navy Dept.,

Washington, DC (Apr 1911); cdr, 2nd Battleship Div., Atl.Flt., *Louisiana* (May-Dec 1911); aide for inspection, Navy Dept., Washington, DC (Dec 1911-Jan 1913); cdr, Atl.Flt., *Wyoming*, (Jan-Mar 1913), *Connecticut* (Mar 1913-Apr 1914), *Arkansas* (Apr-May 1914), and *Wyoming* (May-Sep 1914); member, Gen Bd., Washington, DC (Sep 1914-Aug 1915); additional duty, member, Army-Navy Joint Bd., Washington, DC (Sep 1914-Aug 1915); placed on Ret.Lst. (6 Aug 1915); chairman, Gen Bd., Washington, DC (Aug 1915-Feb 1921).

Career Highlights Served on Greely Relief Expd. in 1884. Received Distinguished Service Medal on 11 Nov 1920 for service as chairman of Gen Bd. during World War I.

FRANK HARVEY BAILEY Born in Elk Creek, PA, on 29 Jun 1851, son of James and Sarah Ann (Hurd) Bailey. Received B.S. degree from Scio College, OH, in 1873. Married Anna J. Markham on 28 Dec 1881. Died in El Paso, TX, on 9 Apr 1921.

Ranks Cadet Engr. (1 Oct 1873); Asst.Engr. (1 Jul 1877); PAsst.Engr. (7 Oct 1884); PAsst.Engr with rel. rank of Ltjg (1 Oct 1893); Chief Engr. (27 Jun 1896); rank changed to LCdr (3 Mar 1899); Cdr (24 Aug 1904); Capt (1 Jul 1908); RAdm (13 Feb 1913); placed on Ret.Lst. (29 Jun 1913).

Career Summary Received appointment from NY (1 Oct 1873); USNA (Oct 1873-Jun 1875); w.o. (Jun-Sep 1875); *Alert*, Asia.Sqdn. (Sep 1875-Sep 1878); home and w.o. (Sep 1878-Jan 1879); spec. duty, Morgan Iron Works, NY (Jan-Sep 1879); w.o. (Sep-Oct 1879); *Constellation*, spec. cruise (Oct-Dec 1879); *Trenton*, Eur.Sqdn. (Dec 1879-Oct 1881); w.o. (Oct-Nov 1881); l.o.a. (Nov 1881-Mar 1882); *Iroquois*, Pac.Sta. (Mar 1882-May 1885); return and l.o.a. (May-Aug 1885); spec. duty, inst. of marine engineering, Cornell Univ., Ithaca, NY (Aug 1885-Aug 1888); w.o. (Aug-Oct 1888); USNA (Oct 1888-Jan 1889); *Chicago*, Sqdn. of Evol. (Jan 1889-Oct 1891); Bur. of Steam Engineering, Washington, DC (Oct 1891-Aug 1896); *Newark*, N.Atl.Sta. (Aug 1896-Mar 1897); *Raleigh*, Asia.Sta. (Mar 1897-Dec 1898); *Baltimore*, on trials (Dec 1898-May 1899); flgs., *Olympia*, Asia. Sta. (May-Oct 1899); Bur. of Steam Engineering, Washington, DC (Oct 1899-May 1903); *Brooklyn*, Eur.Flt. (May-Jun 1903); flt.engr., Eur.Flt., *Brooklyn* (Jun 1903-Aug 1904); home and w.o. (Aug-Nov 1904); *Connecticut* and Navy Yard, NY (Nov 1904-Jan 1910); gen insp. of machinery, USN, and senior member, all bds. on changes of machinery on Atl.cst., Philadelphia (Jan 1910-May 1911); insp. of engineering material and ord., Eastern NY and NJ Dists. (May 1911-Jun 1913); placed on Ret.Lst. (29 Jun 1913); in charge, computing dept., Bur. of Steam Engineering, Washington, DC (May 1917-Nov 1918).

Career Highlights Served at Battle of Manila, being advanced three numbers for highly distinguished conduct.

GEORGE WASHINGTON BAIRD Born in Washington, DC, on 22 Apr 1843, son of Matthew and Ophelia (Cauthorn) Baird. Married Lyle Jane Prather in 1873. Died at his home in Washing-

FRANK HARVEY BAILEY
1851-1921

ton, DC, on 4 Oct 1930. Buried in Arlington National Cemetery.

Ranks Act. 3rd Asst.Engr. (19 Sept 1862); 3rd Asst.Engr. (8 Sept 1863); 2nd Asst.Engr. (25 Jul 1866); PAsst.Engr. (17 Jun 1874); Chief Engr. (22 Jun 1892); Chief Engr. with rel. rank of Cdr (11 Oct 1898); Cdr (3 Mar 1899); Capt (2 Dec 1902); transferred to Ret.Lst. with rank of RAdm (22 Apr 1905).

Career Summary Received appointment from Washington, DC (19 Sept 1862); *Calhoun* and *Kensington*, W.Gulf Blk.Sqdn. (Sept 1862-Sept 1863); *Pensacola*, W.Gulf Blk.Sqdn. (Oct 1863-May 1864); Bur. of Steam Engineering, Washington, DC (May 1864-May 1865); *Pensacola*, Navy Yard, NY (May 1865-Apr 1866); *Shamrock*, W.Ind. and Eur.Sqdns. (Apr 1866-Jul 1868); w.o. (Jul-Oct 1868); *Tallapoosa*, Navy Yard, Washington, DC (Oct 1868-Sept 1869); Navy Yard, Mare Island, CA (Sept 1869-Dec 1870); *Pensacola*, Pac.Sqdn. (Dec 1870-Aug 1873); home and w.o. (Aug-Sept 1873); Bur. of Steam Engineering, Washington, DC (Sept 1873-Feb 1877); flgs., *Trenton*, Eur.Sqdn. (Feb-Nov 1877); *Vandalia*, Eur.Sqdn. (Nov 1877-Feb 1880); w.o. (Feb-Mar 1880); in charge of machinery, *Montauk*, Philadelphia (Mar 1880-Oct 1881); in charge of machinery, *Passaic*, Philadelphia (Jul-Oct 1881); temp. duty, *Standish*, Philadelphia (Oct 1881); *Montauk* and *Passaic*, Philadelphia (Oct 1881-Jun 1882); superintending engr., Fish Commission (Jun-Nov 1882); act.chief engr., Fish Commission steamer, *Albatross* (Nov 1882-Oct 1887); spec. duty, War and Navy Building, Washington, DC (Oct 1887-Mar 1892); *Dolphin*, Sqdn. of Evol. (Mar 1892-Jul 1895); temp. duty, Dept. of Interior, Washington, DC (Jul-Aug 1895); spec. duty, War and Navy Building, Washington, DC (Jul 1895-Jan 1906); chief engr., Navy Yard, Washington, DC (Apr 1898-Jan 1906); transferred to Ret.Lst. (22 Apr 1905).

References

Writings: a) "The U.S. Ship *Trenton*," U.S. Naval Institute *Proceedings* 4 (1877): 5-20; 9 (1879): 443-47. b) "The Ventilation of Ships," U.S. Naval Institute *Proceedings* 13 (1880): 237-63; 14 (1880): 348.

GEORGE HOLCOMB BARBER Born on 15 Nov 1864 in Glastonbury, CT, son of Ralph and Mary Henrietta (Holcomb) Barber. Received two B.S. degrees in 1885, one from MA Agricultural College, the other from Boston Univ. In 1888, received medl. degree from the College of Physicians and Surgeons (Columbia Univ.). Remained unmarried. Died in San Francisco on 23 Aug 1926.

Ranks Asst.Surg. (23 May 1889); PAsst.Surg. (5 Mar 1897); PAsst.Surg. with rank of Lt (3 Mar 1899); Surg. (7 Jun 1900); Surg. with rank of LCdr (3 Mar 1903); Medl.Insp. (17 Sep 1911); Medl.Dir. with rank of Capt (2 Oct 1916); Medl.Dir. with rank of RAdm (15 Oct 1917); died (23 Aug 1926).

Career Summary Received appointment from CT (23 May 1889); rec. ship, *Vermont*, NY (Jun 1889-Aug 1890); *Pensacola*, en route to Pac. (Aug 1890); flgs., *Charleston*, Pac., then Asia.Sqdns. (Aug 1890-Feb 1892); rec. ship, *Minnesota*, NY

(Feb-Jul 1892); Naval Hosp., NY (Jul 1892-Feb 1893); *Miantonomoh*, NY (Feb-Jun 1893); cst.surv. duty (Jul 1893-Dec 1895); *New York*, Eur.Sqdn. (Dec 1895-Aug 1896); USNA (Sep 1896-Jun 1898); Naval Hosp., Philadelphia (Jun-Jul 1898); *Glacier*, N.Atl.Flt. (Jul 1898-Mar 1899); USNA (Mar 1899-May 1900); *Monongahela*, Atl. Training Sqdn. (May 1900-Apr 1903); Training Sta., Newport, RI (May 1903-Feb 1905); flgs., *Ohio*, Asia.Sta. (Mar 1905-Jan 1906); *Wisconsin*, Asia.Sta. (Jan-Aug 1906); *Ohio*, Asia.Sta. (Aug-Dec 1906); *Baltimore*, Asia.Sta. (Dec 1906-May 1907); *Kearsarge*, spec.serv., "Great White Flt." (May-Dec 1907); Naval Hosp., Boston (Dec 1907-Apr 1908); Naval Medl. School, Washington, DC (Apr-Jun 1908); Naval Hosp., Boston (Jun 1908-Mar 1910); cdr, Naval Hosp., Olongapo, P.I. (Apr 1910-Jun 1912); additional duty as senior medl.off., Naval Sta., Olongapo, P.I. (Sep 1910-Jun 1912); home and w.o. (Jun-Oct 1912); Marine Recruiting Sta., Boston (Oct-Nov 1912); medl.off. in command of Naval Hosp., Las Animas (Ft. Lyon), CO (Dec 1912-May 1920); temp. duty, Training Sta., Great Lakes, IL (Apr 1917); temp. duty, Washington, DC (Apr-May 1917); w.o. (May-Aug 1920); spec. duty, Bur. of Medicine and Surgery, Navy Dept., Washington, DC (Aug-Nov 1920); medl.off. in command of Naval Hosp., and of Naval Medl. Supply Depot, Canacos, P.I., and insp., medl. dept. activities, Asia.Sta. (Jan 1921-Aug 1923); insp. of medl. dept. activities, 12th Naval Dist., San Francisco (Sep 1923-Aug 1926); died (23 Aug 1926).

CHARLES JAMES BARCLAY Born in Philadelphia on 8 Sep 1843. Married to Annie T. Barclay. Died at his home in Brookline, MA, on 26 Sep 1909. Buried in a rural cemetery in New Bedford, MA.

Ranks Act.Midn (21 Sep 1860); title changed to Midn (16 Jul 1862); Act.Ens (1 Oct 1863); Ens (21 Dec 1865); Mstr (10 May 1866); Lt (21 Feb 1867); LCdr (12 Mar 1868); Cdr (25 Nov 1881); Capt (1 Oct 1896); RAdm (11 Sep 1903); placed on Ret.Lst. (8 Sep 1905).

Career Summary Received appointment from PA (21 Sep 1860); USNA (Sep 1860-Oct 1863); *Wachusett*, spec. duty, Braz.cst. (Oct 1863-Dec 1864); l.o.a. and w.o. (Dec 1864-Mar 1865); *Kearsarge*, Eur.Sqdn. (Mar 1865-Aug 1866); w.o. (Aug-Oct 1866); *Susquehanna*, spec.serv. (Oct 1866-Jan 1867); w.o. (Jan-May 1867); *Minnesota*, spec.serv. (Jun 1867-Jan 1868); w.o. (Jan-Mar 1868); *Michigan*, on Great Lakes (Apr 1868-Jun 1869); *Resaca*, Pac.Sqdn. (Sep 1869-Jan 1872); w.o. (Feb-Apr 1872); rec. ship, *Sabine*, Portsmouth, NH (Apr-May 1872); ord. duty, Navy Yard, NY (May 1872-Jul 1873); w.o. (Jul-Aug 1873); Torp.Sta., Newport, RI (Sep 1873-Apr 1874); w.o. (Apr-May 1874); exec.off., *Saugus*, N.Atl.Sta. (May-Nov 1874); sick lv. (Nov 1874-Mar 1875); exec.off., *Dictator*, N.Atl.Sta. (Apr 1875-Apr 1876); exec.off., *Saugus*, N.Atl.Sqdn. (Apr-Jul 1876); w.o. (Jul 1876-Mar 1877); l.o.a. (Mar-Aug 1877); cdr, storeship, *Onward*, S.Pac.Sqdn. (Sep 1877-Dec 1879); w.o. and l.o.a. (Dec 1879-Nov 1880); Navy Yard, Portsmouth, NH (Dec 1880-Oct 1882); w.o.

CHARLES JAMES BARCLAY
1843-1909

(Oct 1882-Sep 1883); cdr, *Alert*, Asia.Sta. (Oct 1883-Sep 1886); w.o. and l.o.a. (Sep 1886-Oct 1887); ord.off., Navy Yard, Portsmouth, NH (Oct 1887-Sep 1890); insp., 8th L.h. Dist., New Orleans (Sep 1890-Jan 1891); s.a. and w.o. (Jan-Oct 1891); Navy Yard, Portsmouth, NH (Nov 1891-May 1893); cdr, training ship, *Portsmouth* (May 1893-May 1894); l.o.a. (May-Jul 1894); insp. of ord., Navy Yard, Boston (Jul 1894-Oct 1896); home and w.o. (Oct-Nov 1896); cdr, *Raleigh*, N.Atl.Sqdn. (Jan-Mar 1897); cdr, *Amphitrite*, N.Atl.Sqdn. (Mar 1897-Oct 1899); home and w.o. (Oct 1899-May 1900); NWC (Jun-Oct 1900); w.o. (Oct-Dec 1900); capt.yd., Navy Yard, Boston (Jan 1901-May 1903); comdt., Navy Yard, Bremerton, WA (Jun 1903-Aug 1905); w.o. (Aug-Sep 1905); placed on Ret.Lst. (8 Sep 1905).

WILLIAM JAY BARNETTE Born in Morrisville, NY, on 2 Feb 1847, son of Dr. Milton and Caroline (Shepherd) Barnette. Married Evelyn G. Hutchins on 29 Nov 1877. Died at Naval Medl. Hosp. in Washington D.C. on 19 Apr 1909. Buried at Arlington National Cemetery.

Ranks Midn (26 Jul 1864); Ens (19 Apr 1869); Mstr (12 Jul 1870); Lt (28 Dec 1872); LCdr (16 Apr 1894); Cdr (3 Mar 1899); Capt (11 Oct 1903); RAdm (1 Aug 1908); retired (31 Jan 1909).

Career Summary Received appointment from NY (26 Jul 1864); USNA (Jun 1864-Jun 1868); l.o.a. (Jun-Aug 1868); *Piscataqua* [renamed *Delaware*], Asia.Sta. (Aug 1868-Aug 1869); *Iroquois*, Asia.Sta. (Aug 1869-Apr 1870); home and w.o. (Apr-Jun 1870); signal duty (Jun 1870); sick lv. (Jun-Sep 1870); torp. duty, Newport, RI (Nov 1870-Apr 1871); w.o. (Apr-Sep 1871); flgs., *Wabash*, Eur.Sqdn. (Oct 1871-Apr 1874); home and w.o. (Apr-Jun 1874); l.o.a. (Jun-Sep 1874); Hydrographic Office, Washington, DC (Sep-Dec 1874); Navy Yard, Washington, DC (Dec 1874-Jan 1875); *Benicia*, Mare Island, CA (Jan-Aug 1875); flag lt, N.Pac.Sta., *Pensacola* (Aug 1875-Apr 1878); w.o. (Apr-Jul 1878); USNA (Sep 1878-Sep 1881); training ship, *Saratoga* (Sep 1881-Aug 1884); USNA (Sep 1884-Sep 1888); *Richmond*, N.Atl.Sqdn. (Sep-Dec 1888); *Galena*, N.Atl.Sqdn. (Dec 1888-Jul 1890); l.o.a. (Jul-Aug 1890); rec. ship, *Minnesota*, NY (Sep-Dec 1890); exec.off., schoolship, *St. Mary's* (Dec 1890-Jan 1894); w.o. (Jan-Mar 1894); exec.off., schoolship, *Raleigh*, Navy Yard, Norfolk, VA (Apr 1894-Mar 1897); l.o.a. (Apr-May 1897); cst.surv. duty (Apr 1897-Apr 1898); spec. duty, office of asst. sec., Navy Dept., Washington, DC (Apr-May 1898); cdr, *Dorothea*, N.Atl.Flt. (Jun-Aug 1898); Naval Hosps., Key West, FL, and Portsmouth, NH (Aug 1898); sick lv. (Aug-Oct 1898); cdr, schoolship, *Saratoga* (Oct 1898-Jan 1902); duty with Gen Bd., bd. of examiners, and other duties, Washington, DC (Jan 1902-Jun 1904); member, Army-Navy Joint Bd., Washington, DC (Jul 1903-Jun 1904); cdr, *Kentucky*, N.Atl.Flt. (Jun 1904-Dec 1905); member, Gen Bd. and Army-Navy Joint Bd., Washington, DC (Jan 1906-Dec 1907); supt., Naval Observatory, Washington, DC (Dec 1907-Apr 1909); retired (31 Jan 1909).

WILLIAM JAY BARNETTE
1847-1909

EDWARD BUTTEVANT BARRY Born in NY City on 20 Oct 1849, son of Paymstr. Garrett Robert (USN) and Sarah Agnes (Glover) Barry. Married Mary Wycliff Clitz on 7 Apr 1875. One daughter. Died on 27 Nov 1938 in Baltimore. Buried in Arlington National Cemetery.

Ranks Midn (21 Jul 1865); Ens (12 Jul 1870); Mstr (29 Jan 1872); Lt (6 Apr 1875); LCdr (21 Mar 1897); Cdr (9 Mar 1900); Capt (31 Mar 1905); RAdm (1 Feb 1909); transferred to Ret.Lst. (13 Jan 1911); resigned (27 Jan 1911).

Career Summary Received appointment by virtue of being the son of an officer (21 Jul 1865); USNA (Jul 1865-Jun 1869); *Sabine*, spec. cruise (Jun 1869-Jul 1870); w.o. (Jul-Nov 1870); signal duty, Washington, DC (Nov 1870-Feb 1871); w.o. (Feb 1871); *Worcester*, spec. cruise with supplies to France (Feb-Sep 1871); *Wabash*, then flgs., *Brooklyn*, then *Wachusett*, Eur.Sta. (Oct 1871-Jun 1874); l.o.a. (Jun-Sep 1874); rec. ship, *Vermont*, NY (Sep 1874-Feb 1875); *Roanoke*, NY (Feb-Jun 1875); training ship, *Minnesota* (Jun 1875-Jul 1876); storeship, *New Hampshire*, Port Royal, SC (Jul 1876-Apr 1878); *Alaska*, Pac.Sta. (Apr 1878-Jul 1880); home and w.o. (Jul-Sep 1880); *Richmond* and *Monocacy*, Asia.Sqdn. (Oct 1880-Apr 1883); home and w.o. (Apr-Aug 1883); USNA (Sep 1883-Jun 1886); *Alliance*, S.Atl.Sta. (Jun 1886-Aug 1889); w.o. (Aug-Nov 1889); Bur. of Nav., Washington, DC (Nov 1889-Mar 1891); *Lancaster*, Asia.Sqdn. (Mar 1891-Nov 1892); exec.off., *Marion*, Asia.Sqdn. (Nov 1892-Jul 1894); l.o.a. (Jul-Oct 1894); Office of Naval Intelligence, Washington, DC (Oct 1894-Aug 1897); *Cincinnati*, S.Atl.Sta. (Aug 1897-Feb 1899); exec.off., rec. ship, *Franklin*, Norfolk, VA (Mar-Apr 1899); exec.off., training ship, *Amphitrite* (May 1899-Jan 1900); cdr, *Marcellus*, Atl.Flt. (Jan-May 1900); Navy Yard, Washington, DC (May 1900); NWC (Jun-Aug 1900); cdr, *Vicksburg*, Asia.Sqdn. (Aug 1900-Dec 1902); home and w.o. (Dec 1902-Feb 1903); spec. duty (Feb-Mar 1903); Navy Yard, NY (Apr 1903-Dec 1905); cdr, *Kentucky*, N.Atl.Flt. (Dec 1905-Nov 1907); in charge, Navy Recruiting Sta., NY (Nov-Dec 1907); supervisor, Naval Auxiliaries, Atl.cst., NY (Dec 1907-Apr 1909); cdr, 2nd Div., 1st Sqdn., *West Virginia*, Pac.Flt. (May 1909-Nov 1910); cdr, *West Virginia*, Pac.Flt. (Nov 1910-Jan 1911); transferred to Ret.Lst. (13 Jan 1911); resigned (27 Jan 1911).

References

Writings: translated, Capt Chabaud-Arnault, "The Combats on the Min River," U.S. Naval Institute *Proceedings* 33 (1885): 295-320.

EDWARD BUTTEVANT BARRY
1849-1938

JOHN RUSSELL BARTLETT Born in NY City on 26 Sep 1843, son of John R. and Eliza A. (Rhodes) Bartlett. Early education in Cambridge, MA. Received D.Sc. degree in 1898 from Brown Univ. Married Jeanie R. Jenckes on 6 Feb 1872. Died on 22 Nov 1904 in St. Louis. Buried in Providence, RI.

Ranks Act.Midn (28 Nov 1859); title changed to Midn (16 Jul 1862); Ens (22 Jul 1863); Lt (22 Feb 1864); LCdr (25 Jul 1866); Cdr (25 Apr 1877); Capt (1 Jul 1892); transferred to Ret.Lst. (12

JOHN RUSSELL BARTLETT
1843-1904

Jul 1897); RAdm on Ret.Lst. (9 Feb 1903).

Career Summary Received appointment from RI (28 Nov 1859); USNA (Nov 1859-Dec 1861); *Brooklyn,* W.Gulf Blk.Sqdn. (Dec 1861-May 1863); USNA (May-Jul 1863); *Brooklyn,* S.Atl. Blk.Sqdn. (Aug 1863-Jun 1864); *New Ironsides,* N.Atl.Blk.Sqdn. (Jun-Jul 1864); *Susquehanna* and *Nipsic,* N.Atl.Blk.Sta. and spec.serv. (Jul 1864-Oct 1867); w.o. (Oct-Dec 1867); USNA (Dec 1867-May 1869); *Sabine,* spec. cruise (May 1869-Jul 1870); w.o. (Jul-Sep 1870); Tehuantepec and Nicaraguan Surv.Expd. (Sep 1870-Aug 1871); in charge, Tehuantepec and Nicaraguan Surv.Expd. (Aug 1871-Feb 1872); l.o.a. (Feb-Nov 1872); ord. duty, Navy Yard, Boston (Nov 1872-Oct 1874); l.o.a. (Oct 1874-Mar 1876); Hydrographic Office, Washington, DC (Mar 1876-Oct 1877); Bur. of Equip. and Recruiting, Washington, DC (Oct 1877-Oct 1878); cst.surv. duty (Oct 1878-Oct 1882); Hydrographic Office, Washington, DC (Nov 1882-Jun 1883); in charge, Naval Hydrographic Office, Washington, DC (Jun 1883-Jun 1888); l.o.a. and w.o. (Jun 1888-Mar 1891); cdr, *Marion,* Asia.Sqdn. (Apr 1891-Jul 1892); w.o. (Aug-Dec 1892); cdr, *Minnesota,* spec. duty (Jan-May 1893); cdr, *Atlanta,* N. Atl.Sqdn. (May-Jul 1893); w.o. and l.o.a. (Jul 1893-Mar 1894); cdr, *Atlanta,* N.Atl.Sqdn. (Apr-Dec 1894); sick lv. (Dec 1894-Jun 1895); spec. duty, NWC (Jul-Nov 1895); member, L.h. Bd., Washington, DC (Nov 1895-Dec 1896); cdr, *Puritan,* Chester, PA (Dec 1896-Jul 1897); transferred to Ret.Lst. (12 Jul 1897); in charge, Office of Naval Intelligence, Washington, DC (Apr-Oct 1898); supt., U.S. Cst. Signal Serv., Washington, DC (May-Oct 1898); Chief, U.S. Auxiliary Naval Force (Jul-Oct 1898); Bur. of Nav., Washington, DC (Apr 1901-May 1902).

References

Writings: "The Recent Investigations of the Gulf Stream by the U.S. Coast and Geodetic Steamer *Blake,*" U.S. Naval Institute *Proceedings* 15 (1881): 25-39; 20 (1882): 221-31.

JOHN KENNEDY BARTON
1853-1921

JOHN KENNEDY BARTON Born in Philadelphia on 7 Apr 1853, son of Joseph and Margaret Barton. Married Mildred S. Scott in 1898. At least one son. Died on 23 Dec 1921 at Philadelphia Naval Hosp. Buried in Westminster Cemetery in Philadelphia.

Ranks Cadet Engr. (1 Oct 1871); 2nd.Asst.Engr. (23 Jan 1874); Asst.Engr. (24 Feb 1874); PAsst. Engr. with rel. rank of Ltjg (1 Nov 1879); PAsst.Engr. with rel. rank of Lt (7 Jan 1890); Chief Engr. (15 Jan 1895); rank changed to LCdr (3 Mar 1899); Cdr (4 Jan 1903); Capt (8 Jul 1907); Chief Engr. with rank of RAdm (10 Dec 1908); transferred to Ret.Lst. (10 Dec 1908).

Career Summary Received appointment from PA (1 Oct 1871); USNA (Oct 1871-May 1873); w.o. (May-Jul 1873); *Benicia,* N.Pac.Sqdn. (Jul 1873-Dec 1874); home and w.o. (Dec 1874-Feb 1875); l.o.a. (Feb-Jun 1875); spec. duty, Chester, PA (Jun-Nov 1875); *Marion,* N.Atl. and Eur.Stas. (Dec 1875-May 1878); return and w.o. (May-Sep 1878); spec. duty, engr. exam.bd., Philadelphia (Sep 1878-Aug 1879); *Shenandoah,*

S.Atl.Sta. (Sep 1879-May 1882); w.o. (May-Aug 1882); inst., USNA (Sep 1882-Jun 1886); *Essex*, Asia.Sta. (Jul 1886-Oct 1887); *Palos*, Asia.Sta. (Oct 1887-Nov 1888); *Essex*, Asia.Sqdn. and en route home (Nov 1888-May 1889); w.o. (May-Jul 1889); inst., USNA (Jul 1889-Jun 1893); insp. of machinery, *Castine*, Bath Iron Works, Bath, ME (Jul-Nov 1894); spec. duty, *Columbia*, William Cramp and Sons Iron Works, Philadelphia (Mar-Apr 1894); *Columbia*, N.Atl.Sta. (Apr 1894-Mar 1895); *Mohican*, Pac.Sta. (Mar-May 1895); *Bennington*, Pac.Sta. (May 1895-May 1897); member, trial bd., *Oregon*, San Francisco (May-Jul 1897); member and recorder, engr.exam.bd., Philadelphia (Jul 1897-Oct 1898); additional duty, rec. ship, *Richmond*, League Island, PA (Mar-Jun 1898); chief engr., Navy Yard, Boston (Oct 1898-Mar 1900); training ship, *Pensacola* (Mar-Apr 1900); *Newark*, Asia.Sta. (Apr-Dec 1900); Naval Hosp., Yokohama, Japan (Dec 1900-Apr 1901); flt.engr., Asia.Sta., *Brooklyn* (Apr 1901-Mar 1902); *Brooklyn*, Asia.Sta. (Mar-Aug 1902); USNA (Aug 1902-Jun 1907); head, dept. of steam engineering, Navy Yard, League Island, PA (Jun 1907-Jun 1908); engr.-in-chief and chief, Bur. of Steam Engineering, Washington, DC (Jun-Dec 1908); transferred to Ret.Lst. (22 Dec 1908); member, naval exam. bd., Washington, DC (Jan 1909-May 1910).

References
Writings: a) *Internal Combustion Engines: An Elementary Treatise on Gas, Gasoline and Oil Engines for the Instruction of Midshipmen at the U.S. Naval Academy* (Annapolis: 1907, 1914). b) *Naval Engines and Machinery: A Text-book for the Instruction of Midshipmen at the U.S. Naval Academy* (Annapolis: 1904).

ALEXANDER BERRY BATES Born in Brooklyn, NY, on 25 Nov 1842, son of John A. and Anna M. (Berry) Bates. Educated at Milton Academy in MD. Married Fannie J. Everts. One son and one daughter. Died at his home in Binghamton, NY, on 19 Feb 1917. Buried in that town's Spring Forest Cemetery.

Ranks 3rd Asst.Engr. (16 Jan 1863); 2nd Asst.Engr. (28 May 1864); 1st Asst.Engr. (1 Jan 1874); title changed to PAsst.Engr. (24 Feb 1874); Chief Engr. (12 Apr 1892); Chief Engr. with rel. rank of Cdr (6 Aug 1898); Cdr (3 Mar 1899); Capt (17 Sep 1902); retired with rank of RAdm (13 Jul 1903).

Career Summary Received appointment from MD (16 Jan 1863); w.o. (Jan-Feb 1863); *Sagamore*, N.Atl.Blk.Sqdn. (Feb-Sep 1863); w.o. (Sep-Oct 1863); *Mattabesett*, N.Atl.Sta. (Oct 1863-May 1865); w.o. (May-Aug 1865); *Ticonderoga*, Eur.Sta. (Sep 1865-Oct 1868); *Franklin*, Eur.Sta. (Oct-Dec 1868); home and w.o. (Dec 1868-Apr 1869); *Galena*, N.Atl.Sta. (Apr-May 1869); w.o. (May-Jun 1869); *Dictator*, N.Atl.Sta. (Jun 1869-Aug 1870); home and l.o.a. (Aug 1870-Jun 1871); Navy Yard, Mare Island, CA (Jun 1871-Apr 1873); Navy Yard, League Island, PA (Apr-Nov 1873); *Dictator*, N.Atl.Sta. (Nov 1873-Dec 1874); home and l.o.a. (Dec 1874-Nov 1875); *Montauk*, N.Atl.Sta. (Nov 1875-Jul 1876); Navy Yard, Mare Island, CA (Aug 1876-Aug 1878); *Lackawanna*, Pac.Sta. (Aug 1878-Sep 1881); w.o. (Sep

1881-Mar 1882); experimental bd., NY (Mar-Oct 1882); w.o. (Oct 1882-Nov 1883); *Vandalia*, N.Atl.Sta. (Nov 1883-Aug 1884); w.o. (Aug 1884-Apr 1885); Navy Yard, Portsmouth, NH (Apr 1885-Feb 1886); *Vandalia*, Pac.Sta. (Feb 1886-Jan 1889); *Mohican*, Pac.Sta. (Jan-Mar 1889); home and w.o. (Mar-May 1889); rec. ship, *Minnesota*, NY (May 1889-May 1892); w.o. (May-Sep 1892); rec. ship, *Independence*, Mare Island, CA (Sep-Oct 1892); *Yorktown*, Spec.Serv.Sqdn. (Oct 1892-Oct 1894); *Bennington*, Pac.Sta. (Oct 1894-Apr 1895); hosp. and sick lv. (Apr-Oct 1895); rec. ship, *Franklin*, Norfolk, VA (Nov 1895-Sep 1897); chief engr., *Texas*, N.Atl.Flt. (Sep 1897-Jan 1899); flt.engr., Pac.Sta., *Philadelphia* (Jan-Jun 1899); insp. of engineering material, Midvale Steel Works, Nicetown, PA (Jul-Sep 1899); Navy Yard, League Island, PA (Sep 1899-Jul 1903); retired (13 Jul 1903).

Career Highlights While chief engr. on *Texas* during Spanish-American War, advanced three numbers for "eminent and conspicuous conduct in battle" during the Battle of Santiago.

References

Personal Papers: papers of his father, Purser John A. Bates (1849-53) in NHF,LC.

WARNER BALDWIN BAYLEY
1845-1928

WARNER BALDWIN BAYLEY Born in Baldwinsville, NY, on 9 Sep 1845. Married Annette Williamson in October 1890. One son. Died at his home in Washington, DC, on 22 Apr 1928. Buried at Arlington National Cemetery.

Ranks Act. 3rd Asst.Engr. (4 Aug 1864); mustered out (28 Apr 1869); 2nd Asst.Engr. (2 Sep 1870); title changed to Asst.Engr. (24 Feb 1874); PAsst.Engr. with rel. rank of Mstr (21 Sep 1877); Chief Engr. (25 May 1894); LCdr (3 Mar 1899); Cdr (3 Mar 1901); Capt (1 Jul 1905); retired with rank of RAdm (18 Apr 1906).

Career Summary Received appointment from NY (4 Aug 1864); *Glacia*, N.Atl.Blk.Sqdn. (Aug-Nov 1864); *Rhode Island* and *Octorara*, N.Atl.Blk. and W.Gulf Blk.Sqdns. (Nov 1864-Aug 1865); l.o.a. (Aug-Sep 1865); *Miantonomoh*, N.Atl.Sqdn. (Sep-Dec 1865); *De Soto*, N.Atl.Sqdn. (Dec 1865-Feb 1866); *Madawaska*, NY (Feb 1866-Feb 1867); w.o. (Feb-Apr 1867); flgs., *Franklin*, Eur.Sta. (Apr 1867-Oct 1868); flgs., *Ticonderoga*, Eur.Sta. (Oct 1868-Apr 1869); mustered out (28 Apr 1869); received appointment from NY (2 Sep 1870); *Ajax*, N.Atl.Sta. (Sep 1870-Jun 1871); spec. duty, Baldwinsville, NY (Jun 1871-Apr 1872); *Lancaster*, S.Atl.Sta. (May 1872-Mar 1874); *Powhatan*, Home Sqdn. (Mar-Dec 1874); Bur. of Steam Engineering, Washington, DC (Dec 1874-Mar 1878); *Monocacy*, Asia.Sta. (Apr 1878-Nov 1879); *Palos*, Asia.Sta. (Nov 1879-Apr 1881); home and w.o. (Apr-Aug 1881); Bur. of Steam Engineering, Washington, DC (Aug 1881-Sep 1883); spec. duty, State, War, and Navy Building, Washington, DC (Sep 1883-Mar 1885); *Pensacola*, Eur.Sta. (Mar 1885-Feb 1888); w.o. (Feb-Apr 1888); duty with Fish Commission (Apr 1888-Apr 1892); *Ranger*, Mare Island, CA (Mar-Jun 1892); Naval Hosp., Mare Island, CA

(Jun-Aug 1892); sick lv. (Aug-Dec 1892); Navy Yard, NY (Dec 1892-Mar 1893); *Atlanta*, N.Atl.Sqdn. (Mar-Jul 1893); *Baltimore* (Jul-Aug 1893); *Machias*, N.Atl.Sta. (Aug 1893-Mar 1894); *Alert*, Pac.Sqdn. (Apr 1894-Jun 1895); *Monterey*, Pac.Sqdn. (Jul 1895-Apr 1896); l.o.a. (Apr-Jun 1896); Bur. of Steam Engineering, Washington, DC (Jun 1896-May 1897); Civil Serv. Commission, Washington, DC (Aug 1896-Jan 1898); *Massachusetts*, N.Atl.Flt. (Jan 1898-May 1899); flt.engr., N.Atl.Flt., *New York* (May 1899-Nov 1900); inspection duty, Bur. of Steam Engineering, Washington, DC (Nov 1900-Sep 1903); member, board of inquiry for *Maine* (Sep-Nov 1903); member, naval exam. bd. (Nov 1903-Nov 1905); sick lv. (Oct 1905-Apr 1906); retired (18 Apr 1906).

Career Highlights Advanced two numbers for "eminent and conspicuous conduct in battle" while with *Massachusetts* during the Spanish-American War.

References

Personal Papers: papers covering 1846-1906 in NL.

FRANK EDMUND BEATTY Born in Azatlan, Jefferson County, WI, on 26 Nov 1853, son of Edmund and Annette (Brayton) Beatty. Married Anne Meem Peachy on 29 Apr 1891. One daughter and one son. Died on 16 Mar 1926 in Charleston, SC.

Ranks Cadet Midn (23 Sep 1871); Ens (18 Jul 1876); Mstr (19 Jun 1882); title changed to Ltjg (3 Mar 1883); Lt (23 Mar 1889); LCdr (3 Mar 1899); Cdr (18 Mar 1904); Capt (1 Jul 1908); RAdm (27 Apr 1912); placed on Ret.Lst. (26 Nov 1915).

Career Summary Received appointment from MN (23 Sep 1871); USNA (Sep 1871-Jun 1875); w.o. (Jun-Oct 1875); *Tuscarora*, N.Pac.Sta. (Oct 1875-Aug 1877); home and w.o. (Aug 1877-Jan 1878); USNA (Jan 1878); w.o. (Jan-Feb 1878); temp. duty, training ship, *Minnesota* (Feb-Sep 1878); flgs., *Richmond*, Asia.Sta. (Oct 1878-Sep 1881); home and w.o. (Sep 1881-Jan 1882); training ship, *Minnesota* (Jan-Aug 1882); *Despatch*, spec.serv. (Aug 1882-Nov 1883); *Tallapoosa*, S.Atl.Sta. (Nov 1883-Oct 1889); Library and War Records Office, Washington, DC (Oct 1889-Apr 1892); *Ranger*, Mare Island, CA (Apr-Oct 1892); *Miantonomoh*, N.Atl.Sta. (Oct 1892-Sep 1894); *Vesuvius*, N.Atl.Sqdn. (Sep 1894-Feb 1895); USNA (Feb 1895-Aug 1897); duty with, then exec.off., *Adams*, Pac.Sqdn. (Aug 1897-Mar 1898); *Monterey*, Pac. and Asia.Sqdns. (Mar 1898-Aug 1899); exec.off., *Wheeling*, Asia.Sqdn. (Aug 1899-Apr 1900); Navy Yard, Mare Island, CA (May 1900); home and w.o. (May 1900); Navy Yard, Washington, DC (Jun 1900-Jan 1902); cdr, schoolship, *Saratoga*, Philadelphia (Jan-Nov 1902); cdr, *Gloucester*, S. Atl.Sqdn. (Nov 1902-May 1904); comdt., Naval Base, Culebra Island, Puerto Rico (Feb-May 1904); home and w.o. (May-Jun 1904); asst., then insp., 9th L.h. Dist., Chicago (Jun 1904-Jun 1905); supt., Naval Gun Factory, Navy Yard, Washington, DC (Jul 1905-Mar 1907); Bur. of Ord., Washington, DC (Mar 1907); cdr, *Columbia*, Atl. Training Sqdn. (Mar-Apr 1907); temp. duty,

FRANK EDMUND BEATTY
1853-1926

Bur. of Ord., Washington, DC (May-Jun 1907); cdr, *Charleston*, Pac.Sqdn. (Jun 1907-Jul 1908); cdr, *Wisconsin*, "Great White Flt." (Jul 1908-Jan 1910); home and l.o.a. (Jan-Feb 1910); spec. temp. duty, Bur. of Ord., Washington, DC (Feb-Mar 1910); comdt., Navy Yard, and supt., Naval Gun Factory, Washington, DC (Mar 1910-Jan 1913); cdr, 4th Div., Atl.Flt., *Minnesota* (Jan-Oct 1913), then *Connecticut* (Oct-Dec 1913); cdr, 1st Div., Atl.Flt., *Virginia* (Dec 1913-Jan 1914), then *Florida* (Jan-Feb 1914); cdr, 3rd Div., Atl.Flt., *Virginia* (Feb-Dec 1914); cdr, Navy Yard and Naval Station, Norfolk, VA (Jan-Jun 1915); placed on Ret.Lst. (26 Nov 1915); comdt., 5th Naval Dist., Norfolk, VA (Nov-Dec 1916); comdt., 6th Naval Dist., Charleston, SC (Feb 1917-Oct 1919).

Career Highlights Important figure in improvement of naval artillery practice. Was instrumental in development of electronic range finder and the telescopic sight. Commanded battleship *Wisconsin* as part of "Great White Flt."

EDWARD BELLOWS Born on 28 Apr 1840 at Newport, RI. Died on 20 May 1903 at Walpole, NH.

Ranks Asst.Paymstr. (11 Jun 1862); Paymstr. (20 Feb 1866); dismissed (28 Jan 1869); dismissal declared illegal and thus revoked (22 Jan 1880); Pay Insp. (5 Jul 1889); Pay Dir. (10 Jul 1898); placed on Ret.Lst. as Pay Dir. with rank of RAdm (28 Apr 1902).

Career Summary Private, 8th Regiment, NY State Militia (20 Apr 1861); discharged (2 Aug 1861); received appointment from NH (11 Jun 1862); *Sonoma*, "Flying Sqdn." (Jul 1862-Aug 1863); s.a. and w.o. (Aug-Dec 1863); *Osceola*, N.Atl.Blk.Sqdn. (Dec 1863-May 1865); s.a. and w.o. (May-Sep 1865); *Shamokin*, S.Atl.Sqdn. (Sep 1865-Jul 1866); *Pawnee*, S.Atl.Sqdn. (Jul 1866-Jan 1869); dismissed (28 Jan 1869); restored to duty (22 Jan 1880); w.o. (Jan-Oct 1880); insp. of provisions and clothing, Navy Yard, Mare Island, CA (Nov 1880-Feb 1881); *Alaska*, Pac.Sqdn. (Mar-Jun 1881); s.a. and w.o. (Jun 1881-Oct 1883); *Shenandoah*, Pac.Sqdn. (Nov 1883-Feb 1885); suspended (Feb-Jul 1885); w.o. (Jul 1885-Feb 1888); *Swatara* and *Marion*, S.Atl. and Asia.Sqdns. (Mar 1888-May 1890); s.a. and w.o. (May-Jul 1890); general storekeeper, Navy Yard, Norfolk, VA (Jul 1890-Jul 1891); s.a. and w.o. (Jul 1891-Aug 1893); in charge, Pay Office, San Francisco (Sep 1893-Nov 1896); s.a. and w.o. (Nov 1896-Mar 1897); Training Sta., Newport, RI (Mar-Sep 1897); s.a. and w.o. (Sep-Oct 1897); flt.paymstr., Asia.Flt., *Baltimore* (Oct 1897-Jan 1899); s.a. and w.o. (Jan-May 1899); gen storekeeper, Navy Yard, Portsmouth, NH (Jun 1899-Dec 1901); purchasing pay off., Navy Dept., Washington, DC (Jan-Apr 1902); placed on Ret.Lst. (28 Apr 1902).

WILLIAM SHEPHERD BENSON Born in Macon, GA, on 25 Sep 1855, son of Richard Aaron and Catherine Elizabeth (Brewer) Benson. Early education at the Alexander School in Macon. Married Mary Augusta Wyse on 6 Aug 1879. Two sons, Howard Hartwell James Benson and Francis Wyse Benson, both of whom

EDWARD BELLOWS
1840-1903

WILLIAM SHEPHERD BENSON
1855-1932

served as naval officers, and a daughter. Another child died at an early age. Died on 20 May 1932 in Washington, DC. Buried in Arlington National Cemetery.

Ranks Cadet Midn (23 Sep 1872): Midn (18 Jun 1879); Ens (27 Jul 1881); Ltjg (28 May 1888); Lt (27 Jun 1893); LCdr (1 Jul 1900); Cdr (1 Jul 1905): Capt (24 Jul 1909): Chief of Naval Operations with rank of RAdm (11 May 1915): RAdm (26 Nov 1915); Chief of Naval Operations with rank of Adm (29 Aug 1916); placed on Ret.Lst. with rank of RAdm (25 Sep 1919); Adm on Ret.Lst. (21 Jun 1930).

Career Summary Received appointment from GA (23 Sep 1872); USNA (Sep 1872-Jun 1877); w.o. (Jun-Aug 1877); flgs., *Hartford*, S.Atl.Sqdn. (Aug 1877-Jan 1879); *Essex*, S.Atl.Sqdn. (Jan-May 1879); USNA (May-Jun 1879); w.o. (Jun-Oct 1879); training ship, *Constitution* (Oct 1879-Jun 1881); Navy Yard, NY (Jul 1881-Jan 1882); *Alliance*, Home Sta. (Jan-May 1882); *Yantic*, Home Sta. (May 1882-Aug 1884); naval advisory bd., Boston (Aug 1884-Mar 1885); branch hydrographic office, Baltimore (Mar 1885-Jan 1886); Fish Commission steamer, *Albatross* (Jan 1886-Nov 1887); w.o. (Nov 1887-Jan 1888); *Dolphin*, Pac. and N.Atl.Stas. (Jan 1888-Sep 1890); USNA (Sep 1890-Sep 1893); torp. instruction (Oct 1893); ord. duty, Navy Yard, Washington, DC (Oct 1893-Jan 1894); cst.surv. duty (Jan 1894-Nov 1895); *Dolphin*, spec.serv. (Nov 1895-Apr 1896); cst.surv. duty (Apr-Jun 1896); USNA (Aug 1896-May 1898); exec.off., training ship, *Monongahela* (May 1898); USNA (May-Jun 1898); rec. ship, *Vermont*, NY (Jul-Dec 1898); flgs., *Chicago*, N.Atl.Flt. (Dec 1898-Sep 1899); aide to cdr, N.Atl.Flt., *New York* (Oct 1899-Oct 1900), then *Kearsarge* (Oct 1900-Apr 1901); in charge, branch hydrographic office, NY (Apr-Jun 1901); USNA (Jun 1901-Oct 1903); exec.off., *Iowa*, N.Atl.Sta. (Oct 1903-Aug 1905); asst.insp., 3rd L.h. Dist., NY (Sep 1905); asst., then insp., 6th L.h. Dist., Charleston, SC (Sep 1905-Jun 1907); Bur. of Nav., Washington, DC (Jul 1907); comdt. of midshipmen, USNA (Jul 1907-Sep 1908); cdr, *Albany*, Pac.Flt. (Oct 1908-Jul 1909); chief of staff, Pac.Flt., *Tennessee* (Jul 1909-Feb 1910); naval exam. and ret. bds., Washington, DC (Feb-Apr 1910); cdr, *Missouri*, Navy Yard, Boston (May-Oct 1910); gen insp., *Utah*, Philadelphia (Oct 1910-Aug 1911); cdr, *Utah*, Atl.Flt. (Aug 1911-Aug 1913); temp. duty, cdr, 1st Div., Atl.Flt., *Utah* (Jan-Jun 1913); home and w.o. (Jun-Jul 1913); comdt., Navy Yard, Philadelphia (Aug 1913-May 1915); supervisor, 3rd, 4th, and 5th Dists. (Aug 1913-Oct 1914); Chief of Naval Operations, Navy Dept., Washington, DC (May 1915-Sep 1919); placed on Ret.Lst. (25 Sep 1919).

Career Highlights Served on the *Yantic* as part of the Greely Relief Expd. in 1883. Became first Chief of Naval Operations, organizing and thereby centralizing the navy's administration in time for America's entry in World War I. Was a principal American adviser at Versailles, helping to conclude the naval side of the Armistice in 1919. Received numerous medals, foreign and American, including the Navy Distinguished Service Medal, the Army Distinguished Service Medal, the Grand Cross of St.

Michael and St. George (Britain), the Grand Cross of the Legion of Honor (France), and the Grand Cross of the Order of the Rising Sun (Japan).

References

Personal Papers: 14,000 items (1791-1941) in LC.

Writings: a) *The Merchant Marine* (NY: 1923). b) "Our New Merchant Marine," U.S. Naval Institute *Proceedings* 284 (Oct 1926): 1941-50.

Additional References: a) Mary Klachko and David F. Trask, *Admiral William Shepherd Benson: First Chief of Naval Operations* (Annapolis: 1980).

ALBERT GLEAVES BERRY
1848-1938

ALBERT GLEAVES BERRY Born in Nashville, TN, on 16 Sep 1848, son of William Tyler and Mary Margaret (Tannehill) Berry. Married Lillian Reed Merriman on 28 Sep 1881. Two children, Mary Lillian and LCdr Albert Gleaves Berry, Jr, USN (ret). Died in Coronado, CA, on 12 May 1938. Buried in USNA Cemetery, Annapolis.

Ranks Midn (25 Jul 1865); Ens (12 Jul 1870); Mstr (27 Sep 1872); Lt (20 Oct 1875); LCdr (21 Jul 1897); Cdr (1 Jul 1900); Capt (16 Jun 1905); RAdm (18 Jun 1909); placed on Ret.Lst (16 Sep 1910).

Career Summary Received appointment at large (25 Jul 1865); USNA (Jul 1865-Jun 1869); training ship, *Sabine*, then flgs., *Franklin*, Eur.Sta. (Jun 1869-Nov 1871); w.o. (Nov 1871-Mar 1872); *Lancaster* and *Wasp*, S.Atl.Sta. (Apr 1872-Jan 1876); w.o. (Feb-May 1876); torp. instruction, Newport, RI (Jun-Sep 1876); w.o. (Sep 1876-Feb 1877); *Franklin*, Norfolk, VA (Feb 1877); rec. ship, *Colorado*, NY (Feb-Mar 1877); training ship, *Monongahela* (Mar 1877-Nov 1879); w.o. (Nov 1879-Apr 1880); rec. ship, *Passaic*, Washington, DC (Apr-Jul 1880); Hydrographic Office, Washington, DC (Jul 1880-Jun 1881); *Despatch*, spec.serv. (Jun-Nov 1881); ord. instruction, Navy Yard, Washington, DC (Nov 1881-May 1882); Signal Office, Washington, DC (May 1882-Aug 1883); *Trenton* and *Palos*, Asia.Sqdn. (Sep 1883-Sep 1886); w.o. (Sep-Oct 1886); ord. duty, Navy Yard, Washington, DC (Nov 1886-Aug 1889); l.o.a. (Sep 1889-Oct 1890); spec. duty, Mare Island, CA (Nov 1890); *San Francisco*, S.Pac.Sqdn. (Nov 1890-Jun 1893); torp. instruction, Newport, RI (Jun-Jul 1893); l.o.a. (Jul-Oct 1893); training ship, *Richmond* (Sep-Nov 1893); l.o.a. (Nov 1893-Nov 1894); training ship, *Minnesota* (Nov 1894-Oct 1895); rec. ship, *Vermont*, NY (Oct 1895-Jul 1896); *New York*, N.Atl.Sta. (Jul 1896-Jul 1897); member, labor bd., Navy Yard, NY (Jul-Aug 1897); exec.off., *Amphitrite*, N.Atl.Sta. (Aug 1897-May 1899); asst., then insp., 3rd L.h. Dist., Tompkinsville, NY (May 1899-Oct 1900); in charge, Puerto Rico L.h. Serv. (Oct 1900-Nov 1901); cdr, prac. ship, *Puritan* (Dec 1901-Apr 1903); home and w.o. (Apr-May 1903); NWC (Jun-Jul 1903); insp. of ord., Bethlehem Steel Company, S.Bethlehem, PA (Jul 1903-May 1906); gen insp., *Tennessee*, Philadelphia (Jan-Jul 1906); cdr, *Tennessee*, spec. cruise (Jul 1906-Oct 1907); home and w.o. (Oct-Nov 1907); cdr, rec. ship,

Lancaster, Philadelphia (Nov 1907-Jun 1909); senior member, bd. to conduct survs. of Pac.cst. vessels, and comdt., Pac.Naval Dist., San Francisco (Jun 1909-Apr 1910); member, naval exam. and ret. bds. (Apr-Sep 1910); retired (16 Sep 1910).

References
Personal Papers: covering 1865-1910 in TN State Lib. and Archives, Nashville, TN.

ROBERT MALLORY BERRY Born at "Beechlands" in Henry County, KY, on 28 Jan 1846, son of Edmund Taylor and Sarah Francis (Taylor) Berry. Married Mary Augusta Brady on 9 Oct 1895. No issue. Died on 19 May 1929 in Tryon, NC. Buried in Arlington National Cemetery.

Ranks Act.Midn (31 Jan 1862); title changed to Midn (16 Jul 1862); Ens (12 Mar 1868); Mstr (26 Mar 1869); Lt (21 Mar 1870); LCdr (4 Feb 1886); Cdr (2 Feb 1895); Capt (11 Feb 1901); RAdm (29 Jun 1906); placed on Ret.Lst. (28 Jan 1908).

ROBERT MALLORY BERRY
1846-1929

Career Summary Received appointment from KY (31 Jan 1862); USNA (Jan 1862-Jun 1866); l.o.a. (Jun-Oct 1866); prac. ship, *Sabine* (Nov 1866); *Gettysburg*, spec.serv. (Dec 1866-Feb 1867); w.o. (Feb-Apr 1867); flgs., *Guerriere*, *Huron*, and *Kansas*, S.Atl.Sta. (May 1867-Sep 1869); w.o. (Sep 1869-Jan 1870); *Ossipee*, *Cyane*, then *Pensacola*, Pac.Sqdn. (Feb 1870-Feb 1873); w.o. (Mar-Jun 1873); *Tigress*, spec. relief expd. (Jun-Nov 1873); w.o. (Nov-Dec 1873); *Minnesota*, Navy Yard, NY (Dec 1873); *Dictator*, N.Atl.Sta. (Dec 1873-Mar 1874); flgs., *Franklin*, Eur.Sqdn. (Mar 1874-Jan 1877); w.o. (Jan-May 1877); torp. instruction, Newport, RI (Jun-Sep 1877); w.o. (Sep 1877-Jan 1878); ord. instruction, Navy Yard, Washington, DC (Feb-Apr 1878); exec.off., training ship, *Saratoga* (Apr 1878-Dec 1880); w.o. (Dec 1880-Jan 1881); equip. duty, Navy Yard, Washington, DC (Jan-Apr 1881); cdr, *Mary and Helen*, [renamed *Rodgers*], spec. duty (Apr 1881-Dec 1882); exec.off., nautical schoolship, *St. Mary's* (Dec 1882-Apr 1886); w.o. (Apr-May 1886); exec.off., *Atlanta*, N.Atl.Sta. (Jun 1886-Nov 1888); sick lv. (Apr-Jul 1888); w.o. (Nov 1888-Apr 1889); torp. instruction, Newport, RI (May-Aug 1889); NWC (Aug-Oct 1889); w.o. (Oct-Nov 1889); insp., 16th L.h. Dist., Memphis, TN (Dec 1889-Dec 1892); w.o. (Dec 1892-Mar 1893); cdr, *Michigan*, on Great Lakes (Mar 1893-Dec 1894); w.o. (Dec 1894-Mar 1895); temp. duty, NY (Mar 1895); ord. instruction, Navy Yard, Washington, DC (Mar-May 1895); NWC (Jun-Jul 1895); Navy Yard, NY (Jul 1895-Dec 1896); cdr, *Castine*, S.Atl.Sta. (Dec 1896-Feb 1899); home and w.o. (Feb-Apr 1899); Naval Home, Philadelphia (May 1899-Feb 1901); member, naval exam. bd., Washington, DC (Feb-May 1901); NWC (Jun-Jul 1901); cdr, training ship, *Dixie* (Jul 1901-Jul 1902); capt.yd., Navy Yard, Norfolk, VA (Aug 1902-Feb 1903); cdr, *Kentucky*, Asia.Sta. (Feb 1903-Jun 1904); chief of staff, Asia.Sta., *Kentucky* (Mar 1904-Jun 1904); home and w.o. (Jun-Aug 1904); comdt., Naval Station, and cdr, 6th Naval Dist., Charleston, SC (Sep 1904-Mar 1905); comdt., Navy Yard, and cdr, 8th Naval Dist., Pensacola, FL (May 1905-Jul 1906);

comdt., Navy Yard, and cdr, 5th Naval Dist., Norfolk, VA (Jul 1906-Dec 1907); home and l.o.a. (Dec 1907-Jan 1908); placed on Ret.Lst. (28 Jan 1908); cdr, U.S. naval unit, Univ. of MI, Ann Arbor, MI (Sep 1918-Jan 1919).

GEORGE AUGUSTUS BICKNELL
1846-1925

GEORGE AUGUSTUS BICKNELL Born on 15 May 1846 in Batsto, NJ, son of George and Elizabeth Haskins (Richards) Bicknell. Early education in private schools. Married Annie Sloan on 22 May 1878. Died in New Albany, IN, on 27 January 1925. Buried in New Albany's Fairview Cemetery.

Ranks Act.Midn (2 Dec 1861); title changed to Midn (16 Jul 1862); Ens (12 Mar 1868); Mstr (26 Mar 1869); Lt (21 Mar 1870); LCdr (19 May 1886); Cdr (6 Jan 1896); Capt (12 May 1901); RAdm (8 Feb 1907); placed on Ret.Lst. (15 May 1908).

Career Summary Received appointment from IN (2 Dec 1861); USNA (Dec 1861-Jun 1866); found deficient and put back (Oct 1865); l.o.a. and w.o. (Jun-Dec 1866); *Iroquois*, Asia.Sqdn. (Jan 1867-Apr 1870); w.o. (Apr-Sep 1870); USNA (Sep 1870-Dec 1871); flgs., *Worcester*, N.Atl.Sqdn. (Dec 1871-Feb 1875); home and w.o. (Feb-May 1875); Torp.Sta., Newport, RI (Jun-Oct 1875); Hydrographic Office, Washington, DC (Oct 1875); *Richmond*, S.Pac. and S.Atl.Stas. (Nov 1875-Sep 1877); w.o. (Sep 1877-Mar 1878); l.o.a. (Mar 1878-May 1879); *Wachusett*, S.Atl.Sta. (May 1879-Jan 1880); flgs., *Shenandoah*, S.Atl.Sqdn. (Jan-Aug 1880); *Marion*, S.Atl.Sqdn. (Aug 1880-Dec 1882); w.o. (Dec 1882-Oct 1883); Navy Yard, League Island, PA (Oct-Dec 1883); spec. duty, Chester, PA (Dec 1883-May 1886); w.o. (May-Jun 1886); exec.off., *Essex*, Asia.Sta. (Jun 1886-May 1889); w.o. (May-Jul 1889); Navy Yard, NY (Aug 1889-May 1891); suspended from active duty (May 1891-Jan 1892); exec.off., rec. ship, *Franklin*, Norfolk, VA (Jan-Dec 1892); exec.off., *Atlanta*, N.Atl.Sqdn. (Dec 1892-Jul 1893); rec. ship, *Franklin*, Norfolk, VA (Jul 1893-Sep 1894); cdr, *Fern*, spec.serv. (Oct 1894-Dec 1895); cdr, Naval Station, Port Royal, SC (Jan 1896-Aug 1897); insp., 14th L.h. Dist., Cincinnati (Aug 1897-Apr 1898); cdr, supply ship, *Niagara* (Apr-May 1898); cdr, *Saturn*, Atl.Flt. (Jun-Nov 1898); cdr, *Monocacy*, Atl.Flt. (Dec 1898-May 1900); Navy Yard, Mare Island, CA (Jun-Jul 1900); NWC (Jul-Oct 1900); Navy Yard, Norfolk, VA (Oct 1900-Aug 1902); comdt., Naval Sta., and cdr, 7th Naval Dist., Key West, FL (Aug 1902-Aug 1904); home and w.o. (Aug-Oct 1904); cdr, flgs., *Texas*, U.S. Cst.Sqdn. (Oct 1904-Jun 1906); comdt., Navy Yard and Sta., and cdr, 8th Naval Dist., Pensacola, FL (Jul 1906-Feb 1907); comdt., Navy Yard, and cdr, 1st Naval Dist., Portsmouth, NH (Feb 1907-May 1908); placed on Ret.Lst. (15 May 1908).

References

Personal Papers: a) covering 1892-1925 in IN Historical Society Lib., Indianapolis. b) Journal kept on *Iroquois* (1866-67) in Lilly Lib., IN Univ., Bloomington.

LUTHER GUITEAU BILLINGS Born in Remsen, NY, on 27 Dec 1842, son of Andrew and Abbie (Sheldon) Billings. Married with one son. Died on 30 Dec 1920 in Eagle Rock, CA. Buried in Arlington National Cemetery.

Ranks Act.Asst.Paymstr. (24 Oct 1862); Asst.Paymstr. (3 Mar 1865); Paymstr. (4 May 1866); Pay Insp. (26 Dec 1882); Pay Dir. (9 Jan 1895); retired (14 Mar 1898); promoted to Pay Dir. with rank of RAdm on Ret.Lst. (29 Jun 1906).

Career Summary Received appointment from NY (24 Oct 1862); w.o. (Oct-Dec 1862); *Water Witch*, S.Atl.Blk.Sqdn. (Dec 1862-Jun 1864); prisoner-of-war (3 Jun-16 Oct 1864); w.o. (Oct 1864-Jan 1865); *Connecticut*, W.Indies (Jan-Aug 1865); s.a. and w.o. (Aug-Oct 1865); l.o.a. (Oct 1865-Mar 1866); *Wateree*, S.Pac.Sqdn. (Jun 1866-Sep 1868); s.a. and w.o. (Sep 1868-Jan 1869); rec. ship, *New Hampshire*, Norfolk, VA (Feb 1869-Jan 1872); s.a. and w.o. (Jan-Feb 1872); *Powhatan*, N.Atl.Sta. (Feb 1872-Jan 1875); s.a. and w.o. (Jan-Mar 1875); Navy Yard, NY (Apr 1875-May 1877); rec. ship, *Colorado*, NY (May 1877-Jul 1879); s.a. and w.o. (Jul-Aug 1879); insp. of provisions, Navy Yard, NY (Aug 1879-Mar 1880); *Constellation*, spec.serv. (Mar-Jun 1880); USNA (Jul 1880-Aug 1884); s.a. and w.o. (Aug-Oct 1884); USNA (Oct 1884); w.o. (Oct-Dec 1884); l.o.a. and w.o. (Dec 1884-Oct 1885); duty, advisory bd. (Oct-Nov 1885); Delaware River Shipbuilding Works, Chester, PA (Nov 1885-Dec 1886); spec. duty, Washington, DC (Dec 1886-Feb 1887); Bur. of Provisions and Clothing, Washington, DC (Feb-Nov 1887); l.o.a. (Nov 1887-May 1888); sick lv. (May 1888-Sep 1889); *Pensacola*, spec.serv. (Sep 1889-Jun 1890); flt.paymstr., N.Atl.Sta., *Baltimore* (Jul-Aug 1890), then *Philadelphia* (Aug 1890-Sep 1892); s.a. and l.o.a. (Sep-Dec 1892); in charge, Pay Office, NY (Jan 1893-Jan 1896); spec. bd. duty, Navy Yard, NY (Jan 1896-Mar 1897); spec. duty, Bur. of Supplies and Accounts, NY (Mar-Sep 1897); gen insp., Pay Corps, Washington, DC (Sep 1897-Mar 1898); retired (14 Mar 1898); Cst. Signal Serv. (May-Oct 1898); purchasing off., Eastern Dist., Pay Office, Baltimore (Mar 1917-Feb 1919).

Career Highlights During Civil War, was on *Water Witch* when boarded on 4 Jun 1864 in Ossabaw Sound by Confederates. Wounded and taken prisoner, was eventually exchanged, receiving advance of fifteen numbers in his grade. Served on *Wateree* at Arica, Peru, in Aug 1868 when area badly hit by an earthquake and subsequent tidal wave, putting vessel far inland. Commended for his courageous actions during the emergency.

References
Personal Papers: covering 1865-1900 in NHF,LC.

JOHN VAN BENTHUYSEN BLEECKER Born in Glen Cove, NY, on 16 Aug 1847, son of navy paymstr. John Van Benthuysen and S. Rosalie (Lynch) Bleecker. Died at New Orleans on 20 Feb 1922.

Ranks Midn (10 Oct 1863); Ens (18 Dec 1868); Mstr (21 Mar 1870); Lt (21 Mar 1871); LCdr (30 Jun 1891); Cdr (5 Dec 1897); Capt (3 Jun 1902); retired as RAdm (27 Jun 1905).

Career Summary Received appointment by virtue as being the son of an officer (9 Oct 1863); USNA (Oct 1863-Jun 1867); training ship, *Minnesota*, then *Powhatan*, S.Pac.Sqdn. (Jul 1867-Feb 1869); sick lv. (Feb-Jul 1869); Navy Yard, NY (Jul 1869-Jan 1870); *Congress*, N.Atl.Sqdn., and *Brooklyn*, spec. cruise (Feb 1870-Jul 1873); w.o. (Jul-Aug 1873); Torp.Sta., Newport, RI (Sep 1873-Jun 1874); *Colorado*, N.Atl.Sta. (Jun-Aug 1874); sick lv. (Aug-Nov 1874); Navy Yard, Boston (Nov 1874-Jul 1875); *Frolic*, S.Atl.Sta. (Aug 1875-Oct 1877); w.o. (Oct-Nov 1877); ord. instruction, Navy Yard, Washington, DC (Dec 1877-Aug 1878); USNA (Aug 1878-Jun 1881); training ship, *Minnesota* (Jun-Aug 1881); training ship, *New Hampshire* (Aug 1881-Jun 1882); *Kearsarge*, N.Atl.Sta. (Jun 1882-May 1883); training ship, *Minnesota* (May 1883-Mar 1884); *Hartford*, Pac.Sta. (Apr 1884-Nov 1886); w.o. (Nov 1886-Jul 1887); insp. of steel for new cruisers, Pittsburgh, PA (Jul 1887-Sep 1888); training ship, *New Hampshire* (Oct 1888-Apr 1889); Torp.Sta., Newport, RI (May-Aug 1889); NWC (Aug-Oct 1889); Torp.Sta., Newport, RI (Oct 1889-Apr 1890); *Essex*, S.Atl.Sta. (Apr 1900-Apr 1893); l.o.a. (May-Aug 1893); Navy Yard, Boston (Aug 1893-Jul 1896); temp. duty, Torp.Sta., Newport, RI (Jun-Sep 1894); exec.off., *San Francisco*, N.Atl.Sta. (Jul 1896-Dec 1897); cdr, *Bancroft*, Eur. Sqdn. (Dec 1897-Apr 1898); Naval Hosp., Boston (Apr-Jun 1898); sick lv. (Jun-Aug 1898); ord.off., Navy Yard, Portsmouth, NH (Aug 1898-Oct 1899); cdr, *Isla de Luzon*, and senior insp., gunboats, Hong Kong, China (Nov 1899-May 1901); cdr, *Marietta*, Asia.Sta. (May-Oct 1901); ord.off., Navy Yard, Portsmouth, NH (Nov 1901-Sep 1902); NWC (Oct-Dec 1902); capt.yd., Navy Yard, Puget Sound, WA (Dec 1902-May 1905); cdr, *Columbia*, Atl. Training Sqdn. (Jun 1905); retired (27 Jun 1905).

GOTTFRIED BLOCKLINGER
1847-1930

GOTTFRIED BLOCKLINGER Born on 23 Oct 1847 in Dubuque, IA, son of Gottfried Blocklinger. Early education was in Dubuque. Married Ella Mugel Blocklinger. Died in Dubuque on 18 May 1930. Buried in that city's Linwood Cemetery.

Ranks Midn (21 Jul 1863); Ens (19 Apr 1869); Mstr (12 Jul 1870); Lt (2 Apr 1874); LCdr (21 May 1895); Cdr (3 Mar 1899); Capt (1 Jun 1904); RAdm (30 Oct 1908); placed on Ret.Lst. (23 Oct 1909).

Career Summary Received appointment from IA (21 Jul 1863); USNA (Jul 1863-Jun 1868); found deficient and turned back (Jun 1864); w.o. (Jun-Sep 1868); *Kearsarge*, Pac.Sqdn. (Oct 1868-Oct 1869); home and w.o. (Oct 1869-Feb 1870); *Ossipee*, Pac.Sqdn. (Mar 1870-Nov 1872); w.o. (Nov 1872-Oct 1873); *Kearsarge*, Asia.Sqdn. (Nov 1873-Aug 1876); w.o. (Aug-Dec 1876); l.o.a. (Dec 1876-Jul 1877); torp. duty, Newport, RI (Jul-Sep 1877); w.o. (Sep 1877-Apr 1878); spec. duty, *Enterprise* (Apr-Oct 1878); sick lv. (Oct 1878-Aug 1879); *Adams*, Pac.Sta. (Aug 1879-Aug 1882); w.o. (Aug 1882-Jan 1883); cst.surv. duty (Feb 1883-Mar 1886); w.o. (Mar-Apr 1886); *Alliance*, N.Atl. Sqdn. (Apr 1886); w.o. (Apr-Dec 1886); Hydrographic Office, Washington, DC (Dec 1886-Nov 1887); insp., 7th L.h. Dist.,

Pensacola, FL (Nov 1887-Dec 1889); *Alliance*, Asia.Sqdn. (Jan-Dec 1890); sick lv. (Dec 1890-Dec 1891); training ship, *Richmond* (Dec 1891-Mar 1892); *Baltimore,* spec. duty (Apr 1892-Jun 1893); exec.off., *Yorktown,* Spec.Serv.Sqdn. (Jun-Jul 1893); ord. instruction, Navy Yard, Washington, DC (Oct 1893-Jan 1894); home and w.o. (Jan-Apr 1894); ord. duty, Navy Yard, Washington, DC (Apr 1894-Nov 1895); exec.off., *Boston,* Asia.Sta. (Nov 1895-Oct 1896); sick lv. (Nov 1896-Jun 1897); Navy Yard, Mare Island, CA (Jul-Sep 1897); *Baltimore,* Hawaiian Islands (Sep 1897-Jan 1898); Navy Yard, Mare Island, CA (Jan-May 1898); exec.off., *Charleston,* Asia.Sta. (May 1898-Jul 1899); home and w.o. (Jul-Oct 1899); in charge, Recruiting Rndv. Office, Chicago (Oct 1899-Jun 1901); cdr, training ship, *Alert* (Jul 1901); cdr, *Concord,* Pac.Sqdn. (Jul-Dec 1901); home and w.o. (Dec 1901-Feb 1902); *Wheeling,* Pac.Sqdn. (Mar-Jun 1902); Naval Hosp., Mare Island, CA (Jun-Jul 1902); sick lv. (Jul-Nov 1902); *Vicksburg,* Asia.Flt. (Dec 1902-May 1903); cdr, flgs., *New Orleans,* Asia.Flt. (May-Nov 1903); home and w.o. (Nov 1903-Mar 1904); Navy Yard, Norfolk, VA (Mar-Oct 1904); Navy Yard, NY (Oct 1904-Jun 1906); cdr, *Illinois,* N.Atl.Flt. (Jun 1906-Nov 1907); Navy Yard, NY (Nov 1907-May 1908); member, naval exam. and ret. bds. (May 1908-Oct 1909); placed on Ret.Lst. (23 Oct 1909).

EDWARD STRONG BOGERT Born in Geneva, NY, on 7 May 1836, son of Stephen Van Rensselaer and Amanda (Strong) Bogert. Educated at Dwight's High School in Brooklyn, NY. Married Helen Hart on 6 Jun 1866. One son, Capt Edward Strong Bogert, USN (1867-1924) and a daughter. Died on 16 Feb 1911 in NY City. Buried in USNA Cemetery.

Ranks Asst.Surg. (10 Jun 1861); PAsst.Surg. (22 Jun 1864); Surg. (7 Apr 1866); Medl.Insp. (10 Sep 1882); Medl.Dir. (28 Nov 1889); transferred to Ret.Lst. (7 May 1898); promoted to Medl.Dir. with rank of RAdm (29 Jun 1906).

Career Summary Received appointment from NY (10 Jun 1861); Naval Hosp., NY (Jun-Jul 1861); w.o. (Jul-Aug 1861); *Congress,* Atl.Blk.Sqdn. (Aug-Dec 1861); *Cayuga,* W.Gulf Blk.Sqdn. (Dec 1861-Nov 1863); return and w.o. (Nov-Dec 1863); Naval Hosp., NY (Dec 1863-May 1864); *Niagara,* spec.serv. (May 1864-Sep 1865); w.o. (Sep-Oct 1865); Naval Hosp., NY (Oct 1865-May 1866); Naval Hosp., Norfolk, VA (Jun-Dec 1866); Naval Laboratory, NY (Dec 1866-May 1870); *Congress,* spec.serv. (Jul 1870-May 1873); home and w.o. (May-Aug 1873); MB, and recorder, bd. of examiners, Washington, DC (Sep 1873-Feb 1874); MB, Brooklyn, NY (Feb 1874-Sep 1876); w.o. (Sep-Dec 1876); rec. ship, *Franklin,* Norfolk, VA (Dec 1876-Feb 1877); w.o. (Feb-Aug 1877); *Monongahela,* Asia.Sqdn. (Aug 1877-Nov 1879); w.o. (Nov-Dec 1879); MB, NY (Dec 1879-Jun 1882); Navy Yard, Norfolk, VA (Jun 1882-Aug 1883); *Trenton,* Asia.Sta. (Sep 1883-Aug 1884); flt. surg., Asia.Sta., *Trenton* (Aug 1884-Sep 1886); Navy Yard, NY (Sep 1886-Sep 1889); pres., medl.exam.bd., NY (Oct 1889-Apr 1892);

in charge, Naval Hosp., NY (Apr 1892-Nov 1895); spec. duty, NY (Nov 1895-May 1898); Marine Recruiting office, NY (Apr-Dec 1898); transferred to Ret.Lst. (7 May 1898); spec. duty, NY (May 1898-Jan 1899); temp. duty, Marine Recruiting Rndv., NY (Oct 1900-Mar 1901); Navy Yard, Boston (Apr-Sep 1901).

LAWRENCE GEDNEY BOGGS Born in Washington, DC, on 5 Apr 1846. Married to Anne G. Boggs. Died in Paris on 22 Nov 1915.

Ranks Paymaster's Clerk, Volunteer Service (1 Oct 1862); discharged (Mar 1868); Asst.Paymstr. (24 Sep 1869); PAsst. Paymstr. (25 Oct 1874); Paymstr. (28 Jan 1886); Paymstr. with rel. rank of LCdr (7 Feb 1893); Pay Insp. (12 Nov 1899); Pay Dir. (28 Sep 1902); transferred to Ret.Lst as RAdm (5 Apr 1908).

Career Summary Paymaster's Clerk (1 Oct 1861); discharged (Mar 1868); received appointment from DC (24 Sep 1869); temp. duty, Navy Dept., Washington, DC (Oct 1869-Feb 1870); Bur. of Provisions and Clothing, Washington, DC (Feb-Nov 1870); *Tallapoosa*, spec.serv. (Nov 1870-Jan 1872); *Frolic*, spec.serv. (Jan 1872-Oct 1873); s.a. and w.o. (Oct-Nov 1873); *Despatch*, spec.serv. (Dec 1873-Dec 1875); *Marion*, Eur.Sta. (Dec 1875-Feb 1879); s.a. and w.o. (Feb-Mar 1879); Bur. of Provisions and Clothing, Washington, DC (Mar 1879-Apr 1880); Naval Sta., New London, CT (May 1880-Jan 1881); s.a. and w.o. (Jan-Feb 1881); Bur. of Provisions and Clothing, Washington, DC (Feb-Sep 1881); training ship, *Saratoga* (Sep 1881-Oct 1884); s.a. and w.o. (Oct 1884-Mar 1886); rec. ship, *Dale*, Washington, DC (Mar 1886-May 1889); rec. ship, *New Hampshire*, Newport, RI (Jun 1889-Oct 1890); training ship, *Richmond* (Oct 1890-Mar 1891); s.a. and w.o. (Mar-Jun 1891); *Bennington*, S.Atl.Sta. (Jun 1891-Oct 1894); s.a. and l.o.a. (Oct 1894-Jun 1895); w.o. (Jun-Nov 1895); Navy Yard, NY (Dec 1895-Sep 1897); Torp.Sta., Newport, RI (Sep 1897-Mar 1898); *Columbia*, N.Atl.Flt. (Mar-Sep 1898); s.a. and w.o. (Sep 1898); *Massachusetts*, N.Atl.Flt. (Oct 1898-Mar 1900); s.a. and sick lv. (Mar-Jul 1900); paymstr., Navy Yard, NY (Sep 1900-Jul 1903); purchasing pay off., Navy Yard, NY (Jul 1903-Jun 1908); transferred to Ret.Lst. (5 Apr 1908).

CLIFFORD JOSEPH BOUSH Born on 13 Aug 1854 in Portsmouth, VA, son of George Richard and Adele Virginia (Bilisoli) Boush. Early education at Phillips Academy in Portsmouth, VA. Married to Anna Booker Camm on 30 Nov 1882. One son and one daughter. Died in Gloucester, VA, on 24 Jul 1936. Buried in Arlington National Cemetery.

Ranks Midn (25 Jun 1870); title changed to Cadet Midn (15 Jul 1870); dismissed (14 Oct 1871); Cadet Midn (6 Jun 1872); Midn (20 Jun 1876); Ens (1 Dec 1877); Ltjg (3 Nov 1884); Lt (31 Jul 1890); LCdr (25 Mar 1899); Cdr (12 Jan 1905); Capt (20 Jul 1908); RAdm (26 Mar 1913); placed on Ret.Lst. (13 Aug 1916).

CLIFFORD JOSEPH BOUSH
1854-1936

Career Summary Received appointment from VA (25 Jun 1870); USNA (Jun 1870-Oct 1871); dropped for hazing (14 Oct 1871); received appointment from VA (6 Jun 1872); USNA (Jun 1872-Jun 1876); w.o. (Jun-Aug 1876); *Tennessee*, Asia.Sqdn. (Sep 1876-Jul 1878); w.o. (Jul-Aug 1878); rec. ship, *Franklin*, Norfolk, VA (Aug 1878-Mar 1879); USNA (Mar-Apr 1879); w.o. (Apr-May 1879); rec. ship, *Franklin*, Norfolk, VA (May-Sep 1879); *Constellation* (Oct 1879); *Trenton*, Eur.Sta. (Oct 1879-Oct 1881); w.o. (Oct 1881-Jan 1882); training ship, *Minnesota* (Jan-Apr 1882); torp. instruction, Newport, RI (May-Aug 1882); rec. ship, *Franklin*, Norfolk, VA (Aug-Nov 1882); w.o. (Nov 1882-Feb 1883); Fish Commission steamer, *Albatross* (Feb 1883-Dec 1885); USNA (Dec 1885-Jun 1887); *Trenton*, Navy Yard, Norfolk, VA (Jun 1887); *Lancaster*, S.Atl. and Eur.Stas. (Jun 1887-Aug 1889); Bur. of Ord., Washington, DC (Sep 1889-Oct 1892); *Yorktown*, Spec.Serv.Sqdn. (Oct 1892-Oct 1894); *Ranger*, Pac.Sqdn. (Nov 1894-Aug 1895); USNA (Sep 1895-Jul 1897); *Annapolis*, on trials and N.Atl.Sqdn. (Jul 1897-Aug 1898); Naval Hosp., NY (Aug 1898); *Yankee*, League Island, PA (Sep-Dec 1898); *Yosemite*, spec. duty (Jan 1899-Apr 1900); *Concord*, Asia.Sta. (Apr-Jun 1900); *Solace*, spec. duty (Jun-Jul 1900); Navy Yard, Mare Island, CA (Jul 1900); home and w.o. (Jul-Aug 1900); Hydrographic Office, Washington, DC (Aug 1900-Jun 1902); cdr, *Scorpion*, N.Atl.Sqdn. (Jul 1902-Jul 1904); home and w.o. (Jun-Aug 1904); NWC (Sep 1904-Sep 1905); *Concord*, Asia.Sta. (Sep 1905-Aug 1907); home and w.o. (Aug-Oct 1907); insp., 2nd L.h. Dist., Boston (Oct 1907-Oct 1908); capt.yd., Navy Yard, Portsmouth, NH (Oct 1908-May 1909); cdr, *Ohio*, NY Naval Militia (May-Nov 1909); cdr, *North Carolina*, Atl.Flt. (Nov 1909-Jun 1911); home and w.o. (Jun 1911); member, naval exam. and ret. bds., Washington, DC (Jul 1911-Oct 1913); cdr, 3rd Div., Atl.Flt., *Rhode Island* (Oct-Nov 1913); cdr, 2nd Div., Atl.Flt., *Louisiana* (Nov 1913-Oct 1914), then *Utah* (Oct 1914-Jun 1915); comdt., Naval Sta., Honolulu, Territory of HI (Jul 1915-Aug 1916); placed on Ret.Lst. (13 Aug 1916); comdt., Navy Yard, Portsmouth, NH (Sep 1917-Oct 1919).

FRANCIS TIFFANY BOWLES Born in Springfield, MA, on 7 Oct 1858, son of Benjamin F. and Mary E. (Bailey) Bowles. Married Adelaide Hay Savage on 17 Nov 1886. One son and one daughter. After resignation from navy, was pres. of Fore River Shipbuilding Company of Quincy, MA; manager of the div. of construction, then asst. gen manager, U.S. Shipping Bd. of Emergency Flt. Corporation in Washington, D.C. from 1917 to 1919. Died in Barnstable, MA, on 3 Aug 1927.

Ranks Cadet Engr. (15 Sep 1875); resigned (31 Oct 1881); Asst. Naval Const. (1 Nov 1881); Naval Const. (10 Oct 1888); Naval Const. with rel. rank of Cdr (23 Jun 1898); Capt (3 Mar 1899); Chief Const. and Chief, Bur. of Construction and Repair with rank of RAdm (4 Mar 1901); resigned with rank of RAdm (31 Oct 1903).

Career Summary Received appointment from MA (15 Sep 1875); USNA (Sep 1875-Jun 1879); w.o. (Jun-Sep 1879); *Trenton*, Med.Sqdn. (Sep-Oct 1879); spec. duty, Royal Naval College, Greenwich, England (Oct 1879-Jun 1882); resigned (31 Oct 1881); received appointment from MA as Asst.Naval Const. (1 Nov 1881); l.o.a. (Jun-Oct 1882); Bur. of Construction and Repair, Washington, DC (Oct 1882-Sep 1886); Navy Yard, Norfolk, VA (Sep 1886-Jul 1895); Navy Yard, NY (Aug 1895-Mar 1901); chief const., and chief, Bur. of Construction and Repair, Washington, DC (Mar 1901-Oct 1903); resigned (31 Oct 1903).

References

Personal Papers: 5 vols. (1885-96) in NYPL.

Writings: a) "Towing Experiments on Models to Determine the Resistance of Full-Sized Ships," U.S. Naval Institute *Proceedings* 23 (1883): 81-98. b) "Our New Cruisers," U.S. Naval Institute *Proceedings* 26 (1883): 595-631. c) "Notes on Bilge Keels," U.S. Naval Institute *Proceedings* 32 (1885): 119-36.

JOHN MARSHALL BOWYER
1853-1912

JOHN MARSHALL BOWYER Born in Cass County, IN, on 19 Jun 1853, son of Lewis Franklin and Naomi Emeline (Pugh) Bowyer. Married Cora McCarter on 29 Oct 1879. One daughter. Died in Tampa, FL, on 15 Mar 1912.

Ranks Cadet Midn (30 Sep 1870); Midn (15 Oct 1874); Ens (17 Jul 1875); Mstr (28 May 1881); title changed to Ltjg (3 Mar 1883); Lt (26 May 1887); LCdr (3 Mar 1899); Cdr (21 Mar 1903); Capt (8 Nov 1907); transferred to Ret.Lst. with rank of RAdm (25 Oct 1911).

Career Summary Received appointment from IA (30 Sep 1870); USNA (Sep 1870-Oct 1874); w.o. (Oct-Dec 1874); *Powhatan* and *Alaska*, Eur.Sta. (Dec 1874-Sep 1876); w.o. (Sep-Oct 1876); USNA (Oct-Nov 1876); home and w.o. (Nov 1876-Jan 1877); *Monongahela*, Asia.Sta. (Jan-Aug 1877); *Michigan*, on Great Lakes (Aug 1877-May 1880); w.o. (May-Sep 1880); rec. ship, *Independence*, Mare Island, CA (Sep 1880-Jun 1881); *Wachusett*, Pac.Sta. (Jun 1881-Jul 1884); home and w.o. (Jul-Aug 1884); *Michigan*, on Great Lakes (Aug 1884-May 1887); torp. instruction, Newport, RI (Jun-Sep 1887); NWC (Sep-Dec 1887); torp. instruction, Newport, RI (Dec 1887-Feb 1888); *Pensacola*, Navy Yard, Norfolk, VA (Mar 1888); *Omaha*, Asia.Sta. (Apr 1888-Jun 1891); l.o.a. (Jun-Sep 1891); USNA (Sep 1891-Jul 1894); *Detroit*, Norfolk, VA (Jul-Aug 1894); *Raleigh*, N.Atl.Sqdn. (Aug 1894-Sep 1896); *Maine*, N.Atl.Sqdn. (Sep 1896-Jun 1897); home and w.o. (Jun 1897); Bur. of Ord., Washington, DC (Jul-Aug 1897); Navy Yard, Washington, DC (Aug 1897-Apr 1898); exec.off., *Princeton*, N.Atl.Flt. (May 1898-Dec 1899); exec.off., *Yorktown*, Asia.Sta. (Dec 1899-Sep 1900); exec.off., flgs., *Brooklyn*, Asia.Sta. (Sep 1900-Apr 1901); home and w.o. (Apr-May 1901); l.o.a. (May-Jul 1901); Naval Gun Factory, Navy Yard, Washington, DC (Jul 1901-Jul 1905); additional duty, Bur. of Yards and Docks, Washington, DC (Jan 1902-Jul 1905); additional duty, asst. to supt., Naval Gun Factory, Navy Yard,

Washington, DC (Jun-Jul 1905); cdr, *Columbia*, Atl. Training Sqdn. (Jul 1905-Mar 1907); aide to sec. of navy, Navy Dept., Washington, DC (Mar-Nov 1907); cdr, *Illinois*, "Great White Flt." (Nov 1907-Apr 1909); cdr, flgs., *Connecticut*, Asia.Flt. (Apr-Jun 1909); supt., USNA (Jun 1909-May 1911); duty connected with Gen Bd., Washington, DC (May-Jun 1911); spec. duty, Navy Dept., Washington, DC (Jun-Nov 1911); transferred to Ret.Lst. (25 Oct 1911).

Career Highlights Served during war with Spain in waters off Cuba, against insurrectionists in P.I., and against Boxers in China. Commanded *Illinois* with "Great White Flt."

ROYAL BIRD BRADFORD Born in Turner, ME, on 22 Jul 1844, son of Phillips and Mary Brett (Bird) Bradford. Married Harriet Stanhope Engs on 26 May 1875. Died on 4 Aug 1914 at the Naval Hosp. in Chelsea, MA. Buried in Washington, D.C.

Ranks Act.Midn (27 Nov 1861); title changed to Midn (16 Jul 1862); Ens (1 Dec 1866); Mstr (12 Mar 1868); Lt (26 Mar 1869); LCdr (30 Nov 1878); Cdr (26 Mar 1889); Capt (3 Mar 1899); temp. RAdm (3 Mar 1899); RAdm (23 Nov 1904); transferred to Ret.Lst. (22 Jul 1906).

Career Summary Received appointment from ME (27 Nov 1861); USNA (Nov 1861-Oct 1865); *Swatara*, W.Ind.Sqdn. (Oct 1865-Dec 1866); *Iroquois*, then flgs., *Delaware*, Asia.Sta. (Jan 1867-Nov 1870); w.o. and l.o.a. (Nov 1870-Mar 1871); sick lv. (Mar 1871-Jan 1872); Torp.Sta., Newport, RI (Jan 1872-Jun 1873); w.o. (Jun-Jul 1873); flgs., *Wabash* and flgs., *Franklin*, Eur.Sta. (Aug 1873-Apr 1875); w.o. (Apr-May 1875); Torp.Sta., Newport, RI (May 1875-Dec 1876); exec.off., *Alliance*, Eur.Sta. (Dec 1876-Jan 1880); Torp.Sta., Newport, RI (Jan 1880-May 1883); spec. duty (May-Jun 1883); exec.off., flgs., *Trenton*, Asia.Sta. (Jun 1883-Jun 1885); sick lv. (Jun-Aug 1885); spec. duty, NWC and Navy Dept., Washington, DC (Aug 1885-Jan 1887); insp., electrical lighting in ships (Jan-Oct 1887); asst. chief of Bur. of Nav., Washington, DC (Nov 1887-Jun 1891); cdr, *Bennington*, N.Atl., S.Atl., and Eur.Stas. (Jun 1891-Jul 1893); l.o.a. and w.o. (Jul-Nov 1893); member, bd. of inspection and surv. and various other bd. duties (Nov 1893-Jun 1896); cdr, *Montgomery*, N.Atl.Sta. (Jul 1896-Jul 1897); chief, Bur. of Equip. and Recruiting, Washington, DC (Sep 1897-Oct 1903); naval attaché, Paris Peace Commission (Sep 1898-Jan 1899); cdr, *Illinois*, N.Atl.Sqdn. (Oct 1903-Oct 1904); cdr, Atl. Training Sqdn., *Minneapolis* (Nov 1904-Mar 1905); cdr, 3rd Sqdn., Atl.Flt., *Olympia* (Apr 1905-Jul 1906); transferred to Ret.Lst. (22 Jul 1906).

Career Highlights Exceptional naval administrator as well as technician. Prepared new *Navy Regulations*, organized a naval electrical dept., served as first insp. of electrical lighting, and sat on many boards dealing with naval technology. Researched and wrote much on torpedoes.

References

Writings: a) *History of Torpedo Warfare* (Newport, RI: 1882).

ROYAL BIRD BRADFORD
1844-1914

b) *Notes on Moveable Torpedoes* (Newport, RI: 1882). c) *Notes on the Spar Torpedo* (Newport, RI: 1882). d) *Notes on Towing Torpedoes* (Newport, RI: 1882).

WILLIAM CLARENCE BRAISTED
1864-1941

WILLIAM CLARENCE BRAISTED Born in Toledo, OH, on 9 Oct 1864, son of Frank and Helen Maris (Fiske) Braisted. Married Lillian Mulford Phipps on 2 Apr 1886. One son, navy Capt Frank Alfred Braisted. Graduated with a Bachelor of Pharmacy degree from Univ. of MI in 1883. Received M.D. degree with honors in 1886 from Columbia Univ.'s College of Physicians and Surgeons. Interned at Bellevue Hospital, NY City. Practiced privately in Detroit from 1888 to 1890. Died in West Chester, PA on 17 Jan 1941.

Ranks Asst.Surg. with rank of Ltjg (24 Sep 1890); PAsst.Surg. (24 Sep 1893); PAsst.Surg. with rel. rank of Lt (3 Mar 1899); Surg. (26 Jan 1902); Surg. with rel. rank of LCdr (3 Mar 1903); Medl.Insp. (20 Oct 1913); Surg.Gen and Chief, Bur. of Medicine and Surgery with rank of RAdm (11 Feb 1914); Medl.Dir. (29 Aug 1916); retired (29 Nov 1920).

Career Summary Received appointment from MI (24 Sep 1890); spec. duty, Hot Springs, AR (Oct 1890-Feb 1891); *Vesuvius*, N.Atl.Sqdn. (Feb 1891-Mar 1893); rec. ship, *Vermont*, NY (Mar-Jul 1893); Naval Hosp., NY (Jun 1893-Apr 1894); *Columbia*, N.Atl.Sqdn. (Apr 1894-Jan 1897); Naval Hosp., Newport, RI (Jan 1897-May 1899); home and w.o. (May-Jun 1899); *Detroit*, N.Atl.Sqdn. (Jun 1899-May 1900); home and w.o. (May-Jun 1900); *Massachusetts*, N.Atl.Sqdn. (Jun-Aug 1900); *Topeka*, spec.serv. (Aug 1900-Jan 1902); Naval Hosp., NY (Jan 1902-May 1904); *Relief*, Mare Island, CA (May-Aug 1904); training ship, *Pensacola* (Aug-Sep 1904); *Ohio*, on trials (Sep 1904-Jan 1905); spec. duty, Tokyo (Feb-Jul 1905); Bur. of Medicine and Surgery, Washington, DC (Aug 1905-Feb 1906); Naval Medl. School, Washington, DC (Feb-Oct 1906); asst., Bur. of Medicine and Surgery, Washington, DC (Oct 1906-Dec 1909); spec. duty, Bur. of Medicine and Surgery, Washington, DC (Dec 1909-Feb 1910); asst., Bur. of Medicine and Surgery, Washington, DC (Feb 1910-May 1912); temp. duty, Bur. of Medicine and Surgery, Washington, DC (May-Jun 1912); flt.surg., Atl.Flt., *Connecticut* (Jun-Oct 1912), *Utah* (Oct 1912-Jan 1913), *Wyoming* (Jan-Feb 1913), *Connecticut* (Feb-Mar 1913), and *Wyoming* (May 1913-Feb 1914); surg.gen and chief, Bur. of Medicine and Surgery, Washington, DC (Feb 1914-Nov 1920); retired (29 Nov 1920).

Career Highlights While asst. to chief of Bur. of Medicine and Surgery, reorganized entire bur., helping to found *U.S. Naval Medical Bulletin.* Served with Dr. Presley Marion Rixey [*q.v.*] as attending physician at White House from 1906 to 1907. Was instrumental in reorganizing Hospital Corps, getting rank and pay increases for members, and assisting in establishing a corps for women nurses, the forerunner of the Nurse Corps. Selected in 1913 as pres. of Association of Military Surgeons. While Surg.Gen and Chief of Bur. of Medicine and Surgery, oversaw construction and updating of many hospitals; established special medl. training schools; and was instrumental in design, construction, and launching of first hospital ship, USS *Relief*. During World War I, was responsible for all naval medl. affairs, for which he received Distinguished Service Medal. Held honorary degrees of LL.D. from Univ. of MI (1917), D.Sc., Northwestern Univ. (1918), LL.D., Jefferson Medical College, Philadelphia (1920), and D.Sc., Columbia Univ. (1927).

References

Writings: with Capt. William Hemphill Bell, *The Life Story of Presley Marion Rixey. Biography and Autobiography* (Strasbourg, VA: 1930).

CARLO BONAPARTE BRITTAIN Born in Pineville, KY, on 16 Jan 1867, son of Carlo Bonaparte and Lydia Swan (Burch) Brittain. Educated at Cumberland College in Barbourville, KY, before entering the Naval Academy. Married Mary Elizabeth Baldwin on 27 Jun 1897. One son, Thomas B. Brittain, who was an ensign at time of father's death. Died on 22 Apr 1920 while commanding the *Pennsylvania* in Cuban waters. Buried in hometown of Richmond, KY.

Ranks Naval Cadet (19 May 1884); Ens (1 Jul 1890); Ltjg (6 Feb 1898); Lt (3 Mar 1899); LCdr (1 Jul 1905); Cdr (3 Sep 1909); Capt (1 Jul 1914); temp. RAdm (21 Sep 1918); died (22 Apr 1920).

Career Summary Received appointment from KY (19 May 1884); USNA (May 1884-Jun 1888); *Omaha*, Asia.Sta. (Jul 1888-Apr 1889); *Marion*, Asia.Sta. (Apr 1889-May 1890); USNA (May-Jun 1890); w.o. (Jun-Oct 1890); *Atlanta*, N.Atl.Sta. (Oct 1890-Jul 1893); *Detroit*, on trials (Jul-Oct 1893); l.o.a. and w.o. (Oct 1893-Mar 1894); *Alert*, Pac.Sqdn. (Apr-Aug 1894); *Petrel*, Asia.Sta. (Aug 1894-Mar 1896); *Charleston*, Asia.Sta. (Mar 1896); *Monocacy*, Asia.Sta. (Mar 1896-Jan 1897); *Detroit*, Asia.Sta. and return to NY (Jan-May 1897); l.o.a. (May-Aug 1897); USNA (Aug 1897-May 1898); *Newark*, N.Atl.Sqdn. (May-Aug 1898); *Brooklyn*, Navy Yard, NY (Aug 1898); *Badger*, N.Patrol Sqdn., Atl.Flt. (Aug-Sep 1898); USNA (Sep 1898-May 1899); home and w.o. (May 1898); gunnery training ship, *Lancaster* (Jun-Oct 1899); sick lv. (Oct 1899-Apr 1900); *Iowa*, Pac.Sqdn. (May-Jul 1900); en route to Asia.Sta. (Jul-Aug 1900); *Newark*, Asia.Sta. (Aug-Sep 1900); *Marietta*, Asia.Sta. (Sep 1900-May 1901); *Kentucky*, flgs., Southern Sqdn., Asia.Flt. (May 1901-Apr 1903); *Yorktown*, Asia.Flt, and en route home (Apr-Jun 1903); USNA (Jul 1903-Mar 1905); aide to cdr. in chief, RAdm Robley D. Evans, Atl.Flt., *Maine* (Mar 1905-Apr 1907), then *Connecticut* (Apr-Sep 1907); USNA (Sep 1907-May 1910); cdr., practice ship, *Massachusetts* (May-Dec 1910); cdr., *Wheeling*, N.Atl.Sta. (Jan 1911-May 1912); member, bd. of inspection and surv., Navy Dept., Washington, D.C. (May 1912-May 1913); asst. to chief, Bur. of Nav., Navy Dept., Washington, D.C. (May 1913-Nov 1915); cdr, *Michigan*, Div. 5, Battleship Force 2, Atl.Flt. (Dec 1915-Jun 1918); cdr, forces afloat, 5th Naval Dist., Norfolk,

CARLO BONAPARTE BRITTAIN
1867-1920

VA (Jun-Sep 1918); cdr, Battleship Force 1, Atl.Flt., *Alabama* (Sep 1918-Jul 1919), then *Pennsylvania* with additional duty as chief of staff, Atl.Flt. (Jun 1919-Apr 1920); died (22 Apr 1920).

Career Highlights Awarded Sampson Medal for engagement at Santiago, Cuba while on *Newark*; received West Indian Campaign Badgeand Philippine Campaign Badge.

References

Writings: *Elements of Naval Warfare; A Treatise Prepared for Use as a Text-Book at the U.S. Naval Academy* (Annapolis: 1909).

WILLIAM BENTHAM BROOKS
1832-1910

WILLIAM BENTHAM BROOKS Born on 27 Nov 1832 in Portsmouth, VA, son of William and Mary Elizabeth (Benthall) Brooks. Educated in private schools and by private tutors. Married Amelia Wright on 23 Sep 1858, having four children, including army LtCol John C. W. Brooks. Died at his home in Erie, PA, on 23 Aug 1910.

Ranks 3rd Asst.Engr. (16 Feb 1852); 2nd Asst.Engr. (27 Jun 1855); 1st Asst.Engr. (21 Jul 1858); Chief Engr. (16 Oct 1861); placed on Ret.Lst. as Chief Engr. with rel. rank of Capt (1 Mar 1892); Chief Engr. with rank of RAdm on Ret.Lst. (20 Dec 1906).

Career Summary Received appointment from VA (16 Feb 1852); *Michigan,* on Great Lakes (Apr 1852-Sep 1855); flgs., *San Jacinto,* Asia.Sqdn. (Nov 1855-Aug 1858); l.o.a. (Aug-Sep 1858); racing schooner, *America* (Sep-Nov 1858); temp. duty, Navy Yard, NY (Nov-Dec 1858); *Brooklyn,* spec. duty and W.Gulf Blk.Sqdn. (Jan 1859-Sep 1861); exam. and w.o. (Sep-Nov 1861); *Brooklyn,* W.Gulf Blk.Sqdn. (Nov 1861-Aug 1863); spec. duty, NY (Aug 1863-Aug 1866); *Sacramento,* spec.serv. and N.Pac. Sqdn. (Sep 1866-Mar 1868); w.o. (Mar-Sep 1868); Navy Yard, Portsmouth, NH (Oct 1868-Mar 1869); w.o. (Mar 1869-Jan 1870); *Michigan,* on Great Lakes (Jan 1870-Jun 1872); Navy Yard, Norfolk, VA (Jun 1872-Mar 1874); flt.engr., Eur.Sqdn., *Franklin* (Mar 1874-Apr 1877); home and w.o. (Apr 1877-May 1879); member, bd. of inspection and surv. (May 1879); Navy Yard, Washington, DC (May 1879-Mar 1882); member, engr. exam.bd. (Apr-Sep 1882); flt.engr., N.Atl.Sta., *Tennessee* (Dec 1882-Dec 1884); w.o. (Dec 1884-Feb 1885); Navy Yard, Portsmouth, NH (Feb 1885-Jun 1888); w.o. (Jun-Dec 1888); temp. duty, West Point Foundry, Cold Spring, NY (Dec 1888-Aug 1889); insp. of machinery, *Texas,* Richmond Locomotive and Machine Works, Norfolk, VA (Aug 1889-Feb 1892); placed on Ret.Lst. (1 Mar 1892).

WILLARD HERBERT BROWNSON
1845-1935

WILLARD HERBERT BROWNSON Born in Lyons, NY, on 8 Jul 1845, son of Morton and Harriet (Taft) Brownson. Married Isabella King Roberts on 10 Jul 1872. Three children, Roswell Roberts, Harriet Hussey, wife of RAdm Charles H. Hussey, USN, and Caroline Hart, wife of RAdm Thomas C. Hart, USN. Died on 16 Mar 1935 in Washington, DC. Buried in Arlington National Cemetery.

Ranks Act.Midn (29 Nov 1861); title changed to Midn (16 Jul

1862); Ens (1 Dec 1866); Mstr (12 Mar 1868); Lt (26 Mar 1869); LCdr (14 Dec 1880); Cdr (19 May 1891); Capt (3 Mar 1899); RAdm (6 May 1905); placed on Ret.Lst. (8 Jul 1907).

Career Summary Received appointment from NY (29 Nov 1861); USNA (Nov 1861-Oct 1865); training ship, *Sabine*, Norfolk, VA (Nov-Dec 1865); *Rhode Island*, W.Ind.Sta. (Dec 1865-Jan 1867); *Susquehanna*, N.Atl.Sta. (Jan 1867-Jan 1868); flgs., *Wampanoag*, N.Atl.Sta. (Jan-Apr 1868); w.o. (Apr-Jul 1868); *Dacotah*, *Mohican*, *St. Mary's*, and *Ossipee*, Pac.Sqdn. (Jul 1868-Nov 1871); w.o. (Nov 1871-Jan 1872); torp. duty, Newport, RI (Jan-Jul 1872); w.o. (Jul-Sep 1872); asst.inst. of math., USNA (Sep 1872-Jun 1875); *Kearsarge* and *Tennessee*, Asia.Sta. (Jul 1875-Jul 1878); asst. to comdt. of cadets, USNA (Aug 1878-Jun 1881); w.o. (Jul-Aug 1881); cst.surv. duty (Aug 1881-Dec 1884); exec.off., *Powhatan*, N.Atl.Sta. (Dec 1884-Jun 1885); cst.surv. duty (Jun-Oct 1885); Hydrographic Insp., cst.surv. (Oct 1885-Jul 1889); duty with, then cdr, *Petrel*, N.Atl.Sta. (Jul 1889-Jul 1891); l.o.a. (Jul-Oct 1891); gen insp., cruiser No. 10 (Oct 1891-Mar 1892); cdr, *Dolphin*, Sqdn. of Evol. (Mar 1892-Jan 1893); temp. duty, *Detroit*, Baltimore (Mar-Jul 1893); cdr, *Detroit*, S.Atl.Sqdn. (Jul 1893-Jul 1894); l.o.a. and w.o. (Jul-Nov 1894); cdr, prac. ship, *Bancroft* (Nov 1894-May 1895); cdr, prac. ship, *Monongahela* (May-Aug 1895); comdt. of cadets, USNA (Sep-Nov 1895); l.o.a. (Nov 1895-Dec 1896); member, bd. of inspection and surv. (Dec 1896-Apr 1898); cdr, *Yankee*, N.Atl.Flt. (Apr-Sep 1898); l.o.a. (Sep 1898-Apr 1899); bd. and insp. duties (Apr 1899-Oct 1900); cdr, *Alabama*, N.Atl.Flt. (Oct 1900-Nov 1902); supt., USNA (Nov 1902-Jun 1905); cdr, 4th Div., Atl.Flt., *West Virginia* (Jul 1905-Aug 1906); cdr, Spec.Serv.Sqdn. (Aug-Oct 1906); cdr, Asia.Flt., *West Virginia* (Oct 1906-Mar 1907); chief, Bur. of Nav., Washington, DC (May-Dec 1907); placed on Ret.Lst. (8 Jul 1907).

References

Personal Papers: 49 items (1894-1931) in NHF,LC.

Writings: *From Frigate to Dreadnought*, compiled by Caroline Brownson Hart; Louise Powers Benesch, research editor (Sharon, CT: c.1973).

Additional Sources: George E. Gelm, "The Admirals and the Viceroy," U.S. Naval Institute *Proceedings* 840 (Feb 1973): 82-84.

GEORGE ELI BURD Born in Belfast, ME, on 27 Apr 1857, son of Samuel F. and Rebecca (Brown) Burd. Married Frances A. Goodwin on 3 Aug 1882. Three children. Died on 18 Feb 1924 in Brooklyn, NY.

Ranks Cadet Engr. (1 Oct 1874); Asst.Engr. (20 Jun 1880); Asst.Engr. with rel. rank of Lt (28 Oct 1890); PAsst.Engr. (4 May 1891); PAsst.Engr. with rel. rank of Lt (1 Mar 1895); Chief Engr. (8 Nov 1898); Lt (3 Mar 1899); LCdr (12 Jul 1901); Cdr (12 Jun 1906); Capt (1 Jul 1910); RAdm (29 Aug 1916); placed on Ret.Lst. (27 Apr 1921).

Career Summary Received appointment from MA (1 Oct 1874); USNA (Oct 1874-Jun 1878); w.o. (Jun-Jul 1878); *Alert*,

N.Atl.Sta. and spec.serv. (Aug 1878-Apr 1882); home and w.o. (Apr-Sep 1882); rec. ship, *Passaic*, Washington, DC (Sep-Dec 1882); w.o. (Dec 1882-Jan 1883); Navy Yard, Boston (Jan-Nov 1883); *Shenandoah*, Pac.Sqdn. (Nov 1883-Oct 1886); w.o. (Oct 1886-Jan 1887); Navy Yard, Boston (Jan 1887-Mar 1889); *Chicago*, Chester, PA (Mar-Apr 1889); *Yorktown*, on trials and Sqdn. of Evol. (Apr 1889-Jun 1890); *Atlanta*, Sqdn. of Evol. (Jun 1890-Nov 1891); l.o.a. (Nov 1891-Jan 1892); inspection duties (Jan 1892-May 1894); *Cincinnati*, spec.serv. in W.Indies and Med. (May 1894-Jul 1897); l.o.a. (Jul-Aug 1897); Navy Yard, NY (Aug 1897-Jun 1898); *Badger*, N.Patrol Sqdn., N.Atl.Flt. (Jun-Dec 1898); insp. of machinery, Continental Iron Works, Brooklyn, NY (Dec 1898-Feb 1899); rec. ship, *Vermont*, NY (Feb-Sep 1899); Navy Yard, NY (Sep 1899-Mar 1900); *Philadelphia*, Pac.Sqdn. (Apr 1900-Sep 1902); *Boston*, Pac.Sqdn. (Sep 1902-Jun 1903); asst.insp. of machinery, Union Iron Works, San Francisco (Jun 1903-Mar 1904); in charge, dept. of steam engineering, Navy Yard, Puget Sound, WA (Mar 1904-Jan 1905); *Pennsylvania*, Philadelphia, and Atl.Flt. (Jan 1905-Mar 1906); flt.engr., Atl.Flt., *Pennsylvania* (Mar-Jun 1906); duty with Naval Auxiliaries, Atl.cst., Baltimore (Jul 1906-Jan 1907); head, dept. of steam engineering, Navy Yard, Boston (Jan 1907-May 1910); head, dept. of steam engineering, Navy Yard, NY (Jun 1910-Nov 1914); industrial manager, Navy Yard, NY (Nov 1914-Apr 1921); placed on Ret.Lst. (27 Apr 1921).

Career Highlights As industrial manager at NY Navy Yard, was in charge of all alteration, reconstruction, engineering, and repair work on 723 vessels assigned to 3rd Naval Dist., including all troop transports based at NY, viz., some 40 percent of all armed forces sent to Europe during World War I.

ARTHUR BURTIS
1841-1908

ARTHUR BURTIS Born in Oxford, NY, on 29 Jun 1841, son of Reverend Arthur and Grace Ewing (Phillips) Burtis. Educated at private schools in Buffalo, NY, then at Union College and Hobart College. Married Ida Thomas in 1884. Died in Buffalo, NY, on 22 Oct 1908. Buried in Forest Lawn Cemetery in Buffalo.

Ranks Asst.Paymstr. (14 Jul 1862); Paymstr. (4 May 1866); Pay Insp. (21 Sep 1891); Pay Dir. with rank of Capt (5 May 1899); retired with rank of RAdm (21 Nov 1902).

Career Summary Received appointment from NY (14 Jul 1862); sick lv. (Aug-Nov 1862); *Connecticut*, spec.serv. and N.Atl.Blk.Sqdn. (Dec 1862-Oct 1864); s.a. and w.o. (Oct-Dec 1864); *Muscoota*, under construction and Gulf Sqdn. (Dec 1864-Sep 1866); s.a. and w.o. (Sep 1866-Jan 1867); rec. ship, *St. Louis*, League Island, PA (Jan 1867-Feb 1870); s.a. and w.o. (Feb-July 1870); *Brooklyn*, Eur.Sqdn. (Aug 1870-Jan 1873); s.a. and w.o. (Jan-Oct 1873); member, bd. of examiners, Washington, DC (Oct 1873-Jan 1874); insp. of provisions and clothing, Navy Yard, Philadelphia (Jan 1874-Jan 1877); s.a. and w.o. (Jan-Oct 1877); l.o.a. (Dec 1877-Dec 1878); Navy Yard, League Island, PA (Jan 1879-Jan 1880); s.a. and w.o. (Jan-Jun 1880); prac. ship, *Constellation* (Jun-Aug 1880); s.a. and w.o. (Aug 1880-Jun 1881);

spec. duty, Navy Yard, NY (Jun-Sep 1881); s.a. and w.o. (Sep-Oct 1881); sick lv. (Oct 1881-Sep 1883); *Galena*, N.Atl.Sqdn. (Sep 1883-May 1886); s.a. and w.o. (May-Jun 1886); paymstr., Navy Yard, NY (Jun 1886-May 1889); rec. ship, *Vermont*, NY (May-Dec 1889); s.a. and w.o. (Dec 1889-Jan 1890); flt.paymstr., Pac.Sta., *Charleston* (Jan 1890-Mar 1891) and *San Francisco* (Mar 1891-Jan 1892); s.a. and w.o. (Jan-Mar 1892); general store-keeper, Navy Yard, Norfolk, VA (Mar-Sep 1892); l.o.a. (Sep-Dec 1892); Navy Yard, NY (Dec 1892-Dec 1895); s.a. and w.o. (Dec 1895-Jan 1896); member, bd. of inspection and surv. (Jan 1896-Jun 1897); flt.paymstr., N.Atl.Sta., *New York* (Jul 1897-Jul 1899); s.a. and w.o. (Jul-Nov 1899); in charge, Pay Office, Boston (Dec 1899-May 1902); s.a. (May-Jul 1902); in charge, Pay Office, NY (Jul 1902-Jul 1903); retired (21 Nov 1902).

WILLIAM TURNBULL BURWELL Born in Vicksburg, MS, on 19 Jul 1846, son of Armistead B. and Priscilla Withers (Manlove) Burwell. Married Ella Tazewell Bradford. Died on 4 Jan 1910 in Llandudno, Wales. Buried in USNA Cemetery in Annapolis.

Ranks Midn (30 Sep 1862); Ens (12 Mar 1868); Mstr (26 Mar 1869); Lt (21 Mar 1870); LCdr (23 Sep 1885); Cdr (7 Sep 1894); Capt (29 Nov 1900); RAdm (6 Jun 1906); placed on Ret.Lst. (19 Jul 1908).

Career Summary Received appointment from MO (30 Sep 1862); USNA (Sep 1862-Jun 1866); l.o.a. and w.o. (Jun-Oct 1866); *Susquehanna*, N.Atl.Sqdn. (Oct 1866-Jan 1867); *Tacony*, N.Atl.Sqdn. (Jan-Sep 1867); w.o. (Sep-Oct 1867); *Idaho*, then *Monocacy*, Asia.Sqdn. (Oct 1867-Dec 1870); l.o.a. and w.o. (Dec 1870-Sep 1871); rec. ship, *Vermont*, NY (Sep-Oct 1871); *Severn*, Navy Yard, Boston (Oct-Dec 1871); flgs., *Worcester*, N.Atl.Sqdn. (Dec 1871-Feb 1876); Navy Yard, NY (Feb 1876-Aug 1877); *Trenton*, Eur.Sta. (Oct 1877-Oct 1881); USNA (Oct 1881-Dec 1885); *Juniata*, Asia.Sta. (Dec 1885-Apr 1888); cdr, *Juniata*, Asia.Sta. (Apr 1888-Feb 1889); w.o. (Feb-Mar 1889); nav., then ord.off., Navy Yard, Norfolk, VA (Apr 1889-Jan 1893); cdr, *Pinta*, N.Pac.Sqdn. (Feb 1893-Sep 1894); home and w.o. (Sep-Oct 1894); equip.off., Navy Yard, Norfolk, VA (Nov 1894-Dec 1895); cdr, *Dolphin*, Spec.Serv.Sqdn. (Dec 1895-Apr 1896); NWC (Jun 1896); insp., 16th L.h. Dist., Memphis, TN (Jun 1896-May 1898); cdr, *Alexander*, N.Atl.Flt. (May-Oct 1898); cdr, *Wheeling*, N.Pac.Sqdn. (Nov 1898-May 1900); home and w.o. (May-Jun 1900); comdt., Navy Yard, Puget Sound, WA (Jul 1900-Aug 1902); cdr, *Oregon*, Asia.Sta. (Aug 1902-Aug 1904); home and w.o. (Aug-Oct 1904); cdr, rec. ship, *Independence*, Mare Island, CA (Nov 1904-Sep 1905); cdr, Navy Yard, Puget Sound, WA (Sep 1905-Jul 1908); placed on Ret.Lst. (19 Jul 1908).

WILLIAM BANKS CAPERTON Born in Spring Hill, TN, on 30 Jun 1855, son of Samuel B. and Mary Jane (Childress) Caperton. Early education at Spring Hill Academy. Married Georgie Washington Langhorn Blalock. One daughter. Died on

WILLIAM BANKS CAPERTON
1855-1941

21 Dec 1941 at Naval Hosp. in Newport, RI.

Ranks Cadet Midn (13 Jun 1871); Midn (17 Sep 1875); Ens (3 Aug 1877); Ltjg (13 Oct 1883); Lt (24 Oct 1889); LCdr (3 Mar 1899); Cdr (31 Aug 1904); Capt (1 Jul 1908); RAdm (13 Feb 1913); Act.Adm (19 Jul 1916); placed on Ret.Lst. (30 Jun 1919); Adm on Ret.Lst. (21 Jun 1930).

Career Summary Received appointment from TN (13 Jun 1871); USNA (Jun 1871-Sep 1875); w.o. (Sep-Nov 1875); *Hartford* and *Powhatan*, N.Atl.Sta. (Nov 1875-Jul 1877); w.o. (Jul 1877-Jan 1878); USNA (Jan 1878); w.o. (Jan-Mar 1878); training ship, *Constellation* (Mar-Jul 1878); w.o. (Jul-Sep 1878); flgs., *Powhatan*, N.Atl.Sqdn. (Sep 1878-Dec 1879); flgs., *Tennessee*, N.Atl.Sqdn. (Dec 1879-Jan 1880); l.o.a. (Jan-Nov 1880); cst.surv. duty (Nov 1880-Nov 1883); w.o. (Nov 1883-Jan 1884); *Ossipee*, Asia.Sta. (Jan 1884-Dec 1884); *Trenton*, Asia.Sta. (Dec 1884-Mar 1887); w.o. (Mar-Apr 1887); insp. of steel for new cruisers, Pittsburgh, PA (Apr 1887-Nov 1888); steel inspection duty, Washington, DC (Nov 1888-Feb 1891); l.o.a. (Feb-Mar 1891); w.o. (Mar-May 1891); recorder, naval exam. bd., Norfolk, VA (May-Oct 1891); *Miantonomoh*, N.Atl.Sqdn. (Oct 1891-Jun 1893); *Vesuvius*, N.Atl.Sqdn. (Jul-Dec 1893); training ship, *Essex* (Feb-Nov 1894); l.o.a. (Nov 1894-Feb 1895); Office of Naval Intelligence, Washington, DC (Feb 1895-Nov 1896); NWC (Jun-Oct 1895); *Brooklyn*, spec.cruise (Dec 1896-Aug 1897); *Marietta*, Pac. and N.Atl.Sqdns. (Sep 1897-Oct 1899); home and w.o. (Oct-Dec 1899); insp. of ord., Naval Gun Factory, Navy Yard, Washington, DC (Dec 1899-Jul 1901); exec.off., training ship, *Prairie* (Aug 1901-Jun 1904); w.o. (Jun 1904); NWC (Jul-Oct 1904); insp., 15th L.h. Dist., St. Louis, MO (Oct 1904-Apr 1907); cdr, *Denver*, Asia. Flt. (Apr 1907-Jul 1908); cdr, *Maine* "Great White Flt.," and flgs., 3rd Sqdn., Atl.Flt. (Jul 1908-Aug 1909); w.o. (Aug-Oct 1909); sec., L.h. Bd., Washington, DC (Oct 1909-Jun 1910); NWC (Jul-Sep 1910); member, naval exam. and ret. bd., Navy Yard, Washington, DC (Sep 1910-May 1912); comdt., Naval Sta., and 2nd Naval Dist., Newport and Narragansett Bay, RI (May 1912-Nov 1913); cdr, Atl. Reserve Flt., *Alabama* (Nov 1913-May 1914), *Wisconsin* (May 1914), *Alabama* (May-Nov 1914); cdr, Cruiser Sqdn., Atl.Flt., *Washington* (Nov 1914-Feb 1916), *Tennessee* (Feb 1916), *Dolphin* (Feb-Jul 1916); cdr, Pac.Flt., *San Diego* (Jul 1916-Feb 1917), *Pittsburgh* (Feb 1917-Apr 1919); Office of Naval Operations, Washington, DC (May-Jun 1919); placed on Ret.Lst. (30 Jun 1919).

Career Highlights While commanding Atl.Flt., it was his command that intervened in Haiti in 1915 and 1916, at Vera Cruz in 1915, and during the Santo Domingo Revolution in 1916. During World War I, commanded U.S. Pac.Flt., patrolling east coast of S.America.

References

Personal Papers: ½ box (1875-1951) at NWC. b) 700 items (1873-1937) in NHF,LC. c) Caperton Papers in The TN State Museum, Nashville, TN.

WASHINGTON LEE CAPPS Born in Portsmouth, VA, on 31 Jan 1864, son of Washington Tazewell and Frances (Bernard) Capps. Received B.S. degree in 1888 and a D.Sc. in Jun 1912 from the Univ. of Glasgow. Married Edna Ward, daughter of RAdm Aaron Ward [*q.v.*] in 1911. Died at his home in Washington, DC, on 31 May 1935. Buried in Arlington National Cemetery.

WASHINGTON LEE CAPPS
1864-1935

Ranks Cadet Engr. (1 Oct 1880); Ens (1 Jul 1886); resigned (5 Jun 1888); Asst. Naval Const. (6 Jun 1888); Naval Const. (28 Jan 1895); Naval Const. with rel. rank of Cdr (5 Aug 1899); Chief Const., USN, and Chief, Bur. of Construction and Repair with rank of RAdm (1 Nov 1903); Chief Const. with rank of PAdm (1 Oct 1910); transferred to Ret.Lst. (31 Jan 1928).

Career Summary Received appointment from VA (1 Oct 1880); USNA (Oct 1880-Jun 1884); *Tennessee,* N.Atl.Sqdn. (Jun 1884-Apr 1886); w.o. (Apr-Aug 1886); spec. duty, Glasgow, Scotland (Sep 1886-May 1889); resigned (5 Jun 1888); received appointment as asst. Maval const. (6 Jun 1888); Navy Dept., Washington, DC (May-Jul 1889); duty, William Cramp and Sons Iron Works, Philadelphia (Aug-Sep 1889); Navy Yard, NY (Sep 1889-Jul 1892); Bur. of Construction and Repair, Washington, DC (Jul 1892-Jan 1896); supt. of construction, Union Iron Works, San Francisco (Feb 1896-May 1898); spec. duty, flgs., *Olympia,* Asia.Sta. (Jun 1898-Oct 1899); Bur. of Construction and Repair, Washington, DC (Oct-Nov 1899); member, bd. of inspection and surv., Washington, DC (Oct 1899-Mar 1901); head, construction and repair dept., Navy Yard, NY (Mar 1901-Oct 1903); chief const., and chief, Bur. of Construction and Repair, Washington, DC (Nov 1903-Oct 1910); senior member, bd. on hull changes, Atl.cst. Philadelphia (Oct-Nov 1910); spec, inspection duty, Naval Stas., Cavite and Olongapo, P.I. (Dec 1910-Jul 1911); spec. duty, *Maine* investigation (Sep-Oct 1911); l.o.a. (Nov 1911-Sep 1912); pres., bd. on hull changes, Atl.cst. Washington, DC (Sep 1912-May 1935); U.S. commissioner, international maritime conference, London (Oct 1913-Feb 1914); general manager, Emergency Flt. Corporation (Jul-Dec 1917); member, Navy Yard Commission (1916-May 1935); pres., naval war claims bd. (1917-May 1935); transferred to Ret.Lst. (31 Jan 1928).

Career Highlights The navy's chief const. for many years. During war with Spain and while attached to Asia.Sqdn., supervised the raising of several Spanish vessels sunk during Battle of Manila Bay. Awarded Distinguished Service Medal for his services during World War I. Received special commendation for services on naval compensation bd.

FRENCH ENSOR CHADWICK Born in Morgantown, [W.]VA, on 28 Feb 1844, son of Daniel Clark and Margaret Eliza (Evans) Chadwick. Educated at Monongalia Academy in Morgantown. Married Cornelia J Miller on 20 Nov 1878. No issue. Died on 27 Jan 1919 in NY City. Buried in Morgantown, WV.

FRENCH ENSOR CHADWICK
1844-1919

Ranks Act.Midn (28 Sep 1861); title changed to Midn (16 Jul

1862); Ens (1 Nov 1866); Mstr (1 Dec 1866); Lt (12 Mar 1868); LCdr (26 Mar 1869); Cdr (12 Dec 1884); Capt (7 Nov 1897); Chief, Bur. of Equip. and Recruiting with rank of Commo (1 Jul 1893); RAdm (11 Oct 1903); placed on Ret.Lst. (28 Feb 1906).

Career Summary Received appointment from VA (28 Sep 1861); USNA (Sep 1861-Nov 1864); w.o. (Nov 1864-Feb 1865); Navy Yard, NY (Feb-Apr 1865); flgs., *Susquehanna*, spec.serv. and S.Atl.Sqdn. (Apr 1865-Oct 1866); *Juniata*, S.Atl.Sqdn. (Nov 1866-Jun 1867); w.o. (Jun-Sep 1867); training ship, *Sabine* (Oct 1867-Apr 1868); *Tuscarora*, S.Pac. and N.Atl.Sqdns. (Apr 1868-Feb 1870); sick lv. (Feb-Mar 1870); torp. duty, Newport, RI (Mar-Jul 1870); *Guerriere*, Eur.Sqdn. (Aug 1870-Mar 1872); w.o. and l.o.a. (Mar-Sep 1872); inst. of math., USNA (Sep 1872-May 1875); exec.off., *Powhatan*, N.Atl.Sta. (May 1875-Nov 1878); w.o. and l.o.a. (Nov 1878-May 1879); spec. duty (May-Aug 1879); l.o.a. (Aug-Dec 1879); Navy Yard, NY (Dec 1879-Jul 1880); spec. L.h. duty, 3rd Dist., Tompkinsville, NY (Jul 1880-Jul 1882); naval attaché, London (Oct 1882-Apr 1889); cdr, *Yorktown*, Sqdn. of Evol. (Apr 1889-Jul 1891); spec. duty, Navy Dept., Washington, DC (Jul 1891-Aug 1892); chief, Office of Naval Intelligence, Washington, DC (Aug 1892-Jun 1893); chief, Bur. of Equip. and Recruiting, Washington, DC (Jul 1893-Sep 1897); l.o.a. (Sep-Nov 1897); cdr, flgs., *New York*, N.Atl.Sqdn. (Dec 1897-Dec 1899); chief of staff, N.Atl.Sqdn., *New York* (Mar 1898-Jan 1900); NWC (Jan-Oct 1900); pres., NWC (Oct 1900-Nov 1903); comdt., 2nd Naval Dist. (Mar-Nov 1903); bd. duties, Washington, DC (Nov 1903-Mar 1904); cdr, S.Atl.Sqdn., *Brooklyn* (Apr-Nov 1904); home and w.o. (Nov 1904-Feb 1906); placed on Ret.Lst. (28 Feb 1906).

Career Highlights Served for seven years as first naval attaché at American Embassy in London. Was Chief of Staff to RAdm William T. Sampson during Spanish-American War, participating in many of the important actions of that war and being advanced five numbers in rank for eminent and conspicuous conduct in battle.

References
Personal Papers: a) 12 boxes (1886-88) in NYHS. b) 6 items (1898-1911) in NWC. c) 2 items, 1 box (1903-14) in WV Univ.Lib., Morgantown.

Writings: a) "The Training of Seamen," U.S. Naval Institute *Proceedings* 11 (1880): 17-36. b) "Aids to Navigation," U.S. Naval Institute *Proceedings* 17 (1881): 255-96. c) "Our Merchant Marine: The Causes off Its Decline, and the Means to be Taken for Its Revival," U.S. Naval Institute *Proceedings* 19 (1882): 75-120. d) *et.al.*, *Ocean Steamships* (NY, 1891). e) "Naval Department Organization U.S. Naval Institute *Proceedings* 71 (1894): 493-525. f) "Explanation of Course at the Naval War College, June 4, 1901," U.S. Naval Institute *Proceedings* 98 (Jun 1901): 301-1O. g) "Opening Address Delivered by the President of the War College, June 4, 1902," U.S. Naval Institute *Proceedings* 102 (Jun 1902): 251-68. h) "Causes of the Civil War, 1859-1861," *The American Nation*, ed. Albert Bushnell Hart, 28 vols. (NY: 1904-18). i) *The Relations of the United States and Spain: Diplomacy* (NY: 1909; reprint, 1969). j) *The Relations of the United States and Spain: The Spanish-American War* (NY: 1911; reprint, 1968). k) *The American Navy* (Garden City, NJ: 1915). l) *The Graves Papers and Other Documents Relating to the Naval Operations of the Yorktown Campaign* (NY: 1916).

Additional Sources: a) Paolo E. Coletta, "French Ensor Chadwick: The Scholarly Warrior, 1844-1919," *Shipmate* 40, no. 7 (Sep 1977): 31-33. b) William J. Hourihan, "Marlinspike Diplomacy: The Navy in the Mediterranean, 1904," U.S. Naval Institute *Proceedings* 911 (Jan 1979): 42-51. c) Paolo E. Coletta, "French Ensor Chadwick: The First American Naval Attaché, 1882-1889," *The Neptune* 39, no. 2 (1979): 126-41. d) Paolo E. Coletta, *French Ensor Chadwick. Scholarly Warrior* (Lanham, MD: 1980). e) Doris D. Maguire, *French Ensor Chadwick: Selected Letters and Papers.* (Washington, DC: 1981). f) Paolo E. Coletta, "The 'Newes' of the New Navy," *The American Neptune* 38, no. 2 (1987): 122-30.

COLBY MITCHELL CHESTER Born in New London, CT, on 29 Feb 1844, son of Melville and Frances E. (Harris) Chester. Married Melancia Antoinette Tremaine on 25 Nov 1873. Two sons. Died on 4 May 1932 in Rye, NY. Buried in Arlington National Cemetery.

COLBY MITCHELL CHESTER
1844-1932

Ranks Act.Midn (31 Oct 1859); title changed to Midn (16 Jul 1862); Act.Ens (1 Oct 1863); Ens (21 Dec 1865); Mstr (10 May 1866); Lt (21 Feb 1867); LCdr (12 Mar 1868); Cdr (15 Oct 1881); Capt (12 Jun 1896); RAdm (10 Aug 1903); placed on Ret.Lst. (28 Feb 1906).

Career Summary Received appointment from CT (31 Oct 1859); USNA (Oct 1859-Sep 1863); turned back (9 Jun 1860); *Richmond*, W.Gulf Blk.Sqdn. (Oct 1863-Jul 1865); temp. duty, *Kickapoo*, W.Gulf Blk.Sqdn. (Apr 1865); w.o. (Jul-Sep 1865); flgs., *Powhatan*, S.Pac.Sta. (Sep 1865-Nov 1867); w.o. (Dec 1867-Jan 1868); sick lv. (Jan-Apr 1868); flgs., *Contoocook* [renamed *Albany*], N.Atl.Sta. (Apr-May 1868); exec.off., *Gettysburg*, spec.serv. (May 1868-Oct 1869); w.o. (Oct-Nov 1869); *Alaska*, Asia.Sta. (Dec 1869-Feb 1873); w.o. (Feb-Aug 1873); Torp.Sta., Newport, RI (Sep 1873-Jun 1874); sick lv. (Jun-Jul 1874); USNA (Aug 1874-Aug 1877); w.o. (Aug-Oct 1877); cst.surv. duty (Oct 1877-Oct 1885); Hydrographic Office, Washington, DC (Dec 1880-Oct 1881); cdr, *Galena*, spec.serv. (Oct 1885-Dec 1888); member, commission to select Pac.cst Navy Yard (Dec 1888-Sep 1889); member, bd. on organization, tactics, and drill (Jul 1889); Bur. of Nav., Navy Dept., Washington, DC (Jul 1890-Mar 1891); comdt. of cadets, USNA (Apr 1891-Nov 1894); Navy Yard, NY (Nov 1894-Dec 1895); cdr, rec. ship, *Richmond*, Philadelphia (Jan-Nov 1896); cdr, *Newark*, N.Atl.Sqdn. (Dec 1896-Mar 1897); home and w.o. (Mar-May 1897); cdr, *Minneapolis*, Eur.Sqdn. (May-Jul 1897); cdr S.Atl.Sta., *Cincinnati* (Nov 1,897-Apr 1898); cdr, *Cincinnati*, N.Atl.Flt. (Apr 1898-Feb 1899); general insp., *Kentucky*, Newport News, VA (Feb 1899-May 1900); cdr,

Kentucky, NY and Asia.Sta. (May 1900-Mar 1901); NWC (Jun 1901-Aug 1902); supt., Naval Observatory, Washington, DC (Aug 1902-Feb 1906); placed on Ret.Lst. (28 Feb 1906).

Career Highlights While with the *Alaska,* commanded steam launches surveying Salee River in Korea; fired upon from fortifications guarding that river's entrance in Jun 1871. Became prof. of naval science at Yale Univ. in 1917, then supt. of naval units at Yale, Columbia, and Brown Universities.

References

Personal Papers: a) 300 items (1913-28) in NHF,LC. b) Journal of *Macedonian* (1863) in Weston Public Lib., Weston, MA.

Selected Writings: a) "Curves of Stability," U.S. Naval Institute *Proceedings* 24 (1883): 257-85. b) "Some Early Geographers of the United States," *National Geographic Magazine* 15 (1904): 392-404. c) "The Work of the Naval Observatory," U.S. Naval Institute *Proceedings* 110 (Jun 1904): 265-88. d) "The Panama Canal," *National Geographic Magazine* 16 (1905): 445-67. e) "Preliminary Results of the United States Observatory Eclipse Expedition in 1905," *Astrophysical Journal* 23, no. 2 (1906). f) "The Coming of Explosive Engines for Naval Purposes," U.S. Naval Institute *Proceedings* 119 (Sept 1906): 1031-41. g) "Haiti: A Degenerating Island," *National Geographic Magazine* 19 (1908): 200-17. h) "Diplomacy of the Quarter-Deck," *American Journal of International Law* 3 (1914): 443-76.

CHARLES EDGAR CLARK 1843-1922

CHARLES EDGAR CLARK Born at Bradford, VT, on 10 Aug 1843, son of James Dayton and Mary (Sexton) Clark. Educated at the Bradford dist. school and at Bradford Academy. Married Louisa Davis on 8 Apr 1868. Two daughters, Mary Louise and Caroline Russell, who married future admirals Samuel S. Robison and C. F. Hughes, respectively. Received LL.D. degree from Univ. of PA in 1905. Died on 1 Oct 1922 in Long Beach, CA.

Ranks Act.Midn (29 Sep 1860); title changed to Midn (16 Jul 1862); Act.Ens (1 Oct 1863); designation "Act." discontinued (21 Dec 1865); Mstr (10 May 1866); Lt (21 Feb 1867); LCdr (12 Mar 1868); Cdr (15 Nov 1881); Capt (21 Jun 1896); RAdm (16 Jun 1902); placed on Ret.Lst. (10 Aug 1905).

Career Summary Received appointment from VT (29 Sep 1860); USNA (Sep 1860-Oct 1863); *Ossipee,* W.Gulf Blk.Sqdn. (Oct 1863-Jun 1865); w.o. (Jun-Sep 1865); *Vanderbilt,* Pac.Sta. (Sep 1865-Feb 1867); *Suwanee,* Pac.Sta. (Feb 1867-Aug 1868); w.o. (Aug-Sep 1868); rec. ship, *Vandalia,* Portsmouth, NH (Oct 1868-Mar 1869); *Seminole,* N.Atl.Sta. (Apr-May 1869); rec. ship, *Vermont,* NY (May-Jun 1869); *Dictator,* N.Atl.Sta. (Jul 1869-Aug 1870); w.o. (Aug-Sep 1870); USNA (Sep 1870-Jul 1873); w.o. (Jul-Nov 1873); exec.off., *Mahopac,* N.Atl.Sta. (Nov 1873-Feb 1874); home and to next duty (Feb-Jun 1874); *Hartford* and *Monocacy,* Asia.Sta. (Jun 1874-Apr 1877); home and w.o. (Apr-Aug 1877); Navy Yard, Boston (Aug 1877-Nov 1880); w.o. and l.o.a. (Nov 1880-Jul 1881); exec.off., flgs. *New Hampshire,*

Apprentice Training Sqdn. (Jul-Dec 1881); w.o. (Dec 1881-Mar 1882); cdr, flgs., *New Hampshire,* Apprentice Training Sqdn. (Mar 1882-Apr 1883); Torp.Sta., Newport, RI (Apr-Jul 1883); w.o. (Jul-Sep 1883); *Ranger,* surv. duty (Oct 1883-Oct 1886); spec. duty preparing surv. report (Oct 1886-Jan 1887); insp., 9th L.h. Dist., Chicago (Feb 1887-Apr 1891); ord. duty, Navy Yard, Mare Island, CA (May 1891-Nov 1893); cdr, *Mohican,* Pac.Sqdn. (Nov 1893-Dec 1894); home and l.o a. (Dec 1894-Jan 1895); various bd. duties (Jan 1895-Sep 1896); cdr, rec. ship, *Independence,* Mare Island, CA (Nov 1895-Sep 1896); cdr, *Monterey,* Pac.Sqdn. (Sep 1896-Mar 1898); cdr, *Oregon,* Pac. and N.Atl.Sqdns. (Mar 1898-Aug 1899); chief of staff, E.Sqdn., N.Atl.Flt. (Jul-Aug 1898); sick lv. (Aug 1898-Feb 1899); capt.yd., Navy Yard, League Island, PA (Mar 1899-Sep 1901); gov., Naval Home, Philadelphia (Sep 1901-Jul 1904); member, Gen Bd., Washington, DC (Jul 1904-Aug 1905); pres., naval exam. and ret. bds. (Jul 1904-May 1905); placed on Ret.Lst. (10 Aug 1905).

Career Highlights During Civil War, participated in Battle of Mobile Bay in Aug 1864. Commanded the bon on her epic voyage from the Pac. in time to participate in Battle of Santiago in Jul 1898, being advanced six numbers in rank for his conduct.

References

Personal Papers: a) 1 envelope (1898-1904) at The Essex Institute, James Duncan Philips Lib., Salem, MA. b) 24 items (1898-1900) in S. Wier Mitchell Papers, NYPL.

Writings: a) *Prince and Boatswain Sea Tales from the Recollections of Rear Admiral Charles E. Clark as Related to James Morris Morgan and John Philip Marquand* (Greenfield, MA: 1915). b) *My Fifty Years in the Navy* (Boston: 1917; reprint, 1984).

GEORGE RAMSEY CLARK Born in Monroe, OH, on 20 Mar 1857, son of Peter Williamson and Louisa Jane (Boyd) Clark. Married Mary Winchell Brown on 29 Oct 1889. One daughter. Died at his home in Washington, DC, on 14 Dec 1945.

Ranks Cadet Midn (9 Jun 1874); Midn (4 Jun 1880); Ensjg (3 Mar 1883); Ens (24 Aug 1883); Ltjg (16 Feb 1890); Lt (19 Aug 1894); LCdr (1 Jul 1901); Cdr (6 Jun 1906); Capt (4 May 1910); Act.RAdm (20 Mar 1918); Judge Advocate Gen with rank of RAdm (12 Jul 1918); RAdm (20 Jul 1918); retired (6 Feb 1921).

Career Summary Received appointment from OH (9 Jun 1874); USNA (Jun 1874-Jun 1878); w.o. (Jun-Sep 1878); rec. ship, *Independence,* Mare Island, CA (Sep-Oct 1878); *Tuscarora,* Pac.Sta. (Oct 1878-Feb 1880); home and w.o. (Feb-May 1880); USNA (May-Jun 1880); w.o. (Jun 1880-Apr 1881); *Wachusett,* Pac.Sta. (May 1881-May 1884); home and w.o. (May-Jul 1884); *Michigan,* on Great Lakes (Jul 1884-May 1887); *Trenton,* S. Atl.Sta. (May-Sep 1887); *Lancaster,* S.Atl.Sta. (Sep 1887); *Alliance,* S.Atl.Sta. (Sep 1887-Jul 1888); *Lancaster,* Eur.Sta. (Jul 1888-Sep 1889); w.o. (Sep-Oct 1889); spec. duty, electric lights, William Cramp and Sons Iron Works, Philadelphia (Oct 1889-Apr 1890); *Michigan,* on Great Lakes (Apr 1890-Apr 1892); *Richmond,* Training Sta., Newport, RI (Apr-Dec 1892); *Atlanta,*

GEORGE RAMSEY CLARK
1857-1945

N.Atl.Sta. (Dec 1892-Jul 1893); *Machias,* N.Atl.Sta. (Jul 1893-Feb 1894); training ship, *Essex* (Mar 1894-Jul 1895); *Amphitrite,* N.Atl.Sqdn. (Aug-Sep 1895); USNA (Sep 1895-Mar 1898); *Puritan,* N.Atl.Sqdn. (Mar-Oct 1898); *Adams,* Navy Yard, Mare Island, CA (Oct-Nov 1898); *Yorktown,* Asia. Flt. (Nov 1898-Jun 1900); *Monocacy,* Asia.Flt. (Jun-Jul 1900); Naval Hosp., Yokohama, Japan (Jul-Oct 1900); home and w.o. (Oct-Nov 1900); sick lv. (Nov 1900-Feb 1901); Compass Office, Bur. of Equip. and Recruiting, Washington, DC (Feb-Mar 1901); temp. duty, Hydrographic Office, Washington, DC (Mar 1901); in charge, branch hydrographic office, Cleveland, OH (Apr 1901-May 1902); exec.off., training ship, *Monongahela* (May 1902-May 1904); home and w.o. (May 1904); exec. off., training ship, *Prairie* (Jun 1904-Jul 1905); home and l.o.a. (Jul 1905); aide to comdt., Navy Yard, Norfolk, VA (Jul 1905-Aug 1906); cdr, *Texas,* Cst.Sqdn., Atl.Flt. (Aug 1906-Aug 1907); USNA (Aug 1907-Aug 1910); cdr, *Iowa,* Atl. Reserve Flt. (Aug 1910-Apr 1911); cdr, *Minnesota,* N.Atl.Flt. (Apr 1911-Nov 1912); home and w.o. (Nov 1912-Jan 1913); supervisor, 3rd, 4th, and 5th Naval Dists., Philadelphia (Jan-Feb 1913); comdt., Training Sta., and supervisor, 9th, 10th, and 11th Naval Dists., Great Lakes, IL (Feb 1913-Sep 1914); aide for education, Navy Dept., Washington, DC (Sep 1914-Jun 1915); member, naval exam. and ret. bds., and other bd. duties, Washington, DC (Jun 1915-Jun 1916); comdt., Naval Sta., Honolulu, Territory of HI (Aug 1916-Jun 1918); Judge Advocate Gen., USN, Washington, DC (Jul 1918-Apr 1921); transferred to Ret.Lst. (6 Feb 1921).

Career Highlights Served in Spanish-American War, Philippine Insurrection, and Boxer Rebellion, receiving Decorated Navy Cross and the Distinguished Service Medal. Served as Judge Advocate for the Navy from 1918 to 1921.

References

Writings: a) "The Training Service. A Few Notes," U.S. Naval Institute *Proceedings* 74 (1895): 335-38. b) "On Other Duty," U.S. Naval Institute *Proceedings* 129 (Mar 1909): 127-36. c) "Protecting American Interests," U.S. Naval Institute *Proceedings* 130 (Jun 1909): 393-403. d) with William O. Stevens, Carroll S. Alden, and Herman F. Krafft, *The Navy, 1775-1909,* 2 vols. (Baltimore: 1910). e) *A Short History of the United States Navy* (Philadelphia: 1911, 1914, 1927, 1939). f) "Loyalty," U.S. Naval Institute *Proceedings* 156 (Mar-Apr 1915): 429-31. g) "History Versus Prophecy," U.S. Naval Institute *Proceedings* 160 (Nov-Dec 1915): 1989-91. h) "When the Navy Railroaded in China," U.S. Naval Institute *Proceedings* 294 (Aug 1927): 846-52. i) "Birds of Ebony," U.S. Naval Institute *Proceedings* 297 (Nov 1927): 1184-85. j) "Here and There. Sketches from a Naval Officer's Notebook," U.S. Naval Institute *Proceedings* 322 (Dec 1929): 1052-56. k) "This and That," U.S. Naval Institute *Proceedings* 343 (Sep 1931): 1205-12.

RICHARDSON CLOVER
1846-1919

RICHARDSON CLOVER Born in St. James' College, Hagerstown, MD, on 11 Jul 1846, son of Reverend Lewis P. and

47 DEWITT COFFMAN

Sarah Ann (Ackerman) Clover. Married Mary Eudora Miller on 19 May 1886. Died on 14 Oct 1919 in WY while en route between San Francisco and Washington, DC.

Ranks Midn (29 Jul 1863); Ens (18 Dec 1868); Mstr (21 Mar 1870); Lt (21 Mar 1871); LCdr (19 May 1891); Cdr (16 Sep 1897); Capt (11 Apr 1902); RAdm (8 Nov 1907); placed on Ret.Lst. (11 Jul 1908).

Career Summary Received appointment from MO (29 Jul 1863); USNA (Jul 1863-Jun 1867); *Susquehanna*, W.Indies (Jun 1867-Jan 1868); w.o. (Jan-Mar 1868); flgs., *Contoocook* [renamed *Albany*], N.Atl.Sqdn. (Mar 1868-Oct 1869); Naval Observatory, Washington, DC (Oct 1869-Mar 1870); signal duty (Mar-Jul 1870); *Michigan*, on Great Lakes (Jul 1870-Jan 1871); *Ticonderoga*, S.Atl.Sta. (Jan 1871-Feb 1874); w.o. (Feb-Apr 1874); *Michigan*, on Great Lakes (Apr-May 1874); cst.surv. duty (Jun 1874-Nov 1877); w.o. (Nov 1877-Jan 1878); Hydrographic Office, Washington, DC (Jan-Feb 1878); *Wyoming*, Eur.Sta. (Feb 1878-Jun 1881); w.o. (Jun-Jul 1881); cst.surv. duty (Jul 1881-Mar 1886); l.o.a. (Mar 1886-Feb 1887); cst.surv. duty (Feb-Mar 1887); w.o. (Mar-May 1887); Torp.Sta., Newport, RI (Jun-Sep 1887); NWC (Sep-Dec 1887); w.o. (Dec 1887-Feb 1888); *Pensacola*, N.Atl.Sta. (Mar-Dec 1888); exec.off., *Dolphin* (Dec 1888-Nov 1889); w.o. (Nov-Dec 1889); Hydrographic Office, Washington, DC (Dec 1889-Jun 1891); hydrographer, Bur. of Nav., Washington, D.C. (Jun 1891-May 1893); l.o.a. (May 1893-Feb 1894); exec. off., *Chicago*, Eur.Sta. (Mar 1894-May 1895); l.o.a. (May-Jun 1895); w.o. (Jun-Nov 1895); member, bd. to revise navy regulations, Navy Dept., Washington, DC (Dec 1895-Apr 1896); cdr, *Dolphin*, Spec.Serv.Sqdn. (Apr 1896-May 1897); l.o.a. (May-Oct 1897); chief, Office of Naval Intelligence, Washington, DC (Nov 1897-May 1898); member, War and Strategy Bd., Washington, DC (March-May 1898); cdr, *Bancroft*, N.Atl.Sqdn. (May-Sep 1898); chief, Office of Naval Intelligence, Washington, DC (Oct 1898-Mar 1900); naval attaché, U.S. Embassy, London (Apr 1900-Jun 1903); home and w.o. (Jun-Nov 1903); cdr, *Wisconsin*, Asia.Flt. (Jan 1904-Dec 1905); chief of staff, Asia.Flt., *Wisconsin* (Mar 1904-Dec 1905); w.o. (Jan 1906-Jan 1907); member, then pres., bd. of inspection and surv. (Feb 1907-Jul 1908); placed on Ret.Lst. (11 Jul 1908).

References
Personal Papers: 1 journal (1880) in NHF,WNY.

DEWITT COFFMAN Born at Mount Jackson, VA, on 28 Nov 1854. Married with one son. Died in Jamestown, RI, on 27 Jun 1932. Buried in USNA Cemetery, Annapolis, MD.

Ranks Cadet Midn (8 Jun 1872); Midn (20 Jun 1876); Ens (10 Jul 1879); Ltjg (19 Apr 1886); Lt (27 Sep 1891); LCdr (8 Jul 1899); Cdr (16 Jun 1905); Capt (1 Feb 1909); RAdm (12 Dec 1914): temp. VAdm (19 Jun 1916); placed on Ret.Lst. as RAdm (28 Nov 1918); VAdm on Ret.Lst. (21 Jun 1930).

Career Summary Received appointment from VA (8 Jun 1872); USNA (Jun 1872-Jun 1876); w.o. (Jun-Oct 1876); flgs.,

DEWITT COFFMAN
1854-1932

Pensacola, Pac.Sta. (Nov 1876-Sep 1877); training ship, *Portsmouth* (Sep 1877-Jan 1879); w.o. (Jan-Mar 1879); USNA (Mar-Apr 1879); w.o. (Apr-May 1879); rec. ship, *Franklin,* Norfolk, VA (Jun-Sep 1879); *Constellation,* spec.serv. (Oct-Dec 1879); flgs., *Trenton,* Eur.Sta. (Dec 1879-Oct 1881); w.o. (Oct-Dec 1881); rec. ship, *Colorado,* NY (Dec 1881-May 1882); duty with Fish Commission (May-Nov 1882); w.o. (Nov 1882-Jan 1883); training ship, *New Hampshire* (Jan-Sep 1883); rec. ship, *Franklin,* Norfolk, VA (Sep 1883-Jan 1884); *Yantic,* spec.serv. (Jan 1884-Sep 1885); sick lv. (Sep 1885-Mar 1886); cst.surv. duty (Mar 1886-Nov 1887); w.o. (Nov-Dec 1887); Hydrographic Office, Washington, DC (Dec 1887-Jul 1890); flgs., *Pensacola,* S.Atl., then S.Pac.Stas. (Jul 1890-Mar 1892); *Adams,* Bering Sea (Apr-Dec 1892); *Boston,* Hawaiian Islands (Jan-Jul 1893); l.o.a. (Jul-Sep 1893); USNA (Sep 1893-Jul 1896); *Texas,* N Atl.Sqdn. (Jul-Nov 1896); *Columbia,* N.Atl.Sqdn. (Nov 1896-Jul 1897); *Terror,* N.Atl.Sqdn. (Jul 1897-Jun 1898); Naval Hosp., NY (Jun-Jul 1898); sick lv. (Jul-Oct 1898); *Prairie,* Fore River, MA (Oct 1898-Jan 1899); *Marblehead,* Navy Yard, Boston, and spec. cruise (Jan-Apr 1899); training ship, *Indiana* (Apr-Jul 1899); home and w.o. (Jul-Aug 1899); USNA (Sep 1899-May 1901); NWC (Jun-Aug 1901); exec.off., training ship, *Essex* (Aug 1901-Dec 1903); home and w.o. (Dec 1903-Jan 1904); spec. duty to Mare Island, CA (Jan 1904); Navy Yard, Norfolk, VA (Feb-Sep 1904); in charge, Naval Recruiting Sta., Baltimore (Sep 1904-Oct 1905); cdr, *Boston,* Pac.Sqdn. (Nov 1905-Jun 1907); insp. of ord., and in charge, naval magazine, Ft. Mifflin, PA (Jul 1907-Jul 1908); in charge, naval magazine, St. Julien's Creek, VA (Jul 1908-May 1909); cdr, *New Jersey,* drill duty and in reserve (May 1909-Mar 1911); comdt., Navy Yard and Sta., Boston (Mar 1911-Nov 1914); NWC (Nov-Dec 1914); cdr, 3rd Div., Atl.Flt. *New Jersey* (Dec 1914-May 1916); cdr, 6th Div., Atl.Flt., *New York* (May-Jun 1916); 2nd in command, Atl.Flt., and cdr, Battleship Force, *Arkansas* (Jun-Nov 1916), then *Wyoming* (Nov 1916-Aug 1917); cdr, Atl.Flt. (Aug-Oct 1917); cdr, Battleship Force Two, Atl.Flt., and cdr, Sqdn. Four, and Div. Eight, *Wyoming* (Aug 1917-Aug 1918); cdr, 5th Naval Dist. and Naval Operating Base, Hampton Roads, VA (Aug-Nov 1918); placed on Ret.Lst. (28 Nov 1918); member, bd. of awards, medals and honors, Washington, DC (Nov 1918-Oct 1919).

Career Highlights   One of the leading naval commanders during World War I.

JOSEPH BULLOCK COGHLAN
1844-1908

JOSEPH BULLOCK COGHLAN   Born in Frankfort, KY, on 9 Dec 1844, son of Cornelius and Lavinia (Fouke) Coghlan. Married Julia Barbour in Oct 1868. One son. Died on 5 Dec 1908 in New Rochelle, NY. Buried in Arlington National Cemetery.

Ranks   Act.Midn (27 Sep 1860); title changed to Midn (16 Jul 1862); Act.Ens (28 May 1863); Mstr (10 Nov 1865); Lt (10 Nov 1866); LCdr (12 Mar 1868); Cdr (4 Feb 1882); Capt (18 Nov 1896); RAdm (11 Apr 1902); placed on Ret.Lst. (9 Dec 1906).

Career Summary Received appointment from IL (27 Sep 1860); USNA (Sep 1860-May 1863); *Sacramento*, spec.serv. (Jul 1863-Aug 1865); w.o. (Aug-Sep 1865); flgs., *Brooklyn*, S. Atl.Sqdn. (Oct 1865-Oct 1867); exec. off., *Pawnee, Guerriere*, and *Portsmouth*, S.Atl.Sqdn. (Oct 1867-Oct 1868); Navy Yard, League Island, PA (Oct-Dec 1868); *Richmond*, Eur.Sqdn. (Jan 1869-Nov 1871); w.o. (Nov-Dec 1871); Hydrographic Office, Washington, DC (Jan 1872-Mar 1873); sick lv. (Mar 1873-Feb 1875); cdr, *Saugus*, N.Atl.Sta. (Feb 1875-Apr 1876); suspended (Apr 1876-Jul 1877); rec. ship, *Colorado*, NY (Jul-Aug 1877); exec.off., *Monongahela*, Asia.Sta. (Aug 1877-Nov 1879); exec.off., rec. ship, *Independence*, Mare Island, CA (Nov 1879-Feb 1882); w.o. (Feb 1882-Aug 1883); cdr, *Adams*, Pac.Sta. (Sep 1883-Sep 1884); w.o. and l.o.a. (Sep 1884-Apr 1886); equip.off., Navy Yard, Mare Island, CA (Apr 1886-Aug 1888); cdr, *Mohican*, Pac.Sta. (Aug 1888-Feb 1890); under arrest (Mar-Apr 1890); w.o. (Apr 1890-Jan 1891); insp. of ord., Navy Yard, League Island, PA (Jan 1891-Feb 1894); insp., 8th L.h.Dist., New Orleans (Feb 1894-Feb 1897); cdr, rec. ship, *Richmond*, Philadelphia (Feb-Mar 1897); cdr, *Raleigh*, Asia. Flt. (Mar 1897-Jun 1899); comdt., Naval Station, Bremerton, WA (Jul 1899-Jul 1900); sick lv. (Jul 1900-May 1901); NWC (Jun-Sep 1901); capt.yd., Navy Yard, NY (Sep 1901-May 1902); 2nd in command, N.Atl.Flt., *Brooklyn* (Jun-Sep 1902), then *Olympia* (Sep 1902-Apr 1904); home and w.o. (Apr-Oct 1904); comdt., Navy Yard, NY (Oct 1904-Jun 1907); placed on Ret.Lst. (9 Dec 1906).

Career Highlights Commanded the *Raleigh* in Battle of Manila Bay for which he was advanced six numbers in rank for eminent and conspicuous conduct.

JAMES KELSEY COGSWELL Born in Milwaukee, WI, on 27 Sep 1847, son of George and Celestia Anne Jeannette (Stone) Cogswell. Educated at public schools, St. Aloysius Academy, and Milwaukee Univ. to 1860. He attended Racine College Grammar School from 1860-62. Married Annie Miller Hatch on 16 Jul 1884. Two daughters. Died at South Jacksonville, FL, on 12 Aug 1908. Buried at Forest Home Cemetery in Milwaukee.

Ranks Midn (25 Sep 1863); Ens (19 Apr 1869); Mstr (12 Jul 1870); Lt (8 Dec 1874); LCdr (15 Jun 1895); Cdr (3 Mar 1899); Capt (4 Feb 1904); retired with rank of RAdm. (25 Mar 1904).

Career Summary Received appointment from WI (25 Sep 1863); USNA (Sep 1863-Jun 1868); found deficient and turned back (Jan 1866); w.o. (Jun-Sep 1868); *Powhatan*, S.Pac.Sta. (Oct 1868-Jan 1870); home and w.o. (Jan-Mar 1870); *Saginaw*, Pac.Sqdn. (Mar 1870-May 1871); return and sick lv. (May-Nov 1871); *Saranac* and *Pensacola*, Pac.Sta. (Nov 1871-Feb 1873); under sentence and w.o. (Feb-Jul 1873); suspended (Jul 1873-Apr 1874); w.o. (Apr-May 1874); *Ticonderoga*, N.Atl.Sta. (May-Oct 1874); w.o. (Oct-Nov 1874); rec. ship, *Vermont*, NY (Nov 1874-Jun 1875); *Monongahela*, S.Atl.Sta. (Jun 1875-Jul 1876); w.o. (Jul-Sep 1876); *Essex*, N. and S.Atl.Stas. (Oct 1876-Sep 1878); w.o. (Sep-Oct 1878); l.o.a. (Oct 1878-Mar 1879); torp.

JAMES KELSEY COGSWELL
1847-1908

instruction, Newport, RI (Jun-Sep 1879); w.o.(Sep 1879); Hydrographic Office, Washington, DC (Oct 1879-Mar 1880); *Constellation*, spec.serv. (Mar-Jun 1880); w.o. (Jun 1880-Jan 1881); rec. ship, *Colorado*, NY (Jan-Jun 1881); *Vandalia*, N. Atl.Sta. (Jun 1881-Jun 1884); w.o. (Jun-Aug 1884); Navy Yard, Portsmouth, NH (Aug 1884-May 1886); torp. instruction, Newport, RI (May-Sep 1886); NWC (Sep-Nov 1886); ord.instruction, Navy Yard, Washington, DC (Nov 1886-Feb 1887); insp. of ord., S.Boston Iron Works, Boston (Feb 1887-Oct 1888); *Kearsarge*, spec.serv. (Nov 1888-Jan 1889); *Tallapoosa*, S.Atl.Sta. (Jan 1889-Jan 1892); spec. duty (Jan-Mar 1892); l.o.a. (Mar-May 1892); Navy Yard, Portsmouth, NH (May 1892-Apr 1895); ord. instruction, Navy Yard, Washington, DC (Apr-Jul 1895); w.o. (Jul-Sep 1895); exec.off., *Marion*, Pac.Sqdn. (Sep 1895-Jul 1897); exec.off., *Oregon*, Pac.Sqdn. and N.Atl.Flt. (Jul 1897-Aug 1898); home and w.o. (Aug-Sep 1898); insp., 1st L.h.Dist., Portland, ME (Oct 1898-Mar 1901); cdr, *Marietta*, Asia.Sta. (Apr-May 1901); cdr, *Isla de Luzon*, Asia.Sta. (May 1901-Jan 1902); Naval Hosp., Mare Island, CA (Feb-Mar 1902); home, w.o., and sick lv. (Mar-May 1902); Navy Yard, Portsmouth, NH (May 1902-Nov 1903); cdr, *Cleveland*, N.Atl.Sta. (Nov 1903-Jan 1904); home and w.o. (Jan 1904); bd. duties (Jan-Mar 1904); retired (25 Mar 1904).

Career Highlights Advanced five numbers in rank for services as exec.off. of the *Oregon* during that ship's famous voyage to participate in Battle of Santiago Bay in Jul 1898.

HARRISON GRAY OTIS COLBY
1846-1926

HARRISON GRAY OTIS COLBY Born in New Bedford, MA, on 28 Jan 1846, son of Harrison Gray Otis and Jane Standish (Parker) Colby. Married Mary Catherine Thompson on 20 Apr 1881. One son. Died on 3 Nov 1926 in Boston, MA.

Ranks Midn (25 Nov 1862); Ens (18 Dec 1868); Mstr (21 Mar 1870); Lt (21 Mar 1871); LCdr (20 Nov 1891); Cdr (27 Apr 1898); Capt (18 Jun 1902); placed on Ret.Lst. with rank of RAdm (28 Jan 1908).

Career Summary Received appointment from MA (25 Nov 1862); USNA (Nov 1862-Oct 1867); found deficient and turned back (Jun 1864); *Piscataqua*, then flgs., *Iroquois*, Asia.Sta. (Nov 1867-Apr 1870); home and w.o. (Apr-Jul 1870); exec.off., nautical schoolship, *America*, USNA (Jul-Oct 1870); Navy Yard, Boston (Oct 1870-Feb 1871); *Worcester*, spec.serv. (Feb-Sep 1871); *Congress*, N.Atl.Sta. (Sep-Oct 1871); *Shenandoah*, *Plymouth*, and flgs., *Wabash*, Eur.Sqdn. (Oct 1871-Apr 1874); w.o. (Apr-May 1874); Bur. of Nav., Washington, DC (May-Jun 1874); torp. duty, Newport, RI (Jul-Oct 1874); w.o. (Oct-Dec 1874); surv. expd. to Panama (Dec 1874-Apr 1875); Naval Rndv., Boston (Apr-Jun 1875); flgs., *Tennessee*, Asia.Sqdn. (Jun-Oct 1875); sick lv. (Oct 1875-Apr 1876); Hydrographic Office, Washington, DC (Apr-Jun 1876); naval attaché, U.S. Centennial Commission, Philadelphia (Jun-Nov 1876); Naval Observatory, Washington, DC (Dec 1876-May 1877); l.o.a. (May-Jul 1877); *Marion*, Eur.Sta. (Jul 1877-Mar 1878); flag lt, Eur.Sta., *Trenton*

(Mar 1878-Mar 1880); w.o. (Mar-Oct 1880); cst.surv. duty (Oct 1880-Dec 1882); exec. off., training ship, *Saratoga* (Dec 1882-Oct 1885); asst.insp., 2nd L.h. Dist., Boston (Oct 1885-Apr 1889); exec.off., *Yorktown*, Eur.Sta., spec.serv., and Sqdn. of Evol. (Apr 1889-Aug 1891); office of asst. sec. of navy, Washington, DC (Aug-Dec 1891); asst.insp. , 2nd L.h. Dist. Boston (Dec 1891-Jun 1895); cst.surv. duty (Jul 1895-Apr 1896); Hydrographic Insp., cst.surv., Washington, DC (Apr-Dec 1896); insp., 2nd L.h Dist., Boston (Jan 1897-Jun 1898); cdr, 1st Dist. Cst. Defense System, Portsmouth, NH (Apr 1898); cdr, 2nd Dist. Cst. Defense System, Boston (Apr-Jun 1898); cdr, *Hannibal*, N.Atl.Flt. (May-Oct 1898); insp. 2nd L.h. Dist., Boston (Oct 1898-Mar 1899); s.a. and w.o. (Mar-Apr 1899); cdr, *Marblehead*, Asia.Sqdn. (Apr 1899-Apr 1900); cdr, *Concord*, Asia.Sqdn. (Jun 1900-Apr 1901); home and w.o. (Apr-May 1901); NWC (Jun-Sep 1901); in charge, Naval Recruiting Rndv., Boston (Sep 1901-Dec 1903); cdr, *Olympia*, N.Atl. and Eur.Sqdns. (Dec 1903-Jun 1905); temp. cdr, N. Atl.Sqdn., *Olympia* (Nov 1904-May 1905); home and w.o. (Jun-Jul 1905); capt.yd., Navy Yard, Boston (Jul-Oct 1905); in charge, Naval Recruiting Rndv., Boston, and New England Dist. (Oct 1905-Jan 1908); placed on Ret.Lst. (28 Jan 1908).

GEORGE PARTRIDGE COLVOCORESSES   Born in Norwich, VT, on 3 Apr 1847, son of George M. and Eliza Freelon (Halsey) Colvocoresses. His father served with the Wilkes Expd. Married Mary D. Baldwin. One daughter and two sons. Received an honorary A.M. degree from Norwich Univ. in 1898. Died at his home in Litchfield, CT, on 10 Sep 1932. Buried in that town's New East Cemetery.

Ranks Captain's Clerk (24 Jun 1861); discharged (15 Aug 1862); Captain's Clerk (14 Apr 1863); discharged (25 May 1864); Midn (28 Sep 1864); Ens (12 Jul 1870); Mstr (18 Jun 1872); Lt (1 Jul 1875); LCdr (4 Jun 1897); Cdr (30 Jun 1900); Capt (21 Feb 1905); retired as RAdm (30 Jun 1907).

Career Summary Captain's clerk, *Supply*, Blk.Sqdns. (Jun 1861-Aug 1862); captain's clerk, *Saratoga*, spec. serv., and S.Atl.Blk.Sqdn. (Apr 1863-May 1864); received appointment by virtue of being the son of an officer (28 Sep 1864); USNA (Sep 1864-Jun 1869); found deficient and turned back (Jun 1866); flgs., *Lancaster*, and *Portsmouth*, S.Atl.Sta. (Jul 1869-Nov 1871); w.o. (Nov 1871-Mar 1872); *Lackawanna*, Navy Yard, Mare Island, CA (Apr-Jun 1872); temp. duty, Wilmington, DE (Aug-Sep 1872); *Hartford* and *Lackawanna*, Asia.Sta. (Oct 1872-May 1875); w.o. (May-Jun 1875); l.o.a. (Jun-Oct 1875); Hydrographic Office, Washington, DC (Nov 1875-Sep 1876); *Gettysburg* and *Enterprise*, Eur.Sta. (Sep 1876-Apr 1879); home and w.o. (Apr-May 1879); l.o.a. (May-Sep 1879); Hydrographic Office, Washington, DC (Oct 1879-Jun 1882); *Hartford*, Pac.Sta. (Jul 1882-Apr 1884); l.o.a. (Apr-Oct 1884); training ship, *Saratoga* (Oct 1884-May 1886); USNA (May 1886-Jun 1890); exec .off. *Enterprise*, N.Atl.Sta. (Jul 1890-Sep 1891); temp. duty, Bur. of Nav., Washington, DC (Sep-Nov 1891); *Atlanta*, Sqdn. of Evol.

GEORGE PARTRIDGE
COLVOCORESSES
1847-1932

(Nov 1891-Jun 1892); *Concord*, W.Indies (Jun 1892-Jun 1893); USNA (Jun 1893-May 1897); exec.off., *Concord*, Asia. Flt. (May 1897-Dec 1898); exec.off., flgs., *Olympia*, Asia. Flt. (Dec 1898-Nov 1899); home and l.o.a. (Nov-Dec 1899); Office of Naval War Records, Navy Dept., Washington, DC (Dec 1899-May 1901); NWC (Jun-Sep 1901); Office of Naval War Records, Navy Dept., Washington, DC (Oct-Nov 1901); cdr, training ship, *Lancaster* (Nov 1901-May 1903); training ship, *Yankee* (May-Dec 1903); w.o. (Dec 1903-Jan 1904); asst. to capt.yd., Navy Yard, NY (Jan-Apr 1904); bd. duties, Navy Yard, NY (Jan-Jul 1904); comdt., Naval Sta., and cdr, 7th Naval Dist., Key West, FL (Aug 1904-May 1905); home and w.o. (May-Jun 1905); comdt. of midshipmen, USNA (Jun 1905-Jun 1907); temp. cdr, training ship, Newark (May-Aug 1906); retired (30 Jun 1907).

Career Highlights While exec.off. of *Concord*, participated in Battle of Manila Bay, being advanced five numbers for his conduct in battle.

References

Personal Papers: 1 vol. (1840) at Sterling Memorial Lib. Yale Univ.

Writings: a) assisted in compiling with E. K. Rawson and C. W. Stewart, *Official Records of the Union and Confederate Navies*, ser. I, vols. 11-14, (Washington, DC: 1900-1902). b) "Admiral Porter," U.S. Naval Institute *Proceedings* 125 (Mar 1908): 309-14.

SAMUEL PANCOAST COMLY Born in Woodbury, NJ, on 13 Jul 1849, son of Nathan Folwell and Mary (Wood) Comly. Married Laura L. Carpenter on 17 Dec 1884. Married a second time to Mrs. Hannah L. Hamill on 14 Aug 1895. Died in Philadelphia, PA, on 10 Apr 1918.

Ranks Midn (26 Jul 1865); Ens (12 Jul 1871); Mstr (3 Aug 1873); Lt (26 Apr 1878); LCdr (10 Aug 1898); Cdr (3 Mar 1901); Capt (1 Jul 1905); RAdm (23 Oct 1909); placed on Ret.Lst. (13 Jul 1911).

Career Summary Received appointment from NJ (26 Jul 1865); USNA (Jul 1865-Jun 1869); training ship, *Sabine* (Jun 1869-Jul 1870); w.o. (Jul-Nov 1870); USNA (Nov-Dec 1870); *Tennessee*, Navy Yard, NY (Jan 1871); *Ticonderoga* and *Ossipee*, S.Atl. and Pac.Sqdns. (Jan 1871-Nov 1872); w.o. (Nov 1872-Jan 1873); rec. ship, *Potomac*, League Island, PA (Jan-May 1873); *Juniata*, Polaris Expd. (May-Nov 1873); *Canonicus* and *Dictator*, N.Atl.Sta. (Dec 1873-May 1875); w.o. (May 1875); l.o.a. (May-Aug 1875); *Intrepid*, Navy Yard, NY (Aug 1875-Jul 1876); w.o. (Jul-Aug 1876); *Adams*, Pac.Sta. (Aug 1876-Aug 1879); w.o. (Jul-Oct 1879); l.o.a. (Nov 1879-Jun 1880); torp. instruction, Newport, RI (Jun-Sep 1880); w.o. (Sep 1880); rec. ship, *St. Louis*, League Island, PA (Sep 1880-Jul 1882); *Nantucket*, spec. cruise (Jul-Dec 1882); temp. duty, Navy Yard, League Island, PA (Dec 1882-Jan 1883); training ship, *Portsmouth* (Jan 1883-Oct 1885); w.o. (Oct-Nov 1885); Navy Yard, League Island, PA (Nov 1885-May 1886); asst.insp., Midvale Steel Works, Nicetown, PA (May 1886-Sep 1889); w.o. (Sep 1889-Jan 1890); *Alliance*, Asia.

and Pac.Stas. (Jan 1890-Aug 1891); home and w.o. (Aug-Oct 1891); l.o.a. (Oct-Nov 1891); *Alliance*, Asia. and Pac.Sqdns. (Dec 1891-Apr 1893); l.o.a. (Apr-Aug 1893); rec. ship, *St. Louis*, League Island, PA (Aug 1893-Jun 1894); rec. ship, *Richmond*, Philadelphia (Jun 1894-Nov 1895); *Indiana*, training cruise, and N.Atl.Sta. (Nov 1895-Oct 1898); rec. ship, *Richmond*, Philadelphia (Oct 1898-Apr 1901); cdr, training ship, *Alliance* (Apr 1901-Jan 1903); asst., then insp., 4th L.h. Dist., Philadelphia (Jan 1903-Sep 1905); home and w.o. (Sep-Nov 1905); court-martial duty, USNA (Nov-Dec 1905); cdr, *Alabama*, N.Atl.Sta. (Dec 1905-Oct 1907); home and w.o. (Oct 1907); member, L.h. Bd. , Washington, DC (Nov 1907-Jun 1909); cdr, 4th Div., Atl.Flt., *Virginia* (Jun-Dec 1909); cdr, 3rd Div., Atl.Flt., *Georgia* (Dec 1909-Oct 1910); court-martial, and various bd. duties, Navy Yard, Philadelphia (Oct 1910-Jul 1911); placed on Ret.Lst. (13 Jul 1911).

GEORGE ALBERT CONVERSE Born in Norwich, VT, on 13 May 1844, son of Shubael and Luvia (Morrill) Converse. Educated in Norwich public schools from 1852 to 1858, then Norwich Univ. from 1858 to 1861, receiving B.S. degree. Married Laura Shelby Blood in Dec 1871. Two daughters. Died at his home in Washington, DC, on 29 Mar 1909. Buried in Arlington National Cemetery.

GEORGE ALBERT CONVERSE
1844-1909

Ranks Act.Midn (29 Nov 1861); title changed to Midn (16 Jul 1862); Ens (1 Dec 1866); Mstr (12 Mar 1868); Lt (26 Mar 1869); LCdr (12 Jul 1878); Cdr (23 Mar 1889); Capt (3 Mar 1899); RAdm (16 Nov 1903); placed on Ret.Lst. (13 May 1906).

Career Summary Received appointment from VT (29 Nov 1861); USNA (Nov 1861-Oct 1865); *Canandaigua* and *Frolic*, Eur.Sqdn. (Nov 1865-May 1869); w.o. (May-Aug 1869); spec. duty, Bur. of Nav. Washington, DC (Aug-Oct 1869); torp. serv., Newport, RI (Oct 1869-Feb 1872); flgs., *Hartford*, Asia.Sta. (Feb 1872-Dec 1873); home and w.o. (Dec 1873-May 1874); inst., Torp.Sta., Newport, RI (Jun 1874-Oct 1877); *Marion*, Eur.Sta. (Oct 1877-Jul 1879); sick lv. (Jul 1879-Jan 1883); *Lancaster*, Eur.Sta. (Mar 1883-Sep 1884); return and w.o. (Sep-Dec 1884); Bur. of Ord., Washington, DC (Dec 1884-Jan 1885); inst., Torp.Sta., Newport, RI (Jan 1885-Jan 1889); insp. of Torp. Boats, Bristol, RI (Jan 1889-Jun 1890); cdr, *Enterprise*, spec.serv. (Jul 1890-Jul 1891); Bur. of Ord., Washington, DC (Aug 1891-Dec 1892); in charge, Torp.Sta., Newport, RI (Jan 1893-Jun 1897); cdr, *Montgomery*, N.Atl.Sqdn. (Jul 1897-Apr 1899); Bur. of Nav., Washington, DC (Apr 1899-Sep 1901); general insp., *Illinois* (Jan-Sep 1901); cdr, *Illinois*, unassigned (Sep-Nov 1901); Naval Sta., New Orleans (Nov 1901-Oct 1903); chief, Bur. of Equip. and Recruiting, Washington, DC (Oct 1903-Mar 1904); chief, Bur. of Ord., Washington, DC (Mar-Jul 1904); chief, Bur. of Nav., Washington, DC (Aug 1904-May 1907); placed on Ret.Lst. (13 May 1906).

Career Highlights An expert on ord. and torps., spent much time at the Newport Torp.Sta., being in charge of it from 1892 until 1897. Served as chief of three bureaus in succession from 1903 to 1907.

References

Personal Papers: a) 250 items (1895-1908) in NHF,LC. b) 400 items, 52 vols. (1861-97) in DeGolyer Foundation Lib., Southern Methodist Univ., Dallas, TX.

Writings: *Notes on Torpedo Fuses* (Newport, RI: 1875).

FRANCIS AUGUSTUS COOK
1843-1916

FRANCIS AUGUSTUS COOK Born in Northampton, MA, on 10 May 1843, son of MA Militia Gen Benjamin E. and Elizabeth Christine (Griffin) Cook. Married Carrie Earle on 2 Sep 1868. Two sons, both of whom served in navy. Died in Northampton, MA, on 8 Oct 1916. Buried in USNA Cemetery, Annapolis, MD.

Ranks Act.Midn (20 Sep 1860); title changed to Midn (16 Jul 1862); Act.Ens (1 Oct 1863); Ens (21 Dec 1865); Mstr (10 Nov 1866); Lt (21 Feb 1867); LCdr (12 Mar 1868); Cdr (12 Oct 1881); Capt (28 Feb 1896); RAdm (21 Mar 1903); retired (5 Sep 1903).

Career Summary Received appointment from MA (20 Sep 1860); USNA (Sep 1860-Oct 1863); *Seminole* and *Lackawanna*, W.Gulf Blk.Sqdn. (Oct 1863-Jul 1865); w.o. (Jul-Sep 1865); flgs., *Vanderbilt*, N.Pac.Sqdn. and *Saranac*, N.Atl.Sqdn. (Sep 1865-Aug 1868); home and w.o. (Aug-Oct 1868); USNA (Oct 1868-Oct 1870); rec. ship, *Independence*, Mare Island, CA (Nov 1870-Mar 1871); *Saranac*, and flgs., *Richmond*, Pac.Sqdn. (Mar 1871-Jul 1874); w.o. (Jul-Nov 1874); exec.off., rec. ship, *Sabine*, Portsmouth, NH (Nov 1874-Aug 1876); w.o. (Aug-Sep 1876); exec. off., *Plymouth*, N.Atl.Sta. (Oct 1876-May 1879); w.o. (May-Jun 1879); USNA (Jul 1879-Aug 1883); asst., then insp., 11th L.h. Dist., Detroit (Sep 1883-Sep 1886); cdr, *Ranger*, N.Pac.Sta. (Oct 1886-Oct 1889); w.o. (Oct 1889-Feb 1890); member, L.h. Bd., Washington, DC (Feb-Mar 1890); insp. of ord., Navy Yard, Boston (Mar 1890-Feb 1892); equip.off., Navy Yard, Boston (Feb 1892-May 1893); asst. to chief, Bur. of Nav., Washington, DC (May 1893-Nov 1896); chief of staff and cdr, flgs., *Brooklyn*, "Flying Sqdn." (Dec 1896-Apr 1899); member, naval exam. and ret. bds. and various bd. duties (May 1899-Feb 1903); sick lv. (Feb-Sep 1903); retired (5 Sep 1903).

Career Highlights Served on the *Seminole* at Battle of Mobile Bay on 5 Aug 1864. Commanded *Brooklyn* and served as chief of staff to RAdm Winfield S. Schley during Spanish-American War. Participated in Battle of Santiago Bay, receiving the surrender of Spanish ship *Cristobal Colon*. Subsequently advanced five numbers "for eminent and conspicuous conduct" in that action.

GEORGE HENRY COOKE
1836-1924

GEORGE HENRY COOKE Born in Philadelphia, PA, on 12 Dec 1836, son of Christopher and Dorothea Cooke. Educated in Philadelphia public schools, graduated from Central High School with the A.B. and A.M. degrees. Received M.D. degree from Philadelphia Medical College. Married Mrs. Sarah Lyon Atkinson on 16 Oct 1873. One daughter. Married later to Kate W. Boyd.

Resided in Waverly, AL, where he died on 15 Feb 1924. Buried in Woodlands Cemetery in Philadelphia.

Ranks Act.Asst.Surg. (9 Sep 1862); Asst.Surg. (22 Sep 1862); PAsst.Surg. (20 Jan 1866); Surg. (20 Feb 1870); Medl.Insp. (15 Sep 1888); Medl.Dir. (29 Sep 1895); transferred to Ret.Lst. (21 Nov 1898); RAdm on Ret.Lst. (29 Jun 1906).

Career Summary Received appointment from NJ (9 Sep 1862); Naval Hosp., Norfolk, VA (Sep-Dec 1862); *St. Lawrence, James L. Davis, Somerset, Sagamore,* and *Tioga,* E.Gulf Blk.Sqdn. (Dec 1862-Jul 1864); l.o.a. (Jul-Aug 1864); Navy Yard, Philadelphia (Aug 1864-Apr 1865); *Onondaga,* Navy Yard, NY (Apr 1865); *Mendota,* N.Atl.Blk.Sqdn. (Apr-May 1865); Naval Hosp., NY (May-Aug 1865); *Massachusetts,* S.Atl.Sqdn. and Navy Yard, NY (Aug-Dec 1865); w.o. (Dec 1865-Feb 1866); rec. ship, *Ohio,* Boston (Feb-May 1866); USNA (May-Sep 1866); *Resaca,* Pac. Sqdn. (Sep 1866-Oct 1868); USNA (Oct 1868-Aug 1870); Naval Sta., Mound City, IL (Aug 1870-Nov 1871); prac. ship, *Constellation* (Nov 1871-Feb 1872); *Terror,* N.Atl.Sta. (Mar 1872-Feb 1873); return and w.o. (Feb-Mar 1873); spec. duty, Bur. of Medicine and Surgery, Washington, DC (Mar-Sep 1873); Marine Rndv., Philadelphia (Sep-Dec 1873); w.o. (Dec 1873-Apr 1874); Naval Hosp., Norfolk, VA (Apr 1874-Sep 1875); w.o. (Sep 1875-Jan 1876); *Vandalia,* Eur.Sqdn. (Jan 1876-Feb 1879); w.o. (Feb-May 1879); Navy Yard, League Island, PA (Jun 1879-Jun 1882); pres., bd. for physical exam. of engineers (Jun-Sep 1882); w.o. (Sep 1882-Jan 1883); sick lv. (Jan-Oct 1883); l.o.a. (Oct 1883-Aug 1884); medl.exam.bd., USNA (Aug-Oct 1884); *Lackawanna,* Pac.Sta. (Nov 1884-Mar 1885); Naval Hosp., Mare Island, CA (Mar-May 1885); *Mohican,* spec. cruise, Pac.Ocean (May 1885-Oct 1887); return and w.o. (Oct 1887-May 1888); Navy Yard, League Island, PA, and pres., medl.exam.bd., Philadelphia (May 1888-Jul 1890); flt.surg., S.Atl. and S.Pac.Stas., *Pensacola* (Jul 1890-Jul 1891), then *Baltimore,* Spec.Serv.Sqdn. (Jul 1891-May 1893); home and l.o.a. (May-Jul 1893); Navy Yard, League Island, PA (Jul-Nov 1893); pres., medl.exam.bd., League Island, PA (Aug-Oct 1893); spec. duty, Philadelphia (Oct 1893-Aug 1896); in charge, Naval Hosp. Philadelphia (Aug 1896-Jan 1899); transferred to Ret.Lst. (21 Nov 1898); Naval Receiving Office, Philadelphia (Feb 1903-Mar 1907).

Career Highlights Served on six ships that were hit by various epidemics at one time or another. While on *Mohican,* participated in the explorations of some S.Pac. Islands during 1885-86, including Easter Island, upon which he wrote.

References

Writings: *TePito te Henua, known as Rasa Nui: commonly called Easter Island, South Pacific Ocean ... U.S. National Museum Annual Report. 1897.* part I: 689-723 (Washington, DC: 1899).

ROBERT EDWARD COONTZ Born in Hannibal, MO, on 11 Jun 1864, son of Benton and Mary Bacon (Brewington) Coontz. Received early education at Ingleside College in Palmyra, MO,

ROBERT EDWARD COONTZ
1864-1935

from 1878 to 1879 and then at Hannibal College from 1879 to 1880. Married Augusta Cohen on 31 Oct 1890. Three children. After retirement, received honorary LL.D. degree from Univ. of MO in 1926. Became dir. of naval science at PA Military Academy in 1930, receiving honorary Doctor of Naval Science degree from that institution in 1931. Died at Naval Hosp. in Bremerton, WA, on 26 Jan 1935. Buried in Hannibal, MO.

Ranks Cadet Midn (28 Sep 1881); Naval Cadet (5 Aug 1882); Ens (1 Jul 1887); Ltjg (5 Sep 1896); Lt (3 Mar 1899); LCdr (1 Jan 1905); Cdr (7 Jan 1909); Capt (1 Jul 1912); RAdm (25 Dec 1917); temp. Adm (24 Oct 1919); placed on Ret.Lst. as RAdm (11 Jun 1928); Adm on Ret.Lst. (21 Jun 1930).

Career Summary Received appointment from MO (28 Sep 1881); USNA (Sep 1881-Jun 1885); *Mohican*, Pac.Sqdn. (Jun-Aug 1885); Naval Hosp., NY (Sep 1885); sick lv. (Sep 1885-Feb 1886); *Juniata*, N.Atl.Sqdn. (Feb-Jul 1886); *Galena*, N.Atl.Sqdn. (Jul-Dec 1886); *Atlanta*, on trials (Dec 1886-May 1887); USNA (May-Jun 1887); w.o. (Jun-Jul 1887); Bur. of Nav., Washington, DC (Aug-Dec 1887); *Pinta*, Alaskan waters (Feb 1888-Nov 1890); home and l.o.a. (Nov 1890-Mar 1891); Naval Observatory, Washington, DC (Mar-Jun 1891); *Pinta*, Alaskan waters (Jul 1891-Apr 1892); l.o.a. (Apr-Jun 1892) *Pinta*, Alaskan waters (Jun 1892-Oct 1893); l.o.a. (Oct-Dec 1893); *Michigan*, on Great Lakes (Dec 1893-Nov 1894); home and w.o. (Nov 1894); Bur. of Nav., Washington, DC (Nov 1894-Sep 1895); torp. instruction, Newport, RI (Sep-Oct 1895); *Katahdin*, New London, CT (Oct-Nov 1895); Bur. of Nav., Washington, DC (Nov 1895-Feb 1896); flgs., *Philadelphia*, Pac.Sta. (Mar 1896-Oct 1897); *Baltimore*, Navy Yard, Mare Island, CA (Oct 1897); cst.surv. duty (Oct 1897-May 1898); *Charleston*, Asia.Sqdn. (May 1898-May 1899); *Boston*, Asia.Sqdn. and Mare Island, CA (May-Sep 1899); home and w.o. (Sep 1899); l.o.a. (Sep-Nov 1899); *Enterprise*, Maritime School, Commonwealth of MA (Nov 1899-Nov 1901); *Philadelphia*, Pac.Sta. (Dec 1901-Aug 1902); *Boston*, Navy Yard, Mare Island, CA (Aug 1902); training ship, *Adams*, Pac cst. (Sep 1902-Jun 1904); *Wheeling*, Pac.Sta. (Jun-Aug 1904); *Buffalo*, Pac.Sta. (Aug-Dec 1904); home and w.o. (Dec 1904); temp. duty, Naval Sta., Honolulu, Territory of HI (Jan 1905); home and w. o. (Jan-Feb 1905); temp. duty, Norfolk, VA, and Schenectady, NY (Feb-Apr 1905); inspection duty, Seattle, and at Bur. of Equip. and Recruiting, Washington, DC (Apr 1905-Jun 1907); exec.off., *Nebraska*, "Great White Flt." (Jul 1907-Sep 1909); comdt. of midshipmen, USNA (Sep 1909-Aug 1911); w.o. (Aug-Sep 1911); Bur. of Nav., Washington, DC (Sep-Oct 1911); Member, bd. of inspection and surv., Washington, DC (Oct 1911-Mar 1912); naval gov., and comdt., Naval Sta., Guam (Apr 1912-Sep 1913); cdr, *Georgia*, Atl.Flt. (Dec 1913-Jun 1915); comdt., 13th Naval Dist., and comdt., Navy Yard, Puget Sound, WA (Jul 1915-Jan 1919); cdr, Div. 7, Atl.Flt., *Wyoming* (Jan-Jun 1919); cdr, Div. 6, Pac.Flt., *Wyoming* (Jun-Oct 1919); chief of naval operations, and member, Army-Navy Joint Bd., Washington, DC (24 Oct 1919-21 Jul 1921); cdr, U.S. Flt., *Seattle* (Aug 1923-Oct 1925);

comdt., 5th Naval Dist., Norfolk, VA, and comdt., Naval Operating Base, Hampton Roads, VA (Oct 1925-Jun 1928); placed on Ret.Lst. (11 Jun 1928).

Career Highlights   In Spanish-American War, was on *Charleston*, which captured Guam. Subsequently served during Philippine Insurrection. Was exec.off. of *Nebraska* with "Great White Flt." Commanded the *Georgia* at Vera Cruz, Mexico, and on Haiti in 1914. During World War I, served as act. chief of naval operations during Adm William S. Benson's [*q.v.*] absence in Europe, then commanded a division of the Atl.Flt. As chief of naval operations and member of Joint Bd. from 1919 to 1923, played a key role during naval reductions brought on by Washington Naval Conference.

References

Personal Papers: Coontz MSS in possession of the admiral's grandson, Capt Robert J. Coontz, USN (Washington, DC).

Writings: a) "Across the Continent with an Insane Man," U.S. Naval Institute *Proceedings* 225 (Nov 1921): 1749-54. b) "The Navy and Business," U.S. Naval Institute *Proceedings* 232 (Jun 1922): 987-1004. c) "The Navy," U.S. Naval Institute *Proceedings* 243 (May 1923): 747-57.   d) *From the Mississippi to the Sea* (Philadelphia: 1930). e) *True Anecdotes of an Admiral* (Philadelphia: 1934). f) "The Spirit of the Navy," U.S. Naval Institute *Proceedings* 828 (Feb 1972): 82-83.

Other Sources: Lawrence H. Douglas, "Robert Edward Coontz," in *The Chiefs of Naval Operations*, ed. Robert W. Love, Jr. (Annapolis: 1980), pp. 23-35.

PHILIP HENRY COOPER   Born in Camden, NY, on 5 Aug 1844, son of Hiram H. and Delia A. (Murdock) Cooper. Married three times. First wife was Etta Lou Cooper who he married about 1866 but who died in 1869. Married Sarah Lawrence Stuart, daughter of BGen David Stuart, USA, on 3 Oct 1871. Two sons, Stuart and Philip Benson. Married Katherine Jordena (Foote) Salter on 24 Jun 1884. A daughter, Dorothy Bradford, and a son, Leslie Bradford. Resided in Morristown, NJ, where he died on 29 Dec 1912 and where he was buried.

Ranks   Act.Midn (28 Sep 1860); title changed to Midn (16 Jul 1862); Ens (28 May 1863); Mstr (10 Nov 1865); Lt (10 Nov 1866); LCdr (12 Mar 1868); Cdr (1 Nov 1879); Capt (11 Apr 1894); RAdm (9 Feb 1902); placed on Ret.Lst. (5 Aug 1904).

Career Summary   Received appointment from NY (28 Sep 1860); USNA (Sep 1860-May 1863); *Macedonian*, W.Ind.Sqdn. (May-Oct 1863); *Richmond*, W.Gulf Blk.Sqdn. (Oct 1863-Jul 1865); *Powhatan*, S.Pac.Sqdn. (Jul 1865-Nov 1867); w.o. (Nov-Dec 1867); USNA (Dec 1867-Apr 1869); *Sabine,* spec. cruise (May 1869-Jul 1870); Tehuantepec and Nicaraguan Surv. Expd. (Sep 1870-May 1871); equip. dept., Navy Yard, NY (Jul-Sep 1871); *Congress* and *Plymouth*, spec.serv. and Eur.Sta. (Sep 1871-Jun 1873); w.o. (Jun-Jul 1873); USNA (Aug 1873-Nov 1874); l.o.a. (Dec 1874-Jul 1875); Torp.Sta., Newport, RI (Jul-Aug 1875); Experimental Battery, Annapolis (Aug 1875-Aug

PHILIP HENRY COOPER
1844-1912

1876); sick lv. (Aug 1876-May 1878); w.o. (May-Jun 1878); Cst.Surv. Office, Washington, DC (Jun-Nov 1878); spec. duty, Bur. of Nav., Washington, DC (Nov 1878-Mar 1881); temp. duty, torp. instruction, Newport, RI (Jun-Aug 1880); cdr, *Alliance*, Eur.Sta. (Mar-Jun 1881); w.o. (Jun-Oct 1881); spec. duty, Bur. of Nav., Washington, DC (Oct 1881); cdr, *Swatara*, Asia.Sta. (Dec 1881-May 1884); w.o. (May 1884-Apr 1886); Navy Yard, Norfolk, VA (Apr 1886-Jun 1888); w.o. (Jun 1888-Jan 1890); court-martial duties (Apr-May, Aug-Sep 1889); cdr, flgs., *Swatara*, Asia.Sqdn. (Mar 1890-Feb 1891); l.o.a. and various bd. duties (Feb 1891-Jul 1894); cdr, *San Francisco*, Navy Yard, NY (Jul-Nov 1894); supt., USNA (Nov 1894-Jul 1898); cdr, *Chicago*, Eur.Sta. (Dec 1898-Oct 1899); l.o.a. (Oct 1899-May 1900); cdr, *Iowa*, Pac.Sqdn. (Jun 1900-Jun 1901); various bd. duties (Jun-Nov 1901); w.o. (Nov 1901-Jun 1902); supt., 2nd Naval Dist., Newport, RI (Jun 1902-Jan 1903); cdr, Cruiser Sqdn., Asia. Flt., *New Orleans* (Feb-Dec 1903); cdr, Asia. Flt., *Kentucky* (Mar-Jun 1904); placed on Ret.Lst. (5 Aug 1904).

Career Highlights Was present at the Battle of Mobile May in 1864. Served three tours at the USNA, the last as superintendent.

FRANK CARVILL COSBY Born in Louisville, KY, on 10 Apr 1840, son of Fortunatus and Ellen (Blake) Cosby. Educated in KY and in Washington, DC. Served as a rec. teller for U.S. Treasury from 1854 to 1857. Married Charlotte M. Spencer on 6 Dec 1864. Died in Washington, DC, on 8 Feb 1905. Buried in Arlington National Cemetery.

Ranks Captain's Clerk (17 May 1857); Asst.Paymstr. (24 Aug 1861); Paymstr. (14 Apr 1862); Pay Insp. (12 Apr 1877); Pay Dir. (5 Jul 1889); Gen.Insp., Pay Corps with rank of Capt (16 Mar 1898); placed on Ret.Lst. as Pay Dir. with rank of RAdm (10 Apr 1902).

Career Summary Received appointment from KY (17 May 1857); flgs., *Cumberland*, Afr.Sqdn., and flgs., *Richmond*, Med. Sqdn. (May 1857-Aug 1861); w.o. (Aug-Oct 1861); Bur. of Provisions and Clothing, Washington, DC (Oct-Dec 1861); flt.paymstr., Potomac Flot. (Dec 1861-Mar 1863); w.o. (Mar-May 1863); in charge of stores, S.Atl.Blk.Sqdn., *Vermont* (May 1863-Aug 1864); s.a. and w.o. (Aug-Dec 1864); in charge of stores, rec. ship, *Allegheny*, Baltimore (Dec 1864-Jan 1868); additional duty, in charge of stores, and paymstr., USNA (Jun-Nov 1865); s.a. and w.o. (Jan-Mar 1868); in charge of stores, Honolulu, Sandwich Islands (Mar 1868-Mar 1869); rec. ship, *Independence*, Mare Island, CA (Jun-Jul 1869); s.a. and w.o. (Jul-Nov 1869); flgs., *Saranac*, Pac.Sqdn. (Nov 1869-Oct 1872); s.a. and w.o. (Oct 1872-Nov 1873); *Franklin*, N.Atl.Sta. (Nov 1873-Mar 1874); *Wabash*, N.Atl.Sta. (Mar-May 1874); s.a. and w.o. (May-Jul 1874); Bur. of Provisions and Clothing, Washington, DC (Jul 1874-Jan 1875); Navy Yard, Washington, DC (Jan-May 1875); *Triana*, Navy Yard, Washington, DC (May-Jun 1875); *Alarm*, spec.serv. (Jun 1875); w.o. (Jun 1875-Dec 1876);

spec. duty, *Wyoming*, Navy Yard, Washington, DC (Dec 1876-Jul 1877); spec. duty, Navy Dept., Washington, DC (Jul-Aug 1877); flt.paymstr., Eur.Sta., *Trenton* (Oct 1877-Jan 1881); s.a. (Jan-Feb 1881); insp. of provisions and clothing, Navy Yard, Washington, DC (Feb 1881-Mar 1884); s.a. and w.o. (Mar-Sep 1884); spec. duty, Bur. of Provisions and Clothing, Washington, DC (Sep-Dec 1884); spec. duty, Navy Dept., Washington, DC (Dec 1884-Feb 1885); Pay Office, Baltimore (Feb-Sep 1885); s.a. and w.o. (Sep 1885-May 1886); insp. of provisions and clothing, Navy Yard, Portsmouth, NH (Jun-Dec 1886); general storekeeper, Navy Yard, Portsmouth, NH (Dec 1886-Jun 1889); s.a. and w.o. (Jun-Oct 1889); l.o.a. (Oct 1889-Jul 1891); general storekeeper, Navy Yard, Norfolk, VA (Jul 1891-Mar 1892); s.a. and w.o. (Mar-Jun 1892); Bur. of Provisions and Clothing, Washington, DC (Jun-Jul 1892); duty, World's Columbian Exposition, Chicago (Jul 1892-Jul 1894); w.o. (Jul-Sep 1894); in charge, Pay Office, Washington, DC (Oct 1894-Jul 1897); member, bd. of inspection and surv., Navy Dept., Washington, DC (Jul 1897-Mar 1898); general insp., Pay Corps, Washington, DC (Mar 1898-Apr 1902); placed on Ret.Lst. (10 Apr 1902).

VINCENDON LAZARUS COTTMAN Born in Riverside, Ascension Parish, LA, on 13 Feb 1852, son of Dr. Thomas Edmond Huff and Marie Louise (de Tournillon) Cottman. Educated at Mt. St. Mary's College in MD. Married to Elizabeth Klink Cottman. Resided in Seattle, WA. Died on 15 Mar 1917 in Washington, DC. Buried in Arlington National Cemetery.

Ranks Midn (25 Sep 1868); title changed to Cadet Midn (15 Jul 1870); Midn (1 Jun 1872); Ens (15 Jul 1873); Mstr (9 May 1878); title changed to Ltjg (3 Mar 1883); Lt (8 Jan 1885); LCdr (3 Mar 1899); Cdr (3 Jun 1902); Capt (8 Feb 1907); RAdm (7 Nov 1910); placed on Ret.Lst. (13 Feb 1914).

Career Summary Received appointment from NY (25 Sep 1868); USNA (Sep 1868-Jun 1872); *Tuscarora*, S.Pac.Sta. (Jun 1872-Nov 1873); *Kearsarge*, Asia.Sta., and *Tuscarora*, N.Pac.Sta. (Nov 1873-Aug 1875); w.o. (Aug-Oct 1875); l.o.a. (Nov 1875-Jan 1876); rec. ship, *Colorado*, NY (Jan-Jul 1876); storeship, *Supply* (Jul-Sep 1876); w.o. (Sep-Dec 1876); *Alliance*, Eur.Sta. (Jan 1877-Jan 1879); w.o. (Jan 1879-Apr 1880); rec. ship, *Colorado*, NY (Apr 1880-Aug 1881); *Richmond* and *Monocacy*, Asia.Sta. (Sep 1881-Aug 1884); w.o. (Aug 1884-Jan 1885); branch hydrographic office, NY (Jan 1885-Mar 1889); schoolship, *St. Mary's* (Mar 1889-Mar 1890); sec., international marine conference, Washington, DC (Mar-Nov 1890); spec. duty, Navy Dept., Washington, DC (Nov 1890-Feb 1891); *Concord*, spec.serv. and Asia.Sta. (Feb 1891-Feb 1894); *Marion*, Asia.Sta. (Feb-Jul 1894); home and l.o.a. (Jul-Oct 1894); equip. duty, Navy Yard, NY (Oct 1894-Dec 1896); *Monterey*, Pac.Sqdn. (Dec 1896-Jan 1898); exec.off. *Alert*, Asia.Sta. (Mar-May 1898); *Brutus*, spec.serv. and Pac.Sta. (May 1898-Oct 1899); spec. duty, Manila, P.I. (Oct 1899); *Monterey* and additional duty, nautical schoolship, Manila, P.I. (Oct-Dec 1899); Navy Yard, Mare Island, CA

VINCENDON LAZARUS COTTMAN
1852-1917

(Jan 1900); home and w.o. (Jan-Feb 1900); Hydrographic Office, Washington, DC (Feb-Mar 1900); Bur. of Nav. Washington, DC (Mar 1900-Nov 1902); duty with, then cdr, *Wyoming*, Pac.Sqdn. (Nov 1902-Jan 1905); home and w.o. (Jan-Mar 1905); Navy Yard, Mare Island, CA (Apr-Jun 1905); capt.yd., Navy Yard, Puget Sound, WA (Jun 1905-Nov 1907); cdr, *California*, 2nd Div., Pac.Flt. (Nov 1907-Sep 1909); capt.yd., Navy Yard, Puget Sound, WA (Sep 1909-Jul 1910); comdt., Navy Yard, Puget Sound, WA (Jul 1910-Feb 1914); comdt., 13th Naval Defense Dist., Puget Sound, WA (Sep 1910-Feb 1914); additional temp. duty, cdr, Pac. Reserve Flt. (Aug-Oct 1912); placed on Ret.Lst. (13 Feb 1914).

ALBERT REYNOLDS COUDEN
1846-1923

ALBERT REYNOLDS COUDEN Born in Michigan City, IN, on 30 Oct 1846, son of Reynolds and Margaret S. (Marshall) Couden. Married but later divorced. One son. Died in the Naval Hosp. in Washington, DC, on 7 Apr 1923.

Ranks Midn (26 Sep 1863); Ens (18 Dec 1868); Mstr (21 Mar 1870); Lt (21 Mar 1871); LCdr (31 Mar 1889); Cdr (14 Mar 1897); Capt (15 Jan 1902); RAdm (12 Jul 1907); placed on Ret.Lst (30 Oct 1908).

Career Summary Received appointment from UT (26 Sep 1863); USNA (Sep 1863-Jun 1867); training ship, *Minnesota* (Jul-Dec 1867); flgs., *Franklin*, Eur.Sqdn. (Dec 1867-Jan 1869); *Kenosha* [renamed *Plymouth*], Eur.Sta. (Jan 1869-Feb 1870); w.o. (Feb-Apr 1870); signal duty (May-Jul 1870); *Guard*, Darien Expd. (Jul 1870-Jul 1871); w.o. (Jul-Oct 1871); *Wyoming*, N.Atl.Flt. (Oct 1871-Apr 1874); w.o. (Apr-Jun 1874); Torp.Sta., Newport, RI (Jul-Oct 1874); *Canonicus*, spec.serv. (Oct 1874-May 1875); Torp.Sta., Newport, RI (Jun 1875-Sep 1878); *Palos, Ashuelot*, and *Richmond*, Asia.Sta. (Oct 1878-Sep 1881); w.o. (Sep 1881-Feb 1882); Bur. of Ord., Washington, DC (Feb 1882-Nov 1888); exec.off., *Atlanta*, spec.serv. (Nov 1888-Apr 1891); Bur. of Ord., Washington, DC (Apr 1891-Aug 1894); cdr, *Pinta*, Alaskan waters (Sep 1894-Oct 1896); insp. of ord., Indian Head Proving Ground, MD (Nov 1896-Jan 1900); w.o. (Jan-Feb 1900); temp. duty, Bur. of Ord., Washington, DC (Feb-Apr 1900); cdr, *Wheeling*, Asia.Sta. (May 1900-Jan 1901); cdr, training ship, *Mohican* (Jan 1901-Oct 1902); comdt., Naval Sta., Cavite, P.I. (Nov 1902-Aug 1904); home and w.o. (Aug-Oct 1904); temp. inspection duties (Oct-Nov 1904); general insp. of ord., USN, Washington, DC (Nov 1904-May 1906); additional duty, general insp., *Louisiana*, Newport News, VA (Dec 1905-Jun 1906); cdr, *Louisiana*, spec. cruise (Jun 1906-Jul 1907); various bd. duties (Jul 1907-Apr 1908); general insp. of ord., USN, Washington, DC (Apr 1908-Jul 1909); placed on Ret.Lst. (30 Oct 1908); Bur. of Ord., war industries and U.S. shipping bds., Washington, DC (Sep 1917-Nov 1918).

SAMUEL FRANKLIN COUES Born in NH on 17 Sep 1825. Married with a son. Died on 1 May 1916 at Cambridge, MA. Buried in Mt. Auburn Cemetery, Mt. Auburn, MA.

SAMUEL FRANKLIN COUES
1825-1916

Ranks Asst.Surg. (25 Feb 1851); PAsst.Surg. (9 Apr 1856); Surg. (26 Apr 1861); Medl.Insp. (3 Mar 1871); Medl.Dir. (13 Aug 1876); placed on Ret.Lst. (17 Sep 1887); Medl.Dir. with rank of RAdm on Ret.Lst. (29 Jun 1906).

Career Summary Received appointment from NH (25 Feb 1851); w.o. (Feb-May 1851); cst.surv. duty (May-Oct 1851); *Portsmouth*, Pac.Sqdn. (Oct 1851-Apr 1855); temp. duty, Bur. of Medicine and Surgery, Washington, DC (Apr-Jul 1855); Naval Hosp., Chelsea, MA (Jul-Oct 1855); l.o.a. and w.o. (Oct 1855-Apr 1856); cst.surv. duty (Apr-Aug 1856); w.o. (Aug-Dec 1856); Naval Hosp., Chelsea, MA (Jan-Jul 1857); Naval Laboratory, NY (Jul 1857-Jul 1859); *Saginaw* and *Hartford*, E.Ind.Sqdn. (Aug 1859-Dec 1861); l.o.a. and w.o. (Dec 1861-Mar 1862); rec. ship, *Ohio*, Boston (Mar-Jun 1862); *Housatonic*, S.Atl.Blk.Sqdn. (Jun-Dec 1862); sick lv. and w.o. (Dec 1862-Apr 1863); *Saranac*, Pac.Sqdn. (Jun 1863-Jul 1865); return and w.o. (Jul-Sep 1865); Naval Hosp., Chelsea, MA (Sep 1865-Oct 1868); w.o. (Oct-Dec 1868); *Richmond*, Eur.Sqdn. (Jan 1869-Aug 1871); l.o.a. and w.o. (Aug 1871-Feb 1873); Navy Yard, Portsmouth, NH (Feb-Nov 1873); *Colorado*, N.Atl.Sta. (Dec 1873-May 1874); Navy Yard, Portsmouth, NH (May 1874-Apr 1875); w.o. (Apr 1875); flt.surg., N.Atl.Sta., *Worcester* (Apr 1875-Aug 1876); Naval Hosp., NY (Aug 1876-Oct 1879); spec. duty, Boston (Oct 1879-Apr 1880); Naval Laboratory, NY (May 1880-Mar 1883); w.o. (Mar 1883-Feb 1884); pres., medl.exam.bd., Philadelphia (Feb 1884-Jun 1885); in charge, Naval Hosp., Chelsea, MA (Mar 1885-Sep 1887); placed on Ret.Lst. (17 Sep 1887).

FRANK COURTIS Born in Cincinnati, OH, on 18 Jun 1844, son of James F. and Jane (Cook) Courtis. Educated in schools in Cincinnati from 1850 to 1859, then in Oakland, CA, from 1859 to 1862. Married Maude Carleton on 17 Apr 1883. Died in Washington, DC, on 20 Jan 1908. Buried in Arlington National Cemetery.

Ranks Midn (25 Sep 1862); Ens (12 Mar 1868); Mstr (26 Mar 1869); Lt (21 Mar 1870); LCdr (2 Mar 1885); Cdr (10 Jul 1894); Capt (23 Jul 1900); retired with rank of RAdm (27 Sep 1901).

Career Summary Received appointment from CA (25 Sep 1862); USNA (Sep 1862-Jun 1866); w.o. and l.o.a. (Jun-Dec 1866); *Pawnee*, S.Atl.Sta. (Jan 1867-Jul 1869); w.o. (Jul-Sep 1869); *Resaca*, Pac.Sta. (Sep 1869-Jan 1871); *Ossipee*, Pac.Sta. (Jan 1871-Nov 1872); w.o. (Nov 1872-Jan 1873); rec. ship, *Independence*, Mare Island, CA (Jan-Jul 1873); l.o.a. and w.o. (Jul 1873-Jan 1874); rec. ship, *Independence*, Mare Island, CA (Jan-Feb 1874); cst.surv. duty (Feb 1874-Feb 1878); w.o. (Feb-Mar 1878); ord. instruction, Navy Yard, Washington, DC (Mar-May 1878); torp. instruction, Newport, RI (Jun-Sep 1878); Navy Yard, Mare Island, CA (Sep-Oct 1878); *Tuscarora*, spec. surv. duty (Oct 1878-May 1880); w.o. (May-Sep 1880); *Ranger*, Navy Yard, Mare Island, CA (Sep 1880-Aug 1881); w.o. (Aug-Sep 1881); Navy Yard, Washington, DC (Sep 1881-Jul 1882); *Montauk*, Philadelphia (Jul-Dec 1882); equip. duty, Navy Yard,

FRANK COURTIS
1844-1908

Washington, DC (Dec 1882-Apr 1885); exec.off., *Omaha*, Asia.Sta. (Apr 1885-Mar 1887); cdr, *Omaha*, Asia.Sta. (Mar 1887-Mar 1888); *Pensacola*, Navy Yard, Norfolk, VA (Mar-May 1888); w.o. and l.o.a. (May-Sep 1888); steel inspection duty, Pittsburgh, PA (Sep 1888-Jun 1890); member, steel inspection bd., Washington, DC (Jun 1890-Jun 1893); cdr, *Vesuvius*, N.Atl.Sqdn. (Jun 1893-Aug 1894); insp. of steel, Pittsburgh, PA (Aug 1894-Aug 1895); insp., 12th L.h. Dist., San Francisco (Sep 1895-Apr 1898); sick lv. (Apr-Aug 1898); cdr, training ship, *Essex* (Aug 1898-Apr 1900); Navy Yard, Washington, DC (Apr-May 1900); NWC (Jun-Oct 1900); sick lv. (Nov 1900-Sep 1901); placed on Ret.Lst. (27 Sep 1901).

THOMAS JEFFERSON COWIE Born in Montezuma, IA, on 15 Feb 1857, son of George and Margaret (Duffus) Cowie. Educated in public and private schools in Washington, DC. Married Susie Ada Gedney on 15 Feb 1881. Two daughters. Died on 16 Jul 1936. Buried in Arlington National Cemetery.

Ranks Engineer's Yeoman (8 Jan 1877); dismissed (19 Oct 1878); Paymaster's Yeoman (21 Oct 1878); dismissed (23 Aug 1879); Asst.Paymstr. (16 Jun 1880); PAsst. Paymstr. (26 Mar 1889); PAsst.Paymstr. with rel. rank of Lt (23 Apr 1895); Paymstr. (11 Sep 1895); Paymstr. with rel. rank of LCdr (22 Sep 1901); Pay Insp. (5 Jan 1903); Pay Dir. (2 May 1908); Paymstr. Gen. and Chief, Bur. of Supplies and Accounts, with rank of RAdm (1 Jul 1910); transferred to Ret.Lst. (15 Feb 1921).

Career Summary Received appointment from IA (16 Jun 1880); w.o. (Jun-Jul 1880); Paymaster's Office, Navy Dept., Washington, DC (Jul 1880-May 1881); prac. ship, *Standish* (May-Sep 1881); s.a. and w.o. (Sep 1881); training ship, *Standish*, USNA (Sep-Nov 1881); w.o. (Nov-Dec 1881); temp. duty, Pay Office, Washington, DC (Dec 1881-May 1882); prac. ship, *Dale* (Jun-Aug 1882); s.a. and w.o. (Aug-Nov 1882); training ship, *New Hampshire*, Newport, RI (Nov 1882-Oct 1886); s.a. and w.o. (Oct 1886); training ship, *Saratoga* (Oct 1886-Oct 1888); s.a. and wo. (Oct-Nov 1888); l.o.a. (Nov-Dec 1888); w.o. (Jan-Mar 1889); general storekeeper, Torp.Sta., Newport, RI (Apr 1889-Oct 1891); *Petrel*, Asia.Sqdn. (Oct 1891); suspended from duty (Oct 1891-Sep 1893); w.o. (Sep-Dec 1893); *Monocacy*, Asia.Sta. (Feb 1894-Apr 1897); s.a. and w.o. (Apr-Jul 1897); Training Sta., Newport, RI (Jul 1897-Apr 1902); flgs., *Chicago*, Eur.Sta. (May 1902-Jul 1903); flt.paymstr., Eur.Flt., *Brooklyn* (Jul 1903-Apr 1904); s.a. and w.o. (Apr-Jun 1904); l.o.a. (Jun-Dec 1904); w.o. (Dec 1904-Jan 1905); pay off. and general storekeeper, USNA (Jan 1905-Jul 1910); paymstr. general, and chief, Bur. of Supplies and Accounts, Washington, DC (Jul 1910-Jul 1914); pres., naval exam. bd., Washington, DC (Aug-Nov 1914); NWC (Nov 1914-Mar 1917); disbursing off., 2nd Naval Dist., Newport, RI (Mar-Oct 1917); w.o. (Oct-Nov 1917); temp. duty, purchasing off., Naval Sta., Newport, RI (Nov 1917-Jan 1918); disbursing off., Bur. of Supplies and Accounts, Washington, DC (Feb 1918-Feb 1921); additional duty, contract off., Bur. of Supplies

THOMAS JEFFERSON COWIE
1857-1936

and Accounts, Washington, DC (Mar 1918-Feb 1921); transferred to Ret.Lst. (15 Feb 1921)

WALTER CLEVELAND COWLES Born in Farmington, CT, on 11 Jul 1853, son of Thomas and Elizabeth (Sheffield) Cowles and brother of RAdm William Sheffield Cowles, USN (1846-1923) [*q.v.*]. Married Mary Ada Johnston on 3 Jul 1892. One son, William B. Cowles, who served in the navy. Died on 25 Nov 1917 in Redlands, CA.

Ranks Midn (22 Sep 1869); title changed to Cadet Midn (15 Jul 1870); Midn (31 May 1873); Ens (16 Jul 1874); Mstr (2 Aug 1879); title changed to Ltjg (3 Mar 1883); Lt (1 Dec 1885); LCdr (3 Mar 1899); Cdr (14 Jun 1902); Capt (19 Mar 1907); RAdm (14 Jan 1911); placed on Ret.Lst. (11 Jul 1915).

Career Summary Received appointment from CT (22 Sep 1869); USNA (Sep 1869-May 1873); w.o. (May-Sep 1873); *Monongahela*, Atl.Sta. (Sep 1873-Oct 1875); home and w.o. (Oct 1875-Feb 1876); *Juniata*, Baltimore (Feb-Sep 1876); w.o. (Sep-Oct 1876); rec. ship, *Colorado*, NY (Oct 1876-Jan 1877); w.o. (Jan-Feb 1877); *Trenton* and training ship, *Constellation*, Asia.Sta. (Feb 1877-Jan 1880); w.o. (Jan-Mar 1880); Hydrographic Office, Washington, DC (Mar 1880-Mar 1882); w.o. (Mar-Apr 1882); torp. instruction, Newport, RI (May-Aug 1882); *Kearsarge*, Eur.Sta. (Aug 1882-Oct 1885); home and w.o. (Oct-Dec 1885); ord. duty, Navy Yard, Washington, DC (Dec 1885-Jan 1887); insp. of steel for new cruisers (Jan-Aug 1887); ord. duty, Navy Yard, Washington, DC (Sep 1887-Apr 1889); *Kearsarge*, N.Atl. Sta. (Apr 1889-Aug 1890); *Boston* (Aug-Oct 1890); insp. of steel, Homestead Steel Works, Wellman Iron and Steel Co., and Carnegie, Phipps and Co. (Oct 1890-Aug 1893); l.o.a. (Aug-Oct 1893); torp. instruction, Newport, RI (Oct-Nov 1893); w.o. (Nov 1893-Feb 1894); *Marblehead*, N.Atl. and Eur.Stas. (Mar 1894-Apr 1897); l.o.a. (Apr-Jun 1897); Bur. of Equip. and Recruiting, Washington, DC (Jul 1897-Oct 1899); cdr, *Petrel*, Asia.Sta. (Dec 1899-Jun 1900); ord.off., Naval Sta., Cavite, P.I. (Dec 1899-Jan 1901); exec.off., *Newark*, Asia.Sta. (Jan-Apr 1901); flgs., *Brooklyn*, Asia.Sta. (Apr 1901-Jun 1902); home and who. (Jun-Jul 1902); member, bd. of inspection and surv. (Aug 1902-Jan 1905); temp. duty, Naval Sta., Cavite, P.I. (Feb-Mar 1905); cdr, *Monocacy*, Asia.Sta. (Mar-May 1905); cdr, *Rainbow*, Asia.Sta. (May 1905-Feb 1906); chief of staff, Asia.Sta., *Ohio* (Feb-Aug 1906); home and w. o. (Aug 1906-Jan 1907); cdr, rec. ship, *Franklin*, Norfo.k, VA (Jan-Nov 1907); cdr, *Kentucky*, "Great White Flt." (Nov 1907-Apr 1909); cdr, *Kansas*, Navy Yard, Philadelphia (Apr-May 1909); cdr, flgs., *Connecticut*, "Great White Flt." (Jun-Nov 1909); cdr, rec. ship, *Hancock*, NY (Nov 1909-Nov 1910); comdt., Naval Sta., Honolulu, Territory of HI (Dec 1910-Mar 1913); cdr, Pac.Flt., *California* (Apr-Dec 1913), and *Pittsburgh* (Dec 1913-Feb 1914); cdr, Asia. Flt., *Saratoga* (May 1914-Jul 1915); placed on Ret.Lst. (11 Jul 1915).

WILLIAM SHEFFIELD COWLES Born in Farmington, CT,

WALTER CLEVELAND COWLES
1853-1917

WILLIAM SHEFFIELD COWLES
1846-1923

on 1 Aug 1846, son of Thomas and Elizabeth (Sheffield) Cowles, and brother of RAdm Walter Cleveland Cowles, USN (1853-1917) [*q.v.*]. Married Anna Roosevelt, daughter of future pres. Theodore Roosevelt, 25 Oct 1895. One son, William Sheffield Cowles, Jr. Died in Farmington, CT, on 1 May 1923. Buried in Riverside Cemetery in Farmington.

Ranks Midn (22 Jul 1863); Ens (18 Dec 1868); Mstr (21 Mar 1870); Lt (21 Mar 1871); LCdr (5 May 1892); Cdr (5 Jun 1898); Capt (2 Nov 1902); RAdm (23 Apr 1908); place on Ret.Lst. (1 Aug 1908).

Career Summary Received appointment from CT (22 Jul 1863); USNA (Jul 1863-Jun 1867); *Minnesota, Pensacola,* and *Saginaw,* Med. and N.Pac.Sqdns. (Jul 1867-Oct 1870); w.o. (Oct 1870-Jan 1871); Naval Observatory, Washington, DC (Jan-May 1871); Torp.Sta., Newport, RI (Jun 1871-Jan 1872); prac. ship, *Constellation* (Feb 1872-Mar 1873); w.o. (Mar-Jul 1873); *Alaska,* Med., W.Indies Sqdns., and Afr.cst. (Aug 1873-Sep 1876); w.o. (Sep-Dec 1876); *Tennessee* and *Monocacy,* Asia.Sta. (Mar 1877-Mar 1880); home and w.o. (Mar-Aug 1880); Navy Yard, NY (Aug 1880-Apr 1882); flag lt, N.Atl.Sqdn., *Tennessee* (May 1882-Jul 1884); w.o. (Jul-Oct 1884); member, bd. of inspection, merchant vessels, NY (Oct 1884-Apr 1885); flgs., *Tennessee,* N.Atl.Sqdn. (Apr-May 1885); member, bd. of inspection, merchant vessels, NY (May 1885-Jan 1887); cdr, training ship, *Despatch* (Jan 1887-Nov 1891); l.o.a. (Nov-Dec 1891); aide to sec. of navy in charge of naval militia, Navy Dept., Washington, DC (Dec 1891-Dec 1892); naval attaché, U.S. Embassy, London (Jan 1893-Mar 1897); cdr, *Fern,* N.Atl.Sqdn. (Apr 1897-Apr 1898); cdr, *Topeka,* N.Atl.Flt. (May 1898-Feb 1899); home and w.o. (Feb-Sep 1899); asst., Bur. of Nav., Washington, DC (Sep 1899-Nov 1903); naval aide to pres. Theodore Roosevelt, Washington, DC (Sep 1901-Jan 1910); cdr, *Missouri,* N.Atl.Sta. (Dec 1903-Nov 1905); spec. duty, Navy Dept., Washington, DC (Nov 1905); spec. duty, Bur. of Equip. and Recruiting, Washington, DC (Nov 1905-Jan 1906); chief, Bur. of Equip. and Recruiting, Washington, DC (Jan 1906-Jan 1910); placed on Ret.Lst. (1 Aug 1908).

References
Personal Papers: NYHS.

JOSEPH EDGAR CRAIG Born in Medina, NY, on 24 Feb 1845, son of Joseph and Elizabeth Warren (Herring) Craig. Married Alethe Lowber on 29 Jul 1868. One daughter. Died in Washington, DC, on 21 Jun 1925. Buried in Arlington National Cemetery.

Ranks Act.Midn (29 Nov 1861); title changed to Midn (16 Jul 1862); Ens (1 Dec 1866); Mstr (12 Mar 1868); Lt (26 Mar 1869); LCdr (13 Mar 1880); Cdr (3 Jan 1890); Capt (3 Mar 1899); RAdm (28 Dec 1904); placed on Ret.Lst. (24 Feb 1907).

Career Summary Received appointment from NY (29 Nov 1861); USNA (Nov 1861-Oct 1865); *Monogahela,* W.Ind.Sqdn. (Nov 1865-Jul 1868); l.o.a. (Jul-Dec 1868); *Portsmouth,* S.

JOSEPH EDGAR CRAIG
1845-1925

Atl.Sqdn. (Jan 1869-Nov 1871); w.o. (Nov-Dec 1871); USNA (Dec 1871-Jun 1874); Naval Observatory, Washington, DC (Jul-Oct 1874); spec. duty, astronomer, N.Pac. Survey, *Narragansett* (Nov 1874-Jul 1875); Hydrographic Office, Washington, DC (Jul 1875-Nov 1877); l.o.a. and w.o. (Nov 1877-Apr 1878); *Alaska*, Pac.Sta. (Apr 1878-Apr 1881); return and w.o. (Apr-May 1881); inst. in astronomy, nav., and surveying, then head of dept. of English studies, history, and law, USNA (Jun 1881-Sep 1885); w.o. (Sep 1885-Feb 1886); flgs., *Vandalia*, Pac.Sta. (Feb 1886-Apr 1887); cdr, *Palos*, Asia.Sta. (May 1887-Mar 1890); home and l.o.a. (Mar-Jun 1890); head, dept. of English studies, history, and law, USNA (Jun 1890-Aug 1894); w.o. (Aug-Oct 1894); cdr, *Concord*, Asia.Sta. (Dec 1894-May 1896); home and w.o. (May-Jun 1896); Navy Yard, NY (Jul 1896-Apr 1897); hydrographer, Hydrographic Office, Washington, DC (Apr 1897-Jan 1900); duty with, then cdr, *Albany*, Asia.Sta. (Feb 1900-Oct 1902); home and w.o. (Oct-Dec 1902); capt.yd., Navy Yard, Norfolk, VA (Feb 1903-Dec 1904); member, bd. of examiners (Jan-Mar 1905); comdt., Navy Yard, League Island, PA (Mar 1905-Feb 1907); placed on Ret.Lst. (24 Feb 1907).

References
Writings: a) *Azimuth, A Treatise on the Subject...* (NY: 1887). b) "Negative-Reciprocal Equations," U.S. Naval Institute *Proceedings* 66 (1893): 201-12.

ARENT SCHUYLER CROWNINSHIELD Born in Seneca Falls, NY, on 14 Mar 1843, son of Jacob and Mary Miller (Schuyler) Crowninshield. Married Mary Bradford on 27 Jul 1870. One son. Died in Philadelphia, PA, on 27 May 1908. Buried in Arlington National Cemetery.

Ranks Act.Midn (21 Sep 1860); title changed to Midn (16 Jul 1862); Ens (28 May 1863); Mstr (10 Nov 1865); Lt (12 Nov 1866); LCdr (10 Mar 1868); Cdr (25 Mar 1880); Capt (21 Jul 1894); RAdm (16 Mar 1902); retired (20 Mar 1903).

Career Summary Received appointment from NY (21 Sep 1860); USNA (Sep 1860-May 1863); *Juniata*, W.Ind.Sqdn. (Jun-Dec 1863); w.o. (Dec 1863-Feb 1864); *Ticonderoga*, N. Atl.Blk.Sqdn. (Feb 1864-May 1865); Navy Yard, NY (May-Jun 1865); w.o. (Jun-Jul 1865); *Hartford*, E.Ind.Sqdn. (Jul 1865-Aug 1868); w.o. (Aug-Sep 1868); USNA (Oct-Dec 1868); *Richmond*, Eur.Sqdn. (Jan 1869-Nov 1871); l.o.a. (Nov 1871-Mar 1872); ord. duty, Navy Yard, Boston (Mar-Jul 1872); l.o.a. (Jul 1872-May 1873); *Lackawanna*, Asia.Sta. (May 1873-Apr 1875); l.o.a. (May-Oct 1875); ord. duty, then insp. of ord. Navy Yard, Washington, DC (Oct 1875-Jul 1878); cdr, training ship, *Portsmouth* (Aug 1878-Jul 1881); member, naval advisory bd. (Jun-Nov 1881); w.o. (Nov 1881-Jan 1882); Signal Office, Washington, DC (Jan-May 1882); l.o.a. (May-Sep 1882); insp., 1st L.h. Dist., Portland, ME (Sep 1882-Nov 1885); member, naval advisory bd. Washington, DC (Nov 1885-Dec 1886); cdr, training ship, *St. Mary's* (Jan 1887-Jan 1890); w.o. (Jan 1890-Oct 1891); ord. duty, Navy Yard, NY (Oct 1891-Mar 1892); cdr,

**ARENT SCHUYLER
CROWNINSHIELD**
1843-1908

Kearsarge, N.Atl.Sta. (Mar 1892-Nov 1893); senior member, bd. of inspection, Navy Yard, NY (Nov 1893-Dec 1894); cdr, rec. ship, *Richmond*, Philadelphia (Dec 1894-Sep 1895); cdr, *Maine*, N.Atl.Sta. (Sep 1895-Apr 1897); chief, Bur. of Nav., Washington, DC (Apr 1897-Apr 1902); cdr, Eur.Sta., *Illinois*, then *Chicago* (Apr 1902-Mar 1903); retired (20 Mar 1903).

Career Highlights During the Spanish-American War, he served on the Bd. of Strategy and, as chief, of Bur. of Nav., thus in charge of the assignments and movements of officers and ships.

CHARLES HENRY DAVIS
1845-1921

CHARLES HENRY DAVIS Born in Cambridge, MA, on 28 Aug 1845, son of RAdm Charles Henry Davis, USN (1807-77) and Harriette Blake (Mills) Davis. Raised in Cambridge, married Louisa Quakenbush on 31 Mar 1875. One daughter and a son, Cdr Charles Henry Davis, Jr., USN. Brother-in-law of Henry Cabot Lodge. Died on 27 Dec 1921 in Washington, D.C.

Ranks Act.Midn (29 Nov 1861); title changed to Midn (16 Jul 1862); Ens (1 Nov 1866); Mstr (1 Dec 1866); Lt (12 Mar 1868); LCdr (30 Jun 1869); Cdr (30 Oct 1885); Capt (10 Aug 1898); RAdm (24 Aug 1904); placed on Ret.Lst. (28 Aug 1907).

Career Summary Received appointment from MA (29 Nov 1861); USNA (Nov 1861-Nov 1864); rec. ship, *Vermont*, NY (Nov 1864-Feb 1865); Navy Yard, NY (Feb-Apr 1865); flgs., *Colorado*, and *Augusta*, Eur.Sqdn. (Apr 1865-Aug 1867); w.o. (Jul-Sep 1867); *Idaho*, *Guerriere*, *Kenosha*, and *Portsmouth*, S.Atl. and Eur.Stas. (Oct 1867-Sep 1870); home and w.o. (Sep 1870-May 1871); spec. duty, Key West, FL (May-Jun 1871); rec. ship, *New Hampshire*, Norfolk, VA (Aug 1871-Jul 1872); *Omaha* and *Pensacola*, S.Atl. and Pac.Stas. (Aug 1872-Nov 1874); w.o. (Dec 1874-Feb 1875); Naval Observatory, Washington, DC (Mar-May 1875); torp. duty, Newport, RI (Jun-Oct 1875); Naval Observatory, Washington, DC (Oct 1875-Oct 1877); spec. duty, Europe (Oct 1877-Nov 1878); Hydrographic Office, Washington, DC (Nov 1878-May 1879); spec. duty, Europe (May-Oct 1879); Bur. of Nav., Washington, DC (Oct 1879-Mar 1881); *Palos*, Asia.Sta. (May 1881-Mar 1882); Bur. of Nav., Washington, DC (Mar 1882-Feb 1883); spec. duty, Galveston, TX (Feb-Sep 1883); in charge, expd. to Latin American w.cst. (Sep 1883-Jun 1885); *Powhatan*, N.Atl.Sqdn. (Jun-Nov 1885); ord. instruction, Navy Yard, Washington, DC (Dec 1885-May 1886); cdr, Training Sqdn., *Saratoga* (May 1886-Aug 1888); cdr, *Quinnebaug*, Eur.Sta. (Sep 1888-Jun 1889); special duty, Bur. of Nav., Washington, DC (Jun-Sept 1889); in charge, Office of Naval Intelligence, Navy Dept., Washington, DC (Sep 1889-Aug 1892); additional duty, general insp., *Montgomery* and various bd. duties (Dec 1891-Aug 1892); torp. duty, Newport, RI (Aug 1892-Mar 1893); special duty (Mar-Jul 1893); l.o.a. and w.o. (Jul-Aug 1893); special duty, Columbia Iron Works, Baltimore (Sep 1893-Jun 1894); cdr, *Montgomery*, N.Atl.Sta. (Jun 1894-Jul 1896); member, bd. of inspection and surv., and other bd. duties (Jul 1896-Jul 1897); supt., Naval Observatory, Washington, DC (Jul 1897-Apr 1898); cdr, *Dixie*, N.Atl.Sqdn. (Apr-Sep 1898); supt., Naval Observatory,

Washington, DC (Nov 1898-Nov 1902); cdr, *Alabama*, N.Atl.Sta. (Nov 1902-Sep 1904); div. cdr, Battleship Sqdn., N.Atl.Flt., *Alabama* (Sep 1904-Aug 1907); spec. duty, U.S. commissioner, international commission of inquiry on North Sea incident, Paris (Dec 1904-Mar 1905); placed on Ret.Lst. (28 Aug 1907).

Career Highlights Was also a notable scientist like his father, working on astronomical and geodetic activities. Involved with several expds. to determine differences of longitude by laying submarine telegraph cables. Served as chief of naval intelligence and, for lengthy period, supt. of Naval Observatory. During war with Spain, commanded converted cruiser *Dixie*, which received surrender of Ponce, Puerto Rico, in Jul 1898. Sat on international commission at Paris that investigated "Dogger Bank Incident." While cdr of 2nd Sqdn. of N.Atl.Flt., assisted in relief of earthquake victims in Jamaica in Jan 1907.

References

Personal Papers: RHTRL.

Writings: a) *Chronometer Rates as Affected by Changes of Temperature and Other Causes*, Navy Scientific Paper, no. 6 (Washington, DC: 1877). b) *Telegraphic Determination of Longitude*, 3 vols. (Washington, DC: 1880, 1883, 1885). c) *Life of Charles Henry Davis, Rear Admiral, 1807-1877* (Boston: 1899).

WILLIAM PLUMMER DAY Born in NY City on 30 Sep 1848, son of William Harrison and Mercy Carter (Church) Day. Married Jeanetta Maria Eliza Grace Master of Bath, England, on 3 Mar 1873. One son. Died on 28 Dec 1919 in Nice, France.

Ranks Apprentice (23 Jul 1863); Midn (21 Jul 1865); Ens (12 Jul 1870); Mstr (31 Oct 1871); Lt (23 Jan 1875); LCdr (1 Jan 1897); Cdr (12 Dec 1899); Capt (12 Jan 1905); retired (11 Jun 1906); RAdm on Ret.Lst. (13 Apr 1911) to rank from 11 Jun 1906.

Career Summary Apprentice (23 Jul 1863); training ship, *Sabine* (Jul 1863-Jul 1865); received appointment by pres. as enlisted boy (21 Jul 1865); USNA (Jul 1865-Jun 1869); *Juniata* and *Franklin*, Eur.Sta. (Jul 1869-Nov 1871); w.o. (Nov 1871-Mar 1872); *Powhatan*, N.Atl.Sqdn. (Mar 1872-Jan 1873); l.o.a. (Jan-Jul 1873); *Wyoming* and *Dictator*, N.Atl.Sta. (Jul 1873-Apr 1875); w.o. (Apr-May 1875); rec. ship, *Vermont*, NY (Jun 1875); rec. ship, *Colorado*, NY (Jun-Jul 1875); exec.off., *Despatch*, spec.serv. (Jul 1875-Apr 1877); w.o. (Apr-Jul 1877); *Wyandotte*, N.Atl.Sta. (Jul 1877); *Passaic*, N.Atl.Sta. (Jul-Aug 1877); *Hartford*, S.Atl.Sta. (Aug 1877-Dec 1879); l.o.a. (Dec 1879-Jun 1881); w.o. (Jun 1881); *Quinnebaug*, Eur.Sta. (Jun 1881-Jun 1884); *Powhatan*, N.Atl.Sta. (Jun-Aug 1884); w.o. (Aug-Sep 1884); l.o.a. (Nov 1884-Nov 1885); *Yantic*, N.Atl.Sta. (Nov 1885); sick lv. (Nov-Dec 1885); l.o.a. (Jan-Jul 1886); *Alliance*, S.Atl.Sta. (Jul 1886-Aug 1889); w.o. (Aug-Sep 1889); l.o.a. (Oct 1889-Nov 1890); Bur. of Equip. and Recruiting, Washington, DC (Nov-Dec 1890); w.o. (Dec 1890-May 1891); l.o.a. (Jun-Dec 1891); rec. ship, *Franklin*, Norfolk, VA (Dec 1891-Mar 1892); temp. duty, *Passaic*, USNA (May-Jun 1892); rec. ship, *Franklin*,

Norfolk, VA (Jun-Sep 1892); temp. duty, NWC (Sep 1892); rec. ship, *Franklin*, Norfolk, VA (Sep 1892-Feb 1893); exec.off., training ship, *Bancroft* (Mar-Jul 1893); exec.off., *Machias*, Navy Yard, Portsmouth, NH, and N.Atl.Sqdn. (Jul 1893-Mar 1894); rec. ship, *Franklin*, Norfolk, VA (Mar-Sep 1894); exec.off., *Machias*, Asia.Sqdn. (Sep 1894-Oct 1896); home and l.o.a. (Oct 1896-Jun 1897); exec.off., rec. ship, *Richmond*, Philadelphia (Jun 1897-May 1898); *New Orleans*, N.Atl.Flt. (May 1898-Jul 1899); home and w.o. (Jul-Aug 1899); sick lv. (Aug-Nov 1899); cdr, *Vixen*, N.Atl.Sta. (Nov 1899-Apr 1900); asst., then insp., 13th L.h. Dist., Portland, OR (May 1900-Oct 1902); cdr *Mohican*, spec.serv. (Oct 1902-Feb 1904); asst., then insp., 12th L.h. Dist., San Francisco (Feb 1904-Mar 1905); Navy Yard, Mare Island, CA (Apr 1905-Mar 1906); l.o.a. (Mar-May 1906); retired (11 Jun 1906).

JAMES HENRY DAYTON Born in South Bend, IN, on 25 Oct 1846, son of Daniel and Anna M. Dayton. Remained unmarried. Died in South Bend, IN, on 15 Nov 1938.

Ranks Midn (27 Sep 1862); Ens (12 Mar 1868); Mstr (26 Mar 1869); Lt (21 Mar 1870); LCdr (8 Nov 1884); Cdr (23 Jan 1894); Capt (29 Mar 1900); RAdm (28 Feb 1906); placed on Ret.Lst. (25 Oct 1908).

Career Summary Received appointment from IN (27 Sep 1862); USNA (Sep 1862-Jun 1866); l.o.a. and w.o. (Jun-Oct 1866); *Ossipee*, Pac.Sqdn. (Oct 1866-Sep 1867); *Pensacola* and *Cyane*, N.Pac.Sqdn. (Sep 1867-Mar 1869); return and w.o. (Mar-Nov 1869); *Miantonomoh*, spec.serv. (Nov 1869-Jul 1870); *Plymouth*, Eur.Flt. (Jul 1870-Jun 1873); w.o. and l.o.a. (Jun-Nov 1873); *Powhatan*, *Franklin*, *Dictator*, and *Worcester*, N.Atl.Sta. (Nov 1873-Apr 1875); USNA (Apr 1875-Aug 1878); w.o. (Aug-Sep 1878); *Quinnebaug*, Eur.Sta. (Sep 1878-Jun 1881); w.o. (Jun-Aug 1881); Hydrographic Office, Washington, DC (Sep-Oct 1881); w.o. (Oct 1881-Jan 1882); ord. duty, Navy Yard, Washington, DC (Jan-Apr 1882); torp. instruction, Newport, RI (May-Aug 1882); ord. duty, Navy Yard, Washington, DC (Aug 1882-Jan 1883); spec. duty, Midvale Steel Works, Nicetown, PA (Jan 1883-Oct 1884); *Dolphin*, spec. duty (Oct 1884-May 1885); *Mohican*, Pac.Sta. (May 1885-Aug 1888); w.o. (Aug-Nov 1888); Naval Ord. Proving Ground, Annapolis (Dec 1888-Jan 1892); w.o. (Jan-Mar 1892); exec.off., rec. ship, *Vermont*, NY (Mar 1892-Jan 1893); cdr, *Petrel*, Asia.Sta. (Feb 1893-Mar 1894); l.o.a. (Mar-Apr 1894); insp., 9th L.h. Dist., Chicago (Apr 1894-May 1897); s.a. and w.o. (May-Jun 1897); cdr, *Detroit*, W.Indies (Jul 1897-Aug 1899); home and w.o. (Aug-Sep 1899); comdt., Naval Sta., San Juan, Puerto Rico (Oct 1899-Oct 1900); w.o. (Oct 1900-Mar 1901); cdr, flgs., *Chicago*, S.Atl. and Eur.Stas. (May 1901-May 1903); home and w.o. (May-Jun 1903); NWC (Jul-Oct 1903); spec. duty, Gen Bd., Washington, D.C. (Oct 1903-Feb 1904); pres., bd. of inspection and surv. (Feb 1904-Feb 1906); cdr, Philippine Sqdn. (soon, 3rd Sqdn.), Asia.Flt., *Rainbow* (Mar 1906-Apr 1907); cdr, Pac.Flt., *West Virginia* (Apr 1907-Jul 1908);

home and w.o. (Jul-Oct 1908); placed on Ret.Lst (25 Oct 1908); various bd. duties (Jan 1918-Apr 1919).

RICHARD CRAIN DEAN Born in Harrisburg, PA, on 27 May 1833, son of Alexander Tracy and Mary Adeline (Crain) Dean. Studied at Yale Univ., and received M.D. from Jefferson Medical College in 1854. Received honorary A.M. from Yale in 1854. Married Anna Mulford in 1856 and then Sarah Elizabeth Bingham in 1888. Died at his home in Washington, DC, on 9 Jun 1910.

Ranks Asst.Surg. (17 Apr 1856); PAsst.Surg. (25 Mar 1861); Surg. (1 Aug 1861); Medl.Insp. (8 Jun 1873); Medl.Dir. (10 Jun 1880); placed on Ret.Lst. (27 May 1895); Medl.Dir. on Ret.Lst. with rank of RAdm (29 Jun 1906).

Career Summary Received appointment from NJ (17 Apr 1856); w.o. (Apr 1856-Mar 1857); *Dale*, Afr.cst. (Apr 1857-May 1859) l.o.a. (May-Aug 1859); *Crusader*, Home Sqdn. (Aug 1859-Mar 1861); Naval Hosp., NY (Apr-May 1861); *Wyandotte*, Gulf Blk.Sqdn., and Navy Yard, NY (Jun-Sep 1861); w.o. (Sep-Oct 1861); Naval Rndv., Philadelphia (Oct-Nov 1861); *Tuscarora*, spec.serv., and N.Atl.Blk.Sqdn. (Dec 1861-Jan 1863); w.o. (Feb-Apr 1864); spec. duty, Baltimore (Apr 1864); w.o. (Apr-Jun 1864); spec. duty, Parks Barracks, NY (Jun-Aug 1864); Naval Rndv., Camden, NJ (Aug-Oct 1864); USNA (Oct 1864-Sep 1866); *Sacramento*, spec.serv. (Sep 1866-Nov 1867); w.o. (Nov 1867-Mar 1868); bd. duties, Philadelphia (Mar-Nov 1868); *Michigan*, on Great Lakes (Nov 1868-Dec 1869); spec. duty, Bur. of Medicine and Surgery, Washington, DC (Dec 1869-Feb 1870); asst. to chief, Bur. of Medicine and Surgery, Washington, DC (Feb 1870-Feb 1874); member, medl.exam.bd. (Mar-Jul 1874); *Congress*, Eur.Sta. (Aug 1874-Jul 1876); flt.surg., N.Atl.Flt., *Hartford* (Aug 1876-Jul 1877); w.o. (Jul 1877); senior member, naval exam. and ret. bds. (Jul 1877-Apr 1879); member, bd. of inspection and surv. (Apr 1879-Apr 1880); Naval Hosp., Philadelphia (May 1880-Mar 1883); Naval Hosp., NY (Mar 1883-Oct 1886); member, naval exam. and ret. bds. (Oct 1886-Sep 1887); Naval Hosp., Chelsea, MA (Sep 1887-Jan 1891); member, naval exam. and ret. bds. (Jan 1891-Jun 1893); spec. duty, Medl. Congress, Europe (Jun-Dec 1893); pres., medl.exam.bd. (Dec 1893-May 1895); placed on Ret.Lst. (27 May 1895); pres., naval exam. bd., Washington, DC (Nov 1902-Mar 1903); member, naval ret. bd., Washington, DC (Apr 1903-Aug 1904).

FRANCIS HENRY DELANO Born in Mt. Carmel, OH, on 14 Apr 1848, son of Henry Franklin and Maria (Carter) Delano. Married Evelina Paine on 29 Jan 1874. One son, Maj Frederick H. Delano, USMC (ret). Died in Annapolis on 31 Jan 1929. Buried in Annapolis.

Ranks Midn (23 Sep 1863); Ens (18 Dec 1868); Mstr (21 Mar 1870); Lt (6 Feb 1873); LCdr (22 Jun 1894); Cdr (3 Mar 1899); Capt (11 Oct 1903); retired (29 Jun 1905); RAdm on Ret.Lst.

RICHARD CRAIN DEAN
1833-1910

FRANCIS HENRY DELANO
1848-1929

(13 Apr 1911) to rank from 29 Jun 1905.

Career Summary Received appointment from MA (23 Sep 1863); USNA (Sep 1863-Jun 1867); flgs., *Susquehanna*, N.Atl.Sta. (Jun 1867-Jan 1868); flgs., *Contoocook*, and *Yantic*, N.Atl.Sta. (Mar 1868-Nov 1869); w.o. (Nov 1869-Mar 1870); signal duty, Washington, DC (Mar-Jun 1870); *Mohican*, Pac.Sta. (Jul 1870-Oct 1871); *Ashuelot*, Asia.Sta. (Nov 1871-Nov 1873); home and w.o. (Nov 1873-Mar 1874); *Portsmouth*, N.Pac.Sta. (Mar 1874-Feb 1875); w.o. (Feb-Aug 1875); rec. ship, *Sabine*, Portsmouth, NH (Aug 1875-Aug 1876); w.o. (Aug-Sep 1876); *Shawmut*, N.Atl.Sta. (Sep 1876-Jan 1877); w.o. (Jan-Feb 1877); Hydrographic Office, Washington, DC (Feb-Apr 1877); *Supply*, spec.serv. (May-Sep 1877); l.o.a. (Sep-Dec 1877); rec. ship, *Wyoming*, Washington, DC (Dec 1877-Jan 1878); *Supply*, spec.serv. (Jan 1878-Apr 1879); w.o. (Apr-Aug 1879); cdr, *Intrepid*, Navy Yard, NY (Sep 1879-Jun 1882); flgs., *Pensacola*, Pac.Sta. (Jul 1882-Oct 1883); flgs., *Richmond*, Asia.Sta. (Oct 1883-Aug 1884); w.o. (Aug 1884-Jan 1885); Navy Yard, Portsmouth, NH (Jan-May 1885); Torp.Sta., Newport, RI (Jun-Sep 1885); NWC (Sep 1885); Navy Yard, Portsmouth, NH (Sep 1885-May 1887); *Ossipee*, N.Atl.Sta. (May 1887-Nov 1889); w.o. (Nov-Dec 1889); Navy Yard, Portsmouth, NH (Dec 1889-May 1892); exec.off., training ship, *Portsmouth* (Jun 1892-May 1894); home and l.o.a. (May-Sep 1894); ord. instruction, Navy Yard, Washington, DC (Sep 1894); exec.off., rec. ship, *Wabash*, Boston (Oct 1894-May 1896); exec.off., flgs., *Olympia*, Asia.Sta. (Jun 1896-Sep 1897); home and l.o.a. (Sep-Nov 1897); exec.off., *Minneapolis*, N.Atl.Flt. (Nov 1897-Jul 1898); cdr, *Fish Hawk*, N.Atl.Flt. (Jul-Sep 1898); ord.off., Navy Yard, Boston (Oct 1898-Dec 1899); cdr, *Alliance*, N.Atl.Flt. (Dec 1899-Jun 1900); NWC (Jun-Jul 1900); duty with, then cdr, *Topeka*, N.Atl.Flt. (Jul 1900-Jul 1901); w.o. (Jul-Sep 1901); cdr, training ship, *Marietta*, N.Atl.Flt. (Oct 1901-Jan 1902); sick lv. (Jan-Mar 1902); Navy Yard, League Island, PA (Mar-Dec 1902); ord.off., Navy Yard, Portsmouth, NH (Dec 1902-May 1903); NWC (Jun-Sep 1903); duty with, then cdr, *Dixie*, N.Atl.Flt. (Sep-Nov 1903); w.o. (Nov-Dec 1903); court-martial duty, Navy Yard, League Island, PA (Jan 1904-Jun 1905); cdr, rec. ship, *Lancaster*, League Island, PA (Oct 1903-Jun 1905); retired (29 Jun 1905).

References

Personal Papers: papers covering 1901-27 in U.S. Army Military History Institute, Carlisle Barracks, PA.

HENRY MARTYN DENNISTON Born in Washingtonville, NY, on 13 Jun 1840, son of Robert and Mary (Scott) Denniston. Educated at home and then at Yale Univ. from 1858 to 1861 when he left at beginning of final year to enter service. Subsequently received A.B. degree in 1862 and A.M. degree in 1892. Married Emma J. Dusenbury on 21 Jan 1869. One son. Resided in Dobbs Ferry, NY, where he died on 23 May 1922. Buried in Washingtonville, NY.

Ranks Asst.Paymstr. (9 Sep 1861); Paymstr. (14 Apr 1862);

HENRY MARTYN DENNISTON
1840-1922

Pay Insp. (19 Aug 1876); Pay Dir. (31 Jul 1884); placed on Ret.Lst. as Pay Dir. with rank of RAdm (13 Jun 1902).

Career Summary Received appointment from NY (9 Sep 1861); w.o. (Sep-Oct 1861); Bur. of Provisions and Clothing, Washington, DC (Oct-Nov 1861); *Winona*, W.Gulf Blk.Sqdn. (Nov 1861-Aug 1862); w.o. (Aug-Sep 1862); *San Jacinto*, E.Gulf Blk.Sqdn. (Sep 1862-Mar 1863); *Ticonderoga*, S.Atl.Blk.Sqdn. (Mar 1863-May 1865); s.a. and w.o. (May-Aug 1865); *Onward*, S.Atl.Sqdn. (Aug 1865-Oct 1866); naval storekeeper, Rio de Janeiro (Oct 1866-Jun 1868); s.a. and w.o. (Jun-Sep 1868); *Michigan*, on Great Lakes (Sep 1868-Sep 1871); s.a. and w.o. (Sep 1871-Aug 1872); flt.paymstr., N.Atl.Sqdn., *Worcester* (Sep 1872-Aug 1874); s.a. and w.o. (Aug 1874-Aug 1875); Navy Yard, Philadelphia (Sep-Dec 1875); Navy Yard, League Island, PA (Dec 1875-Jan 1879); s.a. and w.o. (Jan-Jun 1879); spec. duty, Navy Yard, Washington, DC (Jun-Aug 1879); w.o. (Aug 1879-Jan 1880); member, bd. of inspection and surv. (Feb 1880-Jun 1882); flt.paymstr., Pac.Sqdn., *Hartford* (Jun 1882-Jun 1884); s.a. and w.o. (Jun-Aug 1884); insp. of provisions and clothing, Navy Yard, Mare Island, CA (Oct 1884-Dec 1886); general storekeeper, Navy Yard, Mare Island, CA (Jan-Jul 1887); in charge, Pay Office, San Francisco (Jul 1887-May 1888); s.a. and w.o. (May 1888-Mar 1889); Naval Home, Philadelphia (Mar 1889-Feb 1892); in charge, Pay Office, Philadelphia (Feb 1892-May 1895); s.a. (May-Jun 1895); l.o.a. and w.o. (Jun 1895-Mar 1896); general storekeeper, Navy Yard, Portsmouth, NH (Mar 1896-Jun 1899); paymstr., Navy Yard, Portsmouth, NH (Aug-Nov 1897); in charge, Pay Office, NY (Jun 1899-Jul 1902); placed on Ret.Lst. (13 Jun 1902).

FRANCIS WILLIAM DICKENS Born in Beckmanville, Duchess County, NY, on 2 Nov 1844, son of George and Eunice (Pearce) Dickens. Married twice: to Marguerite Bates, who died in 1899; then to Edith Pratt on 9 Apr 1902. No children. Resided in Washington, DC. Died on 15 Sep 1910 in NY City. Buried in Arlington National Cemetery.

Ranks Act.Midn (20 Sep 1861); title changed to Midn (16 Jul 1862); Ens (1 Nov 1866); Mstr (1 Dec 1866); Lt (12 Mar 1868); LCdr (12 Jun 1869); Cdr (23 Sep 1885); Capt (3 Jul 1898); RAdm (17 Jun 1904); placed on Ret.Lst. (2 Nov 1906).

Career Summary Received appointment from CT (20 Sep 1861); USNA (Sep 1861-Nov 1864); l.o.a. (Nov 1864-Feb 1865); rec. ship, *North Carolina*, NY (Feb-Apr 1865); flgs., *Colorado*, Eur.Sqdn. (Apr 1865-Mar 1867); *Augusta*, Eur.Sqdn. (Mar-Jul 1867); w.o. (Jul-Sep 1867); training ship, *Sabine* (Oct 1867-Apr 1868); *Tuscarora*, S.Pac. and W.Ind.Sqdns. (May 1868-Feb 1871); w.o. and l.o.a. (Feb-Jun 1871); Torp.Sta., Newport, RI (Jun 1871-Jan 1872); rec. ship, *Vermont*, NY (Jan-Mar 1872); sick lv. (Mar-Oct 1872); exec.off., *Kansas*, Canal Surveying Expd. (Oct 1872-Apr 1873); sick lv. (May-Aug 1873); exec.off., *Monocacy*, Asia.Sta. (Oct 1873-Jan 1875); exec.off., *Kearsarge*, Asia.Sqdn. (Jan-Apr 1875); exec.off., *Yantic*, Asia.Sta. (Apr-Jul 1875);

FRANCIS WILLIAM DICKENS
1844-1910

Kearsarge, Asia.Sta. (Jul 1875-Mar 1876); *Yantic*, Asia.Sta. (Mar-Apr 1876); cdr, *Yantic*, Asia.Sta. (Apr-Nov 1876); home and l.o.a. (Dec 1876-Jan 1878); inst. of seamanship, USNA (Feb 1878-Jul 1880); w.o. (Jul-Dec 1880); member, bd. on naval officers' precedence, Navy Dept., Washington, DC (Jan-Mar 1881); w.o. (Mar-May 1881); exec.off., flgs., *Constitution*, Apprentice Training Sqdn. (May-Oct 1881); sick lv. (Oct-Dec 1881); Hydrographic Office, Washington, DC (Dec 1881-May 1882); exec.off., *Kearsarge*, N.Atl.Sta. (Jun-Oct 1882); l.o.a. (Oct 1882-Jun 1883); cdr, storeship, *Onward*, S.Pac.Sqdn. (Jul 1883-Nov 1884); general court-martial duty (Dec 1884-May 1887); cdr, *Tallapoosa*, S.Atl.Sta. (Jul 1887-Oct 1889); w.o. (Nov 1889-Jan 1890); general court-martial duty, Navy Yard, NY (Jan 1890); w.o. (Jan-Sep 1890); duties of civil engineer, Navy Yard, Washington, DC (Sep 1890-Jun 1892); temp. duty, gen court-martial (Jun-Sep 1892); duties as civil engineer, Navy Yard, Washington, DC (Sep 1892-Jul 1893); temp. spec. duty (Jan-Mar 1893); temp. spec. duty with State Dept., Washington, DC (Jan-Jul 1893); cdr, training ship, *Monongahela* (Jul 1893-Jan 1894); cdr, training ship, *Essex*, Home Sqdn. (Jan-Jul 1894); cdr, Training Sta., Newport, RI and training ship, *Constellation* (Aug 1894-Dec 1896); asst. to chief, Bur. of Nav., Navy Dept., Washington, DC (Dec 1896-Sep 1899); cdr, *Indiana*, in reserve (Oct 1899-Nov 1900); cdr, *Oregon*, Naval Sta., Puget Sound, WA (Nov 1900-Mar 1901); cdr, flgs., *Brooklyn*, Asia.Sta. (Apr-Dec 1901); home and w.o. (Dec 1901-Mar 1902); member, naval exam. bd. (Mar-May 1902); NWC (Jun-Jul 1902); cdr, rec. ship, *Independence*, Mare Island, CA (Aug 1902-Jun 1903); comdt., Navy Yard, and comdt., Gulf Naval Dist., Pensacola, FL (Jul 1903-May 1904); comdt., Navy Yard, League Island, PA (May 1904-Mar 1905); cdr, Cst.Sqdn., N.Atl.Flt., *Texas* (Mar 1905-Apr 1906); spec. temp. duty, Bur. of Nav. (Apr-Jul 1906); w.o. (Jul-Nov 1906); placed on Ret.Lst. (2 Nov 1906).

Career Highlights Served as President's spec. naval representative to attend funeral of former Pres. Rutherford B. Hayes in Fremont, OH, in 1893. Later that year, was on spec. duty with State Dept. in charge of courtesies to Duke of Veragua, the lineal descendant of Christopher Columbus during celebration of Columbus's voyage. Subsequently received Knight of the Cross of Naval Merit by King Alphonso XIII of Spain.

References
Personal Papers: 8 items (1788-1905) in NHF,LC.

ALBERT CALDWELL
DILLINGHAM
1848-1925

ALBERT CALDWELL DILLINGHAM Born in Philadelphia on 3 Jun 1848, son of Simeon and Mary Elizabeth (Raymond) Dillingham. Early education in Philadelphia public schools. Married Grace Gillmor on 21 Jun 1897. One son. Resided in Norfolk, VA, where he died on 6 Dec 1925.

Ranks Private and Musician, 7th PA Infantry (12 Sep 1862); Midn (21 Jul 1865); Ens (13 Jul 1871); Mstr (4 Jun 1874); Lt (14 Dec 1880); LCdr (3 Mar 1899); Cdr (12 Jul 1901); Capt (19 Feb 1906); RAdm (4 Dec 1910); placed on Ret.Lst. (3 Jun 1910).

Career Summary Served with 7th PA Regiments of Volunteers (12-26 Sep 1862, 18 Jun-1 Aug 1863); received appointment from PA (21 Jul 1865); USNA (Jun 1865-Jun 1870); found deficient and turned back (Jun 1866); *Plymouth*, Eur.Sta. (Jul 1870-Jun 1873); w.o. (Jun-Nov 1873); *Powhatan*, N.Atl.Sta. (Nov-Dec 1873); *Kansas* and *Ossipee*, N.Atl.Sta. (Dec 1873-Mar 1875); w.o. (Mar-May 1875); Torp.Sta., Newport, RI (Jun-Oct 1875); l.o.a. (Oct 1875-Jan 1876); *Nantucket*, N.Atl.Sta. (Jan-May 1876); w.o. (May-Aug 1876); cst.surv. duty (Aug 1876-Sep 1879); *Wachusett*, S.Atl.Sta. (Sep 1879-Oct 1882); w.o. (Oct-Dec 1882); Navy Yard, Norfolk, VA (Dec 1882-Sep 1883); USNA (Sep 1883-Jun 1886); w.o. (Jun-Jul 1886); flgs., *Tennessee*, N.Atl.Sta. (Jul 1886); *Richmond*, N.Atl.Sta. (Jul 1886-Sep 1888); *Pensacola*, Eur.Sta. and en route home (Sep-Dec 1888); flgs., *Richmond*, N.Atl.Sta. (Dec 1888); rec. ship, *Vermont*, NY (Dec 1888-Oct 1889); rec. ship, *Dale*, Washington, DC (Oct 1889-Jun 1892); training ship, *Portsmouth* (Jun 1892-Jul 1894); *Cincinnati*, spec.serv. (Jul 1894-Jun 1895); l.o.a. (Jun-Aug 1895); Navy Yard, NY (Aug 1895-Aug 1897); NWC (Aug-Sep 1896); exec.off., *Nashville*, N.Atl.Flt. (Sep 1896-Sep 1899); exec.off., *Texas*, N.Atl.Flt. (Oct 1899-Jan 1900); exec.off., *Indiana*, N.Atl.Flt. (Jan-Sep 1900); insp., 16th L.h. Dist., Memphis (Sep 1900-Sep 1902); additional temp. duty, asst., then insp., 8th L.h. Dist., New Orleans (Feb-Apr 1901); cdr, *Detroit*, W.Indies (Sep 1902-Jul 1904); cdr, rec. ship, *Franklin*, and Training Sta., Norfolk, VA (Jul 1904-Jan 1907); supt., Naval Training Service, Newport, RI (Jan 1907-Apr 1908); cdr, rec. ship, *Franklin*, Norfolk, VA (May 1908-Nov 1909); member, naval exam. and ret. bds., Washington, DC (Nov 1909-Jun 1910); placed on Ret.Lst. (3 Jun 1910); in charge, developing Naval Operating Base, Hampton Roads, VA (Jun 1917-Jun 1919).

Career Highlights During war with Spain, was promoted for "gallant and conspicuous conduct" for temporarily commanding the *Nashville* when commanding officer was wounded during action off Cienfuegos, Cuba. In 1904, directed affairs in Santo Domingo waters, helping to establish a stable government and to secure lives, commerce, and property of foreigners. Returning to active duty with World War I, received Navy Cross for service in developing Naval Operating Base at Hampton Roads.

References

Writings: a) "Methods Employed at Training Stations for Training Apprentice Seamen for the Fleet," U.S. Naval Institute *Proceedings* 121 (Mar 1907): 137-51. b) "How Shall We Induce Our Men to Continue in the Navy?" U.S. Naval Institute *Proceedings* 132 (Dec 1909): 1019-28. c) "U.S. Naval Training Service," U.S. Naval Institute *Proceedings* 134 (Jun 1910): 343-74. d) "Training of the Personnel of the Fleet for Battle," U.S. Naval Institute *Proceedings* 137 (Mar 1911): 209-15. e) "Flag Officers in the United States Navy," U.S. Naval Institute *Proceedings* 140 (Dec 1911): 1383-88. f) "A Personnel Reserve for the Naval Service," U.S. Naval Institute *Proceedings* 166 (Nov-Dec 1916): 1889-1922. g) "What Steps in Organization and Training Should be Taken to Maintain and Increase the Efficiency of the Navy at the Close of the Present War?" U.S. Naval Institute *Proceedings* 193 (Mar 1919): 317-31. h) "Our Divided Personnel," U.S. Naval Institute *Proceedings* 214 (Dec 1920): 1921-24.

ROBERT MORRIS DOYLE
1853-1925

ROBERT MORRIS DOYLE Born in Dyersburg, TN, on 5 May 1853, son of James Henry and Jane (Sampson) Doyle. Married Kate Amelia Snowden on 19 Oct 1882. One son, LCdr Robert M. Doyle Jr., USN. Died on 15 Dec 1925 in Cocoanut Grove, FL. Buried in Arlington National Cemetery.

Ranks Cadet Midn (30 Sep 1870); Midn (21 Jun 1875); Ens (9 Sep 1876); Mstr (29 Nov 1882); title changed to Ltjg (3 Mar 1883); Lt (12 May 1889); LCdr (3 Mar 1899); Cdr (16 Jun 1904); Capt (1 Jul 1908); RAdm (7 Jun 1912); placed on Ret.Lst. (5 May 1915); recalled to active duty (25 May 1918); retired (13 Jun 1919).

Career Summary Received appointment from TN (30 Sep 1870); USNA (Sep 1870-Jun 1875); found deficient and turned back (Jun 1871); w.o. (Jun-Nov 1875); *Marion*, N.Atl.Sta. (Dec 1875-Oct 1877); home and w.o. (Oct 1877-Jan 1878); USNA (Jan 1878); w.o. (Jan-Feb 1878); training ship, *Minnesota* (Feb 1878-Jan 1879); *Vandalia*, N.Atl.Sta. (Feb 1879-May 1881); w.o. (May-Jul 1881); rec. ship, *Colorado*, NY (Jul 1881-Jan 1882); training ship, *Minnesota* (Jan-Aug 1882); Hydrographic Office, Washington, DC (Aug 1882-Nov 1883); *Galena*, N.Atl.Sta. (Dec 1883-Jan 1886); *Tennessee*, N.Atl.Sta. (Jan-Aug 1886); USNA (Sep 1886-Jun 1889); w.o. (Jun-Sep 1889); training ship, *New Hampshire* (Sep-Oct 1889); spec. duty in connection with new ships (Oct 1889-Jan 1890); *Baltimore*, spec.serv. (Jan 1890-Mar 1893); member, general court-martial, NY (Mar-May 1893); l.o.a. (May-Jul 1893); USNA (Jul 1893-Jul 1896); *Texas*, N.Atl.Sta. (Jul 1896-Apr 1897); training ship, *Alliance* (Apr 1897-Apr 1898); nav.off., *Dixie*, N.Atl.Flt. (Apr-Sep 1898); *Puritan*, N.Atl.Flt. (Sep-Dec 1898); *Resolute*, N.Atl.Flt. (Dec 1898-Jan 1899); *Texas*, N.Atl.Flt. (Jan-Sep 1899); home and w.o. (Sep-Oct 1899); insp. of ord., Navy Yard, Washington, DC (Oct 1899); inspection duty, Bur. of Ord. and Bur. of Steam Engineering, Washington, DC (Oct 1899-Sep 1901); exec.off., *Wisconsin*, Pac.Sta. (Sep 1901-Apr 1902); sick lv. (Apr-Sep 1902); cdr, *Culgoa*, N.Atl.Sqdn. (Sep 1902-Aug 1904); cdr, rec. ship at Philadelphia (Aug 1904-Dec 1906); additional temp. duty, equip.off., Navy Yard, Puget Sound, WA (Aug 1904-Dec 1905); cdr, *Chicago*, Pac.Sta. (Dec 1906-May 1908); capt.yd., Navy Yard, Portsmouth, NH (May-Jun 1908); cdr, *Missouri*, 2nd Sqdn., Atl.Flt. ["Great White Flt."] (Jun 1908-Jan 1910); insp., 3rd L.h. Dist., Tompkinsville, NY (Jan 1910-Jun 1911); temp. duty, Navy Dept., Washington, DC (Jun 1911); capt.yd., Navy Yard, Norfolk, VA (Jun-Nov 1911); comdt., Navy Yard, and 5th Naval Dist., Norfolk, VA (Nov 1911-Feb 1913); Navy Dept., Washington, DC (Feb-Nov 1913); cdr, Pac. Reserve Flt., *Colorado* (Dec 1913), *West Virginia* (Dec 1913-Apr 1914); spec. duty, Pac.Flt. (May-Jul 1914); cdr, Pac. Reserve Flt., *West Virginia* (Jul 1914-Feb 1915),

South Dakota (Feb-Apr 1915); home and w.o. (Apr-May 1915); placed on Ret.Lst. (5 May 1915); comdt., 14th Naval Dist. and U.S. Naval Sta., Pearl Harbor, Territory of HI (Jun 1918-May 1919).

Career Highlights Commanded the *Missouri* with the "Great White Flt."

FRANKLIN JEREMIAH DRAKE Born in Yates, NY, on 4 Mar 1846, son of Caleb Drake. Early education in Gosport, NY. Married but widowed. Died in Washington, DC, on 30 Jan 1929. Buried in Arlington National Cemetery.

Ranks Midn (23 Feb 1863); Ens (19 Apr 1869); Mstr (12 Jul 1870); Lt (15 Nov 1872); LCdr (1 Oct 1893); Cdr (3 Mar 1899); Capt (11 Sep 1903); retired as RAdm (10 Dec 1906).

FRANKLIN JEREMIAH DRAKE
1846-1929

Career Summary Received appointment from NY (23 Feb 1863); USNA (Feb 1863-Jun 1868); found deficient and turned back (Jan 1866); w.o. (Jun-Sep 1868); *Gettysburg*, W.Ind.Sqdn. (Oct 1868-Jun 1869); home and w.o. (Jul-Sep 1869); *Frolic*, Navy Yard, NY (Sep-Dec 1869); signal duty, Washington, DC (Dec 1869-Mar 1870); *Colorado, Benicia,* and *Monocacy,* Asia.Sqdn. (Mar 1870-Mar 1873); home and w.o. (Mar-Aug 1873); Torp. Sta., Newport, RI (Sep-Nov 1873); *Terror*, N.Atl.Sta. (Dec 1873); torp. instruction, Newport, RI (Dec 1873-Mar 1874); *Portsmouth*, N.Pac.Sqdn. (Apr-Dec 1874); nautical schoolship, *Jamestown* (Dec 1874-May 1875); rec. ship, *Independence*, Mare Island, CA (May-Jun 1875); ord. duty, Navy Yard, Mare Island, CA (Jun 1875-Sep 1876); cst.surv. duty (Sep 1876-Jun 1878); w.o. (Jun-Jul 1878); *Powhatan*, N.Atl.Sta. (Jul-Oct 1878); *Ticonderoga*, spec.serv. (Nov 1878-Sep 1881); w.o. (Sep-Nov 1881); Navy Yard, NY (Nov 1881-Aug 1883); ord. instruction, Navy Yard, Washington, DC (Aug 1883); spec. duty, naval advisory bd. and insp. of material (Aug 1883-Mar 1885); *Pensacola* and *Quinnebaug*, Eur.Sta. (Mar 1885-Feb 1888); w.o. (Feb-May 1888); insp. of construction of torpedo boats (May 1888-Jan 1889); insp. of ord., Providence, RI (Jan 1889-Jan 1893); spec. duty, Bur. of Ord., World's Fair, Chicago (May-Jun 1893); asst.insp. of construction, *Montgomery*, Columbia Iron Works, Baltimore (Jun-Nov 1893); Navy Yard, Boston (Nov 1893-Mar 1894); cdr, Fish Commission steamer, *Albatross* (Apr 1894-May 1896); duty with, then exec.off., *Oregon*, Pac.Sqdn. (May 1896-Jul 1897); l.o.a. (Jul-Oct 1897); insp. of ord., Navy Yard, Mare Island, CA (Oct 1897-Dec 1900); additional duty, cdr, *Pensacola*, Mare Island, CA (May 1898-Dec 1900); cdr, *Culgoa*, Asia.Sqdn. (Mar-May 1901); Naval Sta., Cavite, P.I. (May-Jul 1901); cdr, *Monterey*, Asia.Sqdn. (Jul 1901-Jan 1903); home and w.o. (Jan-Apr 1903); ord.off., Navy Yard, Mare Island, CA. (May 1903-Mar 1905); capt.yd., Navy Yard, Mare Island, CA (Mar-Oct 1905); cdr, *Wisconsin*, Asia.Flt. (Dec 1905-Nov 1906); home and w.o. (Nov-Dec 1906); retired (10 Dec 1906).

Career Highlights Commanded a company during assault on Korean forts at Seoul in 1871, receiving commendation for conspicuous conduct. Was a specialist in construction. Was insp.

of construction of navy's first torp. boat, *Cushing,* in 1888. Became insp. of construction of navy's new automatic torpedo. After retirement, became technical expert for Hague Tribunal from 1913-15. From 1918-20, involved with revisions of Navy's regulations.

References

Writings: a) "Automobile Torpedoes. The Howell Torpedo, Present and Future Efficiency of Automobiles in General, and Probable Type of Future Torpedo Cruiser and Destroyer," U.S. Naval Institute *Proceedings* 65 (1893): 1-52.

ANDREW DUNLAP
1844-1914

ANDREW DUNLAP Born in Ovid, NY, on 7 Oct 1844, son of Andrew and Hannah (Kinne) Dunlap. Married Ellen Grace Derby Adams on 13 Oct 1875. Died in Washington, DC, on 11 Apr 1914. Buried in Arlington National Cemetery.

Ranks Act.Midn (23 Apr 1862); title changed to Midn (16 Jul 1862); Ens (18 Dec 1868); Mstr (21 Mar 1870); Lt (21 Mar 1871); LCdr (2 Aug 1891); Cdr (1 Feb 1898); Capt (8 Jun 1902); retired with rank of RAdm. (27 Jun 1905).

Career Summary Received appointment from NY (23 Apr 1862); USNA (Apr 1862-Jun 1867); found deficient and put back (27 Feb 1865); *Minnesota, Mohican, Mohongo,* and *Jamestown,* spec. cruise and Pac.Sta. (Jul 1867-Oct 1870); w.o. (Nov 1870-Mar 1871); signal duty, Washington, DC (Mar-Jul 1871); ord. duty, Navy Yard, Boston (Aug 1871); flgs., *Worcester,* N.Atl.Flt. (Aug 1871-Aug 1874); w.o. (Aug-Oct 1874); Hydrographic Office, Washington, DC (Nov 1874-May 1875); rec. ship, *Sabine,* Portsmouth, NH (May 1875-Aug 1876); w.o. (Aug 1876-Feb 1877); rec. ship, *Wyoming,* Washington, DC (Feb-Apr 1877); Hydrographic Office, Washington, DC (Apr-Sep 1877); *Ossipee,* N.Atl.Sta. (Sep 1877-May 1878); *Powhatan,* N.Atl.Sta. (Jun 1878-Oct 1880); w.o. (Oct-Dec 1880); ord. instruction, Navy Yard, Washington, DC (Dec 1880-May 1881); Torp.Sta., Newport, RI (Jun-Sep 1881); ord. instruction and duty, Navy Yard, Washington, DC (Oct 1881-Aug 1882); asst.insp., 3rd L.h. Dist., Tompkinsville, NY (Aug 1882-Jun 1883); *Kearsarge,* Eur.Sta. (Jun 1883-Feb 1884); *Lancaster,* Eur. and S.Atl.Stas. (Feb 1884-Sep 1886); home and w.o. (Sep-Dec 1886); ord. duty, Navy Yard, Washington, DC (Jan 1887-Nov 1889); *Dolphin,* N.Atl.Sta. (Nov 1889-May 1891); l.o.a. (May-Jun 1891); exec.off., *Bennington,* S.Atl.Sta. (Jun 1891-May 1893); l.o.a. (May-Aug 1893); Navy Yard, Washington, DC (Aug 1893-May 1896); cst.surv. duty (May 1896-Apr 1898); cdr, hosp. ship, *Solace* (Apr 1898-Apr 1900); NWC (Jun-Jul 1900); equip.off., Navy Yard, Norfolk, VA (Jul-Oct 1900); insp., 10th L.h. Dist., Buffalo, NY (Oct 1900-Oct 1902); comdt., Naval Sta., San Juan, Puerto Rico, (Oct 1902-Jun 1906); retired (27 Jun 1906).

HERBERT OMAR DUNN
1857-1930

HERBERT OMAR DUNN Born in Westerly, RI, on 29 May 1857, son of Edward Maxson and Desire Anne (Gavitt) Dunn. Married Elizabeth Amanda Webb on 30 Jul 1890. One son. First wife died in 1907. Married again to Eleanor Cameron Warwick

Palmer on 22 Jun 1919. Died on 13 Feb 1930 in Baltimore.

Ranks Cadet Midn (9 Jun 1873); Midn (18 Jun 1879); Ens (12 Mar 1881); Ltjg (1 Jul 1887); Lt (17 Feb 1893); LCdr (1 Jul 1900); Cdr (1 Jul 1905); Capt (1 Jul 1909); RAdm (6 Aug 1915); placed on Ret.Lst. (29 May 1921).

Career Summary Received appointment from RI (6 Jun 1873); USNA (Jun 1873-Jun 1877); w.o. (Jun-Aug 1877); *Hartford,* S.Atl.Sqdn. (Aug 1877-Apr 1879); home and to USNA (May-Jun 1879); w.o. (Jun-Jul 1879); training ship, *Minnesota* (Jul 1879-Aug 1881); l.o.a. in Paris to study language (Aug 1881-Apr 1882); *Iroquois, Essex, Palos,* and *Juniata,* Pac. and Asia.Sqdns. (Apr 1882-Jan 1886); w.o. (Jan-Feb 1886); Bur. of Equip. and Recruiting, Washington, DC (Mar 1886-Apr 1889); torp. instruction, Newport, RI (May-Jul 1889); flgs., *Baltimore,* N. Atl.Sqdn. (Aug 1889-Oct 1892); l.o.a. (Oct-Dec 1892); in charge, branch hydrographic office, Baltimore (Dec 1892-Jul 1895); l.o.a. (Jul-Sep 1895); *Lancaster,* S.Atl.Sta. (Sep 1895-Dec 1897); *Terror,* N.Atl.Sta. (Dec 1897-Sep 1898); in charge, branch hydrographic office, Baltimore (Sep 1898-Mar 1900); training ship, *Buffalo* (Apr 1900-Mar 1901); exec.off., *Glacier,* Asia.Sta. (Mar 1901-Nov 1902); *Don Juan de Austria,* Asia.Sta. (Nov-Dec 1902); exec.off., *Vicksburg,* Asia.Sta. (Dec 1902); cdr, *Frolic,* Asia.Sta. (Dec 1902-May 1903); w.o. (May-Dec 1903); temp. duty, in charge, Naval Recruiting Sta. and branch hydrographic office, Chicago (Dec 1903-Jan 1904); inspection duty, Bur. of Steam Engineering (Jan 1904-Apr 1905); exec.off., then temp. cdr, *Columbia,* Atl. Training Sqdn. (Apr-Aug 1905); NWC (Aug-Oct 1905); in charge, Naval Recruiting Sta., Baltimore (Oct 1905-May 1906); cdr, *Dixie,* W.Indies (Jun-Aug 1906); cdr, *Yankee,* Auxiliary Service (Aug-Sep 1906); cdr, *Prairie,* Auxiliary Service (Sep 1906-Jul 1907); duty with supt., Naval Auxiliaries, Atl.cst. (Sep-Nov 1907); in charge, Naval Recruiting Sta., Baltimore (Nov 1907-Apr 1909); additional duty, in charge, Naval Recruiting Sta., Philadelphia (Jun 1908-Apr 1909); Navy Yard, NY (Apr-Oct 1909); cdr, *Idaho,* "Great White Flt." (Oct 1909-Nov 1911); home and w.o. (Nov-Dec 1911); spec. duty, Navy Dept., Washington, DC (Dec 1911-Oct 1913); supervisor of harbor, NY (Nov 1913-Jan 1915); cdr, *Wyoming,* Atl.Flt. (Jan-Aug 1915); w.o. (Aug-Oct 1915); court-martial duty, Boston (Oct-Nov 1915); cdr, 4th Div., Atl.Flt., *Louisiana* (Nov 1915-May 1916); cdr, 5th Div., Atl.Flt., *Minnesota* (May-Jun 1916); cdr, 5th Div., Battleship Force, Atl.Flt., *Minnesota* (Jun-Oct 1916), then *Connecticut* (Oct 1916-Nov 1917); cdr, Azores Detachment, Atl.Flt., Naval Base, Punta Delgada, Azores (Jan 1918-Apr 1919); cdr, 1st Naval Dist., Boston (May 1919-May 1921); placed on Ret.Lst. (29 May 1921).

Career Highlights Invented the "Dunn Anchor" in 1889 which became navy's standard anchor. During Spanish-American War, commanded *Terror* on blockade off Havana and Cardenas. Participated in actions against Puerto Rico. Commanded the *Idaho* with the "Great White Flt." Commanded naval base in the Azores during American participation in World War I.

References

Personal Papers: Journal from *Hartford* (1877) in NHF,WNY.
Writings: a) "Notes on the Department's Proposed Personnel Bill," U.S. Naval Institute *Proceedings* 144 (Dec 1912): 1569-93. b) "Discipline in the 'Old Navy,'" U.S. Naval Institute *Proceedings* 165 (Sep-Oct 1916): 1603-5. c) "Gallagher Makes an Estimate of the Situation," U.S. Naval Institute *Proceedings* 275 (Jan 1926): 103-7.

NEHEMIAH MAYO DYER
1839-1910

NEHEMIAH MAYO DYER Born in Provincetown, MA, on 19 Feb 1839, son of Henry and Sally (Mayo) Dyer. Educated in public schools. Served in Merchant Marine from 1854 to 1859 followed by mercantile employment until 1861. Remained unmarried. Resided in Melrose, MA, where he died on 27 Jan 1910.

Ranks Act.Master's Mate (4 Apr 1862); Act.Ens (20 May 1863); Act.Mstr (12 Jan 1864); Act.Volunteer Lt (22 Apr 1865); Lt (12 Mar 1868); LCdr (18 Dec 1868); Cdr (23 Apr 1883); Capt (13 Jul 1897); transferred to Ret.Lst. with rank of RAdm (19 Feb 1901).

Career Summary Company A, 13th Regiment, MA Volunteers (1861-Apr 1862); transferred to volunteer navy (4 Apr 1862); Navy Yard, Boston (Apr-Jul 1862); *R. R. Cuyler*, W.Gulf Blk.Sqdn. (Jul 1862-Dec 1863); cdr, *Eugenie* [renamed *Glasgow*], blockade and despatch duty (Dec 1863-Jul 1864); *Metacomet*, W.Gulf Blk.Sqdn. (Jul-Aug 1864); l.o.a. (Aug-Oct 1864); w.o. (Oct 1864-Jan 1865); cdr, *Rodolph*, W.Gulf Blk.Sqdn. (Jan 1865-May 1865); cdr, *Elk*, Gulf Sqdn. (Jun 1865); cdr, *Stockdale*, Mississippi River (Jul-Sep 1865); *Mahaska*, Appalachicola, FL (Sep-Oct 1865); cdr, *Glasgow*, Pensacola, FL (Oct 1865-Apr 1866); Bur. of Nav., Washington, DC (May 1866-May 1868); w.o. (May-Jul 1868); *Dacotah*, S.Pac.Sqdn. (Jul 1868-Sep 1869); cdr, *Cyane*, Sitka, AK (Sep 1869-Mar 1870); *Pensacola*, Mare Island, CA (Mar-Jul 1870); *Ossipee*, S.Pac.Sta. (Jul 1870-Aug 1871); home and w.o. (Sep-Nov 1871); Navy Yard, Boston (Nov 1871-Aug 1873); Torp.Sta., Newport, RI (Sep-Nov 1873); cdr, *Mayflower*, N.Atl.Sta. (Nov 1873-Apr 1874); cdr, *Pinta*, N.Atl. Sta. (Apr 1874-Feb 1876); exec.off., rec. ship, *New Hampshire*, Norfolk, VA (Feb-Nov 1876); w.o. (Nov 1876-Aug 1877); equip. duty, Navy Yard, Boston (Aug 1877-Sep 1878); exec.off., rec. ship, *Wabash*, Boston (Sep 1878-Jun 1881); exec.off., *Tennessee*, N.Atl.Sta. (Jun 1881-May 1883); w.o. (May-Aug 1883); asst., then insp., 10th L.h. Dist., Buffalo, NY (Sep 1883-Aug 1887); s.a. and w.o. (Aug 1887); NWC (Sep-Nov 1887); spec. duty to Panama (Nov 1887); cdr, *Marion*, Asia.Sta. (Nov 1887-May 1890); home and w.o. (May-Oct 1890); Navy Yard, Portsmouth, NH (Oct 1890-Apr 1893); w.o. (Apr-May 1893); member, court of inquiry (May-Jun 1893); w.o. (Jun 1893-May 1894); torp. instruction, Newport, RI (May-Oct 1894); w.o. (Oct 1894-Mar 1895); ord. instruction, Navy Yard, Washington, DC (Mar-Jun 1895); Navy Yard, Boston (Jun 1895-Jun 1896); insp., 1st L.h. Dist., Portland, ME (Jun 1896-Aug 1897); cdr, flgs., *Philadelphia*,

Pac.Sqdn. (Aug-Oct 1897); cdr, *Baltimore*, Pac. and Asia.Sqdns. (Oct 1897-Mar 1899); home and w.o. (Mar-Jul 1899); sick lv. (Jul-Sep 1899); l.o.a. (Sep-Oct 1899); sick lv. (Nov 1899-Jan 1900); Navy Yard, Boston (Feb 1900-Jan 1901); home and w.o. (Jan-Feb 1901); transferred to Ret.Lst. (19 Feb 1901).

Career Highlights Saw action on the *Metacomet* during Battle of Mobile Bay in Aug 1864, personally receiving surrender of the Confederate *Selma*. Participated in Battle of Manila Bay on 1 May 1898 as cdr of the *Baltimore*, receiving an advance of seven numbers in rank for eminent and conspicuous conduct.

CHARLES WILSON DYSON Born in Morristown, PA, on 2 Dec 1861, son of Reverend John Dyson. Early public education in Morristown. Resided in Washington, DC. Married with two sons and a daughter. Died on 25 Oct 1930 in Washington. Buried in Arlington National Cemetery.

Ranks Cadet Engr. (15 Sep 1879); title changed to Naval Cadet (5 Aug 1882); Asst.Engr. (1 Jul 1885); Asst.Engr. with rel. rank of Ltjg (2 Feb 1895); PAsst.Engr. (1 Jun 1895); PAsst.Engr. with rel. rank of Lt (23 Apr 1898); Lt (3 Mar 1899); LCdr (31 Dec 1903); Cdr (15 May 1908); Capt (1 Jul 1911); RAdm (15 Oct 1917); placed on Ret.Lst. (2 Dec 1925).

Career Summary Received appointment from PA (15 Sep 1879); USNA (Sep 1879-Jun 1883); w.o. (Jun-Aug 1883); flgs., *Trenton*, Asia.Sta. (Sep 1883-Mar 1885); return and w.o. (Mar-Oct 1885); *Adams*, Pac.Sqdn. (Nov 1885-Mar 1889); Navy Yard, Mare Island, CA (Mar 1889-Feb 1890); Navy Yard, Boston (Feb 1890-Aug 1892); w.o. (Aug-Sep 1892); Fish Commission steamer, *Fish Hawk* (Sep 1892-Sep 1895); home and l.o.a. (Sep-Oct 1895); duty, Fish Commission (Oct 1895-Apr 1898); *San Francisco*, N.Atl.Flt. (Apr-Oct 1898); home and w.o. (Oct-Nov 1898); *Machias*, N.Atl.Sta. (Nov 1898-Aug 1900); *Massachusetts*, N.Atl.Sta. (Aug 1900-Jun 1901); Bur. of Steam Engineering, Washington, DC (Jun 1901-Aug 1903); *Monocacy*, Asia.Flt. (Aug-Sep 1903); *Raleigh*, Asia.Flt. (Sep 1903-Jul 1904); *Oregon*, Asia.Flt. (Jul 1904-Jan 1906); flt.engr., Asia.Flt., *Ohio* (Jan-Jun 1906); home and w.o. (Jun-Jul 1906); Bur. of Steam Engineering, Washington, DC (Aug 1906-Mar 1913); insp. of machinery, New York Shipbuilding Company, Camden, NJ (Mar 1913-Dec 1914); in charge, naval machinery, Bur. of Steam Engineering (Dec 1914-Mar 1922); insp. general of engineering, Bur. of Steam Engineering, Washington, DC (Mar 1922-Dec 1925); placed on Ret.Lst. (2 Dec 1925); member, navy war claims bd., Navy Dept., Washington, DC (Mar 1926-Oct 1930).

Career Highlights Served for many years in the design div. of the Bur. of Steam Engineering and was navy's chief designer. Thus, oversaw all machinery plans for every U.S. naval vessel. Awarded Navy Cross and Distinguished Service Medal for this service.

References
Writings: a) with John Kennedy Barton, *Naval Reciprocating Engines and Auxiliary Machinery*, 3rd ed. (Washington, DC: 1914).

b) *Screw Propellers and Estimation of Power for Propulsion of Ships. Also Airship Propellers . . .*, 3rd ed. (NY: 1924).

JOHN ROBIE EASTMAN
1836-1913

JOHN ROBIE EASTMAN Born in Andover, NH, on 29 Jul 1836, son of Royal Friend and Sophronia (Mayo) Eastman. Educated at Dartmouth College where he received his M.A. in 1862 and Ph.D. in 1877. Married Mary J. Ambrose on 25 Dec 1866. Retired to Andover, NH. Died on 26 Sep 1913 in Franklin, NH. Buried in Andover.

Ranks Prof. of Math. with rel. rank of Cdr (17 Feb 1865); transferred to Ret.Lst. with rel. rank of Capt (29 Jul 1898); Prof. of Math. with rank of RAdm on Ret.Lst. (29 Jun 1906).

Career Summary Asst., Naval Observatory, Washington, DC (1861-Feb 1865); received appointment from NH (17 Feb 1865); prof. of math., Naval Observatory, Washington, DC (Feb 1865-Oct 1898); transferred to Ret.Lst. (29 Jul 1898).

Career Highlights Career was devoted to astronomical observation and research, publishing most of his work on the volumes of the government observatory. First pres. of the Washington Academy of Sciences. From 1874 to 1891, in charge of the Meridian Circle work at Naval Observatory. Traveled extensively in order to observe and study solar eclipses.

References

Writings: a) *Transit Circle Observations of the Sun, Moon, Planets, and Comets* (Washington, DC: 1903). b) *History of the Town of Andover, N.H., 1851-1906)* (1910). c) [Most of his studies were published in annual volumes of the Naval Observatory.]

JOSEPH GILES EATON
1847-1913

JOSEPH GILES EATON Born near Selma, AL, on 29 Jan 1847, son of William Pitt and Sarah Farwell (Brazer) Eaton. Early education was in private schools in Lockport, NY, and at Union Academy in Worcester, MA. Married Mary Anne Varnum on 8 Aug 1871. Two daughters. A widower, married Mrs. Jennie Harrison Ainsworth. Died in Assinippi, MA, on 8 Mar 1913. Buried at Lowell, MA.

Ranks Midn (24 Sep 1863); Ens (18 Dec 1868); Mstr (21 Mar 1870); Lt (21 Mar 1871); LCdr (19 Jun 1888); Cdr (10 Nov 1896); Capt (28 Sep 1901); retired with rank of RAdm (30 Jun 1905).

Career Summary Received appointment from MA (24 Sep 1863); USNA (Sep 1863-Jun 1867); *Minnesota*, Eur.Sqdn. (Jul-Sep 1867); *Guard*, Eur.Sqdn. (Sep-Oct 1867); *Ticonderoga*, Eur.Sqdn. (Oct 1867-Oct 1868); *Franklin*, Eur.Sqdn. (Oct 1868-Jan 1869); *Richmond*, Eur.Sqdn. (Jan 1869-Jan 1870); *Guard*, Darien Expd. (Jan-Jul 1870); w.o. (Jul-Aug 1870); flgs., *Severn*, N.Atl.Sta. (Sep-Oct 1870); *Saginaw*, Darien Expd. (Nov 1870-Jul 1871); w.o. (Jul-Aug 1871); l.o.a. (Aug-Oct 1871); ord. duty, Navy Yard, Boston (Oct 1871-Mar 1872); w.o. (Mar-Apr 1872); l.o.a. (Apr-Dec 1872); spec. duty, Darien Expd. (Dec 1872-May 1873); l.o.a. (May-Aug 1873); temp. duty, asst. to exec.off., Navy Yard, Boston (Aug-Dec 1873); *Dictator*, N.Atl.Sta.

(Dec 1873-Mar 1874); *Franklin*, N.Atl.Sta. (Mar 1874); *Wyoming*, N.Atl.Sta. (Mar-Apr 1874); w.o. (Apr-Aug 1874); *Worcester*, N.Atl.Sta. (Aug-Nov 1874); spec. duty, NY (Nov-Dec 1874); spec. duty, Darien Expd. (Jan-Nov 1875); *Marion*, N.Atl., then Eur.Sta. (Dec 1875-Aug 1877); rec. ship, *Wabash*, Boston (Sep 1877-Apr 1878); *Alaska*, Pac.Sta. (Apr 1878-Apr 1881); w.o. (Apr-May 1881); USNA (Jun 1881-Jun 1884); *Nantucket*, spec.serv. (Jun-Sep 1884); exec.off., *Ranger*, Pac.Sta. (Oct 1884-Sep 1887); w.o. (Sep-Oct 1887); insp. of steel, Pittsburgh, PA (Oct 1887-Sep 1888); w.o. (Sep-Oct 1888); insp. of ord., S.Boston Iron Works, Boston (Oct 1888-Oct 1890); insp. of steel, Nashua Steel Works, Boston (Oct 1890-Mar 1891); exec.off., *Monongahela*, Training Sqdn. (Mar 1891-Jun 1893); member, steel inspection bd. (Jun 1893-Nov 1895); cdr, nautical training ship, *Enterprise* (Nov 1895-Apr 1898); cdr, *Resolute*, N.Atl.Sta. (Apr 1898-Sep 1899); w.o. (Sep-Oct 1899); Navy Yard, Boston (Oct 1899-Jan 1902); additional duty, cdr, *Chesapeake*, Boston (Nov 1899-Jan 1902) and ord.off., Boston (Dec 1899-Jan 1902); cdr, *Oregon*, Navy Yard, Puget Sound, WA (Feb-Aug 1902); temp. duty, member, naval exam. and ret. bds., Washington, DC (Nov 1902-May 1903); cdr, *Massachusetts*, N.Atl.Flt. (May 1903-Nov 1904); w.o. (Nov 1904-Feb 1905); capt.yd., Navy Yard, Boston (Feb-Jun 1905); retired (30 Jun 1905).

Career Highlights During Spanish-American War from the *Resolute*, commanded landing party at Guatanamo Bay. Present at Battle of Santiago, participating in chase of Spanish ship, *Colon*, receiving on board 545 Spanish officers and crew as prisoners. Participated in bombardment of Monzanillo on 12 Aug. Was first American warship to enter Havana Harbor after armistice signed, flying flag of RAdm William T. Sampson.

References

Writings: a) "Notes on Steel Inspection of Structural and Boiler Material," U.S. Naval Institute *Proceedings* 47 (1888): 641-53. b) "Domestic Steel for Naval Purposes," U.S. Naval Institute *Proceedings* 49 (1889): 317-37. c) *The "Chesapeake" and the "Shannon"* (Boston: 1901). d) *The last Exploit of Old Ironsides: or the Action between the "Constitution" and the "Cyane" and the "Levant"* (Boston: 1901). e) *Perry's Victory on Lake Erie* (Boston: 1901).

JOHN RICHARD EDWARDS Born in Pottsville, PA, on 9 Jul 1853, son of Richard and Margaret (Williams) Edwards. Married Harriet DeWolf Allen on 25 Jan 1888. Four children. Retired to Bristol, RI, where he died on 2 Dec 1922. Buried in Bristol.

Ranks Cadet Engr. (1 Oct 1871); Asst.Engr. (26 Feb 1875); PAsst.Engr. (11 Sep 1881); Chief Engr. (5 Nov 1895); LCdr (3 Mar 1899); Cdr (23 Sep 1903); Capt (3 Jan 1908); RAdm (14 Sep 1911); placed on Ret.Lst. (9 Jul 1915).

Career Summary Received appointment from PA (1 Oct 1871); USNA (Oct 1871-May 1874); turned back (8 Jun 1872); *Wachusett*, N.Atl.Sta. (Jun-Dec 1874); w.o. (Dec 1874-Jan 1875);

JOHN RICHARD EDWARDS
1853-1922

Plymouth, N.Atl.Sta. (Jan-Dec 1875); *Worcester,* N.Atl.Sta. (Dec 1875-Feb 1876); *Pensacola,* Pac.Sta. (Feb 1876-May 1879); return and w.o. (May-Jul 1879); member, experimental bd., NY (Jul 1879-Sep 1880); l.o.a. (Sep-Nov 1880); w.o. (Nov 1880-Mar 1881); *Despatch,* spec.serv. (Mar 1881-Jan 1883); *Ossipee,* Asia.Sta. (Jan 1883-Apr 1884); rec. ship, *Franklin,* Norfolk, VA (Apr-Jun 1884); *Nantucket,* spec.serv. (Jun-Sep 1884); w.o. (Sep 1884-Feb 1885); *Palos,* Asia.Sta. (Apr 1885-Nov 1887); home and w.o. (Nov 1887-Mar 1888); rec. ship, *Franklin,* Norfolk, Va (Mar-Aug 1888); spec. duty, Univ. of SC, Columbia, SC (Aug 1888-Jul 1891); *Bennington,* Sqdn. of Evol. (Jul-Sep 1891); *Petrel,* Asia.Sta. (Sep 1891-Oct 1894); home and l.o.a. (Oct 1894-May 1895); Bur. of Steam Engineering, Washington, DC (May 1895-Oct 1897); home and sick lv. (Oct-Nov 1897); *Lancaster,* Navy Yard, Boston (Nov-Dec 1897); home and w.o. (Dec 1897-Jan 1898); *Puritan,* N.Atl.Flt. (Jan-May 1898); Naval Hosp., Philadelphia, then home and sick lv. (May-Jul 1898); Naval Sta., Key West, FL (Jul-Aug 1898); *Badger,* N.Atl.Flt. (Aug 1898); *Vulcan,* N.Atl.Flt. (Aug 1898); hosp. ship, *Solace,* N.Atl.Flt. (Aug-Sep 1898); Navy Yard, Boston (Sep-Nov 1898); *Glacier,* N.Atl.Flt. (Nov 1898); *Cincinnati,* N.Atl.Flt. (Nov 1898-Feb 1899); *Texas,* N.Atl.Sta. (Feb 1899-Nov 1900); Bur. of Steam Engineering, Washington, DC (Nov 1900-Jul 1904); Chief Engr., Navy Yard, Portsmouth, NH (Aug 1904-Aug 1908); insp. of machinery, William Cramp and Sons Iron Works, Philadelphia (Aug 1908-Jun 1911); general insp. of machinery, Navy Dept., Washington, DC (Jun 1911-Sep 1912); chairman, American delegation to international radio-telegraphic conference, London (Jun-Aug 1912); pres., bd. of inspection and surv., Washington, DC (Sep 1912-Sep 1914); spec. duty, Navy Dept., Washington, DC (Sep-Oct 1914); comdt., Navy Yard, and supervisor, 6th Naval Dist., Charleston, SC (Oct 1914-Jul 1915); placed on Ret.Lst. (9 Jul 1915); spec. duty, Brown Univ., Providence, RI (May 1918-Oct 1919); comdt., Naval Unit, Brown Univ., Providence, RI (Oct-Dec 1918).

References

Writings: *Strategical Importance of Our Naval Stations* (Washington, DC: 1916).

CHARLES HENRY ELDREDGE Born in Dedham, MA, on 21 Sep 1839, son of Nathaniel T. and Mary H. (Haven) Eldredge. Married Genevieve Redfield on 2 Feb 1881. One son and one daughter. Resided in Norfolk, VA, dying on 16 Jul 1916. Buried in Brooklyn, NY.

Ranks Asst. Paymstr. (10 Jul 1861); Paymstr. (6 Feb 1862); Pay Insp. (3 Jul 1871); Pay Dir. (31 Aug 1881); placed on Ret.Lst. as Pay Dir. with rank of RAdm (21 Sep 1901).

Career Summary Received appointment from NY (10 Jul 1861); *Supply,* N.Atl. and Gulf Blk.Sqdns. (Jul 1861-Feb 1862); s.a. and w.o. (Feb-Jun 1862); *Canandaigua,* S.Atl.Blk.Sqdn. (Jun 1862-Nov 1864); s.a. and w.o. (Nov 1864-May 1865); spec. duty, Navy Yard, NY (May-Oct 1865); w.o. (Oct 1865-Jan 1866);

CHARLES HENRY ELDREDGE
1839-1916

Idaho, Navy Yard, NY (Jan-May 1866); w.o. (May-Aug 1866); Navy Yard and Naval Sta., Pensacola, FL (Aug 1866-Aug 1868); s.a. and w.o. (Aug 1868-Jan 1869); storekeeper, Asia.Sta. (Feb 1869-Jan 1872); s.a. and w.o. (Jan-Jun 1872); Pay Office, Navy Yard, Portsmouth, NH (Jul 1872-Jul 1875); s.a. and w.o. (Jul-Aug 1875); flt.paymstr., S.Pac.Sta., *Richmond* (Sep 1875-Sep 1877); s.a. and w.o. (Sep 1877-Dec 1878); insp. of provisions and clothing, Navy Yard, Norfolk, VA (Jan 1879-Aug 1882); s.a. and w.o. (Aug 1882-Apr 1884); paymstr., Navy Yard, NY (Apr 1884-Jan 1886); Pay Office, Philadelphia (Feb 1886-Feb 1889); s.a. and w.o. (Feb-Jun 1889); general storekeeper, Navy Yard, Norfolk, VA (Jul 1889-Apr 1890); in charge, Pay Office, Navy Yard, Norfolk, VA (Apr 1890-Apr 1893); s.a. and w.o. (Apr-May 1893); in charge, Pay Office, Baltimore (May 1893-Jun 1896); s.a. and l.o.a. (Jun-Jul 1896); w.o. (Jul-Oct 1896); in charge, Pay Office, Norfolk, VA (Nov 1896-Feb 1901); placed on Ret.Lst. (21 Sep 1901); in charge, Pay Office, Norfolk, VA (Oct 1902-Sep 1904).

WILLIAM HEMSLEY EMORY   Born in Washington, DC, on 17 Dec 1846, son of army BGen William H. and Matilda Wilkins (Bache) Emory. Married. Died on 14 Jul 1917 in Newport, RI. Buried at Arlington National Cemetery.

Ranks   Midn (23 Sep 1862); Ens (12 Mar 1868); Mstr (26 Mar 1869); Lt (21 Mar 1870); LCdr (26 May 1887); Cdr (29 Dec 1895); Capt (14 Apr 1901); RAdm (2 Nov 1906); placed on Ret.Lst. (17 Dec 1908).

Career Summary   Received appointment by virtue of being the son of an officer (23 Sep 1862); USNA (Sep 1862-Jun 1866); l.o.a. and w.o. (Jun-Dec 1866); *Iroquois*, Asia.Sqdn. (Jan 1867-Apr 1870); Prac.Sqdn. (May-Sep 1870); w.o. (Sep-Dec 1870); Naval Observatory, Washington, DC (Dec 1870-Apr 1871); rec. ship, *Relief*, Washington, DC (Apr-Sep 1871); w.o. (Sep-Oct 1871); training ship, *Constellation*, Washington, DC (Nov 1871-Jan 1872); flgs., *Hartford*, Asia.Sta. (Apr 1872-Jun 1874); return and w.o. (Jun-Sep 1874); cst.surv. duty (Sep-Dec 1874); temp. duty, *Powhatan*, N.Atl.Sqdn. (Dec 1874); flgs., *Franklin*, Eur.Sta. (Dec 1874-Jun 1876); w.o. (Jul-Sep 1876); centennial duty (Sep-Dec 1876); USNA (Jan 1877-Feb 1879); w.o. (Feb-Jun 1879); l.o.a. (Jun 1879-Mar 1880); flag lt, and aide to cdr, Eur.Sta., *Trenton* (Mar 1880-Oct 1881); w.o. (Oct-Nov 1881); spec. duty, Washington, DC (Nov 1881-Feb 1884); cdr, *Bear*, Greely Relief Expd. (Feb-Nov 1884); w.o. (Nov 1884-Jan 1885); cdr, *Despatch*, spec.serv. (Feb 1885-Jan 1886); cdr, *Thetis*, spec.serv., N.Pac. (Jan 1886-Mar 1889); w.o. (Mar-Apr 1889); duty at U.S. Naval Legation, London (Apr-Dec 1889); naval attaché, U.S. Embassy, London (Dec 1889-Jan 1893); home and l.o.a. (Feb 1893-Mar 1894); cdr, *Petrel*, Asia.Sta. (Mar 1894-May 1896); l.o.a. (Jun 1896-May 1897); chief of staff, *Brooklyn*, N.Atl.Sqdn. (May-Jul 1897); member, bd. of inspection and surv. (Jul 1897-Apr 1898); cdr, *Yosemite*, E.Sqdn., Atl.Flt. (May-Sep 1898); member, bd. of inspection and surv. (Oct 1898-Mar 1900); temp. duty, Navy

WILLIAM HEMSLEY EMORY
1846-1917

Yard, NY (Mar-May 1900); NWC (Jun-Oct 1900); temp. comdt.,
Naval Sta., Key West, FL (Oct-Nov 1900); home and w.o.
(Nov-Dec 1900); cdr, training ship, *Monongahela* (Dec 1900-Aug
1901); cdr, training ship, *Indiana* (Aug 1901-May 1902); insp.,
merchant vessels, NY (May-Jul 1902); NWC (Jul-Aug 1902); cdr,
training ship, *Indiana* (Aug 1902-Dec 1903); home and w.o. (Dec
1903-Jan 1904); cdr, practice ship, *Hancock* (Feb 1904-Nov
1906); home and w.o. (Nov 1906-Jan 1907); cdr, 2nd Sqdn.,
Atl.Flt., *Ohio* (Jan 1907-May 1908); cdr, 3rd Div., 2nd Sqdn.,
Atl.Flt., *Louisiana* (May-Nov 1908); home and w.o. (Nov-Dec
1908); placed on Ret.Lst. (17 Dec 1908).

References
Personal Papers: 2,100 items (1877-1948) in NHF,LC.
Writings: USS *"Yosemite": Orders (diary) of the YOSEMITE: 5
May 1898-14 July 1898* (Washington, DC: 1898).
Additional References: Albert Gleaves, ed., *The Life of an
American Sailor: Rear Admiral William Hemsley Emory, United
States Navy* . . . (NY: c.1923).

ROBLEY DUNGLISON EVANS
1846-1912

ROBLEY DUNGLISON EVANS Born in Floyd County, VA,
on 18 Aug 1846, son of Dr. Samuel Andrew Jackson and Sally
Ann (Jackson) Evans. Moved to Washington, DC, at early age.
Educated in public schools there. Established residency in UT to
receive appointment to USNA. Married Charlotte Taylor, sister
of RAdm Henry Clay Taylor [q.v.], and classmate at USNA, in
1877. Two daughters and a son, navy Capt Frederick Taylor
Evans. Died in Washington, DC, on 3 Jan 1912. Buried in
Arlington National Cemetery.

Ranks Act.Midn (20 Sept 1860); resigned (14 Jun 1861);
reinstated (1 Jul 1861); title changed to Midn (16 Jul 1862);
Act.Ens (1 Oct 1863); medl. retirement with rank of Ens (21 Dec
1865); Mstr on Ret.Lst. (10 May 1866); Lt on Ret.Lst. (10 Aug
1866); reinstated on Active List as Lt (25 Jan 1867) to date from
25 Jul 1866; LCdr (12 Mar 1868); Cdr (12 Jul 1878); Capt (27
Jun 1893); RAdm (11 Feb 1901); placed on Ret.Lst. (18 Aug
1908).

Career Summary Received appointment from UT Territory
(20 Sept 1860); USNA (Sept 1860-Jun 1861); resigned (14 Jun
1861); reinstated (1 Jul 1861); USNA (Jul 1861-Oct 1863);
Powhatan, W.Indies and N.Atl.Blk.Sqdns. (Oct 1863-Jan 1865);
Naval Hosp., Norfolk, VA, and sick lv. (Jan-Sept 1865); Navy
Yard, Philadelphia (Sept 1865-Mar 1866); placed on Ret.Lst. (1
Dec 1865); Naval Observatory, Washington, DC (May-Aug
1866); ord. duty, Navy Yard, Washington, DC (Aug 1866-Oct
1867); reinstated on Active List (25 Jan 1867); flgs., *Piscataqua*
[renamed *Delaware*], Asia.Sqdn. (Oct 1867-Nov 1870); w.o.
(Nov-Dec 1870); ord. duty, Navy Yard, Washington, DC (Dec
1870-Jul 1871); l.o.a. (Jul-Sept 1871); inst., USNA (Sept
1871-Jun 1872); exec.off., *Shenandoah*, Eur.Sqdn. (Jul 1873-Mar
1874); exec.off., *Congress*, Eur.Sqdn. (Mar 1874-Jul 1876); w.o.
(Jul-Oct 1876); signal duty, Navy Yard, Washington, DC (Oct
1876-Mar 1877); cdr, training ship, *Saratoga* (Mar 1877-Dec

1880); equip.off., Navy Yard, Washington, DC (Dec 1880-Apr 1882); asst., then insp., 5th L.h. Dist., Baltimore (May 1882-Jan 1887); insp. of steel for new vessels (Jan-Sept 1887); sec., L.h. Bd., Washington, DC (Sept 1887-Mar 1889); spec. temp. duty, NY (May-Nov 1888); l.o.a. (Mar-Sept 1889); cdr, *Ossipee*, N.Atl.Sta. (Sept-Oct 1889); l.o.a. and on furlough (Oct 1889-May 1891); bd. duties (May-Jul 1891); cdr, *Yorktown*, N.Atl. Sqdn. (Jul 1891-Oct 1892); sec., L.h. Bd., Washington, DC (Nov 1892-Aug 1894); cdr, *New York*, S.Atl.Sta. (Aug 1894-Sep 1895); spec. duty, William Cramp and Sons Iron Works, Philadelphia (Oct-Nov 1895); cdr, *Indiana*, N.Atl.Sqdn. (Nov 1895-Dec 1896); member, L.h. Bd. (Jan 1897-Mar 1898); cdr, *Iowa*, Atl.Flt. (Mar-Sep 1898); member, bd. of inspection and surv. (Oct 1898-Mar 1901); pres., bd. of inspection and surv. (Mar 1901-Feb 1902); cdr, flgs., *Illinois*, spec.serv. (Feb-Mar 1902); senior sqdn. cdr, Asia.Sqdn., *Kentucky* (Apr-Oct 1902); cdr, Asia.Sqdn, *Kentucky* (Oct 1902-Mar 1904); home and w.o. (Mar-Jun 1904); chairman, L.h. Bd. and member, Gen Bd., Washington, DC (Jun 1904-Mar 1905); cdr, N.Atl.Flt., *Maine* (Mar 1905-Apr 1907), *Connecticut* (Apr 1907-May 1908); duty, Gen Bd., Washington, DC (May-Jun 1908); sick lv. (May-Aug 1908); placed on Ret.Lst. (18 Aug 1908); duty, Gen Bd., Washington, DC (Aug 1908-Jan 1910); pres., general court-martial, Norfolk, VA (Mar-Apr 1911).

Career Highlights Nicknamed "Fighting Bob" Evans. Commanded company of marines during assault on Fort Fisher, NC, on 15 Jan 1865, receiving severe wounds in the attack. Retired by a medl. bd., eventually recovered, and successfully appealed bd.'s decision, thereby returning to active duty. In 1882, appointed to the new Naval Advisory Bd. As navy's chief insp. of steel in 1885, assisted in building the new steel ships. In Aug 1891, captained gunboat *Yorktown* sent to Valparaiso, Chile, where he skillfully handled the diplomatic crisis over the killing of two American sailors from USS *Baltimore* and the use of the American legation as an asylum for political refugees. During Spanish-American War, commanded the *Iowa* at Puerto Rico and in Battle of Santiago, being advanced in numbers for eminent conduct in battle. Command the "Great White Flt." during its voyage around the world, a command cut short by ill health.

References
Personal Papers: a) 5 items (1901-50) in NHF,LC. b) Franklin D. Roosevelt Lib., Hyde Park, NY.
Writings: a) *A Sailor's Log: Recollections of Forty Years of Naval Life* (NY: 1901) b) *An Admiral's Log: Being Continued Reflections of Naval Life* (NY: 1910). c) chapter in Sir William Athelstane Meredith Good, *With Sampson through the War* (NY: 1899).
Additional Sources: a) Edwin Albert Falk, *Fighting Bob Evans* (NY: 1931). b) C. Douglas Kroll, "'Fighting Bob' Evans and the America's Cup Patrol Fleet," U.S. Naval Institute *Proceedings* 909 (Nov 1978): 94-95.

WILLIAM HENRY EVERETT Born in NY City on 6 Mar 1847, son of William Moore and Charlotte M. Everett. Married

Bessie Bell Hackett on 6 Aug 1885. Lived in Newport, RI, where he died on 10 Jun 1912. Buried in Arlington National Cemetery.

Ranks Midn (23 Jul 1863); Ens (19 Apr 1869); Mstr (12 Jul 1870); Lt (12 Dec 1873); LCdr (6 Dec 1894); Cdr (3 Mar 1899); Capt (17 Feb 1904); retired with rank of RAdm (9 Oct 1906).

Career Summary Received appointment from CT (23 Jul 1863); USNA (Jul 1863-Jun 1868); found deficient and turned back (Feb 1864); w.o. (Jun-Sep 1868); *Pawnee, Portsmouth,* and *Guerriere,* S.Atl.Sta. (Oct 1868-Jul 1869); w.o. (Aug-Oct 1869); *Nantasket,* and *Congress,* N.Atl.Sqdn., Greenland Polar Expd., and Eur.Sqdn. (Oct 1869-Mar 1874); *Wyoming* (Mar-Apr 1874); l.o.a. (Apr-Nov 1874); equip. duty, Navy Yard, NY (Nov 1874-May 1875); *Alert,* N.Atl.Sta. (May 1875-Jan 1876); flgs., *Tennessee,* Asia.Sta. (Feb 1876-Jul 1878); w.o. (Jul-Oct 1878); Nautical Almanac Office, Washington, DC (Nov 1878-Nov 1879); ord. duty, Navy Yard, NY (Dec 1879-May 1881); sick lv. (May 1881-Jun 1882); *Tallapoosa,* N.Atl.Sta. (Jun 1882-Aug 1884); flag lt, N.Atl.Sta., *Tennessee* (Sep 1884-Apr 1886); sick lv. (Apr-Jul 1886); ord. duty, Navy Yard, Portsmouth, NH (Jul 1886-Oct 1887); exec.off., then cdr, training ship, *Saratoga* (Oct 1887-Oct 1888); w.o. (Oct-Dec 1888); flgs., *Richmond,* S.Atl.Sta. (Dec 1888-Sep 1890); in charge, branch hydrographic office, Boston (Sep 1890-Sep 1893); l.o.a. (Sep-Nov 1893); ord. duty, Navy Yard, Washington, DC (Nov 1893-Feb 1894); w.o. (Feb-Mar 1894); exec.off., rec. ship, *Minnesota,* NY (Mar-May 1894); exec.off., *Montgomery,* N.Atl.Sta. (Jun 1894-Aug 1895); exec.off., *Cincinnati,* spec.serv. (Aug 1895-May 1896); NWC (Jun-Oct 1896); home and l.o.a. (Oct-Nov 1896); member, steel bd., Washington, DC (Nov 1896-Jan 1897); Hydrographic Office, Washington, DC (Jan 1897-Feb 1898); cdr, *Michigan,* on Great Lakes (Mar-Apr 1898); cdr, *Mangrove,* N.Atl.Flt. (Apr-Jun 1898); Naval Hosp., Portsmouth, NH (Jun-Aug 1898); cdr, *Michigan,* on Great Lakes (Sep 1898-Mar 1899); cdr, *Iris,* Asia.Sta. (May-Dec 1899); cdr, *Culgoa,* Asia.Sta. (Dec 1899-Mar 1900); cdr, *Glacier,* Asia.Sta. (Mar-Jul 1900); Naval Hosp., Portsmouth, NH (Aug-Oct 1900); w.o. (Oct 1900-Jan 1901); Navy Yard, Boston (Feb 1901-Aug 1902); ord.off., Navy Yard, Norfolk, VA (Aug 1902-Dec 1903); cdr, training ship, *Buffalo* (Dec 1903-Apr 1905); home and w.o. (Apr-May 1905); NWC (Jun-Oct 1905); capt.yd., Navy Yard, Boston (Oct 1905-Oct 1906); retired (9 Oct 1906).

OSCAR WALTER FARENHOLT Born near San Antonio, TX, on 2 May 1843. Educated in public schools in San Antonio, New Orleans, and in Pittsburgh. Married to Ella Mortimer (Ames) Farenholt. One son, Capt Ammen Farenholt, MC, USN. Died on 30 Jun 1920 at Mare Island, CA.

Ranks Seaman (18 Apr 1861); discharged for medl. reasons (22 Jan 1863); re-entered as seaman for one year (10 Feb 1863); re-enlisted as seaman for one year (20 Feb 1864); Act.Ens (19 Aug 1864); Ens (12 Mar 1868); Mstr (18 Dec 1868); Lt (21 Mar 1870); LCdr (11 May 1882); Cdr (19 Jun 1892); Capt (25 Sep 1899); retired with rank of RAdm (1 Sep 1901).

OSCAR WALTER FARENHOLT
1843-1920

Career Summary Entered navy at NY (18 Apr 1861); flgs., *Wabash*, S.Atl.Blk.Sqdn. (Apr 1861-Oct 1862); Naval Hosp., NY (Oct 1862-Jan 1863); discharged (22 Jan 1862); re-entered (10 Feb 1863); *Catskill*, and *Home*, S.Atl.Blk.Sqdn. (Apr 1863-Feb 1864); on furlough (Feb-Aug 1864); Navy Yard, NY (Aug-Sep 1864); cdr, *Henry Jones*, S.Atl.Blk.Sqdn. (Sep 1864-Jun 1865); l.o.a. (Jun-Jul 1865); *Shawnee*, Boston (Jul-Nov 1865); Navy Yard, Boston (Nov 1865-Mar 1866); *J. C. Kuhn* [renamed *Purveyor*], Navy Yard, NY (Mar-Oct 1866); flgs., *Susquehanna*, N.Atl.Sqdn. (Oct 1866-Jan 1867); w.o. (Jan-Feb 1867); rec. ship, *New Hampshire*, Norfolk, VA (Feb 1867); rec. ship, *Ohio*, Boston (Feb-Sep 1867); *Idaho*, Asia.Sqdn. (Oct 1867-Oct 1870); w.o. and l.o.a. (Nov 1870-Apr 1871); Navy Yard, Norfolk, VA (May-Nov 1871); cdr, *Standish*, Home Sta. (Nov 1871-Jul 1873); *Shenandoah*, Eur.Sta. (Jul 1873-Apr 1874); w.o. (Apr-May 1874); Hydrographic Office, Washington, DC (May 1874); cdr, rec. ship, *Relief*, Navy Yard, Washington, DC (Jun 1874-May 1875); training ship, *Minnesota* (May 1875-Jun 1876); exec.off., training ship, *Supply* (Jun-Sep 1876); Navy Yard, Norfolk, VA (Oct 1876-Jun 1877); in charge, Naval Nitre Depot, Malden, MA (Jun 1877-Oct 1879); w.o. (Oct-Dec 1879); exec.off., *Monocacy* (May 1880-Apr 1882); Navy Dept., Washington, DC (Apr-Jul 1882); w.o. (Jul-Aug 1882); exec.off., rec. ship, *Wabash*, Boston (Sep 1882-Mar 1885); exec.off., training ship, *Portsmouth* (Mar-Nov 1885); exec.off., *Swatara*, Home Sqdn. (Nov 1885-Oct 1886); exec.off., rec. ship, *Wabash*, Boston (Oct 1886-Sep 1889); cdr, *Pinta*, Alaskan waters (Sep 1889-Sep 1891); home and l.o.a. (Sep-Nov 1891); equip. duty, Navy Yard, Boston (Nov 1891-Jul 1892); insp., 13th L.h. Dist., Portland, OR (Jul 1892-Jun 1896); s.a., home and w.o. (Jun-Aug 1896); cdr, *Monocacy*, Asia.Sta. (Nov 1896-Jan 1899); home and w.o. (Jan-Mar 1899); Navy Yard, NY (Mar-Jul 1899); Navy Yard, Boston (Jul 1899-Jul 1900); comdt., Naval Sta., Cavite, P.I. (Aug-Sep 1900); sick lv., Naval Hosp., Yokohama, Japan (Sep-Dec 1900); cdr, *Monadnock*, Asia.Sta. (Dec 1900-Jul 1901); home and w.o. (Jul-Sep 1901); retired (1 Sep 1901).

Career Highlights As a sailor, participated in actions at Fort Hatteras, Port Royal, and Fort Pulaski. Badly wounded at Battle of Pocotaglio, SC, on 22 Oct 1862 and discharged from the service. Recovered and re-enlisted, saw action against defenses of Charleston from Apr 1863 to following Apr, being with the unsuccessful attack to storm Fort Sumter in Sep 1863. Upon exam. in 1867 for entry into the regular navy, became first man to begin his career as an enlisted sailor and complete his career as a RAdm without attending the USNA.

References

Writings: a) "The United States Ship *Idaho*. Reminiscences, 1866-1870," U.S. Naval Institute *Proceedings* 144 (Dec 1912): 1451-65. b) "U.S.S. *Oneida*: Lost January 24, 1870, in Yeddo (Tokyo) Bay, Japan," U.S. Naval Institute *Proceedings* 152 (Jul-Aug 1914): 1109-18. c) "The Volunteer Navy in the Civil War," U.S. Naval Institute *Proceedings* 200 (Oct 1919): 1691-94.

d) "Some Autobiographical Notes Concerning the Service of the Late O. W. Farenholt, Rear Admiral, U.S. Navy, Retired," U.S. Naval Institute *Proceedings* 310 (Dec 1928): 1047-50; 312 (Feb 1929): 139-40.

EDWARD FARMER Born on 1 Mar 1836 in Perkinsville, VT, son of Edward and Lydia A. Farmer. Educated in public schools and by private tutors. Married Louise Buttrick on 1 Jun 1869. Resided in Boston after his retirement, dying there on 20 Feb 1918. Buried in Mt. Auburn Cemetery in Cambridge, MA.

Ranks 3rd Asst.Engr (3 May 1859); 2nd Asst.Engr (16 Oct 1861); 1st Asst.Engr (20 May 1863); Chief Engr (4 Mar 1871); Chief Engr with rel. rank of Cdr (2 Dec 1887); Chief Engr with rel. rank of Capt (15 Jan 1895); placed on Ret.Lst. (1 Mar 1898); RAdm. on Ret.Lst. (29 Jun 1906).

Career Summary Received appointment from MA (3 May 1859); w.o. (May-Oct 1859); *Mohican,* Home and S.Atl. Blk.Sqdns. (Oct 1859-Sep 1861); exam. and w.o. (Sep-Nov 1861); spec. duty, Bridgeport, CT (Nov 1861); *Kanawha,* W.Gulf Blk.Sqdn. (Nov 1861-Feb 1864); w.o. (Feb-Mar 1864); temp. duty, *Saco* (Mar-May 1864); *Alabama,* N.Atl.Sta. (May-Jun 1864); w.o. (Jun 1864-Oct 1865); *Shenandoah,* E.Ind.Sta. (Oct 1865-Apr 1869); w.o. (Apr-Jun 1869); Navy Yard, Boston (Jun 1869-May 1871); w.o. (May-Jun 1871); *Ticonderoga,* S.Atl.Sta. (Jun 1871-Apr 1874); in charge of stores, Navy Yard, Boston (Apr 1874-Apr 1877); additional duty, S.Boston Iron Works, Boston (Aug 1876-Apr 1877); l.o.a. (May 1877-Mar 1878); temp. duty, Navy Yard, Boston (Mar-Jul 1878); *Alert,* Asia.Sta. (Aug 1878-Jul 1881); w.o. (Jul-Dec 1881); USNA (Dec 1881-Aug 1888); *Chicago,* Sqdn. of Evol. (Sep 1888-Nov 1891); Navy Yard, Portsmouth, NH (Dec 1891-Jul 1893); Navy Yard, Boston (Jul 1893-Aug 1895); Navy Yard, NY (Aug 1895-Feb 1898); home and w.o. (Feb-Mar 1898); placed on Ret.Lst. (1 Mar 1898); insp. of machinery, Bur. of Steam Engineering, Washington, DC (May 1898-Jan 1899).

AUGUSTUS FRANCIS FECHTELER Born in Paderborn, Prussia, on 1 Sep 1857, son of Joseph and Elizabeth (Lucken) Fechteler. Emigrated to U.S. in 1865. Graduated from the LaSalle Institute of NY in 1873. Married Maud Morrow on 16 Oct 1893. Two sons, including Adm William Morrow Fechteler, USN (1896-1967) and three daughters. Died on 26 May 1921 at Norfolk, VA, Navy Yard.

Ranks Cadet Midn (9 Jun 1873); Midn (18 Jun 1879); Ens (23 Nov 1880); Ltjg (6 Mar 1887); Lt (21 Jul 1892); LCdr (27 Mar 1900); Cdr (1 Jul 1905); Capt (1 Jul 1909); RAdm (11 Jul 1915); died (26 May 1921).

Career Summary Received appointment from NY (9 Jun 1873); USNA (Jun 1873-Jun 1877); w.o. (Jun-Sep 1877); flgs., *Trenton,* Eur.Sta. (Oct 1877-Apr 1879); USNA (Apr-Jun 1879); w.o. (Jun-Sep 1879); *Shenandoah,* S.Atl.Sqdn. (Sep 1879-May 1882); w.o. (May-Jun 1882); cst.surv. duty (Jun 1882-Sep 1885);

EDWARD FARMER
1836-1918

AUGUSTUS FRANCIS FECHTELER
1857-1921

rec. ship, *Vermont*, NY (Sep-Dec 1885); training ship, *Jamestown* (Dec 1885-Apr 1886); training ship, *Portsmouth* (Apr-Jun 1886); *Essex*, Asia.Sta. (Jul 1886-Nov 1888); home and w.o. (Nov 1888-Jan 1889); Bur. of Nav., Washington, DC (Jan-Jul 1889); l.o.a. (Jul-Oct 1889); Bur. of Nav., Washington, DC (Oct 1889-May 1890); l.o.a. (May-Nov 1890); Office of Naval Intelligence, Washington, DC (Nov 1890-Jan 1892); spec. duty (Jan-Feb 1892); *Mohican*, Pac.Sqdn. (Feb 1892-Jan 1893); Fish Commission steamer, *Albatross*, Bering Sea (Jan 1893-Oct 1894); in charge, branch hydrographic office, San Francisco (Oct 1894-Sep 1896); *Monterey*, Asia.Sqdn. (Oct 1896-Dec 1898); *Concord*, Asia.Sqdn. (Dec 1898-Aug 1899); hosp. ship, *Solace*, spec.serv. (Aug-Oct 1899); aide to comdt., Navy Yard, Mare Island, CA (Oct 1899-Aug 1901); navigator, then exec.off., *Iowa*, Pac.Sqdn., then Atl.Sqdn. (Aug 1901-Jul 1903); inspection duty, Union Iron Works, San Francisco (Aug 1903-Mar 1904); Office of Naval Intelligence, Navy Dept., Washington, DC (Mar 1904-Jun 1905); cdr, *Dubuque*, N.Atl.Sqdn. (Jun 1905-Dec 1906); home and w.o. (Dec 1906-Jan 1907); ord. instruction, Navy Yard, Washington, DC (Jan-May 1907); NWC (Jun-Sep 1907); home and l.o.a. (Sep-Oct 1907); duty connected with, then member, bd. of inspection and surv., Washington, DC (Nov 1907-Jan 1910); general insp., *South Carolina*, Philadelphia (Oct 1909-Mar 1910); cdr, *South Carolina*, Atl.Flt. (Mar 1910-Nov 1911); pres., bd. of inspection and surv., Washington, DC (Nov 1911-Nov 1913); aide for inspections to sec. of navy, Navy Dept., Washington, DC (Nov 1913-Nov 1914); NWC (Nov 1914-Jul 1915); cdr, 2nd Div., Atl.Flt., *Florida* (Jul 1915-May 1916); cdr, 7th Div., Atl.Flt., *Florida* (May-Jun 1916); cdr, 6th Div., Battleship Force, Atl.Flt., *New York* (Jun 1916-Nov 1917), then *Utah* (Nov 1917-Feb 1918); comdt, Navy Yard, and 5th Naval Dist., Norfolk, VA (Feb 1918-May 1921); died (26 May 1921).

Career Highlights Awarded Navy Cross for services as div. cdr of Atl.Flt. and as cdr of Norfolk, VA, Navy Yard.

WELLS LAFLIN FIELD Born in St. Louis on 31 Jan 1846, son of Matthew D. and Clarissa (Laflin) Field. Married Ruth Dunning Clark on 8 Nov 1894. One son and one daughter. Died in Washington, DC, on 27 Nov 1914. Buried in Arlington National Cemetery.

Ranks Midn (20 Nov 1862); Ens (18 Dec 1868); Mstr (21 Mar 1870); Lt (21 Mar 1871); LCdr (5 Nov 1891); Cdr (27 Apr 1898); Capt (16 Jun 1902); retired with rank of RAdm (20 Nov 1902).

Career Summary Received appointment from NY (20 Nov 1862); USNA (Nov 1862-Jun 1867); found deficient and put back (Feb and Nov 1863); w.o. (Jun-Sep 1867); *Piscataqua* [renamed *Delaware*], Asia.Sqdn. (Oct 1867-Nov 1870); w.o. (Dec 1870-Feb 1871); *Supply*, spec.serv. (Feb-Jul 1871); rec. ship, *Vermont*, NY (Jul 1871); cst.surv. duty (Jul 1871-Jan 1872); w.o. (Jan-Mar 1872); *Lackawanna*, Asia.Sqdn. (Mar 1872-Oct 1873); Bur. of Nav., Washington, DC (Oct 1873-Mar 1874); *Franklin*,

N.Atl.Sta. (Mar 1874-Jan 1877); w.o. (Jan-Apr 1877); spec. L.h. duty, Staten Island, NY (Apr 1877-Jun 1880); temp. duty, cdr, L.h. steamer, *Manzanita* (Nov 1879-Jan 1880); w.o. (Jun-Aug 1880); flag lt, Asia.Flt., *Richmond* (Sep 1880-Nov 1883); return and l.o.a. (Nov 1883-May 1884); in charge, branch hydrographic office, NY (May 1884-Mar 1886); training ship, *St. Mary's* (Apr 1886-Mar 1889); w.o. (Mar-Apr 1889); Torp.Sta., Newport, RI (May-Aug 1889); NWC (Aug-Oct 1889); Bur. of Equip. and Recruiting, Washington, DC (Oct-Nov 1889); flgs., *Charleston*, Pac.Sqdn. (Dec 1889-Jun 1893); l.o.a. (Jun-Sep 1893); exec.off., training ship, *Minnesota*, NY (Sep 1893-Mar 1894); cdr, training ship, *St. Mary's* (Mar 1894-Apr 1897); l.o.a. (Mar-Jun 1897); in charge, recruiting office, NY (Jun 1897-Apr 1898); in charge, 2nd, then 3rd, Dist. Cst. Defense System ["Mosquito Flt."] (Apr-Jul 1898); cdr, *Justin*, spec.serv. (Jul 1898-Feb 1899); cdr, *Scindia*, Asia.Flt. (Feb-May 1899); asst., then insp., 13th L.h. Dist., Portland, OR (Jun-Oct 1899); cdr, *Ranger*, spec.serv. (Nov 1899-Oct 1901); home and w.o. (Oct 1901-Jan 1902); asst.insp., 6th L.h. Dist., Charleston, SC (Jan-Sep 1902); home and w.o. (Oct 1902); temp. duty, Bur. of Equip. and Recruiting, Washington, DC (Oct-Nov 1902); retired (20 Nov 1902); spec. duty, Navy Dept., Washington, DC (Oct 1904-Aug 1905); spec. duty, Dept. of Commerce and Labor, Washington, DC (Oct 1904-Dec 1907).

BRADLEY ALLEN FISKE
1854-1942

BRADLEY ALLEN FISKE Born in Lyons, NY, on 13 Jun 1854, son of Reverend William Allen and Susan (Bradley) Fiske. Spent his youth in NY, then in Cleveland and Cincinnati. Married Josephine Harper in 1882. One daughter, Caroline Harper Fiske. Died in NY City on 6 Apr 1942.

Ranks Cadet Midn (24 Sep 1870); Midn (1 Jun 1874); Ens (17 Jul 1875); Mstr (2 Feb 1881); Ltjg (3 Mar 1883); Lt (26 Jan 1887); LCdr (3 Mar 1899); Cdr (7 Mar 1903); Capt (28 Aug 1907); RAdm (3 Aug 1911); placed on Ret.Lst. (13 Jun 1916).

Career Summary Received appointment from OH (24 Sep 1870); USNA (Sep 1870-Jun 1874); w.o. (Jun-Jul 1874); *Pensacola*, N.Pac.Sqdn. (Aug 1874-Aug 1876); home and w.o. (Aug-Oct 1876); USNA (Oct-Nov 1876); w.o. (Nov 1876); l.o.a. (Nov 1876-Apr 1877); rec. ship, *Wyoming*, Washington, DC (Apr-Jun 1877); torp. instruction, Newport, RI (Jul-Sep 1877); w.o. (Sep-Oct 1877); *Plymouth*, Pac.Sqdn. (Oct 1877-Mar 1878); equip. duty, Navy Yard, NY (Mar-May 1878); experimental duty, rec. ship, *Colorado*, NY (Jun 1878-Apr 1879); *Powhatan*, N.Atl.Sqdn. (Apr 1879-Aug 1880); w.o. (Aug-Sep 1880); rec. ship, *Colorado*, NY (Sep 1880-Oct 1881); temp. duty, training ship, *Saratoga* (Oct-Nov 1881); training ship, *Minnesota* (Nov 1881-Sep 1882); l.o.a. (Oct 1882-Sep 1883); *Constellation*, and Bur. of Ord., Washington, DC (Sep 1883-Oct 1885); *Brooklyn*, S.Atl.Sqdn. (Oct-Dec 1885); spec. duty, Bur. of Ord., Washington, DC (Dec 1885-May 1886); supervisor for installation of new ord., *Atlanta*, on trials, and N.Atl.Sqdn. (Jul 1886-Nov 1888); spec. duty, acceptance trials, *Vesuvius* (Nov 1888-Apr 1890);

electric light duty, new ships, Philadelphia (Apr-Sep 1890); on
furlough (Sep 1890-Oct 1891); *Yorktown*, Pac.Sqdn. (Oct
1891-Jul 1893); flgs., *San Francisco*, N.Atl.Sqdn. (Jul 1893-Oct
1894); home and l.o.a. (Oct 1894-Apr 1895); Bur. of Ord.,
Washington, DC (Apr 1895-Dec 1896); navigator and exec.off.,
Petrel, Asia.Flt. (Dec 1896-Dec 1898): navigator, *Monadnock*,
Asia.Flt. (Dec 1898-May 1899); exec.off., *Yorktown*, Asia.Flt.
(May 1899-Jan 1900); Navy Yard, Mare Island, CA (Jan-Feb
1900); home and w.o. (Feb-Mar 1900); insp. of ord., E. W. Bliss
& Company, NY (Mar 1900-Feb 1902); exec.off., *Massachusetts*,
N.Atl.Flt. (Feb 1902-May 1903); home and w.o. (May-Jun 1903);
NWC (Jun-Aug 1903); insp. of ord., William Cramp and Sons
Iron Works, Philadelphia, and New York Shipbuilding Company,
plus other bd. duties (Sep 1903-Mar 1906); member, naval
wireless telegraph bd. (Oct 1904-Mar 1906); cdr, training ship,
Minneapolis (Mar-Nov 1906); cdr, training ship, *Arkansas* (Nov
1906-Aug 1907); home and w.o. (Aug-Dec 1907); temp. duty, in
charge, recruiting office, NY (Dec 1907-Mar 1908); capt.yd.,
Navy Yard, League Island, PA (Mar-Jun 1908); cdr, *Tennessee*,
Pac.Flt. (Jul 1908-Aug 1910); NWC (Aug 1910); member, Gen
Bd., Washington, DC (Aug 1910-Oct 1911); member, Army-
Navy Joint Bd., Washington, DC (Oct 1909-Oct 1910); cdr, 5th
Div., Atl.Flt., *Washington* (Oct 1911-Apr 1912); cdr, 3rd Div.,
Atl.Flt., *Georgia* (Apr-Aug 1912); cdr, 1st Div., Atl.Flt., *Florida*
(Aug 1912-Jan 1913); aide for inspections to sec. of navy, Navy
Dept., Washington, DC (Jan 1912-Feb 1913); aide for operations
to sec. of navy, Navy Dept., Washington, DC (Feb 1913-May
1915); member, Army-Navy Joint Bd., Washington, DC (Apr
1913-May 1915); NWC (Jul 1915-Jun 1916); placed on Ret.Lst.
(13 Jun 1916); member, naval exam. bd., Narragansett Bay, RI
(Jun 1916); temp. duties, Navy Dept., Washington, DC (Mar-Apr
1920, Oct-Nov 1924, Mar-Apr 1925).

Career Highlights Was probably the U.S.'s greatest naval
inventor as well as one of the most progressive and reform-minded
officers. Some of his inventions included a system for lowering and
detaching boats, an electrical mechanism for turning gun turrets,
an electric range-finder and telescopic sights for naval guns, a
hoist for ammunition, a speed and direction finder, the stadimeter,
a shipboard electric communication system, a submarine detection
device, torpedo design improvements and, in 1912, the means for
creating the torpedo-launching airplane. All in all, he had over
sixty patents. In addition to his talents for mechanical and
electrical inventions, urged creation of a naval general staff and
a national security council that would encompass all national
policies into one centralized body. Through much of Fiske's
recommendations, office of chief of naval operations was created.
Urged that the naval bureaus be consistently ready for war with
specific plans. A prolific writer who associated other reform-
minded men, used his position as pres. of Naval Institute from
1911 to 1923 as a means to publish many works.

References

Personal Papers: a)Two diaries (26 Sep 1914-5 Mar 1917; 6

Mar 1917-18 Sep. 1918) in LC. b) One diary (6 Jan 1913-25 Sep 1914) in USNAM.

Selected Writings: a) *Electricity in Theory and Practice* (Washington, DC: 1883); at least 21 subsequent editions. b) "Electricity in Naval Life," U.S. Naval Institute *Proceedings* 78 (1896): 323-428. c) "A Useful Little Change in the Pelorus," U.S. Naval Institute *Proceedings* 98 (Jun 1901): 371-72. d) "The Fiske Semaphone System," U.S. Naval Institute *Proceedings* 107 (Sep 1903): 679-97. e) "A Naval Telescope and Mount," U.S. Naval Institute *Proceedings* 107 (Sep 1903): 699-700. f) "War Signals," U.S. Naval Institute *Proceedings* 108 (Dec 1903): 931-34. g) "American Naval Policy," U.S. Naval Institute *Proceedings* 113 (Mar 1905): 1-80. h) "Compromiseless Ships," U.S. Naval Institute *Proceedings* 115 (Sep 1905): 549-53. i) "Why Togo Won," U.S. Naval Institute *Proceedings* 116 (Dec 1905): 807-9. j) "The Stadimeter in Fire Control," U.S. Naval Institute *Proceedings* 116 (Dec 1905): 973-74. k) "The Civil and the Military Authority," U.S. Naval Institute *Proceedings* 117 (Mar 1906): 127-30. l) "The Horizometer," U.S. Naval Institute *Proceedings* 119 (Sep 1906): 1043-55. m) "Fleet Telephony," U.S. Naval Institute *Proceedings* 121 (Mar 1907): 239-42. n) "The Naval Profession," U.S. Naval Institute *Proceedings* 122 (Jun 1907): 475-578. o) "Navigating without Horizon," U.S. Naval Institute *Proceedings* 123 (Sep 1907): 955-57. p) "Courage and Prudence," U.S. Naval Institute *Proceedings* 125 (Mar 1908): 277-307. q) "To Adjust Range Finders before Battle," U.S. Naval Institute *Proceedings* 127 (Sep 1908): 1043-44. r) "To Find the Fleet Speed and Corresponding Revolutions," U.S. Naval Institute *Proceedings* 127 (Sep 1908): 1045-46. s) "A Fair Basis for Competition in Battle Practice," U.S. Naval Institute *Proceedings* 128 (Dec 1908): 1188-97. t) "A Curious Fact about Spotting," U.S. Naval Institute *Proceedings* 128 (Dec 1908): 1297. u) "The Sight Bar Range," U.S. Naval Institute *Proceedings* 129 (Mar 1909): 113-18. v) "A Simple Electric Steering Gear," U.S. Naval Institute *Proceedings* 129 (Mar 1909): 263-65. w) "The Invention and Development of the Naval Telescope Sight," U.S. Naval Institute *Proceedings* 130 (Jun 1909): 405-24. x) "To Find the Tactical Curves," U.S. Naval Institute *Proceedings* 130 (Jun 1909): 561. y) "An Unprecedented Rescue," U.S. Naval Institute *Proceedings* 136 (Dec 1910): 957-64. z) "Incorrect Adjustment of Range Finders," U.S. Naval Institute *Proceedings* 136 (Dec 1910): 1069. aa) "A Suggestion about Charts," U.S. Naval Institute *Proceedings* 136 (Dec 1910): 1071. bb) "Naval Power," U.S. Naval Institute *Proceedings* 139 (Sep 1911): 683-736. cc) "The Relative Importance of Turret and Telescope Sight," U.S. Naval Institute *Proceedings* 142 (June 1912): 595-602. dd) "The Mean Point of Impact," U.S. Naval Institute *Proceedings* 143 (Sep 1912): 1001-9. ee) *War Time in Manila* (Boston: 1913). ff) "The Diplomatic Responsibility of the United States Navy," U.S. Naval Institute *Proceedings* 151 (May-Jun 1914): 799-802. gg) "The Paramount Duty of the Army and Navy," U.S. Naval Institute *Proceedings* 152 (Jul-Aug 1914): 1073-74. hh) "The Effectiveness of Skill," U.S. Naval Institute

Proceedings 155 (Jan-Feb 1915): 67-70. ii) *The Navy as a Fighting Machine*, (NY: 1916, 1918). jj) "Naval Strategy," U.S. Naval Institute *Proceedings* 162 (Mar-Apr 1916): 387-407. kk) "Admiral Dewey: An Appreciation," U.S. Naval Institute *Proceedings* 169 (Mar 1917): 433-36. ll) "Air Power," U.S. Naval Institute *Proceedings* 174 (Aug 1917): 1701-4. mm) "Stephen B. Luce: An Appreciation," U.S. Naval Institute *Proceedings* 175 (Sep 1917): 1935-40. nn) "Strategy, Tactics, Logistics and Invention," U.S. Naval Institute *Proceedings* 178 (Sep 1917): 1935-40. oo) "The United States Naval Institute," U.S. Naval Institute *Proceedings* 192 (Feb 1919): 197-200. pp) *From Midshipman to Rear Admiral* (NY: 1919). qq) "The Roosevelt Memorial," U.S. Naval Institute *Proceedings* 198 (Aug 1919): 1303-4. rr) *The Art of Fighting: Its Evolution and Progress* . . . (NY: 1920). ss) "The Warfare of the Future," U.S. Naval Institute *Proceedings* 216 (Feb 1921): 157-67. tt) "Disarmament and Foreign Trade," U.S. Naval Institute *Proceedings* 224 (Oct 1921): 1539-42. uu) "Torpedo Plane and Bomber," U.S. Naval Institute *Proceedings* 235 (Sep 1922): 1473-78. vv) "The Navy and Marine Memorial," U.S. Naval Institute *Proceedings* 235 (Mar 1924): 386-88. ww) (posthumously) "Air Power, 1913-43," U.S. Naval Institute *Proceedings* 471 (May 1942): 686-94.

Additional Sources: a) Paolo E. Coletta, *Admiral Bradley A. Fiske and the American Navy* (Lawrence, KS: 1979). b) _____. "Bradley Allen Fiske," *Shipmate* 39, no. 3 (Apr 1976): 19-23. c) _____. "The 'Nerves' of the New Navy," *The American Neptune* 38, no. 2 (1978): 122-30. d) _____. "The Perils of Invention: Bradley A. Fiske and the Torpedo Plane," *The American Neptune* 37, no. 2 (Apr 1977): 111-27.

EDWIN FITHIAN Born in NJ on 13 Dec 1820. Married, his home was Bridgeton, NJ, where he died on 29 Aug 1908 and where he was buried.

Ranks 3rd Asst.Engr (31 Oct 1848); 2nd Asst.Engr (26 Feb 1851); 1st Asst.Engr (21 May 1855); Chief Engr (23 Oct 1859); transferred to Ret.Lst. (13 Dec 1882); advanced to Chief Engr with rank of RAdm on the Ret.Lst (29 Jun 1906).

Career Summary Received appointment from PA (31 Oct 1848); w.o. (Oct 1848-Mar 1849); spec. duty, *Saranac*, Boston (Mar 1849-Aug 1850); l.o.a. and w.o. (Aug 1850-Sep 1851); *Susquehanna*, E.Ind.Sqdn. (Sep 1851-Mar 1855); l.o.a. (Mar-Jun 1855); spec. duty, *Roanoke* and *Colorado*, Richmond, VA (Jun 1855-Mar 1856); *Susquehanna*, Eur.Sqdn. (Apr 1856-Apr 1858); spec. duty, *Lancaster* and *Wyoming*, Philadelphia (Jun 1858-May 1859); w.o. (May-Jun 1859); *Wyoming*, Philadelphia (Jun-Sep 1859); *Narragansett*, Pac.Sqdn. (Sep 1859-Jul 1861); superintended construction of machinery, NY (Aug 1861-Apr 1863); *Roanoke*, N.Atl.Blk.Sqdn. (Apr 1863-Jan 1865); w.o. (Jan-Jul 1865); spec. duty, NY, Chattanooga, TN, and Philadelphia (Jul 1865-Apr 1869); flt.engr., Eur.Sqdn., *Franklin* (Apr 1869-Nov 1871); w.o. (Nov-Dec 1871); Navy Yard, Washington, DC (Dec 1871-Feb 1876); spec. temp. duty, Bur. of Steam Engineering,

EDWIN FITHIAN
1820-1908

Washington, DC (Jan 1876-Feb 1877); additional duty, Centennial Exhibition, Philadelphia (Mar-Oct 1876); flt.engr., Eur.Sqdn., *Trenton* (Feb 1877-Nov 1879); return and w.o. (Nov 1879-Feb 1880); spec. duty, NY (Mar 1880); w.o. (Mar-Jun 1880); spec. duty, Morgan Iron Works, NY (Jun 1880-Dec 1882); placed on Ret.Lst. (13 Dec 1882).

Career Highlights One of the earliest engineers in the navy. Oversaw much construction of machinery of navy's earliest steam vessels. Was with Commo Perry's famous expd. to open Japan to western commerce. Escorted frigate *Niagara* during first attempt at laying a cable across the Atlantic.

FRANK FRIDAY FLETCHER
1855-1928

FRANK FRIDAY FLETCHER Born in Oskaloosa, IA, on 23 Nov 1855, son of James Duncan and Nancy Power (Jack) Fletcher. Married Susan Hunt Stetson on 23 Feb 1895. Two daughters. Died in NY City on 28 Nov 1928. Buried in Arlington National Cemetery.

Ranks Cadet Midn (23 Sep 1870); Midn (21 Jun 1875); Ens (18 Jul 1876); Mstr (1 Apr 1882); title changed to Ltjg (3 Mar 1883); Lt (19 Feb 1889); LCdr (3 Mar 1899); Cdr (12 Mar 1904); Capt (15 May 1908); RAdm (17 Oct 1911); Adm (10 Mar 1915); placed on Ret.Lst. (23 Nov 1919).

Career Summary Received appointment from IA (23 Sep 1870); USNA (Sep 1870-Jun 1875); w.o. (Jun-Oct 1875); *Tuscarora*, Pac.Sta. (Oct 1875-Aug 1876): *Portsmouth*, Pac.Sta. (Aug-Sep 1876); *Plymouth*, Pac.Sqdn. (Sep 1876-Jan 1877); *Lackawanna* (Jan-Aug 1877); w.o. (Aug 1877-Jan 1878); USNA (Jan 1878); w.o. (Jan-Mar 1878); *Constellation*, spec.serv., Paris Exposition, Paris (Mar-Jul 1878); w.o. (Jul-Oct 1878); *Ticonderoga*, spec.serv. (Nov 1878-Sep 1881); w.o. (Sep-Dec 1881); rec. ship, *Passaic*, Washington, DC (Dec 1881-May 1882); Hydrographic Office, Washington, DC (May 1882-Sep 1883); spec.serv., expd. to determine longitudes (Sep 1883-Jun 1884); *Powhatan*, N.Atl.Sqdn. (Jun-Jul 1884); *Quinnebaug*, Eur.Sta. (Jul 1884-Sep 1887); w.o. (Sep-Oct 1887); ord. instruction, Navy Yard, Washington, DC (Nov-Dec 1887); Bur. of Ord., Washington, DC (Dec 1887-Dec 1892); cdr, *Cushing*, Torp.Sta., Newport, RI (Dec 1892-Aug 1895); w.o. (Aug-Sep 1895); Torp.Sta., Newport, RI (Sep 1895); *Maine*, N.Atl.Sqdn. (Sep 1895-Sep 1896); l.o.a. (Sep-Oct 1896); Torp.Sta., Newport, RI (Oct 1896-Mar 1898); Bur. of Ord., Washington, DC (Apr-May 1898); asst. chief, Bur. of Ord., Washington, DC (May-Jul 1898); rec. ship, *St. Louis*, League Island, PA (Jul 1898); cdr, *Kanawha*, N.Atl.Flt. (Jul-Oct 1898); cdr, *Eagle*, surv. duty (Oct 1898-Jul 1901); home and w.o. (Jul-Aug 1901); Navy Yard, Washington, DC (Sep 1901-May 1902); ord. insp., and in charge, Torp.Sta., Newport, RI (Jun 1902-Nov 1904); member, bd. of torp. vessels (Oct 1904-Mar 1905); flgs., *Ohio*, Asia.Sta. (Mar-Nov 1905); chief of staff, Asia.Sta., *Ohio* (May-Nov 1905); cdr, *Raleigh*, Asia.Sta. (Nov 1905-Feb 1907); home and w.o. (Feb-May 1907); NWC (Jun-Oct 1907); member, spec. bd. on naval ord. (Oct 1907-Sep 1908); duty connected with Gen Bd., Washington, DC (Dec 1907-Sep

1908); cdr, *Vermont*, Atl.Flt. (Nov 1908-Feb 1910); Navy Dept., Washington, DC (Feb-Mar 1910); aide to sec. of navy for div. of material, Navy Dept., Washington, DC (Mar 1910-Jul 1912); cdr, 4th Div., Atl.Flt, *Missouri* (Aug-Sep 1912), then *Ohio* (Sep-Oct 1912), then *Minnesota* (Oct 1912-Jan 1913); cdr, 2nd Div., Atl. Flt., *Vermont* (Jan-Jun 1913), then *Louisiana* (Jun-Oct 1913); cdr, 3rd Div., Atl.Flt., *Rhode Island* (Nov 1913-Feb 1914); cdr, 1st Div., Atl.Flt., *Florida* (Feb-May 1914), then *Arkansas* (May-Sep 1914); cdr, Atl.Flt., *Wyoming* (Sep-Oct 1914), then *New York* (Oct 1914-Jan 1915), then *Wyoming* (Jan 1915-Jun 1916); member, Gen Bd., Navy Dept., Washington, DC (Jun 1916-Nov 1919); member, Army-Navy Joint Bd., Washington, DC (Nov 1916-Nov 1919); placed on Ret.Lst. (23 Nov 1919).

Career Highlights Served on board the *Ticonderoga*, which sailed around the world to open new commercial ties and to expand existing ones. While with Bur. of Ord., contributed to the design and manufacturing of gun mechanisms, which increased the speed of rapid-fire guns. Campaigned for the implementation of range lights for all naval vessels, which the navy adopted in 1890. In 1893, developed first doctrine on use of torpedo warfare. Commanded the *Vermont* as part of "Great White Flt." As cdr of forces off w.cst. of Mexico in Apr 1914, ordered by Pres. Wilson to seize the customs house at Vera Cruz, subsequently being awarded the Medal of Honor. During World War I, served valuable role as member of Army-Navy Joint Bd. and as a member of the War Industries Bd. Also won Distinguished Service Medal for the Navy and Distinguished Service Medal for Army.

References

Personal Papers: ca. 7500 items (1873-1928) in Univ. of VA Lib., Charlottesville, VA.

Writings: a) "Range Lights on Seagoing Ships," U.S. Naval Institute *Proceedings* 39 (1886): 463-76. b) "War Time Control of Industry," U.S. Naval Institute *Proceedings* 246 (Aug 1923): 1237-42.

WILLIAM MAYHEW FOLGER Born in Massillon, OH, on 19 May 1844, son of Robert and Amelia (Heyden) Folger. Married twice: to Annie W. Merrill on 8 Apr 1875, and to Mary Eleanor Gilmour on 20 Oct 1899. Two children. Died on Cornish, NH, on 22 Jul 1928. Buried in Mt. Auburn Cemetery, Cambridge, MA.

Ranks Act.Midn (21 Sep 1861); title changed to Midn (16 Jul 1862); Ens (1 Nov 1866); Mstr (1 Dec 1866); Lt (12 Mar 1868); LCdr (27 Apr 1868); Cdr (1 Mar 1885); Chief, Bur. of Ord. with rank of Commo (12 Feb 1890); Capt (6 Feb 1898); RAdm (1 Jun 1904); retired (30 Jun 1905).

Career Summary Received appointment from OH (21 Sep 1861); USNA (Sep 1861-Nov 1864); l.o.a. (Nov 1864-Feb 1865); rec. ship, *North Carolina*, NY (Feb-Jun 1865); *Sabine*, New London, CT (Jun-Jul 1865); flgs., *Hartford*, Asia.Sqdn. (Jul 1865-Aug 1868); w.o. (Aug-Oct 1868); rec. ship, *New Hampshire*, Navy Yard, Norfolk, VA (Oct-Dec 1868); flgs., *Franklin*, Eur.

WILLIAM MAYHEW FOLGER
1844-1928

Sqdn. (Dec 1868-Jan 1872); w.o. (Jan-Feb 1872); ord. duty, Pittsburgh (Feb 1872-Apr 1875); l.o.a. (Apr 1875-Mar 1876); exec.off., *Marion*, Eur.Sta. (Mar 1876-Dec 1877); w.o. (Dec 1877-Jan 1878); ord. duty, Navy Yard, Washington, DC (Feb-Jun 1878); USNA (Jun 1878-Mar 1879); cdr, training ship, *Mayflower* (Mar-Sep 1879); spec. duty, Springfield, MA (Sep-Dec 1879); exec.off., *Swatara*, Asia.Sta. (Dec 1879-Jul 1882); w.o. (Jul-Oct 1882); Bur. of Ord., Washington, DC, and ord. duty, USNA (Oct 1882-Dec 1885); l.o.a. (Dec 1885-Oct 1886); insp. of ord., Navy Yard, Washington, DC (Oct 1886-Mar 1887); cdr, *Quinnebaug*, Eur.Sta. (Apr 1887-Sep 1888); insp. of ord., Navy Yard, Washington, DC (Oct 1888-Feb 1890); chief, Bur. of Ord., Washington, DC (Feb 1890-Jan 1893); l.o.a. (Jan-Nov 1893); Compass Office, Navy Dept., Washington, DC (Nov 1893-Jan 1894); cdr, *Yorktown*, Pac. and Asia.Stas. (Jan 1894-Oct 1895); home and l.o.a. (Oct 1895-Jan 1896); w.o. (Jan-Apr 1896); insp., 11th L.h. Dist., Detroit (Apr 1896-Jan 1898); insp., 3rd L.h. Dist., Tomkinsville, NY (Feb-Apr 1898); cdr, *New Orleans*, N.Atl.Flt. (Apr 1898-Feb 1899); general insp., *Kearsarge*, N.Atl.Flt. (Feb 1899-Feb 1900); cdr, *Kearsarge*, N.Atl.Flt. (Feb 1900-May 1901); chief of staff, N.Atl.Flt., *Kearsarge* (Nov 1900-May 1901); insp., 3rd L.h. Dist., Tompkinsville, NY (May 1901-Mar 1904); cdr, Philippine Sqdn., Asia.Flt., *Rainbow, New Orleans*, then *Baltimore* (May 1904-Mar 1905); cdr, Asia.Flt., *Wisconsin* (Mar 1905); home and w.o. (Mar-Jun 1905); retired (30 Jun 1905).

References

Writings: a) "On Recent Modifications of the Explosive Force of Gunpowder," U.S. Naval Institute *Proceedings* 7 (1879): 99-117. b) *Machine Guns and the Adaptability of the Gatlin Gun for Naval Purposes* (Washington, DC: 1880).

JOHN DONALDSON FORD Born in Baltimore on 19 May 1840, son of Thomas C. and Isabella (Logie) Ford. Received education in the Baltimore public schools. Graduated from the Maryland Institute School of Design in 1861. He received the first Peabody Prize. Graduated from the Potts School of Mechanical Engineering in Jun 1862. Married Laura Jane Darling on 30 Apr 1866. One son and four daughters. Resided in Baltimore, dying there on 8 Apr 1918. Buried in Baltimore's Greenwood Cemetery.

Ranks 3rd Asst.Engr. (30 Jul 1862); 2nd Asst.Engr. (14 Feb 1864); 1st Asst.Engr. (6 Jun 1868); title changed to PAsst.Engr. (14 Feb 1874); Chief Engr. (27 Dec 1890); Chief Engr. with rel. rank of Cdr (29 Jul 1897); Cdr (3 Mar 1899); Capt (5 Mar 1902); placed on Ret.Lst. with rank of RAdm (19 May 1902).

Career Summary Received appointment from MD (30 Jul 1862); *Richmond*, W.Gulf Blk.Sqdn. (Oct 1862-Jun 1864); in charge of machinery, prize steamer, *Donegal*, Philadelphia (Jun 1864); *Richmond*, W.Gulf Blk.Sqdn. (Jul-Aug 1864); in charge of machinery, former prize *Tennessee*, W.Gulf Blk.Sqdn. (Aug 1864); in charge of machinery, former prize *Selma*, W.Gulf Blk.Sqdn. (Aug 1864-Feb 1865); *Arizona*, Mississippi River Flot. (Feb 1865); flgs., *Estrella*, W.Gulf Blk.Sqdn. (Mar-Jul 1865); *Sebago*, W.Gulf

JOHN DONALDSON FORD
1840-1918

Blk.Sqdn. (Jul 1865); w.o. (Jul-Oct 1865); experimental duty, *Pensacola*, Baltimore (Oct 1865-May 1866); w.o. (May-Jul 1866); experimental duty, *Guerriere*, Boston (Jul-Oct 1866); *Sacramento*, spec.serv. (Oct 1866-Nov 1867); home and w.o. (Nov 1867-Feb 1868); in charge, machinery afloat, Navy Yard, Norfolk, VA (Feb-Dec 1868); *Swatara*, Eur.Sqdn. (Dec 1868-Jun 1869); l.o.a. (Jun-Oct 1869); *Miantonomoh*, spec.serv. and N.Atl.Sqdn. (Oct 1869-Jul 1870); w.o. (Jul 1870-Sep 1871); Navy Yard, Norfolk, VA (Sep 1871-Sep 1872); *Hartford*, Asia.Sqdn. (Oct 1872-Oct 1875); w.o. (Oct 1875-Jan 1876); member, naval exam. bd., Washington, DC (Jan-Aug 1876); w.o. (Aug-Sep 1876); member, naval exam. bd. (Oct 1876-Mar 1878); spec. duty, Bur. of Steam Engineering, Washington, DC (Mar 1878-Nov 1879); flgs., *Tennessee*, W.Ind. and N.Atl.Stas. (Nov 1879-Apr 1883); w.o. (Apr-May 1883); Bur. of Steam Engineering, Washington, DC (May 1883-Mar 1884); spec. duty, Manual Training School, Baltimore (Mar 1884-Jul 1890); trial duty, *San Francisco*, San Francisco (Aug-Sep 1890); rec. ship, *Independence*, Mare Island, CA (Sep-Oct 1890); *Alert*, Bering Sea and N.Atl.Sta. (Oct 1890-Oct 1893); l.o.a. (Oct 1893-Jan 1894); member and recorder, engr.exam.bd., Philadelphia (Jan-Feb 1894); organizer and inst., Mechanical Engineering, Maryland Agriculture and Mechanical College, Baltimore (Feb 1894-Aug 1896); *Brooklyn*, William Cramp and Sons Iron Works, Philadelphia (Aug-Dec 1896); *Brooklyn*, N.Atl.Sqdn. (Dec 1896-Jan 1898); flt.engr, Pac.Flt., then Asia.Flt., *Baltimore* (Feb-Dec 1898); flt.engr, Asia.Flt, *Olympia* (Dec 1898-May 1899); home and w.o. (May-Jun 1899); insp. of machinery and ord., Columbia Iron Works, Baltimore, and Maryland Steel Company, Sparrow's Point, MD (Jun 1899-Dec 1907); transferred to Ret.Lst. (19 May 1902).

Career Highlights Instrumental in establishing the Baltimore Manual Technical School in 1884 and in beginning a course in mechanical engineering at the Maryland Agricultural and Mechanical College. Was flt.engr. for Asia.Sqdn. in 1898, taking part in Battle of Manila Bay, in capture of forts on Corregidor, and in capture of Manila.

References
Writings: *An American Cruiser in the East: Travels and Studies in the Far East* (NY: 1898).

CHARLES THOMAS FORSE Born in Pittsburgh on 29 Dec 1846, son of William and Marianne (Boyer) Forse. Remained unmarried. Retired to Pittsburgh, where he died on 13 Apr 1925. Buried in Pittsburgh's Homewood Cemetery.

Ranks Midn (24 Sep 1863); Ens (19 Apr 1869); Mstr (12 Jul 1870); Lt (11 Feb 1873); LCdr (22 Jun 1894); Cdr (3 Mar 1899); Capt (11 Oct 1903); retired (26 Dec 1903); RAdm (13 Apr 1911) to rank from 26 Dec 1903.

Career Summary Received appointment from KY (24 Sep 1863); USNA (Sep 1863-Jun 1868); found deficient and turned back (Jun 1866); l.o.a. (Jun-Sep 1868); *Jamestown*, Pac.Sqdn. (Oct 1868-Aug 1869); home and w.o. (Aug-Nov 1869); *Alaska*,

Asia.Sqdn. (Dec 1869-Sep 1873); *Ossipee*, Pac.Sta. (Oct 1873-Sep 1876); w.o. (Sep-Oct 1876); l.o.a. (Oct 1876-Nov 1877); *Pensacola*, Pac.Sta. (Nov 1877); *Lackawanna*, Pac.Sta. (Nov-Dec 1877); rec. ship, *Independence*, Mare Island, CA (Dec 1877-Jan 1878); *Tuscarora*, spec.serv. (Jan 1878-Mar 1880); w.o. (Mar 1880-Jan 1881); *Ranger*, surv. duty (Jan 1881-Mar 1884); home and w.o. (Mar-Jul 1884); cst.surv. duty (Jul 1884-Dec 1887); insp. of steel, new cruisers, Philadelphia (Dec 1887-Jun 1892); *Kearsarge*, N.Atl.Sta. (Jul 1892-Mar 1894); home and w.o. (Mar 1894); spec. duty (Mar-Apr 1894); insp. of steel, Homestead Steel Works, Munhall, PA (Apr 1894-Jun 1897); cst.surv. duty (Jun 1897-Apr 1898); Navy Yard, NY (Apr 1898); cdr, *Lebanon*, N.Atl.Flt. (Apr 1898-Mar 1899); insp., 14th L.h. Dist., Cincinnati (Mar 1899-Jul 1900); cdr, *Celtic*, Asia.Flt. (Aug 1900-Jul 1902); Naval Hosp., Yokohama, Japan (Jul-Sep 1902); home and w.o. (Sep 1902-Jan 1903); Navy Yard, Pensacola, FL (Jan-Dec 1903); retired (26 Dec 1903).

JAMES MCQUEEN FORSYTH
1842-1915

JAMES MCQUEEN FORSYTH   Born on Long Island, Bahamas, British W.Indies, on 1 Jan 1842, son of James and Catherine Ann (Taylor) Forsyth. Emigrated to U.S. in 1853. Graduated from Central High School in Philadelphia in Feb 1858. Served at sea as a sailor before the mast from 1858 to 1861 when entering volunteer navy. Received an honorary M.A. in 1886. Married Mary J. M. Perkins on 1 Aug 1871. After her death, married Caroline A. Helfenstein on 7 Oct 1903. Resided in Shamokin, PA, where he died on 3 Aug 1915. Buried in Arlington National Cemetery.

Ranks   Volunteer 2nd Class Pilot (1 Aug 1861); Act.Master's Mate (25 Sep 1861); Act.Ens (5 Sep 1862); Act.Mstr (26 Aug 1864); Mstr (12 Mar 1868); Lt (18 Dec 1868); LCdr (9 May 1878); Cdr (12 Feb 1889); Capt (3 Mar 1899); retired (25 Sep 1901); RAdm on Ret.Lst. (13 Apr 1911) to rank from 25 Sep 1901.

Career Summary   Received appointment as Act.Master's Mate (25 Sep 1861); *Water Witch*, *Nantucket*, and *Columbia*, S. and N.Atl.Blk.Sqdns. and W.Gulf Blk.Sqdn. (Sep 1861-Jun 1865); l.o.a. (Jun-Jul 1865); exec.off., *Nyack*, Pac.Sqdn. (Jul 1865-Apr 1868); received appointment from PA as Mstr (12 Mar 1868); w.o. (Apr-Jun 1868); exec.off., *Purveyor*, spec.serv. (Jun 1868-Apr 1869); w.o. (Apr-May 1869); rec. ship, *Potomac*, Philadelphia (May 1869-Apr 1870); exec.off., *Saugus*, then *Ajax*, N.Atl.Sqdn. (May 1870-Jun 1871); Navy Yard, Philadelphia (Jun 1871-Dec 1872); exec.off., *Supply*, spec.serv., Vienna Exposition (Jan-Nov 1873); w.o. (Nov-Dec 1873); rec. ship, *Potomac*, League Island, PA (Dec 1873); Navy Yard, Philadelphia (Dec 1873-Feb 1874); navigator, *Powhatan*, N.Atl.Sqdn. (Feb 1874-Feb 1877); sick lv. (Feb-Jun 1877); torp. instruction, Newport, RI (Jun-Sep 1877); navigation duty, Navy Yard, League Island, PA (Sep 1877-Mar 1880); exec.off., *Constellation*, spec.serv. (Mar-Jun 1880); w.o. (Jun 1880-Mar 1881); exec.off., rec. ship, *Colorado*, NY (Mar-Jun 1881); w.o. (Jun-Aug 1881); *Lancaster*, Eur.Sta. (Aug 1881-Jun

1884); home and w.o. (Jul-Nov 1884); l.o.a. (Nov 1884-Jun
1885); Navy Yard, League Island, PA (Jun 1885-Apr 1886);
Naval Asylum, Philadelphia (Apr 1886-Jul 1889); cdr, *Tallapoosa,*
S.Atl.Sta. (Oct 1889-Mar 1892); l.o.a. (Mar-Jun 1892); Naval
Home, Philadelphia (Jun 1892-Jun 1895); cdr of monitors,
Richmond, VA (Jun-Aug 1895); cdr, Naval Sta., Key West, FL
(Aug 1895-Oct 1898); sick lv. and convalescence, Naval Hosp.,
Philadelphia (Oct 1898-Jan 1899); w.o. (Jan-Mar 1899); Naval
Home, Philadelphia (Mar-Apr 1899); cdr, *Baltimore,* Asia.Sqdn.
(May 1899-Feb 1900); chief of staff, U.S. Naval Force, Asia.Sta.,
Brooklyn (Aug-Dec 1899); cdr, *Brooklyn,* and chief of staff, U.S.
Naval Force, Asia.Sta. (Feb-Apr 1900); cdr, *Baltimore,* Asia.Sta.
(Apr-Sep 1900); home and w.o. (Sep-Nov 1900); cdr, training
ship, *Indiana* (Nov 1900-May 1901); capt.yd., Navy Yard, Mare
Island, CA (Jun-Aug 1901); home and w.o. (Aug-Sep 1901);
retired (25 Sep 1901).

Career Highlights During the Civil War, participated in
captures of forts Clarke and Hatteras, and in actions on Lower
Mississippi River from forts Jackson and St. Philip through to
Vicksburg. Saw action against the forts guarding Charleston
Harbor. Was in charge of the Key West Naval Sta. when the
Maine blew up in Havana Harbor, continuing as such throughout
the Spanish-American War, and receiving special commendation
for his efforts in successfully supplying American naval forces with
quantities of coal.

JOSEPH FOSTER Born in Gloucester, MA, on 17 Jun 1841,
son of Joseph and Adelaide Coues (Spalding) Foster. Educated in
public and private schools in Portsmouth, NH. Married Helen
Dickey on 7 Oct 1875. Four children. Married a second time on
17 Mar 1906 to Josephine Hunt of Broxbourne, Hertfordshire,
England. Died on 18 May 1930 in Portsmouth, NH.

Ranks Captain's Clerk (3 Oct 1862); Act.Asst.Paymstr. (19
Oct 1863); Asst.Paymstr. (23 Jul 1866); PAsst.Paymstr. (10 May
1867); Paymstr. (23 Feb 1877); Pay Insp. (15 Jun 1898); Pay Dir.
with rank of Capt (27 Aug 1901); transferred to Ret.Lst. with
rank of RAdm (9 Dec 1902).

Career Summary Received appointment from NH (3 Oct
1862); *Augusta,* S.Atl.Blk.Sqdn. (Nov 1862-Sep 1863); w.o.
(Oct-Nov 1863); *Acacia,* S.Atl.Blk.Sqdn. (Nov 1863-May 1865);
s.a. (May-Jul 1865); *Commodore McDonough,* S.Atl.Blk.Sqdn.
(Jul-Aug 1865); s.a. and w.o. (Aug-Oct 1865); *Tallapoosa,* Gulf
Sqdn. (Oct 1865-Aug 1866); s.a. and w.o. (Aug-Dec 1866);
Marblehead, N.Atl.Sqdn. (Dec 1866); *Aroostook,* Asia.Sta. (Dec
1866-Sep 1869); s.a. and w.o. (Sep 1869-Mar 1871); *Shawmut,*
N.Atl.Sta. (Mar 1871-May 1875); s.a. and w.o. (May-Sep 1875);
Torp.Sta., Newport, RI (Sep 1875-Oct 1879); s.a. and w.o. (Oct
1879); *Monocacy,* Asia.Sta. (Dec 1879-Nov 1882); s.a. and w.o.
(Nov 1882-Sep 1883); Naval Asylum, Philadelphia (Sep 1883-
Oct 1886); s.a. and w.o. (Oct-Nov 1886); spec. duty and asst. to
general storekeeper, Navy Yard, Portsmouth, NH (Feb 1887-Feb
1888); *Pensacola,* N.Atl.Sta. (Mar-Dec 1888); s.a. (Dec 1888);

JOSEPH FOSTER
1841-1930

general storekeeper, Navy Yard, Norfolk, VA (Dec 1888-Jul 1889); s.a. (Jul 1889-Jul 1890); paymstr. and purchasing off., Navy Yard, Portsmouth, NH (Jul 1890-Jul 1893); s.a. and w.o. (Jul-Sep 1893); *San Francisco*, N.Atl., S.Atl., and Eur.Stas. (Oct 1893-Oct 1896); s.a. and w.o. (Oct-Nov 1896); paymstr. and purchasing off., Navy Yard, Portsmouth, NH (Nov 1896-May 1898); paymstr., purchasing off., general storekeeper, and pay off., auxiliary vessels, Naval Sta., Key West, FL (May-Jun 1898); s.a. and w.o. (Jun-Jul 1898); paymstr. and purchasing off., Navy Yard, Portsmouth, NH (Jul 1898-Jun 1899); flt.paymstr, N.Atl.Flt., *New York* (Jun 1899-Nov 1900), then *Kearsarge* (Dec 1900-Jul 1901); s.a. and w.o. (Jul-Dec 1901); general storekeeper, Navy Yard, Portsmouth, NH (Dec 1901-Oct 1903); transferred to Ret.Lst. (9 Dec 1902).

References
Writings: *The Graves We Decorate* (Storer Post, G.A.R., Portsmouth, NH: 1893).

CHARLES EBEN FOX
1851-1916

CHARLES EBEN FOX Born in Chelsea, MA, on 20 Sep 1851, son of navy surg. John Lawrence and Elizabeth Amory (Morris) Fox. Maternal grandfather was Commo Charles Morris, USN. Married Nelly Beckwith on 10 Jun 1884. At least one son. Resided in Washington, DC, where he died on 12 Feb 1916. Buried in Arlington National Cemetery.

Ranks Midn (25 Jun 1868); title change to Cadet Midn (15 Jun 1870); Midn (1 Jun 1872); Ens (15 Jul 1873); Mstr (25 Nov 1877); title changed to Ltjg (3 Mar 1883); Lt (2 Aug 1884); LCdr (3 Mar 1899); Cdr (16 Mar 1902); Capt (5 Aug 1906); RAdm (16 Sep 1910); retired (2 Aug 1911).

Career Summary Received appointment as the son of an officer (25 Jun 1868); USNA (Jun 1868-Jun 1872); w.o. (Jun-Sep 1872); *Hartford*, Asia.Sta. (Oct 1872-Oct 1875); Hydrographic Office, Washington, DC (Nov 1875-Sep 1876); *Hartford*, NY (Oct-Nov 1876); *Adams*, N.Atl.Sta. (Nov 1876-Mar 1878); home and w.o. (Mar-May 1878); l.o.a. (May-Aug 1878); cst.surv. duty (Aug 1878-Jul 1879); w.o. (Jul-Oct 1879); *Nipsic*, Eur.Sta. (Nov 1879-Mar 1883); spec. duty, Bur. of Nav., Washington, DC (Apr 1883-Mar 1884); aide to Adm David D. Porter, Washington, DC (Mar 1884-Mar 1886); *Iroquois*, Pac.Sta. (Apr 1886-May 1887); *Vandalia*, Pac.Sta. (May 1887-Jan 1889); *Mohican*, Pac.Sta. (Jan-Mar 1889); home and w.o. (Mar-May 1889); l.o.a. (Jun-Oct 1889); Office of Naval Intelligence, Navy Dept., Washington, DC (Oct 1889-Dec 1892); flag lt, Pac.Sta., *Mohican* (Jan-May 1893), then *Boston* (May-Sep 1893), then *Philadelphia* (Sep-Nov 1893); flag lt, Asia.Sta., *Lancaster* (Dec 1893-Jan 1894), then *Baltimore* (Jan-Jul 1894); l.o.a. (Jul-Aug 1894); staff duty, Pac.Sta., *Philadelphia* (Aug 1894-Dec 1895); home and l.o.a. (Dec 1895-Feb 1896); Bur. of Nav., Washington, DC (Feb-Aug 1896); Library and War Records Office, Washington, DC (Sep 1896-Mar 1897); Naval Observatory, Washington, DC (Mar-Oct 1897); exec.off., *Vicksburg*, on trials and N.Atl.Sta. (Oct 1897-Apr 1898); insp., *Morris*, Bristol, RI (Apr-May 1898); cdr, *Morris*,

N.Atl.Flt. (May-Nov 1898); *Olympia,* Asia.Sta. (Dec 1898-May 1899); *Helena,* Asia.Sta. (May 1899-Mar 1900); cdr, *General Alava,* Asia.Sta. (Mar-Sep 1900); home, w.o., and l.o.a. (Sep-Nov 1900); Naval Observatory, Washington, DC (Nov 1900-Aug 1902); duty with, then cdr, training ship, *Adams* (Aug 1902-Jun 1904); cdr, *Wheeling,* Puget Sound, WA (Jun-Aug 1904); home and l.o.a. (Aug-Oct 1904); aide to comdt., Navy Yard, Norfolk, VA (Oct 1904-May 1905); asst., then insp., 11th L.h. Dist., Detroit (May 1905-Sep 1906); s.a., home, and w.o. (Sep-Nov 1906); court-martial duty, Navy Yard, Washington, DC (Nov 1906-Aug 1907); duty with, then cdr, *South Dakota,* Pac.Flt. (Aug 1907-Nov 1908); Naval Hosp., Mare Island, CA, and l.o.a. (Nov-Dec 1908); cdr, rec. ship, *Wabash,* Boston (Jan 1908-Dec 1909); cdr, rec. ship, *Lancaster,* Philadelphia (Dec 1909-Mar 1910); Navy Yard, Charleston, SC (Apr-Jun 1910); comdt., Navy Yard, Charleston, SC (Jun 1910-Oct 1911); retired (2 Aug 1911).

LEONARD AUGUSTUS FRAILEY Born in Washington, DC, on 8 Aug 1843, son of Charles S. and Caroline M. B. Frailey. Received education at Union Academy, Gonzaga College, and Young Commercial College. Married Helen Watson Freeman on 28 Sep 1869. Made his home in Washington, DC, where he died on 31 Dec 1913. Buried in Arlington National Cemetery.

Ranks Act.Asst.Paymstr. (20 Aug 1864); PAsst.Paymstr. (23 Jul 1866); Paymstr. (29 Jan 1869); Pay Insp. (24 May 1894); Pay Dir. (29 Aug 1899); transferred to Ret.Lst. with rank of RAdm (17 Feb 1905).

Career Summary Received appointment from Washington, DC (20 Aug 1864); *Quaker City,* N.Atl. and W.Gulf Blk.Sqdns. (Sep 1864-May 1865); s.a. (May-Jun 1865); *Nyack,* Pac.Sqdn. (Jun 1865-Apr 1867); home and w.o. (Apr-Aug 1867); spec. duty, Navy Yard, Washington, DC (Sep 1867-Jun 1868); w.o. (Jun-Sep 1868); insp. of provisions and clothing, Naval Sta., Mound City, IL (Oct 1868-Apr 1871); s.a. and w.o. (Apr-May 1871); *Wachusett,* Eur.Sqdn. (Jun 1871-Mar 1874); *Wyoming,* N.Atl.Sta. and Navy Yard, Washington, DC (Mar-May 1874); s.a. and w.o. (May 1874-Jan 1875); Bur. of Provision and Clothing, Washington, DC (Jan-Dec 1875); Navy Yard, Norfolk, VA (Jan 1876-Jan 1879); s.a. and w.o. (Jan 1879-Mar 1880); training ship, *Dale* (Jun 1880); s.a. and w.o. (Jun 1880-Mar 1881); training ship, *Constitution* (Apr-Dec 1881); s.a. and w.o. (Dec 1881); Navy Yard, Norfolk, VA (Jan 1882-Jan 1885); s.a. and w.o. (Jan 1885); *Marion,* Asia.Sqdn. (Jan 1885-Sep 1886); *Ossipee,* Asia.Sqdn. (Sep 1886-Mar 1887); s.a. and w.o. (Mar-Apr 1887); spec. duty, Navy Dept., Washington, DC (Apr 1887-Mar 1891); flt.paymstr., Asia.Sqdn., *Lancaster* (Mar-Oct 1891); *Lancaster,* Asia.Sqdn. (Oct 1891-Feb 1892); flt.paymstr., Asia.Sqdn., *Lancaster* (Feb 1892-Jun 1894); s.a. and l.o.a. (Jun-Dec 1894); Bur. of Supplies and Accounts, Washington, DC (Dec 1894-Jul 1895); Navy Yard, Washington, DC (Jul 1895-Jun 1898); Naval Sta., Key West, FL (Jun 1898); *Lancaster,* N.Atl.Flt. (Jun-Sep 1898); s.a. and w.o. (Sep-Oct 1898); spec. duty, Bur. of Supplies and Accounts,

LEONARD AUGUSTUS FRAILEY
1843-1913

Washington, DC (Oct-Nov 1898); Navy Yard, Washington, DC (Nov-Dec 1898); Bur. of Supplies and Accounts, Washington, DC (Dec 1898-Apr 1899); gen storekeeper, Navy Yard, Washington, DC (Apr 1899-Nov 1901); Pay Office, Washington, DC (Nov 1901-Jun 1905) transferred to Ret.Lst. (17 Feb 1905).

JOHN CHARLES FREMONT Born in San Francisco on 19 Apr 1851, son of MGen John Charles (USA) and Jessie (Benton) Fremont. His father was the famous explorer, territorial governor and Senator of CA. Married Sally Anderson on 27 May 1877. Two daughters and one son. Died at the Boston Navy Yard on 7 Mar 1911. Buried at Sparkhill, NY.

Ranks Midn (25 Jun 1868); title changed to Cadet Midn (15 Jul 1870); Midn (1 Jun 1872); Ens (15 Jul 1873); Mstr (25 Nov 1877); title changed to Ltjg (3 Mar 1883); Lt (2 Sep 1884); LCdr (3 Mar 1899); Cdr (11 Apr 1902); Capt (10 Oct 1906); RAdm (22 Sep 1910); died (7 Mar 1911).

Career Summary Received appointment by being son of officer (25 Jun 1868); USNA (Jun 1868-Jun 1872); w.o. (Jun-Aug 1872); l.o.a. (Aug-Oct 1872); *Wabash*, Eur.Sta. (Nov 1872-Mar 1874); l.o.a. (Mar 1874-Apr 1875); resigned (30 Jun 1875); resignation revoked (1 Jul 1875); w.o. (Jul-Nov 1875); *Powhatan*, spec.serv. (Nov 1875-Jul 1878); spec. duty, 3rd L.h. Dist., Tompkinsville, NY (Jul 1878-Oct 1880); *Shenandoah*, S.Atl.Sta. (Dec 1880-Mar 1881); home and w.o. (Mar-May 1881); cst.surv. duty (May 1881-Jul 1884); *Lackawanna*, Pac.Sta. (Aug-Sep 1884); *Hartford*, Pac.Sta. (Sep 1884-Jan 1887); w.o. (Jan-Mar 1887); Hydrographic Office, Washington, DC (Mar 1887-Dec 1888); recorder, bd. of inspection (Dec 1888-Apr 1889); torp. instruction, Newport, RI (May-Aug 1889); NWC (Aug-Oct 1889); ord. instruction, Navy Yard, Washington, DC (Oct 1889-Apr 1890); w.o. (Apr-Jul 1890); flgs., *Philadelphia*, N. Atl.Sta., and Naval Review Flt. (Jul 1890-Jun 1893); l.o.a. (Jun-Sep 1893); asst. to insp., NY Harbor (Sep 1893-Nov 1895); *Indiana*, Navy Yard, Philadelphia (Nov 1895-Nov 1896); cdr, *Cushing*, spec.serv. (Nov 1896-Feb 1897); cdr, *Porter*, on trails, and N.Atl.Sqdn. (Feb 1897-Aug 1898); supervisor, NY Harbor (Aug 1898-Jul 1900); Asia.Sta. (Jul-Aug 1900); temp. duty, Naval Sta., Cavite, P.I. (Aug-Dec 1900); cdr, *Culgoa*, Asia.Sta. (Dec 1900-Mar 1901); *Celtic*, Asia.Sta. (Mar-Apr 1901); capt.yd., Naval Sta., Cavite, P.I. (Apr 1901); Naval Sta., Cavite, P.I. (Apr-Dec 1901); insp. of colliers, Hong Kong, then P.I. (Jan 1902); insp. of vessels, Bur. of Cst. Guard and Transportation under U.S.A. (Jan-Sep 1902); home and w.o. (Sep-Oct 1902); member, bd. of engineers to install search lights for cst. defense, NY (Oct 1902-May 1903); cdr, *Florida*, Cst.Sqdn. (Jun 1903-Oct 1905); member, bd. of inspection and surv., Washington, DC (Oct 1905-Aug 1906); naval attaché, Paris, and St. Petersburg, Russia (Aug 1906-Jan 1908); Bur. of Nav., Washington, DC (Feb 1908); cdr, *Mississippi*, League Island, PA (Feb 1908-Dec 1909); comdt., Navy Yard, Boston (Dec 1909-Mar 1911); died (7 March 1911).

JOHN CHARLES FREMONT
1851-1911

WILLIAM FREELAND FULLAM Born in Pittsford, NY, on 20 Oct 1855, son of Nathan Seymour and Rhoda Ann (Stowits) Fullam. Married Mariana Winder on 15 Apr 1885. Two daughters. Died in Washington, DC, on 23 Sep 1926. Buried in USNA Cemetery.

Ranks Cadet Midn (25 Sep 1873); Midn (18 Jun 1879); Ens (13 Mar 1880); Ltjg (7 Oct 1886); Lt (28 May 1892); LCdr (29 Dec 1899); Cdr (1 Jul 1905); Capt (24 Jun 1909); RAdm (15 Dec 1914); placed on Ret.Lst. (20 Oct 1919).

Career Summary Received appointment from NY (25 Sep 1873); USNA (Sep 1873-Jun 1877); w.o. (Jun-Sep 1877); *Marion,* and *Trenton,* Eur.Sta. (Oct 1877-Apr 1879); USNA (May-Jun 1879); w.o. (Jun-Dec 1879); *Swatara,* Asia.Sta. (Dec 1879-Dec 1882); w.o. (Dec 1882-Jan 1883); USNA (Jan 1883-May 1887); *Boston,* spec.serv. (May 1887-Feb 1889); *Vesuvius,* Navy Yard, Philadelphia (Feb-Oct 1889); *Yorktown,* Sqdn. of Evol. (Oct 1889-Jun 1890); *Chicago,* Sqdn. of Evol. (Jun 1890-Jan 1891); l.o.a. (Jan-Feb 1891); spec. duty, Navy Dept., Washington, DC (Feb-Mar 1891); USNA (Mar 1891-May 1894); *Raleigh,* Sqdn. of Evol. (May 1894-Apr 1897); *Amphitrite,* N.Atl.Sta. (Apr-Jun 1897); USNA (Jul 1897-Apr 1898); *New Orleans,* N.Atl.Flt. (Apr-Oct 1898); USNA (Oct 1898-Jun 1899); training ship, *Lancaster* (Jul 1899-Jun 1902); NWC (Jun-Aug 1902); USNA (Aug 1902-Apr 1905); cdr, prac. ship, *Terror* (May-Sep 1905); cdr, *Glacier,* Spec.Serv.Sqdn. (Sep-Nov 1905); home and w.o. (Nov 1905-Mar 1906); Navy Dept., Washington, DC (Mar-May 1906); cdr, *Marietta,* W.Indies (May 1906-Jul 1907); comdt., Training Sta., and cdr, *Constellation,* Newport, RI (Jul 1907-Dec 1909); cdr, *Mississippi,* Atl.Flt. (Dec 1909-Nov 1911); comdt., Training Sta., Great Lakes, IL (Nov 1911-Feb 1913); additional duty, comdt., 9th, 10th, and 11th Naval Dists. (Jun 1912-Feb 1913); aide for inspections, Navy Dept., Washington, DC (Feb-Nov 1913); aide for personnel, Navy Dept., Washington, DC (Nov 1913-Feb 1914); supt., USNA (Feb 1914-Sep 1915); cdr, Pac. Reserve Flt., *Milwaukee, Maryland, Pittsburgh,* and *Colorado* (Oct 1915-May 1917); cdr, Patrol Force, Pac.Flt. (May-Aug 1917); cdr, 2nd Div., Pac.Flt., *Saratoga* (Aug 1917-Jul 1919); home and w.o. (Jul-Oct 1919); placed on Ret.Lst. (20 Oct 1919).

Career Highlights Graduated at top of class from USNA. Served as supt. of USNA, concluding his career as cdr in chief of Pac.Flt. Received, amongst others, the Navy Cross, and the Order of the Rising Sun (Japan).

References

Personal Papers: 3850 items (1877-1919) in NHF,LC.

Writings: a) "The System of Naval Training and Discipline Required to Promote Efficiency and Attract Americans," U.S. Naval Institute *Proceedings* 55 (1890): 473-95. b) "Street Riot Drill," U.S. Naval Institute *Proceedings* 69 (1894): 169-80. c) "The Organization, Training, and Discipline of the Navy Personnel as Viewed from the Ship," U.S. Naval Institute *Proceedings* 77 (1896): 83-116. d) *Hand Book of Infantry and Artillery, United States Navy* (Washington, DC: 1899). e) "The Employment of

WILLIAM FREELAND FULLAM
1855-1926

Petty Officers in the Navy," U.S. Naval Institute *Proceedings* 103 (Sep 1902): 467-73. f) "The Training of Landsmen for the Navy," U.S. Naval Institute *Proceedings* 103 (Sep 1902): 475-84. g) *Text-Book of Ordnance and Gunnery* (Washington, DC: 1903). h) *The Recruits' Handy Book, U.S. Navy* (Washington, DC: 1903). i) "'Reports of Fitness' in the Case of Naval Academy Graduates," U.S. Naval Institute *Proceedings* 107 (Sep 1903): 661-78. j) *The Petty Officers' Drill Book, U.S. Navy* (Washington, DC: 1904). k) "Absence over Leave in the Fleet," U.S. Naval Institute *Proceedings* 140 (Dec 1911): 1103-12. l) "Co-ordinating the Army and Navy," U.S. Naval Institute *Proceedings* 251 (Jan 1924): 14-17.

Additional Sources: John G. Miller, "William Freeland Fullam's War with the Corps," U.S. Naval Institute *Proceedings* 873 (Nov 1975): 37-45.

PERRY GARST
1848-1939

PERRY GARST   Born in Dayton, OH, on 11 Jul 1848, son of Michael Garst. Early education in Champaign, IL. Married to Elizabeth O. Garst. One daughter. Died in Bradenton, FL, on 29 Aug 1939. Buried in USNA Cemetery, Annapolis.

Ranks   Midn (25 Jul 1863); Ens (19 Apr 1869); Mstr (12 Jul 1870); Lt (5 Apr 1874); LCdr (7 Jun 1895); Cdr (3 Mar 1899); Capt (17 Jun 1904); retired with rank of RAdm (30 Jun 1907).

Career Summary   Received appointment from IL (25 Jul 1863); USNA (Jul 1863-Jun 1868); found deficient and turned back (Sep 1868); w.o. (Jun-Sep 1868); *Kearsarge*, Pac.Sqdn. (Oct 1868-Oct 1869); w.o. (Oct 1869-Apr 1870); *Saranac*, N.Pac. Sqdn. (Apr 1870-Sep 1873); w.o. (Sep-Dec 1873); *Terror*, League Island, PA (Dec 1873); rec. ship, *Potomac*, League Island, PA (Dec 1873-Jan 1874); *Frolic*, spec.serv. (Jan-Apr 1874); w.o. (Apr-Jul 1874); *Palos*, Asia.Sqdn. (Aug 1874-Apr 1878); l.o.a. and w.o. (Apr 1878-Mar 1879); rec. ship, *Franklin*, Norfolk, VA (Mar-Aug 1879); cst.surv. duty (Sep 1879-Jul 1882); w.o. (Jul-Sep 1882); exec.off., rec. ship, *Passaic*, Washington, DC (Sep-Dec 1882); rec. ship, *Franklin*, Norfolk, VA (Dec 1882-Oct 1883); *Shenandoah*, Pac.Sta. (Nov 1883-Oct 1886); home and w.o. (Oct-Dec 1886); ord. duty, Navy Yard, Washington, DC (Jan 1887-May 1888); Judge Advocate Gen's office, Navy Dept., Washington, DC (May 1888-May 1890); training ship, *Jamestown* (Jun 1890-Jun 1892); l.o.a. (Jun-Aug 1892); USNA (Sep 1892-Jul 1896); exec.off., *Newark*, N.Atl.Sta. (Jul 1896-Mar 1897); exec.off., *Raleigh*, N.Atl.Sta. (Mar-Apr 1897); exec.off., *Terror*, N.Atl.Sta. (Apr 1897-Oct 1898); USNA (Oct 1898-Mar 1900); ord. instruction, Navy Yard, Washington, DC (Mar-Apr 1900); Navy Yard, Norfolk, VA (Apr-Jun 1900); cdr, *Isla de Cuba*, Asia.Sta. (Aug 1900-Feb 1902); Naval Hosp., Yokohama, Japan (Feb-Apr 1902); home and sick lv. (Apr-May 1902); NWC (Jun-Jul 1902); court-martial duty (Aug 1902); asst., then insp., 10th L.h. Dist., Buffalo, NY (Aug 1902-Oct 1904); capt.yd., Navy Yard, Portsmouth, NH (Nov 1904-Oct 1905); general insp., then cdr, *Rhode Island*, Quincy, MA, and shakedown cruise (Oct 1905-Jun 1906); suspended (Jun-Dec 1906); w.o. (Dec 1906-Feb 1907); bd. duties (Feb-Dec 1907); retired (30 Jun 1907).

EDWARD HICKMAN GHEEN Born in Delaware County, PA, on 11 Dec 1845, son of Edward and Phebe (Hickman) Gheen. Married Florence Monfort on 17 Oct 1883. Two daughters. Died in Atlantic City, NJ, on 10 Aug 1920.

Ranks Midn (25 Sep 1862); Ens (18 Dec 1868); Mstr (21 Mar 1870); Lt (21 Mar 1871); LCdr (2 Oct 1891); Cdr (28 Mar 1898); Capt (14 Jun 1902); placed on Ret.Lst. (1 Dec 1902); RAdm on Ret.Lst. (13 Apr 1911) to rank from 1 Dec 1902.

Career Summary Received appointment from PA (25 Sep 1862); USNA (Sep 1862-Jun 1867); found deficient and put back (Jun 1864); w.o. (Jun-Sep 1867); *Piscataqua*, and *Delaware*, Asia.Sta. (Oct 1867-Nov 1870); home and w.o. (Dec 1870-Mar 1871); signal duty, Washington, DC (Mar-Jul 1871); w.o. (Jul 1871-Jan 1872); *Mahopac*, N.Atl.Sta. (Jan-Mar 1872); rec. ship, *New Hampshire*, Norfolk, VA (Mar-Apr 1872); *Supply*, spec.serv. (Apr-May 1872); flgs., *Lancaster*, S.Atl.Sta. (May 1872-Jul 1875); w.o. (Jul-Aug 1875); rec. ship, *Potomac*, Philadelphia (Aug 1875-Dec 1876); training ship, *Constitution* (Dec 1876-Jan 1877); *Alliance*, Eur.Sta. (Jan 1877-Jan 1880); w.o. (Jan-Apr 1880); Navy Yard, League Island, PA (Apr 1880-May 1881); Torp.Sta., Newport, RI (Jun-Sep 1881); Navy Yard, League Island, PA (Sep-Dec 1881); flgs., *Tennessee*, N.Atl.Sta. (Dec 1881-Sep 1883); USNA (Sep 1883-Jun 1887); exec.off., *Yantic*, spec.serv. (Jul 1887-Jul 1890); l.o.a. (Jul-Oct 1890); insp. of steel, Pittsburgh and Thurlow, PA (Oct 1890-May 1891); in charge, branch hydrographic office, Philadelphia (May 1891-Jun 1892); l.o.a. (Jun 1892-Mar 1893); Navy Yard, League Island, PA (Apr 1893-Sep 1894); exec.off., *Miantonomoh*, N.Atl.Sta. (Oct-Nov 1894); rec. ship, *Richmond*, Philadelphia (Nov-Dec 1894); exec.off., *Minneapolis*, N.Atl. and Eur.Stas. (Dec 1894-Oct 1896); l.o.a. (Oct-Dec 1896); Hydrographic Office, Washington, DC (Jan 1897-Jun 1898); cdr, *Frolic*, N.Atl.Sta. (Jun-Sep 1898); Hydrographic Office, Washington, DC (Oct 1898-Jun 1899); cdr, *Marietta*, Asia.Sta. (Jun 1899-Apr 1901); cdr, *Petrel*, Asia.Sta. (May-Sep 1901); home and w.o. (Sep 1901-Feb 1902); asst., then insp., 11th L.h. Dist., Detroit (Feb-Sep 1902); in charge, Naval Recruiting Office, and branch hydrographic office, Chicago (Sep 1902-Feb 1903); placed on Ret.Lst. (1 Dec 1902).

EDWARD HICKMAN GHEEN
1845-1920

THOMAS AUGUSTUS GILL Born in Philadelphia on 8 Feb 1840, son of John Stokes and Sarah (Boggs) Gill. Attended Bucknell Univ., receiving A.B., A.M., B.D., and D.D. degrees, his studies being interrupted by two enlistments in the volunteer army during the Civil War. Ordained a Baptist minister in 1868, becoming the pastor of the 1st Baptist Church in Germantown PA, to 1871. Married twice: to Marie Antoinette Nevin on 8 Apr 1875, and Rachel Hurst Souderl. Two children. Died in Littleton, NH, on 1 Aug 1926. Buried in West Laurel Hill Cemetery, Philadelphia.

Ranks Chaplain (Baptist) (22 Dec 1874); Chaplain with rel. rank of Cdr (18 Oct 1897); Capt (9 Jun 1901); placed on Ret.Lst. (8 Feb 1902); RAdm on Ret.Lst. (13 Apr 1911) to rank

THOMAS AUGUSTUS GILL
1840-1926

from 8 Feb 1902.

Career Summary Received appointment from PA (22 Dec 1874); rec. ship, *Sabine*, Portsmouth, NH (May-Oct 1875); Navy Yard, Portsmouth, NH (Oct 1875-Jan 1876); w.o. (Jan 1876-Feb 1877); Navy Yard, Mare Island, CA (Feb 1877-Jun 1878); w.o. (Jun 1878-Jan 1880); flgs., *Tennessee*, N.Atl.Sta. (Jan 1880-Dec 1882); w.o. (Dec 1882-Feb 1883); rec. ship, *St. Louis*, League Island, PA (Feb 1883-Feb 1887); w.o. (Feb 1887-Oct 1888); training ship, *Constellation* (Oct 1888-Apr 1889); training ship, *Jamestown* (Apr 1889-Jun 1890); w.o. (Jun-Oct 1890); training ship, *Portsmouth* (Oct 1890-Oct 1891); rec. ship, *St. Louis*, League Island, PA (Nov 1891-Jun 1894); rec. ship, *Richmond*, Philadelphia (Jun-Nov 1894); w.o. (Nov 1894-Aug 1895); *Lancaster*, S.Atl.Sqdn. (Sep 1895-Oct 1896); home and sick lv. (Oct 1896-Feb 1897); w.o. (Feb-Oct 1897); rec. ship, *Richmond*, Philadelphia (Oct 1897-Jun 1899); training ship, *Essex* (Jul 1899-Aug 1901); home and sick lv. (Aug 1901-Feb 1902); placed on Ret.Lst. (8 Feb 1902).

Career Highlights Was U.S.'s first navy chaplain to become a RAdm.

FERNANDO PADILLO GILMORE
1847-1904

FERNANDO PADILLO GILMORE Born in Steubenville, OH, on 15 Aug 1847, son of David Gilmore. Remained unmarried. Died in NY City on 24 Sep 1904. Buried in Annapolis.

Ranks Midn (28 Feb 1863); Ens (18 Dec 1868); Mstr (21 Mar 1870); Lt (21 Mar 1871); LCdr (23 Mar 1889); Cdr (1 Jan 1897); Capt (28 Sep 1901); retired with rank of RAdm (6 Nov 1902).

Career Summary Received appointment from OH (28 Feb 1863); USNA (Feb 1863-Jun 1867); *Minnesota*, and *Canandaigua*, spec. cruise and Eur.Sta. (Jul 1867-Feb 1869); w.o. (Feb-Apr 1869); rec. ship, *New Hampshire*, Norfolk, VA (Apr-Jun 1869); *Pensacola*, Pac.Sta. (Jul 1869-Jan 1873); home and w.o. (Jan-Jul 1873); *Frolic*, sta. ship, NY (Jul-Dec 1873); *Minnesota*, Navy Yard, NY (Dec 1873); *Dictator*, N.Atl.Sta. (Dec 1873-Mar 1874); flgs., *Franklin*, Eur.Sta. (Mar 1874-Dec 1876); w.o. (Dec 1876-May 1877); torp. duty, Newport, RI (Jun-Sep 1877); l.o.a. (Sep 1877-Jan 1879); Hydrographic Office, Washington, DC (Jan-Dec 1879); *Swatara*, and *Monocacy*, Asia.Sta. (Dec 1879-Nov 1882); home and w.o. (Nov 1882-Feb 1883); l.o.a. (Feb-Aug 1883); ord. duty, Navy Yard, Washington, DC (Aug-Sep 1883); duty with new cruisers (Sep-Dec 1883); *Richmond*, and *Trenton*, Asia.Sta. (Dec 1883-Aug 1885); *Monocacy*, Asia.Sta. (Aug 1885-Jan 1887); home and w.o. (Jan-Feb 1887); spec. duty, Washington, DC (Feb-Mar 1887); insp. of steel (Mar 1887-Sep 1890); l.o.a. (Sep 1890-Feb 1891); exec.off., flgs., *Lancaster*, Asia.Sqdn. (Mar 1891-Oct 1892); home and l.o.a. (Oct 1892-Feb 1893); member, bd. of inspection (Feb 1893-May 1895); NWC (Jun-Sep 1895); cdr, *Yantic*, spec.serv. (Oct 1895-Jan 1897); home and l.o.a. (Jan-Apr 1897); Navy Yard, NY (Apr 1897-Sep 1898); comdt., Naval Sta., Key West, FL (Oct 1898-Oct 1899); duty with Asia.Flt., and cdr, *Isla de Cuba* (Nov 1899-Jul 1900); Naval

Hosp., Mare Island, CA (Aug 1900); home and sick lv. (Sep-Oct 1900); equip.off., Naval Sta., Puget Sound, WA (Nov 1900); cdr, rec. ship, and prison, *Nipsic,* Navy Yard, Puget Sound, WA (Nov-Dec 1900); cdr, *Glacier,* Asia.Sta. (Jan 1901-Nov 1901); cdr, *Monadnock,* Asia.Sta. (Nov 1901-Jul 1902); home and w.o. (Jul-Oct 1902); temp. bd. duties (Oct-Nov 1902); retired (6 Nov 1902).

References
Writings: "Ship-Building and Its Interests on the Pacific Coast," U.S. Naval Institute *Proceedings* 50 (1889): 443-49.

HENRY GLASS Born in Hopkinsville, KY, on 7 Jan 1844, son of Henry and Martha K. Glass. Married Ella M. Johnson on 15 Mar 1881. Died in Paso Robles, CA, on 1 Sep 1908. Buried in Mountain View Cemetery in Oakland, CA.

HENRY GLASS
1844-1908

Ranks Act.Cadet Midn (24 Sep 1860); title changed to Midn (16 Jul 1862); Ens (28 May 1863); Mstr (10 Nov 1865); Lt (10 Nov 1866); LCdr (12 Mar 1868); Cdr (27 Oct 1879); Capt (23 Jan 1894); RAdm (9 Oct 1901); placed on Ret.Lst. (7 Jan 1906).
Career Summary Received appointment from IL (24 Sep 1860); USNA (Sep 1860-May 1863); *Canandaigua,* S.Atl.Blk. Sqdn. (Jun 1863-Jun 1865); w.o. (Jun-Jul 1865); *Powhatan,* Pac.Sqdn. (Jul 1865-Nov 1867); w.o. (Nov-Dec 1867); *Dacotah,* and *Tuscarora,* S.Pac.Sqdn. (Dec 1867-Aug 1869); w.o. (Sep-Oct 1869); equip. duty, Navy Yard, Philadelphia (Nov 1869-May 1870); l.o.a. (May-Jun 1870); *Mohican,* then cdr, *Nyack,* Pac. Sqdn. (Jul 1870-Feb 1871); staff duty, *St. Mary's,* Pac.Sqdn. (Mar 1871-Jul 1872); w.o. (Jul 1872-Jan 1873); chief of staff, Asia.Sta., *Iroquois,* then *Hartford* (Feb 1872-Jul 1874); l.o.a. (Jul-Sep 1874); fitting out and commanding, schoolship, *Jamestown* (Sep 1874-May 1875); exec.off., rec. ship, *Independence,* Mare Island, CA (May-Sep 1875); w.o. (Sep 1875-Feb 1876); cdr, schoolship, *Jamestown* (Feb 1876-Jan 1879); w.o. (Jan-Jul 1879); in charge, Naval Rndv., San Francisco (Jul-Dec 1879); w.o. (Dec 1879-Aug 1880); cdr, schoolship, *Jamestown,* and senior officer in AK (Sep 1880-Sep 1881); cdr, *Wachusett,* Pac.Sta. (Oct 1881-Mar 1882); w.o. (Apr 1882-Sep 1883); Navy Yard, Mare Island, CA (Sep 1883-Feb 1886); cdr, *Monocacy,* Asia.Sta. (Apr 1886-Sep 1888); w.o. (Oct 1888-Feb 1889); bd. duties (Feb-Oct 1889); USNA (Sep 1889-Apr 1891); ord. instructions, Navy Yard, Washington, DC (Apr 1891); member, naval exam. and ret. bds. (May 1891-Mar 1892); equip.off., Navy Yard, Mare Island, CA (Mar 1892-Oct 1893); capt.yd., Navy Yard, Mare Island, CA (Aug 1893-May 1894); cdr, *Cincinnati,* N.Atl.Sta. (Jun 1894-Aug 1895); cdr, *Texas,* N.Atl.Sta. (Aug 1895-Mar 1897); capt.yd., Mare Island, CA (May 1897-Apr 1898); cdr, *Pensacola,* Navy Yard, Mare Island, CA (Apr-May 1898); cdr, *Charleston,* Asia.Sta. (May-Dec 1898); capt. of port, Manila, P.I. (Aug-Oct 1898); home and w.o. (Oct 1898-Jan 1899); comdt., Training Sta. and Navy Yard, Mare Island, CA (Jan 1899-Feb 1903); cdr, Pac.Sta., *Marblehead* (Feb 1903-Jul 1904); comdt., Pac. Naval Dist., San Francisco (Sep 1904-Sep 1908); placed on Ret.Lst. (7 Jan 1906).

Career Highlights Graduated first in his class. During Civil War, saw considerable action against the forts and batteries guarding Charleston Harbor from Jul through Sep 1863. During war with Spain, took part in capture in May 1898 of the Ladrone Islands and in the capture of Manila in following Aug.

References

Writings: a) *Marine International Law* (Annapolis: 1883). b) "Some Suggestions for Manning our Future Naval Vessels," U.S. Naval Institute *Proceedings* 37 (1886): 41-52. c) "Naval Administration in Alaska," U.S. Naval Institute *Proceedings* 52 (1890): 1-19.

ALBERT GLEAVES
1858-1937

ALBERT GLEAVES Born in Nashville, TN, on 1 Jan 1858, son of Henry Albert and Eliza (Tannehill) Gleaves. Attended the Hume School in Nashville. Married Evelina M. Heap on 12 Jun 1889. Two daughters, Mrs. Anne Heap Van Metre, wife of navy Commo T. L. Van Metre (1887-1973), and Mrs. Evelina Porter Cohen. Resided in Haverford, PA, where he died on 6 Jan 1937. Buried in Arlington National Cemetery.

Ranks Cadet Midn (12 Jun 1873); Midn (18 Jun 1879); Ens (1 Jan 1881); Ltjg (26 May 1887); Lt (9 Jan 1893); LCdr (25 May 1900); Cdr (1 Jul 1905); Capt (1 Jul 1909); RAdm (29 Jul 1915); temp. VAdm (4 Dec 1918); temp. Adm (1 Sep 1919); reverted to RAdm (4 Feb 1921); transferred to Ret.Lst. (1 Jan 1922); Adm on Ret.Lst. (21 Jun 1930).

Career Summary Received appointment from TN (12 Jun 1873); USNA (Jun 1873-Jun 1877); w.o. (Jun-Aug 1877); flgs., *Hartford*, S.Atl.Sqdn. (Aug 1877-Oct 1878); home and l.o.a. (Oct 1878-Feb 1879); *Plymouth*, N.Atl.Sqdn. (Mar-Apr 1879); USNA (May-Jun 1879); *Nipsic*, Eur.Sqdn. (Nov 1879-Mar 1883); w.o. (Mar-Apr 1883); l.o.a. (Apr-Aug 1883); *Trenton*, Asia.Sqdn. (Sep 1883-May 1884); *Monocacy*, Asia.Sta. (May 1884-May 1886); *Trenton*, returning home (May-Sep 1886); w.o. (Sep-Nov 1886); ord. duty, Navy Yard, Washington, DC (Nov 1886-Feb 1887); Naval Ord. Proving Ground, Indian Head, MD (Feb 1887-Nov 1889); *Dolphin*, W.Indies (Nov 1889-Apr 1891); l.o.a. (Apr-May 1891); *Boston*, Pac.Sta. (May 1891-Dec 1892); home and w.o. (Dec 1892-Feb 1893); l.o.a. (Feb-Mar 1893); ord. duty, Navy Yard, Washington, DC (Mar 1893-Aug 1895); *Texas*, N.Atl.Sqdn. (Aug 1895-Jan 1896); spec. duty, Navy Yard, Mare Island, CA (Feb 1896); rec. ship, *Independence*, Mare Island, CA (Feb 1896); *Monadnock*, Pac.Sta. (Feb-Jul 1896); *Texas*, N.Atl.Sqdn. (Jul 1896-May 1897); cdr, *Cushing*, Newport, RI, and N.Atl.Flt. (May 1897-Sep 1898); Navy Yard, Washington, DC (Sep 1898-Apr 1900); *Alabama*, Philadelphia (May-Jun 1900); navigator, training ship, *Indiana* (Jun 1900-Nov 1901); cdr, presidential yacht, *Dolphin* (Nov 1901-Jun 1902); cdr, presidential yacht, *Mayflower* (Jun 1902-Nov 1904); cdr, Torp.Sta., Newport, RI (Nov 1904-Apr 1908); cdr, *St. Louis*, Pac.Flt. (Apr 1908-Nov 1909); aide to asst. sec. of navy, and member, Gen Bd., Washington, DC (Nov 1909-Jul 1910); cdr, *North Dakota*, Atl.Flt. (Jul 1910-Nov 1911); comdt., Naval Sta. and 2nd Naval Dist., Newport, RI (Nov

1911-May 1912); comdt., Navy Yard, NY (May 1912-Sep 1914); cdr, 3rd Naval Dist., NY (Jun 1912-Sep 1914); cdr, *Utah*, Atl.Flt. (Sep 1914-Jul 1915); temp. cdr, 2nd Div., Atl.Flt., *Utah* (Jun-Jul 1915); w.o. (Jul-Oct 1915); cdr, Torp.Flot., later, Destroyer Force, Atl.Flt., *Birmingham*, then *Seattle* (Nov 1915-Jul 1917); cdr, Cruiser and Transport Force, Atl.Flt, *San Diego*, then *Seattle* (Jul 1917-Sep 1919); cdr, Asia.Sta., *South Dakota* [renamed *Huron*] (Sep 1919-Feb 1921); spec. duty, Washington, DC (Mar-May 1921); comdt., 1st Naval Dist. and Navy Yard, Boston (May 1921-Jan 1922); transferred to Ret.Lst. (1 Jan 1922); recalled to active duty as gov., Naval Home, Philadelphia (Sep 1928-Sep 1931).

Career Highlights   Instrumental in the improvement of torpedoes. Important figure in the convoying of American troops and supplies to Europe during World War I. A naval reformer, was recipient of many awards and recognitions, including the Victory Medal with star, the navy's and the army's Distinguished Service Medals and four foreign decorations.

References

Personal Papers: a) 6000 items (1803-1946) in NHF,LC. b) 1 item (1897) in NHF,WNY. c) 1 vol. (1917) in USNAM. d) 1 item (1917) in Porter Collection, USMA Lib. e) letter from P. F. Harrington on S. B. Luce in WPL. f) see: U.S. Library of Congress, *Albert Gleaves; A Register of His Papers in the Library of Congress* (Washington, DC: 1968).

Writings: a) "The Result of the Bombardment of Fort Mex, Alexandria. Preparations for Flooding Lake Mareotis," U.S. Naval Institute *Proceedings* 22 (1882): 549-60. b) "The Naval Ordnance Proving Ground," U.S. Naval Institute *Proceedings* 50 (1889): 451-61. c) "The Influence of Range-Finders Upon Modern Ordnance, Gunnery, and War-Ship Construction," U.S. Naval Institute *Proceedings* 62 (1892): 259-64. d) "The Howell Torpedo. An Elementary Description," U.S. Naval Institute *Proceedings* 71 (1894): 125-29. e) "The Problem of Torpedo Discharge," U.S. Naval Institute *Proceedings* 74 (1895): 339-48. f) *James Lawrence, Captain, United States Navy.* (NY: 1904). g) "The Bagdad Railway and Why It Is of Interest to the United States," U.S. Naval Institute *Proceedings* 142 (Jun 1912): 499-517. h) "An Officer of the Old Navy: Rear-Admiral Charles Steedman, U.S.N. (1811-1890)," U.S. Naval Institute *Proceedings* 145 (Mar 1913): 197-210.   i) "Some Foreign and Other Views of War and Conduct of War," U.S. Naval Institute *Proceedings* 153 (Sep-Oct 1914): 1301-21. j) "The Cost of Building a Battleship in a Navy-Yard," U.S. Naval Institute *Proceedings* 162 (Mar-Apr 1916): 439-45. k) *Addresses and After Dinner Naval Talks, 1913-1919* (s.l., 1920?). l) *A History of the Cruiser and Transport Service* (NY: 1921). m) "The Affair of the Blanche (October 7, 1862). An Incident of the Civil War," U.S. Naval Institute *Proceedings* 236 (Oct 1922): 1661-76. n) *The Life of an American Sailor: Rear Admiral William Hemsley Emory* (NY: 1923). o) *Life and Letters of Rear Admiral Stephen B. Luce, Founder of the Naval War College* (NY: 1925). p) "A Close Call," U.S. Naval Institute

Proceedings 286 (Dec 1926): 2470-72. q) "Dedication of the St. Nazaire Memorial," U.S. Naval Institute *Proceedings* 287 (Jan 1927): 13-16. r) "The DeHaven Arctic Expedition. A Forgotten Page in American Naval History," U.S. Naval Institute *Proceedings* 305 (Jul 1928): 379-91. s) "The United States Naval Home, Philadelphia," U.S. Naval Institute *Proceedings* 338 (Apr 1931): 473-84. t) "Leadership," U.S. Naval Institute *Proceedings* (Jan 1932): 9-14. u) "Has Sea Power Passed?" *Scientific American* 129 (Nov 1923): 313-14, 372-73. v) "The Battle of Shanghai," *Current History* 36 (Apr 1932): 47-52. w) *The Admiral: The Memoirs of Albert Gleaves, Admiral USN* (Pasadena: 1985).

Additional Sources: Evelina Gleaves Cohen, *Family Facts and Fairy Tales* (1953).

JAMES HENRY GLENNON
1857-1940

JAMES HENRY GLENNON   Born in French Gulf, Shasta County, CA, on 11 Feb 1857, son of John and Ann (Kenny) Glennon. Married Susan Davenport Blair on 12 Aug 1884. Five children. Died in Washington, DC, on 29 May 1940. Buried in Arlington National Cemetery.

Ranks Cadet Midn (24 Sep 1874); Midn (4 Jun 1880); Ens (4 Feb 1882); Ltjg (26 Mar 1889); Lt (26 Dec 1893); LCdr (22 Jan 1901); Cdr (8 Jul 1905); Capt (25 Oct 1909); RAdm (10 Aug 1916); placed on Ret.Lst. (11 Feb 1921).

Career Summary Received appointment from CA (24 Sep 1874); USNA (Sep 1874-Jun 1878); w.o. (Jun-Oct 1878); *Lackawanna*, Pac.Sqdn. (Oct 1878-Jan 1879); *Alaska*, Pac.Sqdn. (Jan-Nov 1879); *Pensacola*, Pac.Sqdn. (Nov 1879-Mar 1880); home and w.o. (Mar-May 1880); USNA (May-Jun 1880); w.o. (Jun 1880-Jan 1881); *Ranger*, surv. duty, Pac.cst. (Jan 1881-Aug 1885); USNA (Sep 1885-Jun 1889); Navy Yard, Mare Island, CA (Aug 1889-Jan 1890); *Charleston*, Pac.Sta. (Jan 1890-Mar 1893); l.o.a. (Mar-Apr 1893); USNA (Apr 1893-Jul 1896); *Newark*, N.Atl.Sqdn. (Jul-Aug 1896); *Massachusetts*, N.Atl.Sqdn. and Flt. (Aug 1896-Dec 1898); Naval Sta., Havana, Cuba (Dec 1898-Aug 1899); USNA (Sep 1899-Sep 1900); exec.off., *Vicksburg*, Asia.Sta. (Oct 1900-Jun 1902); cdr, *General Alava*, Asia.Sta. (Jun-Sep 1902); in charge, Nautical School, Manila, P.I. (Sep-Nov 1902); exec.off., *Monterey*, Asia.Sta. (Dec 1902-Aug 1903); home and w.o. (Aug 1903-Jan 1904); exec.off., rec. ship, *Independence*, Mare Island, CA (Jan-Dec 1904); additional duty, asst. equip.off., Navy Yard, Mare Island, CA (May-Dec 1904); Bur. of Ord., Washington, DC (Jan 1905-Jun 1907); cdr, *Yorktown*, Pac.Flt. (Aug 1907-Dec 1908); home and w.o. (Dec 1908-Jan 1909); insp. of ord., Navy Yard, NY (Feb 1909-Jan 1910); cdr, *Virginia*, Atl.Flt. (Jan 1910-Dec 1911); home and w.o. (Dec 1911-Jan 1912); member, various bds. (Jan 1912-Dec 1913); cdr, *Florida*, Atl.Flt. (Dec 1913); cdr, *Wyoming*, Atl.Flt. (Dec 1913-Jan 1915); member, various bds. (Jan-Sep 1915); comdt., Navy Yard, and supt., Naval Gun Factory, Washington, DC (Sep 1915-Sep 1917); naval representative, special mission to Russia, *Buffalo* (May-Aug 1917); cdr, Sqdn. One, Battleship Force One, and Div. Two, Atl.Flt. (Sep 1917-Feb 1918); Cdr, 5th Div., Atl.Flt.,

Connecticut (Feb-Apr 1918), then *South Carolina* (Apr-Aug 1918), then *Vermont* (Aug-Sep 1918); comdt., 13th Naval Dist., Seattle (Sep 1918-Mar 1919); comdt., 3rd Naval Dist., NY (Mar 1919-Feb 1921); placed on Ret.Lst (11 Feb 1921).

References

Writings: a) "Velocities and Pressures in Guns," U.S. Naval Institute *Proceedings* 45 (1888): 395-418. b) "Powder in Guns," U.S. Naval Institute *Proceedings* 52 (1890): 21-30. c) "Velocity of Combustion of an Explosive Under Variable Pressure," U.S. Naval Institute *Proceedings* 68 (1893): 449-51. d) "Elastic Strength of Guns," U.S. Naval Institute *Proceedings* 73 (1895): 175-86.

CASPAR FREDERICK GOODRICH Born in Philadelphia on 7 Jan 1847, son of William and Sarah A. (Beardon) Goodrich. Married twice; to Eleanor Milnor on 4 Sep 1873, and to Sarah M. Hayes. One son, Lt Caspar Goodrich, USN (1881-1907), and two daughters. Died on 26 Dec 1925 at his home in Princeton, NJ. Buried in USNA Cemetery, Annapolis.

CASPAR FREDERICK GOODRICH
1847-1925

Ranks Act.Midn (10 Dec 1861); title changed to Midn (16 Jul 1862); Ens (1 Nov 1866); Mstr (1 Dec 1866); Lt (12 Mar 1868); LCdr (26 Mar 1869); Cdr (27 Sep 1884); Capt (16 Sep 1897); RAdm (17 Feb 1904); placed on Ret.Lst. (7 Jan 1909).

Career Summary Received appointment from CT (10 Dec 1861); USNA (Dec 1861-Nov 1864); l.o.a. (Nov 1864-Feb 1865); Navy Yard, NY (Feb-Aug 1865); flgs., *Colorado,* and *Frolic,* Eur.Sqdn. (Aug 1865-Oct 1868); w.o. (Nov-Dec 1868); *Portsmouth,* S.Atl.Sqdn. (Jan 1869-Nov 1871); inst., physics and chemistry, USNA (Dec 1871-Jun 1874); l.o.a. and w.o. (Jun 1874-Apr 1875); flgs., *Tennessee,* and *Kearsarge,* Asia.Sqdn. (Apr 1875-Jan 1878); w.o. (Jan-Feb 1878); Torp.Sta., Newport, RI (Feb 1878-Nov 1880); l.o.a. (Nov 1880-Jul 1881); spec. duty, then exec.off., *Lancaster,* Eur.Sta. (Jul 1881-Feb 1884); *Alert,* San Francisco (Feb-Apr 1884); spec. duty (May-Aug 1884); insp. of ord., Navy Yard, Washington, DC (Aug 1884-Mar 1885); spec. insp. of ord. and member, Endicott bd. of fortifications (Mar 1885-Aug 1886); in charge, Torp.Sta., Newport, RI (Sep 1886-Jan 1889); pres., NWC (Jan 1889-Jul 1892); l.o.a. and on furlough (Nov 1889-Sep 1891); cdr, training ship, *Jamestown* (Nov 1891-Sep 1892); cdr, training ship, *Constellation* (Sep 1892-May 1893); bd. duties (May-Jun 1893); cdr, *Concord,* Asia.Sqdn. (Jun 1893-Dec 1894); home and l.o.a. (Dec 1894-Mar 1895); lecturer, NWC (Mar 1895-Dec 1896); pres., NWC (Dec 1896-Apr 1898); cdr, *St. Louis,* N.Atl.Flt. (Apr-Aug 1898); cdr, *Newark,* N.Atl.Flt. and spec.serv. (Aug 1898-Sep 1899); cdr, *Iowa,* Pac.Sta. (Sep 1899-Jun 1900); lecturer, NWC (Jun 1900-Aug 1901); capt.yd., Navy Yard, League Island, PA (Sep-Dec 1901); cdr, rec. ship, *Richmond,* Philadelphia (Dec 1901-Apr 1902); cdr, rec. ship, *Minneapolis,* League Island, PA (Apr 1902-May 1903); cdr, rec. ship, *Puritan,* League Island, PA (May 1903-Jul 1904); cdr, Pac.Flt., *New York* (Aug 1904-Aug 1906); home, bd. duties and w.o. (Aug 1906-Jun 1907); comdt., Navy Yard, NY (Jun 1907-Jun 1909); placed on Ret.Lst. (7 Jan

1909).

Career Highlights One of the brightest naval officers during the period of naval expansion. Graduated first in his class. While an inst. at USNA, was instrumental in helping found the Naval Institute, serving as that body's pres. from 1904-9. Also helped found NWC in 1884, serving twice as pres. as well as being a regular lecturer there. Served as naval attaché to Gen Sir Garnet Wolsley during the bombardment of Alexandria, Egypt, in 1882, participating also as an assault cdr. In 1884, brought home to NY City the Greely relief ship, *Alert*. During war with Spain, participated in action at Santiago Bay. Was the navy's delegate to the Historical Convention at Saragossa, Spain in 1908, and from 1914 to 1916 served as pres. of the Naval Historical Society.

References

Personal Papers: 2 boxes (1863-1909) in NYHS.

Writings: "Hygienic Notes on Ships' Bilges," U.S. Naval Institute *Proceedings* 6 (1876): 93-99. b) "Naval Education," U.S. Naval Institute *Proceedings* 9 (1879): 323-44. c) "Torpedoes--Their Disposition and Radius of Destructive Effect," U.S. Naval Institute *Proceedings* 10 (1879): 479-91. e) *Report of the British Naval and Military Operations in Egypt, 1882* (Washington, DC: 1885). e) "Howe and D'Estaing. A Study in Coast Defense," U.S. Naval Institute *Proceedings* 79 (1896): 577-86. f) "The Sailor in the Revolution," U.S. Naval Institute *Proceedings* 83 (1897): 469-94. g) "Naval War College. Closing Address, Session of 1897," U.S. Naval Institute *Proceedings* 84 (1897): 679-87. h) "Esprit de Corps--A Tract for the Times," U.S. Naval Institute *Proceedings* 85 (1898): 1-24. i) "Naval Raids: A Cursory Examination and a Concrete Example," U.S. Naval Institute *Proceedings* 86 (1898): 321-48. j) "The St. Louis as a Transport," U.S. Naval Institute *Proceedings* 89 (Mar 1899): 1-9. k) "The St. Louis' Cable-Cutting," U.S. Naval Institute *Proceedings* 93 (March 1900): 157-66. l) *The Naval Side of the Revolutionary War* (Boston: 1900). m) "Some Points in Coast-Defence Budget Brought Out by the War with Spain," U.S. Naval Institute *Proceedings* 98 (Jun 1901): 223-46. n) "Naval Intelligence During War," U.S. Naval Institute *Proceedings* 106 (Jun 1903): 357-68. o) "Scouts," U.S. Naval Institute *Proceedings* 107 (Sep 1903): 569-80. p) "Historical Instances of Scouting," U.S. Naval Institute *Proceedings* 108 (Dec 1903): 917-25. q) "Cable Cutting," U.S. Naval Institute *Proceedings* 109 (Mar 1904): 109-20. r) "The Camp of Sanitation at League Island, 1903," U.S. Naval Institute *Proceedings* 110 (Jun 1904): 289-312. s) "The *Korea*'s Wardroom Mess. A True Story," U.S. Naval Institute *Proceedings* 112 (Dec 1904): 695-708. t) "Memorabilia of the Old Navy," U.S. Naval Institute *Proceedings* 112 (Dec 1904): 823-30. u) "Desertions in the Navy. A Contribution to the Discussion of the Question," U.S. Naval Institute *Proceedings* 116 (Dec 1905): 811-21. v) "For the Broader Study of Tactics," U.S. Naval Institute *Proceedings* 118 (Jun 1906): 673-74. w) "Aids to Contentment in the Navy," U.S. Naval Institute *Proceedings* 123 (Sep 1907): 905-16. x) "Aids to Contentment. A Home for the Fleet," U.S. Naval Institute

Proceedings 124 (Dec 1907): 1357-66. y) "The School of the Captain," U.S. Naval Institute *Proceedings* 129 (Mar 1909): 119-26. z) "Another View of Alma Mater," U.S. Naval Institute *Proceedings* 131 (Sep 1909): 631-56. aa) "Random Notes on a Lake Freighter," U.S. Naval Institute *Proceedings* 136 (Dec 1910): 943-56. bb) "On the Desirability of a Uniform Type in Battleships," U.S. Naval Institute *Proceedings* 137 (Mar 1911): 157-61. cc) "Scientific Ship Designing," U.S. Naval Institute *Proceedings* 146 (Jun 1913): 715-20. dd) "The *Frolic* in the Baltic, 1867. A Reminiscence," U.S. Naval Institute *Proceedings* 156 (Mar-Apr 1915): 473-80. ee) "Our Navy and the West Indian Pirates. A Documentary History," U.S. Naval Institute *Proceedings* 164 (Jul-Aug 1916): 1171-92; 165 (Sep-Oct 1916): 1161-83; 166 (Nov-Dec 1916): 1923-39; 167 (Jan 1917): 83-98; 168 (Feb 1917): 313-24; 169 (Mar 1917): 483-96; 170 (Apr 1917): 683-98; 171 (May 1917): 973-84; 172 (Jun 1917): 1197-1206; 173 (Jul 1917): 1449-61; 174 (Aug 1917): 1727-38; 175 (Sep 1917): 2023-35. ff) "'Alvarado Hunter' A Biographical Sketch," U.S. Naval Institute *Proceedings* 181 (Mar 1918): 495-514. gg) "The Founding of Our New Navy," U.S. Naval Institute *Proceedings* 184 (Jun 1918): 1267-68. hh) "The Princeton Naval Unit," U.S. Naval Institute *Proceedings* 197 (Jul 1919): 1227-32. ii) "The Navy's Paper Work," U.S. Naval Institute *Proceedings* 241 (Mar 1923): 465-68. jj) "Farragut," U.S. Naval Institute *Proceedings* 250 (Dec 1923): 1961-86. kk) "America's Past in Founding the German Navy," U.S. Naval Institute *Proceedings* 252 (Feb 1924): 208-13. ll) "Two Episodes in Sicard's Life," U.S. Naval Institute *Proceedings* 258 (Aug 1924): 1278-80. mm) *Rope Yarns from the Old Navy* (NY: 1931).

CHARLES AUGUSTUS GOVE Born in Concord, NH, on 5 Jul 1854, son of Col Jesse Augustus and Maria Louise (Sherburne) Gove. Married Minnie Webster on 23 May 1887. Resided in San Francisco, dying at the Naval Hosp. at Mare Island, CA, on 10 Sep 1933.

Ranks Cadet Midn (9 Jun 1871); Midn (21 Jun 1876); Ens (29 Mar 1879); Ltjg (4 Mar 1886); Lt (4 Aug 1891); LCdr (1 Jul 1899); Cdr (6 May 1905); Capt (7 Jan 1909); RAdm (11 Jul 1914); retired (11 Dec 1914).

Career Summary Received appointment at large (9 Jun 1871); USNA (Jun 1871-Jun 1876); w.o. (Jun-Oct 1876); *Pensacola*, Pac.Sqdn. (Nov 1876-Sep 1877); *Portsmouth*, spec.serv. (Sep 1877-Mar 1878); w.o. (Mar-Apr 1878); flgs., *Powhatan*, N.Atl. Sta. (Apr-Aug 1878); rec. ship, *Wabash*, Boston (Aug-Nov 1878); w.o. (Nov 1878-Mar 1879); USNA (Mar-Apr 1879); w.o. (Apr-May 1879); *Wachusett*, Navy Yard, Boston (May 1879); *Lackawanna*, Pac.Sqdn. (May 1879-May 1882); home and w.o. (May-Aug 1882); rec. ship, *Wabash*, Boston (Aug 1882-Jul 1883); spec. duty, Concord, NH (Jul-Aug 1883); *Trenton*, Asia.Sta. (Sep 1883-Sep 1886); w.o. (Sep 1886-Jan 1887); Hydrographic Office, Washington, DC (Jan-Apr 1887); l.o.a. (May-Jun 1887); branch hydrographic office, Boston (Jun 1887-Mar 1888); cst.surv. duty

CHARLES AUGUSTUS GOVE
1854-1933

(Mar 1888-Apr 1891); USNA (Jun 1891-Jun 1894); *Cincinnati*, spec.serv. (Jun 1894-Jul 1897); home and l.o.a. (Jul-Sep 1897); USNA (Sep 1897-May 1898); *Topeka*, N.Atl.Sqdn. (May-Sep 1898); USNA (Sep 1898-Jul 1899); Torp.Sta., Newport, RI (Jul-Aug 1899); *Massachusetts*, N.Atl.Sqdn. (Aug 1899-Jan 1900); *Kentucky*, Newport News, VA (Jan-Feb 1900); compass instruction, Bur. of Equip., Washington, DC (Mar 1900); court-martial duty (Mar-May 1900); *Kentucky*, Asia.Sta. (May 1900-Apr 1903); home and w.o. (Apr-Jun 1903); NWC (Jul-Nov 1903); Bur. of Equip., Washington, DC (Nov 1903-Jul 1906); general insp., then cdr, *Milwaukee*, San Francisco, and Pac.Flt. (Jul 1906-May 1908); member, naval exam. and ret. bds., Mare Island, CA (May-Aug 1908); comdt. of midshipmen, USNA (Sep 1908-Apr 1910); cdr, *Delaware*, 1st Div., Atl.Flt. (Apr 1910-Nov 1911); home and w.o. (Nov 1911-Jan 1912); member, naval exam. bd., Navy Yard, Washington, DC (Jan-Feb 1912); duty, Gen Bd., Washington, DC (Feb-Mar 1912); cdr, Training Sta., San Francisco (Mar 1912-Oct 1914); Naval Hosp., Washington, DC (Oct-Dec 1914); retired (11 Dec 1914); duty connected with, then cdr, naval unit, Univ. of CA, Berkeley (Aug 1918-Jan 1919).

Career Highlights Commanded the *Delaware*, then the largest warship, off Spithead at Naval Review for King George V's Coronation in 1910.

References

Personal Papers: Gove Family: 7 items (1848-1911) in NHF,LC.

Writings: a) *An Aid for Executive and Division Officers* (Annapolis: 1899). b) "Watch, Quarter and Station Bill, 'An Aid to Executive and Division Officers,'" U.S. Naval Institute *Proceedings* 91 (Oct 1899): 479-513. c) "The *Centurion*'s Anchor," U.S. Naval Institute *Proceedings* 158 (Jul-Aug 1915): 1157.

ALBERT WESTON GRANT Born in East Benton, ME, on 14 Apr 1856, son of E. B. Grant. His youth was spent in Stevens Point, WI. Married Florence Southall Sharp on 6 May 1866. Three sons. Retired to Philadelphia. Died at Naval Hosp. at League Island, PA, on 30 Sep 1930. Buried in Norfolk, VA.

Ranks Cadet Midn (10 Jun 1873); Midn (18 Jun 1879); Ens (17 May 1881); Ltjg (1 Nov 1887); Lt (9 May 1893); LCdr (1 Jul 1900); Cdr (1 Jul 1905); Capt (1 Jul 1909); RAdm (7 Sep 1915); Act.VAdm (20 Jul 1917); placed on Ret.Lst. as RAdm (14 Apr 1920); VAdm on Ret.Lst. (posthumously) (21 Jun 1930).

Career Summary Received appointment from WI (10 Jun 1873); USNA (Jun 1873-Jun 1877); w.o. (Jun-Sep 1877); *Pensacola*, Pac.Sqdn. (Sep 1877-Sep 1878); *Lackawanna*, Pac. Sqdn. (Sep 1878-Feb 1879); Naval Hosp., Mare Island, CA (Feb-Mar 1879); w.o. (Mar-May 1879); USNA (May-Jun 1879); w.o. (Jun-Dec 1879); *Alliance*, surv. duty, Grand Banks (Jan-Sep 1880); w.o. (Sep-Dec 1880); rec. ship, *Passaic*, Washington, DC (Jan 1881-Mar 1882); *Iroquois*, Pac.Sta. (Apr 1882-May 1885); home and w.o. (May-Aug 1885); Navy Yard, Norfolk, VA (Aug 1885-May 1886); torp. instruction, Newport, RI (Jun-Sep 1886);

ALBERT WESTON GRANT
1856-1930

NWC (Sep-Nov 1886); Navy Yard, Norfolk, VA (Nov 1886-May 1887); *Trenton*, spec.serv. (May 1887-Jan 1888); *Richmond*, N.Atl.Sta. (Jan 1888); training ship, *Saratoga* (Jan-Jul 1888); spec. duty, San Francisco (Jul-Sep 1888); duty connected with *Yorktown*, Philadelphia (Sep-Oct 1888); *Pensacola*, Eur.Sta. (Oct-Dec 1888); spec. duty, electric lights, *Charleston*, San Francisco (Dec 1888-Dec 1890); electric lighting duty, Bur. of Equip. and Recruiting, Washington, DC (Dec 1890-Feb 1891); *Concord*, spec.serv. (Feb 1891-Jun 1893); *San Francisco*, N.Atl.Sta. (Jun 1893-Jul 1894); l.o.a. (Jul-Sep 1894); USNA (Sep 1894-Jul 1897); *Helena*, N.Atl.Sqdn. (Jul-Dec 1897); *Massachusetts*, N.Atl.Flt. (Dec 1897-Sep 1898); *Machias*, N.Atl.Flt. (Sep 1898-Aug 1900); USNA (Aug 1900-May 1901); training ship, *Indiana* (May-Aug 1901); USNA (Aug 1901-Jun 1902); exec.off., *Oregon*, Puget Sound, WA, and Asia.Sta. (Jun 1902-Aug 1903); cdr, *Frolic*, Asia.Sta. (Aug 1903-May 1905); home and w.o. (May-Jun 1905); USNA (Aug 1905-Jul 1907); NWC (Jul-Oct 1907); USNA (Oct-Nov 1907); cdr, *Arethusa*, Pac.Flt. (Nov 1907-Apr 1908); chief of staff, Atl.Flt., *Connecticut* (May 1908-Nov 1909); cdr, flgs., *Connecticut*, Atl.Flt. (Nov 1909-Mar 1910); comdt., 4th Naval Dist. and Navy Yard, Philadelphia (Mar 1910-Jan 1913); additional duty, cdr, Atl. Reserve Flt., *Maine* (Nov 1912-Jan 1913); supervisor, 3rd, 4th, and 5th Naval Dists., Philadelphia (Feb-Aug 1913); spec. duty connected with *Texas*, Newport News, VA, and Atl.Flt. (Jul 1913-Mar 1914); cdr, *Texas*, Atl.Flt. (Mar 1914-Jun 1915); cdr, Submarine Force, Atl.Flt., *Prairie*, then *Chicago* (Jun 1915-Jul 1917); cdr, Battleship Force One, Sqdn. Two, and Div. Four, Atl.Flt., *Minnesota* (Jul 1917-Apr 1919); comdt., Navy Yard, and supervisor, Naval Gun Factory, Washington, DC (Apr 1919-Apr 1920); placed on Ret.Lst. (14 Apr 1920).

Career Highlights Served as chief of staff during "Great White Fleet's" cruise around the world in 1908-9. Rose rapidly to become one of the highest ranking officers in the service during World War I. Received Distinguished Service Medal and the Navy Cross.

References

Personal Papers: 3 Boxes (1872-1930) at State Hist. Society of WI.

Writings: *School of the Ship, etc. prepared for Midshipmen . . .* (Annapolis: 1907).

CARY TRAVERS GRAYSON Born in "Salubria," Culpeper County, VA, on 11 Oct 1878, son of Dr. John Cooke and Adelena (Pettus) Grayson. Attended William and Mary College, Williamsburg, VA, from 1895 to 1898, then studied at the Univ. of the South in Sewanee, TN, where he received the M.D. degree in 1902. Attended the Medical College of VA and graduated from the U.S. Naval Medical School in 1904. Held an honorary LL.D. from William and Mary College. Married Alice Gertrude Gordon on 24 May 1916. Three sons. Served an internship at Columbia Hosp. for Women in Washington, DC, from 1902 to

CARY TRAVERS GRAYSON
1878-1938

1903 before entering the service. Resided in Washington, DC, where he died on 15 Feb 1938. Buried in Arlington National Cemetery.

Ranks Act.Asst.Surg. (14 Jul 1903); Asst.Surg. (28 Jun 1904); PAsst.Surg. (28 Jun 1907); Medl.Dir. with rank of RAdm (29 Aug 1916); retired (20 Dec 1928).

Career Summary Received appointment from VA (14 Jul 1903); w.o. (Jul-Nov 1903); Naval Hosp., Washington, DC (Nov 1903-Sep 1904); Museum of Hygiene and Medl. School, Washington, DC (Sep 1904-May 1905); *Maryland*, Atl.Flt. (May 1905-May 1907); home and w.o. (May-Nov 1907); Naval Dispensary, Washington, DC (Nov 1907-Apr 1909); Naval Medl. School, Washington, DC (Apr-Oct 1909); presidential yacht *Mayflower*, spec.serv. (Oct 1909-Dec 1912); Bur. of Medicine and Surgery, Washington, DC (Dec 1912-Jan 1913); duty at, then in charge, Naval Dispensary, Washington, DC (Jan 1913-Dec 1928); retired (20 Dec 1928).

Career Highlights Served on the *Maryland* as part of "Great White Fleet." Became Pres. Woodrow Wilson's physician. Member of the Public Health Commission of the National Food Administration, and medl. member of Council of National Defense. Became chairman of American Red Cross in 1935. Decorated with Navy Cross, Belgium's Commander Order of Leopold, and France's Commander of the Legion of Honor.

References
Writings: *Woodrow Wilson, An Intimate Memoir* (NY: 1960).

JAMES GILCHRIST GREEN Born in Jamaica Plains, MA, on 27 Jun 1841, son of Matthews W. and Margaret Augusta Green. Educated in NH and MA. Married Cornelia F. Bond on 19 Jan 1864. Died at Edenton, NC, on 16 Feb 1909.

Ranks Act.Master's Mate, volunteer navy (11 May 1861); Act.Ens (27 Nov 1862); Act.Mstr (11 Aug 1864); Mstr (12 Mar 1868); Lt (18 Dec 1868); LCdr (3 Jul 1870); Cdr (6 Mar 1887); Capt (3 Mar 1899); retired with rank of RAdm (11 May 1901).

Career Summary Received appointment from MA (11 May 1861); *Mississippi*, W.Gulf Blk.Sqdn. (May 1861-Jan 1862); *Katahdin*, W.Gulf Blk.Sqdn. (Jan 1862-Oct 1863); *Wyalusing*, Philadelphia (Jan 1864-Jan 1865); *Belle*, N.Atl.Blk.Sqdn. (Jan-Jun 1865); l.o.a. (Jun-Oct 1865); w.o. (Oct-Nov 1865); *New Hampshire*, S.Atl.Sqdn. (Nov 1865-Sep 1866); *Don*, spec.serv., NY (Sep 1866-May 1867); *Osceola*, N.Atl.Sqdn. (May-Sep 1867); *Maumee*, Washington, DC (Sep-Oct 1867); rec. ship, *Vermont*, NY (Oct 1867-Apr 1868); rec. ship, *Potomac*, Philadelphia (Apr-Sep 1868); *Piscataqua*, Asia.Sqdn. (Dec 1868-Sep 1869); *Delaware*, Asia.Sqdn. (Sep-Oct 1869); *Ashuelot*, Asia.Flt. (Oct 1869-Aug 1871); home and w.o. (Aug 1871-Feb 1872); rec. ship, *Ohio*, Boston (Feb 1872-Aug 1873); *Saco*, Asia.Sqdn. (Aug 1873-Apr 1874); *Ashuelot*, Asia.Sqdn. (Apr 1874-Jun 1876); home and w.o. (Jun 1876-Oct 1877); Navy Yard, Norfolk, VA (Oct 1877-May 1878); cdr, *Palos*, Asia.Sta. (May 1878-May 1881); w.o. (Jun-Aug 1881); Hydrographic Office, Washington, DC (Sep 1881-Oct 1883);

JAMES GILCHRIST GREEN
1841-1909

Galena, N.Atl.Sta. (Oct 1883-Jun 1886); w.o. (Jun 1886-May 1887); Torp.Sta., Newport, RI (Jun-Sep 1887); NWC (Sep-Dec 1887); w.o. (Dec 1887-Jul 1888); NWC (Aug-Nov 1888); w.o. (Nov-Dec 1888); cdr, *Alert*, Pac.Sta. (Jan 1889-Feb 1890); cdr, *Adams*, Pac.Sta. (Apr-Jul 1890); l.o.a. (Jul-Aug 1890); insp., 6th L.h. Dist., Charleston, SC (Aug 1890-Jun 1893); insp., 10th L.h. Dist., Buffalo, NY (Jul 1893-Aug 1894); s.a., w.o., and l.o.a. (Aug-Oct 1894); ord. instruction, Washington, DC (Oct 1894-Feb 1895); member, general court-martial, Navy Yard, Washington, DC (Jan-Feb 1895); w.o. (Feb-Aug 1895); member, court of inquiry, NY (Aug-Dec 1895); equip.off., Navy Yard, Norfolk, VA (Dec 1895-Mar 1896); cdr, *Marion*, Pac.Sqdn. (Mar 1896-May 1897); w.o. (May-Jun 1897); comdt., Naval Sta., Puget Sound, WA (Jun 1897-Jun 1899); bd. duties and w.o. (Jun-Nov 1899); comdt., Naval Sta., Havana, Cuba (Nov 1899-Apr 1900); w.o. (Apr-May 1900); Naval Recruiting Rndv., Philadelphia (May-Jun 1900); training sta., San Francisco (Jun 1900); cdr, *New Orleans*, Asia.Sta. (Jun-Dec 1900); w.o. (Dec 1900-May 1901); retired (11 May 1901).

ROBERT STANISLAUS GRIFFIN Born in Fredericksburg, VA, on 27 Sep 1857, son of Patrick and Mary Griffin. Married twice; to Helena M. Laubey on 7 Jul 1866, then to her sister, Emma Laubey in 1896. One son, VAdm Robert Melville Griffin, USN (ret.) and a daughter. Received D.Sc. from Columbia Univ. in 1915 and a D.Engineering from the Stevens Institute of Technology. Resided in Washington, DC, dying on 21 Feb 1933 at the Naval Hosp. there. Buried in Arlington National Cemetery.

Ranks Cadet Engr. (1 Oct 1874); Asst.Engr. (20 Jun 1880); PAsst.Engr. (25 Aug 1889); PAsst.Engr. with rel. rank of Lt (1 Mar 1895); Chief Engr. (1 Mar 1898); Lt (3 Mar 1899); LCdr (3 Mar 1901); Cdr (22 Jan 1906); Capt (9 Jan 1910); Engr.-in-Chief with rank of RAdm (29 Aug 1916); RAdm (17 May 1913); placed on Ret.Lst. (27 Sep 1921).

Career Summary Received appointment from VA (1 Oct 1874); USNA (Oct 1874-Jun 1878); w.o. (Jun-Oct 1878); *Quinnebaug*, Eur.Sta. (Oct-Dec 1878); *Richmond*, Boston (Dec 1878-Jan 1879); *Alliance*, Navy Yard, Boston (Feb 1879); *Quinnebaug*, Eur.Sta. (Feb 1879-Jun 1881); w.o. (Jun-Dec 1881); *Tennessee*, N.Atl.Sta. (Dec 1881-Dec 1884); w.o. (Dec 1884-Feb 1885); temp. duty, advisory bd. (Feb 1885-Jan 1886); Bur. of Nav., Washington, DC (Jan 1886-Jun 1888); Bur. of Steam Engineering, Washington, DC (Jun 1888-Jul 1890); flgs., *Philadelphia*, N.Atl.Sqdn. (Jul 1890-Nov 1892); asst. insp. of machinery, *Bancroft*, Elizabethport, NJ (Nov 1892-Mar 1893); training ship, *Bancroft* (Mar-Jul 1893); Bur. of Steam Engineering, Washington, DC (Jul 1893-Oct 1897); *Vicksburg*, N.Atl.Sqdn. (Oct 1897-Mar 1898); *Mayflower*, N.Atl.Flt. (Apr 1898-Feb 1899); *Dolphin*, spec.serv. (Feb-Sep 1899); Bur. of Steam Engineering, Washington, DC (Sep 1899-Nov 1901); *Illinois*, spec.serv. (Nov 1901-May 1902); *Chicago*, Eur.Sta. and spec.serv. (May 1902-Dec 1903); *Iowa*, N.Atl.Flt. (Dec 1903-Sep 1904); flt.engr., N.Atl.Flt.,

ROBERT STANISLAUS GRIFFIN
1857-1933

Kearsarge (Sep 1904-Apr 1905); Bur. of Steam Engineering, Washington, DC (Apr 1905-Jul 1908); asst. to chief, Bur. of Steam Engineering, Washington, DC (Jul 1908-May 1913); temp. duty, Bur. of Steam Engineering, Washington, DC (May 1913); engr.-in-chief, and chief, Bur. of Steam Engineering, Washington, DC (May 1913-Sep 1921); placed on Ret.Lst. (27 Sep 1921).

Career Highlights As chief engr. and head of Bur. of Steam Engineering from 1913 to 1921, Griffin led in the shift from coal to oil and to electric drive for the navy. Received the Distinguished Service Medal and was a cdr, Legion of Honor (France).

References

Writings: *History of the Bureau of Engineering, Navy Department, during the World War* (Washington, DC: 1922).

FRANCIS MACKALL GUNNELL
1827-1922

FRANCIS MACKALL GUNNELL Born in Washington, DC, on 27 Nov 1827, son of James and Helen (Mackall) Gunnell. Received A.B. degree from Georgetown Univ. in 1845, A.M. in 1848, and M.D. from Columbian (now George Washington Univ.) in 1846. Later received an honorary A.M. in 1852 and an LL.D. degree from George Washington Univ. in 1911. Married Harriet Patterson Chew on 1 Jun 1891. No children. Died on 10 Jun 1922 in Washington, DC. Buried in Arlington National Cemetery.

Ranks Asst.Surg. (22 Mar 1849); PAsst.Surg. (7 Apr 1854); Surg. (23 Apr 1861); Medl.Insp. (3 Mar 1871); Medl.Dir. (3 Feb 1875); placed on Ret.Lst. with rel. rank of Commo (27 Nov 1889); Medl.Dir. with rank of RAdm on Ret.Lst. (29 Jun 1906).

Career Summary Received appointment from DC (22 Mar 1849); w.o. (Mar-Apr 1849); *Falmouth*, Pac.Sqdn. (Apr 1849-Jan 1852); l.o.a. (Jan-Mar 1852); Navy Yard, and MB, Washington, DC (Mar 1852-Dec 1853); w.o. (Dec 1853-Jul 1854); *Vixen*, Navy Yard, NY (Jul 1854); w.o. (Jul-Aug 1854); *Independence*, Pac.Sqdn. (Sep 1854-Oct 1856); *St. Mary's*, and *Independence*, Pac.Sqdn. (Oct 1856-Oct 1857); l.o.a. (Oct 1857-Feb 1858); *Niagara*, Atl. Cable Expd. (Feb-Aug 1858); l.o.a. (Aug-Oct 1858); rec. ship, *North Carolina*, NY (Nov 1858-Jul 1859); *Fulton*, spec.serv., W.Indies (Jul-Oct 1859); *Pensacola*, spec.serv. (Nov 1859-Jan 1860); w.o. (Jan-May 1860); *Pawnee*, N. and S.Atl. Blk.Sqdns. (Jun 1860-Dec 1862); w.o. (Dec 1862-Jan 1863); temp. duty, Naval Hosp., Washington, DC (Jan 1863-Oct 1865); *Ticonderoga*, and *Franklin*, Eur.Sqdn. (Oct 1865-Dec 1868); w.o. (Dec 1868-Jan 1869); spec. duty, Washington, DC (Jan-Feb 1869); Naval Hosp., Washington, DC (Feb 1869-Mar 1872); member, naval exam. bd. (Mar-May 1872); *Frolic*, NY (Jun 1872-Nov 1873); *Franklin*, N.Atl.Flt. (Nov-Dec 1873); flt.surg., N.Atl.Flt., *Franklin* (Dec 1873-Mar 1874), then *Wabash* (Mar-Apr 1874); *Roanoke*, Navy Yard, NY (May 1874-Mar 1875); member, naval exam. bd., Washington, DC (Mar-Oct 1875); Naval Hosp., Washington, DC (Oct 1875-May 1879); pres., medl.exam.bd. (May-Oct 1879); flt.surg., Asia.Flt., *Richmond* (Dec 1879-Mar 1881); return and w.o. (Mar-May 1881); member, naval ret. bd. (May 1881-Sep 1882); pres., medl.exam.bd.,

Washington, DC (Sep 1882-Apr 1883); member, naval ret. bd., Washington, DC (Apr 1883-Jul 1884); chief surg., and chief, Bur. of Medicine and Surgery, Washington, DC (Mar 1884-Mar 1888); l.o.a. (Mar-Jul 1888); pres., medl.exam.bd., Washington, DC (Jul 1888-Nov 1889); placed on Ret.Lst (27 Nov 1889).

REYNOLD THOMAS HALL Born in Philadelphia on 5 Nov 1858, son of Edward Smyth and Katherine Piercy (Romney) Hall. Graduated from the Episcopal Academy in Philadelphia in 1875, and was enrolled in a technical course at the Franklin Institute in Philadelphia. Married Anne Martin on 15 Dec 1887, making his home in Wynnewood, PA. Died on 10 Feb 1934. Buried in Arlington National Cemetery.

REYNOLD THOMAS HALL
1858-1934

Ranks Asst.Engr. (22 Apr 1880); PAsst.Engr. (9 Jan 1889); PAsst.Engr. with rel. rank of Ltjg (1 Oct 1893); Chief Engr. (7 Feb 1898); Lt (3 Mar 1899); LCdr (11 Jan 1900); Cdr (1 Jul 1905); Capt (18 Jun 1909); RAdm (12 Dec 1914); placed on Ret.Lst. (5 Nov 1922).

Career Summary Received appointment from PA (22 Apr 1880); *Alliance*, spec.serv. and N.Atl.Sqdn. (May 1880-May 1883); w.o. (May-Jun 1883); *Puritan*, Chester, PA (Jun 1883-Jun 1884); *Nantucket*, spec.serv. (Jun-Sep 1884); *Powhatan*, N.Atl. Sqdn. (Sep 1884-May 1886); w.o. (May-Jun 1886); Navy Yard, Norfolk, VA (Jun 1886-Mar 1887); *Ossipee*, N.Atl.Sta. (Mar-Dec 1887); w.o. (Dec 1887-Feb 1888); William Cramp and Sons Iron Works, Philadelphia (Feb 1888-Mar 1889); inspection duty, Thurloe, PA (Mar 1889-Aug 1890); *Philadelphia*, NY (Aug 1890); *Pensacola*, Pac.Sqdn. (Aug 1890-Apr 1892); rec. ship, *Independence*, Mare Island, CA (Apr-Jun 1892); *Baltimore*, Pac. and N.Atl.Sqdns. (Jun 1892-Jul 1893); prac. ship, *Miantonomoh* (Jul-Aug 1893); l.o.a. (Aug-Sep 1893); Navy Yard, NY (Sep 1893-Jul 1896); *Texas*, N.Atl.Sqdn. (Jul-Dec 1896); chief engr., *Petrel*, Asia.Flt. (Dec 1896-Nov 1898); *Concord*, Asia.Sta. (Dec 1898-May 1899); *Boston*, Asia.Sta. (May-Sep 1899); home and w.o. (Sep-Oct 1899); Navy Yard, NY (Oct 1899-Dec 1901); *Olympia*, N.Atl.Flt. (Dec 1901-Apr 1902); flgs., *Kearsarge*, N.Atl.Flt. (Apr-Jul 1902); *Olympia*, N.Atl.Flt. (Jul 1902-Aug 1903); sqdn.engr., Caribbean Sqdn., N.Atl.Flt., *Olympia* (Aug 1903-Apr 1904); flt.engr., Eur.Flt., *New York* (Apr 1904-Feb 1905); *Alliance*, Culebra Island, Puerto Rico (Feb-Apr 1905); home and w.o. (Apr-Jun 1905); asst.insp. of machinery, Newport News Shipbuilding and Drydock Company, Newport News, VA (Jun 1905-Dec 1906); head, dept. of steam engineering, Navy Yard, NY (Dec 1906-Sep 1908); insp. of machinery, Newport News Shipbuilding and Drydock Company, Newport News, VA (Oct 1908-Nov 1909); insp. of naval materials, Mosher Boiler Company, Ossining, NY (Nov 1909-Jun 1911); insp. of naval machinery, William Cramp and Sons Iron Works, Philadelphia (Jun 1911-Nov 1922); insp. of naval machinery, New York Shipbuilding Company, Camden, NJ (1920-Nov 1922); placed on Ret.Lst. (5 Nov 1922).

Career Highlights Was chief engr. on the *Petrel* during Battle of Manila, being advanced three numbers in rank for "eminent and conspicuous conduct" and receiving the Dewey Medal.

References

Personal Papers: 1 vol (1881) in NHF,WNY.

FRANKLIN HANFORD Born in Chili, NY, on 8 Nov 1844, son of William Haynes and Abbey (Pixley) Hanford. Early education was in Scottsville and Rochester, NY. Married Sara A. Crosby on 6 Nov 1878. One son and two daughters. Resided in Scottsville, NY, where he died on 8 Feb 1928 and where he was buried.

Ranks Midn (29 Nov 1862); dropped on account of age (5 Dec 1862); restored by order of the pres. (22 Dec 1862); Ens (12 Mar 1868); Mstr (26 Mar 1869); Lt (21 Mar 1870); LCdr (30 Oct 1885); Cdr (30 Sep 1894); Capt (29 Jan 1901); retired (3 Jan 1903); RAdm on Ret.Lst. (13 Apr 1911) to rank from 3 Jan 1903.

Career Summary Received appointment from NY (29 Nov 1862); USNA (Nov 1862-Jun 1866); l.o.a. and w.o. (Jun-Oct 1866); *Saco*, W.Indies (Oct 1866-Oct 1867); w.o. (Oct-Dec 1867); *Kearsarge*, S.Pac.Sta. (Jan-Sep 1868); *Tuscarora*, S.Pac. and W.Ind.Stas. (Sep 1868-Feb 1871); w.o. and l.o.a. (Feb-Sep 1871); flgs., *Wabash*, Eur.Sta. (Oct 1871-Apr 1874); torp. duty, Newport, RI (Jun-Aug 1874); w.o. (Aug-Nov 1874); rec. ship, *Vermont*, NY (Nov 1874-Apr 1875); flgs., *Tennessee*, and *Ashuelot*, Asia.Sta. (Apr 1875-Jul 1878); w.o. and l.o.a. (Jul 1878-Jan 1879); ord. duty, Navy Yard, NY (Feb 1879-Jun 1881); navigator, flgs., *Pensacola*, Pac.Sta. (Jul 1881-May 1884); w.o. (May-Oct 1884); ord. duty, Navy Yard, Washington, DC (Nov 1884-May 1886); insp. of ord., West Point Foundry, Cold Spring, NY (May 1886-Mar 1888); exec.off., *Pensacola*, spec. duty, S.America, U.S. Atl.cst., and Afr.cst. (Mar 1888-Apr 1891); home and l.o.a. (Apr 1891-Apr 1892); senior aide to comdt., Navy Yard, NY (Apr 1892-Jun 1895); cdr, *Alert*, Pac.Sta. (Jul 1895-Aug 1897); home and l.o.a. (Aug-Dec 1897); asst., then insp., 10th L.h. Dist., Buffalo, NY (Jan 1898-Oct 1900); comdt., U.S. Naval Sta., and cdr, *Yosemite*, Cavite, P.I. (Oct 1900-Sep 1902); home and w.o. (Sep 1902-Jan 1903); placed on Ret.Lst. (3 Jan 1903).

Career Highlights As navigator of the *Pensacola*, sailed on that vessel's circumnavigation of the globe from 1882-84, taking observations and recordings for the determination of compass variations. Again with the same vessel, conveyed a scientific expd. to W.Afr. from 1889-90. While cdr of the *Alert*, protected American interests during the revolutions in Nicaragua and Ecuador.

References

Personal Papers: 1 box, 1 vol. (1881-1927) at NYPL.

Writings: a) *Notes on the Visits of American and British Naval Vessels to the Genessee River, 1809-1814* (Rochester, NY: 1911). b) "How I Entered the Navy. Including a Personal Interview with Abraham Lincoln," U.S. Naval Institute *Proceedings* 748 (Jun 1965): 75-87.

JOHN FORSYTH HANSCOM Born in Eliot, ME, on 21 May 1842. Served during Civil War with 62nd ME Volunteers from 10 Sep 1862 to his discharge on 17 Jul 1863. Then worked as a draftsman at the Navy Yards in Norfolk, Washington, and Boston. Married to Margaret E. Hanscom with five children. Died at his home in Philadelphia on 30 Sep 1912.

Ranks Asst.Naval Const. (29 Jul 1875); Naval Const. (10 Oct 1888); Naval Const. with rel. rank of Cdr (4 Apr 1893); transferred to Ret.Lst. with rank of RAdm (21 May 1904).

Career Summary Received appointment from MA (29 Jul 1875); Navy Yard, Boston (Jul-Nov 1875); Bur. of Construction and Repair, Washington, DC (Nov 1875-Apr 1876); Navy Yard, Boston (Apr 1876-Oct 1877); Navy Yard, League Island, PA (Oct 1877-Jul 1878); Navy Yard, Boston (Jul 1878-Jul 1883); spec. duty, naval advisory bd., Chester, PA (Jul 1883-Jun 1887); member, naval advisory bd., Navy Yard, NY (Jun 1887-Jun 1888); insp. of hull work, William Cramp and Sons Shipyard, Philadelphia, and Navy Yard, League Island, PA (Jul 1888-May 1903); member, bd. of changes, Navy Dept., Washington, DC (May 1903-Aug 1910); transferred to Ret.Lst. (21 May 1904).

GILES BATES HARBER Born in Youngstown, OH, on 24 Sep 1849, son of Joseph and Ann Eliza (Darrow) Harber. Married Jeannette Thurston Manning on 25 Apr 1889. Died in Youngstown on 29 Dec 1925. Buried in Arlington National Cemetery.

Ranks Midn (24 Jul 1865); Ens (12 Jul 1870); Mstr (12 Jul 1871); Lt (19 Sep 1874); LCdr (4 Sep 1896); Cdr (25 Sep 1899); Capt (30 Sep 1904); RAdm (12 Nov 1908); placed on Ret.Lst. (24 Sep 1911).

Career Summary Received appointment from OH (24 Jul 1865); USNA (Jul 1865-Jun 1869); *Sabine,* and *Franklin,* Eur.Sqdn. (Jun 1869-Nov 1871); w.o. (Nov 1871-Feb 1872); *Iroquois,* and *Monocacy,* Asia.Sta. (Feb 1872-Feb 1875); return and w.o. (Feb-Oct 1875); *Omaha,* S.Pac.Sta. (Oct 1875-Apr 1878); w.o. (Apr-Oct 1878); ord. duty, Navy Yard, Washington, DC (Nov 1878-May 1879); torp. instruction, Newport, RI (Jun-Sep 1879); w.o. (Sep-Nov 1879); *Tennessee,* N.Atl.Sta. (Dec 1879-May 1881); *Alarm,* N.Atl.Sta. (May 1881-Feb 1882); cdr, *Jeannette* Search Expd., *Alarm* (Feb 1882-Feb 1884); home and w.o. (Feb-Mar 1884); Bur. of Nav., Washington, DC (Mar-May 1884); home and w.o. (May-Sep 1884); ord. duty, Navy Yard, Washington, DC (Oct 1884-Oct 1885); training ship, *Saratoga* (Nov 1885-Apr 1886); *Tallapoosa,* S.Atl.Sta. (May 1886-Oct 1888); home and w.o. (Oct 1888-Jan 1889); USNA (Jan 1889-Jan 1892); cst.surv. duty (Jan 1892-Apr 1895); home and l.o.a. (Apr-Jul 1895); Bur. of Equip. and Recruiting, Washington, DC (Jul 1895-Jan 1898); exec.off., *Texas,* N.Atl.Flt. (Jan 1898-Oct 1899); home and w.o. (Oct-Nov 1899); spec. duty, Navy Yard, NY (Dec 1899-Jan 1900); spec. duty, Office of Naval Intelligence, Washington, DC (Jan-Apr 1900); naval attaché, Paris, and St. Petersburg, Russia (Jun 1900-Aug 1903); home and w.o. (Aug-Sep 1903); *New Orleans,* Asia.Sta. (Nov 1903-Feb

GILES BATES HARBER
1849-1925

1905); home and w.o. (Feb-May 1905); NWC (Jun-Sep 1905); cdr, rec. ship, *Independence*, Mare Island, CA (Oct 1905-Jul 1907); cdr, *Maine*, spec.serv., and "Great White Flt." (Jul 1907-Jul 1908); cdr, 3rd Sqdn., Pac.Flt., *Charleston* (Jul 1908-Jan 1910); home and w.o. (Jan-Feb 1910); cdr, Pac.Flt., *California* (Feb-Nov 1910); home and w.o. (Nov-Dec 1910); member, then pres., naval exam. and ret. bds., and other bd. duties, Washington, DC (Dec 1910-Oct 1911); placed on Ret.Lst. (24 Sep 1911); comdt. of naval units, Georgetown and George Washington Universities, Washington, DC (Sep-Dec 1918).

Career Highlights Commanded the search expd. for survivors of the *Jeannette* Expd. from 1882-84, returning with the bodies of ten members of the expd. Served on the *Texas* during the war with Spain, being advanced five numbers for his conduct in battle. From 1900 to 1903, he served as naval attaché to France and to Russia.

References

Writings: *Report of Lt. Giles B. Harber, U.S.N., of His Search for the Missing People of the Jeannette Expedition* (Washington, DC: 1884).

PURNELL FREDERICK
HARRINGTON
1844-1937

PURNELL FREDERICK HARRINGTON Born in Dover, DE, on 6 Jun 1844, son of Samuel M. and Mary (Lofland) Harrington. Married Mia N. Ruan of St. Croix, Danish W.Indies, on 5 Aug 1868. Four children, including Col Samuel Milby Harrington, USMC. Resided in Yonkers, NY, where he died on 20 Oct 1937.

Ranks Act.Midn (20 Sep 1861); title changed to Midn (16 Jul 1862); Act.Ens (1 Oct 1863); Ens (21 Dec 1865); Mstr (10 May 1866); Lt (21 Feb 1867); LCdr (12 Mar 1868); Cdr (28 May 1881); Capt (1 Mar 1895); RAdm (21 Mar 1903); placed on Ret.Lst. (6 Jun 1906).

Career Summary Received appointment from DE (20 Sep 1861); USNA (Sep 1861-Oct 1863); *Ticonderoga*, N.Atl.Blk.Sqdn. (Oct 1863-Jan 1864); *Niagara*, spec.serv. (Jan-Jun 1864); *Monongahela*, W.Gulf Blk.Sqdn. (Jun 1864-Apr 1865); w.o. (Apr-Nov 1865); *Monongahela*, N.Atl.Sqdn. (Nov 1865-Jul 1868); l.o.a. (Jul-Oct 1868); USNA (Oct 1868-May 1870); w.o. (May-Jul 1870); temp. torp. duty (Aug-Nov 1870); *California*, then, exec.off., flgs., *Pensacola*, Pac.Flt. (Dec 1870-Aug 1873); USNA (Sep 1873-Sep 1876); w.o. (Sep 1876-Jan 1877); exec.off., flgs., *Hartford*, S.Atl.Sta. (Jan 1877-Dec 1879); w.o. (Dec 1879-Jan 1880); USNA (Jan 1880-Feb 1883); cdr, *Juniata*, Asia.Sta. (Mar 1883-Jan 1886); comdt. of cadets, USNA (Jan 1886-Jul 1889); suspended (Jul 1889-Apr 1890); asst., then insp., 4th L.h. Dist., Philadelphia (May 1890-Jul 1893); cdr, *Yorktown*, Pac.Sqdn. (Jul 1893-Jan 1894); home and l.o.a. (Jan-Mar 1894); spec. duty, Navy Dept., Washington, DC (Mar-Sep 1894); pres., steel bd. (Sep 1894-Apr 1896); cdr, *Terror*, N.Atl.Sqdn. (Apr 1896-Jul 1897); cdr, *Puritan*, N.Atl.Sqdn. (Jul 1897-Jun 1898); w.o. (Jun-Oct 1898); capt.yd., Navy Yard, Portsmouth, NH (Nov 1898-Oct 1901); court-martial duty and w.o. (Oct 1901-May 1902); capt.yd., Navy Yard, NY (May 1902-Mar 1903); comdt.,

Navy Yard, Norfolk, VA (Mar 1903-Jul 1906); placed on Ret.Lst. (6 Jun 1906); duty connected with Jamestown Exposition (Jul 1906-Jan 1908).

Career Highlights Participated in Battle of Mobile Bay on 5 Aug 1864.

References

Personal Papers: a) 100 items (1861-85) in NHF,LC. b) ½ box (1884-1919) in GARL. c) ½ ft. (1879-1920) at Rutherford B. Hayes Lib., Fremont, OH. e) 1 ltr. to RAdm Albert Gleaves among Gleaves papers in WRPL.

Writings: a) "The Chronodeik," U.S. Naval Institute *Proceedings* 13 (1880): 306-9. b) "The Coefficient of Safety in Navigation, U.S. Naval Institute *Proceedings* 18 (1882): 385-95. c) *Personal Log of Commander P. F. Harrington, Commandant of Cadets, USNA (1886-1889).* d) *Notes of Navigation and the Determination of Meridian Distances for the Use of Naval Cadets at the U.S. Naval Academy* (Washington, DC: 1882).

FREDERIC ROBERT HARRIS Born in NY City on 10 Apr 1875, son of Siegmund and Rose (Leeberg) Harris. Received the M.E. from Stevens Institute of Technology in Hoboken, NJ, in 1896 and an honorary E.D. in 1921. Married twice, his second wife being Dena Sperry, whom he married on 4 Mar 1931. Was in private engineering business from 1896 to 1903. Lived in New York and died there on 20 Jul 1949. Buried in Arlington National Cemetery.

Ranks Civil Engr. with rank of Ltjg (3 Jan 1903); Civil Engr. with rank of Lt (17 Mar 1906); Civil Engr. with rank of LCdr (1 Jul 1913); Chief, Bur. of Yards and Docks, with rank of RAdm (17 Jan 1916); RAdm (29 Aug 1916); placed on Ret.Lst. (5 Apr 1927).

Career Summary Received appointment from NY (3 Jan 1903); w.o. (Jan-Feb 1903); Navy Yard, NY (Feb-Jul 1903); Naval Sta., Charleston, SC (Jul 1903-Mar 1906); Naval Sta., Guantanamo Bay, Cuba (Mar 1906-Apr 1907); Bur. of Yards and Docks, Washington, DC (Apr 1907-Nov 1909); public works off., Navy Yard, NY (Nov 1909-Jan 1915); public works off., Navy Yard, Philadelphia (Jan 1915-Jan 1916); chief, Bur. of Yards and Docks, Washington, DC (Jan 1916-Jan 1918); public works off., Navy Yard, Norfolk, VA (Jan 1918-Jun 1920); public works off., Navy Yard, Philadelphia (Jul 1920-Nov 1923); public works off., Navy Yard, and 3rd Naval Dist., NY (Nov 1923-Apr 1927); placed on Ret.Lst. (5 Apr 1927).

Career Highlights Was in charge of the navy's war construction and shore program both in the U.S. and abroad from 1915-17. Was general manager, Emergency Fleet Corporation, U.S. Shipping Board, and thus in charge of the emergency merchant marine construction. Received Navy Cross for his efforts during World War I. After retirement, was pres. of Frederick R. Harris, Inc., and was consulting engineer to the navy from 1939-45. Designed waterfront facilities, floating drydocks, including the world's largest to that time, and was a construction

FREDERIC ROBERT HARRIS
1875-1949

engr. to British admiralty.
References
Writings: a) with W. G. Groesbeck, "Future Development of the New York Navy Yard," U.S. Naval Institute *Proceedings* 139 (Sep 1911): 853-64. b) *Operating Procedures for Floating Dry Docks*, 3rd ed. (NY: 1945). c) with H. Gard Knox and Husband E. Kimmel, "Naval Bases--Past and Present," U.S. Naval Institute *Proceedings* (Oct 1945): 1147-53.

HENRY TUDOR BROWNELL
HARRIS
1843-1920

HENRY TUDOR BROWNELL HARRIS Born in Hartford, CT, on 10 Mar 1843. Died on 12 Jul 1920 in Southampton, England. Buried in Arlington National Cemetery.

Ranks Captain's Clerk (Mar 1863); Act.Asst.Paymstr. (1 Nov 1864); discharged (13 Sep 1865); Asst.Paymstr. (21 Feb 1867); PAsst. Paymstr. (17 Feb 1869); Paymstr. (18 Jan 1881); Pay Insp. (29 Aug 1899); Pay Dir. (13 Jun 1902); Paymstr. Gen, and Chief, Bur. of Supplies and Accounts with rank of RAdm (31 Jul 1904); transferred to Ret.Lst. as Pay Dir. with rank of RAdm (10 Mar 1905).

Career Summary Captain's Clerk, *Ino*, spec.serv. (Mar 1863-Oct 1864); received appointment from NY (1 Nov 1864); *Naubuc*, spec.serv. (Nov 1864-Jan 1865); *Napa* [never commissioned] Wilmington, DE (Jan-Jul 1865); s.a. and l.o.a. (Aug-Sep 1865); discharged (13 Sep 1865); received commission as asst.paymstr. (21 Feb 1867); w.o. (Feb-Mar 1867); *Nyack*, S.Pac.Sta. (Mar 1867-Oct 1869); s.a. and w.o. (Nov 1869-Jan 1870); l.o.a. (Jan-Apr 1870); w.o. (Apr 1870-Feb 1871); *Supply*, Eur. and Braz.Sqdns. (Feb-Jul 1871); s.a. and w.o. (Jul-Sep 1871); l.o.a. (Sep 1871-Mar 1872); *Supply*, spec.serv. (Apr-Aug 1872); s.a. and w.o. (Aug-Dec 1872); l.o.a. (Dec 1872-Aug 1873); *Frolic*, spec.serv. (Oct 1873-Apr 1874); s.a. and w.o. (Apr-May 1874); temp. duty, *Roanoke*, Navy Yard, NY (May 1874-May 1875); in charge of stores, Honolulu, Territory of HI (May 1875-May 1877); home and w.o. (May 1877-Feb 1878); in charge of stores, Rio de Janeiro, Brazil (Mar 1878-Aug 1879); s.a. and w.o. (Aug-Dec 1879); *Swatara*, Asia.Sta. (Dec 1879-Dec 1882); s.a. and w.o. (Dec 1882-Jan 1884); training ship, *Minnesota* (Feb 1884-Jan 1887); spec. duty, Navy Yard, NY (Feb-May 1887); *Galena*, N.Atl.Sta. (May-Nov 1887); s.a. and w.o. (Nov-Dec 1887); spec. duty, Navy Yard, NY (Dec 1887-Apr 1888); naval storekeeper, USNA (Apr 1888-Oct 1889); *Boston*, Sqdn. of Evol. (Oct 1889-Jan 1891); asst. general storekeeper, Navy Yard, NY (Jan 1891-Dec 1892); *Miantonomoh*, N.Atl.Sta. (Dec 1892-Nov 1894); s.a. and w.o. (Nov 1894-Apr 1895); general storekeeper, Navy Yard, Norfolk, VA (May 1895-Jul 1897); s.a. and w.o. (Jul-Aug 1897); rec. ship, *Vermont*, NY (Aug 1897-May 1900); flt.paymstr, Asia.Flt., *Brooklyn* (Jul 1900-Jan 1902); flt.paymstr, Eur.Flt., *Chicago* (Feb-May 1902); s.a. and w.o. (May-Aug 1902); paymstr., Navy Yard, League Island, PA (Aug 1902-Mar 1903); s.a. and w.o. (Mar-Jun 1903); paymstr. gen and chief, Bur. of Supplies and Accounts, Washington, DC (Jul 1903-Nov 1906); transferred to Ret.Lst. (10 Mar 1905).

URIAH ROSE HARRIS   Born in Columbus, IN, on 14 Sep 1849, son of John and Abigail (Rose) Harris. Married Sophia Ann Simonton on 8 Feb 1878. Died at the Naval Hosp. in Washington, DC, on 20 Jun 1930.

Ranks   Midn (22 Jul 1865); Ens (12 Jul 1870); Mstr (1 Jan 1872); Lt (11 Feb 1875); LCdr (22 Feb 1879); Cdr (31 Dec 1899); Capt (21 Feb 1905); RAdm (7 Jan 1909); placed on Ret.Lst. (14 Sep 1911).

Career Summary   Received appointment from IN (22 Jul 1865); USNA (Jul 1865-Jun 1869); *Sabine,* spec. cruise (Jul 1869-Aug 1870); w.o. (Aug-Oct 1870); flgs., *Ossipee,* S.Pac.Sta. (Oct 1870-Nov 1872); w.o. (Nov 1872-Feb 1873); flgs., *Frolic,* port adm, NY (Feb-Jul 1873); *Narragansett,* spec.surv. duty, Pac.Ocean (Sep 1873-Jul 1875); *Benicia,* Pac.Sta. (Jul-Aug 1875); w.o. (Aug-Oct 1875); cst.surv. duty (Oct 1875-Jul 1876); w.o. (Jul-Aug 1876); *Portsmouth,* NY (Aug 1876); w.o. (Aug-Sep 1876); Navy Yard, Mare Island, CA (Oct 1876-Apr 1877); cst.surv. duty, Puget Sound, WA (May 1877-Mar 1879); w.o. (Mar-Aug 1879); flgs., *Shenandoah,* S.Atl.Sta. (Sep 1879-May 1882); w.o. (May-Jul 1882); Naval Observatory, Washington, DC (Jul 1882-Jul 1884); Navy Yard, Mare Island, CA (Jul 1884-Sep 1887); exec.off., *Ranger,* surv. duty (Sep 1887-Sep 1890); home and w.o. (Sep-Nov 1890); USNA (Nov 1890-Aug 1894); w.o. (Aug-Dec 1894); exec.off., *Ranger,* Pac.Sta. (Jan-Dec 1895); exec.off., *Adams,* Pac.Sta. and training serv. (Dec 1895-Aug 1897); home and l.o.a. (Aug-Sep 1897); Navy Yard, Boston (Sep 1897-Mar 1899); flgs., *Chicago,* S.Atl.Sta. (Apr-Nov 1899); excc.off., training ship, *Monongahela* (Nov-Dec 1899); excc.off., *Indiana,* in reserve (Dec 1899-Jan 1900); insp., 15th L.h. Dist., St. Louis (Feb 1900-Apr 1902); comdt., Naval Sta., Olongapo, and gov., Subic Bay Naval Reserve, P.I. (May-Nov 1902); *Wilmington,* Asia.Sta. (Nov 1902-Apr 1904); home and w.o. (Apr-Jul 1904); equip.off., Navy Yard, Boston (Jul 1904-Oct 1906); capt.yd., Navy Yard, Boston (Oct 1906-Jan 1907); comdt., Naval Stas., Olongapo and Cavite, P.I. (Mar 1907-Feb 1909); home and w.o. (Feb-May 1909); comdt., Navy Yard, Philadelphia (May 1909-Mar 1910); gov., Naval Home, Philadelphia (Apr 1910-Sep 1911); placed on Ret.Lst (14 Sep 1911).

URIAH ROSE HARRIS
1849-1930

JAMES ALBERT HAWKE   Born in Bristol, PA, on 31 Jan 1841. Received medl. degree in Mar 1863 from the Univ. of PA. Served first as an asst.surg., then a surg., in the army during the Civil War, seeing action at Chancellorsville, Gettysburg, the Wilderness, and Petersburg. Practicing in his native Bristol between service during the Civil War and his entry into the navy, married Mary Whilldin Halfmann on 29 Jan 1868. Five children. Died in Washington, DC, on 25 Jul 1910. Buried in Bristol, PA.

Ranks   Asst.Surg., 114th PA Volunteers (28 Mar 1863); Surg., 215th PA Volunteers (25 Apr 1865); mustered out (31 Jul 1865); Asst.Surg. (24 Jun 1867); PAsst.Surg. (26 Feb 1873); Surg. (1 May 1879); Medl.Insp. (8 Jun 1895); Medl.Dir. (24 Sep 1899); transferred to Ret.Lst. with rank of RAdm (31 Jan 1903).

JAMES ALBERT HAWKE
1841-1910

Career Summary Received appointment from PA (24 Jun 1867); rec. ship, *Potomac*, League Island, PA (Jul-Sep 1867); Naval Asylum, Philadelphia (Sep 1867-Jul 1868); *Nyack*, *Pensacola*, and *Powhatan*, Pac.Sqdn. (Aug 1868-Mar 1869); *Pensacola*, and *St. Mary's*, Pac.Sqdn. (Mar 1869-Aug 1871); *Ossipee*, Pac.Sqdn. (Aug-Oct 1871); return and w.o. (Oct 1871-Mar 1872); Naval Hosp., Philadelphia (Mar-Sep 1872); Navy Yard, Philadelphia (Sep 1872-Apr 1873); *Wasp*, S.Atl.Sqdn. (May 1873-Jan 1876); return and w.o. (Jan-Jul 1876); Naval Hosp., Philadelphia (Aug 1876-Feb 1879); w.o. (Feb-Sep 1879); *Constellation*, spec. cruise (Oct 1879-Jan 1880); w.o. (Jan-Mar 1880); spec. duty, Philadelphia (Mar-Jul 1880); *Monocacy*, Asia.Sta. (Sep 1880-Nov 1881); *Swatara*, Asia.Sta. (Nov 1881-Dec 1882); w.o. (Dec 1882-Feb 1883); rec. ship, *Wabash*, Boston (Feb 1883-May 1886); w.o. (May-Jun 1886); *Essex*, Asia.Sta. (Jul 1886-May 1889); w.o. (May 1889-Jun 1890); in charge, Naval Hosp., Widow's Island, ME (Jun 1890-Dec 1893); training ship, *Richmond* (Dec 1893-Jan 1894); w.o. (Jan-Apr 1894); rec. ship, *Independence*, Mare Island, CA (Apr-Aug 1894); *Charleston*, Asia.Sqdn. (Aug 1894-Jan 1895); flt.surg., Pac.Sta., *Baltimore* (Jan 1895-Feb 1896), then *Philadelphia* (Feb 1896-Jun 1897); senior medl.off., Navy Yard, NY (Jul 1897-Oct 1900); in charge, Naval Hosp., Mare Island, CA (Oct 1900-Apr 1903); transferred to Ret.Lst. (31 Jan 1903).

JOHN MITCHELL HAWLEY Born in Northampton, MA, on 28 Jul 1846, son of army quartermaster William A. Hawley. Early education in Springfield, MA. Married Ella S. Moore on 17 Jun 1874. One daughter. Died on 9 Feb 1925 in Washington, DC. Buried in Arlington National Cemetery.

Ranks Midn (23 Jul 1863); Ens (19 Apr 1869); Mstr (12 Jul 1870); Lt (6 Jan 1874); LCdr (9 Dec 1894); Cdr (3 Mar 1899); Capt (15 Mar 1904); retired with rank of RAdm (30 Jun 1907).

Career Summary Received appointment from MA (23 Jul 1863); USNA (Jul 1863-Jun 1868); found deficient and turned back (Jun 1864); w.o. (Jun-Sep 1868); *Guerriere*, S.Atl.Flt. (Sep 1868-Jul 1869); w.o. (Jul-Aug 1869); ord. duty, Navy Yard, Boston (Sep 1869-Jan 1870); *Guard*, Eur.Sqdn. (Jan 1870-Jul 1871); w.o. (Jul-Nov 1871); *Wyoming*, N.Atl.Sta. (Nov 1871-Oct 1872); spec. duty, Nicaraguan Surv.Expd. (Oct 1872-Jul 1873); l.o.a. (Jul-Dec 1873); training ship, *Minnesota* (Dec 1873); rec. ship, *Vermont*, NY (Dec 1873-Jan 1874); *Ticonderoga*, S.Atl.Sta. (Jan-May 1874); w.o. (May-Jun 1874); torp. duty, Newport, RI (Jul-Oct 1874); cst.surv. duty (Oct 1874-Apr 1879); w.o. (Apr-May 1879); *Wachusett*, S.Atl.Sta. (May 1879-Feb 1881); *Pensacola*, S.Atl.Sta. (Feb-Jun 1881); *Wachusett*, S.Atl.Sta. (Jun 1881-Jan 1882); training ship, *Jamestown* (Jan-Jun 1882); w.o. (Jun-Dec 1882); Hydrographic Office, Washington, DC (Dec 1882-Dec 1883); in charge, branch hydrographic office, Baltimore (Dec 1883-Mar 1885); cst.surv. duty (Mar 1885-May 1887); *Trenton*, spec.serv. (May-Jun 1887); Naval Hosp., Chelsea, MA (Jun-Oct 1887); exec.off., *Nipsic*, Pac.Sta. (Oct 1887-Oct 1890);

JOHN MITCHELL HAWLEY
1846-1925

USNA (Nov 1890-Jun 1894); exec.off., *Detroit*, Asia.Sta. (Jun 1894-Aug 1896); home and l.o.a. (Aug-Nov 1896); Hydrographic Office, Washington, DC (Nov 1896); Bur. of Nav., Washington, DC (Dec 1896-Sep 1899); cdr, training ship, *Hartford* (Oct 1899-Nov 1901); War Records Office, Washington, DC (Dec 1901-Mar 1902); asst., then insp., 5th L.h. Dist., Baltimore (Mar 1902-Apr 1904); cdr, flgs., *Brooklyn*, N.Atl.Sqdn. (Apr-Jun 1904); chief of staff, N.Atl.Sqdn., *Kearsarge* (Jun 1904-Sep 1905); Naval Hosp., Boston (Sep-Oct 1905); home and sick lv. (Oct-Dec 1905); member, general court-martial, Navy Yard, Washington, DC (Dec 1905); cdr, rec. ship, *Wabash*, Boston (Jan 1906-Jun 1907); retired (30 Jun 1907).

Career Highlights Was exec.off. of the *Nipsic* when she was hit by the Mar 1899 hurricane at Apia, Samoa. For outstanding bravery and efforts in getting that ship afloat after being beached, received a commendation from the Navy Dept. and a vote of thanks from the MA Legislature. Was first naval officer to establish recruiting stations in the western U.S. with hope of bringing more westerners into the service. Subsequently in charge of all recruiting stations in the west and southwest during the war with Spain.

References
Writings: "The Samoan Hurricane of 1889," U.S. Naval Institute *Proceedings* 442 (Dec 1939): 1756-66; 444 (Feb 1940): 308-9.

LEWIS CASS HEILNER Born in Tamaqua, PA, on 29 Jan 1849, son of Benjamin Heilner. Married to Susie H. Heilner. At least one daughter. Died at the Naval Hosp. in Brooklyn, NY, on 25 Jan 1912. Buried in Arlington National Cemetery.

Ranks Midn (24 Jul 1866); Ens (13 Jul 1871); Mstr (27 Sep 1873); Lt (2 Jun 1879); LCdr (9 Dec 1898); Cdr (2 May 1901); Capt (7 Jan 1906); RAdm (16 Nov 1909); placed on Ret.Lst. (29 Jan 1911).

Career Summary Received appointment from PA (24 Jul 1866); USNA (Jul 1866-Jun 1870); *Saco,* and *Palos,* Eur. and Asia.Sqdns. (Jul 1870-Dec 1873); home and w.o. (Dec 1873-Aug 1874); *Brooklyn,* S.American waters (Sep 1874-Mar 1876); *Ossipee,* N.Atl.Sta. (Mar 1876-Sep 1877); w.o. (Sep-Nov 1877); rec. ship, *Colorado,* NY (Nov 1877-Dec 1878); cst.surv. duty (Dec 1878-Feb 1882); w.o. (Feb-Apr 1882); temp. duty, rec. ship, *Colorado,* NY (Apr 1882-Jan 1883); training ship, *Portsmouth* (Jan 1883-Oct 1885); w.o. (Oct 1885-Jan 1886); Naval Observatory, Washington, DC (Jan 1886-Apr 1889); *Pensacola,* N.Atl.Sqdn. (Apr 1889-May 1892); l.o.a. (May-Aug 1892); Naval Observatory, Washington, DC (Aug 1892); NWC (Sep-Oct 1892); Naval Observatory, Washington, DC (Nov 1892-Aug 1895); *Texas,* N.Atl.Sqdn. (Aug 1895-Jan 1896); home and w.o. (Jan-Feb 1896); *Texas,* N.Atl.Sqdn. and Flt. (Feb 1896-Jan 1899); w.o. (Jan-Mar 1899); Navy Yard, NY (Mar 1899-Apr 1902); cdr, training ship, *Essex* (Apr 1902-Nov 1903); additional duty, comdt. of base and sta., Guantanamo Bay, Cuba (Nov 1903); cdr,

LEWIS CASS HEILNER
1849-1912

training ship, *Yankee* (Dec 1903-Jun 1904); home and w.o. (Jun 1904); l.o.a. (Jun-Aug 1904); asst., then insp., 13th L.h. Dist., Portland, OR (Aug 1904-Feb 1906); capt.yd., Navy Yard, League Island, PA (Mar-Dec 1906); temp. additional duty, cdr, *Brooklyn*, League Island, PA (Sep-Oct 1906); cdr, flgs., *Ohio*, Asia.Flt. (Dec 1906-Nov 1907); home and w.o. (Nov-Dec 1907); Navy Yard, NY (Dec 1907-Jan 1908); comdt., Navy Yard and 8th Naval Dist., Pensacola, FL (Jan 1908-Apr 1909); NWC (Jun-Sep 1908); supervisor, naval auxiliaries, Atl.cst., NY (May 1909-Feb 1911); member, court of inquiry, Navy Yard, Norfolk, VA (Dec 1910-Mar 1911); placed on Ret.Lst. (29 Jan 1911).

Career Highlights Served as nav. on the *Texas* during Battle of Santiago in Jul 1898 during the Spanish-American War.

JAMES MEREDITH HELM Born in Grayville, IL, on 16 Dec 1855, son of John Jacob and Mary Walden (Gray) Helm. Died in Tacoma Park, MD, on 28 Oct 1927. Buried in Arlington National Cemetery.

Ranks Cadet Midn (30 Sep 1871); Ens (18 Jul 1876); Mstr (25 Nov 1881); title changed to Ltjg (3 Mar 1883); Lt (1 Jun 1888); LCdr (3 Mar 1899); Cdr (11 Oct 1903); Capt (28 Jan 1908); RAdm (14 Sep 1911); placed on Ret.Lst. (16 Dec 1919).

Career Summary Received appointment from TN (30 Sep 1871); USNA (Sep 1871-Jun 1875); *Tennessee*, N.Atl.Sqdn. (Jun 1875-Aug 1877); *Kearsarge*, spec.serv. (Aug 1877-Jan 1878); USNA (Jan 1878); w.o. (Jan-May 1878); *Alaska*, Pac.Sqdn. (May 1878-Jan 1879); *Tuscarora*, Pac.Sqdn. (Jan 1879-May 1880); w.o. (May 1880-Jan 1881); *Ranger*, spec.serv. (Jan 1881-Aug 1883, Sep-Oct 1884); w.o. (Oct 1884-Feb 1885); cst.surv. duty (Feb 1885-Nov 1886); l.o.a. (Nov 1886-Nov 1887); training ship, *Saratoga* (Nov 1887-Aug 1888); cst.surv. duty (Sep 1888-Feb 1892); l.o.a. (Feb-Apr 1892); *Michigan*, on Great Lakes (Apr 1892-May 1894); *Columbia*, Asia.Sta. (May 1894-Mar 1896); temp. torp. instruction, Newport, RI (Aug-Sep 1895); *Terror*, N.Atl.Sqdn. (Apr-Sep 1896); l.o.a. (Sep 1896-Jan 1897); bd. of inspection and surv., NY (Jan 1897); *Puritan*, N.Atl.Flt. (Jan-Mar 1897); cst.surv. duty (Mar 1897-Apr 1898); cdr, *Hornet*, N.Atl. Flt. (Apr-Nov 1898); rec. ship, *Richmond*, Philadelphia (Nov-Dec 1898); insp., 16th L.h. Dist., Memphis, TN (Dec 1898-Sep 1900); additional duty, in charge, 15th L.h. Dist., St. Louis (Dec 1899-Feb 1900); cdr, *Dorothea*, League Island, PA, and on loan, IL Naval Militia (Oct 1900-Mar 1902); L.h. duty, P.I. (Mar 1902-Feb 1903); capt. of port, Manila, P.I. (Mar 1903-Jan 1906); cdr, *Baltimore*, Asia.Sqdn. (Jan 1906-Feb 1907); cdr, *Galveston*, Asia.Sqdn. (Feb-Aug 1907); home and w.o. (Aug-Sep 1907); naval sec., L.h. Bd., Washington, DC (Sep 1907-Oct 1908); cdr, *Idaho*, spec.serv. (Nov 1908-Oct 1909); capt.yd., Navy Yard, Boston (Oct-Dec 1909); cdr, rec. ship, *Wabash*, Boston (Dec 1909-Dec 1910); comdt., Naval Sta., New Orleans (Dec 1910-Sep 1911); court-martial duty, Atl.Flt. (Sep-Oct 1911); comdt., Naval Sta. and 6th Naval Dist., Charleston, SC (Oct 1911-Oct 1914); w.o. (Oct-Nov 1914); cdr, Atl. Reserve Flt., *Alabama*

JAMES MEREDITH HELM
1855-1927

(Nov 1914-Sep 1916); additional duty, comdt., 4th Naval Dist. (Sep 1916-Dec 1918); placed on Ret.Lst. (16 Dec 1919).

Career Highlights Considered an expert on yards and shore establishments; commanded the *Hornet* during war with Spain, participating in Battle of Manzanilla on 30 Jun 1898 for which he was advanced five numbers for conspicuous conduct in battle.

JOSEPH NEWTON HEMPHILL Born in Ripley, OH, on 18 Jun 1847, son of Samuel and Sarah (Campbell) Hemphill. Married Oro E. Stark in Dec 1873. One daughter. Married again in Aug 1893 to Mrs. Dora A. Hancock. Died on 8 Jul 1931 in Washington, DC.

JOSEPH NEWTON HEMPHILL
1847-1931

Ranks Midn (29 Sep 1862); Ens (12 Mar 1868); Mstr (26 Mar 1869); Lt (21 Mar 1870); LCdr (26 Jan 1887); Cdr (15 Jun 1895); Capt (3 Mar 1891); RAdm (5 Aug 1906); placed on Ret.Lst. (18 Jun 1909).

Career Summary Received appointment from OH (27 Sep 1862); USNA (Sep 1862-Jun 1866); found deficient and put back (Feb 1864); l.o.a. and w.o. (Jun-Oct 1866); *Tacony*, Navy Yard, Boston (Oct-Nov 1866); *Osceola*, Navy Yard, Boston (Nov 1866-Jan 1867); *Monongahela*, W.Ind.Sqdn. (Jan-Dec 1867); *De Soto*, N.Atl.Sqdn. (Dec 1867-Sep 1868); w.o. (Sep-Oct 1868); Navy Yard, League Island, PA (Oct 1868-Jan 1869); *Kenosha* [renamed *Plymouth*], Eur.Sta. (Jan 1869-Apr 1870); w.o. (Apr 1870); flgs., *Plymouth*, Eur.Sta. (Apr 1870-Jun 1872); w.o. (Jun 1872-Jul 1873); l.o.a. (Jul 1873-Jan 1874); nav. duty, Navy Yard, Norfolk, VA (Jan-Dec 1874); l.o.a. (Dec 1874-Apr 1875); navigator, *Tuscarora*, Pac.Sqdn. (May 1875-Aug 1876); *Portsmouth*, NY (Aug 1876); w.o. (Aug-Dec 1876); cst.surv. duty (Dec 1876-Sep 1877); *Swatara*, N.Atl.Sqdn. (Sep 1877-Jul 1878); l.o.a. (Jul-Nov 1878); ord. instruction, Navy Yard, Washington, DC (Nov 1878-Jan 1879); Naval Observatory, Washington, DC (Jan 1879-Oct 1880); *Powhatan*, N.Atl.Sta. (Oct 1880-Sep 1883); w.o. (Sep 1883-Apr 1884); torp. duty, Newport, RI (Apr-Aug 1884); w.o. (Aug-Sep 1884); ord. duty, Navy Yard, Washington, DC (Sep 1884-Jul 1887); l.o.a. (Jul-Dec 1887); exec.off., training ship, *Jamestown* (Dec 1887-Aug 1888); exec.off., training ship, *Constellation* (Sep 1888-Apr 1889); exec.off., training ship, *Jamestown* (Apr 1889-Aug 1890); w.o. (Aug-Sep 1890); member, bd. of inspection and surv. (Sep 1890-Oct 1893); cdr, supply ship, *Fern* (Nov 1893-Oct 1894); Bur. of Yards and Docks, Washington, DC (Oct 1894-Mar 1898); Bur. of Nav., Washington, DC (Mar-Aug 1898); *Buffalo*, Navy Yard, NY (Aug 1898); cdr, *Buffalo*, spec.serv. (Sep 1898-Jul 1899); home and w.o. (Jul 1899); cdr, *Detroit*, N.Atl.Sqdn. (Aug 1899-Jan 1900); home and w.o. (Jan-Mar 1900); member, bd. of inspection and surv. (Mar 1900-May 1902); cdr, *Kearsarge*, N.Atl.Flt. (May 1902-Apr 1904); chief of staff, N.Atl.Flt. (Aug 1902-Apr 1904); capt.yd., Navy Yard, NY (Jun 1904-Aug 1906); pres., bd. of inspection and surv. (Sep 1906-May 1907); cdr, 3rd Sqdn., Pac.Flt., *Rainbow* (May 1907-Aug 1908); home and w.o. (Aug 1908-Jan 1909); pres., naval exam. and ret. bds. (Jan-Jun 1909); placed on Ret.Lst.

(18 Jun 1909).

GEORGE ELLSWORTH HENDEE Born in Roxbury, MA, on 30 Jun 1841, son of Charles J. and Adeline (Davis) Hendee. Educated in public and private schools. Married Elsie S. Lewis on 21 Apr 1870. Resided in Brookline, MA. Died on 10 Sep 1916. Buried in Boston's Forest Hills Cemetery.

Ranks Paymaster's Clerk (11 Oct 1861); discharged (30 Nov 1862); Paymaster's Clerk (20 Aug 1863); discharged (5 Mar 1864); Act.Asst.Paymstr. (25 Mar 1864); PAsst.Paymstr. (23 Jul 1866); Paymstr. (27 Feb 1869); Pay Insp. (9 Jan 1895); Pay Dir. (1 Sep 1899); transferred to Ret.Lst. with rank of RAdm (30 Jun 1902).

Career Summary Received appointment as paymaster's clerk (10 Oct 1861); storeship, *Brandywine*, Chesapeake Bay, and N.Atl.Blk.Sqdn. (Oct 1861-Nov 1862); discharged (30 Nov 1862); received appointment as Paymaster's clerk (20 Aug 1863); *Pinola*, W.Gulf Blk.Sqdn. (Aug 1863-Mar 1864); w.o. (Mar-May 1864); flgs., *Don*, Potomac Flot. (May 1864-Feb 1866); s.a. and l.o.a. (Feb-Apr 1866); w.o. (Apr-Oct 1866); *Ossipee*, N.Pac.Sqdn. (Oct 1866-Jul 1869); s.a. and w.o. (Jul-Dec 1869); rec. ship, *Independence*, Mare Island, CA (Jan 1870-Sep 1871); *Pensacola*, Pac.Sqdn. (Oct 1871-Feb 1872); s.a. and w.o. (Feb-May 1872); l.o.a. (May-Nov 1872); *Richmond*, W.Ind.Sqdn. (Nov 1872-Jan 1874); *Saranac*, Pac.Sqdn. (Jan 1874-May 1875); s.a. and w.o. (May-Oct 1875); Bur. of Provisions and Clothing, Washington, DC (Oct 1875-Jan 1876); Pay Office, Norfolk, VA (Jan-Sep 1876); s.a. and w.o. (Sep 1876-Jun 1877); rec. ship, *Independence*, Mare Island, CA (Aug 1877-Aug 1878); Navy Yard, Mare Island, CA (Aug 1878-Aug 1880); s.a. and w.o. (Aug 1880-Jan 1881); training ship, *Minnesota* (Feb 1881-Feb 1884); s.a. and w.o. (Feb-Aug 1884); *Powhatan*, N.Atl.Sqdn. (Aug 1884-May 1886); s.a. and w.o. (May-Jul 1886); rec. ship, *Franklin*, Norfolk, VA (Jul 1886-Jan 1888); general storekeeper, Navy Yard, League Island, PA (Feb 1888-Nov 1891); s.a. and w.o. (Nov 1891-Jun 1892); Navy Yard, NY (Jun-Sep 1892); *Philadelphia*, N.Atl.Sta. (Sep 1892-Nov 1893); flt.paymstr., Pac.Sta., *Philadelphia* (Nov 1893-Feb 1895); s.a. and w.o. (Feb-Mar 1895); general storekeeper, Navy Yard, Portsmouth, NH (Mar 1895-Mar 1896); general storekeeper, Navy Yard, Boston (Mar 1896-Apr 1899); paymstr., Navy Yard, Boston (Apr 1899-Apr 1902); in charge, Pay Office, Boston (May 1902-Jul 1903); transferred to Ret.Lst. (30 Jun 1902).

WILLIAM WOODBURY HENDRICKSON Born in Mt. Joy, PA, on 21 Jun 1844, son of James William and Ellen (Woodbury) Hendrickson. Married Eleanor M. Hendrickson on 18 Apr 1867. Resided in Annapolis, dying at the Naval Hosp. there on 1 Jun 1920.

Ranks Act.Midn (26 Sep 1860); dismissed (21 May 1863); reinstated (27 May 1863); title changed to Midn (16 Jul 1862); Act.Ens (1 Oct 1863); Mstr (10 Nov 1865); Lt (10 Nov 1866);

WILLIAM WOODBURY
HENDRICKSON
1844-1920

LCdr (12 Mar 1868); resigned (21 Mar 1873); Prof. of Math. (21 Mar 1873); Prof. of Math. with rel. rank of Capt (13 Mar 1897); transferred to Ret.Lst. (21 Jun 1906); Prof. of Math. with rank of RAdm on Ret.Lst. (13 Apr 1911) to rank from 21 Jun 1906.

Career Summary Received appointment from OH (26 Sep 1860); USNA (Sep 1860-May 1863); dismissed (21 May 1863); reinstated (27 May 1863); w.o. (May-Dec 1863); *Brooklyn*, Navy Yard, NY (Dec 1863-Feb 1864); flgs., *Lancaster*, Pac.Sqdn. (Feb 1864-Mar 1867); w.o. (Mar-May 1867); *Portsmouth*, spec.serv. (Jun 1867-Oct 1868); w.o. (Oct-Dec 1868); *Kenosha* [renamed *Plymouth*], Eur.Sta. (Jan 1869-Jul 1870); USNA (Jul 1870-Mar 1873); resigned (21 Mar 1873); received appointment from OH as prof. of math. (21 Mar 1873); USNA (Mar 1873-Nov 1890); Nautical Almanac Office, Washington, DC (Nov 1890-Mar 1897); dir., Nautical Almanac Office, Washington, DC (Mar-Jun 1897); USNA (Jul 1897-Jun 1906); transferred to Ret.Lst. (21 Jun 1906).

ICHABOD GOODWIN HOBBS Born in North Berwick, ME, on 13 Mar 1843, son of Wilson and Sarah Eliot (Goodwin) Hobbs. Received A.B. degree in 1864 and A.M. degree in 1865 from Dartmouth College. Married Helen M. Hazard on 29 Jun 1882. Three sons, all of whom served in the navy. Made his home in Newport, RI, dying there on 2 Dec 1918.

Ranks Act.Asst.Paymstr. (31 Aug 1864); discharged (18 Jul 1865); Asst.Paymstr. (21 Feb 1867); PAsst.Paymstr. (16 Sep 1868); Paymstr. (15 May 1879); Pay Insp. (7 May 1899); Pay Dir. (28 Apr 1902); transferred to Ret.Lst. (13 Mar 1905); Pay Dir. on Ret.Lst. with rank of RAdm (13 Apr 1911) to date from 13 Mar 1905.

Career Summary Received appointment from ME (31 Aug 1864); Navy Yard, NY (Sep 1864); *Unadilla*, N.Atl.Sta. (Sep 1864-Jun 1865); l.o.a. (Jun-Jul 1865); discharged (18 Jul 1865); received appointment from ME (21 Feb 1867); w.o. (Feb-Nov 1867); *Ascutney*, spec.serv. (Nov 1867-Aug 1868); *Tallapoosa*, spec.serv. (Aug 1868-Nov 1870); s.a. and w.o. (Nov 1870-May 1871); Bur. of Provisions and Clothing, Washington, DC (May 1871-May 1872); *Tuscarora*, Pac.Sta. (May 1872-Aug 1875); s.a. and w.o. (Aug-Nov 1875); *Despatch*, Eur.Sqdn. (Dec 1875-Oct 1878); s.a. and w.o. (Oct 1878-Sep 1879); Torp.Sta., Newport, RI (Oct 1879-Sep 1882); s.a. and w.o. (Sep-Oct 1882); *Juniata*, Asia.Sta. (Oct 1882-Dec 1885); s.a. and w.o. (Dec 1885-Jun 1886); rec. ship, *New Hampshire*, Newport, RI (Jul 1886-Jul 1889); s.a. and w.o. (Jul 1889-Apr 1890); spec. duty, *Constellation* (Apr-Sep 1890); s.a. and w.o. (Sep 1890-Jan 1891); *Boston*, Pac.Sta. (Jan 1891-Nov 1893); s.a. and l.o.a. (Nov 1893-Mar 1894); Naval Sta., Newport, RI (Mar 1894-Nov 1896); *Brooklyn*, spec.serv. (Dec 1896-Oct 1899); additional duty, flt.paymstr, "Flying Sqdn.," N.Atl.Flt., *Brooklyn* (May 1898-Oct 1899); s.a. and w.o. (Oct 1899-May 1900); flgs., *Kearsarge*, N.Atl.Sqdn. (May-Jul 1900); Pay Office, Newport, RI (Jul 1900-Mar 1905); additional duty, pay off. and general storekeeper, Torp.Sta.,

ICHABOD GOODWIN HOBBS
1843-1918

Newport, RI (Dec 1900-Aug 1901, Oct 1902-Apr 1903); transferred to Ret.Lst. (13 Mar 1905).

ADOLPH AUGUST HOEHLING
1839-1920

ADOLPH AUGUST HOEHLING Born in Philadelphia on 5 Mar 1839. Married with a son and two daughters. Resided in Chevy Chase, MD, where he died on 25 Apr 1920. Buried in Arlington National Cemetery.

Ranks Asst.Surg. (14 Aug 1861); PAsst.Surg. (24 Apr 1865); Surg. (2 Oct 1867); Medl.Insp. (31 Jan 1885); Medl.Dir. (11 May 1893); retired (14 Jun 1895); RAdm on Ret.Lst. (29 Jun 1906).

Career Summary Received appointment from PA (14 Aug 1861); w.o. (Aug-Oct 1861); Navy Yard, Washington, DC (Oct-Dec 1861); *T. A. Ward,* and *Dan Smith,* Bomb and Potomac Flots. (Dec 1861-Jan 1863); *Jacob Bell,* N.Atl.Blk.Sqdn. (Jan-Jul 1863); *Roanoke,* Hampton Roads, VA (Jul 1863-Jun 1864); w.o. (Jun-Jul 1864); Naval Asylum, Philadelphia (Jul 1864-May 1865); *Dacotah,* W.Indies and Pac.Sqdn. (May 1865-Dec 1867); return and w.o. (Dec 1867-Dec 1868); member, ret. bd., Navy Yard, Philadelphia (Dec 1868-Mar 1869); w.o. (Mar-May 1869); rec. ship, *New Hampshire,* Norfolk, VA (May-Sep 1869); *Frolic,* spec.serv. (Sep 1869-Nov 1870); spec. duty, Navy Yard, NY (Nov 1870-Feb 1871); w.o. (Feb-Apr 1871); prac. ship, *Constellation* (May-Nov 1871); Navy Yard, League Island, PA (Nov 1871-Feb 1873); *Juniata,* Navy Yard, Boston (Feb 1873); sick lv. (Feb-Jun 1873); USNA (Jun-Sep 1873); *Monongahela,* S.Atl.Sta. (Sep-Dec 1873); flt.surg., S.Atl.Sta., *Monongahela* (Dec 1873-Feb 1876); w.o. (Feb-Apr 1876); Navy Yard, League Island, PA (Apr 1876-Jun 1879); w.o. (Jun-Aug 1879); spec. duty, Navy Yard, Washington, DC (Aug 1879-Feb 1884); *Powhatan,* N.Atl.Sqdn. (Feb 1884-Mar 1885); *Pensacola,* Eur.Sta. (Mar 1885-Mar 1888); w.o. (Mar-Apr 1888); in charge, Naval Hosp., Washington, DC (Apr 1888-Jul 1890); Navy Yard, League Island, PA (Jul 1890-May 1891); w.o. (May-Aug 1891); member, naval exam. bd., NY (Sep 1891-May 1893); w.o. (May-Aug 1893); bd. duties (Aug-Dec 1893); w.o. (Dec 1893-Mar 1894); temp. duty, U.S. Senate, Washington, DC (Mar-Apr 1894); w.o. (Apr-May 1894); pres., medl.exam.bd., USNA (May-Aug 1894); in charge, Naval Hosp., Chelsea, MA (Aug 1894-Feb 1895); l.o.a. (Feb-Jun 1895); retired (14 Jun 1895).

JOHN HOOD
1859-1919

JOHN HOOD Born on 3 Dec 1859 in Florence, AL, son of John Murray and Mary Cornelia (Heslap) Hood. Married Rosalie Caswell, daughter of RAdm Thomas Thompson Caswell, Pay Corps, USN, on 28 Jan 1890. After retirement, resided in Annapolis, MD, dying in the naval hospital there on 11 Feb 1919.

Ranks Cadet Midn (12 Jun 1874); dismissed (10 Feb 1875); reappointed Cadet Midn (10 Sep 1875); Midn (10 Jun 1881); Ensjg (3 Mar 1883); Ens (26 Jun 1884); Ltjg (5 Dec 1890); Lt (28 Apr 1895); LCdr (22 Sep 1901); Cdr (1 Jul 1906); Capt (1 Jul 1910); RAdm (29 Aug 1916); retired (19 Mar 1918).

Career Summary Received appointment from AL as Cadet

Midn (12 Jun 1874); USNA (Jun 1874-Feb 1875); dismissed (10 Feb 1875); Reappointed Cadet Midn (10 Sep 1875); USNA (Sep 1875-Jun 1879); w.o. (Jun-Aug 1879); *Shenandoah*, flgs., S.Atl. Sta., then *Wachusett*, S.Atl. and Pac.Stas. (Sep 1879-Mar 1881); w.o. (Mar-May 1881); USNA (May-Jun 1881); w.o. (Jun-Jul 1881); *New Hampshire*, flgs., Training Sqdn., Norfolk, VA (Jul-Nov 1881); *Brooklyn*, S.Atl.Sta. (Nov 1881-Oct 1884); w.o. (Oct-Nov 1884); USNA (Jan 1885-Apr 1886); *Vandalia*, flgs., Pac. Sqdn. (Apr 1886-Apr 1887); *Mohican*, Pac.Sqdn. (Apr 1887-Aug 1888); USNA (Sep 1888-Jun 1892); training ship, *Jamestown* (Jun-Sep 1892); *Constellation*, spec.serv. to Eur. (Sep 1892-Mar 1893); practice ship, *Bancroft* (Mar-Jul 1893); *Kearsarge*, N.Atl. Sqdn. (Aug 1893-Mar 1894); w.o. (Mar 1894); *Atlanta*, N. Atl.Sqdn. (Apr 1894-Jun 1895); w.o. (Jun-Aug 1895); in charge, branch hydrographic office, Baltimore (Aug 1895-Jun 1896); USNA (Jun-Jul 1896); l.o.a. (Jul-Sep 1896); USNA (Sep 1896-Jun 1897); l.o.a. (Jun-Jul 1897); *Annapolis*, on trials (Jul-Oct 1897); *Maine*, N.Atl.Sqdn. (Oct 1897-Feb 1898); home and w.o. (Mar-Apr 1898); cdr, *Hawke*, N.Atl.Sqdn. (Apr-Sep 1898); *Topeka*, spec.serv., Boston, Philadelphia, then Caribbean (Sep 1898-Feb 1899); *Nero*, Navy Yard, Mare Island, Ca (Mar 1899-Mar 1900); home and l.o.a. (Mar-Apr 1900); spec.temp. duty, Hydrographic Office, Washington, D.C. (Apr-Jul 1900); *Massachusetts*, N.Atl.Sqdn. (Jul 1900); Naval Hosp., New York (Jul-Sep 1900); USNA (Sep 1900-May 1901); nav., training ship, *Indiana* (May-Sep 1901); USNA (Sep 1901-May 1902); en route to Asia. Sta. (May-Jul 1902); executive officer, *New Orleans*, flgs, Cruiser Sqdn., Asia.Flt. (Jul 1902-Apr 1903); cdr, *Elcano*, Yangtze River Patrol (Apr 1903-Apr 1905); home and w.o. (Apr-Jun 1905); NWC (Jul-Aug 1905); insp, 7th L.h. Dist., Key West, FL (Aug 1905-Dec 1907); cdr, *Tacoma*, spec.serv., Caribbean (Dec 1907-Jun 1909; cdr, *Severn* and other ships, USNA (Jun 1909-May 1910); w.o. (May-Jun 1910); NWC (Jun-Sep 1910: cdr, *Rhode Island*, Div 4, Sqdn. 1, Atl.Flt. (Oct 1910-Nov 1911); cdr, *Delaware*, Atl.Flt. (Nov 1911-Oct 1912); member, Gen Bd., Navy Dept., Washington, D.C. (Oct 1912-Jun 1915); cdr, *Texas*, Atl.Flt. (Jun 1915-Aug 1916); NWC (Aug-Oct 1916); cdr, Reserve Force, Atl.Flt., *Minnesota* (Oct 1916-Apr 1917); cdr. Div. 4, Atl.Flt., *Minnesota* (Apr 1917); naval hosp., Washington, D.C. and sick lv. (Apr 1917-Mar 1918); retired (19 Mar 1918).

Career Highlights On board *Kearsarge* when wrecked on 2 Feb 1894 in Caribbean off Nicaragua; on *Maine* when exploded in Havana on 15 Feb 1898; took the important news of arrival of Spanish fleet in Santiago, Cuba to commander of Flying Squadron at Cienfuegos and delivered orders to him to proceed to Santiago; made survey for Pacific Ocean cable, 1899-1900; commanded *Elcano* in Chinese waters during the Russo-Japanese War of 1904-05. Received the Spanish Campaign Medal, the Sampson Medal, and the Victory Medal.

References
Writings: a) "The Pacific Submarine Cable--Some Remarks on the Military Necessity and the Advantages of a National Cable,"

U.S. Naval Institute *Proceedings* 95 (Sep 1900): 477-88. b) translated J.Depelley, "Telegraph Cables in Time of War," U.S. Naval Institute Proceedings 96 (Dec 1900): 663-75. c) "Naval Administration and Organization," U.S. Naval Institute *Proceedings* 97 (Mar 1901): 1-27. d) "The School of the Officer," U.S. Naval Institute *Proceedings* 102 (Jun 1902): 195-206. e) "Some Remarks on the Administration of Justice in the Navy," U.S. Naval Institute *Proceedings* 111 (Sep 1904): 589-92. f) "Desertion from the Navy," U.S. Naval Institute *Proceedings* 114 (Jun 1905):367-81. g) "Draft of a Bill for Increasing the Commissioned Personnel of the Line of the Navy, establishing a Commensurate Engineering Branch, and Promoting the Efficiency of the Navy, U.S. Naval Institute *Proceedings* 115 (Sep 1905): 565-83. h) "Some Remarks Called Forth by the Able Essay of Pay Inspector Mudd--and a Plea," U.S. Naval Institute *Proceedings* 129 (Mar 1909): 385-91 i) "The Monroe Doctrine: Its Meaning and Application at the Present Day," U.S. Naval Institute *Proceedings* 131 (Sep 1909): 657-66. j) "The Organization of the Fleet. Administrative: Tactical: For War," U.S. Naval Institute *Proceedings* 135 (Sep 1910): 825-34. k) "Naval Policy as it Relates to the Shore Establishment, and the Maintenance of the Fleet," U.S. Naval Institute *Proceedings* 150 (Mar-Apr 1914): 319-44.

JOHN ADRIAN HOOGEWERFF
1860-1933

JOHN ADRIAN HOOGEWERFF Born in Howard County, MD, on 27 Nov 1860, son of Samuel Evans and Mary Elizabeth (Duval) Hoogewerff. Was a student at the PA Military Academy from 1875-76. Married Edwardine L. Hiester on 10 Oct 1889. Died at Pearl Harbor, Territory of HI, on 13 Feb 1933.

Ranks Cadet Midn (27 Jun 1877); Naval Cadet (5 Aug 1882); Ensjg (1 Jul 1883); Ens (26 Jun 1884); Ltjg (5 Nov 1893); Lt (21 Jul 1897); LCdr (3 Mar 1903); Cdr (6 Jul 1907); Capt (4 Mar 1911); temp. RAdm (31 Aug 1917); RAdm (1 Jul 1918); placed on Ret.Lst. (27 Nov 1924).

Career Summary Received appointment at large (27 Jun 1877); USNA (Jun 1877-Jun 1881); w.o. (Jun-Aug 1881); *Lancaster*, Eur.Sta. (Aug 1881-Apr 1883); USNA (Apr-Jun 1883); w.o. (Jun-Jul 1883); Naval Observatory, Washington, DC (Jul 1883-Oct 1885); *Brooklyn*, S.American waters (Oct 1885-May 1889); in charge, magnetic observatory, Naval Observatory, Washington, DC (Jun 1889-Jun 1892); spec. duty, Mare Island, CA (Jun-Jul 1892); *Charleston*, Spec.Serv.Sqdn. (Jul 1892-Aug 1894); *Philadelphia*, Pac.Sqdn. (Aug 1894-Jul 1895); l.o.a. (Jul 1895); USNA (Jul 1895-Jul 1897); *Cincinnati*, S.Atl.Sta. (Jul 1897-Feb 1898); *Amphitrite*, N.Atl.Flt., and training ship (Feb 1898-Aug 1900); USNA (Aug 1900-Jun 1902); training ship, *Dixie* (Jun-Jul 1902); training ship, *Panther* (Jul 1902-Sep 1903); exec.off., *Minneapolis*, spec.serv. (Sep 1903-Jun 1905); USNA (Aug 1905-Sep 1908); Asia.Sta. (Oct-Nov 1908); Naval Sta., Olongapo, P.I. (Nov-Dec 1908); cdr, *Monadnock*, then *Monterey*, Asia.Sta. (Dec 1908-Feb 1909); cdr, *Galveston*, Asia.Sta. (Feb 1909-Mar 1910); member, Gen Bd., Washington, DC (Apr 1910-Apr 1911); cdr, *Kansas*, N.Atl.Flt. (Apr 1911-May 1913);

NWC (Jun 1913-Jan 1914); supt., Naval Observatory, Washington, DC (Feb 1914-Mar 1917); cdr, *Pennsylvania*, Yorktown, VA (Apr-Sep 1917); cdr, Mine Force, Atl.Flt., *Pennsylvania* (Sep-Nov 1917); cdr, Div. One, Battleship Force One, Atl.Flt., *Alabama* (Nov 1917-Feb 1919); supt., Naval Observatory, Washington, DC (Mar 1919-Jun 1921); comdt., Navy Yard, Puget Sound, WA (Jun 1921-Oct 1924); placed on Ret.Lst. (27 Nov 1924).

Career Highlights Landed with American forces in Alexandria, Egypt, shortly after that city was bombarded by the British in 1882. During war with Spain, served on the *Cincinnati* for which he was awarded medals for the action at Matanzas and the W.Indies campaign. As cdr of a battleship div. of the Atl.Flt. during World War I, received the Victory Medal and the Navy Cross.

References

Writings: *Magnetic Observations* (Washington, DC: 1891).

EDWIN SAMUEL HOUSTON Born in Lancaster, PA, on 13 May 1845, son of William and Mary Henderson Houston. Married with a son. Died on 7 Mar 1905 in Lausanne, Switzerland. Buried in the Sallaz Cemetery in Lausanne.

Ranks Act.Midn (18 Apr 1862); title changed to Midn (16 Jul 1862); Ens (1 Dec 1866); Mstr (12 Mar 1868); Lt (26 Mar 1869); LCdr (29 Mar 1881); Cdr (27 Sep 1891); Capt (3 Mar 1899); retired with rank of RAdm (7 Jun 1902).

Career Summary Received appointment from PA (18 Apr 1862); USNA (Apr 1862-Oct 1865); l.o.a. and w.o. (Oct 1865-Jan 1866); training ship, *Sabine* (Jan-Apr 1866); *Lackawanna*, Pac.Sqdn. (May 1866-Feb 1869); rec. ship, *Vandalia*, Portsmouth, NH (Mar-Aug 1869); flgs., *Severn*, and *Dictator*, N.Atl. Sqdn. (Aug 1869-Jun 1871); l.o.a. and w.o. (Jun 1871-Mar 1872); *Lancaster*, and *Ticonderoga*, S. and N.Atl.Sta. (Apr 1872-Apr 1874); l.o.a. (Apr-Nov 1874); *Benicia*, N.Pac.Sqdn. (Nov 1874-Feb 1875); Naval Rndv., San Francisco (Feb 1875-Jun 1876); w.o. (Jun-Dec 1876); training ship, *Jamestown* (Dec 1876-Jun 1877); w.o. (Jun-Aug 1877); *Hartford*, S.Atl.Sta. (Sep 1877-Dec 1879); w.o. (Dec 1879-Jan 1880); ord. instruction, Navy Yard, Washington, DC (Jan-May 1880); torp. instruction, Newport, RI (Jun-Sep 1880); ord. instruction, Navy Yard, Washington, DC (Sep 1880-Apr 1881); l.o.a. (Apr-Aug 1881); *Richmond*, Asia.Sta. (Sep 1881-Aug 1884); w.o. (Aug-Sep 1884); l.o.a. (Nov 1884-Oct 1885); Navy Yard, Norfolk, VA (Oct 1885-May 1886); exec.off., *Trenton*, spec.serv. (May 1886-Jun 1887); *Lancaster*, S.Atl.Sta. (Jun 1887-Sep 1889); w.o. (Sep-Oct 1889); exec.off., training ship, *Minnesota*, NY (Nov 1889-Oct 1891); ord. instruction, Navy Yard, Washington, DC (Oct 1891-Nov 1892); cdr, rec. ship, *Dale*, Washington, DC (Nov 1892-Aug 1894); cdr, *Machias*, Asia.Sqdn. (Sep 1894-Oct 1896); l.o.a. (Oct-Dec 1896); capt.yd., and cdr, Naval Sta., League Island, PA (Jan 1897-Mar 1899); w.o. (Mar 1899); Navy Yard, Washington, DC (Mar-Sep 1899); cdr, gunnery training ship, *Amphitrite* (Oct 1899-Nov 1901); l.o.a. (Nov-Dec 1901); capt.yd., League Island, PA

EDWIN SAMUEL HOUSTON
1845-1905

(Jan-Jun 1902); retired (7 Jun 1902).

References

Personal Papers: 21 ft. (1877-1940) in HI State Archives, Honolulu, HI.

THOMAS BENTON HOWARD
1854-1920

THOMAS BENTON HOWARD Born in Galena, IL, on 10 Aug 1854, son of Bushrod Brush and Elizabeth (Mackay) Howard. Married Anne J. Claude on 13 May 1879. Three sons and a daughter. Died in Annapolis on 10 Nov 1920. Buried in USNA Cemetery, Annapolis.

Ranks Midn (25 Jun 1869); title changed to Cadet Midn (15 Jul 1870); Midn (31 May 1873); Ens (16 Jul 1874); Mstr (13 Jan 1879); title changed to Ltjg (3 Mar 1883); Lt (7 Nov 1885); LCdr (3 Mar 1899); Cdr (8 Jun 1902); Capt (24 Feb 1907); RAdm (14 Nov 1910); placed on Ret.Lst. (10 Aug 1916).

Career Summary Received appointment at large (25 Jun 1869); USNA (Jun 1869-May 1873); w.o. (May-Jul 1873); *Alaska, Wabash, Juniata,* and *Franklin,* Eur.Sta. (Aug 1873-Aug 1875); home and w.o. (Aug-Oct 1875); USNA (Nov 1875-Jul 1878); *Plymouth,* N.Atl.Sta. (Jul 1878-May 1879); *Kearsarge,* N.Atl.Sta. (May 1879-Jun 1881); prac. ship, *Dale* (Jun-Aug 1881); USNA (Sep 1881-Sep 1884); training ship, *Saratoga* (Sep 1884-Sep 1887); USNA (Sep 1887-Jun 1891); *Bennington,* Sqdn. of Evol., then S.Atl.Sta. (Jun 1891-Jul 1893); *Miantonomoh,* spec.serv. (Jul 1893-Jun 1894); home and l.o.a. (Jun-Aug 1894); USNA (Aug 1894-May 1897); navigator, *Concord,* Alaskan waters, and Asia.Sta. (May 1897-Dec 1898); *Charleston,* Asia.Sta. (Dec 1898-Aug 1899); exec.off., *Monadnock,* Asia.Sta. (Aug 1899-Mar 1900); *Scindia* [renamed *Ajax*], Asia.Sta. (Mar-Aug 1900); home and w.o. (Aug 1900); USNA (Sep 1900-Feb 1903); temp. duty, cdr, *Puritan,* presidential inauguration serv. (Mar-May 1901); *Nevada,* Atl.Flt. (Feb 1903-May 1905); home and w.o. (May 1905); USNA (Jun 1905-Aug 1907); *Olympia,* USNA Sqdn. (Jun-Aug 1907); home and w.o. (Aug-Sep 1907); cdr, *Tennessee,* Pac.Flt. (Oct 1907-Jun 1908); *Ohio,* "Great White Flt." (Jun 1908-May 1909); member, Gen Bd., Washington, DC (May 1909-Oct 1910); cdr, 4th Div., Atl.Flt., *Georgia* (Oct 1910-Jan 1912); cdr, 3rd Div., Atl.Flt., *Virginia* (Jan-Apr 1912); pres., naval exam. and ret. bds., Washington, DC (Apr 1912-Dec 1913); temp. duty, Gen Bd., Washington, DC (Dec 1913-Feb 1914); cdr, Pac.Flt., *California* (Feb 1914-Mar 1915), and *Colorado* (Mar-Sep 1915); pres., naval exam. and ret. bd., Navy Yard, Washington, DC (Sep 1915-Aug 1916); placed on Ret.Lst. (10 Aug 1916); supt., Naval Observatory, Washington, DC (Mar 1917-Mar 1919).

Career Highlights During war with Spain, was at Battle of Manila Bay. Saw service during the Philippine insurrection. Was a participant in the "Great White Fleet's" cruise around the world.

WILLIAM LAURISTON HOWARD
1860-1930

WILLIAM LAURISTON HOWARD Born on 10 Jan 1860 in Plainfield, CT, son of George F. and Mary (Phillips) Howard. Married Louise G. Alden on 23 Nov 1886. One daughter, Helen, who married Capt Charles C. Gill, USN (1885-1948). Resided in Newport, RI, where he died on 3 Feb 1930. Buried in Arlington National Cemetery.

Ranks Cadet Midn (22 Sep 1877); Ens (1 Jul 1884); Ltjg (7 Sep 1894); Lt (10 Mar 1898); Lcdr (11 Oct 1903); Cdr (28 Jan 1908); Capt (1 Jul 1911); temp. RAdm (16 Dec 1918); placed on Ret.Lst. with rank of RAdm (21 Dec 1919).

Career Summary Received appointment from CT as Cadet Midn (22 Sep 1877); USNA (Sep 1877-Jun 1882); w.o. (Jun-Aug 1882); *Yantic*, spec.serv. Greely Relief Expd. (Aug 1882-Feb 1884); *Powhatan*, Navy Yard, Norfolk, VA (Mar-Apr 1884); USNA (Apr-Jun 1884); w.o. (Jun-Jul 1884); *Alarm*, spec.serv. (Jul-Sep 1884); receiving ship, *Vermont*, NY (Sep 1884-Mar 1885); duty in connection with Northern Alaskan Expd. (Mar 1885-Oct 1886); w.o. (Oct-Dec 1886); sick lv. (Jan-Feb 1887); spec.temp. duty, Bur. of Nav., Washington, D.C. (Feb-Jun 1887); sick lv. (Jun-Sep 1887); spec. duty, Bur. of Nav., Washington, D.C. (Sep 1887-Apr 1889); l.o.a. (Apr-Nov 1889); spec. temp. duty connected with International Marine Conference (Nov 1889-Jan 1890); *Thetis*, Navy Yard, Mare Island, Ca, and Pac.Sqdn. (Feb 1890-Feb 1891); cst.surv. duty (Feb 1891-Apr 1893); return and l.o.a. (Apr-Jul 1893); asst. insp. of steel, Carnegie Steel Works, Pittsburgh, PA (Jul 1893-Feb 1895); asst. insp. of steel, Homestead Steel Works, Munhall, PA (Feb-Nov 1895); *Boston*, Asia.Sta. (Nov 1895-Oct 1898); *Nero*, Asia.Sta. and en route home (Oct 1898-Jan 1899); l.o.a. (Jan-Feb 1899); Office of Naval Intelligence, Washington, D.C. (Feb 1899-Oct 1900); exec. officer, and navigator, *Bancroft*, surv. duty, Columbian waters (Oct 1900-Apr 1901); cdr., *Bancroft*, Navy Yard, Boston (Apr-Jun 1901); Hydrographic Office, Washington, D.C. (Jun-Aug 1901); *Illinois*, spec. service, then flgs. of Eur.Sqdn., then N.Atl.Sqdn. (Sep 1901-Jun 1904); home and w.o. (Jun-Jul 1904); spec. temp. duty, Office of Naval Intelligence, Washington, D.C. (Jul-Sep 1904); Naval Attaché, American embassies, Berlin, Rome, and Vienna (Oct 1904-Dec 1906); Naval Attaché, American Embassy, Berlin (Dec 1906-Jan 1908); Bur. of Nav., Washington, D.C. (Jan-Mar 1908); executive officer, *Mississippi*, spec.serv. (Mar 1908-Feb 1909); cdr., *Birmingham*, Atl.Flt. (Feb-Oct 1909); equipment officer, then inspection officer, Navy Yard, Philadelphia (Nov 1909-Nov 1911); cdr., *Idaho*, N.Atl.Sqdn. (Nov 1911-Jul 1913); capt.yd., New York (Jul 1913-Nov 1914); NWC (Dec 1914-Dec 1915); comdt., Navy Yard and Sta., Portsmouth, NH (Dec 1915-Sep 1917); cdr. *Pennsylvania*, flgs., Atl.Flt. (Sep 1917-Sep 1918); comdt., Naval Station, Cavite, P.I. (Sept 1918-Oct 1919); home and w.o. (Oct-Dec 1919); placed on Ret.Lst. (21 Dec 1919).

Career Highlights Received Navy Cross for servies on *Pennsylvania* during World War I, the Cross of the Order of Merit of Duke Frederick Peter Louis of Oldenburg (Germany), and a decoration from the Italian government. In 1927 the U.S. Geographic Board named part of the Brooks Range of mountains in northwestern Alaska the Howard Hills in honor of his partici-

pation in the 1885-86 expd. of that region.
References
Personal Papers: 1 item (1880-1890) in Naval Historical Foundation Repository, Building 210, Washington Navy Yard, Washington, D.C.

JOHN HUBBARD
1849-1932

JOHN HUBBARD Born in South Berwick, ME, on 19 May 1849, son of John and Eleanor Augusta (Tucker) Hubbard. A bachelor, made his home in Washington, DC, where he died on 28 May 1932.

Ranks Midn (25 Jul 1866); Ens (13 Jul 1871); Mstr (15 Sep 1873); Lt (28 Dec 1878); LCdr (6 Oct 1898); Cdr (2 Apr 1901); Capt (8 Jul 1905); RAdm (25 Oct 1909); placed on Ret.Lst. (19 May 1911).

Career Summary Received appointment from AZ (25 Jul 1866); USNA (Jul 1866-Jun 1870); w.o. (Jun-Jul 1870); *Brooklyn*, and *Juniata*, Eur.Sqdn. (Aug 1870-Jul 1872); w.o. (Jul-Sep 1872); l.o.a. (Sep 1872-Jan 1873); *Guard*, spec.serv. (Jan 1873-Apr 1874); w.o. (Apr-May 1874); rec. ship, *Sabine*, Portsmouth, NH (May-Sep 1874); cst.surv. duty (Sep 1874-Oct 1877); Hydrographic Office, Washington, DC (Nov 1877-Jan 1878); *Supply*, spec.serv. (Jan 1878-Apr 1879); w.o. (Apr-May 1879); ord. instruction, Navy Yard, Washington, DC (May-Dec 1879); *Swatara*, Asia.Sta. (Dec 1879-Dec 1882); w.o. (Dec 1882-Jan 1883); l.o.a. (Feb-Apr 1883); Torp.Sta., Newport, RI (Apr-Aug 1883); Bur. of Nav., Washington, DC (Sep 1883-Jul 1884); prac. ship, *Despatch* (Jul-Oct 1884); Bur. of Nav., Washington, DC (Oct-Dec 1884); asst.insp., 5th L.h. Dist., Baltimore (Dec 1884-Oct 1885); insp., 7th L.h. Dist., Pensacola, FL (Oct 1885-Jun 1887); w.o. (Jun-Jul 1887); spec. duty, Bur. of Nav., Washington, DC (Jul 1887-Jan 1889); *Chicago*, Sqdn. of Evol. (Jan 1889-Jun 1892); asst. insp. of ord., E. W. Bliss and Co., Brooklyn, NY (Jul 1892-Jul 1895); duty with, then exec.off., training ship, *Essex* (Jul 1895-Apr 1898); Navy Yard, Portsmouth, NH (Apr 1898); exec.off., *Yankee*, N.Atl.Flt. (Apr-Oct 1898); ord. duty, Navy Yard, NY (Oct 1898-Jan 1900); exec.off., training ship, *Amphitrite*, Boston (Jan 1900-Feb 1901); asst., then insp., 4th L.h. Dist., Philadelphia (Feb 1901-Feb 1903); cdr, *Nashville*, and naval forces, Isthmus of Panama (Feb 1903-May 1904); temp. duty, Bur. of Nav., Washington, DC (May-Jun 1904); cdr, *Boston*, Pac.Sqdn. (Jun-Nov 1904); Bur. of Ord., Washington, DC (Nov 1904-Dec 1906); cdr, *Minnesota*, "Great White Flt." (Jan 1907-Mar 1909); spec. duty, aide to asst. sec. of navy, and member, Gen Bd., Navy Dept., Washington, DC (Mar-Dec 1909); cdr, 3rd Div., Pac.Flt., *Charleston* (Jan 1910); cdr, Asia.Flt., *Charleston* (Feb-Aug 1910), and *New York* [renamed *Saratoga*] (Aug 1910-May 1911); placed on Ret.Lst. (19 May 1911).

Career Highlights Commanded the *Nashville* and naval forces in 1903 at the Isthmus of Panama during the revolt there, which resulted in the independence of Panama from Columbia. Commanded the *Minnesota* with the "Great White Flt.

JOHN JACOB HUNKER Born in Pittsburgh, PA, on 12 Jun 1844, son of Andrew and Margaret (Donaldson) Hunker. Educated at Toledo (OH) High School, finishing there in 1861. Married Mary Monroe on 22 Dec 1875. Married later, his second wife being Eleanor P. Hunker. Died on 16 Dec 1916 in Ashville, NC. Buried in Toledo, OH.

Ranks Private, Co. H., 1st OH Artillery (1861); Act.Midn (18 Apr 1862); title changed to Midn (16 Jul 1862); Ens (12 Mar 1868); Mstr (26 Mar 1869); Lt (21 Mar 1870); LCdr (2 Oct 1885); Cdr (16 Sep 1894); Capt (11 Dec 1900); RAdm (6 Jun 1906); placed on Ret.Lst. (12 Jun 1906).

Career Summary Enlisted as Private, Company H, 1st OH Volunteers (1861); received appointment from OH (18 Apr 1862); USNA (Apr 1862-Jun 1866); l.o.a. and w.o. (Jun-Sep 1866); flgs., *Susquehanna*, N.Atl.Sta. (Oct 1866-Jan 1868); w.o. (Jan-Mar 1868); ord. duty, Navy Yard, Washington, DC (Mar-Nov 1868); flgs., *Franklin*, Eur.Sqdn. (Jan 1869-Nov 1871); w.o. (Nov 1871-Jan 1872); torp.serv., Newport, RI (Jan 1872-May 1873); *Michigan*, on Great Lakes (May 1873-Apr 1874); *Swatara*, N.Atl.Sta. (May 1874-Jul 1875); l.o.a. (Jul-Oct 1875); *Michigan*, on Great Lakes (Oct 1875-Dec 1876); w.o. and l.o.a. (Dec 1876-Jun 1877); torp. duty, Newport, RI (Jul-Sep 1877); w.o. (Sep-Oct 1877); nautical schoolship, *St. Mary's* (Oct 1877-Nov 1880); w.o. (Nov 1880-Aug 1881); *Richmond*, Asia.Sta. (Sep 1881-Aug 1884); w.o. (Aug 1884-Mar 1885); *Michigan*, on Great Lakes (Mar 1885-Sep 1888); w.o. (Sep 1888-Apr 1889); exec.off., *Adams*, Pac.Sta. (Apr 1889-Jul 1890); rec. ship, *Independence*, Mare Island, CA (Jul 1890-Apr 1891); *Marion*, Pac. and Asia.Stas. (Apr 1891-Jul 1892); *Palos*, Asia.Sta. (Jul 1892-Jan 1893); home and l.o.a. (Jan-Jun 1893); exec.off., rec. ship, *Wabash*, Boston (Jun 1893-Oct 1894); insp. of ord., Navy Yard, Portsmouth, NH (Nov 1894-Feb 1895); equip.off., Navy Yard, NY (Feb 1895-Jul 1896); ord.off., Navy Yard, NY (Jul 1896-Jul 1897); cdr, *Annapolis*, N.Atl.Sqdn. and training ship (Jul 1897-May 1899); cdr, training ship and sta., Newport, RI (Jun 1899-Aug 1902); home and w.o. (Aug-Dec 1902); cdr, *New York*, N. Atl.Flt. (Jan 1903-Mar 1905); home and w.o. (Mar-May 1905); NWC (Jun 1905-May 1906); court-martial bd. duties, Newport, RI (May-Jul 1906); placed on Ret.Lst. (12 Jun 1906).

Career Highlights Essentially organized and commanded the convoy fleet at Tampa, FL, in Jun 1898 to carry the army to Santiago, Cuba, during the war with Spain. Also led the successful expd. at Nipe Bay, Cuba, on 21 Jul 1898. Was advanced three numbers for eminent and conspicuous conduct in battle.

References
Writings: a) *Manual for Officers Serving on Board U.S. Cruising Training Ships* (Washington, DC: 1899). b) *Manual of Instruction in Ordnance and Gunnery for the U.S. Naval Training Service* (Washington, DC: 1900).

HARRY MCLAREN PINCKNEY HUSE Born at USMA at West Point, NY, on 8 Dec 1858, son of Col Caleb and Harriet

**HARRY MCLAREN PINCKNEY
HUSE**
1858-1942

(Pinckney) Huse. Early education gained abroad. Married Mary Sheward Whitelock on 14 Sep 1886. One daughter. Retired to Washington, DC. Died on 14 May 1942 at the Naval Hosp. in Bethesda, MD.

Ranks Cadet Midn (30 Sep 1874); Midn (4 Jun 1880); Ens (2 Jun 1882); Ltjg (27 Jun 1889); Lt (13 May 1894); LCdr (3 Mar 1901); Cdr (25 Feb 1907); Capt (4 Dec 1909); RAdm (29 Aug 1916); temp. VAdm (27 Jun 1920); placed on Ret.Lst. (8 Dec 1922); VAdm on Ret.Lst. (21 Jun 1930).

Career Summary Received appointment from NY (30 Sep 1874); USNA (Sep 1874-Jun 1878); w.o. (Jun-Sep 1878); *Pensacola,* Pac.Sqdn. (Oct 1878-Mar 1880); w.o. (Mar-May 1880); USNA (May-Jun 1880); training ship, *Minnesota* (Jul-Nov 1880); *Galena,* Eur. and S.Atl.Sqdns. (Nov 1880-Jun 1883); *Brooklyn,* S.American waters (Jun 1883-Oct 1884); Proving Grounds, Annapolis (Nov 1884-Oct 1885); USNA (Oct 1885-Jul 1888); *Kearsarge,* spec.serv. (Nov 1888-Sep 1889); *Galena,* N.Atl.Sta. (Sep 1889-Aug 1890); flgs., *Philadelphia,* N.Atl.Sta. (Aug 1890-Jul 1891); l.o.a. (Jul-Oct 1891); on furlough (Oct 1891-Apr 1892); USNA (Apr 1892-Jun 1894); *Cincinnati,* Navy Yard, NY (Jun-Sep 1894); *Cushing,* Newport, RI (Sep 1894-Jul 1897); l.o.a. (Jul-Aug 1897); USNA (Aug 1897-May 1898); exec.off., *Gloucester,* N.Atl.Flt. (May-Sep 1898); USNA (Sep 1898-Jun 1900); Naval Torp.Sta., Newport, RI (Jun-Jul 1900); *Newark,* Asia.Sta. (Aug-Sep 1900); *Manila,* Asia.Sta. (Sep-Nov 1900); cdr, *Villalobos,* Asia.Sta. (Nov 1900-Aug 1902); home and w.o. (Aug-Oct 1902); USNA (Oct 1902-Jan 1905); inst. of math., USNA (Jan 1905-May 1907); cdr, *Nevada,* spec.serv. (May 1907-Sep 1908); duty with, then cdr, supply ship, *Celtic,* spec.serv. (Sep 1908-Dec 1909); capt.yd., Navy Yard, Philadelphia (Dec 1909-Nov 1911); cdr, *Vermont,* Atl.Flt. (Nov 1911-Oct 1913); NWC (Nov 1913-Feb 1914); chief of staff, Detached Sqdn., Vera Cruz, Mexico (Feb-Jul 1914); NWC (Jul-Sep 1914); cdr, U.S. Atl.Flt., *New York,* then *Wyoming* (Sep 1914-Nov 1915); home and w.o. (Nov-Dec 1915); NWC (Jan-Dec 1916); member, then pres., naval exam. and ret. bds. (Dec 1916-Jan 1919); cdr, Atl. Training Flt., flgs., *Columbia* (Jan-Dec 1919); senior U.S. naval member, Allied Naval Armistice Commission, Paris (Dec 1919-1920); U.S. Naval HQ, London (1920); senior U.S. naval member, Naval Inter-Allied Commission of Control (1920); cdr, U.S. Naval Forces, Eur. Waters, *Pittsburgh* (May 1920-Jan 1921); comdt., 3rd Naval Dist., NY (Feb-Jul 1921); member, Gen Bd., Navy Dept., Washington, DC (Jul 1921-Dec 1922); placed on Ret.Lst. (8 Dec 1922).

Career Highlights Commanded a landing force from the *Gloucester* to Guanica, Puerto Rico, on 25 Jul 1898, securing a landing place for the army, bringing down the Spanish flag, and hoisting the first U.S. flag over Puerto Rico. For his efforts and actions, was advanced five numbers. Advanced another five places for his conduct in the battle off Santiago. Served on staff of cdr of naval forces off Vera Cruz, Mexico. For heroism displayed on 21 and 22 Apr 1914 in directing affairs during the landing there, was awarded the Medal of Honor. Was an important figure in the post-World War I settlement, serving as senior U.S. naval delegate on the Allied Naval Armistice and Control Commissions. Then served as cdr of American naval forces in European waters. Was also awarded the Gold Life-Saving Medal by the Human Society for diving overboard from his flgs. in order to save a crewman who had fallen overboard.

References

Writings: a) "The Question of Naval Engineers," U.S. Naval Institute *Proceedings* 104 (Dec 1902): 911-16. b) "Logistics--Its Influence upon the Conduct of War and Its Bearing upon the Formulation of War Plans," U.S. Naval Institute *Proceedings* 168 (Feb 1917): 245-53. c) *The Descendants of Abel Huse of Newbury (1602-1690)* (Washington, DC: 1935).

CHARLES THOMAS HUTCHINS Born in Kingston, PA, on 5 Feb 1844, son of Richard and Emily (Little) Hutchins. Married Marion Clementine Borup on 17 Nov 1876. One son, Cdr Charles T. Hutchins, USN. Died on 9 Aug 1920 while in Peking, China. Buried in Arlington National Cemetery.

Ranks Act.Midn (2 Jan 1862); Midn (16 Jul 1862); Ens (12 Mar 1868); Mstr (26 Mar 1869); Lt (21 Mar 1870); LCdr (30 Jun 1887); Cdr (28 Feb 1896); Capt (2 Jul 1901); retired (30 Jun 1905); RAdm on Ret.Lst. (13 Apr 1911) to rank from 30 Jun 1905.

Career Summary Received appointment from PA (2 Jan 1862); USNA (Jan 1862-Jun 1866); found deficient and put back (Feb 1864); l.o.a. and w.o. (Jun-Oct 1866); *Lenapee*, N.Atl.Sta. (Oct 1866-Oct 1867); *Idaho*, spec.serv., Asia.Sqdn. (Oct 1867-Oct 1870); w.o. (Oct 1870-Jan 1871); USNA (Jan-Mar 1871); rec. ship, *Relief*, Washington, DC (Mar-Sep 1871); w.o. (Sep-Oct 1871); *Wyoming*, N.Atl.Sta. (Oct 1871-Mar 1874); *Fortune*, N.Atl.Sta. (Mar-Aug 1874); l.o.a. (Aug-Oct 1874); aide to comdt., Navy Yard, Washington, DC (Oct-Dec 1874); cst.surv. duty (Dec 1874-Aug 1876); cdr, *Lehigh*, N.Atl.Sta. (Sep 1876-May 1877); Hydrographic Office, Washington, DC (May 1877-Jan 1878); navigator, and exec.off., *Supply*, spec.serv., Paris (Jan 1878-Apr 1879); w.o. (Apr-Jun 1879); l.o.a. (Jun-Oct 1879); equip. duty, Navy Yard, Washington, DC (Nov 1879-Apr 1880); asst. to hydrographic off., Cst.Surv. Office, Washington, DC (Apr 1880-Aug 1881); navigator, flgs., *Lancaster*, Eur.Sta. (Aug 1881-Jun 1884); *Powhatan*, spec.serv. (Jun-Aug 1884); w.o. (Aug-Sep 1884); in charge of ships, dept. of seamanship and construction, USNA (Sep 1884-Nov 1887); exec.off., *Marion*, Asia.Sta. (Nov 1887-Jun 1890); l.o.a. (Jun-Jul 1890); asst., Bur. of Equip., Navy Dept., Washington, DC (Jul 1890-Apr 1893); cdr, *Thetis*, Pac.Sqdn. (May 1893-Jun 1895); Bur. of Nav., Washington, DC (Jul-Dec 1895); cdr, schoolship, *Saratoga* (Dec 1895-Feb 1898); asst., then insp., 5th L.h. Dist., Baltimore (Mar-Apr 1898); in charge, 5th Dist. Cst. Defense, and cdr, auxiliary naval force of dist., Baltimore (Apr-Jul 1898); comdt. of cadets, USNA (Aug 1898-Apr 1899); cdr, training ship, *Mononga-*

CHARLES THOMAS HUTCHINS
1844-1920

hela (Apr 1899-Mar 1900); training ship, *Buffalo* (Mar 1900); cdr, *Buffalo*, Asia.Sqdn. (Mar 1900-May 1902); home and w.o. (May 1902); NWC (Jun-Oct 1902); sec., L.h. Bd., Washington, DC (Oct 1902-Nov 1904); cdr, *Maine*, N.Atl.Flt. (Nov 1904-Jun 1905); retired (30 Jun 1905).

Career Highlights In 1871, was on board the *Relief* taking supplies to those starving in France during the Paris Commune. While on board the *Lancaster*, was present at the British bombardment of Alexandria, Egypt, commanding a landing party on shore for five days. With the same vessel, was at Kronstadt for the coronation of the Russian czar in 1884.

References
Writings: a) "The Naval Brigade: Its Organization, Equipment, and Tactics," U.S. Naval Institute *Proceedings* 42 (1887): 303-40. b) "Infantry-fire Tactics, Fire Discipline, and Musketry Instruction, and Practice with Rapid-Firing Cannon," U.S. Naval Institute *Proceedings* 43 (1887): 547-60.

GEORGE ELMORE IDE
1845-1917

GEORGE ELMORE IDE Born in Zanesville, OH, on 6 Dec 1845, son of Dr. William E. and Angelina (Sullivan) Ide. Married Alexandra Louise Bruen on 28 Jul 1889. One son. Retired to NY City where he died on 12 Feb 1917. Buried in Rye, NY.

Ranks Act.Midn (27 Sep 1861); title changed to Midn (16 Jul 1862); Ens (1 Dec 1866); Mstr (12 Mar 1868); Lt (26 Mar 1869); LCdr (12 Oct 1881); Cdr (5 Nov 1891); Capt (25 Mar 1899); retired with rank of RAdm (27 Sep 1901).

Career Summary Received appointment from OH (27 Sep 1861); USNA (Sep 1861-Oct 1865); turned back (Nov 1864); w.o. (Oct 1865-Jan 1866); *Dakotah*, Pac.Sqdn. (Jan 1866-Jun 1868); *Nyack*, Pac.Sqdn. (Jun-Aug 1868); w.o. (Sep-Oct 1868); rec. ship, *Vermont*, NY (Oct-Dec 1868); *Kenosha* [renamed *Plymouth*], Eur.Sta. (Jan-Oct 1869); *Severn*, and *Plymouth*, Eur.Sqdn. (Oct 1869-Apr 1872); l.o.a. (Apr-Dec 1872); rec. ship, *Vermont*, NY (Dec 1872-Jan 1873); *Juniata*, N.Atl.Sqdn. (Jan 1873-Mar 1874); *Ticonderoga*, N.Atl.Sqdn. (Mar-Apr 1874); l.o.a. (Apr-Dec 1874); Hydrographic Office, Washington, DC (Dec 1874-Jul 1875); *Portsmouth*, spec.serv. (Aug-Dec 1875); rec. ship, *Independence*, Mare Island, CA (Jan 1876-Apr 1877); w.o. and l.o.a. (Apr-Oct 1877); Naval Observatory, Washington, DC (Oct 1877-Jan 1879); *Vandalia*, Eur.Sta. (Jan-Jul 1879); w.o. (Jul-Dec 1879); exec.off., *Alliance*, N.Atl.Sta. (Jan 1880-Jun 1881); Naval Hosp., Brooklyn, NY (Jun-Sep 1881); w.o. (Sep-Nov 1881); Navy Yard, NY (Nov 1881-Feb 1882); rec. ship, *Independence*, Mare Island, CA (Mar 1882-May 1883); *Adams*, Pac.Sta. (May 1883-Sep 1884); w.o. and l.o.a. (Sep 1884-May 1885); torp. instruction, Newport, RI (Jun-Sep 1885); NWC (Sep 1885); l.o.a. (Sep 1885-May 1886); exec.off., *Alliance*, S.Atl.Sta. (May 1886-Aug 1889); w.o. and l.o.a. (Aug 1889-Aug 1891); exec.off., rec. ship *Franklin*, Norfolk, VA (Sep-Nov 1891); ord. instruction, Navy Yard, Washington, DC (Dec 1891-Mar 1892); w.o. (Mar-Aug 1892); member, bd. of inspection of merchant vessels, and other bd. duties, NY (Sep 1892-May 1894); torp. instruction, Newport, RI

(Jun-Sep 1894); cdr, *Alert*, Pac.Sqdn. (Oct 1894-Jun 1895); w.o.
(Jun 1895-Nov 1896); ord.off., Navy Yard, Norfolk, VA (Nov
1896-Feb 1898); cdr, Navy Yard, Norfolk, VA (Feb-Apr 1898);
cdr, *Justin*, N.Atl.Flt. (Apr-Jul 1898); Naval Hosps., NY, and
Norfolk, VA (Jul-Aug 1898); w.o. (Aug-Nov 1898); court-martial
bd., League Island, PA (Nov-Dec 1898); cdr, *Yosemite*, Navy
Yards, Norfolk, VA, and NY (Dec 1898-May 1900); cdr, *New
Orleans*, Asia.Sta. (May-Jun 1900); home and w.o. (Jun-Jul 1900);
capt.yd., Navy Yard, Mare Island, CA (Aug 1900-May 1901);
home, sick lv., and w.o. (May-Sep 1901); retired (27 Sep 1901).

Career Highlights Was on the 1873 voyage to Greenland to
retrieve the *Polaris* survivors. In same year, was on board the
vessel that brought back to the U.S. the *Virginius* filibusters from
Santiago, Cuba. During the war with Spain, commanded the
Justin, which participated in the Battle of Santiago.

RICHARD INCH Born in Washington, DC, on 20 Jun 1843,
son of Philip and Mary (O'Neill) Inch. Educated at the East
Washington Seminary and the Washington Seminary before
entering the navy. Married with one son; resided in Washington,
DC, where he died on 21 Apr 1911. Buried in Arlington National
Cemetery.

Ranks 3rd Asst.Engr. (8 Sep 1863); 2nd Asst.Engr. (15 Oct
1865); PAsst.Engr. (28 Sep 1874); Chief Engr. (3 Aug 1892);
Chief Engr. with rel. rank of Cdr (12 Oct 1898); Cdr (3 Mar
1899); Capt (21 Nov 1902); retired with rank of RAdm (29 Jun
1905).

Career Summary Received appointment from Washington, DC
(8 Sep 1863); *Lancaster*, and *Powhatan*, Pac.Sqdn. (Oct 1863-Mar
1867); home and w.o. (Mar-May 1867); Navy Yard, NY (May
1867-Feb 1868); *Nyack*, Pac.Sta. (Mar 1868-Nov 1870); home
and w.o. (Nov 1870-May 1871); *Triana*, and *Fortune*, spec.serv.
(May 1871-Nov 1872); *Richmond*, N.Atl.Sta. (Nov 1872-May
1873); w.o. (May-Jul 1873); training ship, *Tallapoosa* (Jul-Nov
1873); *Gettysburg*, spec.serv. (Nov 1873-Oct 1874); w.o. (Oct
1874-Mar 1875); temp. experimental duty, Navy Yard, Washington, DC (Mar 1875-Aug 1876); w.o. (Aug-Sep 1876); Navy Yard,
Washington, DC (Sep 1876-Dec 1877); *Wyoming*, Eur.Sta. (Jan
1878-May 1881); w.o. (May-Jun 1881); rec. ship, *Passaic*,
Washington, DC (Jun-Jul 1881); spec. duty, exec. mansion,
Washington, DC (Jul-Oct 1881); rec. ship, *Passaic*, Washington,
DC (Oct 1881-Jul 1882); w.o. (Jul 1882-Jun 1883); *Pinta*,
spec.serv. (Jun-Aug 1883); w.o. (Aug 1883-Mar 1884); *Yantic*,
N.Atl.Sta. (Mar 1884-Nov 1886); w.o. (Nov 1886-Mar 1887);
Navy Yard, Washington, DC (Mar 1887-Mar 1890); *Philadelphia*,
Philadelphia (Mar-Aug 1890); l.o.a. and w.o. (Aug 1890-Feb
1891); *Lancaster*, Asia.Sta. (Feb 1891-Feb 1893); *Marion*,
Asia.Sta. (Mar 1893-Jun 1894); w.o. (Jun 1894-Feb 1895); temp.
duty, *Baltimore* (Feb-Apr 1895); insp. of coal, Bur. of Equip. and
Recruiting, Washington, DC (Apr-Aug 1895); w.o. (Aug-Sep
1895); rec. ship, *Independence*, Mare Island, CA (Sep-Oct 1895);
Navy Yard, Mare Island, CA (Oct 1895-Jun 1897); *Concord*,

RICHARD INCH
1843-1911

Alaskan waters, and Asia.Sta. (Jun 1897-Feb 1898); *Boston*, Asia.Sta. (Feb-Dec 1898); *Charleston*, Asia.Sta. (Dec 1898-May 1899); Naval Sta., Cavite, P.I. (May-Dec 1899); home and w.o. (Dec 1899-May 1900); insp. of machinery, Newport News, VA (May 1900-Mar 1905); senior member, bd. of changes, Newport News, VA (Jul 1900-Jul 1905); retired (29 Jun 1905).

ROYAL RODNEY INGERSOLL Born on 4 Dec 1847 in Niles, MI, son of Harmon W. and Rebecca A. (Deniston) Ingersoll. Married Cynthia Eason on 26 Aug 1873. One son, Adm Royal Eason Ingersoll, USN (1883-1976). Retired to La Porte, IN, where he died on 21 Apr 1931. Buried in Pine Lake Cemetery in La Porte.

Ranks Midn (23 Jul 1864); Ens (19 Apr 1869); Mstr (12 Jul 1870); Lt (13 Apr 1872); LCdr (25 Feb 1893); Cdr (3 Mar 1899); Capt (21 Mar 1903); RAdm (11 Jul 1908); placed on Ret.Lst. (4 Dec 1909).

Career Summary Received appointment from MI (23 Jul 1864); USNA (Jul 1864-Jun 1868); w.o. (Jun-Sep 1868); *Ticonderoga*, Eur.Sta. (Oct 1868-Nov 1869); *Miantonomoh*, spec.serv. (Nov 1869-Jul 1870); *Plymouth*, Eur.Sqdn. (Jul 1870-Jun 1873); w.o. (Jun-Oct 1873); *Kansas*, N.Atl.Sta. (Oct 1873-Mar 1874); *Juniata*, Eur.Sqdn. (Mar-Nov 1874); *Yantic*, and *Kearsarge*, Asia.Sta. (Nov 1874-Apr 1876); home and w.o. (Apr-Jun 1876); USNA (Jul 1876-Jun 1879); w.o. (Jun-Jul 1879); *Pensacola*, Pac.Sta. (Jul 1879-Jul 1882); home and l.o.a. (Jul-Oct 1882); Naval Observatory, Washington, DC (Oct 1882-Aug 1883); USNA (Aug 1883-Sep 1887); exec.off., *Enterprise*, Eur.Sta. (Oct 1887-May 1890); l.o.a. (Jun-Dec 1890); USNA (Dec 1890-Jun 1894); cdr, prac. ship, *Bancroft* (Jun-Sep 1894); w.o. (Sep-Oct 1894); exec.off., flgs., *Philadelphia*, Pac.Sqdn. (Nov 1894-Jun 1897); l.o.a. (Jun-Aug 1897); USNA (Sep 1897-May 1898); cdr, *Hist*, N.Atl.Flt. (May-Jun 1898); cdr, *Supply*, spec.serv. (Jul-Sep 1898); USNA (Sep 1898-May 1899); cdr, *Annapolis*, N.Atl.Sqdn., and training duty (May-Sep 1899); USNA (Sep 1899-Feb 1900); ord.off., Navy Yard, Norfolk, VA (Mar-May 1900); insp. of ord., Navy Yard, NY (May 1900-Feb 1901); cdr, *Bennington*, Asia.Sta. (Apr-May 1901); cdr, *Helena*, Asia.Sta. (May 1901-Jan 1903); cdr, *New Orleans*, Asia.Sta. (Jan-May 1903); home and l.o.a. (May-Jun 1903); Bur. of Nav., Washington, DC (Jun 1903); NWC (Jul 1903-Apr 1904); member, naval exam. and ret. bds., and other duties, Washington, DC (Apr 1904-Mar 1905); additional duty, insp., *Maryland*, Newport News, VA (Jan-Apr 1905); cdr, *Maryland*, Atl.Flt. (Apr 1905-Mar 1907); home and w.o. (Mar-May 1907); spec. temp. duty, Navy Dept., Washington, DC (Jun 1907); chief of staff, Atl.Flt., *Connecticut* (Jun 1907-Apr 1908); member, Gen Bd. and other duties, Washington, DC (Apr 1908-Mar 1910); placed on Ret.Lst. (4 Dec 1909); senior member, spec. bd. on naval ord. (Jul 1917-Jan 1919).

Career Highlights Served as Chief of Staff of "Great White Flt." from its departure from Hampton Roads to its arrival in the Pacific. Spent much of his career at the USNA, subsequently

ROYAL RODNEY INGERSOLL
1847-1931

writing much on naval ordnance and ballistics.

References

Personal Papers: a) 40 items (1864-1931) in NHF,LC. b) 1 folder (1907-8) in NHF,WNY.

Writings: a) numerous works on ordnance and gunnery as textbooks for use at USNA. b) "Corrections for Wind, Motion of Gun and Speed of Target, and How to Allow for the Same," U.S. Naval Institute *Proceedings* 33 (1885): 207-23. c) "The Present Course in Ordnance and Gunnery at the Naval Academy," U.S. Naval Institute *Proceedings* 37 (1886): 91-103. d) "The Willson Disc Gun," U.S. Naval Institute *Proceedings* 68 (1893): 415-18.

BENJAMIN FRANKLIN ISHERWOOD Born in NY City on 6 Oct 1822, son of Dr. Benjamin and Eliza (Hicks) Isherwood. Educated at the Albany Academy, famous for its scientific curriculum, until he was expelled in 1836. Worked as a draftsman for the Utica and Schenectady Railroad and then with the civil engineering dept. of the railroad. Following employment on the Crofton Aquaduct and on the Erie Railroad, served as an engineer for the Treasury Dept. working on L.h. construction. Last civilian employment was with the Novelty Iron Works Company of NY. Married Mrs. Anna Hansine (Munster) Ragsdale in 1848. Five children. Died on 19 Jun 1915 in NY City.

BENJAMIN FRANKLIN
ISHERWOOD
1822-1915

Ranks 1st Asst.Engr. (23 May 1844); demoted to 2nd Asst.Engr. (22 Jan 1846); 1st Asst.Engr. (10 Jul 1847); Chief Engr. (31 Oct 1848); Engr.-in-Chief (26 Mar 1861); Engr.-in-Chief, and Chief, Bur. of Steam Engineering with rank of Commo (25 Jul 1862); placed on Ret.Lst. as Chief Engr. with rel. rank of Commo. (6 Oct 1884); Chief Engr. with rank of RAdm on Ret.Lst. (29 Jun 1906).

Career Summary Received appointment from NY (23 May 1844); yd.engr., and *General Taylor*, Navy Yard, Pensacola, FL (Oct 1844-Dec 1845); *Princeton*, and *Spitfire*, Home Sqdn. (Feb 1846-Aug 1847); l.o.a. (Aug 1847-Jan 1848); spec. duty, office of engr.-in-chief, Navy Dept., Washington, DC (Jan-Feb 1848); L.h. serv. (Feb 1848-Dec 1850); spec. duty, Bur. of Construction, Equip., and Repair, Washington, DC (Dec 1850); member, bd. of examiners (Dec 1850-Apr 1851); L.h. duty (Apr-Jun 1851); office of engr.-in-chief, Navy Dept., Washington, DC (Jun 1851-Aug 1853); *Allegheny*, Navy Yard, Washington, DC (Sep-Oct 1853); w.o. (Oct 1853-Mar 1854); *Massachusetts*, spec.serv. (Mar-Nov 1854); w.o. (Nov 1854-Apr 1855); member, bd. of examiners, Washington, DC (May-Jun 1855); *San Jacinto*, E.Ind.Sqdn. (Sep 1855-Aug 1858); spec. duty, *San Jacinto* (Aug 1858-Sep 1859); member, bd. of examiners (Mar-Sep 1859); spec. duty, *Seminole* (Sep 1859); pres., bd. of examiners (Sep 1859-Sep 1860); spec. duty, *Michigan*, Erie, PA, then spec. duty, Washington, DC (Sep 1860-Mar 1861); engr.-in-chief, and chief, Bur. of Steam Engineering, Washington, DC (Mar 1861-Mar 1869); w.o. (Mar-Jul 1869); Navy Yard, Mare Island, CA (Sep 1869-Sep 1871); w.o. and spec. duty, NY (Sep 1871-Jul 1872); w.o. (Jul 1872-Jan 1873); spec. duty, Key West, FL (Jan-Jul 1873); sick lv. (Jul

1873-Feb 1874); spec. duty (Feb 1874-Sep 1875); l.o.a. and spec. duty, Europe (Nov 1875-Apr 1877); spec. duty, experimental bd., NY (Apr-Dec 1877); member, various bds. on engineering, NY (Jan 1878-Jul 1881); member, naval advisory bds. (Jul 1881-Oct 1884); placed on Ret.Lst. (6 Oct 1884).

Career Highlights Often considered mid-nineteenth century's leading marine engr., was very actively involved in designing what would become the foundation of the steel navy. As chief engr, developed many revolutionary types of engines, propellers, and vessels. Wrote prolifically on experiments he conducted. Became chief engr. of the navy just prior to the Civil War and in following year became chief of the newly formed Bur. of Steam Engineering. Served on first naval advisory bd. in 1881.

References

Selected Writings: a) *Engineering Precedents for Steam Machinery* (NY: 1858-59). b) *Experimental Researches in Steam Engineering* (2 vols., Philadelphia: 1863-1865). c) [Numerous other works]

Additional Sources: a) *A Brief Sketch of Some of the Blunders in the Engineering Practice of the Bureau of Steam Engineering, in the U.S. Navy, by an Engineer* (NY: 1868). b) Frank M. Bennett, *The Steam Navy of the United States* (Pittsburgh: 1896). c) George W. Dyson, "Benjamin Franklin Isherwood," U.S. Naval Institute *Proceedings*, 462 (Aug 1941): 1138-46. d) Edward William Sloan, III. *Benjamin Franklin Isherwood, Naval Engineer* (Annapolis: 1965). e) _____, "Isherwood's Masterpiece," U.S. Naval Institute *Proceedings* 754 (Dec 1965): 55-65.

JOSEPH LEE JAYNE
1863-1928

JOSEPH LEE JAYNE Born on 30 May 1863 in Brandon, MS, son of William McAfee and Julia Hamilton (Kennon) Jayne. Married Elizabeth Tilton Eastman on 5 Dec 1894. Two children, Anna Morwell Jayne and Capt John Kennon Jayne, USNR (1897-1957). Studied at Johns Hopkins Univ. from 1885 to 1888, receiving a certificate in applied electricity for which he was awarded the B.Engineering degree in 1927. Resided in Jamestown, RI, dying in Newport, RI, on 24 Nov 1928. Buried in Arlington National Cemetery.

Ranks Cadet Midn (28 Jun 1878); Ens (10 Jul 1884); Ltjg (10 Jul 1894); Lt (17 Dec 1897); LCdr (11 Sep 1903); Cdr (3 Jan 1908); Capt (1 Jul 1911); temp. RAdm (15 Oct 1917); placed on Ret.Lst. with rank of RAdm (10 May 1921).

Career Summary Received appointment from MS as a Cadet Midn (28 Jun 1878); USNA (Jun 1878-Jun 1882); *Tennessee,* N.Atl.Sqdn. (Jun 1882-Apr 1884); USNA (Apr-Jun 1884); w.o. (Jun-Jul 1884); ord. instruction, Navy Yard, Washington, D.C. (Jul-Oct 1884); *Galena,* N.Atl.Sta. (Oct 1884-Oct 1885); spec. duty, Johns Hopkins Univ., Baltimore (Oct 1885-May 1886); prac. ship, *Jamestown* (May-Aug 1886); spec. duty, Johns Hopkins Univ., Baltimore (Sep 1886-Jun 1887); torp. instruction, Newport, RI (Jun-Sep 1887); w.o. (Sep 1887); spec. duty, Johns Hopkins Univ., Baltimore (Oct 1887-Jun 1888); *Atlanta,* N.Atl.Sqdn. (Jun-Nov 1888); on furlough (Nov 1888-Nov 1889); w.o. (Nov-Dec 1889); *Charleston,* Navy Yard, Mare Island, CA (Jan-Apr 1890);

Iroquois, Pac.Sta. (Apr 1890-May 1892); rec. ship *Independence,* Navy Yard, Mare Island, CA (May-Jun 1892); *Gedney,* cst.surv. duty (Jun 1892-Apr 1893); home and l.o.a. (Apr-Aug 1893); Naval Insp. of Electric Lighting, Bur. of Equip., Washington, D.C. (Sep 1893-Oct 1895); *Lancaster,* S.Atl.Sqdn. (Oct 1895-Oct 1896); sick lv. (Nov 1896-May 1897); Torp.Sta., Newport, RI (Jun-Sep 1897); Navy Yard, Washington, D.C. (Sep 1897-Mar 1898); *Rodgers,* Baltimore (Mar-Apr 1898); cdr, *Rodgers,* N.Atl. Sqdn. (Apr-Nov 1898); cdr, *Peoria,* N.Atl.Sta. (Nov 1898-Jun 1899); cdr, *Uncas,* Navy Yards, Philadelphia and Port Royal, SC (Jun-Oct 1899); naval hospitals, Port Royal, SC, and Norfolk, VA (Oct-Nov 1899); sick lv. (Nov 1899-Feb 1900); temp. duty, rec. ship, *Independence,* Navy Yard, Mare Island, CA (Mar 1900); en route to Asia.Sta. (Mar-Apr 1900); *Newark,* flgs., Asia.Sqdn. (Apr-Oct 1900); Navy Yard, Mare Island, CA (Oct-Nov 1900); l.o.a. (Nov 1900-Feb 1901); *Richmond,* League Island, PA (Feb-Mar 1901); rec. ship, *Vermont,* NY (Mar-Apr 1901); *Philadelphia,* Pac.Sta. (Apr-Jul 1901); navigator and engineering officer, *Abarenda,* station ship, Samoa (Jul 1901-Sep 1902); duty, Bur. of Equip., Washington, D.C. (Oct 1902-Jan 1905); navigator, *Colorado,* on trials, Atl.Flt, then Asia.Sta. (Jan 1905-Feb 1907): cdr, *Elcano,* Yangtze Patrol, and Cavite, P.I. (Feb-Nov 1907); temp. cdr, *Rainbow,* flgs. Philippine Sqdn., Atl.Flt. (Nov-Dec 1907); return and w.o. (Dec 1907-Feb 1908); Sec., Gen Bd., Washington, D.C. (Mar 1908-Mar 1910); cdr, *New York,* Asia.Flt. [name changed on 16 Feb 1911 to *Saratoga*] (Mar 1910-Jun 1911); spec. temp. duty, Navy Dept., Washington, D.C. (Jul 1911); spec. duty, NWC (Jul-Sep 1911); supt., Naval Observatory, Washington, D.C. (Oct 1911-Feb 1914); cdr, *New Jersey,* Atl.Flt. (Feb 1914-Jan 1916); NWC (Jan-Dec 1916); comdt., Naval Aeronautic Sta., Pensacola, FL (Jan-Oct 1917); duty with, then cdr, *Mississippi,* Newport News, VA (Nov 1917-Jan 1918); cdr, Div. 3, Battleship Force, Atl. Flt., *Virginia* (Feb-Sep 1918); temp. duty with Chief of Naval Operations, Navy Dept., Washington, D.C. (Sep-Oct 1918); comdt., 12th Naval Dist., San Francisco (Oct 1918-Sep 1920); cdr, *Minneapolis,* flgs., Pac. Flt. (Oct 1920-Mar 1921); Naval Hosp., Mare Island, CA (Mar 1921); w.o. (Mar-May 1921); placed on Ret.Lst. (10 May 1921).

Career Highlights Commanded *New Jersey* during the intervention in Vera Cruz, Mexico, in 1914. Received Navy Cross for services as a battleship division commander as well as Spanish Campaign Medal, Philippione Campaign Medal, China Relief Expd. Medal, and Victory Medal. Also received Insignia of Diploma "Al Merito," First Class from government of Chile and was named Cdr of Order of Leopold (Belgium).

References

Writings: a) "The Naval Observatory Time Service and How Jewelers May Make Use of its Radio Signals," *American Jeweler* 33 (1913): 424-32. b) "A Naval Pooh-Bah," U.S. Naval Institute *Proceedings* 244 (Jun 1923): 983-1001.

THEODORE FRELINGHUYSEN JEWELL Born in George-

**THEODORE FRELINGHUYSEN
JEWELL
1844-1932**

town, Washington, DC, on 5 Aug 1844, son of Thomas and Eleanor (Spencer) Jewell. Married Elizabeth Lindsay, daughter of RAdm Charles H. Poor, USN, on 15 Jun 1871. One son, Cdr Charles T. Jewell, USN (ret). Resided in Washington, DC, where he died on 26 Jul 1932. Buried in Arlington National Cemetery.

Ranks Act.Midn (29 Nov 1861); title changed to Midn (16 Jul 1862); Ens (1 Nov 1866); Mstr (1 Dec 1866); Lt (12 Mar 1868); LCdr (26 Mar 1869); Cdr (26 Jan 1885); Capt (1 Feb 1898); RAdm (15 Mar 1904); retired (22 Nov 1904).

Career Summary Received appointment from VA (29 Nov 1861); USNA (Nov 1861-Nov 1864); spec. duty, Navy Yard, Washington, DC, and Potomac Flot. (Jun-Jul 1863); l.o.a. (Nov 1864-Feb 1865); rec. ship, *Vermont*, NY (Feb-Apr 1865); flgs., *Colorado*, Eur.Sqdn. (Apr 1865-Dec 1866); *Frolic*, and *Canandaigua*, Eur.Sqdn. (Dec 1866-May 1868); w.o. (May-Oct 1868); Hydrographic Office, Washington, DC (Oct 1868-May 1869); training ship, *Sabine* (May 1869-Aug 1870); Naval Observatory, Washington, DC (Sep 1870-Mar 1871); asst., dept. of physics and chemistry, USNA (Mar 1871-May 1872); *Tuscarora*, S.Pac.Sqdn. and spec.serv. (May 1872-Oct 1874); w.o. (Oct-Dec 1874); inst. of physics and chemistry, USNA (Dec 1874-Jun 1878); cst.surv. duty (Jun 1878-Jul 1879); exec.off., apprentice ship, *Constitution* (Aug 1879-May 1881); Torp.Sta., Newport, RI (Jun 1881-Jun 1886); cdr, *Essex*, Asia.Sta. (Jun 1886-May 1889); torp. instruction, Newport, RI (Jun-Aug 1889); NWC (Aug-Sep 1889); l.o.a. (Sep-Oct 1889); member, bd. of organization, Washington, DC (Oct-Nov 1889); insp. of ord. and in charge, Torp.Sta., Newport, RI (Dec 1889-Jan 1893); supt., Naval Gun Factory, Navy Yard, Washington, DC (Jan 1893-Feb 1896); cdr, *Marblehead*, Eur. and N.Atl.Stas. (Mar 1896-Mar 1897); l.o.a. (Mar-Apr 1897); asst., then insp., 10th L.h. Dist., Buffalo, NY (Apr 1897-Mar 1898); cdr, *Minneapolis*, "Flying Sqdn.," N.Atl.Flt. (Mar-Sep 1898); cdr, *Minneapolis*, *Columbia*, and other vessels in reserve, Navy Yard, League Island, PA (Sep 1898-Mar 1899); cdr, *Lancaster*, Boston, and N.Atl.Flt. (Mar-May 1899); cdr, *Brooklyn*, Asia.Sta. (May 1899-Feb 1900); chief of staff, Asia.Sta., and cdr, *Brooklyn* (Oct 1899-Feb 1900); member, naval exam. and ret. bds., and other bd. duties (Mar 1900-May 1901); NWC (Jun-Sep 1901); member, naval exam. and ret. bds., and various other bd. duties (Oct 1901-Mar 1904); cdr, N.Atl. Sqdn., *Olympia* (Mar-Nov 1904); retired (22 Nov 1904).

Career Highlights During the Civil War and while still at the USNA, was despatched to the Washington Navy Yard and to the Potomac Flot. when the Capital's defenses were threatened by Gen Robert E. Lee's forces during the summer of 1863. While on board the *Tuscarora* from 1872-74, assisted in survey of an interoceanic canal route, in that vessel's sounding of the north Pac.Ocean, and commanded a force of sailors and marines in 1873 at Panama to protect American lives and interests there. Also commanded a force from the *Tuscarora* in Feb of 1874 against the mob during the election of King Kalakaua at Honolulu.

References
Writings: Deep Sea Soundings," U.S. Naval Institute *Proceedings* 4 (1877): 37-63.
Additional Sources: William J. Hourihan, "Marlinespike Diplomacy: The Navy in the Mediterranean, 1904," U.S. Naval Institute *Proceedings* 911 (Jan 1979): 42-51.

MORTIMER LAWRENCE JOHNSON Born in Nahant, MA, on 1 Jun 1842, son of Walter Johnson. Died in Portsmouth, NH, on 14 Feb 1913. Buried in Mt. Auburn Cemetery, Cambridge, MA.

Ranks Act.Midn (29 Nov 1859); title changed to Midn (16 Jul 1862); Ens (16 Sep 1862); Lt (22 Feb 1864); LCdr (25 Jul 1866); Cdr (26 Apr 1878); Capt (9 May 1893); RAdm (29 Jan 1901); placed on Ret.Lst. (1 Jun 1904).

Career Summary Received appointment from MA (29 Nov 1859); USNA (Nov 1859-May 1861); *Susquehanna*, S.Atl. Blk.Sqdn. (Jun-Aug 1861); *Sabine*, S.Atl.Blk.Sqdn. (Aug-Nov 1861); *Wabash*, S.Atl.Blk.Sqdn. (Nov 1861-Jul 1863); to exam. and w.o. (Jul-Aug 1863); *Wabash*, S.Atl.Blk.Sqdn. (Aug 1863-Aug 1864); *Colorado*, S.Atl.Blk.Sqdn. (Aug 1864-Mar 1865); flag lt and cdr, *Estrella*, W.Gulf Blk.Sqdn. (Mar-Jul 1865); sick lv. (Jul-Dec 1865); *Dacotah*, and *Wateree*, Pac.Sta. (Dec 1865-Sep 1868); w.o. (Sep-Oct 1868); rec. ship, *Ohio*, Boston (Oct 1868-Jan 1869); *Kenosha* [renamed *Plymouth*], Eur.Sta. (Jan 1869-Jan 1870); ord. duty, then asst. to exec.off., Navy Yard, Portsmouth, NH (Jan 1870-Jul 1871); *Worcester*, spec.serv. (Aug-Dec 1871); w.o. (Dec 1871-Feb 1872); exec.off., *Wyoming*, N.Atl.Sta. (Feb 1872-Aug 1873); w.o. (Aug-Oct 1873); exec.off., rec. ship, *Sabine*, Portsmouth, NH (Oct 1873-Aug 1874); exec.off., *Powhatan*, spec.serv. (Sep 1874-May 1875); exec.off., rec. ship, *Ohio*, Boston (May-Oct 1875); exec.off., rec. ship, *Wabash*, Boston (Oct 1875-Aug 1878); insp. of ord., Navy Yard, Portsmouth, NH (Sep 1878-Feb 1879); cdr, *Ashuelot*, Asia.Sta. (Mar 1879-May 1881); w.o. (Jun 1881-Jan 1882); Navy Yard, Portsmouth, NH (Jan-Apr 1882); torp. instruction, Newport, RI (May-Jul 1882); w.o. (Jul-Sep 1882); bd. duty, Portsmouth, NH (Sep 1882-Jul 1883); w.o. (Jul 1883-Sep 1884); Navy Yard, Boston (Sep 1884-Oct 1887); l.o.a. (Oct 1887-Jun 1889); w.o. (Jun-Aug 1889); court-martial duty (Aug 1889); *Monocacy*, Asia.Sta. (Oct 1889-Sep 1891); l.o.a. and w.o. (Sep 1891-Sep 1892); NWC (Sep-Oct 1892); w.o. (Oct 1892-Mar 1893); equip.off., Navy Yard, Portsmouth, NH (May-Nov 1893); w.o. (Nov 1893-May 1894); cdr, rec. ship, *Franklin*, Norfolk, VA (Apr 1894-Jul 1895); cdr, *Cincinnati*, N.Atl.Sta. (Aug 1895-May 1897); cdr, *San Francisco*, Eur.Sta. (May-Sep 1897); l.o.a. and w.o. (Oct 1897-Mar 1898); cdr, *Miantonomoh*, N.Atl.Sqdn. (Mar-Oct 1898); capt.yd., Navy Yard, Boston (Oct 1898-Jan 1901); comdt., Naval Sta., Port Royal, SC (Jan-Sep 1901); comdt., Navy Yard, Boston (Sep 1901-Jun 1904); placed on Ret.Lst. (1 Jun 1904).

Career Highlights During Civil War, participated in all the operations by the S.Atl.Blk.Sqdn. against Charleston. Also

MORTIMER LAWRENCE JOHNSON
1842-1913

participated in both attacks against Fort Fisher in Dec and Jan 1864-65.

MARBURY JOHNSTON   Born in Albany, GA, on 2 Dec 1860, son of Thomas Henry and Camilla (Hill) Johnston. Remained single. Made his home in Cuthbert, GA, where he died on 15 Mar 1934. Buried in Macon, GA.

Ranks   Cadet Midn (23 Sep 1878); title changed to Naval Cadet (1 Jun 1882); Ens (1 Jul 1884); Ltjg (22 Jun 1894); Lt (7 Nov 1897); LCdr (10 Aug 1903); Cdr (6 Dec 1907); Capt (14 Jun 1911); temp. RAdm (31 Aug 1917); RAdm (28 Nov 1918); placed on Ret.Lst. (2 Dec 1924).

Career Summary   Received appointment from GA (23 Sep 1878); USNA (Sep 1878-Jun 1882); *Yantic*, spec.serv. (Jun 1882-Aug 1883); *Swatara*, Navy Yard, NY (Aug 1883); *Tennessee*, Navy Yard, NY (Aug 1883); *Swatara*, N.Atl.Sta. (Aug 1883-Mar 1884); USNA (Apr-Jun 1884); w.o. (Jun-Jul 1884); training ship, *Portsmouth* (Aug 1884-May 1886); cst.surv. duty (May 1886-Nov 1887); Fish Commission steamer, *Albatross* (Nov 1887-Oct 1890); l.o.a. (Nov 1890-Feb 1891); Office of Naval Intelligence, Navy Dept., Washington, DC (Feb 1891-Apr 1892); *Concord*, spec.serv., and Asia. and N.Pac.Sqdns. (Apr 1892-May 1895); w.o. (May-Sep 1895); rec. ship, *Franklin*, Norfolk, VA (Oct-Nov 1895); NWC (Nov 1895-Aug 1897); *San Francisco*, N.Atl.Sqdn. (Aug 1897-Mar 1898); *New Orleans*, Norfolk, VA (Mar-Apr 1898); *San Francisco*, N.Atl.Flt. (Apr-Sep 1898); exec.off., *Cassius*, N.Atl.Flt. (Sep-Nov 1898); *Justin*, spec.serv. (Nov 1898-Feb 1899); *Nero*, Asia.Sta. (Feb 1899-Mar 1900); spec. duty (Mar-Apr 1900); exec.off., *Prairie*, Naval Militia (Apr 1900-Feb 1901); rec. ship, *Vermont*, NY (Feb-Aug 1901); rec. ship, *Columbia*, NY (Aug 1901-Jul 1902); exec.off., *Dolphin*, Navy Yard, Washington, DC (Jul 1902); rec. ship, *Columbia*, NY (Jul-Aug 1902); navigator, *Montgomery*, Caribbean Div., N.Atl. qdn. (Aug-Dec 1902); asst. to U.S. naval minister, Laguyara, Venezuela (Dec 1902-Jul 1903); additional duty, naval attaché, Caracas, Venezuela (Jan-Jul 1903); temp. duty, Gen Bd., Washington, DC (Sep-Oct 1903); home and w.o. (Oct 1903); cdr, 2nd Torp.Flot., *Whipple* (Nov 1903-Dec 1905); Navy Yard, NY (Jan 1906-Aug 1907); cdr, Fish Commission steamer, *Albatross* (Sep 1907-May 1908); cdr, *Galveston*, Asia.Sta. (Jun 1908-Mar 1909); Navy Yard, Puget Sound, WA (Apr 1909-Aug 1910); additional temp. duty, capt.yd., Puget Sound, WA (July 1909-Aug 1910); capt.yd., Navy Yard, Portsmouth, NH (Aug 1910-Nov 1911); cdr, training ship, *Georgia* (Nov 1911-Dec 1912); NWC (Jan 1913-Dec 1914); comdt., Naval Sta., New Orleans (Jan 1915-Apr 1917); cdr, Sqdn. Four, Patrol Force, Atl.Flt., *Tacoma* (Apr-Jul 1917); cdr, Divs. Three and Four, Sqdn. Two, Cruiser Force, Atl.Flt., *Denver* (Jul 1917-Oct 1918); additional duty, American convoy off., Port of NY (Jul 1917-Oct 1918); comdt., 15th Naval Dist., Panama Canal Zone (Nov 1918-Aug 1921); dir. of naval communications, Navy Dept., Washington, DC (Aug-Dec 1921); pres., naval exam. and ret. bds., Navy Dept., Washington, DC

(Dec 1921-Aug 1924); w.o. (Aug-Dec 1924); placed on Ret.Lst. (2 Dec 1924).

References
Writings: "Discipline in the Navy," U.S. Naval Institute *Proceedings* 143 (Sep 1912): 851-57.

JAMES JOHNSON KANE Born in Ottawa, Ontario, Canada, on 18 Oct 1837, son of Capt Clement (Royal Navy) and Barbara (Price) Kane. Studied at Chambale College for one year and at Montreal College for a year before attending Stonyhurst College in England from 1847 to 1851. Then studied medicine at Toronto where he took the A.M. On account of ill health, went to sea in 1853. Entered the U.S. Navy as a volunteer officer in 1861. Between the end of the Civil War and his appointment in the regular navy, attended the Univ. of Lewisburg (now Bucknell), graduating from the theology dept. there in 1867. Then attended Harvard Law School from 1869 to 1870. Died on 10 Mar 1921 at the Navy Hosp. in Philadelphia. Buried in Arlington National Cemetery.

Ranks Act. Mate (8 Aug 1861); Act.Ens (14 Nov 1862); honorably discharged (31 Aug 1865); Chaplain (Baptist) (6 Jun 1868); retired with rank of Capt (30 Oct 1896); Chaplain with rank of RAdm on Ret.Lst. (29 Jun 1906).

Career Summary Received appointment as Act. Mate (8 Aug 1861); *Tennessee, Maria A. Wood,* and *Pontoosuc,* W.Gulf and N.Atl.Blk.Sqdns. (1861-Aug 1865); discharged (31 Aug 1865); received appointment from NY as chaplain (6 Jun 1868); w.o. (Jun-Aug 1868); flgs., *Contoocook* [renamed *Albany*], N.Atl.Sqdn. (Sep 1868-Oct 1869); w.o. (Oct-Nov 1869); Navy Yard, Portsmouth, NH (Dec 1869-Oct 1870); rec. ship, *Vermont,* NY (Nov 1870-Apr 1872); Navy Yard, Mare Island, CA (May-Dec 1872); w.o. (Dec 1872-Dec 1873); *Minnesota,* Navy Yard, NY (Dec 1873); w.o. (Dec 1873-Jan 1874); *Roanoke,* spec. duty, NY (Jan-Jun 1874); l.o.a. and w.o. (Jun 1874-Dec 1880); rec. ship, *Franklin,* Norfolk, VA (Jan 1881-Jul 1883); w.o. (Jul 1883-Jun 1884); l.o.a. (Aug 1884-Feb 1886); *Pensacola,* Eur.Sta. (Mar 1886-Feb 1888); w.o. and l.o.a. (Feb 1888-Jan 1891); rec. ship, *Franklin,* Norfolk, VA (Jan-Jul 1891); l.o.a. (Jul 1891-Apr 1892); Navy Yard, NY (May 1892-Jun 1894); w.o. and l.o.a. (Jun 1894-Oct 1896); retired (30 Oct 1896).

THEODORE FREDERICK KANE Born in Washington, DC, on 19 Aug 1840, son of Theodore Kane. Married with two sons. Died in NY City on 14 Mar 1908. Buried in Arlington National Cemetery.

Ranks Act.Midn (27 Sep 1855); Midn (9 Jun 1859); Lt (31 Aug 1861); LCdr (22 Sep 1865); Cdr (28 Dec 1872); Capt (19 May 1886); retired (20 Jun 1896); promoted to RAdm on Ret.Lst. (29 Jun 1906).

Career Summary Received appointment from NY (27 Sep 1855); USNA (Sep 1855-Jun 1859); flgs., *Constellation,* and *Mystic,* Afr.Sqdn. (Jun 1859-Oct 1861); exec.off., *Bainbridge,* E.

THEODORE FREDERICK KANE
1840-1908

Gulf Blk.Sqdn. (Nov 1861-Jun 1862); *Sonoma,* James River Flot.
(Jun-Aug 1862); USNA (Aug 1862-Sep 1863); *Neptune,* W.Ind.
Sqdn. (Sep 1863-May 1865); w.o. (May-Jul 1865); apprentice
ship, *Savannah* (Jul-Sep 1865); inst. of gunnery, USNA (Oct
1865-Sep 1868); *Mohongo,* N.Pac.Sta. (Nov 1868-May 1869);
w.o. (May-Jun 1869); *Juniata,* and supply ship, *Supply,* Eur.Sta.
(Jul 1869-Jul 1871); ord. duty, Navy Yard, Washington, DC (Aug
1871-Apr 1872); cdr, *Frolic,* spec.serv. (Apr-May 1872); ord. duty,
Navy Yard, Washington, DC (May 1872-Mar 1873); spec. duty,
aide to Adm David D. Porter, Washington, DC (Mar 1873-Aug
1876); asst.sec., spec. bd., Washington, DC (Oct-Dec 1876); cdr,
Alliance, Eur.Sta. (Dec 1876-Jan 1879); l.o.a. (Jan-Mar 1879);
torp. instruction, Newport, RI (Jun-Sep 1879); Naval Observatory, Washington, DC (Sep 1879-Sep 1880); cdr, *Santee,* USNA
(Oct 1880-Mar 1881); insp. of ord., Navy Yard, Washington, DC
(Apr 1881-Nov 1884); cdr, *Galena,* N.Atl.Sta. (Dec 1884-Oct
1885); w.o. (Oct-Nov 1885); cdr, training ship, *Minnesota* (Dec
1885-Apr 1888); cdr, flgs., *Lancaster,* Eur.Sta. (May 1888-Sep
1889); equip.off., Navy Yard, NY (Oct 1889-Apr 1891); capt.yd.,
Navy Yard, NY (May 1891-Sep 1893); w.o. (Oct-Nov 1893);
pres., bd. of inspection of merchant ships, NY (Nov 1893-Aug
1894); cdr, *Miantonomoh,* spec.serv. (Aug-Nov 1894); w.o. (Nov
1894-Apr 1895); bd. and court-martial duties (May-Sep 1895);
cdr, *Monterey,* Pac.Sqdn. (Sep 1895-Feb 1896); sick lv. (Feb-May
1896); retired (20 Jun 1896); spec. duty, supt., Atl.Cst. Signal
Serv. (Apr-May 1898).

References
Personal Papers: c. 200 pp. (1855-98) in Newport Historical
Society, Newport, RI.

BENJAMIN HARRISON KIDDER Born in Edgartown, MA,
on 23 Jan 1836. His wife was Eugenia N. Kidder. Resided in
Malden, MA. Died on 26 Oct 1909, in Edgartown, where he was
also buried.

Ranks Asst.Surg. (20 Sep 1861); PAsst.Surg. (28 Jun 1865);
Surg. (2 Mar 1868); Medl.Insp. (30 Jan 1887); Medl.Dir. (21 Aug
1893); placed on Ret.Lst. (23 Jan 1898); RAdm on Ret.Lst. (29
Jun 1906).

Career Summary Received appointment from MA (20 Sep
1861); w.o. (Sep-Dec 1861); rec. ship, *Ohio,* Boston (Dec
1861-Jan 1862); *Marblehead,* S.Atl.Blk.Sqdn. (Feb 1862-Feb
1864); Navy Yard, NY (Feb-Sep 1864); flgs., *Colorado,* N.Atl.
Sqdn. (Sep 1864-Feb 1865); USNA (Feb-Jul 1865); *De Soto,*
spec.serv., then N.Atl.Sqdn. (Jul 1865-Jan 1868); w.o. (Jan-Aug
1868); temp. duty, Norfolk, VA (Aug-Oct 1868); w.o. (Oct
1868-May 1869); spec. duty, Boston (May 1869-Nov 1870);
Terror, N.Atl.Sqdn. (Nov 1870-Nov 1871); return and w.o. (Nov
1871-Mar 1872); Naval Hosp., Norfolk, VA (Mar 1872-Aug
1873); USNA (Aug-Sep 1873); *Ossipee,* N.Atl.Sta. (Oct 1873-
Sep 1876); Naval Hosp., Philadelphia (Sep 1876-Sep 1878); depot
ship, *New Hampshire,* Port Royal, SC (Oct 1878-Jun 1881);
Wyoming, Port Royal, SC (Jun-Oct 1881); w.o. (Oct 1881-Feb

1882); member, naval exam. bd., Washington, DC (Feb-Apr 1882); rec. ship, *Wabash*, Boston (Apr-Nov 1882); Naval Sta., Port Royal, SC (Nov 1882-Aug 1883); Navy Yard, Norfolk, VA (Sep 1883-Mar 1885); *Powhatan*, N.Atl.Sta. (May 1885-Jun 1886); flt.surg., N.Atl.Sta., *Tennessee* (Jun 1886-Jun 1888); w.o. (Jun 1888-Jun 1889); USNA (Jun 1889-Oct 1892); Naval Sta., Port Royal, SC (Oct 1892-Sep 1893); w.o. (Sep 1893-Jul 1894); bd. and spec. duties (Aug 1894-Feb 1898); placed on Ret.Lst. (23 Jan 1898).

ANDREW JACKSON KIERSTED   Born in New Point Comfort (Matthews County), VA, on 25 Dec 1832, son of Luke and Catherine Sophia (Myer) Kiersted. Educated in schools in VA and ME. Married Isabella Stuart Henderson on 26 Jan 1866. Retired to Philadelphia, where he died on 10 May 1910.

Ranks   3rd Asst.Engr. (26 Jun 1856); 1st Asst.Engr. (2 Aug 1859); Chief Engr. (12 Nov 1861); placed on Ret.Lst. (25 Dec 1894); RAdm on Ret.Lst. (29 Jun 1906).

Career Summary   Received appointment from MD (26 Jun 1856); *Minnesota*, Navy Yard, Washington, DC (Jul 1856-May 1857); *Minnesota*, E.Ind.Sqdn. (May 1857-May 1859); *Mohican*, Afr.cst. (Oct 1859-Sep 1861); *Tuscarora*, spec.serv., Eur. waters (Oct 1861-Apr 1863); *Tuscarora*, N.Atl.Blk.Sqdn. (Oct 1863-Jun 1865); insp. of machinery being built, Port Richmond Iron Works, and Penn Works, Philadelphia (Sep 1865-Jul 1868); w.o. (Jul 1868-Jun 1869); *Ossipee*, Pac.Sta. (Jun 1869-Jun 1872); member, bd. of examiners, USNA (Mar-Apr 1873); insp. of machinery afloat, Norfolk, VA (Aug-Sep 1873); in charge, engineers' stores, Philadelphia (Sep-Nov 1873); *Franklin*, Navy Yard, Boston (Nov-Dec 1873); in charge, engineers' stores, Philadelphia (Dec 1873-May 1875); additional duty, pres., engr.exam.bd., Philadelphia (Feb-May 1875); pres., engr.exam.bd., NY (May-Nov 1875); *Vandalia*, N.Atl.Sqdn. (Dec 1875-Aug 1876); flt.engr., N.Atl. Sqdn., *Hartford* (Aug 1876-Mar 1877); in charge, engineers' stores, Boston, and insp. of steam boilers, S.Boston Iron Works, Boston (Mar-May 1877); w.o. (Mar 1877-Jan 1878); member, bd. of examiners, USNA (Jan 1878); member, bd. for steam trials, Philadelphia (Feb-Nov 1878); w.o. (Nov 1878-Jul 1879); *Vandalia*, N.Atl.Sqdn. (Jul 1879-Sep 1881); flt.engr., N.Atl.Sqdn., *Tennessee* (Sep 1881-Aug 1882); w.o. (Aug 1882-Feb 1884); spec. duty, Milford, CT (Mar-May 1884); head, dept. of steam engineering, Navy Yard, League Island, PA (May 1884-May 1887); Navy Yard, League Island (May 1887-May 1888); *Trenton*, Pac. Sqdn. (Jun 1888-Mar 1889); *Nipsic*, Pac.Sqdn. (Mar-Oct 1889); insp. of machinery, Southwark Foundry and Machine Company, Philadelphia (Dec 1889-Jul 1893); Navy Yard, Portsmouth, NH (Jul 1893-Dec 1894); placed on Ret.Lst. (25 Dec 1894); duty, Naval Auxiliary Force, Philadelphia (Jun 1898-Mar 1899).

WILLIAM WIRT KIMBALL   Born in Paris, ME, on 9 Jan 1848, son of BGen William King, USA, and Frances Freeland (Rawson) Kimball. His father commanded the 12th ME Infantry

WILLIAM WIRT KIMBALL
1848-1930

from 1862 to 1864. Married Esther Smith Spencer on 18 Jul 1882. Resided in Paris, ME. Died in Washington, DC, on 26 Jan 1930. Buried in Arlington National Cemetery.

Ranks Midn (31 Jul 1865); Ens (12 Jul 1870); Mstr (14 Oct 1871); Lt (18 Dec 1874); LCdr (6 Dec 1896); Cdr (8 Dec 1899); Capt (12 Jan 1905); RAdm (17 Dec 1908); placed on Ret.Lst. (9 Jan 1910).

Career Summary Received appointment by virtue of being the son of an officer (31 Jul 1865); USNA (Jul 1865-Jun 1869); *Sabine*, spec. cruise (Jun 1869-Jul 1870); w.o. (Jul-Oct 1870); torp. instruction, Newport, RI (Nov 1870-Apr 1871); *Shawmut*, N.Atl.Sqdn. (Apr 1871-Aug 1873); Experimental Battery, Annapolis (Sep 1873-Jul 1874); torp.off., *Intrepid*, spec.serv. (Jul-Dec 1874); Experimental Battery, Annapolis (Dec 1874-Oct 1875); *Alert*, Asia.Sta. (Nov 1875-Feb 1879); home and w.o. (Feb-Jul 1879); ord. duty, Navy Yard, Washington, DC (Aug-Dec 1879); spec. duty, Springfield, MA (Dec 1879-Nov 1882); *Tennessee*, N.Atl.Sta. (Nov 1882-Feb 1886); l.o.a. (Feb-Sep 1886); Bur. of Ord., Washington, DC (Sep 1886-Jan 1888); insp. of ord., Hartford, CT, and elsewhere (Jan 1888-Apr 1890); on furlough (Apr 1890-May 1891); training ship, *Monongahela* (May 1891-Jul 1893); *San Francisco*, N.Atl. and S.Atl.Stas. (Jul 1893-Jan 1894); exec.off., *Detroit*, S.Atl.Sta. (Jan-Jun 1894); home and l.o.a. (Jun-Oct 1894); head, Office of Naval Intelligence, Washington, DC (Oct 1894-Jun 1897); *Rodgers*, Baltimore (Jun-Sep 1897); cdr, Atl. Torp. Boat Flot., *Foote* (Sep 1897-Nov 1898); cdr, *Caesar*, N.Atl.Sta. (Dec 1898); cdr, *Glacier*, spec.serv. (Jan 1899); cdr, *Supply*, N.Atl.Sta. (Jan-Apr 1899); cdr, *Vixen*, N.Atl.Sta. (Apr-Nov 1899); ord.off., Navy Yard, Norfolk, VA (Dec 1899-Jan 1900); recorder, bd. of labor employment, Navy Yard, Washington, DC (Jan 1900-May 1901); NWC (Jun-Sep 1901); equip. duty, Navy Yard, Washington, DC (Sep-Dec 1901); cdr, *Concord*, Asia.Sta. (Jan-Feb 1902); cdr, *Wheeling*, Pac.Sta. (Feb-Mar 1902); cdr, *Abarenda*, Pac.Sta. (Apr-Aug 1902); cdr, training ship, *Alert* (Sep 1902-Dec 1903); home and w.o. (Dec 1903-Jan 1904); asst., then insp., 8th L.h. Dist., New Orleans (Feb 1904-Jan 1905); s.a., home, and w.o. (Jan-Mar 1905); member, naval exam. and ret. bds., Washington, DC (Mar 1905-May 1906); general insp., then cdr, *New Jersey*, spec.serv. (May 1906-Nov 1907); member, naval exam. bd., and other bd. duties, Washington, DC (Nov 1907-Nov 1909); cdr, Nicaragua Expd. Sqdn., *Prairie, Dixie, Buffalo*, and *Albany* (Dec 1909-Apr 1910); placed on Ret.Lst. (9 Jan 1910); spec. duty, Nicaraguan Expd. Sqdn. (Apr-May 1910); senior member, naval exam. bd., 3rd Naval Dist., NY (Nov 1917-Jan 1918); in charge, historical section, Office of Naval Intelligence, Navy Dept., Washington, DC (Jun 1918-May 1919).

Career Highlights A long and distinguished career as a pioneer in torpedo boats and in submarines. Was a member of first torpedo class at Newport, RI, in 1871. Assisted in commissioning and sailing first torpedo boats, the *Alarm* and the *Intrepid* in 1874. Organized and commanded first torp. boat flot. in 1897. While at

Office of Naval Intelligence, completed draft of U.S.'s basic
strategy and plans for naval squadrons in the Atlantic and Pacific
for war against Spain. Made very important contributions,
technical as well as political, to the final construction of the first
U.S. submarines being built by John P. Holland.

References

Writings: a) "Magazine Small Arms," U.S. Naval Institute
Proceedings 17 (1881): 231-53. b) "Machine Guns," U.S. Naval
Institute *Proceedings* 18 (1881): 405-35. c) "Notes on an Experimental Ammunition Cart, Constructed for the Ordnance
Department," U.S. Naval Institute *Proceedings* 57 (1891): 51-56.
d) "Torpedo-Boat Organization and Service: Atlantic Coast of the
United States," U.S. Naval Institute *Proceedings* 100 (Dec 1901):
713-23. e) "Submarine Boats. Tactical Value and Strategical
Considerations," U.S. Naval Institute *Proceedings* 100 (Dec 1901):
739-48. f) (supplementary chapter in) Frank T. Cable, *The Birth
and Development of the American Submarine* (NY: 1924).

DAVID KINDELBERGER Born in Smithville, OH, on 2 Sep
1834, son of Dr. Thomas J. and Katherine (Newcomer) Kindelberger. Received A.B. degree from Wittenberg College in Springfield, OH, in 1857. Married Olivia Monsen Bishop on 10 Mar
1906. Died at his home in NY City on 25 Mar 1921.

Ranks Asst.Surg. (20 May 1859); PAsst.Surg. (7 Jun 1862);
Surg. (14 Aug 1862); Medl.Insp. (13 Aug 1876); Medl.Dir. (30
Jan 1887); placed on Ret.Lst. (2 Sep 1896); advance to Medl.Dir.
with rank of RAdm on Ret.Lst. (29 Jun 1906).

Career Summary Received appointment from OH (20 May
1859); *San Jacinto*, Afr.Sqdn. (Jun-Dec 1859); *Portsmouth*,
Afr.Sqdn. (Dec 1859-Oct 1861); l.o.a. (Oct-Nov 1861); Navy
Yard, Philadelphia (Nov-Dec 1861); *Miami*, W.Gulf Blk.Sqdn.
(Feb-May 1862); return and w.o. (May-Jul 1862); Navy Yard,
Philadelphia (Jul-Aug 1862); w.o. (Aug-Dec 1862); *Monongahela*,
N.Atl. and W.Gulf Blk.Sqdns. (Dec 1862-Apr 1865); *Itasca*,
W.Gulf Blk.Sqdn. (May 1865); sick lv. (May-Sep 1865); l.o.a.
(Sep 1865-Apr 1866); w.o. (Apr-Oct 1866); *Bienville*, and *De
Soto*, W.Gulf and N.Atl.Blk.Sqdns. (Oct 1866-Dec 1867); w.o.
(Dec 1867-Apr 1869); Marine Rndv., Washington, DC (May-Jul
1869); rec. ship, *Independence*, Mare Island, CA (Jul-Aug 1869);
Naval Rndv., San Francisco (Aug 1869-Mar 1870); rec. ship,
Independence, Mare Island, CA (Mar 1870-May 1871); *Wachusett*,
Eur.Sta. (Jun 1871-Mar 1874); return and w.o. (Mar-Apr 1874);
member, naval exam. and ret. bds. (Apr 1874-Aug 1877);
flt.surg., Asia.Sta., *Monongahela* (Oct 1877-Dec 1879); return and
w.o. (Dec 1879-Feb 1880); member, naval exam. and ret. bds.,
Washington, DC (Mar 1880-Dec 1883); flgs., *Hartford*, N.Atl.Sta.
(Jan-May 1884); flt.surg., Pac.Sta., *Hartford* (May-Aug 1884);
Naval Hosp., Washington, DC (Sep-Nov 1884); sick lv. (Nov
1884-Feb 1885); member, naval ret. bd. (Feb-Nov 1885); l.o.a.
(Nov 1885-Jun 1886); w.o. (Jul-Aug 1886); Naval Hosp.,
Washington, DC (Oct 1886-Jun 1891); spec. duty, Philadelphia
(Jun 1891-May 1893); in charge, Naval Hosp., Philadelphia (May

DAVID KINDELBERGER
1834-1921

1893-Aug 1896); w.o. (Aug 1896); placed on Ret.Lst. (2 Sep 1896).

THOMAS WRIGHT KINKAID Born in Cincinnati, OH, on 27 Feb 1860, son of William P. and Susan (Monahan) Kinkaid. Married Virginia Lee Cassin on 3 Apr 1883. Three children. Resided in Annapolis, dying at the Naval Hosp. there on 11 Aug 1920. Buried in USNA Cemetery, Annapolis.

Ranks Cadet Engr. (14 Sep 1876); Asst.Engr. (10 Jun 1882); PAsst.Engr. (11 Nov 1892); PAsst.Engr. with rel. rank of Lt (14 Mar 1897); Lt (3 Mar 1899); LCdr (2 Nov 1902); Cdr (1 Jul 1907); Capt (4 Mar 1911); RAdm (15 Oct 1917); died (11 Aug 1920).

Career Summary Received appointment from OH (14 Sep 1876); USNA (Sep 1876-Jun 1880); w.o. (Jun-Sep 1880); *Yantic*, N.Atl.Sta. (Sep 1880-Aug 1882); training ship, *Despatch* (Aug 1882-Nov 1883); *Alliance*, N.Atl.Sqdn. (Nov 1883-Jan 1886); *Swatara*, spec.serv. (Jan-Oct 1886); College of Agriculture, Hanover, NH (Nov 1886-Dec 1888); w.o. (Dec 1888-Feb 1889); *Pinta*, Alaskan waters (Apr 1889-Sep 1891); home and l.o.a. (Sep-Nov 1891); asst. insp. of machinery, William Cramp and Sons Iron Works, Philadelphia (Nov 1891-Jan 1893); Pennsylvania State College, Pennsylvania (Jan 1893-Aug 1895); spec. duty, Norfolk, VA (Aug 1895); *Texas*, N.Atl.Sqdn. (Aug 1895-Jan 1896); home and w.o. (Jan-Feb 1896); *Terror*, Navy Yard, NY (Feb 1896-Mar 1898); *Machias*, N.Atl.Flt. (Mar-Nov 1898); USNA (Nov 1898-Aug 1901); *Oregon*, Navy Yard, Puget Sound, WA (Aug 1901-Mar 1904); flt.engr., Asia.Flt., *Oregon* (Mar-Jul 1904); home and l.o.a. (Jul-Sep 1904); head, dept. of steam engineering, Navy Yard, Norfolk, VA (Sep 1904-Jan 1906); flt.engr., Pac.Sqdn., *Chicago* (Jan-Dec 1906), then *Charleston* (Dec 1906-Jul 1907); home and w.o. (Jul-Aug 1907); insp. of engineering material, Chester, PA (Aug 1907-Apr 1908); head, dept. of steam engineering, Navy Yard, Norfolk, VA (Apr 1908-Dec 1909); Engineering Experimental Sta., USNA (Dec 1909-Sep 1910); head, Engineering Experimental Sta., USNA (Sep 1910-Aug 1920); died (11 Aug 1920).

References

Writings: a) "Should There Be an International Navy?" U.S. Naval Institute *Proceedings* 137 (Mar 1911): 91-93. b) "Examinations for Promotions," U.S. Naval Institute *Proceedings* 153 (Sep-Oct 1914): 1405-7. c) "Superdread-noughts and Supermen," U.S. Naval Institute *Proceedings* 162 (Mar-Apr 1916): 503-7. d) "Naval Corps," U.S. Naval Institute *Proceedings* 169 (Mar 1917): 497-504.

GEORGE WASHINGTON KLINE Born on 4 Jan 1864 in Flemington, NJ. Married to Elizabeth Kline. Resided in Bound Brook, NJ, where he died on 28 Jun 1922. Buried in Readington, NJ.

Ranks Cadet Engr. (1 Oct 1881); Ens (1 Jul 1887); Ltjg (12 Mar 1896); Lt (3 Mar 1899); LCdr (13 Sep 1904); Cdr (1 Aug

GEORGE WASHINGTON KLINE
1864-1922

1908); Capt (1 Jul 1912); temp. RAdm (31 Dec 1918); placed on Ret.Lst. with rank of RAdm (24 Jun 1921).

Career Summary Received appointment from NJ as Cadet Engr. (1 Oct 1881); USNA (Oct 1881-Jun 1885); *Iroquois*, Pac.Sta. (Jun 1885-Mar 1887); return and USNA (Mar-Jun 1887); w.o. (Jun-Oct 1887); *Enterprise*, Atl.Sqdn., and Navy Yard, NY (Oct 1887-May 1890); w.o. (May-Jun 1890); l.o.a. (Jun-Aug 1890); insp. of steel, Homestead Steel Works, Munhall, PA (Aug 1890-Jan 1891); inspection duty, Union Iron Works, Pittsburgh, PA (Jan-Mar 1891); inspection duty, Bolt and Nut Works, Reading, PA (Mar 1891-Apr 1892); *Bache*, cst.surv. duty (Apr 1892-May 1895); PA marine school ship, *Saratoga*, Philadelphia (May 1895-Nov 1897); *Annapolis*, on trials, N.Atl.Sqdn., then training vessel (Nov 1897-May 1899); *Brooklyn*, Hampton Roads, VA, and en route to Asia.Sta. (Jun 1899-Jan 1900); *Marietta*, Asia.Sta. (Jan-Sep 1900); *Caesar*, Asia.Sta. (Nov 1900-Mar 1901); *Richmond*, League Island, PA (Apr 1901-Apr 1902); rec. ship, *Minneapolis*, League Island, PA (Apr-Sep 1902); *San Francisco*, spec.serv., Caribbean, Mediterranean, and Asia.Sta. (Sep 1902-Jun 1904); exec. off., *Raleigh*, Asia.Flt. (Jun 1904-Sep 1905); home and l.o.a. (sep-Dec 1905); Naval Recruiting Sta., New York (Dec 1905-Aug 1907); exec. off., *Georgia*, Atl.Flt. (Aug 1907-Dec 1909); inspection duty, Bur. of Ord., Philadelphia, and Camden, NJ (Dec 1909-Jan 1912); comdt., Naval Sta., Guantanamo, Cuba, and cdr., sta. ship *Cumberland* (Jan 1912-Jan 1913); cdr., *Vermont*, Atl.Flt. (Jan 1913-Jul 1915); member, naval exam. and ret. bds., Navy Yard, Washington, DC (Jul-Dec 1915); member, bd. of inspection and surv., Navy Dept., Washington, DC (Dec 1915-Oct 1919); pres., bd. of inspection and surv., Navy Dept., Washington, DC (Oct 1919-Jun 1921); placed on Ret.Lst. (24 Jun 1921).

References
Writings: with Albert Liscomb Gale, *Bryan the Man, The Great Commoner at Close Range* (St. Louis: 1908).

HARRY SHEPARD KNAPP Born in New Britain, CT, on 27 Jun 1856, son of Frederic and Mary Eunice (Burritt) Knapp. Remained unmarried. Resided in Hartford, CT, where he died on 6 Apr 1923. Cremated with ashes dispersed at sea.

Ranks Cadet Midn (26 Jun 1874); Midn (4 Jun 1880); Ens (16 Feb 1882); Ltjg (31 Mar 1889); Lt (23 Jan 1894); LCdr (11 Feb 1901); Cdr (30 Sep 1905); Capt (20 Nov 1909); RAdm (13 Aug 1916); placed on Ret.Lst. (27 Jun 1920); VAdm (posthumously) on Ret.Lst. (6 Apr 1923).

Career Summary Received appointment from CT (26 Jun 1874); USNA (Jun 1874-Jun 1878); w.o. (Jun-Sep 1878); *Pensacola*, Pac.Sqdn. (Oct 1878-Mar 1880); w.o. (Apr-May 1880); USNA (May-Jun 1880); w.o. (Jun-Jul 1880); training ship, *Minnesota* (Jul 1880-Jan 1882); training ship, *Jamestown* (Feb-Jul 1882); cst.surv. duty (Jul 1882-Nov 1883); spec. duty, Smithsonian Institution, Washington, DC (Dec 1883-Jun 1884); training ship, *Dale*, USNA (Jun-Sep 1884); USNA (Sep 1884-Sep 1888);

HARRY SHEPARD KNAPP
1856-1923

branch hydrographic office, Boston (Sep-Nov 1888); *Atlanta*, N.Atl.Sqdn., Sqdn. of Evol., and spec. cruises (Nov 1888-Aug 1891); USNA (Sep 1891-Jun 1894); *Montgomery*, N.Atl.Sqdn. (Jun 1894-May 1897); USNA (May 1897-May 1898); exec.off., *Dorothea*, N.Atl.Flt. (May-Sep 1898); USNA (Sep 1898-Jun 1899); temp. duty, Bur. of Equip. and Recruiting, Washington, DC (Jun 1899); *Solace*, Pac.Sta. (Jun-Aug 1899); *Baltimore*, Asia.Sta. (Aug 1899-Apr 1900); *Wheeling*, Asia.Sta. (Apr 1900-Jan 1901); training ship, *Mohican* (Jan 1901-Sep 1902); home and w.o. (Sep-Dec 1902); NWC (Dec 1902-Oct 1904); exec.off., *Kentucky*, N.Atl.Flt. (Nov 1904-Dec 1905); home and w.o. (Dec 1905-Jan 1906); NWC (Jan-Nov 1906); Army War College, Washington, DC (Nov 1906-May 1907); NWC (Jun-Nov 1907); chief of staff, Pac.Flt., *West Virginia* (Nov 1907-Jul 1908); cdr, flgs., *Charleston*, Pac.Flt. (Aug 1908-Jul 1909); home and w.o. (Jul-Oct 1909); duty in connection with, then member of, Gen Bd., Navy Dept., Washington, DC (Oct 1909-Nov 1910); member, Army-Navy Joint Board, Washington, DC (Dec 1909-Nov 1910); cdr, *Tennessee*, Pac.Flt. (Aug 1910-Jun 1911); cdr, *Florida*, NY, and flgs., 1st Div., Atl.Flt. (Jun 1911-Oct 1912); member, Gen Bd., Navy Dept., Washington, DC (Nov 1912-Nov 1916); cdr, Cruiser Force, Atl.Flt., *Olympia* (Nov 1916-Mar 1917); military gov., Santo Domingo, and military representative, Haiti (Mar 1917-Nov 1918); spec. duty, Peace Conference, Paris (Dec 1918-Mar 1919); cdr, U.S. Naval Forces, European Waters, *Corsair*, then *Chattanooga* (Mar 1919-Jun 1920); additional duties, naval attaché, London (Mar-Oct 1919); placed on Ret.Lst. (27 Jun 1920); spec. temp. duty, Madrid (Jun-Jul 1920); senior navy representative to Haiti, *Minnesota*, then *New Hampshire* (Sep 1920-Jan 1921); duty, Office of Naval Operations, Navy Dept., Washington, DC (Jan 1921); duty, Navy Yard, Washington, DC (Apr 1921); temp. duty, Office of Naval Operations, Navy Dept., Washington, DC (Aug-Sep 1921); NWC (Jul-Oct 1922).

Career Highlights Won Spanish Campaign Medal, Philippine Campaign Medal, China Relief Medal, and the Victory Medal for World War I. Won the Navy Cross for his services as gov. of Santo Domingo and military representative in Haiti during World War I. Also received France's Legion of Honor in Sep 1919 and Britain's Honorary Knighthood for distinguished service to the Royal Air Service during World War I. Served as military gov. of Santo Domingo and was with Peace Commission at Versailles.

References

Personal Papers: 1 box (1877-1923) at NL.

Writings: a) "Results of Some Special Researches at the Torpedo Station," U.S. Naval Institute *Proceedings* 67 (1893): 249-66. b) "Tests of Southern Coal," U.S. Naval Institute *Proceedings* 76 (1895): 747-52. c) "Graphic Solution in Coast Navigation," U.S. Naval Institute *Proceedings* 103 (Sep 1902): 573-76. d) "The Training of Landsmen," U.S. Naval Institute *Proceedings* 104 (Dec 1902): 895-909. e) "The General Problem of the Relation Between Two Bearings of a Single Object and Its Distance when Abeam," U.S. Naval Institute *Proceedings* 129

(Mar 1909): 185-88. f) "The Real Status of the Panama Canal as Regards Neutralization," U.S. Naval Institute *Proceedings* 133 (Mar 1910): 61-102. g) "Star Identification," U.S. Naval Institute *Proceedings* 144 (Dec 1912): 1529-35. h) "The Panama Canal in International Law," U.S. Naval Institute *Proceedings* 145 (Mar 1913): 95-126. i) "The Navy and the Panama Canal," U.S. Naval Institute *Proceedings* 147 (Sep 1913): 931-48. j) (with Reuben Edwin Bakenhus and Emory R. John), *The Panama Canal* (NY: 1915). k) "An International Outlook," U.S. Naval Institute *Proceedings* 221 (Jul 1921): 1023-27. l) "Onward and Upward," U.S. Naval Institute *Proceedings* 224 (Oct 1921): 1509-17. m) "The Limitation of Armament at the Congress of Washington," U.S. Naval Institute *Proceedings* 243 (May 1923): 767-76. n) "Treaty No. 2 of the Washington Conference," *Political Science Quarterly* 39, no. 2 (Jun 1924). o) "The Naval Officer in Diplomacy," U.S. Naval Institute *Proceedings* 259 (Sep 1924): 1473-91. p) "The Naval Officer in Diplomacy," U.S. Naval Institute *Proceedings* 289 (Mar 1927): 309-17.

AUSTIN MELVIN KNIGHT Born in Ware, MA, on 16 Dec 1854, son of Charles Sanford and Cordelia (Cutter) Knight. Married twice; to Alice Phinney Tobey on 3 Jan 1878, and to Elizabeth Harwood Welsh on 29 Apr 1886. Two daughters, one of whom married future RAdm Forrest Betton Royal (1893-1945), and a son, Cdr Richard Harwood Knight, USN (ret.). Died at the Naval Hosp. in Washington, DC, on 26 Feb 1927. Buried in USNA Cemetery, Annapolis.

Ranks Midn (30 Jun 1869); title changed to Cadet Midn (15 Jul 1870; Midn (31 May 1873); Ens (16 Jul 1874); Mstr (27 Oct 1879); title changed to Ltjg (3 Mar 1883); Lt (19 Dec 1885); LCdr (3 Mar 1899); Cdr (16 Jun 1902); Capt (1 Jul 1907); RAdm (29 Jan 1911); Adm (4 Apr 1917); placed on Ret.Lst. with rank of RAdm (16 Dec 1918); Adm (posthumously) on Ret.Lst. (26 Feb 1927).

Career Summary Received appointment from FL (30 Jun 1869); USNA (Jun 1869-May 1873); w.o. (May-Jul 1873); *Tuscarora, Kearsarge, Palos,* and *Saco,* Asia.Sta. (Jul 1873-Aug 1875); home and w.o. (Aug-Oct 1875); USNA (Oct-Nov 1875); l.o.a. (Dec 1875-Jan 1876); inst., dept. of English, history and law, USNA (Jan 1876-Aug 1878); w.o. (Aug-Sep 1878); *Quinnebaug,* Eur.Sta. (Sep 1878-Aug 1880); *Galena,* and *Brooklyn,* Eur., and S.Atl.Stas. (Aug 1880-Sep 1883); w.o. (Sep-Oct 1883); l.o.a. (Oct-Dec 1883); ord. instruction, Navy Yard, Washington, DC (Jan 1884); Ord. Proving Ground, Annapolis (Jan 1884-Dec 1885); in charge, Ord. Proving Grounds, Annapolis (Dec 1885-Jan 1889); w.o. (Jan-Mar 1889); ord.off., flgs., *Chicago,* Sqdn. of Evol., N.Atl., Eur., and S.Atl.Stas. (Mar 1889-Jun 1892); instructor, dept. of physics and chemistry, USNA (Jun 1892-Jun 1895); torp. instruction, Newport, RI (Jul-Aug 1895); *Lancaster,* S.Atl.Sta. (Sep 1895-Mar 1896); *Castine,* S.Atl.Sta. (Mar-Dec 1896); navigator, *Puritan,* N.Atl.Sta. (Dec 1896-Sep 1898); head, dept. of seamanship, USNA (Sep 1898-Jun 1901);

AUSTIN MELVIN KNIGHT
1854-1927

NWC (Jun-Sep 1901); home and w.o. (Sep-Oct 1901); exec.off., *Olympia*, Navy Yard, Boston (Oct 1901); cdr, *Yankton*, N.Atl. Sqdn. (Oct 1901-Nov 1903); cdr, *Castine*, N.Atl.Sqdn. (Nov 1903-Apr 1904); spec. bd. on naval ord., and pres., joint army-navy bd. on smokeless powders, Washington, DC (Apr 1904-Sep 1907); cdr, *Washington*, Pac.Sta. (Oct 1907-May 1909); pres., spec. bd. on naval ord., and pres., joint army-navy bd. on smokeless powders, Washington, DC (May-Jul 1909); senior member, bd. on Naval Ord. Proving Ground, Indian Head, MD (Jul 1909-Feb 1910); spec. duty, Norfolk, VA (Feb-Mar 1910); member, spec. bd. on naval ord., Washington, DC (Mar 1910-Apr 1912); cdr, Atl. Reserve Flt., *Tennessee* (May 1912-Nov 1912); cdr, Spec.Serv.Sqdn., *Tennessee* (Nov 1912-Feb 1913); cdr, Atl. Reserve Flt., *Wisconsin* (Feb-Nov 1913); comdt., Naval Sta., 2nd Naval Dist., Narragansett Bay, RI, and pres., NWC (Dec 1913-Feb 1917); cdr, Asia.Flt., *Brooklyn* (May 1917-Feb 1919); placed on Ret.Lst. (16 Dec 1918); pres., bd. to award decorations for war service, Washington, DC (Oct 1919-Jun 1920).

Career Highlights As cdr of Reserve Flt. in 1912, was sent to the Eastern Med. to protect American interests there during the 1st Balkans War. Served as pres. of NWC from 1913 to 1917, a period that saw great growth and modernization in the College. As cdr. of Asia.Flt. during World War I, commanded the early phases of American operations at Vladivostok and in Siberia. Was one of the naval intellects during the period of great naval expansion, contributing numerous articles to the Naval Institute during that body's early years. Received the Distinguished Service Medal and several foreign decorations.

References

Writings: a) "A Message Pigeon Service in Connection with Coast Defense," U.S. Naval Institute *Proceedings* 72 (789-94). b) *Modern Seamanship* (NY: 1901) [17 editions]. c) "Professor Philip Rounseville Alger, U.S. Navy. An Appreciation," U.S. Naval Institute *Proceedings* 141 (Mar 1912): 1-5. d) "The Estimate of the Situation," U.S. Naval Institute *Proceedings* 157 (May-Jun 1915): 765-83. e) "Arms and Methods of the War College," U.S. Naval Institute *Proceedings* 158 (Jul-Aug 1915): 1223-37. f) with William D. Puleston, *History of the United States Naval War College* (Newport, RI: 1916).

HARRY KNOX Born in Greenville, OH, on 2 Jul 1848, son of John Reily and Isabel Southgate (Briggs) Knox. Married Mary Gard on 7 Sep 1875. Died while traveling from OH to St. Louis on 29 Aug 1923. Buried in the USNA Cemetery, Annapolis.

Ranks Midn (2 Mar 1863); Ens (18 Dec 1868); Mstr (21 Mar 1870); Lt (21 Mar 1871); LCdr (2 Jan 1888); Cdr (1 Oct 1896); Capt (22 Sep 1901); retired (20 Jun 1905); RAdm on Ret.Lst. (13 Apr 1911) to rank from 20 Jun 1905.

Career Summary Received appointment from OH (2 Mar 1863); USNA (Mar 1863-Jun 1867); flgs., *Franklin*, then *Frolic*, Eur.Sqdn. (Jun 1867-May 1869); w.o. (May-Jul 1869); *Mohican*, Pac.Sqdn. (Sep 1869-Jun 1872); w.o. (Jun-Jul 1872); torp. duty,

HARRY KNOX
1848-1923

Newport, RI (Sep 1872-Sep 1873); *Monongahela*, S.Atl.Sta. (Sep 1873-Jun 1875); home and w.o. (Jun-Aug 1875); USNA (Aug 1875-Jul 1879); *Adams*, Pac.Sta. (Aug 1879-Jun 1882); w.o. (Jun-Aug 1882); USNA (Sep 1882-Oct 1886); w.o. (Oct 1886-Mar 1887); temp. duty, Bur. of Nav., Washington, DC (Mar-Apr 1887); exec.off., *Boston*, spec.serv. (May 1887-Jun 1890); USNA (Jun 1890-Jul 1894); cdr, *Vesuvius*, N.Atl.Sqdn. (Aug 1894-Apr 1895); home and w.o. (Apr-May 1895); cdr, *Thetis*, spec.serv., Pac. Ocean (Jun 1895-Aug 1896); USNA (Sep 1896-Jun 1899); cdr, *Princeton*, Asia.Sta. (Aug 1899-May 1901); cdr, *Concord*, Asia.Sta. (May-Jul 1901); home and sick lv. (Aug-Oct 1901); ord. duty, Navy Yard, Washington, DC (Oct-Dec 1901); bd. duties, Washington, DC (Dec 1901-May 1902); NWC (May-Oct 1902); sick lv. (Oct-Dec 1902); senior asst. in charge, Naval Defense, Pac.Cst. Dist., San Francisco (Dec 1902-Apr 1903); cdr, *Brooklyn*, N.Atl.Flt. (May 1903-Apr 1904); temp. cdr, Eur.Sqdn., *Brooklyn* (Feb-Apr 1904); Naval Hosp., Washington, DC (Apr-Jun 1904); sick lv. (Jun-Oct 1904); bd. duties, Washington, DC (Oct 1904-Jun 1905); retired (20 Jun 1905).

GEORGE FINK KUTZ Born in Wilkes-Barre, PA, on 14 Jun 1835, son of Jacob and Rosanna (Fitzgerald) Kutz. Educated at the Wilkes-Barre Academy and at Wyoming Seminary. Married Mrs. Katherine Makee Bennett on 1 Oct 1874. Resided in Oakland, CA. Died in San Francisco on 9 Aug 1921.

Ranks 3rd Asst.Engr. (26 Jun 1856); 1st Asst.Engr. (2 Aug 1859); Chief Engr. (10 Nov 1861); Chief Engr. with rel. rank of Cdr (23 Jun 1881); Chief Engr. with rel. rank of Capt (25 Aug 1889); placed on Ret.Lst. (26 Jun 1896); Chief Engr. with rank of RAdm on Ret.Lst. (29 Jun 1906).

Career Summary Received appointment from PA (26 Jun 1856); w.o. (Jun 1856-Mar 1857); *Niagara*, Atl. Cable Expd. (Mar-Nov 1857); w.o. (Nov-Dec 1857); *Niagara*, spec.serv. (Dec 1857-Aug 1858); l.o.a. (Aug-Oct 1858); *Caledonia*, spec. duty (Oct 1858); *Atlanta*, Braz.Sqdn. (Oct 1858-May 1859); w.o. (May-Jun 1859); exam. and w.o. (Jun-Aug 1859); *Saginaw*, E.Ind.Sqdn. (Aug 1859-Feb 1862); home and w.o. (Feb-Apr 1862); *Pawnee*, S.Atl.Blk.Sqdn. (Apr-Dec 1862); *Monongahela*, W.Gulf Blk.Sqdn. (Dec 1862-Apr 1865); w.o. (Apr-May 1865); member, bd. of examiners, Philadelphia (May-Aug 1865); *Ticonderoga*, Eur.Sqdn. (Aug 1865-Apr 1869); w.o. (Apr-May 1869); insp. of machinery afloat, Navy Yard, League Island, PA (May 1869-Mar 1870); *Pensacola*, Pac.Sta. (Mar 1870-Aug 1872); *Benicia*, N.Pac.Sta. (Aug 1872-Jul 1874); report and w.o. (Jul 1874-Mar 1875); Naval Rndv., San Francisco (Mar 1875-Jun 1876); flt.engr., Asia.Sta., *Tennessee* (Aug 1876-Mar 1877); home and l.o.a. (Mar-Dec 1877); in charge of stores, Navy Yard, Mare Island, CA (Dec 1877-Apr 1881); flt.engr., Pac.Sta., *Pensacola* (Jun 1881-Sep 1883); w.o. (Sep-Oct 1883); chief engr., Navy Yard, Mare Island, CA (Nov 1883-Jul 1888); insp. of machinery, new cruisers, William Cramp and Sons Iron Works, Philadelphia (Jul 1888-Jun 1889); Union Iron Works, San Francisco (Jul

GEORGE FINK KUTZ
1835-1921

1889-May 1893); chief engr., Navy Yard, Mare Island, CA (May 1893-Jun 1896); placed on Ret.Lst. (26 Jun 1896); insp. of machinery, Wolff and Zwicker Iron Works, Portland, OR (Jun 1898-Jan 1899).

BENJAMIN PEFFER LAMBERTON
1844-1912

BENJAMIN PEFFER LAMBERTON   Born in Cumberland County, PA, on 25 Feb 1844, son of James Finlay and Elizabeth (Peffer) Lamberton. Married Lilla Stedman on 25 Feb 1873. Three children. Resided in Washington, DC, dying there on 9 Jun 1912. Buried in Arlington National Cemetery.

Ranks   Act.Midn (21 Sep 1861); title changed to Midn (16 Jul 1862); Ens (1 Nov 1866); Mstr (1 Dec 1866); Lt (12 Mar 1867); LCdr (27 Apr 1869); Cdr (2 Jun 1885); Capt (11 May 1898); RAdm (11 Oct 1903); placed on Ret.Lst. (25 Feb 1906).

Career Summary   Received appointment from PA (21 Sep 1861); USNA (Sep 1861-Nov 1864); l.o.a. (Nov 1864-Feb 1865); rec. ship, *Vermont*, NY (Feb-Mar 1865); *Susquehanna*, and *Juniata*, S.Atl.Sqdn. (Mar 1865-Jun 1867); w.o. (Jun-Sep 1867); apprentice ship, *Saratoga* (Oct 1867-Jul 1869); sick lv. and w.o. (Jul 1869-Jan 1870); *Mohican*, and *California*, Pac.Sqdn. (Jan 1870-Dec 1872); w.o. (Dec 1872-Feb 1873); USNA (Mar-Dec 1873); *Dictator*, N.Atl.Sqdn. (Dec 1873-Apr 1875); w.o. (Apr-May 1875); torp. duty, Newport, RI (Jun-Oct 1875); Navy Yard, Boston (Nov 1875-Aug 1876); Navy Yard, Portsmouth, NH (Aug 1876-Mar 1878); w.o. (Mar-Apr 1878); *Alaska*, Pac.Sta. (Apr 1878-Jun 1879); w.o. (Jun-Oct 1879); Bur. of Equip. and Recruiting, Washington, DC (Oct 1879-Jun 1882); *Vandalia*, N.Atl.Sta. (Jun 1882-Oct 1884); w.o. (Oct-Dec 1884); asst., then insp., 6th Dist., Charleston, SC (Jan 1885-Jun 1888); equip.off., Navy Yard, Norfolk, VA (Jun 1888-Apr 1889); cdr, training ship, *Jamestown* (Apr 1889-Nov 1891); Bur. of Yards and Docks, Washington, DC (Nov 1891-Oct 1894); insp., 5th L.h. Dist., Baltimore (Oct 1894-Mar 1898); chief of staff, Asia.Sta., *Olympia* (Apr-Nov 1898); cdr, *Olympia*, Asia.Sta. (May 1898-Nov 1899); home and w.o. (Nov 1899-Jan 1900); member, naval exam. and ret. bds. (Jan-Jun 1900); member, L.h. Bd., Washington, DC (Jul 1900-Sep 1903); cdr, S.Atl.Sqdn., *Newark* (Oct 1903-Jan 1904); home and sick lv. (Jan-Apr 1904); NWC (Apr-Dec 1904); w.o. (Dec 1904-Jan 1905); chairman, L.h. Bd., Washington, DC (Jan 1905-Feb 1906); placed on Ret.Lst. (25 Feb 1906).

Career Highlights   Served as chief of staff to Adm George Dewey and cdr of flgs, *Olympia*, during the Battle of Manila Bay on 1 May 1898, for which he was advanced seven numbers "for eminent and conspicuous conduct."

References

Personal Papers: 2 ft. (c.1834-1917) in National Museum of History and Technology, Div. of Naval History, Washington, DC.

ELIJAH LAWS   Born in PA on 20 Mar 1833. Resided in Morristown, NJ, where he died on 25 Sep 1926. Buried in Evergreen Cemetery in Morristown, NJ.

Ranks   3rd Asst.Engr. (19 Mar 1858); 2nd Asst.Engr. (1 Dec 1860); dismissed (27 May 1863); restored (31 Mar 1864); 1st

Asst.Engr. (25 Jul 1866); Chief Engr. (21 Mar 1870); Chief Engr. with rel. rank of Cdr (1 Jul 1887); Chief Engr. with rel. rank of Capt (26 Dec 1894); transferred to Ret.Lst. (20 Mar 1895); Chief Engr. with rank of RAdm on Ret.Lst. (29 Jun 1906).

Career Summary Received appointment from PA (19 Mar 1858); w.o. (Mar-Jun 1858); *Saranac*, Pac.Sqdn. (Jul 1858-Nov 1859); l.o.a. (Nov 1859-Aug 1860); *Powhatan*, Home and Gulf Blk.Sqdns. (Aug 1860-Nov 1861); l.o.a. and w.o. (Nov 1861-Jan 1862); *Dacotah*, N.Atl.Blk.Sqdn. (Jan-Oct 1862); sick lv. (Oct-Dec 1862); *Housatonic*, S.Atl.Blk.Sqdn. (Dec 1862-May 1863); dismissed (27 May 1863); restored (31 Mar 1864); *Itasca*, and *Chickopee*, W.Gulf and N.Atl.Blk.Sqdns. (Apr 1864-Dec 1866); *Marblehead*, W.Ind.Sqdn. (Dec 1866-Sep 1867); sick lv. (Sep-Oct 1867); *Contoocook*, spec. duty (Nov 1867-Jan 1868); *Mosholu*, spec.serv. (Jan-Mar 1868); *Ammonoosuc*, spec. duty (Mar-May 1868); w.o. (May 1868-Mar 1869); *Galena*, spec.serv. (Apr-May 1869); *Resaca*, Pac.Sqdn. (Jun 1869-Jun 1871); w.o. (Jun 1871-Jan 1872); in charge of engine works, Key West, FL (Jan-Apr 1872); *Terror*, Navy Yard, League Island, PA (Apr 1872-Jun 1873); w.o. (Jun-Nov 1873); in charge of stores, engineering dept., Navy Yard, Norfolk, VA (Nov 1873); *Terror*, Navy Yard, League Island, PA (Nov-Dec 1873); in charge of stores, engineering dept., Navy Yard, Norfolk, VA (Dec 1873-Jan 1874); *Roanoke*, Navy Yard, NY (Jan 1874-Apr 1875); training ship, *Minnesota* (Apr-Sep 1875); w.o. (Sep-Dec 1875); in charge of stores, Navy Yard, NY (Dec 1875-Mar 1877); *Enterprise*, spec. duty (Mar 1877-Oct 1878); w.o. (Oct 1878-Oct 1879); Navy Yard, Pensacola, FL (Nov 1879-Oct 1882); w.o. (Oct 1882-Mar 1884); *Lackawanna*, Pac.Sqdn. (May 1884-Mar 1885); *Mohican*, Pac.Sqdn. (Mar 1885-Apr 1887); w.o. (Apr 1887-May 1888); Navy Yard, League Island, PA (May 1888-Jun 1889); w.o. (Jun 1889-Aug 1890); *Pensacola*, S.Atl.Sta. (Aug 1890-Apr 1892); l.o.a. and w.o. (Apr-Jun 1892); South Brooklyn Steam Engine Works, Brooklyn, NY (Jun 1892-May 1893); rec. ship, *Franklin*, Norfolk, VA (May 1893-Mar 1895); transferred to Ret.Lst. (20 Mar 1895).

EUGENE HENRY COZZENS LEUTZE Born in Dusseldorf, Prussia, on 16 Nov 1847, son of Emanuel and Julia Leutze. His father was the painter of the famous picture of George Washington crossing the Delaware. Married Julia Jarvis McAlpine in Mar 1873. Three children. Died in Brooklyn, NY, on 15 Sep 1931. Buried in Arlington National Cemetery.

Ranks Midn (4 Mar 1863); Ens (18 Dec 1868); Mstr (21 Mar 1870); Lt (21 Mar 1871); LCdr (26 Mar 1889); Cdr (5 Jan 1897); Capt (9 Oct 1901); RAdm (6 Jul 1907); placed on Ret.Lst. (16 Nov 1909).

Career Summary Received appointment from Washington, DC (4 Mar 1863); USNA (Mar 1863-Jun 1867); *Minnesota, Canandaigua,* and *Ticonderoga,* Eur.Sqdn. (Jul 1867-Apr 1869); w.o. (Apr-Jun 1869); rec. ship, *Vermont,* NY (Jun-Aug 1869); flgs., *Severn,* N.Atl.Sqdn. (Aug 1869-Dec 1871); flgs., *Worcester,* N.Atl.Sqdn. (Dec 1871-Mar 1872); Nicaraguan Surv.Expd.

EUGENE HENRY COZZENS
LEUTZE
1847-1931

(Mar-Jul 1872); w.o. (Jul-Aug 1872); spec. duty, Washington, DC
(Aug-Sep 1872); w.o. (Sep-Nov 1872); Nicaraguan Surv.Expd.
(Nov 1872-Jul 1873); l.o.a. (Jul 1873-Jan 1874); Hydrographic
Office, Washington, DC (Jan-Dec 1874); Panama Surv.Expd.
(Dec 1874-Apr 1875); Hydrographic Office, Washington, DC
(Apr-Aug 1875); *Tuscarora*, N.Pac.Sqdn. (Sep 1875-Aug 1876);
Portsmouth, spec.serv. (Aug 1876); cst.surv. duty (Aug 1876-Nov
1880); l.o.a. during which employed for surveying duties with the
Tehuantepec Railroad Company (Nov 1880-Jul 1882); *Nantucket*,
spec.serv. (Jul-Oct 1882); exec.off., *Juniata*, spec.serv. (Oct
1882-Dec 1885); w.o. (Dec 1885-Jan 1886); USNA (Jan
1886-Mar 1890); duty with, then exec.off., flgs., *Philadelphia*,
N.Atl.Sqdn. (Mar 1890-Nov 1892); Navy Yard, Washington, DC
(Nov 1892-Apr 1896); cdr, *Michigan*, on Great Lakes (Apr
1896-Apr 1897); asst., then insp., 9th L.h. Dist., Chicago (Apr
1897-Jan 1898); cdr, *Alert*, Navy Yard, Mare Island, CA (Jan-May
1898); *Monterey*, Asia.Sta. (May 1898-Dec 1899); comdt., Navy
Yard, Cavite, P.I. (Oct 1898-Dec 1899); home and w.o. (Dec
1899-Feb 1900); spec. duty, Bur. of Ord., Washington, DC
(Feb-Mar 1900); supt., Naval Gun Factory, Navy Yard, Washington, DC (Mar 1900-Oct 1902); cdr, *Maine*, Philadelphia, and
N.Atl.Sta. (Oct 1902-Nov 1904); member, bd. of inspection and
surv. (Nov 1904-Oct 1905); comdt., Navy Yard, and supt., Naval
Gun Factory, Navy Yard, Washington, DC (Oct 1905-Apr 1910);
placed on Ret.Lst. (16 Nov 1909); comdt., Navy Yard and Sta.,
NY (Mar 1910-Jun 1912).

Career Highlights Involved with several surv. expds., including
Nicaragua (1872-73), Panama (1874-75), a deep-sea sounding
from Honolulu to Brisbane, Australia (1875), the Pac.cst.
(1877-80), and with a private railroad company surveying the
Isthmus of Tehuantepec (1880-82). While cdr of the *Alert* in
1897-98, guarded American interests in Panama during an
insurrection there. During the war with Spain, commanded the
Monterey in taking Manila and participated in actions against the
insurrectionists.

ABRAHAM BRUYN HASBROUCK LILLIE Born in NY
City on 23 Sep 1845, son of Rev Dr. J. Lillie. Early education in
Kingston, NY. Remaining a bachelor, died at his home in NY City
on 11 Dec 1905. Buried at Woodlawn Cemetery in NY.

Ranks Midn (24 Sep 1862); Ens (12 Mar 1868); Mstr (26 Mar
1869); Lt (21 Mar 1870); LCdr (29 Jan 1887); Cdr (1 Sep 1895);
Capt (3 Mar 1901); Retired with rank of RAdm (6 Mar 1903).

Career Summary Received appointment from NY (24 Sep
1862); USNA (Sep 1862-Jun 1866); l.o.a. and w.o. (Jun-Oct
1866); *Saco*, N.Atl.Sta. (Oct 1866); w.o. (Oct 1866-Dec 1867);
Kearsarge, Pac.Sta. (Jan 1868-Oct 1870); w.o. (Oct 1870-Mar
1871); *Shawmut*, N.Atl.Sta. (Mar 1871-Oct 1873); w.o. (Oct-Nov
1873); *Canonicus*, Navy Yard, NY (Dec 1873); *Minnesota*, Navy
Yard, NY (Dec 1873); w.o. (Dec 1873-Jan 1874); *Brooklyn*,
N.Atl. and Braz.Stas. (Jan 1874-Jul 1876); w.o. (Jul-Sep 1876);
rec. ship, *Potomac*, Philadelphia (Oct-Dec 1876); training ship,

Constellation (Dec 1876-Jan 1877); Navy Yard, NY (Jan 1877-Mar 1878); training ship, *Constellation,* spec. duty, Paris Exposition, Paris (Mar-Jul 1878); Navy Yard, NY (Aug 1878-Oct 1879); *Nipsic,* Eur.Sta. (Oct 1879-Mar 1883); w.o. and l.o.a. (Mar-Apr 1883); torp. instruction, Newport, RI (Apr-Jul 1883); rec. ship, *Colorado,* NY (Jul 1883-Dec 1885); *Juniata,* Asia.Sta. (Dec 1885-Apr 1886); *Tennessee,* and *Richmond,* N.Atl.Sta. (Apr 1886-Oct 1888); Navy Yard, NY (Nov 1888-Mar 1892); *Baltimore,* Pac. and N.Atl.Stas. (Mar 1892-May 1893); sick lv. (May-Oct 1893); Navy Yard, Norfolk, VA (Oct 1893-Mar 1894); w.o. (Mar-May 1894); asst., then insp., 15th L.h. Dist., St. Louis (May 1894-Apr 1897); home, s.a., and w.o. (Apr-May 1897); Navy Yard, NY (May-Oct 1897); cdr, *Vicksburg,* N.Atl.Flt. (Oct 1897-May 1899); home and w.o. (May-Jun 1899); Navy Yard, NY (Jul 1899-Mar 1901); additional temp. duty, *Marcellus,* Navy Yard, NY (Nov 1899-Jan 1900); comdt., Naval Station, Key West, FL (Mar 1901-Jun 1902); home and w.o. (Jun-Dec 1902); capt.yd., Navy Yard, League Island, PA (Jan-Mar 1903); placed on Ret.Lst. (6 Mar 1903).

ROBERT PATTON LISLE Born in Philadelphia on 28 Aug 1842. Married to Mary Keating Lisle, he made his home in Philadelphia. Died on 28 Oct 1911 in Devon, PA. Buried in Woodlawn Cemetery in Philadelphia.

Ranks Act.Asst.Paymstr. (2 Nov 1863); Asst.Paymstr. (2 Jul 1864); PAsst.Paymstr. (4 May 1866); Paymstr. (11 Dec 1867); Pay Insp. (19 Jan 1892); Pay Dir. (6 Jun 1899); retired as Pay Dir. with rank of RAdm (3 Nov 1903).

Career Summary Received appointment from PA (2 Nov 1863); spec. duty, Bur. of Provisions and Clothing, Washington, DC (Nov 1863-Feb 1864); w.o. (Feb 1864); *Canonicus,* S.Atl. Blk.Sqdn. (Feb 1864-Apr 1865); home and w.o. (Apr-Nov 1865); *Swatara,* W.Ind.Sqdn. (Nov 1865-Jun 1866); s.a. and w.o. (Jun-Sep 1866); *Resaca,* N.Pac.Sqdn. (Sep 1866-Aug 1869); s.a. and w.o. (Aug 1869-Jan 1870); Navy Yard, League Island, PA (Feb 1870-Apr 1873); s.a. and w.o. (Apr-Jul 1873); *Alaska,* Eur.Sqdn. (Aug 1873-Sep 1876); s.a. and w.o. (Sep 1876-Apr 1877); rec. ship, *St. Louis,* League Island, PA (Apr 1877-Jul 1880); s.a. and w.o. (Jul 1880-Jun 1881); *Powhatan,* N.Atl.Sta. (Jun 1881-Dec 1883); s.a. and w.o. (Dec 1883-Aug 1884); rec. ship, *St. Louis,* League Island, PA (Aug 1884-Apr 1887); s.a. and w.o. (Apr 1887); *Trenton,* spec.serv. (May-Sep 1887); flgs., *Lancaster,* S.Atl., then Eur.Sqdn. (Sep 1887-Sep 1889); s.a. and w.o. (Sep 1889-May 1890); rec. ship, *St. Louis,* League Island, PA (Jun 1890-Aug 1892); general storekeeper, Navy Yard, Norfolk, VA (Sep 1892-May 1895); in charge, Pay Office, Philadelphia (May 1895-Jul 1896); s.a. and w.o. (Jul-Aug 1896); flt.paymstr., Eur.Sta., then 1st Sqdn., N.Atl.Flt., *San Francisco* (Sep 1896-Oct 1898); Naval Home, Philadelphia (Nov 1898-May 1899); general storekeeper, Navy Yard, Norfolk, VA (May-Aug 1899); general storekeeper, Navy Yard, League Island, PA (Aug 1899-Apr 1900); in charge, Pay Office, Philadelphia (Apr 1900-Oct 1903); home and w.o.

WILLIAM NELSON LITTLE, II
1852-1925

(Oct-Nov 1903); retired (3 Nov 1903).

WILLIAM NELSON LITTLE, II Born in Newburgh, NY, on 31 Dec 1852, son of William Nelson and Margaret (Thall) Little. Married Kate Sewell on 23 Nov 1876. Four children. Resided at Mountain Lakes, NJ, where he died on 4 Jan 1925. Buried in Arlington National Cemetery.

Ranks Cadet Engr. (1 Oct 1872); Asst.Engr. (1 Jul 1877); PAsst.Engr. (17 Oct 1885); PAsst.Engr. with rel. rank of Ltjg (1 Oct 1893); Chief Engr. (14 Dec 1896); LCdr (3 Mar 1899); Cdr (30 Sep 1904); Capt (1 Jul 1908); RAdm (26 Mar 1913); placed on Ret.Lst. (31 Dec 1914).

Career Summary Received appointment from GA (1 Oct 1872); USNA (Oct 1872-Jun 1875); w.o. (Jun-Aug 1875); *Swatara*, N.Atl.Sta. (Aug 1875-Oct 1878); w.o. (Oct-Nov 1878); Navy Yard, Pensacola, FL (Nov 1878-May 1880); *Monocacy*, Asia.Sta. (Jul 1880-Jul 1883); return and w.o. (Jul 1883-Jan 1884); Navy Yard, NY (Jan-Aug 1884); temp. duty, *Nina*, spec.serv. (Aug-Sep 1884); Navy Yard, NY (Sep-Nov 1884); cst.surv. duty (Nov 1884-Jan 1885); prof. of mechanical engineering, Worcester Polytechnic Institute, Worcester, MA (Jan 1885-Sep 1886); *Galena*, N.Atl.Sta. (Sep 1886-Aug 1889); USNA (Aug 1889-Aug 1890); Navy Yard, NY (Aug 1890-Nov 1892); *Philadelphia*, N.Atl.Sta. (Nov 1892-Nov 1895); home and l.o.a. (Nov 1895-Mar 1896); Navy Yard, Norfolk, VA (Mar 1896-Sep 1897); rec. ship, *Franklin*, Norfolk, VA (Sep 1897-Mar 1898); chief engr., Naval Sta., Key West, FL (Apr-Jul 1898); *Iris*, Asia.Sta. (Jul 1898-May 1899); *Charleston*, Asia.Sta. (May-Nov 1899); *Baltimore*, Asia.Sta. (Dec 1899-Apr 1900); *New Orleans*, Asia.Sta. (Apr 1900-Mar 1901); *Newark*, Asia.Sta. (Mar-Jul 1901); home and l.o.a. (Jul-Sep 1901); member, bd. of insp., Navy Yard, NY (Sep 1901-Sep 1903); *Dixie*, Navy Yard, NY (Sep 1903); flt.engr., Atl. Training Flt., *Minnesota* (Sep 1903-Sep 1904); insp. of machinery, Babcock and Wilcox Company, Bayonne, NJ (Sep 1904-Oct 1905); insp. of engineering materials, CT Div. (Nov 1905-Jan 1907); Army General Hosp., Ft. Bayard, NM (Jan-Sep 1907); home and sick lv. (Sep-Dec 1907); insp. of engineering materials, Middle West Dist., Shelby, OH (Dec 1907-Jun 1908); insp. of machinery, Bath Iron Works, Bath, ME (Jun 1908-Aug 1910); insp. of machinery, Fore River Shipbuilding Company, Quincy, MA (Aug 1910-Dec 1914); placed on Ret.Lst. (31 Dec 1914); insp. of engines for Bur. of Steam Engineering, Standard Motor Construction Company, Jersey City, NJ (May 1917-Mar 1919).

LEAVITT CURTIS LOGAN Born in Medina, OH, on 30 Jan 1846, son of Samuel Sheldon and Hannah Hall (Curtis) Logan. Married Elizabeth C. Porter on 9 May 1877. Two daughters. Died in Washington, DC, on 23 Nov 1921.

Ranks Midn (28 Feb 1863); Ens (18 Dec 1868); Mstr (21 Mar 1870); Lt (12 Jun 1871); LCdr (16 Dec 1891); Cdr (1 May 1898); Capt (11 Jul 1902); RAdm (28 Jan 1908); placed on

LEAVITT CURTIS LOGAN
1846-1921

Ret.Lst. (30 Jan 1908).

Career Summary Received appointment from OH (28 Feb 1863); USNA (Feb 1863-Jun 1867); *Minnesota*, and *Saginaw*, spec. cruise and Pac.Sqdn. (Jul 1867-Oct 1870); spec. duty, Navy Dept., Washington, DC (Jan-Sep 1871); flgs., *Wabash*, Eur.Sta. (Oct 1871-Apr 1874); w.o. (Apr-Jun 1874); torp. duty, Newport, RI (Jul-Oct 1874); l.o.a. (Oct-Dec 1874); Naval Observatory, Washington, DC (Dec 1874-Apr 1875); *Tennessee*, Asia.Sqdn. (Apr 1875-Dec 1876); home and w.o. (Dec 1876-Feb 1877); Naval Observatory, Washington, DC (Feb-Apr 1877); l.o.a. (Apr-Aug 1877); USNA (Sep 1877-Jun 1880); *Powhatan*, spec. serv. (Jul 1880-Dec 1881); training ship, *Portsmouth* (Dec 1881-Jun 1883); w.o. (Jun-Jul 1883); training ship, *New Hampshire* (Aug 1883-Jan 1885); NWC (Jan 1885-Mar 1887); *Ossipee*, N.Atl.Sta. (Mar 1887-May 1889); recorder, bd. of inspection and surv. (May 1889-Sep 1892); NWC (Sep-Oct 1892); exec.off., *Philadelphia*, Pac.Sta. (Nov 1892-Nov 1894); home and l.o.a. (Nov 1894-Jan 1895); training ship, *Constellation* (Jan 1895-Feb 1898); navy representative, Trans-Mississippi and International Exposition, Omaha, NB (Mar-May 1898); cdr, *Armeria*, N.Atl.Flt. (May-Sep 1898); w.o. (Sep 1898); cdr, *Machias*, N.Atl.Flt. (Oct 1898-Jul 1900); NWC (Aug-Oct 1900); ord. instruction, Navy Yard, Washington, DC (Oct-Dec 1900); Bur. of Equip. and Recruiting, Washington, DC (Dec 1900-Jun 1904); cdr, *Ohio*, Asia.Flt. (Jun 1904-Dec 1906); home and w.o. (Dec 1906-Feb 1907); comdt., 8th Naval Dist. and Naval Sta., Pensacola, FL (Feb 1907-Jan 1908); placed on Ret.Lst. (30 Jan 1908).

EDWIN LONGNECKER Born in Cumberland County, PA, on 19 Feb 1844, son of Hyman Longnecker. Married to Elizabeth H. Longnecker. Resided in Wernersville, PA, dying in Reading, PA, on 13 Nov 1923.

Ranks Act.Midn (24 Sep 1861); title changed to Midn (16 Jul 1862); Ens (1 Dec 1866); Mstr (12 Mar 1868); Lt (26 Mar 1869); LCdr (30 Aug 1881); Cdr (2 Oct 1891); Capt (3 Mar 1899); RAdm (8 Jul 1905); placed on Ret.Lst. (19 Feb 1906).

Career Summary Received appointment from PA (24 Sep 1861); USNA (Sep 1861-Oct 1865); w.o. (Oct-Nov 1865); *Shenandoah*, E.Ind.Sta. (Nov 1865-Apr 1869); w.o. (May-Jun 1869); rec. ship, *Potomac*, Philadelphia (Jun-Nov 1869); *Swatara*, N.Atl.Flt. (Nov 1869-Jan 1872); w.o. (Jan-Feb 1872); spec. duty (Feb 1872); w.o. (Feb-Aug 1872); torp. duty (Sep 1872-Jun 1873); w.o. (Jun-Aug 1873); Torp.Sta., Newport, RI (Aug-Nov 1873); *Colorado*, N.Atl.Sta. (Dec 1873-Mar 1874); *Alaska*, Eur.Sta. (Mar 1874-Sep 1876); w.o. (Sep 1876-Jul 1877); *Wyandotte*, N.Atl.Sqdn. (Jul 1877); exec.off., *Passaic*, spec.serv. (Jul-Aug 1877); w.o. (Aug-Oct 1877); Signal Office, Washington, DC (Oct 1877-Feb 1878); *Wyoming*, spec.serv., Paris Exposition, Paris (Feb-Oct 1878); w.o. (Oct 1878); Naval Observatory, Washington, DC (Nov 1878-May 1882); *Michigan*, on Great Lakes (May 1882-Nov 1883); exec.off., *Shenandoah*, Pac.Sta. (Nov 1883-Oct 1886); w.o. (Oct 1886-Aug 1888); NWC (Aug

1888); rec. ship, *New Hampshire*, Newport, RI (Aug 1888-Oct 1890); training ship, *Richmond* (Oct 1890-Oct 1891); w.o. (Oct 1891-May 1892); temp.cdr, training ship, *Passaic* (May-Jun 1892); w.o. (Jun-Nov 1892); cdr, *Ranger*, N.Pac.Sqdn. (Nov 1892-Dec 1894); l.o.a. (Dec 1894-Mar 1895); ord. instruction, Navy Yard, Washington, DC (Mar-May 1895); NWC (Jun-Aug 1895); insp. of ord., Navy Yard, League Island, PA (Aug 1895-Feb 1898); cdr, Navy Yard, League Island, PA (Feb 1898-Feb 1899); cdr, *New Orleans*, spec.serv. and Asia.Sta. (Feb 1899-Apr 1900); Naval Hosps., Yokohama, Japan, Mare Island, CA, and Philadelphia (Apr-Sep 1900); w.o. (Sep-Dec 1900); Navy Yard, Boston (Jan-Mar 1901); Naval Sta., Port Royal, SC (Mar 1901-Apr 1902); comdt., Naval Sta., Port Royal, SC (Apr 1902-Jun 1903); comdt., Naval Sta., Charleston, SC (Jul 1903-Sep 1904); home and w.o. (Sep-Oct 1904); Navy Yard, Norfolk, VA (Oct-Nov 1904); Navy Yard, League Island, PA (Nov 1904-Feb 1906); placed on Ret.Lst. (19 Feb 1906).

THOMAS HENRY LOOKER
1829-1910

THOMAS HENRY LOOKER Born in Cincinnati, OH, on 23 Nov 1829, son of James H. and Rachel H. Looker. Early education by tutors. Married Lucilia S. Brigham on 19 May 1857. Four children. Died at his home in Washington, DC, on 24 Jul 1910. Buried in Cincinnati.

Ranks Midn (6 Nov 1846); resigned (24 Nov 1852); appointed Purser (31 Aug 1853); Pay Dir. (3 Mar 1871); Paymstr. Gen with rank of Commo (27 Mar 1890); transferred to Ret.Lst. (23 Nov 1891); Pay Dir. with rank of RAdm on Ret.Lst. (29 Jun 1906).

Career Summary Received appointment from Washington, DC (6 Nov 1846); Naval School, Annapolis (Dec 1846-Mar 1847); *Germantown*, Home Sqdn. (Mar 1847-Nov 1849); w.o. (Nov 1849-Apr 1850); *Congress*, and *Relief*, Braz.Sqdn. (Apr 1850-Feb 1852); spec. duty, NY, and Cincinnati, OH, then w.o. (Feb-Sep 1852); on furlough (Oct-Nov 1852); resigned (24 Nov 1852); received appointment from OH as purser (31 Aug 1853); w.o. (Aug-Oct 1853); *Bainbridge*, Braz.Sqdn. (Oct 1853-Sep 1856); s.a. and w.o. (Sep 1856-Jun 1857); *Portsmouth*, E.Ind.Sqdn. (Jul 1857-Jun 1858); s.a. and w.o. (Jun-Dec 1858); *Brooklyn*, Home, Atl., and Gulf Sqdns. (Jan 1859-Oct 1861); s.a. (Oct 1861); paymstr., N.Atl.Blk.Sqdn., *Brandywine* (Nov 1861-Jul 1863); l.o.a. (Jul-Oct 1863); rec. ship, *Allegheny*, Baltimore (Nov 1863-Dec 1864); s.a. and w.o. (Dec 1864-Aug 1865); flt.paymstr., Pac.Sta., *Powhatan* (Aug 1865-Sep 1868); s.a. and w.o. (Sep 1868-Apr 1869); paymstr., Pay Office, Baltimore (Apr 1869-Apr 1872); s.a. and w.o. (Apr-Jun 1872); Navy Yard, Washington, DC (Jul 1872-Jan 1875); s.a. and w.o. (Jan-Mar 1875); paymstr., Pay Office, Baltimore (Mar 1875-Mar 1877); asst. to sec. of navy, Washington, DC (Mar 1877); s.a. and w.o. (Mar 1877-Jul 1878); general insp., and act.chief, Bur. of Provisions and Clothing, Washington, DC (Jul 1878-Apr 1882); w.o. (Apr 1882-Oct 1883); naval pay agent, Pay Office, Washington, DC (Nov 1883-Mar 1888); s.a. and w.o. (Mar-Sep 1888); pres., naval exam. bd. (Sep-Nov 1888); w.o. (Nov 1888-May 1889); general insp., Navy Dept., Washing-

ton, DC (May 1889-Mar 1890); paymstr.gen, and chief, Bur. of
Provision and Clothing, Washington, DC (Mar-May 1890); sick
lv. (May 1890-May 1891); w.o. (May-Nov 1891); transferred to
Ret.Lst. (23 Nov 1891).

NICOLL LUDLOW Born in Islip, NY, on 11 Sep 1842, son of
army Bvt.MGen William Handy and Frances Louise (Nicoll)
Ludlow. His brother was BGen William Ludlow, USA. Married
Frances Mary Thomas on 12 May 1870. Two children. Married
a second time to Mary (McLean) Bugher on 15 Feb 1897. She
was sister of Mrs. George Dewey. Died in NY City on 9 Dec
1915. Cremated in Union Hills, NJ.

Ranks Act.Midn (28 Oct 1859); resigned (2 Oct 1860);
resignation revoked (11 Oct 1860); title changed to Midn (16 Jul
1862); Act.Ens (1 Oct 1863); designation "Act." discontinued (21
Dec 1865); Mstr (10 May 1866); Lt (21 Feb 1867); LCdr (12
Mar 1868); Cdr (1 Oct 1881); Capt (21 May 1895); retired (1
Nov 1899); RAdm on Ret.Lst. (13 Apr 1911) to rank from 1
Nov 1899.

Career Summary Received appointment from NY (28 Oct
1859); USNA (Oct 1859-Oct 1863); failed examination and
resigned (2 Oct 1860); resignation revoked; joined fourth class
(11 Oct 1860); *Wachusett*, spec.serv. (Oct 1863-Jan 1865);
Dictator, N.Atl.Blk.Sqdn. (Jan-Sep 1865); *Monadnock*, spec.serv.
(Sep 1865-Jul 1866); w.o. (Jul-Dec 1866); *Iroquois*, Asia.Sqdn.
(Jan 1867-Apr 1870); w.o. (Apr-Sep 1870); inst. of gunnery,
USNA (Sep 1870-Apr 1873); w.o. (Apr-Sep 1873); exec.off.,
Monongahela, then *Brooklyn*, S.Atl.Sta. (Sep 1873-Apr 1876);
l.o.a. (Apr-Nov 1876); Torp. School, Newport, RI (Nov 1876-Feb
1877); exec.off., flgs., *Trenton*, Eur.Sta. (Feb 1877-Jan 1880); w.o.
(Jan 1880-Apr 1881); insp. of ord., West Point Foundry, Cold
Spring, NY, S.Boston Iron Works, Boston, and Midvale Steel
Works, Nicetown, PA (Apr 1881-Feb 1883); cdr, *Quinnebaug*,
Eur.Sta. (Mar 1883-Dec 1885); sick lv. (Dec 1885-Jun 1886);
w.o. (Jun 1886-Mar 1887); asst., then insp., 12th L.h. Dist., San
Francisco (Mar 1887-Feb 1890); insp. of ord., Navy Yard, Mare
Island, CA (Feb 1890-Apr 1891); insp., 9th L.h. Dist., Chicago
(May 1891-Dec 1892); s.a. and w.o. (Dec 1892-Jan 1893); cdr,
flgs., *Mohican*, Pac.Sqdn. (Jan-Nov 1893); senior off. in command
of Bering Sea Sqdn. (Jan-Nov 1893); l.o.a. and bd. duties (Nov
1893-May 1895); NWC (Jun-Oct 1895); w.o. and bd. duties (Oct
1895-Feb 1896); cdr, *Monterey*, Pac.Sqdn. (Feb-Nov 1896);
member, naval exam. and ret. bds. (Nov 1896-Jul 1897); cdr,
Terror, N.Atl.Sqdn. (Jul 1897-Sep 1898); cdr, *Massachusetts*,
N.Atl.Flt. (Sep 1898-Jun 1899); w.o. (Jun-Nov 1899); retired (1
Nov 1899); gov., Naval Home, Philadelphia (Oct 1904-Nov
1907).

NICOLL LUDLOW
1842-1915

HENRY WARE LYON Born in Charleston, MA, on 8 Nov
1845, son of Dr. Henry Lyon. Married to Liela S. Lyon by whom
he had at least one son, LCdr Henry W. Lyon, Jr., USNR, who
was an aviator. Resided in Paris, ME. Died on 22 Nov 1929 in

HENRY WARE LYON
1845-1929

Washington, DC. Buried in Mount Auburn Cemetery, Boston.

Ranks   Midn (7 Oct 1862); Ens (12 Mar 1868); Mstr (26 Mar 1869); Lt (21 Mar 1870); LCdr (3 Nov 1884); Cdr (1 Oct 1893); Capt (27 Mar 1900); RAdm (19 Feb 1906); placed on Ret.Lst. (8 Nov 1907).

Career Summary   Received appointment from MA (7 Oct 1862); USNA (Oct 1862-Jun 1866); l.o.a. and w.o. (Jun-Sep 1866); *Sacramento,* spec.serv. (Sep 1866-Nov 1867); w.o. (Nov-Dec 1867); ord. duty, Navy Yard, Boston (Jan-Oct 1868); *Guard,* and *Richmond,* Med.Sqdn. (Oct 1868-Jun 1871); *Wabash,* and *Brooklyn,* Eur.Sta. (Jun 1871-Jul 1873); w.o. (Jul-Sep 1873); ord. duty, Navy Yard, Washington, DC (Oct-Nov 1873); *Franklin,* N.Atl.Flt. (Dec 1873-Mar 1874); *Wabash,* Key West, FL (Mar-Apr 1874); w.o. (Apr-May 1874); spec. ord. duty (May 1874-Apr 1875); flgs., *Tennessee,* Eur.Sqdn. (Apr 1875-May 1877); w.o. (May-Sep 1877); spec. ord. duty (Oct 1877-Aug 1880); *Galena,* Eur.Sta. (Aug 1880-Sep 1883); w.o. (Sep-Nov 1883); ord. duty, Navy Yard, Washington, DC (Dec 1883-Feb 1884); S.Boston Iron Works, Boston (Feb 1884-Feb 1887); w.o. (Feb-Apr 1887); exec.off., *Trenton,* Pac.Sta. (May 1887-May 1889); cdr, *Nipsic,* Pac.Sta. (May 1889-Apr 1890); w.o. (Apr-Jun 1890); Torp.Sta. and NWC, Newport, RI (Jun 1890-Mar 1893); cdr, *Yantic,* spec.serv. (May-Dec 1893); w.o. (Dec 1893-Feb 1894); ord. instruction, Navy Yard, Washington, DC (Mar-Apr 1894); Navy Yard, Boston (Apr 1894-May 1897); cdr, *Dolphin,* spec.serv., out of commission, and N.Atl.Flt. (May 1897-Jun 1899); w.o. (Jun-Sep 1899); Navy Yard, NY (Sep 1899-May 1901); *Olympia,* Navy Yard, Boston (Jun 1901-Jan 1902); cdr, *Olympia,* N.Atl. Sqdn. (Jan 1902-Dec 1903); chief of staff, N.Atl.Sta., *Olympia* (May-Aug 1902); bd. duties, Navy Yard, NY (Jan-Feb 1904); capt.yd., Navy Yard, Portsmouth, NH (Feb-Oct 1904); comdt., Naval Sta., Honolulu, Territory of HI (Nov 1904-Jun 1906); comdt., Navy Yard, Mare Island, CA (Jul 1906-Oct 1907); home and w.o. (Oct-Nov 1907); placed on Ret.Lst. (8 Nov 1907).

References

Writings: "Our Rifles Ordnance," U.S. Naval Institute *Proceedings* 11 (1880): 1-15.

CHARLES JENKINS MACCONNELL   Born in Morrisville, PA, on 14 Dec 1837, son of William and Ann S. (Jenkins) MacConnell. Educated at the Model Institute and the State Normal School in Trenton, NJ. Married Louisa B. Small on 13 Dec 1863. Served an apprenticeship in Philadelphia as a mechanical engineer and builder before becoming a prof. of drawing and mechanical engineering at the State Normal School in Trenton. Before being commissioned in the navy, served a few months with Company A, NJ National Guard, at outset of the Civil War. Resided in Brooklyn, NY, where he died on 16 Feb 1909. Buried in Portland, ME.

Ranks   3rd Asst.Engr. (29 Oct 1861); 2nd Asst.Engr. (3 Aug 1863); 1st Asst.Engr. (11 Oct 1866); title changed to PAsst.Engr. (24 Feb 1874); Chief Engr. (2 Dec 1885); Chief Engr. with rel.

CHARLES JENKINS
MACCONNELL
1837-1909

rank of Cdr (5 Jun 1896); Chief Engr. with rel. rank of Capt (10 Aug 1898); retired (19 Jan 1899); RAdm on Ret.Lst. (29 Jun 1906).

Career Summary Received appointment from NJ (29 Oct 1861); *Kineo*, and *Mendota*, W.Gulf and N.Atl.Blk.Sqdns. (Nov 1861-Oct 1863); *Pontoosuc*, N.Atl.Blk.Sqdn. (Nov 1863-Mar 1864); *Mattabesett*, N.Atl.Blk.Sqdn. (Mar 1864-May 1865); w.o. (May-Jun 1865); l.o.a. (Jun-Oct 1865); Navy Yard, League Island, PA (Oct 1865-Apr 1866); *Lackawanna*, Pac.Sqdn. (May 1866-Feb 1869); home and w.o. (Feb-Mar 1869); l.o.a. (Mar-Jun 1869); Navy Yard, Boston (Jun 1869-Dec 1870); *Tennessee*, Navy Yard, NY (Jan 1871); w.o. (Jan 1871-Jan 1872); *Canonicus*, spec.serv. (Jan-Oct 1872); flgs., *Pensacola*, S.Pac.Sqdn. (Nov 1872-Oct 1874); Navy Yard, Mare Island, CA (Oct 1874-Mar 1876); l.o.a. (Mar 1876-Aug 1877); *Monongahela*, Asia.Sqdn. (Aug 1877-Nov 1879); w.o. (Nov 1879-Jan 1880); Navy Yard, Norfolk, VA (Jan-Mar 1880); l.o.a. and w.o. (Mar 1880-Mar 1881); in charge of machinery, *Intrepid*, Navy Yard, NY (Mar-Sep 1881); additional duties, Navy Yard, NY (Jul 1881-Jul 1882); *Nantucket*, spec.serv. (Jul-Dec 1882); w.o. (Dec 1882-Jan 1883); *Swatara*, W.Indies and N.Atl.Sqdn. (Jan 1883-Aug 1885); w.o. (Aug 1885-Apr 1886); l.o.a. (Apr 1886-Mar 1887); rec. ship, *Vermont*, NY (Mar 1887-Mar 1888); l.o.a. (Mar 1888-Mar 1889); *Mohican*, Pac.Sta. (Mar 1889-Apr 1892); l.o.a. (Apr-Jul 1892); training ship, *Richmond*, and in charge, Naval Sta., Newport, RI (Aug 1892-Feb 1894); rec. ship, *Minnesota*, NY (Feb 1894-Jul 1895); *Olympia*, Asia.Sqdn. (Jul-Nov 1895); *Charleston*, Asia.Sqdn. (Nov 1895-Jul 1896); flgs., *Lancaster*, S.Atl.Sqdn. (Sep 1896-Nov 1897); flt.engr., N.Atl.Flt., *New York* (Nov 1897-Aug 1898); Naval Hosp., NY, and sick lv. (Aug 1898-Jan 1899); retired (19 Jan 1899).

Career Highlights As flt.engr. of the N.Atl.Flt. when war with Spain broke out, participated in the blockade of Havana, the bombardments of Puerto Rico, and the Battle of Santiago, being commended for conspicuous conduct and bravery in battle.

MORRIS ROBINSON SLIDELL MACKENZIE Born in Tarrytown, NY, on 5 May 1848, son of Cdr Alexander Slidell, USN, and Catherine Robinson MacKenzie. Father commanded the *Somers* during the famous mutiny on that vessel in 1842. Was a cousin to RAdm Raymond P. Rodgers [*q.v.*]. Remaining single, died in Morristown, NJ, on 16 Jan 1915.

Ranks Midn (29 Sep 1862); Ens (12 Mar 1868); Mstr (26 Mar 1869); Lt (21 Mar 1870); LCdr (26 Dec 1884); Cdr (16 Apr 1894); Capt (1 Jul 1900); RAdm (13 May 1906); retired (28 Jun 1906).

Career Summary Received appointment by virtue of being son of an officer (29 Sep 1862); USNA (Sep 1862-Jun 1866); l.o.a. and w.o. (Jun-Sep 1866); *Sacramento*, spec.serv. (Sep 1866-Nov 1867); ord. duty, Navy Yard, Portsmouth, NH (Nov 1867-Sep 1868); w.o. (Sep-Oct 1868); *Guard*, and flgs., *Franklin*, Eur.Sqdn. (Oct 1868-Nov 1871); w.o. (Nov 1871-May 1872); spec. duty,

MORRIS ROBINSON SLIDELL
MACKENZIE
1848-1915

Wilmington, DE (May-Aug 1872); USNA (Sep 1872-Jun 1875); flgs., *Pensacola*, N.Pac.Sta. (Jul 1875-Aug 1877); USNA (Sep 1877-Jul 1880); w.o. (Jul 1880-Jun 1881); member, naval advisory bd., Washington, DC (Jun-Oct 1881); *Essex*, Asia.Sta. (Nov 1881-Nov 1884); home and l.o.a. (Nov 1884-Sep 1885); asst., then insp., 3rd L.h. Dist., Tompkinsville, NY (Sep 1885-Jan 1889); exec.off., *Chicago*, Eur.Sta. (Jan 1889-Jul 1891); cdr, *Petrel*, Asia.Sta. (Jul 1891-Feb 1893); l.o.a. (Feb-May 1893); insp., 6th L.h. Dist., Charleston, SC (Jun 1893-May 1896); NWC (Jun 1896); w.o. (Jun-Aug 1896); cdr, *Machias*, Asia.Sqdn. (Sep 1896-Mar 1897); home and sick lv. (Apr 1897-Mar 1898); cdr, *Mayflower*, N.Atl.Flt. (Mar 1898-Feb 1899); home and w.o. (Feb-Mar 1899); cdr, *Prairie*, Navy Yard, Philadelphia (Mar 1899); spec. duty, Bur. of Nav., Washington, DC (Mar 1899-May 1900); home and w.o. (May-Jun 1900); cdr, *Texas*, N.Atl.Sta. (Jun-Nov 1900); Navy Yard, NY (Nov 1900-Feb 1901); cdr, flgs., *New York*, Asia.Sta. (Feb 1901-Jan 1903); home and w.o. (Jan-Apr 1903); capt.yd., Navy Yard, Portsmouth, NH (May 1903-Feb 1904); insp., 3rd L.h. Dist., Tompkinsville, NY (Feb 1904-Jun 1906); retired (28 Jun 1906).

DAVID BENTON MACOMB
1827-1911

DAVID BENTON MACOMB Born in Tallahassee, FL, on 27 Feb 1827, son of David Benton and Mary Tiffins (Worthington) Macomb. His maternal grandfather was first gov. of OH. His family moved to TX where his father became the Republic of TX's first adjutant gen. Married Augusta Pope. Two daughters. Retired to North Cambridge, MA. Died at Fordham Heights, NY, on 27 Jan 1911. Buried in Cedar Grove Cemetery, Boston.

Ranks 3rd Asst.Engr. (11 Jan 1849); 2nd Asst.Engr. (26 Feb 1851); 1st Asst.Engr. (26 Jun 1856); Chief Engr. (15 Sep 1861); placed on Ret.Lst. with rel. rank of Commo (27 Feb 1889); Chief Engr. with rank of RAdm on Ret.Lst. (29 Jun 1906).

Career Summary Received appointment from PA (11 Jan 1849); office of engr.-in-chief, Washington, DC (May 1849-May 1850); cst.surv. duty (May 1850-Jan 1851); *San Jacinto*, Navy Yard, NY (Feb-Mar 1851); cst.surv. duty (Mar 1851-Dec 1852); *John Hancock*, N.Pac.Expl.Expd. (Dec 1852-Nov 1855); l.o.a. (Nov 1855-Feb 1856); w.o. (Feb-Aug 1856); flgs., *Wabash*, Home Sqdn. (Aug 1856-Feb 1858); l.o.a. (Feb-Jun 1858); *Saranac*, Pac.Sqdn. (Jul 1858-Nov 1859); l.o.a. (Nov 1859-Apr 1860); *Niagara*, spec. duty (Apr 1860-Jan 1862); spec. duty, NY (May 1862-Jul 1863); *Canonicus*, James River Flot., and N.Atl.Blk. Sqdn. (Jul 1863-Jun 1865); w.o. (Jul-Sep 1865); spec. duty, Philadelphia (Sep-Dec 1865); spec. duty, Baltimore (Dec 1865-May 1866); Navy Yard, Pensacola, FL (May 1866-Oct 1867); spec. duty, Navy Yard, Boston (Oct-Dec 1867); w.o. (Dec 1867-Jan 1868); Navy Yard, Portsmouth, NH (Jan 1868-Jan 1870); *Tennessee*, spec.serv. (Jan 1870-Apr 1871); w.o. (Apr-May 1871); flt.engr., N.Atl.Sqdn., *Severn* (Jun-Dec 1871); flt.engr., N.Atl.Sqdn., *Worcester* (Dec 1871-Jul 1873); w.o. (Jul-Oct 1873); insp. of machinery afloat, Navy Yard, Portsmouth, NH (Oct 1873-Apr 1877); w.o. (Apr-Jun 1877); flt.engr., N.Atl.Sta.,

Powhatan (Jul 1877-Jun 1879); pres., statutory bd. of appraisal and survey, and in charge of stores, Navy Yard, Portsmouth, NH (Jun 1879-Jul 1883); w.o. (Jul 1883-Feb 1884); Navy Yard, Boston (Feb 1884-Feb 1889); placed on Ret.Lst. (27 Feb 1889); temp. duty, Navy Yard, Boston (May 1898); spec. recruiting duty (May-Dec 1898).

ALFRED THAYER MAHAN Born in West Point, NY, on 27 Sep 1840, son of Dennis Hart and Mary Helena (Okill) Mahan. His father was prof. of civil and military engineering at the USMA. Educated at St. James' School in Hagerstown, MD, from 1852 to 1854, then at Columbia College in NY City from 1854 to 1856 before entering the USNA. Married Ellen Lyle Evans on 11 Jun 1872. One son, Lyle, and two daughters, Ellen and Helen. His brother was Commo Dennis Hart Mahan, USN (1849-1925). Retired to Quogue, NY. Died on 1 Dec 1914 at Naval Hosp. in Washington, DC. Buried in Quogue, NY.

Ranks Act.Midn (30 Sep 1856); Midn (9 Jun 1859); Lt (31 Aug 1861); LCdr (7 Jun 1865); Cdr (20 Nov 1872); Capt (23 Sep 1885); retired (17 Nov 1896); promoted to RAdm on Ret.Lst. (29 Jun 1906).

Career Summary Received appointment from NY (30 Sep 1856); USNA (Sep 1856-Jun 1859); *Congress*, Braz.Sqdn. (Jun 1859-Aug 1861); w.o. (Aug 1861); *James Adger*, Navy Yard, NY (Sep 1861); *Pocahontas*, S.Atl.Blk.Sqdn. (Sep 1861-Sep 1862); inst., USNA (Sep 1862-Oct 1863); *Seminole*, W.Gulf Blk.Sqdn. (Oct 1863-Mar 1864); *James Adger*, S.Atl.Blk.Sqdn. (Mar 1864-Jun 1865); w.o. (Jun-Nov 1865); *Muscoota*, Gulf Sqdn. (Nov 1865-Sep 1866); w.o. (Sep-Oct 1866); ord. duty, Navy Yard, Washington, DC (Oct-Dec 1866); *Iroquois*, Asia.Sqdn. (Jan 1867-Sep 1869); cdr, *Aroostook*, Asia.Sqdn. (Sep-Nov 1869); l.o.a. (Nov 1869-Aug 1870); spec. duty, Pittsburgh, PA (Sep 1870); w.o. (Sep-Nov 1870); Navy Yard, NY (Nov 1870-Feb 1871); *Worcester*, spec.serv. (Feb-Aug 1871); w.o. (Aug-Sep 1871); spec.duty, Navy Yard, NY (Sep 1871-Jan 1872); rec. ship, *Vermont*, NY (Jan-May 1872); l.o.a. (May-Dec 1872); cdr, *Wasp*, S.Atl.Sta. (Dec 1872-Jan 1875); l.o.a. (Feb-Aug 1875); Navy Yard, Boston (Sep 1875-Aug 1876); w.o. (Aug-Oct 1876); member, bd. of examiners, USNA (Oct-Nov 1876); w.o. (Nov-Dec 1876); l.o.a. (Dec 1876-Aug 1877); USNA (Aug 1877-Jul 1880); nav. dept., Navy Yard, NY (Jul 1880-Aug 1883); cdr, *Wachusett*, Pac.Sta. (Sep 1883-Sep 1885); lecturer on naval tactics and history, NWC (Oct 1885-Aug 1886); pres., NWC (Aug 1886-Nov 1888); pres., commission to select site for navy yard on northwest cst. (Nov 1888-Aug 1889); spec. duty, Bur. of Nav., Washington, DC (Aug 1889-Jul 1892); pres., NWC and Torp. School, Newport, RI (Jul 1892-May 1893); cdr, *Chicago*, Naval Review Flt., and flgs., Eur.Sta. (May 1893-May 1895); spec. duty connected with NWC (May 1895-Nov 1896); retired (17 Nov 1896); spec. duty, Navy Dept., Washington, DC (Apr-Sep 1898); member, naval war board, Navy Dept., Washington, DC (May 1898-Jan 1899); delegate, Hague Peace Confer-

ALFRED THAYER MAHAN
1840-1914

ence, The Netherlands (1899); member, bd. of visitors, USNA (May 1903); numerous spec. committees and assignments (Nov 1904-Jun 1912).

Career Highlights Probably best known naval figure of period between the Civil War and World War I and a man whose advocacy of sea power had a profound effect on naval strength and competition from 1890 until the present. Became synonymous with naval history and sea power for both U.S. and most world powers. Career became particularly notable when he was called to lecture at the newly established NWC in naval history and strategy. Subsequently served twice as the NWC's pres. Although retiring in 1896, was called back in an advisory capacity on the naval war strategy bd. during the war with Spain in 1898. Received several honorary degrees for his historical studies, including a D.C.L. from Oxford Univ. and an LL.D. from Cambridge Univ. in 1894; an LL.D. from Harvard Univ. in 1895 and from Yale Univ. in 1897; and an LL.D. from McGill Univ. and from Columbia Univ. in 1900. In 1902, was elected pres. of the American Historical Association.

References

Personal Papers: a) 1,000 items (1824-1914) in LC. b) 5 items (1861-1913) in NHF,LC. c) 1 item (1859) in USMA. d) letters from Mahan to Samuel A'Court Ashe in WPL. e) 14 vols., 15 folders (1868-1908) in Naval War College, Newport, RI.

Selected Writings: a) *The Gulf and Inland Waters* (NY: 1883). b) *The Influence of Sea Power upon History, 1660-1783* (Boston: 1890). c) *The Influence of Sea Power upon the French Revolution and Empire* (Boston: 1892). d) *The Life of Admiral Farragut* (NY: 1892). e) *The Life of Nelson: The Embodiment of the Sea Power of Great Britain*, 2 vols. (Boston: 1897). f) *The Interest of America in Sea Power, Present and Future* (Boston: 1897). g) *Lessons of the War with Spain* (Boston: 1898). h) *The Problem of Asia* (Boston: 1900). i) *The South African War* (NY: 1900). j) *Types of Naval Officers* (Boston: 1901). k) *Retrospect and Prospect* (Boston: 1902). l) *Sea Power in Its Relations to the War of 1812* (Boston: 1905). m) *From Sail to Steam* (NY: 1907). n) *Some Neglected Aspects of War* (Boston: 1907). o) *Naval Administration and Warfare* (Boston: 1908). p) *The Harvest Within* (Boston: 1909). q) *Interest of America in International Conditions* (Boston: 1910). r) *Armaments and Arbitration* (NY: 1912). s) *Major Operations of the Navies in the War of American Independence* (Boston: 1913). t) numerous articles and essays. See Hattendorf and Hattendorf below.

Other Sources: a) William D Puleston, *Mahan: The Life and Work of Captain Alfred Thayer Mahan, U.S.N.* (New Haven: 1939). b) _____, "A Re-Examination of Mahan's Concept of Sea Power," U.S. Naval Institute *Proceedings* 451 (Sep 1940): 1229-36. c) William E Livezey, *Mahan on Sea Power* (Norman, OK: 1947). d) J. M. Ellicott, "Sidelights on Mahan," U.S. Naval Institute *Proceedings* 548 (Oct 1948): 1247-49. e) John D. Hayes, "Peripheral Strategy--Mahan's Doctrine Today," U.S. Naval Institute *Proceedings* 609 (Nov 1953): 1185-93. f) Francis

Duncan, "Mahan--Historian with a Purpose," U.S. Naval Institute *Proceedings* 651 (May 1957): 498-503. g) E. G. Campbell, "Mahan's Message on the Merchant Marine," U.S. Naval Institute *Proceedings* 687 (May 1960): 92-95. h) Richard W. Smith, "Mahan's Historical Method," U.S. Naval Institute *Proceedings* 731 (Jan 1964): 49-51. i) Robert Brent, "Mahan--Mariner or Misfit," U.S. Naval Institite *Proceedings* 758 (Apr 1966): 92-103. j) Kenneth Bourne and Carl Boyd, "Captain Mahan's 'War' with Great Britain," U.S. Naval Institute *Proceedings* 785 (Jul 1968): 71-78. k) Robert Seager II and Doris D. Maguire, eds. *Letters and Papers of Alfred Thayer Mahan*, 3 vols. (Annapolis: 1975). l) Robert Seager II, *Alfred Thayer Mahan: The Man and His Letters* (Annapolis: 1977). m) Thomas H. Etzold, "Is Mahan Still Valid?" U.S. Naval Institute *Proceedings* 930 (Aug 1980): 38-43. n) John B. Hattendorf, and Lynn C. Hattendorf, comp., *A Bibliography of the Works of Alfred Thayer Mahan* (Newport, RI: NWC Historical Manuscript Ser. 7, 1986).

HENRY NEWMAN MANNEY Born in La Porte, IA, on 22 Jan 1844, son of Rev. J. W. Manney. Early education in Faribault, MN. Married to Mary A. Manney. One son. Resided in Point Loma, CA, dying in San Diego on 25 Oct 1915. Buried in San Diego.

Ranks Act.Midn (24 Sep 1861); title change to Midn (16 Jul 1862); Ens (12 Mar 1868); Mstr (26 Mar 1869); Lt (21 Mar 1870); LCdr (7 Oct 1886); Cdr (10 May 1895); Capt (3 Mar 1901); Chief of Bur. of Equip. and Recruiting with rank of RAdm (15 Mar 1904); placed on Ret.Lst. with rank of RAdm (22 Jan 1906).

Career Summary Received appointment from MN (24 Sep 1861); USNA (Sep 1861-Jun 1866); found deficient and put back (Oct 1865); l.o.a. and w.o.(Jun-Sep 1866); *Pensacola*, and *Resaca*, Pac.Sqdn. (Sep 1866-Sep 1869); w.o. (Oct 1869-Jan 1870); *Swatara*, N.Atl.Sqdn. (Jan 1870-Jan 1872); w.o. (Jan-Jun 1872); *Michigan*, on Great Lakes (Jun 1872-Jun 1873); rec. ship, *Independence*, Mare Island, CA (Jul-Nov 1873); *Tuscarora*, *Kearsarge*, and *Yantic*, surv. duty, Pac. Ocean, then Asia.Sta. (Nov 1873-Feb 1876); home and w.o. (Feb-Aug 1876); l.o.a. (Aug 1876-Nov 1877); w.o. (Nov 1877-Apr 1878); *Alaska*, Pac.Sta. (Apr 1878-Apr 1881); w.o. (Apr-May 1881); torp. instruction, Newport, RI (Jun-Sep 1881); USNA (Sep 1881-Jun 1884); *Lancaster*, Eur. and S.Atl.Stas. (Jul 1884-Nov 1887); w.o. (Nov 1887-Mar 1888); Hydrographic Office, Washington, DC (Mar-May 1888); l.o.a. (May 1888-May 1889); w.o. (May-Jul 1889); Naval Home, Philadelphia (Jul 1889-Jun 1891); exec.off., *Newark*, spec.serv., and N.Atl.Sqdn. (Jun 1891-Jun 1892); l.o.a. (Jun-Aug 1892); Naval Hosp., Philadelphia (Aug-Sep 1892); Naval Home, Philadelphia (Sep 1892-Oct 1895); cdr, training ship, *Alliance* (Oct 1895-Jan 1898); cdr, Naval Home, Philadelphia (Feb 1898-Mar 1899); Navy Yard, NY (Mar 1899-May 1901); cdr, *Massachusetts*, N.Atl.Sqdn. (May 1901-May 1903); NWC (May 1903-Feb 1904); chief, Bur. of Equip., Washington, DC (Mar

HENRY NEWMAN MANNEY
1844-1915

1904-Jan 1906); placed on Ret.Lst. (22 Jan 1906); spec. duty, Navy Dept., Washington, DC (Jan 1906-Nov 1909).

**HENRY BUCKINGHAM
MANSFIELD
1846-1918**

HENRY BUCKINGHAM MANSFIELD   Born in Brooklyn, NY, on 5 Mar 1846, son of merchant capt Charles and Eliza Maria (Buckingham) Mansfield. Educated in public schools in Sheffield, MA, and at the Hudson River Institute in Claverack, NY. Served at sea in the clipper ship, *Golden State,* from 1861-62. Married Harriet Sheldon on 23 Oct 1872. Two daughters. Resided in Brooklyn, NY, dying there on 17 Jul 1918.

Ranks   Midn (27 Feb 1863); Ens (18 Dec 1868); Mstr (21 Mar 1870); Lt (21 Mar 1871); LCdr (3 Jan 1890); Cdr (16 May 1897); Capt (19 Feb 1902); retired (15 Jun 1905); RAdm on Ret.Lst. (13 Apr 1911) to rank from 15 Jun 1905.

Career Summary   Received appointment from MA (27 Feb 1863); USNA (Feb 1863-Jun 1867); found deficient and put back (Jan 1864); *Minnesota, Marion, Macedonian, Winnipeg, Minnesota,* spec. training serv. (Jul 1867-1868); *Mohongo,* and *Mohican,* spec. expl. duty, and Pac.Sqdn. (1868-Aug 1870); w.o. (Aug-Oct 1870); torp. duty, Newport, RI (Nov 1870-May 1871); spec. duty, Key West, FL (May-Jun 1871); cst.surv. duty (Jul 1871-Mar 1874); w.o. (Mar-May 1874); *Michigan,* on Great Lakes (May 1874-Jun 1875); *Yantic, Saco, Mohongo,* and *Tennessee,* Asia.Sqdn. (Jul 1875-Jul 1878); w.o. (Jul-Oct 1878); Navy Yard, NY (Oct 1878-Mar 1880); *Constellation,* spec.serv. to Ireland (Mar-Jun 1880); Navy Yard, NY (Jun 1880-Feb 1881); cst.surv. duty (Feb 1881-Sep 1884); w.o. (Sep 1884-Mar 1885); *Pensacola,* Eur.Sta. (Mar 1885-Feb 1888); w.o. (Feb-Apr 1888); cst.surv. duty (Apr 1888-Feb 1892); l.o.a. (Feb-May 1892); ord. duty, Navy Yard, NY (May 1892-Jan 1893); exec.off., rec. ship, *Vermont,* NY (Jan 1893-Jan 1896); cdr, *Fern,* spec.serv. (Jan 1896-Apr 1897); asst., then insp., 15th L.h. Dist., St. Louis (Apr 1897-May 1898); cdr, *Celtic,* N.Atl.Sqdn. (May-Sep 1898); Navy Yard, NY (Sep 1898-Jan 1899); insp., 15th L.h. Dist., St. Louis (Jan-Dec 1899); cdr, training ship, *Lancaster* (Dec 1899-Nov 1901); in charge, Naval Recruiting Rndv., NY (Nov 1901-May 1903); cdr, flgs., *Iowa,* S.Atl.Sqdn. (May-Jun 1903); NWC (Jul-Oct 1903); member, naval exam. and ret. bds. (Oct 1903); cdr, *Iowa,* N.Atl.Sqdn. (Oct 1903-Jan 1905); sick lv. (Jan-Feb 1905); Navy Yard, NY (Feb-Jul 1905); retired (15 Jun 1905).

ADOLPH MARIX   Born in Dresden, Saxony, on 10 May 1848, son of Henry and Frederica (Meyer) Marix. Emigrated to the U.S. Married Grace Filkins on 31 May 1896. Resided in NY City, dying in Gloucester, MA, on 11 Jul 1919. Buried in Arlington National Cemetery.

Ranks   Midn (26 Sep 1864); Ens (19 Apr 1869); Mstr (12 Jul 1870); Lt (24 May 1872); LCdr (9 May 1893); Cdr (3 Mar 1899); Capt (21 Mar 1903); RAdm (4 Jul 1908); placed on Ret.Lst. (10 May 1910).

Career Summary   Received appointment from IA (26 Sep 1864); USNA (Sep 1864-Jun 1868); w.o. (Jun-Sep 1868); *Guard,*

**ADOLPH MARIX
1848-1919**

Eur.Sta. (Oct 1868-Oct 1869); ord. duty, Navy Yard, Washington, DC (Oct 1869-Jan 1870); *Congress*, spec.serv. (Feb 1870-Jun 1871); w.o. (Jun-Jul 1871); Naval Observatory, Washington, DC (Jul-Aug 1871); *Iroquois*, spec.serv. (Aug 1871-Jan 1872); *Canandaigua*, and flgs., *Worcester*, N.Atl.Sta. (Jan 1872-Jun 1874); home and w.o. (Jun-Aug 1874); *Saco*, and *Tennessee*, Asia.Sta. (Oct 1874-Jun 1877); home and w.o. (Jun-Aug 1877); *Trenton*, Eur.Sta. (Oct 1877-Aug 1879); w.o. (Aug-Sep 1879); Hydrographic Office, Washington, DC (Sep 1879-Aug 1880); training ship, *Minnesota* (Aug 1880-Dec 1881); rec. ship, *Colorado*, NY (Dec 1881-Apr 1882); *Brooklyn*, S.Atl.Sta. (Jun 1882-Apr 1883); *Richmond*, Asia.Sta. (Apr 1883-Apr 1884); *Monocacy*, Asia.Sta. (Apr-May 1884); *Enterprise*, spec. surv. duty (May 1884-Jun 1885); *Trenton*, Asia.Sta. (Jun-Jul 1885); *Enterprise*, Asia.Sta. (Jul 1885-Apr 1886); l.o.a. (Apr-Nov 1886); judge advocate gen's office, Navy Dept., Washington, DC (Nov 1886-Apr 1888); spec. duty to Australia (Apr 1888-Oct 1889); training ship, *Jamestown* (Nov 1889-Jun 1890); flgs., *Philadelphia*, N.Atl.Sta. (Jun 1890-Jun 1892); in charge, branch hydrographic office, NY (Jun 1892-Jun 1894); exec.off., training ship, *Minnesota* (Jun 1894-Apr 1895); spec. temp. duty, Navy Dept., Washington, DC (Apr-Dec 1895); exec.off., *Maine*, N.Atl.Sqdn. (Sep 1895-Dec 1897); rec. ship, *Vermont*, NY (Dec 1897-Apr 1898); judge advocate, court of inquiry, *Maine* (Feb-Mar 1898); cdr, *Scorpion*, N.Atl.Flt. (Apr-Oct 1898); insp., 4th L.h. Dist., Philadelphia (Oct 1898-Mar 1901); capt. of port, Manila, P.I. (Apr 1901-Feb 1903); in charge, branch hydrographic office, Manila, P.I. (Jul 1901-Feb 1903); home and w.o. (Feb-Apr 1903); capt.yd., Navy Yard, League Island, PA (May-Sep 1903); cdr, *Minneapolis*, spec.serv. (Sep 1903-Jun 1905); supervisor of naval auxiliaries, Atl.cst., Baltimore (Jun 1905-Dec 1907); chairman, L.h. Bd., Washington, DC (Dec 1907-Jun 1910); placed on Ret.Lst. (10 May 1910).

Career Highlights Served as judge advocate on the court of enquiry for the explosion of the *Maine* in 1898. Commanded the *Scorpion* during the war with Spain, being promoted for conspicuous bravery.

WILLIAM ALEXANDER MARSHALL Born in Lancaster, PA, on 17 Oct 1849, son of William Marshall. Early education in Lancaster, PA. Married to Mary Bartlett Marshall. One daughter. Resided in Washington, DC. Died on 10 Jul 1926 in Jamestown, RI.

Ranks Midn (26 Jun 1867); title changed to Cadet Midn (15 Jul 1870); Midn (6 Jun 1871); Ens (14 Jul 1872); Mstr (22 Apr 1875); Lt (15 Apr 1882); LCdr (3 Mar 1899); Cdr (27 Dec 1901); Capt (1 Jul 1906); RAdm (17 Mar 1910); placed on Ret.Lst. (17 Oct 1911).

Career Summary Received appointment from PA (26 Jun 1867); USNA (Jun 1867-Jun 1871); w.o. (Jun-Aug 1871); *Iroquois*, N.Atl.Sta. (Aug 1871-Jan 1872); *Canandaigua*, N. Atl.Sta. (Jan-Sep 1872); *Hartford*, Asia.Sta. (Oct 1872-May 1874); home and w.o. (May 1874-Apr 1875); *Tennessee*, Asia.Sta.

WILLIAM ALEXANDER
MARSHALL
1849-1926

(Apr 1875-Jul 1878); w.o. (Jul-Aug 1878); l.o.a. (Aug 1878-Feb 1879); temp. duty, training ship, *New Hampshire* (Feb 1879-Feb 1880); *Vandalia*, N.Atl.Sta. (Feb 1880-May 1883); w.o. (May-Sep 1883); Navy Yard, Portsmouth, NH (Sep-Oct 1883); in charge, branch hydrographic office, Boston (Oct 1883-May 1886); torp. instruction, Newport, RI (Jun-Aug 1886); NWC (Sep-Nov 1886); l.o.a. (Nov 1886-Jan 1887); *Dolphin*, Pac.Sta., and spec.serv. (Jan 1887-Nov 1889); Torp.Sta., Newport, RI (Dec 1889-Mar 1893); *Charleston*, S.Atl.Sta. (Apr 1893-Mar 1894); *Detroit*, Asia.Sta. (Mar 1894-Nov 1895); *Baltimore*, Asia.Sta., and Navy Yard, Mare Island, CA (Nov 1895-Feb 1896); home and l.o.a. (Feb-May 1896); USNA (May 1896-Oct 1897); l.o.a. (Oct 1897-Apr 1898); Navy Yard, NY (Apr-Jul 1898); Navy Yard, Washington, DC (Jul 1898); Torp.Sta., Newport, RI (Jul-Dec 1898); exec.off., *Resolute*, spec.serv. (Dec 1898-Aug 1899); cdr, *Scorpion*, Isthmian Canal Commission (Aug-Sep 1899); home and w.o. (Sep 1899); aide, N.Atl.Sta., *New York* (Oct 1899-Oct 1900), then *Kearsarge* (Oct 1900-Nov 1901); home and w.o. (Nov-Dec 1901); Navy Yard, Boston (Dec 1901-Mar 1902); asst., then insp., 15th L.h. Dist., St. Louis (Mar 1902-Mar 1903); cdr, *Vicksburg*, Asia.Sta. (Apr 1903-May 1904); cdr, *Raleigh*, Asia.Sta. (May 1904-Mar 1905); home and l.o.a. (Mar-Aug 1905); insp., 2nd L.h. Dist., Boston (Sep 1905-Sep 1906); asst.equip.off., Navy Yard, Boston (Oct 1906-Apr 1907); capt.yd., Navy Yard, Boston (Apr 1907-Mar 1908); general insp., then cdr, *North Carolina*, spec.serv. (Mar 1908-Nov 1909); comdt., Navy Yard, and 5th Naval Dist., Norfolk, VA (Nov 1909-Nov 1911); placed on Ret.Lst. (17 Oct 1911); temp. duty, Bur. of Nav., Washington, DC (Apr 1918-May 1919).

References
Personal Papers: 100 items (1876-1906) in NHF,LC.

NEWTON ELIPHALET MASON   Born in Monroeton, Bradford County, PA, on 14 Oct 1850, son of Gordon Fowler and Mary Ann Mason. Educated at Susquehanna Collegiate Institute in Towanda, PA, before the USNA. Married Dora E. Hancock on 4 Apr 1894. One son and one daughter. Retired to Coronado, CA, dying in San Diego on 23 Jan 1945. Buried in Arlington National Cemetery.

Ranks Midn (24 Jul 1865); Ens (12 Jul 1870); Mstr (12 Jul 1871); Lt (8 Nov 1874); LCdr (10 Nov 1896); Cdr (2 Nov 1899); Capt (30 Sep 1904); RAdm (12 Nov 1908); placed on Ret.Lst. (14 Oct 1912).

Career Summary Received appointment from PA (24 Jul 1865); USNA (Jul 1865-Jun 1869); *Sabine*, spec. cruise (Jun 1869-Jul 1870); w.o. (Jul-Oct 1870); torp. instruction, Newport, RI (Oct 1870-May 1871); w.o. (May-Sep 1871); *Wabash*, and *Brooklyn*, Eur.Sqdn. (Oct 1871-Jul 1873); w.o. (Jul-Nov 1873); *Manhattan*, and *Kansas*, N.Atl.Sta. (Nov 1873-Jul 1875); w.o. (Jul-Nov 1875); *Catskill*, N.Atl.Sta. (Nov 1875-Jul 1876); w.o. (Jul-Aug 1876); *Ossipee*, N.Atl.Sta. (Aug 1876-May 1878); w.o. (May-Sep 1878); rec. ship, *St. Louis*, League Island, PA (Oct

NEWTON ELIPHALET MASON
1850-1945

1878-Mar 1880); *Constellation*, spec. duty (Mar-June 1880); w.o. (Jun-Jul 1880); *Monocacy*, Asia.Sta. (Oct 1880-Mar 1882); *Richmond*, Asia.Sta. (Mar-Nov 1882); *Pensacola*, Asia.Sta. (Nov 1882-Aug 1883); *Richmond*, Asia.Sta. (Aug-Oct 1883); *Pensacola*, Asia.Sta. (Oct 1883-May 1884); w.o. (May-Aug 1884); ord. instruction, Navy Yard, Washington, DC (Aug 1884-Aug 1885); Bur. of Ord., Washington, DC (Aug 1885-Oct 1889); exec.off., *Petrel*, N.Atl.Sta. (Oct 1889-Oct 1891); *Miantonomoh*, N.Atl.Sta. (Oct 1891-Nov 1892); Bur. of Ord., Washington, DC (Nov 1892-Jun 1893); insp. of ord., and in charge, Naval Ord. Proving Ground, Indian Head, MD (Jun 1893-Nov 1896); exec.off., *Brooklyn*, spec. duty, and N.Atl.Flt. (Dec 1896-Feb 1899); insp. of ord., Navy Yard, League Island, PA (Feb-Oct 1899); in charge, Naval Torp.Sta., Newport, RI (Oct 1899-Jun 1902); NWC (Jun-Sep 1902); cdr, *Cincinnati*, spec.serv. and Asia.Sta. (Sep 1902-Apr 1904); spec. duty, Bur. of Ord., Washington, DC (May-Aug 1904); chief, Bur. of Ord., Washington, DC (Aug 1904-May 1911); member, Gen Bd. and other bd. duties, Washington, DC (May 1911-Oct 1912); placed on Ret.Lst. (14 Oct 1912); Bur. of Ord., and member, Priorities Committee, War Industries Bd., and Council of National Defense, Washington, DC (Jun 1917-Jan 1919); pres., spec. bd. on naval ord., Bur. of Ord., Washington, DC (Jan-Nov 1919).

WASHBURN MAYNARD Born in Knoxville, TN, on 5 Dec 1844, son of Horace and Laura Ann (Washburn) Maynard. Married but became a widower. Died at Newton Centre, MA, on 24 Oct 1913. Buried in Island Cemetery, Newport, RI.

Ranks Midn (6 Oct 1862); Ens (12 Mar 1868); Mstr (26 March 1869); Lt (21 Mar 1870); LCdr (27 Sep 1884); Cdr (27 Sep 1893); Capt (9 Mar 1900); retired (1 Nov 1902); promoted to RAdm on Ret.Lst. (13 Apr 1911) to rank from 1 Nov 1902.

Career Summary Received appointment from TN (6 Oct 1862); USNA (Oct 1862-Jun 1866); l.o.a. and w.o. (Jun-Oct 1866); *Susquehanna*, N.Atl.Sqdn. (Oct 1866-Jun 1867); flgs., *Franklin*, and *Frolic*, Eur.Sqdn. (Jun 1867-May 1869); w.o. (May-Sep 1869); *Seminole*, Pac.Sta. (Oct 1869-Feb 1870); USNA (Feb-Mar 1870); torp. duty, Newport, RI (Mar 1870-Aug 1872); *California*, and *Saranac*, Pac.Sqdn. (Oct 1872-Apr 1874); *Richmond*, Pac.Sqdn. (May 1874-Jul 1875); Torp.Sta., Newport, RI (Jul 1875-Jan 1876); exec.off., *Wyandotte*, N.Atl.Sta. (Jan-Jun 1876); cst.surv. duty (Jun 1876-Oct 1877); Torp.Sta., Newport, RI (Oct 1877-Nov 1879); *Tennessee*, N.Atl.Sta. (Dec 1879-Jun 1882); w.o. (Jun-Oct 1882); Torp.Sta., Newport, RI (Oct 1882-Oct 1885); exec.off., *Brooklyn*, N.Atl. and Asia.Stas. (Oct 1885-Sep 1887); w.o. (Sep-Nov 1887); Bur. of Ord., Washington, DC (Nov 1887-Jun 1891); w.o. (Jun-Aug 1891); cdr, *Pinta*, Alaskan waters (Sep 1891-Jan 1893); Bur. of Equip. and Recruiting, Washington, DC (Jan 1893-Aug 1897); cdr, *Nashville*, N.Atl.Flt. (Aug 1897-Jul 1899); home and w.o. (Jul-Sep 1899); insp., 8th L.h. Dist., New Orleans (Sep-Dec 1899); insp., 2nd L.h. Dist., Boston (Dec 1899-Sep 1900); member, naval exam. bd.

WASHBURN MAYNARD
1844-1913

(Oct 1900-Feb 1901); sec., L.h. Bd., Washington, DC (Feb 1901-Nov 1902); retired (1 Nov 1902).

References

Other Sources: Bessie M. Henry, ed., *The Reminiscences and Letters of Rear Admiral Washburn Maynard, 1844-1913* (c. 1975).

HENRY THOMAS MAYO
1856-1937

HENRY THOMAS MAYO Born in Burlington, VT, on 8 Dec 1856, son of Henry and Elizabeth (Elrie) Mayo. Married Carrie Wing on 9 Mar 1881. Two sons, Capt Chester Garst Mayo, SC (USN), and Maj George Mayo, CE (USA). Retired to Burlington. Died in Portsmouth, NH, on 23 Feb 1937. Buried in Burlington, VT.

Ranks Cadet Midn (14 Jun 1872); Midn (20 Jun 1876); Ens (26 Feb 1878); Ltjg (25 Feb 1885); Lt (5 Dec 1890); LCdr (11 Jun 1899); Cdr (21 Feb 1905); Capt (7 Sep 1908); RAdm (15 Jun 1913); temp. VAdm (10 Jun 1915); temp. Adm (22 May 1917); placed on Ret.Lst. with rank of RAdm (8 Dec 1920); Adm on Ret.Lst. (21 Jun 1930).

Career Summary Received appointment from VT (14 Jun 1872); USNA (Jun 1872-Jun 1876); w.o. (Jun-Aug 1876); *Tennessee*, Asia.Sqdn. (Sep 1876-Jul 1878); home and w.o. (Jul 1878-Mar 1879); USNA (Mar-Apr 1879); w.o. (Apr-May 1879); cst.surv. duty (May 1879-Feb 1882); w.o. (Feb-May 1882); cst.surv. duty (May-Jul 1882); *Yantic*, spec.serv., and Greely Relief Expd. (Jul 1882-Oct 1885); w.o. (Oct-Dec 1885); Naval Observatory, Washington, DC (Dec 1885-Apr 1886); cst.surv. duty (Apr 1886-Jun 1889); w.o. (Jun-Jul 1889); l.o.a. (Jul-Oct 1889); training ship, *Jamestown* (Oct 1889-Sep 1892); NWC (Sep-Oct 1892); l.o.a. (Oct-Nov 1892); in charge, branch hydrographic office, Port Townsend, Puget Sound, WA (Dec 1892-May 1895); nav., then exec.off., hydrographic surv. ship, *Bennington*, Pearl Harbor, Territory of HI (May 1895-Jul 1896); temp. duty, *Thetis*, Pac.Sqdn. (Jul 1896-Jul 1897); *Bennington*, Pac.Sqdn. (Jul 1897-Aug 1898); rec. ship, *Independence*, Mare Island, CA (Sept-Oct 1898); inspection duty, Union Iron Works, San Francisco (Oct 1898-Feb 1900); insp., then nav., then exec.off., *Wisconsin*, San Francisco, and flgs., Pac.Sta. (Feb 1900-Mar 1904); home and l.o.a. (Mar-Jun 1904); Navy Yard, Boston (Jun 1904-Mar 1905); asst., then insp., 12th L.h. Dist., San Francisco (Mar 1905-Jul 1906); cdr, *Albany*, Pac.Sqdn. (Jul 1906-Oct 1908); sec., L.h. Bd., Washington, DC (Oct 1908-Aug 1909); cdr, *California*, Pac.Flt. (Sep 1909-Jan 1911); capt.yd., Navy Yard, Mare Island, CA (Jan 1911-Apr 1913); comdt., Navy Yard, Mare Island, CA, and 12th Naval Dist., San Francisco (May-Jul 1911); aide for personnel, Navy Dept., Washington, DC (Apr-Nov 1913); NWC (Nov-Dec 1913); cdr, 4th Div., Atl.Flt., *Connecticut* (Dec 1913-Jun 1914), then *Minnesota* (Jun-Aug 1914), then *Kansas* (Aug-Sep 1914), then *Vermont* (Sep-Oct 1914); cdr, 1st Div., Atl.Flt., *Arkansas* (Oct 1914-Jan 1915), then *New York* (Jan-Jun 1915); cdr, Battleship Sqdn. and 2nd in command, Atl.Flt. with rank of VAdm, *New York* (Jun 1915), then *Arkansas* (Jun 1915-Jun 1916); cdr, Atl.Flt., *Pennsylvania* (Jun 1916-Jun

1919) [command redesignated U.S. Flt. from Jan-Jul 1919];
member, Gen Bd., Navy Dept., Washington, DC (Jul-Oct 1919);
chairman, Gen Bd., Washington, DC (Oct 1919-Feb 1921);
placed on Ret.Lst. (8 Dec 1920); gov., Naval Home, Philadelphia
(Jul 1924-1928).

Career Highlights Served on the *Yantic* as part of the Greely
Relief Expd. of 1883. In Apr 1914, demanded a public apology,
disciplinary action against the citizens responsible, and a twenty-
one gun salute to the American flag when Mexican officials seized
a boat's crew on the Tampico wharf. It was this action and the
refusal of the Mexican government to comply that prompted Pres.
Woodrow Wilson to seize the Mexican customs house at Vera
Cruz, which resulted in the American occupation of that city. In
1916, became cdr of Atl.Flt., thereby cdr of all U.S. naval forces
in Atl. and Eur. waters. Held this important command through
World War I. Represented the U.S. at the allied naval conference
in London in Sep 1917. Awarded Distinguished Service Medal
and a few foreign medals.

BOWMAN HENDRY MCCALLA Born in Camden, NJ, on
19 Jun 1844, son of Auley and Mary Duffield (Hendry) McCalla.
Married Elizabeth Hazard Sargent on 3 Mar 1875. Three
daughters, one of whom married future Commo Dudley W. Knox,
USN (1877-1960) who served as historian of the navy. Resided
in Santa Barbara, CA, where he died on 6 May 1910. Buried in
Arlington National Cemetery.

BOWMAN HENDRY MCCALLA
1844-1910

Ranks Act.Midn (30 Nov 1861); title changed to Midn (16 Jul
1862); Ens (1 Nov 1866); Mstr (1 Dec 1866); Lt (12 Mar 1868);
LCdr (26 Mar 1869); Cdr (3 Nov 1884); Capt (10 Aug 1898);
RAdm (11 Oct 1903); placed on Ret.Lst. (19 Jun 1906).

Career Summary Received appointment from NJ (30 Nov
1861); USNA (Nov 1861-Nov 1864); l.o.a. (Nov 1864-Feb
1865); Navy Yard, NY (Feb-Mar 1865); *Susquehanna*, and flgs.,
Brooklyn, S.Atl.Sqdn. (Mar 1865-Sep 1867); w.o. (Sep-Oct 1867);
training ship, *Sabine*, and *Kearsarge*, S.Pac.Sqdn. (Oct 1867-Apr
1868); *Tuscarora*, S.Pac.Sqdn. (Apr 1868-Feb 1871); l.o.a.
(Feb-Sep 1871); flgs., *Wabash*, and *Wachusett*, Eur.Sqdn. (Oct
1871-Mar 1874); sick lv. (Mar-Aug 1874); inst., USNA (Sep
1874-Aug 1878); w.o. (Aug-Oct 1878); exec.off., *Powhatan*,
N.Atl.Sqdn. (Nov 1878-Oct 1881); w.o. (Oct-Dec 1881); Bur. of
Nav., Washington, DC (Dec 1881-Oct 1887); cdr, *Enterprise*,
Eur.Sta. (Oct 1887-May 1890); suspended (May 1890-Dec 1891);
l.o.a. (Dec 1891-Oct 1893); equip.off., Navy Yard, Mare Island,
CA (Oct 1893-Apr 1897); NWC (Apr-Sep 1897); cdr, *Marble-
head*, N.Atl.Sqdn. (Sep 1897-Oct 1898); cdr, *Vulcan*, Navy Yard,
Norfolk, VA (Nov 1898); capt.yd., Navy Yard, Norfolk, VA (Nov
1898-Aug 1899); cdr, *Newark*, Asia.Sta. (Sep 1899-Jul 1901); cdr,
Kearsarge, and chief of staff, N.Atl.Sta. (Jul 1901-Apr 1902); w.o.,
l.o.a., and bd. duties (Apr 1902-Feb 1903); comdt., Training Sta.,
San Francisco (Feb-Jul 1903); Navy Yard, Mare Island, CA (Jul
1903-Jun 1906); placed on Ret.Lst. (19 Jun 1906).

Career Highlights Frequently led troops into combat during his career, thereby gaining the reputation as a fighting adm. In 1885, led a landing party of Bluejackets and marines which quickly occupied Panama City and helped quell trouble there. In 1890, while commanding the *Enterprise*, struck a mutinous sailor for which he was court-martialled and suspended for three years, a sentence reduced by his recall in 1891. During Spanish-American War, commanded the *Marblehead*, which blockaded Havana and Cienfuegos before participating in the action at Guantanamo Bay, during which he led a force of marines and sailors, establishing and commanding a naval base there for the remainder of the war. Was later advanced six numbers for his action and eventually receive two congressional medals for action at Cienfuegos and at Guantanamo Bay and another Congressional medal for "specially meritorious service other than in battle." During the Boxer Rebellion in China of 1900, he commanded a landing party as part of the column the Royal Navy designed to relieve the legations in Peking. Wounded three times during the expd., was subsequently advanced again three numbers in rank. Received the China War Medal from King Edward VII of Great Britain for his efforts. Also received the Order of the Red Eagle by German Kaiser Wilhelm II.

References

Personal Papers: RAdm Bowman H. McCalla, "Memoirs of a Naval Career" (typescript) in Navy Dept. Lib., Washington Navy Yard, Washington, DC.

Other Sources: Paolo E. Coletta, *Bowman Hendry McCalla: A Fighting Sailor* (Washington, DC: 1979).

JOHN DANIEL MCDONALD Born in Machias, ME, on 1 Nov 1863, son of Patrick McDonald. Early education in Gold Hill, NV, where his father was a miner. Remaining single, he made his home in Oakland, CA, dying at the Naval Hosp. there on 2 Sep 1952.

Ranks Cadet Midn (6 Oct 1880); Ens (1 Jul 1886); Ltjg (1 Sep 1895); Lt (17 Jul 1898); LCdr (4 Feb 1904); Cdr (1 Jul 1908); Capt (14 Sep 1911); temp. RAdm (15 Oct 1917); RAdm (31 Dec 1918); placed on Ret.Lst. (1 Nov 1927); VAdm on Ret.Lst. (21 Jun 1930).

Career Summary Received appointment from NV (6 Oct 1880); USNA (Oct 1880-Jun 1884); *Hartford*, Pac.Sqdn. (Jul 1884); *Lackawanna*, Pac.Sqdn. (Jul 1884-Mar 1885); rec. ship, *Independence*, Mare Island, CA (Mar-May 1885); *Mohican*, Pac.Sqdn. (May 1885-Mar 1886); USNA (Apr-Jun 1886); w.o. (Jun-Jul 1886); cst.surv. duty (Aug 1886-Dec 1889); flgs., *Charleston*, Pac.Sqdn. (Jan-Jul 1890); *Nipsic*, Pac.Sqdn. (Jul-Oct 1890); rec. ship, *Independence*, Mare Island, CA (Oct-Dec 1890); *Mohican*, Pac.Sqdn. (Dec 1890-Oct 1892); home and l.o.a. (Oct 1892-Feb 1893); *Monterey*, Pac.Sqdn. (Mar 1893-May 1896); *Charleston*, Asia.Sqdn. (May-Jul 1896); home and l.o.a. (Jul-Sep 1896); Bur. of Equip. and Recruiting, Washington, DC (Sep-Nov 1896); schoolship, *St. Mary's* (Nov 1896-Jan 1898); *Monadnock*, Pac.Sqdn. (Jan 1898); *Monterey*, Pac. and Asia.Stas. (Jan 1898-

JOHN DANIEL MCDONALD
1863-1952

Aug 1899); *Charleston*, Asia.Sta. (Aug-Nov 1899); temp. duty,
Wheeling, Asia.Sta. (Nov-Dec 1899); *Baltimore*, Asia.Sta. (Dec
1899-Jan 1900); *Castine*, Asia.Sta. (Jan 1900-Apr 1901); *Buffalo*,
spec. duty, Asia.Sta. (Apr 1901-Jun 1904); home and w.o.
(Jun-Jul 1904); Navy Dept., Washington, DC (Jul 1904); home
and w.o. (Jul-Aug 1904); duty connected with Naval Torp.Sta.,
Newport, RI (Aug-Sep 1904); temp. duty and instruction, Naval
Gun Factory, Navy Yard, Washington, DC (Sep-Oct 1904);
Naval Ord. Proving Ground, Indian Head, MD (Oct 1904); Bur.
of Nav., Washington, DC (Oct 1904); flgs., *Ohio*, Asia.Flt. (Oct
1904-Jan 1907); insp., 1st L.h. Dist., Portland, ME (Feb 1907-Sep
1908); cdr, *Castine*, spec.serv. (Oct 1908-Jun 1909); cdr, *Chattanooga*, Pac.Sqdn. (Aug 1909-Sep 1910); insp., 1st L.h. Dist.,
Portland, ME (Oct 1910-Jul 1911); cdr, rec. ship, *Hancock*, NY
(Jul-Dec 1911); cdr, *Virginia*, Atl.Flt. (Dec 1911-Oct 1913); home
and w.o. (Oct-Nov 1913); NWC (Dec 1913-Nov 1915); chief of
staff, Atl.Flt., *Wyoming* (Nov 1915-Jun 1916); duty with, then
cdr, *Arizona*, on trials, and Atl.Flt. (Jun 1916-Feb 1918); comdt.,
Navy Yard, NY (Feb 1918-Jun 1921); cdr, Battleship Force,
Atl.Flt., *Arizona* (Jun 1921-Dec 1922); cdr, Scouting Flt.,
Wyoming (Dec 1922-Jun 1923); comdt., 14th Naval Dist. and
Naval Operating Base, Pearl Harbor, Territory of HI (Jun
1923-Sep 1927); home and w.o. (Sep-Nov 1927); transferred to
Ret.Lst. (1 Nov 1927).

JACKSON MCELMELL Born in Philadelphia on 4 Jun 1834.
Resided in Philadelphia after retirement, where he died on 31
May 1908. Buried in Holy Cross Cemetery, Philadelphia.
   Ranks 3rd Asst.Engr. (2 Aug 1855); 2nd Asst.Engr. (21 Jul
1858); 1st Asst.Engr. (25 Mar 1861); Chief Engr. (2 Feb 1862);
Chief Engr. with rel. rank of Capt (2 Mar 1892); placed on
Ret.Lst. (4 Jun 1896); RAdm on Ret.Lst. (29 Jun 1906).
   Career Summary Received appointment from PA (2 Aug
1855); cst.surv. duty (Apr-Oct 1856); w.o. (Oct 1856-Mar 1857);
Niagara, spec.serv. (Mar-Nov 1857); w.o. (Nov-Dec 1857);
Niagara, spec.serv. (Dec 1857-Aug 1858); l.o.a. (Aug-Oct 1858);
Memphis, Braz.Sqdn. and Paraguay Expd. (Oct-Nov 1858);
Memphis, Paraguay Expd. (Nov 1858-Aug 1859); w.o. (Aug
1859-Mar 1860); *Pawnee*, Navy Yard, Philadelphia (Mar-Aug
1860); *Powhatan*, Home Sqdn. and Gulf Blk.Sqdn. (Aug 1860-
Mar 1861); w.o. (Mar-Apr 1861); *Powhatan*, Gulf Blk.Sqdn.
(Apr-Dec 1861); spec. duty, *Octorara*, mortar flot., N.Atl.Blk.
Sqdn. (Dec 1861-May 1863); exam. and w.o. (Jun-Aug 1863);
Richmond, W.Gulf Blk.Sqdn. (Aug 1863-Jul 1865); w.o. (Jul-Sep
1865); USNA (Sep-Oct 1865); w.o. (Oct-Nov 1865); spec. duty
with ironclads, Navy Yard, League Island, PA (Nov 1865-Dec
1868); w.o. (Dec 1868); *Kenosha* [renamed *Plymouth*], N.Atl.
Sqdn. (Jan 1869-Aug 1871); w.o. (Aug 1871-Jun 1873); spec.
duty, Chester, PA (Jun 1873-May 1875); *Powhatan*, N.Atl.Sqdn.
(May 1875-Aug 1877); w.o. (Aug 1877-Jul 1878); l.o.a. (Aug
1878-Feb 1879); in charge of stores, Navy Yard, League Island,
PA (Feb 1879-Aug 1882); sick lv. and w.o. (Aug 1882-Dec

JACKSON MCELMELL
1834-1908

1884); flt.engr., N.Atl.Sqdn., *Tennessee* (Dec 1884-Dec 1887); w.o. (Dec 1887-Mar 1888); pres., naval exam. bd., Philadelphia (Mar 1888-Jun 1896); placed on Ret.Lst. (4 Jun 1896); senior member, naval exam. bd., Philadelphia (May 1898-Jan 1899).

References
Personal Papers: 3 in. (1854-1908) in Georgetown Univ. Lib. Washington, DC.

GEORGE WIGHTMAN MCELROY Born in Henry, IL, on 19 Mar 1858, son of George B. and Mary (Good) McElroy. Remained unmarried. Resided in Adrian, MI. Died in Orlando, FL, on 6 Jan 1931.

Ranks Cadet Engr. (1 Oct 1874); Asst.Engr. (20 Jun 1880); PAsst.Engr. (28 Jan 1890); PAsst.Engr. with rel. rank of Lt (1 Mar 1895); Chief Engr. (6 Aug 1898); rank changed to Lt (3 Mar 1899); LCdr (3 Mar 1901); Cdr (7 Jan 1906); Capt (27 Dec 1909); RAdm (29 Aug 1916); placed on Ret.Lst. (19 Mar 1922).

Career Summary Received appointment from MI (1 Oct 1874); USNA (Oct 1874-Jun 1878); w.o. (Jun-Oct 1878); *Ticonderoga*, spec.serv. (Nov 1878-Sep 1881); w.o. (Sep-Dec 1881); *Enterprise*, spec. surv. duty (Jan 1882-Jan 1885); home and w.o. (Jan-Oct 1885); Bur. of Steam Engineering, Washington, DC (Nov 1885-Feb 1886); spec. duty, South Carolina College, Columbia, SC (Feb 1886-Aug 1888); asst. insp. of steel, San Francisco (Sep 1888-Apr 1889); *Adams*, Pac.Sta. (Apr 1889-Jul 1890); rec. ship, *Independence*, Mare Island, CA (Jul-Sep 1890); w.o. (Sep-Oct 1890); *San Francisco*, S.Pac.Sqdn. (Nov 1890-May 1893); l.o.a. (May-Aug 1893); Bur. of Steam Engineering, Washington, DC (Aug 1893-Apr 1894); *Alert*, Pac.Sqdn. (Apr-May 1894); *Albatross*, Pac.Sqdn. (May 1894); *Concord*, N.Pac. and Asia.Sqdns. (May-Oct 1894); *Baltimore*, Asia.Sqdn. (Oct 1894-Jan 1896); *Adams*, Pac.Sqdn. (Jan 1896-Jul 1897); l.o.a. (Jul-Oct 1897); insp. of machinery, Torp. Boat #14, Harlan and Hollingsworth Co., Wilmington, DE (Oct 1897-Apr 1898); *Gloucester*, N.Atl.Flt. (May-Oct 1898); insp. of machinery, Monitor #9, and Torp. Boats #29 and #30, Elizabethport, NJ (Oct 1898-Jun 1899); w.o. (Jun-Jul 1899); insp. duty, Bur. of Steam Engineering (Jul 1899-Feb 1901); *Wisconsin*, Pac.Sqdn. (Feb 1901-Feb 1902); flt.engr., Pac.Sqdn., *Wisconsin* (Feb-Dec 1902); flt.engr., Asia Flt., *Wisconsin* (Dec 1902-Mar 1904); flt.engr,, Asia,Sqdn., *Wisconsin* (Mar 1904); home and l.o.a. (Mar-Jul 1904); insp. of machinery and engineering material, American Steel Casting Company, Thurlow, PA (Jul-Nov 1904); in charge, dept. of steam engineering, Naval Sta., Cavite, P.I. (Jan 1905-Jan 1906); Naval Hosp., Yokohama, Japan (Feb-Apr 1906); home and w.o. (Apr-Jun 1906); insp. of machinery, Bath Iron Works, Bath, ME (Jul-Dec 1906); insp. of machinery, Babcock and Wilcox Company, Bayonne, NJ (Dec 1906-May 1908); insp. of machinery, Mosher Company, Ossining, NY (May 1908-Oct 1909); insp. of engineering material, Eastern NY and NJ Dists. (Oct 1909-May 1911); insp. of machinery, New York Shipbuilding Company, Camden, NJ (May 1911-Mar 1913); insp. of engineering material, Pittsburgh, PA Dist. (Mar 1913-Mar 1915); insp. of machinery and ord., Fore River Shipbuilding Company, Quincy, MA (Mar 1915-Jun 1919); insp. of engineering material, Brooklyn, NY Dist. (Jun 1919-Mar 1922); placed on Ret.Lst. (19 Mar 1922).

JOHN MCGOWAN Born in Port Penn, DE, on 4 Aug 1843, son of John and Catherine (Caldwell) McGowan. Educated in public schools in PA from 1848 to 1853, then attended private schools from 1853 to 1859 in Elizabeth, NJ. Married Evelyn Manderson in Oct 1871. One daughter. Made his home in Washington, DC, after retiring. Died on 13 Aug 1915 in Haines Falls, NY. Buried in Arlington National Cemetery.

Ranks Act.Master's Mate, Volunteer Navy (8 Mar 1862); Act.Mstr. (8 May 1862); Mstr. (12 Mar 1868); Lt (18 Dec 1868); LCdr (22 Apr 1870); Cdr (29 Jan 1887); Capt (3 Mar 1899); retired (13 Apr 1901); RAdm on Ret.Lst. (13 Apr 1911) to rank from 13 Apr 1901.

Career Summary Received appointment from NJ (8 Mar 1862); *Wyandank*, Potomac Flot. (Mar 1862-Feb 1863); *Florida*, N.Atl.Sta. (Feb 1863-Nov 1864); *State of Georgia*, N.Atl.Sta. (Nov 1864-Jan 1865); *State of Georgia*, S.Atl.Sta. (Jan-Sep 1865); w.o. (Oct-Nov 1865); *Monongahela*, N.Atl.Sqdn. (Nov 1865-Jan 1867); *Tacony*, Gulf Sqdn. (Feb-Sep 1867); rec. ship, *Potomac*, Philadelphia (Oct 1867-Sep 1868); Asia.Sqdn. (Oct 1868-Jan 1869); *Unadilla*, Asia.Sqdn. (Jan-Nov 1869); *Iroquois*, Asia.Sqdn. (Nov 1869-Apr 1870); ord. duty, Navy Yard, Philadelphia (May-Sep 1870); *Terror*, N.Atl.Sta. (Sep 1870-Aug 1871); l.o.a. (Aug-Nov 1871); ord. duty, Navy Yard, Philadelphia (Nov 1871-Jun 1872); l.o.a. (Jun 1872-May 1873); *Wachusett*, Eur.Sta. (May 1873-Apr 1874); *Juniata*, Eur.Sta. (Apr 1874-Dec 1875); l.o.a. and w.o. (Dec 1875-May 1876); Hydrographic Office, Washington, DC (Jun 1876-Sep 1879); exec.off., *Marion*, S.Atl.Sta. (Sep 1879-Dec 1882); w.o. (Dec 1882-Feb 1883); Navy Yard, League Island, PA (Feb-Jul 1883); Naval Rndv., Philadelphia (Jul 1883-Apr 1884); torp. instruction, Newport, RI (Apr-Aug 1884); Naval Rndv., Philadelphia (Aug 1884-May 1885); l.o.a. (May-Aug 1885); Navy Yard, NY (Sep 1885-Feb 1888); cdr, *Swatara*, S.Atl. and Asia.Stas. (Mar 1888-Apr 1890); sick lv. (Apr-Dec 1890); cdr, training ship, *St. Mary's* (Jan 1891-Mar 1894); ord. instruction, Navy Yard, Washington, DC (Mar-May 1894); cdr, training ship, *Portsmouth* (May 1894-Jan 1895); cdr, training ship, *Alliance* (Jan-Oct 1895); Bur. of Nav., Washington, DC (Oct 1895-Dec 1896); cdr, training ship and Naval Sta., Newport, RI (Dec 1896-Jun 1899); cdr, *Monterey*, Asia.Sta. (Aug 1899-Feb 1900); l.o.a. (Feb-Jun 1900); suspended (Jun-Oct 1900); comdt., Naval Sta., Key West, FL (Dec 1900-Apr 1901); retired (13 Apr 1901).

SAMUEL MCGOWAN Born in Laurens, SC, on 1 Sep 1870, son of Homer L. and Julia Ann (Farrow) McGowan. Received B.A. degree from the Univ. of SC in 1889, LL.B. in 1891, and

JOHN MCGOWAN
1843-1915

SAMUEL MCGOWAN
1870-1934

LL.D. in 1918. Remained unmarried. Resided in Laurens, SC, where he died on 11 Nov 1934.

Ranks Asst.Paymstr. (15 Mar 1894); PAsst. Paymstr. (30 Mar 1895); Paymstr. (5 May 1899); Pay Insp. (11 May 1906); Paymstr. Gen and Chief, Bur. of Supplies and Accounts with rank of RAdm (1 Jul 1914); Pay Dir. with rank of Capt (23 Sep 1915); Pay Dir. with rank of RAdm (29 Aug 1916); retired (31 Dec 1920).

Career Summary Received appointment from SC (15 Mar 1894); w.o. (Mar-May 1894); rec. ship, *Minnesota*, NY (May-Aug 1894); *Dolphin*, spec.serv. (Aug 1894-Feb 1895); *Marblehead*, Eur. and N.Atl.Stas. (Feb 1895-Apr 1897); w.o. (Apr-May 1897); *Michigan*, on Great Lakes (May 1897-Mar 1898); Naval Sta., Port Royal, SC (Apr 1898-Jun 1900); flgs., *Kearsarge*, N.Atl.Sqdn. (Jun-Sep 1900); *Alabama*, N.Atl.Sqdn. (Oct 1900-Nov 1902); sick lv. (Nov 1902-Feb 1903); Navy Yard, NY (Feb-Jun 1903); Bur. of Supplies and Accounts, Washington, DC (Jun 1903-Feb 1904); asst., Bur. of Supplies and Accounts, Washington, DC (Feb 1904-Dec 1906); spec. duty, Bur. of Supplies and Accounts, Washington, DC (Dec 1906-Jun 1908); flt.paymstr., Atl.Flt., *Connecticut* (Jun 1908-Sep 1909); pay off., *Connecticut*, "Great White Flt." (Jun-Aug 1909); purchasing and pay off., Navy Yard, Charleston, SC (Nov 1909-Oct 1910); Pay Office, Philadelphia (Nov 1910-Dec 1912); additional duty, pay off., Naval Home, Philadelphia (Nov 1910-Mar 1912); flt.paymstr., Atl.Flt., *Wyoming* (Dec 1912-Apr 1914), then *Arkansas* (Apr 1914); spec. duty, Navy Dept., Washington, DC (Apr-Jul 1914); paymstr.gen, and chief, Bur. of Supplies and Accounts, Washington, DC (Jul 1914-Dec 1920); retired (31 Dec 1920).

Career Highlights Served as paymstr. gen of the navy and headed Bur. of Supplies and Accounts throughout World War I, being chief supply officer, whereby he instituting many reforms. Was awarded navy's Distinguished Service Medal, became a cdr of the French Legion of Honor and was awarded Greece's Royal Order of the Redeemer.

References

Personal Papers: a) 2000 items (1883-1943) in NHF,LC. b) 2 ft. (1908-20) in NHF,WNY. c) 228 items (1910-35) in WPL. d) 1 vol. (1893-1903) in SCL.

DONALD MCLAREN
1834-1920

DONALD MCLAREN Born in Caledonia, NY, on 7 Mar 1834, son of Rev. Donald Campbell and Jane (Stevenson) McLaren. Received A.B. degree from Union College in 1853, graduated from the Princeton Theological Seminary and was ordained a Presbyterian minister in 1857. Received the D.D. degree from the Univ. of Wooster in 1882. Married Elizabeth Stockton Green on 14 Jul 1858. Served as pastor of Tennent Church in Monmouth, NJ, from 1857 to 1862. After his retirement in 1896, served from 1902 to 1904 as an agent in Puerto Rico for the American Bible Society, for the West Indies from 1905 to 1906 with headquarters in Havana, Cuba, and for VA from 1906 to 1907. He then established the Pac. agency for the American Bible Society at San Francisco from 1907 to 1908. Died on 27 May 1920 at Princeton, NJ.

Ranks   Chaplain (Presbyterian) (10 Mar 1863); placed on Ret.Lst. (7 Mar 1896); RAdm on Ret.Lst. (29 Jun 1906).

Career Summary   Received appointment from NJ (10 Mar 1863); w.o. (Mar-Jun 1863); USNA (Oct 1863-Jul 1865); *Lancaster*, and *Powhatan*, S.Pac.Sqdn. (Jul 1865-Aug 1867); home and w.o. (Aug-Sep 1867); USNA (Sep 1867-Sep 1868); chaplain, USNA (Oct 1868-Nov 1871); Navy Yard, NY (Nov 1871-Apr 1875); *Tennessee*, N.Atl.Sqdn. (Apr 1875-Apr 1876); sick lv. (May 1876-Mar 1880); Navy Yard, League Island, PA (Mar 1880-Oct 1882); w.o. (Oct 1882-Mar 1884); Naval Asylum, Philadelphia (Apr 1884-Nov 1885); *Tennessee*, N.Atl.Sqdn. (Nov 1885); *Richmond*, Navy Yard, NY (Nov 1885-Jan 1887); w.o. (Jan-Apr 1887); Navy Yard, NY (Apr 1887-May 1890); w.o. (May-Aug 1890); rec. ship, *Vermont*, NY (Aug 1890-Aug 1893); *Minnesota*, training ship (Aug 1893-Oct 1895); w.o. (Oct 1895-Feb 1896); placed on Ret.Lst. (7 Mar 1896); Navy Yard, NY (Apr-Dec 1901).

References
Personal Papers: Journal from the *Lancaster* (1865-67) in NJ Historical Society, Newark, NJ.

THOMAS CHALMERS MCLEAN   Born in New Hartford, NY, on 25 Oct 1847, son of Charles and Ann (Waters) McLean. Married Emily Gordon on 29 Dec 1875. Three children. Married again, to Harriet Maynard on 23 Sep 1909. Retired to Utica, NY, dying there on 29 Aug 1919.

Ranks   Midn (21 Sep 1864); Ens (19 Apr 1869); Mstr (12 Jul 1870); Lt (12 Dec 1872); LCdr (11 Apr 1894); Cdr (3 Mar 1899); Capt (23 Sep 1903); RAdm (19 Jul 1908); placed on Ret.Lst. (25 Oct 1909).

Career Summary   Received appointment from NY (21 Sep 1864); USNA (Sep 1864-Jun 1868); w.o. (Jun-Sep 1868); *Tuscarora*, S.Pac. and W.Ind.Sqdns. (Oct 1868-Oct 1869); w.o. (Oct 1869); *Benicia*, and *Idaho*, Asia.Sqdn. (Nov 1869-Feb 1872); sick lv. (Feb-Sep 1872); Torp.Sta., Newport, RI (Sep 1872-Jun 1873); Experimental Battery, Annapolis (Jul 1873-Apr 1875); flgs., *Tennessee*, Asia.Sqdn. (Apr 1875-May 1876); sick lv. (May-Oct 1876); Torp.Sta., Newport, RI (Oct 1876-Dec 1877); l.o.a. (Dec 1877-Oct 1878); ord. duty, Navy Yard, Washington, DC (Oct 1878-Sep 1879); *Constellation*, Navy Yard, NY (Oct 1879); flgs., *Trenton*, Eur.Sta. (Oct 1879-Aug 1881); member, U.S. delegation, International Electrical Congress, and of Commission to Electrical Exhibition, Paris (Aug-Nov 1881); spec. duty for Bur. of Ord., Germany, France, Russia, and Great Britain (Nov 1881-Feb 1882); w.o. (Feb-Mar 1882); Bur. of Ord., Washington, DC (Mar-Jun 1882); inst., Torp.Sta., Newport, RI (Jun 1882-Aug 1883); naval attaché, and U.S. representative, Electrical Exhibition, Vienna (Aug 1883-Oct 1884); *Dolphin*, Chester, PA (Oct 1884-Jul 1885); temp. duty, Washington, DC (Jul-Oct 1885); *Brooklyn*, S.American waters (Oct-Dec 1885); *Dolphin*, N.Atl.Sta.

THOMAS CHALMERS MCLEAN
1847-1919

(Dec 1885-Dec 1888); w.o. (Dec 1888-May 1889); Torp.Sta., Newport, RI (Jun 1889-Feb 1893); duty with, then exec.off., *Detroit*, spec.serv. (Mar 1893-Jan 1894); *San Francisco*, N.Atl. and Eur.Stas. (Jan 1894-Aug 1896); l.o.a. (Aug-Dec 1896); Bur. of Nav., Washington, DC (Dec 1896-May 1897); insp. of ord., Torp.Sta., Newport, RI (Jun 1897-Oct 1899); cdr, *Don Juan de Austria*, Asia.Sta. (Nov 1899-May 1901); *Castine*, Asia.Sta. (May-Oct 1901); home and w.o. (Oct-Nov 1901); duty with, then cdr, *Cincinnati*, Navy Yard, NY, and spec.serv. (Dec 1901-Oct 1902); w.o. (Oct-Nov 1902); in charge, Naval Recruiting Rndv., Baltimore (Nov 1902-Sep 1903); capt.yd., Navy Yard, League Island, PA (Sep 1903-Jan 1905); cdr, *Pennsylvania*, Philadelphia, and Asia.Sta. (Jan 1905-Mar 1907); home and l.o.a. (Mar-May 1907); NWC (Jun-Oct 1907); pres., bd. of inspection and surv. (Oct 1907-Dec 1909); placed on Ret.Lst. (25 Oct 1909).

Career Highlights While on the *Benicia* as part of the Asia.Sqdn. in the early 1870s, he commanded the Bluejackets during the Korean Expd., being commended for gallantry in the assault on Fort duCoude. Several tours with special commissions abroad, including being the naval attaché to Austria in 1883-84.

WALTER MCLEAN Born in Elizabeth, NJ, on 30 Jul 1855, son of George Washington and Rebecca J. (McCormick) McLean. Married Emma Bowne Jarvis on 8 Dec 1887. One daughter. Retired to Lutherville, MD. Died in the Naval Hosp. at Annapolis on 20 Mar 1930.

Ranks Cadet Midn (8 Jun 1872); Midn (20 Jun 1876); Ens (23 Oct 1878); Ltjg (1 Dec 1885); Lt (20 May 1891); LCdr (1 Jul 1899); Cdr (31 Mar 1905); Capt (15 Dec 1908); RAdm (10 Mar 1914); retired (15 Mar 1919).

Career Summary Received appointment at large (8 Jun 1872); USNA (Jun 1872-Jun 1876); w.o. (Jun 1876-Feb 1877); flgs., *Trenton*, Eur.Sta. (Feb 1877-May 1878); l.o.a. (May-Aug 1878); flgs., *Powhatan*, N.Atl.Sqdn. (Aug-Oct 1878); w.o. (Oct 1878-Mar 1879); USNA (Mar-Apr 1879); w.o. (Apr-May 1879); rec. ship, *Colorado*, NY (May-Jul 1879); *Alert*, and *Monocacy*, Asia. Sqdn. (Aug 1879-Jun 1882); home and w.o. (Jun 1882-Mar 1883); ord. instruction, Navy Yard, Washington, DC (Mar 1883); Experimental Battery, Annapolis (Apr 1883-Jul 1884); cst.surv. duty (Jul 1884-Oct 1885); home and w.o. (Oct-Nov 1885); rec. ship, *Vermont*, NY (Nov 1885-Apr 1886); *Alliance*, N.Atl.Sta. (Apr 1886); rec. ship, *Vermont*, NY (Apr 1886-Jan 1887); prac. ship, *Despatch* (Jan 1887-May 1889); l.o.a. (May 1889-May 1890); Naval Ord. Proving Ground, Annapolis (May-Jun 1890); *Enterprise*, spec.serv., W.Indies (Jul 1890-Sep 1891); *Yantic*, S.Atl.Sta. (Sep 1891-Mar 1893); home and w.o. (Mar-May 1893); l.o.a. (May-Aug 1893); Cst.Surv. Office, Washington, DC (Aug 1893-Nov 1895); *Boston*, Asia.Sta. (Nov 1895-Sep 1897); *Monocacy*, Asia.Sta. (Sep 1897-Apr 1898); senior aide, flgs., *Olympia*, Asia.Sta. (May-Sep 1898); *Charleston*, Asia.Sta. (Sep-Nov 1898) home and w.o. (Dec 1898-Feb 1899); l.o.a. (Feb-Mar 1899); Bur.

of Ord., Washington, DC (Mar 1899-Apr 1900); *Prairie*, spec.serv.
(Apr-May 1900); exec.off., *Mayflower*, San Juan, Puerto Rico (Jun
1900-Aug 1901); exec.off. and navigator, *Machias*, spec.serv.,
W.Indies (Aug 1901-Oct 1902); cdr, *Vixen*, N.Atl.Sta. (Oct
1902-Sep 1903); Bur. of Ord., Washington, DC (Oct 1903-May
1906); spec. duty, NWC (Jun-Aug 1906); temp. duty, Bur. of
Ord., Washington, DC (Aug-Nov 1906); comdt., Naval Sta.,
Cavite and Olongapo, P.I. (Feb 1907-Feb 1908); cdr, *Cleveland*,
Asia.Sta. (Feb-Nov 1908); spec. temp. duty, Naval Sta., Olonga-
po, P.I. (Dec 1908); home and w.o. (Dec 1908-Feb 1909); Navy
Yard, Washington, DC (Feb 1909-Mar 1910); cdr, *Vermont*,
N.Atl.Flt. (Mar 1910-Nov 1911); Army War College, Washing-
ton, DC (Nov 1911-May 1912); member, naval exam. and ret.
bds., Navy Dept., Washington, DC (May 1912-Sep 1914); cdr,
4th Div., Atl.Flt., *Minnesota* (Sep 1914-Mar 1915), then *Louisiana*
(Mar-Nov 1915); comdt., Navy Yard and Naval Sta., Norfolk,
VA (Nov 1915-Jan 1918); comdt., 5th Naval Dist., Norfolk, VA
(Nov 1915-Oct 1916, Jan 1917-Aug 1918); w.o. (Aug 1918-Mar
1919); retired (15 Mar 1919).

Career Highlights Served as senior aide to Adm George
Dewey's staff in 1898 and thus at the Battle of Manila during the
Spanish-American War.

References

Writings: (with Lt. B. H. Bennington and Ens. G. C. Foulk),
*Observations upon the Korean Coast, Japanese and Korean Ports and
Siberia . . . June 3 to September 8, 1882* (Washington, DC: 1883).

WILLIAM WIGHTMAN MEAD Born in Burlington, KY, on
8 Feb 1845, son of Sackett and Anna A. Mead. Married Julia B.
Watts. Resided in Wayne, PA. Died on 13 Mar 1930 in Mande-
ville, Jamaica. Buried in Arlington National Cemetery.

Ranks Act.Midn (30 Dec 1861); title changed to Midn (16 Jul
1862); Ens (1 Dec 1866); Mstr (12 Mar 1868); Lt (26 Mar
1869); LCdr (12 Mar 1881); Cdr (2 Aug 1891); Capt (3 Mar
1899); RAdm (1 Jul 1905); placed on Ret.Lst. (8 Feb 1907).

Career Summary Received appointment from KY (30 Dec
1861); USNA (Dec 1861-Oct 1865); w.o. (Oct 1865-Mar 1866);
training ship, *Sabine* (Mar-Apr 1866); *Lackawanna*, N.Pac.Sqdn.
(May 1866-Feb 1869); Naval Sta., Mound City, IL (Mar-May
1869); prac. ship, *Savannah* (May-Sep 1869); w.o. (Sep-Dec
1869); Signal Office, Washington, DC (Dec 1869-Mar 1870);
chief signal off., Asia.Sqdn., *Colorado* (Mar 1870-Mar 1873); w.o.
(Mar-Aug 1873); *Michigan*, on Great Lakes (Aug 1873-Aug
1874); *Canandaigua*, and *Shawmut*, N.Atl.Sta. (Aug 1874-Jan
1877); w.o. (Jan-Apr 1877); l.o.a. (May-Oct 1877); Hydrographic
Office, Washington, DC (Oct 1877-Mar 1879); w.o. (Mar-May
1879); torp. instruction, Newport, RI (Jun-Sep 1879); *Shenandoah*,
S.Atl.Sta. (Sep 1879-May 1881); w.o. (May-Sep 1881); Hydrographic Office, Washington, DC (Sep 1881-Aug 1883); *Miantonomoh*, Navy Yard, Washington, DC (Sep 1883); w.o. (Sep-Nov
1883); exec.off., *Tennessee*, N.Atl.Sta. (Nov 1883-Oct 1885); w.o.
(Oct 1885-Mar 1886); asst., then insp., 8th L.h. Dist., New

WILLIAM WIGHTMAN MEAD
1845-1930

Orleans (Apr 1886-Apr 1890); s.a. and w.o. (Apr-May 1890); exec.off., rec. ship, *Independence*, Mare Island, CA (May 1890-Oct 1891); w.o. (Oct 1891-Jan 1892); ord. instruction, Navy Yard, Washington, DC (Feb-Mar 1892); cdr, training ship, *Essex* (May 1892-Apr 1893); asst., then insp., 11th L.h. Dist., Detroit (May 1893-Apr 1896); also temp. insp., 9th L.h. Dist., Chicago (Feb-Apr 1894); equip.off., Navy Yard, Norfolk, VA (May 1896-Jun 1898); cdr, *Machias*, N.Atl.Flt. (Jun-Sep 1898); cdr, *Marblehead*, N.Atl.Flt. (Oct 1898-Apr 1899); temp.cdr, *Brooklyn*, N.Atl.Sqdn. (Apr-May 1899); home and w.o. (May 1899); capt.yd., Navy Yard, Mare Island, CA (Jun 1899-Feb 1900); cdr, *Philadelphia*, Pac.Sta. (Feb 1900-Jan 1902); w.o. (Jan-Mar 1902); member, bd. of inspection and surv. (Apr-Sep 1902); comdt., Training Sta., Newport, RI, and prac. ship, *Constellation* (Sep 1902-Jul 1904); additional duties, comdt., 2nd Naval Dist., Narragansett Bay, RI (Nov 1903-Jul 1904); comdt., Navy Yard, and comdt., 1st Naval Dist., Portsmouth, NH (Jul 1904-Feb 1907); placed on Ret.Lst. (8 Feb 1907).

JOHN PORTER MERRELL
1846-1916

JOHN PORTER MERRELL Born in Auburn, NY, on 7 Sep 1846, son of John Camp and Jane A. (Allen) Merrell. Married Sarah Frances Tyler on 22 Jan 1872. One daughter, who married navy paymstr, R. H. Johnston. Resided in Washington, DC. Died in New London, CT, on 8 Dec 1916. Buried in Annapolis.

Ranks Midn (20 Jul 1863); Ens (18 Dec 1868); Mstr (21 Mar 1870); Lt (21 Mar 1871); LCdr (28 May 1888); Cdr (1 Nov 1896); Capt (26 Sep 1901); RAdm (19 Mar 1907); placed on Ret.Lst. (7 Sep 1908).

Career Summary Received appointment from MI (20 Jul 1863); USNA (Jul 1863-Jun 1867); *Minnesota, Ticonderoga,* and *Franklin*, Eur.Sqdn. (Jul 1867-Jan 1869); *Kenosha* [renamed *Plymouth*], Eur.Sqdn. (Jan 1869-Apr 1870); w.o. (Apr-May 1870); signal duty, Washington, DC (May-Jul 1870); *Guard*, Darien Expd. (Jul 1870-Jul 1871); w.o. (Jul 1871-Jan 1872); torp. duty, Newport, RI (Jan 1872-Sep 1875); *Swatara*, N.Atl.Sta. (Sep 1875-Aug 1877); w.o. (Aug-Sep 1877); Experimental Battery, Annapolis (Oct 1877-Feb 1879); *Marion*, N. and S.Atl.Stas. (Feb 1879-Oct 1881); *Shenandoah*, S.Atl.Sta. (Oct 1881-May 1882); w.o. (May-Aug 1882); USNA (Sep 1882-Jul 1887); staff member, N.Atl.Sta., *Pensacola* (Aug-Dec 1887), then *Quinnebaug*, (Dec 1887-Apr 1888), and *Lancaster* (Apr 1888-Jun 1889); USNA (Aug 1889-Jun 1893); *Baltimore*, Asia.Sta. (Jun 1893-Nov 1895); spec. duty, member of State Dept. commission investigating anti-foreign riots, Chengtu, Szechuan Province, China (Oct 1895-Mar 1896); *Olympia*, Asia.Sta. (Nov 1895-Mar 1896); spec. duty, staff member, Asia.Sta., *Olympia* (Dec 1895-Mar 1896); home and l.o.a. (Mar-May 1896); asst., then insp., 13th L.h. Dist., Portland, OR (May 1896-Jan 1898); NWC (Jan-May 1898); *Scipio*, N.Atl.Flt. (May-Jul 1898); *Glacier*, N.Atl.Flt. (Jul-Oct 1898); equip.off., Navy Yard, NY (Nov 1898-Mar 1899); cdr, *Montgomery*, S.Atl.Sqdn. (Apr 1899-Sep 1900); equip.off., Navy Yard, Norfolk, VA (Oct 1900-Nov 1901); comdt., Naval Sta.,

New Orleans (Nov 1901-May 1904); temp. duty, NWC (Jun-Oct 1903); bd. duties (Jun 1904); cdr, *Oregon*, Asia.Flt. (Aug 1904-Apr 1906); pres., NWC, and member, Gen Bd., Washington, DC (May 1906-Oct 1909); additional duty, comdt., 2nd Naval Dist., Newport, RI (Jan 1907-Oct 1909); placed on Ret.Lst. (7 Sep 1908).

JOHN FAIRFIELD MERRY Born in Edgecomb, ME, on 5 Mar 1840, son of John and Sarah A. Merry. Educated in public schools in Edgecomb. Married Nancy J. Winslow on 11 Aug 1862. His second wife was Etta C. Merry. Retired to Somerville, MA. Died on 30 May 1916 at the Naval Hosp. in Washington, DC.

Ranks Act.Ens (18 Oct 1862); Act.Mstr (23 Sep 1865); Ens (12 Mar 1868); Mstr (18 Dec 1868); Lt (21 Mar 1870); LCdr (1 Dec 1883); Cdr (9 May 1893); Capt (29 Dec 1899); placed on Ret.Lst. with rank of RAdm (5 Mar 1902).

Career Summary Received appointment from ME (15 Oct 1862); Navy Yard, NY (Oct-Dec 1862); *Morse*, and *Osceola*, N.Atl.Blk.Sqdn. (Dec 1862-Sep 1864); sick lv. (Sep-Oct 1864); Naval Sta., Norfolk, VA, and *Morse*, Potomac Flot. (Oct 1864-Feb 1865); sick lv. (Feb-Sep 1865); *Saratoga*, spec.serv. (Sep 1865); *Portsmouth*, and *Vermont*, spec.serv. and NY (Sep 1865-Feb 1866); rec. ship, *Ohio*, Boston (Feb 1866-Sep 1868); *Idaho*, Asia.Sqdn. (Oct 1868-Nov 1871); home and w.o. (Dec 1871-May 1872); rec. ship, *Sabine*, Portsmouth, NH (May-Aug 1872); Navy Yard, Portsmouth, NH (Aug 1872-Jan 1873); *Juniata*, spec.serv. (Feb-Jun 1873); w.o. (Jun-Sep 1873); Naval Rndv., Boston (Oct 1873-Apr 1875); cdr, rec. ship, *Relief*, Washington, DC (May 1875-Jul 1876); w.o. (Jul-Sep 1876); exec.off., *Gettysburg*, and *Despatch*, spec.serv., Med. Sea (Sep 1876-Jul 1879); w.o. (Jul-Nov 1879); spec.serv., Bur. of Construction and Repair, Washington, DC (Nov 1879-Feb 1880); w.o. (Feb-Apr 1880); exec.off., storeship, *Onward*, Pac.Sta. (May-Sep 1880); w.o. (Oct 1880-May 1881); torp. instruction, Newport, RI (Jun-Jul 1881); *Tallapoosa*, spec.serv. (Aug 1881-Nov 1884); w.o. (Nov-Dec 1884); exec.off., *Marion*, Asia.Sta. (Jan 1885-Nov 1887); home and w.o. (Nov 1887-Sep 1888); exec.off., *Michigan*, on Great Lakes (Sep 1888-Oct 1889); rec. ship, *Wabash*, Boston (Oct 1889-Nov 1892); cdr, schoolship, *Enterprise* (Nov 1892-Nov 1895); home and w.o. (Nov 1895-Jan 1896); temp. duty, Navy Yard, NY (Jan-May 1896); NWC (Jun-Oct 1896); ord. instruction, Navy Yard, Washington, DC (Oct 1896-Jan 1897); w.o. (Jan-Mar 1897); cdr, *Machias*, Asia.Sta. (Apr 1897-Jun 1898); sick lv., Naval Hosp., Chelsea, MA (Jun-Aug 1898); cdr, *Arethusa*, on trials (Aug 1898-Feb 1899); Navy Yard, Boston (Feb-Apr 1899); naval representative, Honolulu, Territory of HI (May-Nov 1899); comdt., Naval Sta., Honolulu, Territory of HI (Nov 1899-Jul 1902); placed on Ret.Lst. (5 Mar 1902); temp. duty, Bur. of Equip. and Recruiting, Washington, DC (Jul-Aug 1902).

ALBERT MERTZ Born in Richwood, WI, on 26 Mar 1851, son of Leonard and Katinka Mertz. Educated in public schools in

JOHN FAIRFIELD MERRY
1840-1916

ALBERT MERTZ
1851-1936

Beaver Dam, WI. Married Mary E. Germain on 11 July 1878. One daughter. Resided in Bonita, CA. Died at the Naval Hosp. in San Diego on 21 Jul 1936. Buried in USNA Cemetery, Annapolis.

Ranks Midn (26 Jun 1867); title changed to Cadet Midn (15 Jul 1870); Midn (1 Jun 1872); Ens (15 Jul 1873); Mstr (26 Nov 1877); title changed to Ltjg (3 Mar 1883); Lt (27 Sep 1884); LCdr (3 Mar 1899); Cdr (11 Apr 1902); Capt (2 Nov 1906); RAdm (20 Oct 1910); placed on Ret.Lst. (26 Mar 1913).

Career Summary Received appointment from WI (26 Jun 1867); USNA (Jun 1867-Jun 1872); found deficient and turned back (Jun 1869); w.o. (Jun-Jul 1872); *Yantic,* Asia.Sqdn. (Aug 1872); *Hartford,* Asia.Sqdn. (Aug 1872-Oct 1875); USNA (Oct-Nov 1875); w.o. (Nov 1875-Jan 1876); *Ajax,* N.Atl.Sqdn. (Jan-Jul 1876); w.o. (Jul-Dec 1876); rec. ship, *Wyoming,* Washington, DC (Dec 1876-Apr 1877); cst.surv. duty (Apr 1877-Jan 1880); sick lv. (Jan-Feb 1880); storeship, *New Hampshire,* Port Royal, SC (Feb-Jun 1880); *Wyoming,* N.Atl.Sta. (Jun 1880-Oct 1882); w.o. (Oct-Dec 1882); l.o.a. (Dec 1882-Jun 1883); *Alliance,* N.Atl.Sta. (Jun-Oct 1883); sick lv. (Nov 1883-Apr 1885); *Omaha,* Asia.Sta. (Apr 1885-Jan 1886); *Marion,* Asia.Sta. (Jan 1886-Nov 1887); home and w.o. (Nov 1887-Mar 1888); training ship, *Minnesota,* NY (Mar 1888-Jan 1891); *Yantic,* N.Atl.Sta. (Jan 1891-Jan 1894); home and l.o.a. (Jan-Jun 1894); training ship, *Minnesota,* NY (Jun 1894-Sep 1895); training ship, *Constellation* (Sep 1895-Mar 1896); *Michigan,* on Great Lakes (Mar-Nov 1896); training ship, *Fern* (Nov 1896-Dec 1897); *Amphitrite,* N.Atl.Flt. (Dec 1897-Oct 1898); exec.off., training ship, *Essex* (Oct 1898-Jan 1899); home and sick lv. (Jan-Mar 1899); *Glacier,* Asia.Sta. (Mar 1899-Mar 1901); *Newark,* Asia.Sta. (Mar-Apr 1901); Naval Hosp., Mare Island, CA (Apr-May 1901); home and sick lv. (May-Oct 1901); exec.off., rec. ship, *Wabash,* Boston (Nov 1901-Apr 1902); Navy Yard, Boston (Apr 1902-Jul 1903); cdr, *Newport,* N.Atl.Sta. (Jul 1903-Apr 1905); Navy Yard, Norfolk, VA (Apr-Jun 1905); insp. of ord., in charge of naval magazine, St. Julien's Creek, VA (Jul 1905-Jul 1908); additional duty, insp. of ord., Navy Yard, Norfolk, VA (Jan 1907-Jul 1908); insp., 3rd L.h. Dist., Tompkinsville, NY (Jul-Aug 1908); cdr, L.h. flot. (Aug 1908-Mar 1909); home and w.o. (Mar-Jun 1909); cdr, rec. ship, *Lancaster,* Philadelphia (Jun-Nov 1909); comdt., Naval Sta., Cavite and Olongapo, P.I. (Dec 1909-Feb 1912); home and w.o. (Feb-Mar 1912); gov., Naval Home, Philadelphia (Mar 1912-May 1913); placed on Ret.Lst. (26 Mar 1913).

JAMES MADISON MILLER Born on 23 May 1847 in Liberty, MO, son of Madison Miller. Married Agnes Watson. Two daughters. Died in Philadelphia on 11 Nov 1908. Buried in Arlington National Cemetery.

Ranks Midn (21 Sep 1863); Ens (18 Dec 1868); Mstr (21 Mar 1870); Lt (21 Mar 1871); LCdr (29 May 1891); Cdr (26 Sep 1897); Capt (29 Apr 1902); RAdm (18 Nov 1907); died (11 Nov 1908).

JAMES MADISON MILLER
1847-1908

Career Summary Received appointment from MO (21 Sep 1863); USNA (Sep 1863-Jun 1867); *Minnesota, Jamestown,* and *Ossipee,* spec. cruise, and Pac.Sqdn. (Jul 1867-Jun 1870); *Kansas,* Tehuantepec and Darien Expds. (Sep 1870-Oct 1872); w.o. (Oct 1872-Aug 1873); *Monongahela,* S.Atl.Sta. (Sep 1873-Feb 1876); w.o. (Feb-May 1876); USNA (Jun 1876-Jul 1879); w.o. (Jul 1879); training ship, *Constitution* (Aug 1879-Dec 1881); training ship, *Minnesota* (Dec 1881-Jun 1882); *Hartford,* Pac.Sta. (Jul 1882-Jan 1884); *Lackawanna,* Pac.Sta. (Jan 1884-Apr 1885); w.o. (Apr-May 1885); spec. torp. serv., Newport, RI (Jun-Sep 1885); USNA (Sep 1885-Mar 1888); *Omaha,* Asia.Sta. (Mar 1888-Jun 1891); l.o.a. (Jun-Aug 1891); ord. duty, Navy Yard, Washington, DC (Aug 1891-Jul 1892); exec.off., *Monocacy,* Asia.Sta. (Aug 1892-Aug 1895); home and l.o.a. (Aug-Dec 1895); exec.off., rec. ship, *Vermont,* NY (Jan-Dec 1896); cdr, *Yantic,* N.Atl.Sta. (Jan-Jul 1897); Navy Yard, NY (Jul 1897-Apr 1898); cdr, *Merrimack,* N.Atl.Flt. (Apr-Jun 1898); cdr, *Pompey,* N.Atl.Flt. (Jun-Dec 1898); cdr, *Badger,* Pac.Sqdn. (Dec 1898-Oct 1899); duty with Naval Militia of CA and OR (Aug-Oct 1899); *Ranger,* spec.serv. (Oct-Nov 1899); cdr, *Scindia,* spec.serv. (Nov 1899-Mar 1901); Navy Yard, NY (Apr 1901-Oct 1903); cdr, *Columbia,* Atl. Training Sqdn. (Oct 1903-Jun 1905); cdr, *Minneapolis,* Spec.Serv.Sqdn. (Jun 1905-Mar 1906); home and w.o. (Mar 1906); cdr, rec. ship, *Lancaster,* Philadelphia (Apr 1906-Nov 1907); gov., Naval Home, Philadelphia (Dec 1907-Nov 1908); died (11 Nov 1908).

ROBERT WILEY MILLIGAN Born in Philadelphia on 8 Apr 1843, son of James and Mary (Thornton) Milligan. Educated in public schools in Philadelphia. Married Sarah Ann DuBois on 17 Feb 1870. Two daughters. Retired to Norfolk, VA, dying in Annapolis on 14 Oct 1909. Buried in USNA Cemetery, Annapolis.

Ranks 3rd Asst.Engr. (3 Aug 1863); 2nd Asst.Engr. (25 Jul 1866); PAsst.Engr. (25 Mar 1874); Chief Engr. (16 May 1892); Chief Engr. with rel. rank of Cdr (10 Aug 1898); Cdr (3 Mar 1899); Capt (7 Nov 1902); placed on Ret.Lst. with rank of RAdm (8 Apr 1905).

Career Summary Received appointment from PA (3 Aug 1863); *Mackinaw,* N.Atl.Sta. (Aug 1863-May 1865); w.o. (May 1865-Jan 1866); spec. duty, *Stonewall,* Navy Yard, Washington, DC (Jan-Mar 1866); USNA (Apr 1866-Jun 1867); w.o. (Jun-Oct 1867); *Powhatan,* Pac.Sqdn. (Oct 1867-Dec 1869); w.o. (Dec 1869-Mar 1870); *Congress,* Philadelphia (Mar-Apr 1870); Navy Yard, League Island, PA (Apr 1870-Oct 1871); *Powhatan,* and *Wyoming,* N.Atl.Sta. (Oct 1871-Jan 1874); home and w.o. (Jan-Apr 1874); Navy Yard, Norfolk, VA (Apr 1874-Jan 1875); w.o. (Jan-Jul 1875); *Brooklyn,* S.Atl.Sta. (Jul 1875-Jul 1876); cst.surv. duty (Aug 1876-Jul 1878); w.o. (Jul 1878-Apr 1879); *Montauk,* Navy Yard, Philadelphia (Apr-May 1879); prac. ship, *Standish* (May-Sep 1879); USNA (Sep 1879-May 1882); prac. ship, *Mayflower* (Jun-Aug 1882); w.o. (Aug-Sep 1882); *Kearsarge,*

ROBERT WILEY MILLIGAN
1843-1909

N.Atl.Sta. (Sep-Nov 1882); *Tennessee*, N.Atl.Sta. (Nov 1882-Aug 1885); USNA (Aug 1885-Jun 1889); *Ranger*, N.Pac.Sta. (Jul 1889-Aug 1891); Navy Yard, Mare Island, CA (Aug 1891-Mar 1892); additional duty, rec. ship, *Independence*, Mare Island, CA (Oct 1891-Mar 1892); *Adams*, Pac.Sta. (Mar 1892-Jan 1893); rec. ship, *Independence*, Mare Island, CA (Jan-Feb 1893); l.o.a. (Feb-Jun 1893); member, engr.exam.bd. (Jun-Oct 1893); member, bd. of inspection and surv. (Oct 1893-Apr 1896); *Monterey*, Pac.Sqdn. (Apr-Jul 1896); *Oregon*, Pac.Sqdn., and N.Atl.Flt. (Jul 1896-Sep 1898); chief engr., N.Atl.Flt., *New York* (Sep 1898-May 1899); w.o. (May-June 1899); chief engr., Navy Yard, Norfolk, VA (Jul 1899-Jan 1905); sick lv. (Jan-Apr 1905); placed on Ret.Lst. (8 Apr 1905).

Career Highlights Was chief engr. on the *Oregon* on her famous voyage from the Pac. to the Atl. in time to participate in the Battle of Santiago Bay, during which he continued as chief engr. of that vessel.

JOHN BROWN MILTON Born in Lexington, KY, on 20 Oct 1848, son of Bushrod T. and Mary A. Milton. Married Harriet B. Steele on 20 Oct 1880. One daughter. Made his home in Annapolis. Died in the Naval Hosp. at Mare Island, CA, on 7 Jan 1931.

Ranks Midn (26 Jul 1866); Ens (13 Jul 1871); Mstr (19 Nov 1874); Lt (14 Sep 1881); LCdr (3 Mar 1899); Cdr (26 Sep 1901); Capt (6 Jun 1906); RAdm (9 Jan 1910); placed on Ret.Lst. (20 Oct 1910).

Career Summary Received appointment from KY (26 Jul 1866); USNA (Jul 1866-Jun 1870); w.o. (Jun-Aug 1870); *Severn*, W.Ind.Sqdn. (Sep 1870-Dec 1871); *Worcester*, N.Atl.Sta. (Dec 1871-Nov 1872); flgs., *Worcester*, N.Atl.Sqdn. (Dec 1872-Sep 1873); w.o. (Sep-Dec 1873); flgs., *Franklin*, and *Juniata*, and *Powhatan*, Eur. and N.Atl.Sqdns. (Dec 1873-Jul 1877); w.o. (Jul-Nov 1877); rec. ship, *Wyoming*, Washington, DC (Nov-Dec 1877); *Tuscarora*, Pac.Sta. (Jan 1878-May 1880); w.o. (May 1880-Jan 1881); *Ranger*, Pac.Sta. (Jan 1881-Jun 1882); w.o. (Jun-Aug 1882); cst.surv. duty (Aug 1882-Jan 1884); in charge, branch hydrographic office, San Francisco (Jan 1884-Aug 1887); w.o. (Aug-Nov 1887); *Ossipee*, N.Atl.Sta. (Nov 1887-Nov 1889); training ship, *Jamestown* (Nov 1889-Sep 1890); USNA (Oct 1890-Oct 1893); *Castine*, Bath, ME (Oct-Dec 1893); rec. ship, *Wabash*, Boston (Dec 1893); training ship, *Essex* (Dec 1893); temp. duty, training ship, *Monongahela* (Dec 1893-Jan 1894); training ship, *Essex* (Jan 1894-Jul 1895); rec. ship, *Independence*, Mare Island, CA (Jul-Aug 1895); *Monterey*, Pac.Sqdn. (Aug 1895-Jan 1897); inspection duty, Union Iron Works, San Francisco (Jan-Apr 1897); Navy Yard, Mare Island, CA (Apr 1897-Apr 1898); rec. ship, *Vermont*, NY (Apr 1898); exec.off., *Prairie*, N.Patrol Sqdn. (Apr 1898); cdr, *Wyandotte*, Boston (Apr-Jun 1898); exec.off., *Vulcan*, N.Atl.Flt. (Jun-Jul 1898); *Scorpion*, N.Atl.Flt. (Jul-Oct 1898); *Newark*, N.Atl.Flt. (Oct-Dec 1898); exec.off., *Yosemite*, League Island, PA (Dec 1898);

exec.off., *Badger*, Pac.Sta. (Dec 1898-Oct 1899); Navy Yard, Mare Island, CA (Nov 1899-Feb 1900); *Wisconsin*, San Francisco (Jan 1900-Feb 1901); cdr, *Wisconsin*, Pac.Sqdn. (Feb-Sep 1901); in charge, branch hydrographic office, San Francisco (Sep-Oct 1901); asst., then insp., 12th L.h. Dist., San Francisco (Oct 1901-Feb 1904); cdr, *Monterey*, Asia.Sqdn. (Apr-Sep 1904); Naval Sta., Cavite, P.I. (Sep 1904-Jan 1906); comdt., Naval Stas., Cavite and Olongapo, P.I. (Jan-Mar 1906); home and w.o. (Mar-May 1906); NWC (Jun 1906-Jan 1907); cdr, *West Virginia*, Asia.Sta. (Mar-Dec 1907); capt.yd,, Navy Yard, Mare Island, CA (Dec 1907-Aug 1908); cdr, rec. ship, *Independence*, Mare Island, CA (Aug 1908-Jan 1910); Training Sta., San Francisco (Jan-Dec 1910); cdr, *Pensacola*, San Francisco (Jan-Feb 1910); placed on Ret.Lst. (20 Oct 1910); pres., naval exam. bd., San Francisco (Jul-Aug 1914); court-martial duty, Naval Sta., New Orleans (Aug 1917-Jan 1920); member, naval exam. bd. (Jan-Jun 1920).

CHARLES BRAINARD TAYLOR MOORE Born in Paris, IL, on 29 Jul 1853, son of army Bvt.BGen and later IL Congressman Jesse H. Moore, USA. Married to Helen Johns Moore. One son, RAdm Charles Johns Moore USN (ret) (1889-1974), and one daughter. Resided in Decatur, IL. Died at the Naval Hosp. at League Island, PA, on 4 Apr 1923. Buried in Decatur.

Ranks Midn (28 Sep 1869); title changed to Cadet Midn (15 Jul 1870); Midn (31 May 1873); Ens (16 Jul 1874); Mstr (14 Dec 1880); title changed to Ltjg (3 Mar 1883); Lt (23 May 1886); LCdr (3 Mar 1899); Cdr (2 Nov 1902); Capt (1 Jul 1907); RAdm (14 Jun 1911); transferred to Ret.Lst. (29 Jul 1915).

Career Summary Received appointment from IL (28 Sep 1869); USNA (Sep 1869-May 1873); w.o. (May-Jul 1873); *Alaska*, Eur.Sta. (Aug 1873-Jan 1874); *Shenandoah*, Eur.Sqdn. (Jan-Apr 1874); w.o. (Apr-Jun 1874); l.o.a. (Apr-Aug 1874); *Pensacola*, N.Pac.Sta. (Aug 1874-Aug 1875); home and w.o. (Aug-Oct 1875); l.o.a. (Oct 1875-Jan 1876); *Passaic*, spec.serv. (Jan-Jul 1876); w.o. (Jul-Dec 1876); *Alliance*, Navy Yard, Norfolk, VA (Jan 1877); training ship, *Monongahela* (Jan 1877); rec. ship, *Wyoming*, Washington, DC (Jan-Jul 1877); *Essex*, S.Atl.Sta. (Jul 1877-Oct 1879); l.o.a. (Oct 1879-Mar 1880); rec. ship, *Franklin*, Norfolk, VA (Mar 1880-Jun 1881); storeship, *Onward*, S.Pac. Sqdn. (Jul 1881-Jul 1883); home and w.o. (Jul-Nov 1883); *Galena*, N.Atl.Sta. (Nov 1883-Aug 1885); sick lv. (Aug-Sep 1885); Navy Yard, Boston (Sep 1885-Dec 1886); *Alert*, Asia.Sta. (Jan 1887-Feb 1890); USNA (Feb 1890-Jul 1893); *Newark*, S.Atl.Sqdn. (Jul 1893-Jul 1896); l.o.a. (Jul-Aug 1896); USNA (Aug 1896-Nov 1897); inst., NWC (Jun-Sep 1897); Naval Sta., Port Royal, SC (Nov 1897-Apr 1898); cdr, *Nantucket*, Port Royal, SC (Apr-Jul 1898); exec.off., *Alexander*, Atl.Flt. (Jul-Aug 1898); exec.off., *Bennington*, Asia.Sqdn. (Aug 1898-May 1900); *Monterey*, Asia.Sqdn. (May 1900-Mar 1901); *Buffalo*, Asia.Sqdn. (Mar-Apr 1901); cdr, *Brutus*, spec.serv. (Apr-Aug 1901); home and w.o. (Aug-Sep 1901); Navy Yard, Mare Island, CA (Oct 1901-Dec 1904); comdt., Naval Sta., and cdr, sta. ships, *Adams*, and

CHARLES BRAINARD TAYLOR
MOORE
1853-1923

Annapolis, and naval gov., Tutuila, Samoa (Jan 1905-May 1908); home and w.o. (May-Jul 1908); capt.yd., Navy Yard, Philadelphia (Aug-Dec 1908); cdr, *Colorado,* Pac. and Asia.Stas. (Dec 1908-Nov 1909); Naval Hosp., Canacao, P.I. (Nov 1909-Mar 1910); home and w.o. (Mar-May 1910); NWC (May-Sep 1910); member, naval exam. and ret. bds. (Sep-Dec 1910); comdt., Training Sta., San Francisco (Dec 1910-Mar 1912); additional duty, comdt., 12th Naval Dist., San Francisco (Jul 1911-Mar 1912); comdt., Training Sta., Cavite and Olongapo, P.I. (May 1912-Jan 1913); asst., then comdt., Training Sta., Territory of HI (Feb 1913-Jul 1915); transferred to Ret.Lst. (29 Jul 1915).

EDWIN KING MOORE
1847-1931

EDWIN KING MOORE Born in Georgetown, OH, on 24 Jul 1847, son of Joseph Austin and Nancy Jane (King) Moore. Married Eva Carleton, daughter of Gen James H. Carleton, USA, on 2 Oct 1877. Died in Atlantic City, NJ, on 1 Sep 1931.

Ranks Midn (1 Oct 1864); Ens (19 Apr 1869); Mstr (12 Jul 1870); Lt (1 Mar 1873); LCdr (10 Jul 1894); Cdr (3 Mar 1899); Capt (11 Oct 1903); RAdm (7 Sep 1908); placed on Ret.Lst. (24 Jul 1909).

Career Summary Received appointment from OH (1 Oct 1864); USNA (Oct 1864-Jun 1868); w.o. (Jun-Oct 1868); *Guard,* Eur.Sqdn. (Oct 1868-Oct 1869); home and w.o. (Oct-Dec 1869); signal duty, Washington, DC (Dec 1869-Mar 1870); *Colorado, Benicia,* and *Monocacy,* Asia.Sta. (Mar 1870-Mar 1873); w.o. (Mar-Jul 1873); *Portsmouth,* surv. duty, Pac. Ocean (Jul 1873-Aug 1876); w.o. (Aug-Oct 1876); cst.surv. duty (Oct 1876-Nov 1880); w.o. (Nov-Dec 1880); Naval Observatory, Washington, DC (Jan 1881-Jul 1884); training ship, *Saratoga* (Jul 1884-Nov 1887); USNA (Dec 1887-Dec 1890); Bur. of Equip. and Recruiting, Washington, DC (Dec 1890-Jan 1891); *Boston,* Pac.Sqdn. (Jan 1891-Apr 1893); *Mohican,* N.Pac.Sqdn. (Apr-Dec 1893); home and l.o.a. (Dec 1893-Jan 1894); Navy Yard, Boston (Jan 1894-Jan 1895); cst.surv. duty (Mar 1895-Mar 1898); USNA (Apr 1898-Jun 1899); cdr, *Helena,* Asia.Sta. (Aug 1899-May 1901); cdr, *Bennington,* Asia.Sta. (May-Sep 1901); home and w.o. (Sep 1901); Navy Yard, Boston (Oct 1901-Aug 1904); duty with, then cdr, flgs., *Chicago,* Pac.Sta. (Aug 1904-Oct 1905); member, naval exam. and ret. bds. (Nov 1905-May 1908); comdt., Navy Yard, Portsmouth, NH (May 1908-Sep 1909); placed on Ret.Lst. (24 Jul 1909).

References

Writings: a) "Method of Testing Chronometers in the U.S. Naval Observatory," U.S. Naval Institute *Proceedings* 29 (1884): 171-86. b) "Competitive Trial of Chronometers at the United States Naval Observatory," U.S. Naval Institute *Proceedings* 32 (1885): 137-39.

JOHN WHITE MOORE
1832-1913

JOHN WHITE MOORE Born in Plattsburg, NY, on 24 May 1832, son of Amasa C. Charlotte E. (Mooers) Moore. Educated at the Plattsburg Academy, the Williston Seminary, and by private instruction. Married Emily Sawyer, daughter of navy Capt

Horace B. Sawyer, on 19 Nov 1863. Five children. Died in Ridgewood, NJ, on 31 Mar 1913. Buried in Bolton, NY.

Ranks 3rd Asst.Engr. (21 May 1853); 2nd Asst.Engr. (27 Jun 1855); 1st Asst.Engr. (21 Jul 1858); Chief Engr. (5 Aug 1861); Chief Engr. with rel. rank of Capt (2 Dec 1887); transferred to Ret.Lst. with rel. rank of Commo (24 May 1894); Chief Engr. with rank of RAdm on Ret.Lst. (29 Jun 1906).

Career Summary Received appointment from NY (21 May 1853); office of chief engr., Navy Dept., Washington, DC (Aug-Nov 1853); *Saranac*, Med.Sqdn. (Nov 1853-Jun 1856); l.o.a. and w.o. (Jun 1856-Mar 1857); *Niagara*, spec. duty, Atl. Cable Expd. (Mar-Nov 1857); w.o. (Nov 1857-Jan 1858); *Colorado*, Home Sqdn. (Jan-Aug 1858); *Roanoke*, Home Sqdn. (Aug 1858-May 1860); l.o.a. (May-Aug 1860); *Richmond*, Med. and W.Gulf Blk.Sqdns. (Sep 1860-Aug 1863); spec. duty, general insp. of ironclad construction, NY (Sep-Oct 1863); member, bd. of examiners, Philadelphia (Oct 1863-Jan 1864); spec. duty, supervising construction, Boston (Jan 1864-May 1867); flt.engr., Eur.Sqdn., *Franklin* (Jun 1867-Dec 1868); w.o. (Dec 1868-Feb 1869); Navy Yard, Portsmouth, NH (Feb 1869-Sep 1872): flt.engr., Asia.Sta., *Hartford* (Oct 1872-Nov 1875); return and w.o. (Nov 1875-Jan 1876); Navy Yard, Washington, DC (Feb 1876-Apr 1879); member, bd. of inspection (Apr 1879-Mar 1882); spec. duty, Providence, RI (Mar-Jun 1882); *Hartford*, Pac.Sta. (Jun 1882-Sep 1884); suspended from serv. (Sep 1884-Mar 1885); w.o. (Mar 1885-Mar 1886); spec. duty, Navy Yard, Washington, DC (Mar-Apr 1886); experimental duty, NY (Apr 1886-Jan 1887); Navy Yard, NY (Jan 1887-Jan 1888); Navy Yard, Mare Island, CA (Jan 1888-May 1893); insp. of machinery for new cruisers, *Olympia* and *Oregon*, San Francisco (May 1893-May 1894); home and w.o. (May 1894); placed on Ret.Lst. (24 May 1894); spec. duty, Navy Yard, NY (May-Dec 1898).

JEFFERSON FRANKLIN MOSER Born in Allentown, PA, on 3 May 1848, son of John B. and Henrietta (Beidelman) Moser. Married Nancy C. McDowell on 20 Oct 1874. Four children, only one daughter, however, surviving him. Retired to Alameda, CA, where he died on 11 Oct 1934.

Ranks Midn (29 Sep 1864); Ens (19 Apr 1869); Mstr (12 Jul 1870); Lt (19 Aug 1872); LCdr (27 Jun 1893); Cdr (3 Mar 1899); Capt (10 Aug 1903); placed on Ret.Lst. (29 Sep 1904); returned to active duty (6 Apr 1917); retired (15 Jun 1919); RAdm on Ret.Lst. (2 Apr 1925) to rank from 29 Sep 1904.

Career Summary Received appointment from PA (29 Sep 1864); USNA (Sep 1864-Jun 1868); w.o. (Jun-Sep 1868); *Swatara, Kenosha,* and *Guard,* Eur.Sqdn. (Oct 1868-Oct 1869); home and w.o. (Oct-Nov 1869); *Nipsic,* S.Atl.Sqdn. (Nov 1869-Jul 1870); w.o. (Jul 1870); *Guerriere,* Eur.Sqdn. (Aug 1870-Feb 1872); spec. duty (Feb-Jul 1872); w.o. (Jul-Aug 1872); spec. duty, Washington, DC (Aug-Nov 1872); spec. duty, Nicaraguan Surv.Expd. (Nov 1872-Nov 1873); exec.off., *Despatch,* N.Atl.Sta. (Nov 1873-Sep 1874); l.o.a. (Oct 1874-Jan 1875);

JEFFERSON FRANKLIN MOSER
1848-1934

Panama surv. duty (Jan-Sep 1875); cst.surv. duty (Sep 1875-Feb 1880); w.o. (Feb-Aug 1880); *Galena*, Eur. and S.Atl.Sqdns. (Aug 1880-Sep 1883); w.o. (Sep 1883-Jan 1884); cst.surv. duty (Jan 1884-Jun 1890); *San Francisco*, Pac.Sqdn. (Jun 1890-Mar 1893); Cst.Surv. Office, Washington, DC (Mar 1893-Apr 1896); cdr, Fish Commission steamer, *Albatross* (May 1896-Apr 1898); L.h. steamer, *Mayflower* (Apr 1898); cdr, *Albatross*, Atl.cst. (Apr-Jul 1898); temp. chief, Auxiliary Naval Force, Pac.Sta., and cdr, *Bennington* (Jul-Aug 1898); cdr, Fish Commission steamer, *Albatross* (Sep 1898-Oct 1901); spec. duty (Oct-Dec 1901); cdr, training ship, *Pensacola* (Jan 1902-May 1904); bd. duties, U.S. Pac.cst. (Sep 1902-May 1904); l.o.a. (May-Sep 1904); placed on Ret.Lst. (29 Sep 1904); returned to active duty (6 Apr 1917); Training Sta., San Francisco (Apr 1917); duty, 12th Naval Dist., San Francisco (Apr 1917-Jun 1919); retired (15 Jun 1919).

References

Writings: a) *The Salmon and Salmon Fisheries of Alaska* (Washington, DC: 1899). b) *Alaska Salmon Investigations* (Washington, DC: 1902).

JOSEPH BALLARD MURDOCK
1851-1931

JOSEPH BALLARD MURDOCK   Born in Hartford, CT, on 13 Feb 1851, son of the Reverend John Nelson and Martha (Ballard) Murdock. Married Anne Dillingham on 26 Jun 1879. Resided in Hill, NH. Died in Manchester, NH, on 20 Mar 1931. Buried in Mt. Auburn Cemetery in Cambridge, MA.

Ranks   Midn (25 Jul 1866); Ens (13 Jul 1871); Mstr (2 Feb 1874); Lt (10 Mar 1880); LCdr (3 Mar 1899); Cdr (16 Jun 1901); Capt (22 Jan 1906); RAdm (20 Nov 1909); placed on Ret.Lst. (13 Feb 1913).

Career Summary   Received appointment from MA (25 July 1866); USNA (Jul 1866-Jun 1870); w.o. (Jun-Jul 1870); *Nipsic*, N.Atl.Sqdn. (Jul 1870-Nov 1872); USNA (Nov-Dec 1872); w.o. (Dec 1872-Mar 1873); rec. ship, *Sabine*, Portsmouth, NH (Mar-Sep 1873); *Monongahela*, S.Atl.Sqdn. (Sep 1873-May 1874); *Lancaster*, S.Atl.Sqdn. (May 1874-Jul 1875); w.o. (Jul-Oct 1875); cst.surv. duty (Oct 1875-Jun 1879); w.o. (Jun-Jul 1879); training ship, *Constitution* (Aug 1879-Sep 1880); inst. of physics, USNA (Sep 1880-Aug 1883); l.o.a. (Aug 1883-Aug 1884); spec. electrical duty, International Exposition, Philadelphia (Aug 1884-Dec 1885); *Dolphin*, N.Atl.Sta. (Dec 1885-Dec 1886); Torp.Sta., Newport, RI (Dec 1886-Feb 1888); *Pensacola*, Navy Yard, NY (Mar-Apr 1888); *Omaha*, Asia.Sta. (Apr 1888-Mar 1891); spec. duty, Europe (May-Nov 1891); asst.equip.off., Navy Yard, NY (Nov 1891-Mar 1894); *Atlanta*, N.Atl.Sta. (Apr-Dec 1894); rec. ship, *Richmond*, Philadelphia (Dec 1894); *Minneapolis*, N.Atl. and Eur.Stas. (Dec 1894-Mar 1897); NWC (Apr 1897-Apr 1898); exec.off., *Panther*, N.Atl.Flt. (Apr-Oct 1898); NWC (Oct 1898-Oct 1899); exec.off., flgs., *New York*, N.Atl.Flt. (Oct 1899-Nov 1900); NWC (Nov 1900-Jan 1903); cdr, training ship, *Alliance* (Jan-Sep 1903); *Denver*, Philadelphia (Sep 1903-May 1904); cdr, *Denver*, spec.serv. (May 1904-Oct 1905); home and w.o. (Oct 1905); l.o.a. (Oct 1905-Feb 1906); Navy Dept.,

Washington, DC (Feb 1906); USNA (Feb-May 1906); member, naval exam. and ret. bds., Washington, DC (Apr 1906-Jul 1907); additional duty, member, Gen Bd., Washington, DC (May-Jul 1907); cdr, *Rhode Island*, "Great White Flt." (Jul 1907-Mar 1909); comdt., Navy Yard, NY (May 1909-Mar 1910); cdr, 2nd Div., Atl.Flt., *Minnesota* (Mar-Jul 1910); cdr, 4th Div., Atl.Flt., *Minnesota* (Jul-Nov 1910); cdr, 3rd Div., Atl.Flt., *Minnesota* (Nov 1910-Apr 1911); cdr, Asia.Flt., *Saratoga* (May 1911-Jul 1912); home and w.o. (Jul-Sep 1912); member, Gen Bd., Washington, DC (Sep 1912-Feb 1913); member, Army-Navy Joint Bd., Washington, DC (Oct 1912-Feb 1913); placed on Ret.Lst. (13 Feb 1913); various bd. duties, Navy Yard, Portsmouth, NH (May 1918-May 1919).

Career Highlights Commanded the *Rhode Island* as part of the "Great White Flt." Subsequently commanded Asia.Flt. After retirement, served in House of Representatives from NH from 1921 to 1923.

References

Writings: a) "The Naval Use of the Dynamo Machine and Electric Light," U.S. Naval Institute *Proceedings* 21 (1882): 343-85. b) "The Cruise of Columbus in the Bahamas, 1492," U.S. Naval Institute *Proceedings* 30 (1884): 449-86. c) *Notes on Electricity and Magnetism* (1884). d) "The Protection of the Hulls of Vessels by Lacquer," U.S. Naval Institute *Proceedings* 55 (1890): 457-72. e) "Noted on Naval Dynamo Machinery," U.S. Naval Institute *Proceedings* 68 (1893): 345-90. f) "Our Need of Fighting Ships," U.S. Naval Institute *Proceedings* 98 (1901): 247-67. g) "Torpedo Tubes in Battleships," U.S. Naval Institute *Proceedings* 107 (Sep 1903): 547-51.

ARTHUR PHILLIPS NAZRO Born in Milwaukee, WI, on 3 Dec 1850, son of Henry J. Nazro. Early education in Dorcester, MA. His wife was Mary Evert Nazro. At least one son. Died at his home in Jamaica Plain, MA, on 16 Feb 1911. Buried in Forest Hills Cemetery, Jamaica Plain.

ARTHUR PHILLIPS NAZRO
1850-1911

Ranks Midn (20 Jul 1865); Ens (12 Jul 1870); Mstr (26 Jul 1871); Lt (19 Nov 1874); LCdr (18 Nov 1896); Cdr (22 Nov 1899); Capt (28 Dec 1904); RAdm (15 Dec 1908); placed on Ret.Lst. (10 May 1910).

Career Summary Received appointment from MA (20 Jul 1865); USNA (Jul 1865-Jun 1869); *Sabine*, and *Franklin*, Med.Sqdn. (Jun 1869-Nov 1871); w.o. (Nov 1871-Jan 1872); ord. duty, Navy Yard, Boston (Jan-Mar 1872); *Portsmouth*, *Lancaster*, *Ticonderoga*, *Colorado*, and *Congress*, S.Atl. and Eur.Stas. (Apr 1872-Sep 1875); home and w.o. (Sep-Nov 1875); *Hartford*, N.Atl.Sta. (Nov 1875-Aug 1876); USNA (Sep 1876-Jul 1879); training ship, *Constitution* (Aug 1879-Dec 1881); training ship, *Minnesota* (Dec 1881-Nov 1882); recorder, bd. of inspection, Navy Dept., Washington, DC (Nov 1882-Apr 1884); Torp.Sta., Newport, RI (Apr-Aug 1884); ord. instruction, Navy Yard, Washington, DC (Aug-Dec 1884); *Powhatan*, N.Atl.Sta. (Jan 1885-Mar 1886); *Tennessee*, N.Atl.Sta. (Mar 1886-Jan 1887);

Richmond, N.Atl.Sta. (Jan 1887-Sep 1888); training ship, *Minnesota*, NY (Sep-Dec 1888); l.o.a. (Dec 1888-Jan 1889); member, bd. of inspection of merchant ships, NY (Jan 1889-Jan 1890); in charge, branch hydrographic office, NY (Jan 1890-Jun 1891); l.o.a. (Jun 1891-Jan 1892); chartered steamer, *Ohio* (Jan 1892); w.o. (Jan-Apr 1892); in charge, branch hydrographic office, NY (Apr-Jun 1892); flgs., *Chicago*, Eur.Sta. (Jul 1892-May 1895); exec.off., training ship, *Enterprise* (May 1895-Jan 1897); exec.off., rec. ship, *Vermont*, NY (Jan-Nov 1897); exec.off., *San Francisco*, N.Atl.Sta. (Dec 1897-Mar 1898); cdr, *New Orleans*, N.Atl.Flt. (Mar-Apr 1898); *San Francisco*, N.Atl.Flt. (Apr-Aug 1898); exec.off., *Oregon*, N.Atl.Flt. and Asia.Sta. (Aug 1898-May 1899); cdr, *Manila*, Asia.Sta. (May 1899-Jul 1900); asst., then insp., 2nd L.h. Dist., Boston (Sep 1900-Nov 1902); additional duty, insp., 1st L.h. Dist., Portland, ME (May 1901-Nov 1902); cdr, *Raleigh*, spec.serv., and Asia.Sta. (Nov 1902-May 1904); cdr, *Vicksburg*, Asia.Sta. (May-Jul 1904); home and w.o. (Jul-Sep 1904); in charge, recruiting sta., Philadelphia (Oct 1904-Jan 1905); capt.yd., Navy Yard, League Island, PA (Jan-Oct 1905); cdr, *Brooklyn*, spec. cruises (Oct 1905-Jul 1907); cdr, rec. ship, *Wabash*, Boston (Jul 1907-Dec 1908); comdt., Naval Sta., Cavite, P.I. (Feb-Dec 1909); additional duty, comdt., Naval Sta., Olongapo, P.I. (Feb-Dec 1909); home and w.o. (Dec 1909-Mar 1910); placed on Ret.Lst. (10 May 1910).

SIMON NEWCOMB Born in Wallace, Nova Scotia, Canada, on 12 Mar 1835, son of John Burton and Emily (Prince) Newcomb. Received little if any formal schooling, although his father was an itinerate school teacher. Apprenticed to a herbalist before moving to MD in 1853. Taught in various county schools, being particularly adept and fascinated by mathematics. Studied occasionally under Joseph Henry of the Smithsonian Institution. In early 1857, and upon Henry's recommendation, he began work in Cambridge, MA, with the *American Epheremis and Nautical Almanac*. Enrolled in the Lawrence Scientific School of Harvard Univ., graduating in 1858 with the B.S. degree. Married Mary Caroline Hassler, granddaughter of the founder of the U.S. Coast and Geodetic Survey, in 1863. Died in Washington, DC, on 11 Jul 1909. Buried in Arlington National Cemetery.

SIMON NEWCOMB
1835-1909

Ranks Prof. of Math. (21 Sep 1861); placed on Ret.Lst. (12 Mar 1897); Prof. of Math. with rank of RAdm on Ret.Lst. (20 Dec 1906) to rank from 29 Jun 1906.

Career Summary Received appointment from MA (21 Sep 1861); Naval Observatory, Washington, DC (Sep 1861-Sep 1877); senior math. prof., and supt., Nautical Almanac Office, Washington, DC (Sep 1877-Mar 1882); duty, Nautical Almanac Office, Washington, DC (Mar 1882-Mar 1897); placed on Ret.Lst. (12 Mar 1897).

Career Highlights One of the most famous American mathmeticians and astronomers. For many years while at Naval Observatory, he corrected many errors of celestial bodies in earlier published volumes of the *Nautical Almanac*. Was instrumental in getting the 26-inch telescope for the Naval Observatory in 1873 and for a number of years led expeditions observing celestial movements. Was editor of the *American Journal of Mathematics* from 1874 to 1901. Helped found in 1899 the American Astronomical Society, serving as the first pres. until 1905. Was prof. of math. and astronomy at Johns Hopkins Univ. in Baltimore from 1884 to 1894. Received many honorary degrees and awards from American and foreign universities and societies.

References

Personal Papers: 46,000 items (1854-1936) in LC.

Writings: a) *A Critical Examination of Our Financial Policy during the Southern Rebellion* (NY: 1865; repr., 1969). b) *Popular Astronomy* (NY: 1878). c) "The Nautical Almanac," U.S. Naval Institute *Proceedings* 7 (1879): 33-49. d) *Astronomy for Schools and Colleges* (NY: 1879). e) *The Elements of the Four Inner Planets and the Fundamental Constants of Astronomy* (Washington, DC: 1895). f) *The Stars* (1901). g) *Astronomy for Everyone* (1902). h) *Reminiscences of an Astronomer* (Boston: 1903). i) *Compendium of Spherical Astronomy* (NY: 1960).

Additional Sources: a) William Wallace Campbell, *Biographical Memoir, Simon Newcomb, 1835-1909* (Washington, DC: 1924). b) Raymond Clare Archibald, *Simon Newcomb, 1835-1909: Bibliography of His Life and Work* (Washington, DC: 1924).

ALBERT PARKER NIBLACK Born in Vincennes, IN, on 25 Jul 1859, son of the Honorable William Ellis and Eliza Ann (Sherman) Niblack. Married Mary A. Harrington on 24 Nov 1903. Died at Nice, France, on 20 Aug 1929.

Ranks Cadet Midn (22 Sep 1876); Mid (22 Jun 1882); Ensjg (3 Mar 1883); Ens (26 Jun 1884); Ltjg (24 Aug 1892); Lt (5 Sep 1896); LCdr (18 Jun 1902); Cdr (1 Jul 1907); Capt (4 Mar 1911); temp. RAdm (31 Aug 1917); RAdm (20 Mar 1918); VAdm (15 Jan 1921); placed on Ret.Lst. with rank of RAdm (25 Jul 1923); advanced posthumously to VAdm (21 Jun 1930).

Career Summary Received appointment from IN (22 Sep 1876); USNA (Sep 1876-Jun 1880); w.o. (Jun-Aug 1880); *Lackawanna,* and *Adams,* Pac.Sqdn. (Sep 1880-Apr 1882); USNA (Apr-Oct 1882); w.o. (Oct 1882); *Yantic,* N.Atl.Sqdn. (Oct-Nov 1882); spec. instruction duty, Smithsonian Institution, Washington, DC (Nov 1882-Jul 1884); cst.surv. duty (Jul 1884-Nov 1887); home and w.o. (Nov 1887-Feb 1888); ord. instruction, Navy Yard, Washington, DC (Feb-Apr 1888); torp. instruction, Newport, RI (May-Jul 1888); w.o. (Jul-Oct 1888); temp. duty, Smithsonian Institution, Washington, DC (Oct 1888-Mar 1889); *Chicago,* Sqdn. of Evol. (Mar 1889-Jan 1892); sick lv. (Jan-May 1892); Bur. of Nav., Washington, DC (May-Sep 1892); home and w.o. (Sep 1892-Feb 1893); cst.surv. duty (Feb-Oct 1893); Office of Naval Intelligence, Navy Dept., Washington, DC (Nov 1893); Bur. of Nav., Washington, DC (Nov 1893-Mar 1894); *Dolphin,* N.Atl.Sta. (Mar-Aug 1894); flag lt., N.Atl.Sta., *Dolphin* (Aug 1894-May 1895); home and w.o. (May 1895); office of asst. sec. of navy, Washington, DC (Jun 1895-Jun 1896); *Dolphin,*

ALBERT PARKER NIBLACK
1859-1929

Spec.Serv.Sqdn. (Jun-Aug 1896); office of asst. sec. of navy, Washington, DC (Aug 1896); naval attaché, Rome, Berlin, and Vienna (Jan 1897-May 1898); rec. ship, *Vermont*, NY (May 1898); *Topeka*, N.Atl.Flt. (May-Aug 1898); cdr, *Winslow*, Navy Yard, NY (Aug-Nov 1898); *Concord*, Asia.Sta. (Dec 1898-Mar 1899); *Oregon*, Asia.Sta. (May 1899-Jan 1900); exec.off., *Castine*, Asia.Sta. (Jan-Dec 1900); flgs., *Brooklyn*, Asia.Sta. (Dec 1900-Apr 1901); sec. to naval commissioner, and dir., naval base hydrographic survs., P.I. (Jul-Aug 1901); flgs., *Kentucky*, S.Sqdn., Asia.Flt. (Apr-May 1901); *Manila*, Asia.Sta. (May-Jun 1901); exec.off., *Culgoa*, Asia.Sta. (Jun-Jul 1901); member, bd. on naval stas., Washington, DC (Aug-Oct 1901); Bur. of Nav., Washington, DC (Oct 1901-Nov 1902); bd. duty (Nov 1902-Jan 1903); Army-Navy Hosp., Ft. Bagard, NM (Jan-Jul 1903); in charge, Naval Sta., Honolulu, Territory of HI (Jul 1903-Apr 1906); additional temp. duty, cdr, *Iroquois*, Midway Island (Aug 1903-Apr 1906); additional duty, asst., then insp., 12th L.h. Dist., San Francisco, and in charge of L.h. establishments, Territory of HI (Dec 1903-Apr 1906); customs insp., Midway Island (Mar 1904-Jan 1906); home and w.o. (Apr-May 1906); exec.off., flgs., *Chicago*, Pac.Sqdn. (May 1906-Jun 1907); member, bd. on HI, Navy Dept., Washington, DC (Jun-Nov 1907); cdr, training ship, *Hartford* (Oct 1907-May 1908); cdr, training ship, *Severn* (May-Sep 1908); cdr, training ships, USNA (Sep 1908-May 1909); cdr, *Tacoma*, spec.serv. (Jun 1909-May 1910); naval attaché, Rio de Janeiro, Buenos Aires, and Santiago, Chile (Jun 1910-Nov 1911); naval attaché, Berlin, and The Hague, Netherlands (Dec 1911-Jul 1913); l.o.a. (Jul-Aug 1913); Office of Naval Intelligence, Navy Dept., Washington, DC (Sep-Oct 1913); NWC (Oct-Nov 1913); cdr, *Michigan*, Atl.Flt. (Dec 1913-Dec 1915); home and w.o. (Dec 1915); NWC (Jan-Dec 1916); member, Gen Bd., Washington, DC (Dec 1916-Apr 1917); cdr, Div. 1, Atl.Flt., *Alabama* (Apr-Nov 1917); temp. duty, office of chief of naval operations, Washington, DC (Nov 1917); spec. duty, London (Nov 1917); cdr, Sqdn. 2, Patrol Force, Atl.Flt., Gibraltar, *Birmingham*, then *Buffalo* (Nov 1917-Jan 1919); cdr, U.S. Naval Forces, Eastern Med. and Adriatic Seas (Jan-Mar 1919); dir. of naval intelligence, Navy Dept., Washington, DC (Apr 1919-Sep 1920); naval attaché, London (Oct 1920-Jan 1921); cdr, U.S. Naval Forces, Eur. waters, *Utah* (Jan 1921-Apr 1922); cdr, 6th Naval Dist. and Navy Yard, Charleston, SC (May 1922-Jul 1923); placed on Ret.Lst. (25 Jul 1923).

Career Highlights During Spanish-American War, commanded a torp. boat, the *Winslow*, off Cuba, then was transferred to the P.I. where he participated in several actions. Served several tours of duty as naval attaché in various capitals of Europe and South America. During the troubles with Mexico in 1914, commanded the *Michigan* and the 3rd Seaman Regiment during the occupation of Vera Cruz. With World War I, commanded several divs. and sqdns. of the Atl.Flt., coordinating the convoy system from Gibraltar. Eventually commanded all naval forces in Eur. waters in 1921. Received numerous awards, including the navy's

Distinguished Service Medal for his services during World War I
and at least a dozen foreign awards and decorations. Served as
Dir. of the International Hydrographic Bur. of Monaco after
retirement. Was a prolific writer, many articles appearing in the
Naval Institute's *Proceedings*.

References

Personal Papers: 167 items (1880-1933) in IN Historical
Society Lib., Indianapolis.

Writings: a) *The Coast Indians of Southern Alaska and Northern
British Columbia* (1888). b) "The Enlistment, Training, and
Organization of Crews for Our New Ships," U.S. Naval Institute
Proceedings 57 (1891): 3-49. c) "Proposed Day, Night, and Fog
Signals for the Navy, with Brief Descriptions of the Artois Night
System," U.S. Naval Institute *Proceedings* 58 (1891): 253-63. d)
"The Signal Question Up to Date," U.S. Naval Institute *Proceed-
ings* 61 (1892): 57-65. e) "Naval Signaling," U.S. Naval Institute
Proceedings 64 (1892): 431-505. f) *Tactical Considerations Involved
in Warship Design* (NY: 1895). g) "The Naval Militia Movement,"
U.S. Naval Institute *Proceedings* 76 (1895): 779-87. h) "The
Tactics of Ships in the Line of Battle," U.S. Naval Institute
Proceedings 77 (1896): 1-28. i) "The Taking of Ilo Ilo," U.S.
Naval Institute *Proceedings* 91 (Oct 1899): 593-606. j) "Tactical
Considerations Involved in the Design of the Torpedo-Boat," U.S.
Naval Institute *Proceedings* 93 (Mar 1900): 167-78. k) "The
Signal Question Once More," U.S. Naval Institute *Proceedings*
103 (Sep 1902): 553-63. l) "The Tactics of the Gun," U.S. Naval
Institute *Proceedings* 104 (Dec 1902): 925-36. m) "The Jane
Naval War Game in the Scientific American," U.S. Naval
Institute *Proceedings* 107 (Sep 1903): 581-94. n) "Colliers and
Coaling Stations," U.S. Naval Institute *Proceedings* 111 (Sep
1904): 567-76. o) "Operations of the Navy and Marine Corps in
the Philippine Archipelago, 1898-1902," U.S. Naval Institute
Proceedings, 30 (Dec 1904): 745-73. p) "The Elements of Fleet
Tactics," U.S. Naval Institute *Proceedings* 118 (Jun 1906):
387-445. q) "An Answer to Criticisms of 'The Elements of Fleet
Tactics,'" U.S. Naval Institute *Proceedings* 119 (Sep 1906):
1065-67. r) "Lieutenant Dewar's Papers on 'Speed in Naval
Tactics' and 'Speed in Battleship Strategy,'" U.S. Naval Institute
Proceedings 124 (Dec 1907): 1385-90. s) "A Plea for Physical
Training in the Navy," U.S. Naval Institute *Proceedings* 129 (Mar
1909): 67-91. t) "The Swedish System--A Further Plea for
Physical Training in the Navy," U.S. Naval Institute *Proceedings*
138 (Jun 1911): 425-45. u) "The Letters of a Retired Rear
Admiral to His Son in the Navy," U.S. Naval Institute *Proceedings*
156 (Mar-Apr 1915): 367-82; 157 (May-Jun 1915): 841-56; 238
(Dec 1922): 2063-69; 240 (Feb 1923): 253-67; 241 (Mar 1923):
571-80. v) "Forms of Government in Relation to Their Efficiency
for War," U.S. Naval Institute *Proceedings* 21 (Sep 1920):
1399-1430. w) *Why Wars Come; or, Forms of Government and
Foreign Policies in Relation to the Causes of War* (Boston: 1922). x)
"Athletics,   Beneficial and Otherwise," U.S. Naval Institute
Proceedings 248 (Oct 1923): 1609-22. y) "The International

Hydrographic Bureau, Monaco," U.S. Naval Institute *Proceedings* 300 (Feb 1928): 135-36. z) *The Office of Naval Intelligence; Its History and Aims* (Washington, DC: 1928). aa) *Putting Cargos Across* (Washington, DC: 1977).

REGINALD FAIRFAX NICHOLSON
1852-1939

REGINALD FAIRFAX NICHOLSON Born in Washington, DC, on 15 Dec 1852, son of navy Capt Somerville Nicholson. Married to Elizabeth Code Nicholson. One daughter, who married Capt Edward H. Durell, USN. Resided in Washington, DC, dying in the Naval Hosp. there on 19 Dec 1939.

Ranks Captain's Clerk (1 Aug 1864); resigned (31 Aug 1864); Midn (30 Sep 1869); title changed to Cadet Midn (15 Jul 1870); Midn (31 May 1873); Ens (16 Jul 1874); Mstr (22 Jan 1880); title changed to Ltjg (3 Mar 1883); Lt (17 Jan 1886); LCdr (3 Mar 1899); Cdr (17 Sep 1902); Capt (1 Jul 1907); Chief, Bur. of Nav. with rank of RAdm (1 Dec 1909); RAdm (19 May 1911); placed on Ret.Lst. (15 Dec 1914).

Career Summary Captain's Clerk, *State of Georgia*, N.Atl.Blk. Sqdn. (Aug 1864); resigned (31 Aug 1864); received appointment from NC (30 Sep 1869); USNA (Sep 1869-May 1873); w.o. (May-Jul 1873); *Alaska*, and *Hartford*, Eur. and Asia.Sqdns. (Aug 1873-Oct 1875); USNA (Oct-Nov 1875); Hydrographic Office, Washington, DC (Nov 1875-Sep 1876); *Hartford*, Navy Yard, NY (Sep 1876-Feb 1877); *Powhatan*, N.Atl.Sta. (Feb-Aug 1877); w.o. (Aug-Sep 1877); ord. instruction, Navy Yard, Washington, DC (Sep 1877-Feb 1879); training ship, *Portsmouth* (Feb 1879-Oct 1882); w.o. (Oct-Nov 1882); Hydrographic Office, Washington, DC (Nov 1882-May 1885); *Mohican*, Pac.Sta. (Jun 1885-Aug 1888); w.o. (Aug-Oct 1888); ord. duty, Navy Yard, Washington, DC (Oct 1888-Aug 1892); Union Iron Works, San Francisco (Sep 1892-Feb 1893); *Monterey*, Pac.Sqdn. (Feb 1893-Sep 1894); *Thetis*, Pac.Sqdn. (Sep 1894-Dec 1895); ord. duty, Navy Yard, Washington, DC (Dec 1895-Dec 1897); *Oregon*, Pac.Sqdn. and N.Atl.Flt. (Dec 1897-Aug 1898); cdr, *Farragut*, San Francisco (Oct 1898-Mar 1899); cdr, torp. boat, *Rowan*, Pac.Sta. (Mar-Jun 1899); cdr, *Farragut*, Pac.Sta. (Jun 1899-Jul 1901); Bur. of Nav., Washington, DC (Jul 1901-Jan 1904); cdr, *Tacoma*, Pac. and N.Atl.Stas., and spec.serv. (Jan 1904-Dec 1905); home and w.o. (Dec 1905-Jan 1906); Bur. of Equip. and Recruiting, Washington, DC (Jan-Jun 1906); Bur. of Nav., Washington, DC (Jun 1906-Jul 1907); asst., Bur. of Nav., Washington, DC (Jul 1907); cdr, *Nebraska*, "Great White Flt." (Aug 1907-May 1909); member, bd. of inspection and surv., Washington, DC (Jun-Dec 1909); chief, Bur. of Nav., Washington, DC (Dec 1909-Jan 1912); temp. duty, Gen Bd., Washington, DC (Jan-Mar 1912); temp. duty, cdr, Asia.Flt. (Mar-Jul 1912); cdr, Asia.Flt., *Rainbow* and *Saratoga* (Apr 1912-May 1914); member, Gen Bd., Washington, DC (Jul-Dec 1914); placed on Ret.Lst. (15 Dec 1914); temp. duty, Office of Naval Intelligence, Washington, DC (Sep-Oct 1917); naval attaché to Santiago, Lima, and Quito, Ecuador (Sep 1917-Nov 1919); temp. duty, Office of Naval Intelligence, Washington, DC (Nov 1919-Jun 1920).

Career Highlights During the Spanish-American War, served on the *Oregon*, from her outset on the Pac.cst. to the Caribbean. Was frequently billeted with the Bur. of Nav., eventually serving as chief. Commanded the *Nebraska* as part of the "Great White Flt." Served as cdr of the Asia.Flt., and he was recalled to active duty as naval attaché to three S.American nations during World War I.

References

Personal Papers: a) 20 items (1873-1939) in NHF,LC.

KOSSUTH NILES Born in Belleville, IL, on 14 Jun 1849, son of Nathaniel and Maria Louisa (Thomas) Niles. Married Elizabeth Challenor on 31 Dec 1873. Retired to Winstead, CT. Died on 6 Dec 1913 in NY City. Buried in Arlington National Cemetery.

Ranks Private, 142nd Regiment, IL Volunteers (Jun 1864); Midn (22 Sep 1865); Ens (12 Jul 1870); Mstr (1 Mar 1873); Lt (30 Sep 1876); LCdr (1 May 1898); Cdr (19 Feb 1901); Capt (1 Jul 1905); RAdm (15 Sep 1909); placed on Ret.Lst. (14 Jun 1911).

KOSSUTH NILES
1849-1913

Career Summary Service with 142nd Regiment, IL Volunteers (Jun-Oct 1864); received appointment from IL (22 Sep 1865); USNA (Sep 1865-Jun 1869); *Sabine*, spec.serv. (Jun 1869-Jul 1870); w.o. (Jul-Nov 1870); USNA (Nov 1870); *Pawnee*, and *Terror*, N.Atl.Sqdn. (Nov 1870-Apr 1872); home and w.o. (Apr-Sep 1872); Naval Sta., Mound City, IL (Sep-Nov 1872); Nicaraguan Surv.Expd. (Nov 1872-Jul 1873); w.o. (Jul-Aug 1873); Torp.Sta., Newport, RI (Sep 1873-Mar 1874); *Frolic*, N.Atl.Sta. (Mar-Apr 1874); w.o. (Apr-Jun 1874); cst.surv. duty (Jun 1874-Aug 1877); w.o. (Aug-Sep 1877); *Michigan*, on Great Lakes (Sep 1877-Mar 1878); *Constellation*, Paris Exposition, Paris (Mar-Jul 1878); *Swatara*, N.Atl.Sqdn. (Jul-Oct 1878); flgs., *Ticonderoga*, spec. cruise around world (Nov 1878-Sep 1881); w.o. (Sep-Nov 1881); ord. duty, Navy Yard, Washington, DC (Nov 1881-Jun 1884); *Powhatan*, Eur.Sta. (Jun-Jul 1884); flgs., *Lancaster*, Eur., then S.Atl.Stas. (Jul 1884-Nov 1887); w.o. (Nov-Dec 1887); ord. duty, Navy Yard, Washington, DC (Dec 1887-Jan 1888); insp. of ord., Midvale Steel Works, Nicetown, PA (Jan-Oct 1888); insp. of ord., armor and steel shafting, Bethlehem Iron Works, Bethlehem, PA, and insp. of armor-piercing projectiles, Carpenter Steel Works, Reading, PA (Oct 1888-Aug 1892); Bur. of Ord., Washington, DC (Aug 1892-Jul 1893); *Detroit*, S.Atl.Sta. (Jul 1893-Feb 1894); exec.off., *Yantic*, S.Atl.Sta. (Mar 1894-Mar 1896); *Newark*, S.Atl.Sta. (Mar-Jul 1896); home and l.o.a. (Jun-Oct 1896); rec. ship, *Vermont*, NY (Oct-Dec 1896); Torp.Sta., Newport, RI (Dec 1896-Mar 1899); exec.off., *Massachusetts*, N.Atl.Sqdn. (Apr 1899-Feb 1901); home and w.o. (Feb 1901); insp., 8th L.h. Dist., New Orleans (Apr 1901-Nov 1903); cdr, *Bennington*, Pac.Sta. (Dec 1903-Nov 1904); cdr, *Boston*, Pac.Sta. (Nov 1904-Nov 1905); home and w.o. (Nov-Dec 1905); spec. temp. duty, Bur. of Ord., Washington, DC (Dec 1905); asst. insp. of ord., NY (Dec 1905-Apr 1906); general insp. of ord., NY (Apr 1906-May 1908); cdr, *Louisiana*, "Great

White Flt." (May 1908-Jun 1909); member, L.h. Bd., Washington, DC (Jun 1909-Jun 1910); general insp. of ord. for navy, Washington, DC (Jun 1910-Jul 1911); member, then pres., naval exam. and ret. bds., Washington, DC (Jun 1910-Jun 1911); placed on Ret.Lst. (14 Jun 1911).

Career Highlights Commanded of the *Louisiana* as part of the "Great White Flt."

NATHAN ERRICK NILES Born in Wellsboro, PA, on 27 Dec 1847, son of Alanson E. and Angeline Niles. Married Blanche Rousseau on 12 Oct 1876. Two daughters. Resided in Washington, DC. Died in Woodberry Forest, VA, on 28 Nov 1930. Buried in Arlington National Cemetery.

Ranks Midn (28 Jul 1864); Ens (19 Apr 1869); Mstr (12 Jul 1870); Lt (7 Jul 1874); LCdr (5 Jan 1896); Cdr (25 Mar 1899); Capt (13 Sep 1904); RAdm (12 Nov 1908); placed on Ret.Lst. (27 Dec 1909).

Career Summary Received appointment from PA (28 Jul 1864); USNA (Jul 1864-Jun 1868); w.o. (Jun-Sep 1868); *Nipsic*, N.Atl.Sqdn. and Darien Surv.Expd. (Oct 1868-Jul 1870); w.o. (Jul-Oct 1870); *Saranac, Resaca*, and *St. Mary's*, Pac.Sqdn. (Dec 1870-May 1873); home and w.o. (May-Nov 1873); *Manhattan*, and *Ossipee*, N.Atl.Sta. (Nov 1873-Mar 1875); home and w.o. (Mar-May 1875); Torp.Sta., Newport, RI (Jun-Oct 1875); rec. ship, *Potomac*, League Island, PA (Oct-Nov 1875); *Marion*, Eur.Sta. (Dec 1875-Nov 1878); l.o.a. (Nov 1878-Sep 1879); ord. duty, Navy Yard, Portsmouth, NH (Oct 1879-Mar 1882); *Iroquois*, Pac.Sta. (Apr 1882-May 1885); home and w.o. (May-Jul 1885); rec. ship, *Wabash*, Boston (Jul-Sep 1885); Hydrographic Office, Washington, DC (Sep 1885-Apr 1888); torp. instruction, Newport, RI (May-Aug 1888); NWC (Aug-Nov 1888); *Atlanta*, Eur.Sta. (Nov 1888-Nov 1891); electric light duty, Navy Yard, Norfolk, VA (Nov 1891-Aug 1895); *Lancaster*, S.Atl.Sqdn. (Sep 1895-Dec 1897); Bur. of Equipment and Recruiting, Washington, DC (Jan-Jun 1898); cdr, *Piscataqua*, N.Atl.Flt. (Jun-Sep 1898); equip.off., Navy Yard, Norfolk, VA (Oct 1898-Jul 1900); cdr, *Nashville*, Asia. and Eur.Stas. (Sep 1900-Feb 1903); home and w.o. (Feb-Mar 1903); Naval Home, Philadelphia (Apr 1903-Jul 1905); cdr, *Maine*, N.Atl.Sqdn. (Jul 1905-Jul 1907); cdr, rec. ship, *Hancock*, NY (Jul 1907-Dec 1908); gov., Naval Home, Philadelphia (Dec 1908-Apr 1910); placed on Ret.Lst. (27 Dec 1909).

References
Personal Papers: 1 vol. (c. 1847-1930) in New England Historic Genealogical Society, Boston, MA.

HAROLD PERCIVAL NORTON Born in NY City on 4 Nov 1855, son of Charles E. and Emily A. (Norton) Norton. Married Mrs. Mary V. (Barbour) McCartney on 27 Dec 1911. Resided in Washington, DC, where he died on 11 Feb 1933. Buried in Arlington National Cemetery.

Ranks Cadet Engr. (1 Oct 1874); Asst.Engr. (10 Jun 1881); PAsst.Engr. (12 Oct 1891); PAsst.Engr. with rel. rank of Ltjg (29

HAROLD PERCIVAL NORTON
1855-1933

May 1892); Chief Engr. (10 Feb 1899); Lt (3 Mar 1899); LCdr (26 Oct 1901); Cdr (10 Oct 1906); Capt (16 Sep 1910); RAdm (1 Jul 1918); placed on Ret.Lst. (4 Nov 1919).

Career Summary Received appointment from NY (1 Oct 1874); USNA (Oct 1874-Jun 1879); w.o. (Jun-Dec 1879); *Swatara*, Asia.Sta. (Dec 1879-Apr 1882); *Alert*, Asia.Sta. (Apr-Jul 1882); w.o. (Jul-Dec 1882); spec. duty, naval advisory bd., Navy Dept., Washington, DC (Dec 1882-May 1886); *Atlanta*, on trials and N.Atl.Sqdn. (Jun 1886-Nov 1887); spec. duty, naval advisory bd., Navy Dept., Washington, DC (Nov-Dec 1887); Bur. of Steam Engineering, Washington, DC (Dec 1887-Apr 1891); *Concord*, N.Atl.Sqdn. (May 1891-May 1894); return and l.o.a. (May-Sep 1894); Bur. of Steam Engineering, Washington, DC (Sep 1894-Aug 1898); insp. of machinery, *Albany*, Elswick, England (Sep 1898-May 1900); *Albany*, Asia. and Eur.Stas. (May 1900-Mar 1904); *Kentucky*, spec.serv. (Mar-Jun 1904); home and l.o.a. (Jun-Sep 1904); Navy Yard, NY (Sep 1904-Jun 1906); Bur. of Steam Engineering, Washington, DC (Jun 1906-Apr 1910); insp. of engineering, Bur. of Steam Engineering (Apr 1910-Oct 1911); spec. duty, Bur. of Steam Engineering, Washington, DC (Oct 1911-Apr 1912); member, bd. of inspection of shore stas. (Apr 1912-Jul 1913); member, naval exam. and ret. bds. (Jul 1913-Nov 1919); retired (4 Nov 1919).

JAMES HARRISON OLIVER Born in Houston County, GA, on 15 Jan 1857, son of Thaddeus and Sarah Penelope (Lawson) Oliver. Attended Washington and Lee Univ. in Lexington, VA, in 1872. Married Marion Carter Oliver on 7 Dec 1893. Resided in Shirley, VA, where he died on 6 Apr 1928.

Ranks Cadet Midn (16 Jun 1873); Midn (18 Jun 1879); Ens (1 Oct 1881); Ltjg (28 Sep 1888); Lt (4 Jul 1893); LCdr (23 Jul 1900); resigned (13 Feb 1902); reinstated (15 Mar 1902); transferred to Ret.Lst. (30 Jun 1905); restored to Active List with rank of Cdr (30 Jun 1906); Capt (1 Jul 1910); RAdm (29 Aug 1916); placed on Ret.Lst. (15 Jan 1921).

Career Summary Received appointment from GA (12 Jun 1873); USNA (Jun 1873-Jun 1877); w.o. (Jun-Aug 1877); *Hartford*, N.Atl.Sta. (Aug 1877-Jan 1879); *Essex*, S.Atl.Sqdn. (Jan-May 1879); USNA (May-Jun 1879); l.o.a. (Jun-Aug 1879); USNA (Aug-Sep 1879); w.o. (Sep-Dec 1879); *Swatara*, and *Ashuelot*, Asia.Sta. (Dec 1879-Dec 1882); w.o. (Dec 1882-Feb 1883); l.o.a. (Feb-May 1883); artillery school, Ft. Monroe, VA (May 1883-Apr 1884); *Lackawanna*, Pac.Sta. (Jun 1884-Mar 1886); *Shenandoah*, Pac.Sta. (Mar 1886); *Mohican*, Pac.Sta. (Mar 1886-May 1887); w.o. (May-Jun 1887); cst.surv. duty (Jun 1887-Feb 1889); Naval Ord. Proving Ground, Annapolis (Mar-Apr 1889); torp. instruction, Newport, RI (May-Aug 1889); NWC (Aug-Sep 1889); *Kearsarge*, spec.serv. (Sep 1889-Dec 1892); l.o.a. (Dec 1892-Jan 1893); ord.insp., Navy Yard, Washington, DC (Jan-Feb 1893); insp. of ord., Providence, RI (Feb 1893-Nov 1894); l.o.a. (Nov-Dec 1894); *Minneapolis*, N.Atl.Sqdn. (Dec 1894-Oct 1896); *San Francisco*, Eur.Sta. (Oct 1896-Dec

JAMES HARRISON OLIVER
1857-1928

1897); l.o.a. (Dec 1897-Feb 1898); Torp.Sta., Newport, RI (Feb 1898-Sep 1899); *Yankton*, spec.serv. (Oct-Nov 1899); hosp. ship, *Solace*, Pac.Sta. (Nov-Dec 1899); *Nashville*, Asia.Sta. (Dec 1899-Dec 1901); home and w.o. (Dec 1901-Feb 1902); resigned (13 Feb 1902); reinstated (15 Mar 1902); NWC (Mar 1902-Dec 1903); cdr, *Glacier*, spec.serv. (Dec 1903-Jul 1904); cdr, *Culgoa*, N.Atl.Sqdn. (Aug 1904-Aug 1905); transferred to Ret.Lst. (30 Jun 1905); asst., then insp., 14th L.h. Dist., Cincinnati, OH (Oct 1905-Apr 1907); additional duties, Naval Recruiting Sta., Cincinnati, OH (Mar 1906-Apr 1907); restored to Active List (30 Jun 1906); NWC (Apr 1907-Jul 1908); chief of staff, Pac.Flt., *West Virginia* (Aug 1908-May 1909); cdr, *Albany*, Pac.Flt. (May 1909-Apr 1910); NWC (May 1910-Nov 1911); cdr, training ship, *New Hampshire* (Nov 1911-Jul 1912); pres., naval ret. bd., Norfolk, VA (Jan-Jul 1912); cdr, *Alabama*, Atl.Flt. (Jul-Sep 1912); cdr, *New Hampshire*, spec.serv. (Sep 1912-Dec 1913); home and w.o. (Dec 1913-Jan 1914); dir. of naval intelligence, Navy Dept., Washington, DC (Jan 1914-Mar 1917); gov., and comdt., Naval Sta., Virgin Islands (Mar 1917-Apr 1919); Navy Dept., Washington, DC (Apr 1919-Jan 1921); placed on Ret.Lst. (15 Jan 1921).

CHARLES O'NEIL Born in Manchester, England, on 15 Mar 1842, son of John and Mary Anne (Francis) O'Neil. On 6 Apr 1869, married Mary C. Frothingham. One son. Resided in Washington, DC. Died on 28 Feb 1927 at the Naval Hosp. in Chelsea, MA. Buried in Arlington National Cemetery.

Ranks Act.Master's Mate (29 Jul 1861); Act.Mstr (1 May 1862); Act.Lt (30 May 1865); Lt (12 Mar 1868); LCdr (18 Dec 1868); Cdr (28 Jul 1884); Capt (21 Jul 1897); Act.RAdm (11 Mar 1899); RAdm (31 Dec 1903); placed on Ret.Lst. (15 Mar 1904).

Career Summary Received appointment from MA (29 Jul 1861); *Cumberland*, N.Atl.Blk.Sqdn. (Jul 1861-May 1862); *Tioga*, N.Atl.Blk.Sqdn. (May 1862-Jul 1864); w.o. (Jul-Aug 1864); *Rhode Island*, N.Atl.Blk.Sqdn. (Aug 1864-Jun 1865); rec. ship, *Princeton*, Philadelphia (Jun 1865-May 1866); *Shamrock*, Eur.Sqdn. (May 1866-Mar 1867); return home (Mar-May 1867); *Guard*, Eur.Sqdn. (May 1867-Oct 1868); rec. ship, *Ohio*, Boston (Oct 1868-Mar 1869); *Galena*, Hampton Roads, VA (Apr-May 1869); rec. ship, *Ohio*, Boston (May-Sep 1869); l.o.a. (Sep 1869-Jan 1870); aide to RAdm Hiram Paulding, Navy Yard, Boston (Jan-Jul 1870); *Dictator*, and *Severn*, N.Atl.Sqdn. (Jul 1870-Jul 1871); w.o. (Jul-Oct 1871); rec. ship, *Ohio*, Boston (Oct 1871-Apr 1872); exec.off., *Supply*, spec.serv. (Apr 1872); flgs., *Lancaster*, and *Wasp*, S.Atl. Sqdn. (Apr 1872-Jan 1876); w.o. (Jan-May 1876); torp. instruction, Newport, RI (Jun-Sep 1876); w.o. (Sep-Oct 1876); exec.off., rec. ship, *Worcester*, Norfolk, VA (Oct-Dec 1876); training ship, *Minnesota* (Dec 1876-Apr 1877); cdr, *Supply*, spec.serv. (Apr-Sep 1877); exec.off., training ship, *Minnesota* (Sep-Nov 1877); exec.off., *Swatara*, Asia.Sqdn. (Nov 1877-Oct 1878); w.o. (Oct 1878-May 1879); ord. duty, Navy Yard, Boston (May 1879-Jun

CHARLES O'NEIL
1842-1927

1882); *Richmond*, Asia.Sta. (Aug 1882-Jun 1884); w.o. (Aug-Nov 1884); spec. ord. duty, West Point Foundry, Cold Spring, NY (Nov 1884-Apr 1886); ord. duty, Navy Yard, NY (Apr 1886-Nov 1889); cdr, *Dolphin*, spec.serv. (Nov 1889-Mar 1890); insp. of ord., Navy Yard, Washington, DC (Mar 1890-Sep 1892); general insp., then cdr, *Marblehead*, Boston, and N.Atl.Sta. (Sep 1892-Mar 1896); supt., Naval Gun Factory, Navy Yard, Washington, DC (Apr 1896-May 1897): chief, Bur. of Ord., Washington, DC (Jun 1897-Mar 1904); placed on Ret.Lst. (15 Mar 1904).

References
Personal Papers: a) 5500 items (1833-1927) in NHF,LC. b) 1 diary (1914) in NHF,WNY. c) ½ ft. (1871-1899) in Rutherford B. Hayes Lib., Fremont, OH.

Writings: "Engagement between the *Cumberland* and *Merrimack*," U.S. Naval Institute *Proceedings* 232 (Jun 1922): 863-93.

Other Sources: a) U.S. Lib. of Congress, *Edmund R. Calhoun; Charles O'Neil: A Register of Their Papers in the Library of Congress*. (Washington, DC: 1967).

HUGO OSTERHAUS Born in Belleville, IL, on 15 Jun 1851, son of Peter Joseph and Mathilde (Born) Osterhaus. Early education in St. Louis schools. Married Mary Willoughby Wilson on 23 Oct 1877. Two sons, including RAdm Hugo Wilson Osterhaus, USN (1878-1972). Died on 11 Jun 1927 at Castle Point, NY. Buried in Arlington National Cemetery.

Ranks Midn (22 Sep 1865); Ens (13 Jul 1871); Mstr (12 Feb 1874); Lt (13 Mar 1880); LCdr (3 Mar 1899); Cdr (2 Jul 1901); Capt (19 Feb 1906); RAdm (4 Dec 1909); placed on Ret.Lst. (15 Jun 1913).

Career Summary Received appointment from MO (22 Sep 1865); USNA (Sep 1865-Jun 1870); found deficient and turned back (Jun 1867); w.o. (Jun 1870); *Plymouth*, Eur.Sqdn. (Jul 1870-Jun 1873); w.o. (Jun-Nov 1873); temp. duty, *Powhatan*, N.Atl.Sta. (Nov-Dec 1873); flgs., *Worcester*, N.Atl.Sta. (Dec 1873-Feb 1876); *Powhatan*, N.Atl.Sta. (Feb 1876-Oct 1877); Hydrographic Office, Washington, DC (Nov 1877-May 1878); Navy Yard, Norfolk, VA (May 1878-Jul 1879); cst.surv. duty (Aug 1879-Nov 1882); *Enterprise*, Asia.Sta. (Dec 1882-Apr 1886); home and w.o. (Apr-May 1886); Navy Yard, Norfolk, VA (May 1886-Nov 1888); l.o.a. (Nov 1888-May 1889); w.o. (May-Jun 1889); judge advocate, court of inquiry, Norfolk, VA (Jun 1889); Navy Yard, Norfolk, VA (Jun-Jul 1889); *Enterprise*, Eur.Sta. (Jul 1889-Apr 1890); rec. ship, *Franklin*, Norfolk, VA (Apr-Jul 1890); *Pensacola*, Navy Yard, NY (Aug 1890); *Baltimore*, N.Atl. and S.Pac.Sqdns. (Aug 1890-Aug 1891); *Atlanta*, S.Atl. Sta. (Aug 1891-Sep 1892); USNA (Sep 1892-May 1894); exec.off., prac. ship, *Monongahela*, USNA (May-Sep 1894); USNA (Sep 1894-Jun 1895); member of staff, N.Atl.Flt., *Cincinnati* (Jun-Jul 1895) and *New York* (Jul 1895-May 1897); home and w.o. (May 1897); NWC, and Torp. School, Newport, RI (Jun-Aug 1897); USNA (Aug 1897-May 1898); exec.off., *Prairie*, N.Atl.Flt. (May-Aug 1898); USNA (Sep 1898-Dec 1899); training ship,

HUGO OSTERHAUS
1851-1927

Monongahela (Dec 1899-May 1900); exec.off., *Kentucky,* Asia.Sta. (May 1900-May 1901); cdr, *Culgoa,* Asia.Sta. (May-Dec 1901); USNA (Oct 1901-May 1902); cdr, training ship, *Chesapeake* (May-Sep 1902); USNA (Sep 1902-Jun 1903); member, naval wireless telegraphy bd., Navy Dept., Washington, DC (Jan-Oct 1903); cdr, *Monterey,* Asia.Sta. (Nov 1903-Apr 1904); *Cincinnati,* Asia.Sta. (Apr 1904-May 1905); home and w.o. (May-Aug 1905); bd. duties, League Island, PA (Aug-Nov 1905); member, bd. of inspection and surv., Washington, DC (Nov 1905-Apr 1907); cdr, flgs., *Connecticut,* Atl.Flt. (Apr 1907-Mar 1909); cdr, 2nd Div., Atl.Flt., *Minnesota* (Mar 1909-Feb 1910); Navy Dept., Washington, DC (Feb-Mar 1910); comdt., Navy Yard, Mare Island, CA (Mar 1910-May 1911); additional duty, comdt., 12th Naval Dist., San Francisco (Nov 1910-May 1911); member, bd. of selection, Navy Dept., Washington, DC (May 1911); cdr, Atl.Flt., *Connecticut* (Jun 1911-May 1912), then *Washington* (May-Oct 1912), then *Utah* (Oct 1912-Jan 1913); member, Gen Bd., Navy Dept., Washington, DC (Jan-Jun 1913); member, Army-Navy Joint Bd., Washington, DC (Feb-Jun 1913); pres., naval exam. and ret. bds. (Mar-Jun 1913); placed on Ret.Lst. (15 Jun 1913); supervisor, naval auxiliaries, Norfolk, VA, and various temp. duties (Apr 1917-Nov 1920).

References

Personal Papers: 5 items (1886-96) in NHF,WNY.

JOSEPH BENSON PARKER
1841-1915

JOSEPH BENSON PARKER Born near Carlisle, PA, on 20 Jun 1841, son of Rev. Joseph and Mary (Sheerer) Parker. Received A.B. degree in 1860 and A.M. degree in 1863 from Dickinson College. Received M.D. from Bellevue Hosp. Medl. College in NY City in 1862. On 15 Oct 1868, married Margaret Johnson Yorke. Two daughters. Resided in Philadelphia, where he died on 21 Oct 1915. Buried in the grounds of St. John's Church, Salem, NJ.

Ranks Act.Asst.Surg. (16 Mar 1863); honorably discharged (12 Oct 1865); Asst.Surg. (24 Nov 1866); PAsst.Surg. (31 Dec 1867); Surg. (13 Aug 1876); Medl.Insp. (30 Nov 1894); Medl. Dir. (18 Jun 1898); placed on Ret.Lst. as Medl.Dir. with rank of RAdm (20 Jun 1903).

Career Summary Received appointment from PA (16 Mar 1863); *Red Rover,* MS Sqdn. (Mar-Apr 1863); Naval Hosp., *Pinkney,* Memphis, TN (Apr 1863-Jul 1865); l.o.a. (Jul-Oct 1865); honorably discharged (12 Oct 1865); received appointment from MD (24 Nov 1866); w.o. (Nov-Dec 1866); USNA (Dec 1866-Nov 1867); w.o. (Nov 1867-Jan 1868); *De Soto,* N.Atl. Sqdn. (Jan-Sep 1868); w.o. (Sep-Nov 1868); Naval Rndv., NY (Nov 1868-Jan 1869); w.o. (Jan-May 1869); *Tallapoosa,* N.Atl. Sqdn. (May-Oct 1869); *Nantasket,* N.Atl.Sqdn. (Oct 1869-Dec 1870); return and w.o. (Dec 1870-Jan 1871); rec. ship, *Potomac,* League Island, PA (Jan-Sep 1871); Naval Hosp., Chelsea, MA (Sep-Nov 1871); rec. ship, *Ohio,* Boston (Nov-Dec 1871); Naval Hosp., Chelsea, MA (Dec 1871-Jan 1872); Naval Hosp., NY (Jan-Jun 1872); *Nantasket,* Navy Yard, Portsmouth, NH (Jul-Aug

1872); *Yantic*, Asia.Sqdn. (Aug 1872-Jun 1875); return and w.o. (Jun-Aug 1875); spec. duty, Bur. of Medicine and Surgery, Washington, DC (Oct 1875-Mar 1877); asst. to chief, Bur. of Medicine and Surgery, Washington, DC (Mar 1877-Sep 1879); *Wachusett*, Pac.Sqdn. (Sep 1879-Dec 1881); return and w.o. (Dec 1881-Jan 1882); l.o.a. and w.o. (Jan 1882-Apr 1883); Torp.Sta., Newport, RI (Apr 1883-Apr 1885); w.o. (Apr-Jul 1885); *Swatara*, N.Atl.Sqdn. (Aug 1885-Oct 1886); w.o. (Oct 1886-Mar 1887); *Ossipee*, N.Atl.Sqdn. (Mar 1887-Jun 1888); w.o. (Jun-Jul 1888); Navy Yard, Boston (Aug 1888-Aug 1891); w.o. (Aug-Sep 1891); bd. duty, USNA (Sep-Oct 1891); w.o. (Oct 1891-Jan 1892); *Charleston*, Spec.Serv.Sqdn. (Jan 1892-Aug 1894); rec. ship, *Independence*, Mare Island, CA (Aug-Sep 1894); home and l.o.a. (Sep-Nov 1894); w.o. (Nov 1894-Jan 1895); spec. duty, Senate Committee investigating Ford's Theatre disaster, Washington, DC (Jan-Mar 1895); in charge, Navy Hosp., Portsmouth, NH (Mar 1895-Jan 1898); member, then pres., medl.exam.bd., Washington, DC (Jan 1898-Apr 1901); in charge, Naval Hosp., Philadelphia (Apr 1901-May 1903); home and w.o. (May-Jun 1903); placed on Ret.Lst. (20 Jun 1903).

CHARLES WELLMAN PARKS Born on 22 Mar 1863 in Woburn, MA, son of Granville and Elizabeth Augusta (Carter) Parks. Attended Woburn High School and graduated from Rensselaer Polytechnic Institute of Troy, NY, receiving Certificate of engineering in 1884. Served as chief engineer of Denver, Memphis and Atlantic Railroad and of Chicago, Burlington and Quincy railroads. Headed dept. of physics at Rensselaer from 1885 to 1894, during which also studied as a graduate student at Gottingen University in Germany and served as electrical engineer for Electric Manufactoring Company of Troy, NY. Received LL.B. degree from Columbian University College of Law in Washington, DC in 1899, and in 1921 received honorary LL.D. degree from George Washington Univ. Served as supt. of liberal arts at Paris Exposition in 1889, and in 1893, was spec. agent for Bur. of Education at Chicago Exposition, where he exhibited a model town library of 5,000 volumes. Married Martha Bessac Frear on 14 Apr 1887. A member of numerous professional societies, resided in Washington, DC, dying on 25 Jun 1930, at Naval Hosp. there. Buried in Arlington National Cemetery.

CHARLES WELLMAN PARKS
1863-1930

Ranks Civil Engr. (19 Jul 1897); Civil Engr. with rel. rank of Ltjg (21 Mar 1898); Civil Engr. with rank of Lt (28 Feb 1901); Civil Engr. with rank of LCdr (18 Oct 1909); Civil Engr. with rank of Cdr (8 Aug 1913); Civil Engr. with rank of Capt (1 Jul 1917); Chief, Bur. of Yards and Docks with rank of RAdm (11 Jan 1918); placed on Ret.Lst. (1 Dec 1921).

Career Summary Received appointment from MA as Civil Engr. (19 Jul 1897); Navy Yard, Norfolk, VA (Jul 1897-Feb 1898); Navy Yard, NY (Feb-Jun 1898); Bur. of Yards and Docks, Washington, DC (Jun 1898-Aug 1899); Naval Sta., San Juan, Puerto Rico (Aug 1899-Jan 1903); Navy Yard, Boston (Jan 1903-Jul 1905); Navy Yard, Portsmouth, NH (Jul 1905-May 1908);

head, Dept. of Yards and Docks, Naval Station, Pearl Harbor, Territory of HI (Jun 1908-Feb 1910); return and Navy Dept., Washington DC (Feb-Apr 1910); inspection duty for Bur. of Yards and Docks with General Electric Company, Schenectedy, NY (Apr 1910-Feb 1912); public works off., Navy Yard, Philadelphia (Feb 1912-Dec 1914): temp. duty, Bur. of Yards and Docks, Navy Dept. Washington, DC (Dec 1914-Jan 1915); public works off., Naval Station, Pearl Harbor, Territory of HI (Jan 1915-Dec 1917); spec. duty, Navy Dept., Washington, DC (Jan 1918); Chief, Bur. of Yards and Docks, Navy Dept., Washington, DC (Jan 1918-Dec 1921); placed on Ret.Lst. (1 Dec 1921); spec.temp. duty, for Bur. of Yards and Docks, Key West, FL (Jan-Feb 1922).

Career Highlights   Most of his career to First World War centered on construction of dry docks for USN. During war, his building expertise was put to many imporant projects, including dirigible hangar at Lakehurst, NJ. For his efforts, received Distinguished Service Medal in 1919, and in 1920, France created him a cdr of Legion of Honor.

References

Writings: *Forestry Education* (Washington, DC: U.S. Bur. of Education, Report, Vol 1 (1893/94): 808-818.

WYTHE MARCHANT PARKS   Born in Norfolk, VA, on 8 Sep 1856, son of John W. and Victoria Parks. Educated at Norwood, VA, and at the Norfolk Academy. Married Lilian Baird on 17 Aug 1882. Two daughters and a son. Died on 17 Sep 1938.

Ranks   Asst.Engr. (8 May 1877); Asst.Engr. with rel. rank of Mstr (3 Mar 1882); PAsst.Engr. (22 Jun 1884); PAsst.Engr. with rel. rank of Ltjg (5 May 1892); Chief Engr. (27 Jun 1896); LCdr (3 Mar 1899); Cdr (6 Aug 1904); Capt (1 Jul 1908); RAdm (13 Feb 1913); placed on Ret.Lst. (8 Sep 1920).

Career Summary   Received appointment from VA (8 May 1877); w.o. (May-Jul 1877); *Hartford*, S.Atl.Sta. (Jul 1877-Dec 1879); w.o. (Dec 1879-Mar 1880); Navy Yard, Norfolk, VA (Mar-May 1880); *Alliance*, N.Atl.Sta. (May 1880-Jul 1882); w.o. (Jul-Aug 1882); USNA (Sep 1882-Aug 1885); *Tennessee,* and *Richmond*, N.Atl.Sta. (Aug 1885-Nov 1887); *Atlanta*, N.Atl.Sta. (Nov 1887-Aug 1888); w.o. (Aug-Nov 1888); Chicago Manual Training School, Chicago (Nov 1888-Jun 1891); w.o. (Jun-Sep 1891); *Atlanta*, S.Atl.Sta. (Sep 1891-Jul 1893); Navy Yard, Norfolk, VA (Jul 1893-Apr 1894); *Atlanta*, N.Atl.Sqdn. (Apr 1894-Jun 1895); home and l.o.a. (Jun-Jul 1895); Navy Yard, Norfolk, VA (Jul-Sep 1895); insp. of machinery, Newport News, VA (Sep 1895-Jan 1896); insp. of machinery, Columbia Iron Works, Baltimore (Jan-Feb 1896); insp. of machinery, Newport News, VA (Feb 1896); insp. of machinery, Columbia Iron Works, Baltimore (Feb 1896-Mar 1898); *Miantonomoh*, Pac.Sqdn. (Mar 1898-Mar 1899); Navy Yard, League Island, PA (Mar 1899); *Iowa*, Navy Yard, Puget Sound, WA, and Pac.Sqdn. (Mar 1899-Jul 1900); flt.engr., Pac.Sqdn., *Iowa* (Jul 1900-Mar 1901);

Bur. of Steam Engineering, Washington, DC (Apr 1901-Sep 1908); head, dept. of steam engineering, Navy Yard, NY (Sep 1908-Jun 1910); member, then pres., naval exam. and ret. bds., Washington, DC (Jun 1910-Jul 1913); additional duty, Civil Service Commission, Washington, DC (Jun 1910-Jul 1913); general insp. of machinery for navy, Philadelphia (Jul 1913-Sep 1920); placed on Ret.Lst. (8 Sep 1920).

References

Writings: a) "Training of Enlisted Men of the Engineers' Force," U.S. Naval Institute *Proceedings* 42 (1887): 341-68. b) "Building a War Ship in the Southern Confederacy," U.S. Naval Institute *Proceedings* 246 (Aug 1923): 1299-1307.

ROBERT EDWIN PEARY Born in Cresson, PA, on 6 May 1856, son of Charles N. and Mary (Wiley) Peary. Received Civil Engineering degree from Bowdoin College in 1877. Subsequently received the Sc.D. in 1894 and two LL.D. degrees from Univ. of Edinburgh and Tufts Univ. Served from 1879 to 1881 with the U.S. Coast and Geodetic Survey. Married Josephine Diebitsch in 1888. One daughter. Died at his home in Washington, DC, on 20 Feb 1920. Buried in Arlington National Cemetery.

ROBERT EDWIN PEARY
1856-1920

Ranks Civil Engr. with rel. rank of Lt (26 Oct 1881); Civil Engr. with rank of LCdr (5 Jan 1901); Civil Engr. with rank of Cdr (6 Apr 1902); Civil Engr. with rank of Capt (20 Oct 1909); transferred to Ret.Lst. (6 Apr 1909); Civil Engr. with rank of RAdm on Ret.Lst. (27 Mar 1911) to rank from 6 Apr 1909.

Career Summary Received appointment from ME (26 Oct 1881); w.o. (Oct-Dec 1881); Navy Yard, Washington, DC (Dec 1881-Nov 1882); spec. duty, Key West, FL (Nov 1882-Jun 1883); w.o. (Jun-Aug 1883); canal surv. duty, Coaster's Harbour Island, Nicaragua (Aug 1883-Aug 1885); spec. duty, Washington, DC (Aug 1885-Apr 1886); l.o.a., exploration of central Greenland (Apr 1886-Jan 1887); Bur. of Yards and Docks, Washington, DC (Jan-Oct 1887); l.o.a., engr.-in- chief, Nicaraguan Surv.Expd. (Oct 1887-Oct 1888); Navy Yard, NY (Oct 1888-Jan 1889); Navy Yard, League Island, PA (Jan 1889-Apr 1891); l.o.a., Greenland exploration (May 1891-Dec 1893); Navy Yard, Norfolk, VA (Dec 1893); l.o.a. (Dec 1893-Nov 1895); Navy Yard, NY (Nov 1895-Apr 1896); w.o. (Apr-May 1896); l.o.a. (May-Oct 1896); Navy Yard, NY (Nov 1896-May 1897); l.o.a. (May 1897-Nov 1902); temp. duty, Bur. of Yards and Docks, Washington, DC (Nov 1902-Sept 1903); member, bd. of barracks, England (Oct 1903-Apr 1904); l.o.a. (Apr 1904-Apr 1907); cst.surv. duty (Apr 1907-Apr 1910); transferred to Ret.Lst. (6 Apr 1909); technical advisor, Dept. of Justice, Washington, DC (Nov 1910-Mar 1911).

Career Highlights Peary's career was more that of a privately financed explorer than a naval officer. Most of his service career was spent on leave during which he made many remarkable explorations into the Arctic regions. Became first man to reach the North Pole on 6 Apr 1909, although his claim was long challenged. Was given the thanks of Congress and promoted to

RAdm on the Ret.Lst. for his efforts. His latter years were spent studying aviation. During World War I, founded National Aerial Coast Patrol Commission, and he chaired the National Committee on Coast Defense by Air. A member of many international organizations and congresses, he was awarded numerous medals and citations.

References

Personal Papers: a) c. 5 vols. (1906) in Chemung County Historical Society, Elmira, NY. b) correspondence with Edward Guild Wyckoff in Cornell Univ. Libraries, Ithaca, NY. c) 172 items (1890-94) in Academy of Natural Sciences Lib., Philadelphia.

Writings: a) *Northward over the "Great Ice"* (NY: 1898). b) *Nearest the Pole* (London: 1907). c) *Boy's Book of the Navy* (NY: 1907). d) *The North Pole* (NY: 1910). e) *Secrets of Polar Travel* (1917).

Other Sources: a) George Borup, *A Tenderfoot with Peary* (NY: 1911). b) Fitzhugh Green, "Rear Admiral Peary, U.S.N., Scientist and Arctic Explorer," U.S. Naval Institute *Proceedings* 231 (Aug 1922): 1315-24. c) Fitzhugh Green, *Peary: The Man Who Refused to Fail* (NY: 1926). d) James G. Hayes, *Robert Edwin Peary: A Record of His Exploits, 1886-1909* (London: 1929). e) Donald B. MacMillan, *How Peary Reached the Pole* (Boston: 1934). f) William H. Hobbs, *Peary* (NY: 1936). g) Hugh C. Mitchell, "Peary at the North Pole," U.S. Naval Institute *Proceedings* 674 (Apr 1959): 64-72. h) John Edward Weems, *Race for the Pole* (NY: 1960). i) _____, *Peary, the Explorer and the Man* (Boston: 1967). j) Dennis Rawlins, "Peary and the North Pole. The Lingering Doubt," U.S. Naval Institute *Proceedings* 808 (Jun 1970): 32-41. k) Theon Wright, *The Big Nail: The Story of the Cook-Peary Feud* (NY: 1970). l) Edward P. Stafford, "Peary and the North Pole: Not the Shadow of a Doubt," U.S. Naval Institute *Proceedings* 826 (Dec 1971): 44-53. m) Wally Herbert, "Commander Robert E. Peary: Did He Reach the Pole?" *National Geographic* 174 (Sep 1988): 387-413.

EDWIN CONWAY PENDLETON Born in Richmond, VA, on 27 May 1847, son of USNA prof. Alexander Garland and Selina Christiana (Dickson) Pendleton. Married Mary Riddle Saxton on 2 Apr 1872. One son. Died in Philadelphia on 28 Sep 1919.

Ranks Midn (10 Oct 1863); Ens (18 Dec 1868); Mstr (21 Mar 1870); Lt (21 Mar 1871); LCdr (4 Aug 1889); Cdr (21 Mar 1897); Capt (21 Jan 1902); RAdm (28 Aug 1907); placed on Ret.Lst. (27 May 1909).

Career Summary Received appointment at large (10 Oct 1863); USNA (Oct 1863-Jun 1867); training ship, *Minnesota*, then *Onward*, Pac.Sqdn. (Jul 1867-Jul 1870); home and w.o. (Jul-Aug 1870); Hydrographic Office, Washington, DC (Aug 1870-Mar 1871); *Portsmouth*, and *Wasp*, spec.serv. (Mar 1871-Jan 1872); home and w.o. (Jan-Mar 1872); ord. duty, Navy Yard, Washington, DC (Mar-Dec 1872); *Supply*, spec.serv. (Jan-Nov

EDWIN CONWAY PENDLETON
1847-1919

215 CHRISTIAN JOY PEOPLES

1873); ord. duty, Navy Yard, Washington, DC (Dec 1873-Mar 1874); *Congress*, Eur.Sta. (Mar 1874-Jul 1876); Navy Yard, Washington, DC (Sep 1876-May 1878); Torp.Sta., Newport, RI (Jun-Sep 1878); ord. duty, Navy Yard, Washington, DC (Sep 1878-Dec 1879); *Swatara*, Asia.Sta. (Dec 1879-Dec 1882); w.o. (Dec 1882-Jan 1883); Naval Observatory, Washington, DC (Jan 1883-Jun 1886); *Atlanta*, N.Atl.Sta. (Jul 1886-Nov 1888); ord. duty, Navy Yard, Washington, DC (Dec 1888-Dec 1892); spec. duty, *Monterey*, San Francisco (Dec 1892-Feb 1893); exec.off., *Monterey*, Pac.Sta. (Feb 1893-Sep 1895); Bur. of Ord., Washington, DC (Oct 1895-May 1897); supt., Naval Gun Factory, Navy Yard, Washington, DC (May 1897-Mar 1900); home and w.o. (Mar-May 1900); NWC (Jun-Sep 1900); cdr, *Atlanta*, S.Atl.Sqdn. (Sep 1900-Aug 1902); home and w.o. (Aug-Sep 1902); temp. duty, Bur. of Ord., Washington, DC (Sep-Oct 1902); supt., Naval Gun Factory, Navy Yard, Washington, DC (Oct 1902-Oct 1905); comdt., Navy Yard, Washington, DC (Jul-Oct 1905); cdr, *Missouri*, N.Atl.Flt. (Nov 1905-May 1907); comdt., Navy Yard, League Island, PA (Jun 1907-May 1909); placed on Ret.Lst. (27 May 1909).

CHRISTIAN JOY PEOPLES Born in Creston, IA, on 17 Oct 1876, son of Robert A. and Lydia (Love) Peoples. Moved to CA. Attended St. Ignatius College, Sacred Heart College, Vallejo High School, and took a special course at the Univ. of CA. Married Leila Warren on 18 Mar 1901. Two daughters. Resided in Washington, DC, and died at the Naval Hosp. there on 3 Feb 1941. Buried in Arlington National Cemetery.

Ranks Asst.Paymstr. (27 Mar 1900); Asst.Paymstr. with rank of Ltjg (1 Jul 1902); PAsst.Paymstr. (3 Mar 1903); Paymstr. (27 Dec 1903); Paymstr. with rank of LCdr (20 Feb 1910); RAdm (1 Jul 1917); placed on Ret.Lst. (1 Nov 1940).

Career Summary Received appointment from CA (27 Mar 1900); asst. general storekeeper, Navy Yard, Mare Island, CA (May-Dec 1900); Naval Sta., Puget Sound, WA (Dec 1900-Mar 1901); hosp. ship, *Solace*, Pac. Ocean (Apr-May 1901); supply off., *Wilmington*, Asia.Sta. (Jun 1901-Feb 1904); home and w.o. (Feb-May 1904); general storekeeper, Navy Yard, Norfolk, VA (May-Sep 1904); Bur. of Supplies and Accounts, Washington, DC (Sep 1904-Feb 1911); l.o.a. (Feb-Mar 1911); supply off., *Utah*, Atl.Flt. (Mar 1911-Aug 1914); general insp., Pay Corps, and asst. to chief, Bur. of Supplies and Accounts, Washington, DC (Aug 1914-May 1921); act.paymstr.gen, Washington, DC (Jan-May 1921); general insp., Supply Corps, for Pac.cst., San Francisco (May 1921-Mar 1930); in charge, Naval Supply Depot, Brooklyn, NY (Mar 1930-Jun 1933); paymstr.gen, and chief, Bur. of Supplies and Accounts, Washington, DC (Jun 1933-Jun 1935); dir., Procurement Div., U.S. Treasury, Washington, DC (Jun 1933-Oct 1939); general insp., Supply Corps for Pac.cst. (Oct 1939-Nov 1940); placed on Ret.Lst. (1 Nov 1940).

Career Highlights As chief of Bur. of Supplies and Accounts, developed the purchase system for the navy, standardized the steaming coal and fuel oil system, and was the navy's representative on the exports control commission during World War I. Also served on the War Industries Board.

THOMAS PERRY
1844-1918

THOMAS PERRY Born in Elmira, NY, on 26 May 1844, son of Guy Maxwell and Elizabeth Asia (Taylor) Perry. Resided in Port Deposit, MD. Died on 7 Mar 1918 at Southern Pines, NC.

Ranks Act.Midn (25 Sep 1861); title changed to Midn (16 Jul 1865); Ens (1 Dec 1866); Mstr (12 Mar 1868); Lt (26 Mar 1869); LCdr (6 Nov 1881); Cdr (10 Jan 1892); Capt (11 Jun 1899); RAdm (8 Sep 1905); placed on Ret.Lst. (26 May 1906).

Career Summary Received appointment from NY (25 Sep 1861); USNA (Sep 1861-Oct 1865); w.o. (Oct-Nov 1865); schoolship, *Sabine* (Nov 1865-Feb 1866); *Chattanooga*, Philadelphia (Feb-Aug 1866); *Pensacola*, N.Pac.Sqdn. (Aug 1866-May 1869); w.o. (May-Jun 1869); *Dictator*, N.Atl.Sta. (Jul-Sep 1869); l.o.a. (Sep-Nov 1869); *Miantonomoh*, spec.serv. (Nov 1869-Jul 1870); *Shenandoah*, Eur.Sqdn. (Aug 1870-Apr 1873); l.o.a. (Apr-Nov 1873); *Manhattan*, N.Atl.Sta. (Nov 1873-Jul 1874); w.o. (Jul-Sep 1874); l.o.a. (Oct 1874-Feb 1875); rec. ship, *Vermont*, NY (Feb-May 1875); *Omaha*, S.Pac.Sqdn. (Jul 1875-Apr 1878); w.o. and l.o.a. (Apr-Oct 1878); Naval Observatory, Washington, DC (Oct 1878-Sep 1879); w.o. (Sep-Dec 1879); *Swatara*, Asia. Sta. (Dec 1879-Dec 1882); w.o. (Dec 1882-Feb 1883); asst.insp., 5th L.h. Dist., Baltimore (Feb 1883-Nov 1884); insp., 14th L.h. Dist., Cincinnati, OH (Nov 1884-Feb 1887); *Boston*, Chester, PA (Feb-May 1887); sick lv. (May-Aug 1887); *Brooklyn*, Asia.Sta. (Sep 1887-May 1889); w.o. (May-Jul 1889); Navy Dept., Washington, DC (Jul-Dec 1889); asst.insp., 3rd L.h. Dist., Tompkinsville, NY (Dec 1889-Jan 1890); insp., 12th L.h. Dist., San Francisco (Feb 1890-Dec 1892); w.o. (Dec 1892-Feb 1894); general insp., then cdr, *Castine*, Bath, ME (Feb-Mar 1894); sick lv. (Mar-May 1894); NWC, and torp. instruction, Newport, RI (May-Sep 1894); cdr, *Castine*, N.Atl.Sqdn. (Oct 1894-Dec 1896); l.o.a. (Dec 1896-Jun 1897); NWC (Jun-Jul 1897); asst., then insp., 1st L.h. Dist., Portland, ME (Jul 1897-May 1898); cdr, *Lancaster*, N.Atl.Flt. (May 1898-Mar 1899); sec., L.h. Bd., Washington, DC (Mar 1899-Mar 1901); cdr, *Iowa*, Pac. and N. Atl.Stas. (Apr 1901-May 1903); capt.yd., Navy Yard, NY (May 1903-May 1904); comdt., Navy Yard, and cdr, 8th Naval Dist., Pensacola, FL (May 1904-May 1905); pres., naval exam. bd. (May 1905-May 1906); placed on Ret.Lst. (26 May 1906).

THOMAS STOWELL PHELPS, JR. Born in Portsmouth, VA, on 7 Nov 1848, son of RAdm Thomas Stowell [1822-1901] and Margaret Riche (Levy) Phelps. Married Elwena Dewees Martin on 18 Oct 1877. One daughter. Resided in Oakland, CA, where he died on 3 Nov 1915.

Ranks Master's Mate (20 Sep 1864); resigned (31 Dec 1864); Captain's Clerk (5 Apr 1865); resigned (20 Jul 1865); Midn (26 Jul 1865); Ens (12 Jul 1870); Mstr (29 Oct 1872); Lt (15 Mar 1876); LCdr (7 Nov 1897); Cdr (19 Aug 1900); Capt (26 Mar

THOMAS STOWELL PHELPS, JR.
1848-1915

1905); RAdm (24 Jul 1909); placed on Ret.Lst. (7 Nov 1910).

Career Summary Master's Mate, cst.surv. steamer, *Corwin* (Sep-Dec 1864); resigned (31 Dec 1864); Captain's Clerk, *Lenapee*, N.Atl.Blk.Sqdn. (Apr-Jul 1865); resigned (20 Jul 1865); received appointment as Midn by virtue of being the son of an officer (26 Jul 1865); USNA (Jul 1865-Jul 1869); *Juniata*, and flgs., *Franklin*, Eur.Sta. (Jul 1869-Nov 1871); w.o. (Nov 1871-Mar 1872); *Lackawanna*, Navy Yard, Mare Island, CA (Mar-Jun 1872); rec. ship, *Independence*, Mare Island, CA (Jun 1872-Nov 1873); *Kearsarge*, Navy Yard, Mare Island, CA (Nov-Dec 1873); sick lv. (Dec 1873-Apr 1874); *Richmond*, N.Pac.Sqdn. (Apr-Oct 1874); *Narragansett*, spec.serv. (Oct 1874-Apr 1875); w.o. (Apr 1875-Feb 1876); rec. ship, *Independence*, Mare Island, CA (Feb-Aug 1876); *Pensacola*, Pac.Sqdn. (Aug 1876-Aug 1879); home and w.o. (Aug-Dec 1879); Naval Rndv., San Francisco (Dec 1879); w.o. (Dec 1879-Sep 1880); Naval Rndv., San Francisco (Sep 1880-Mar 1881); w.o. (Mar-Apr 1881); Navy Yard, Mare Island, CA (Apr 1881-Apr 1882); *Iroquois*, Pac.Sta. (Apr-May 1882); w.o. (May-Jun 1882); Navy Yard, Mare Island, CA (Jun-Sep 1882); *Wachusett*, Pac.Sta. (Oct 1882-Jan 1883); on furlough (Jan-Mar 1883); *Brooklyn*, S.Atl.Sta. (Jun 1883-Oct 1884); w.o. (Oct 1884-Mar 1885); Navy Yard, Mare Island, CA (Mar-May 1885); *Mohican*, Navy Yard, Mare Island, CA (May 1885); *Hartford*, Pac.Sta. (May 1885-Jan 1887); w.o. (Jan-Sep 1887); *Palos*, Asia.Sta. (Oct 1887-Feb 1891); home and w.o. (Feb-Aug 1891); rec. ship, *Independence*, Mare Island, CA (Aug 1891-Feb 1895); *Olympia*, Navy Yard, Mare Island, CA (Feb-Aug 1895); w.o. (Aug-Sep 1895); flgs., *Philadelphia*, Pac.Sqdn. (Sep 1895-Sep 1896); exec.off., *Alert*, Pac.Sqdn. (Sep 1896-Dec 1897); l.o.a. (Dec 1897-Jan 1898); spec. duty, State Dept., Washington, DC (Jan-Feb 1898); w.o. (Feb-Mar 1898); Navy Yard, Mare Island, CA (Mar-Apr 1898); in charge, Recruiting Rndv., San Francisco (Apr-May 1898); exec.off., *Raleigh*, Asia.Sta. (May 1898-Jun 1899); home and w.o. (Jun-Jul 1899); Navy Yard, Mare Island, CA (Aug-Nov 1899); exec.off., rec. ship, *Independence*, Mare Island, CA (Nov 1899-Feb 1900); equip.off., Navy Yard, Mare Island, CA (Feb 1900-Nov 1902); cdr, *Marblehead*, Pac. Sqdn. (Nov 1902-Oct 1904); home and w.o. (Oct-Nov 1904); judge advocate, court of inquiry, Navy Yard, Bremerton, WA (Nov 1904-Jan 1905); bd. duties, Navy Yard, Mare Island, CA (Feb-Apr 1905); in charge, Naval Recruiting Sta., San Francisco (Apr 1905-Nov 1906); Navy Yard, Mare Island, CA (Nov 1906-Jul 1907); cdr, *California*, Pac.Flt. (Aug-Oct 1907); comdt., Navy Yard and Naval Sta., Mare Island, CA (Oct 1907-Mar 1910); senior member, bd. to conduct survs. of Pac.cst. (Apr-Nov 1910); comdt., 13th Naval Dist., Portland, OR (Apr-Sep 1910); comdt., 12th Naval Dist., San Francisco (Apr-Nov 1910); placed on Ret.Lst. (7 Nov 1910).

GEORGE WOOD PIGMAN Born in Delphi, IN, on 19 Dec 1843, son of George W. and Caroline (Swarmstead) Pigman. Married Lillie C. Howard on 7 Nov 1871. Two children, including

GEORGE WOOD PIGMAN
1843-1920

a son, Cdr George W. Pigman, Jr., USN (SC). Resided in Takoma Park, MD. Died in Washington, DC, on 30 Jun 1920.

Ranks Act.Midn (28 Sep 1861); title changed to Midn (16 Jul 1862); Ens (1 Nov 1866); Mstr (1 Dec 1866); Lt (12 Mar 1868); LCdr (28 Oct 1869); Cdr (7 Oct 1886); Capt (3 Mar 1899); RAdm (3 Oct 1904); retired (11 Jan 1905).

Career Summary Received appointment from IN (28 Sep 1861); USNA (Sep 1861-Nov 1864); l.o.a. (Nov 1864-Feb 1865); Navy Yard, NY (Feb-Jun 1865); training ship, *Sabine* (Jun-Sep 1865); flgs., *Brooklyn*, and *Huron*, S.Atl.Sta. (Oct 1865-Sep 1868); w.o. (Sep-Nov 1868); Naval Sta., Mound City, IL (Nov 1868-Apr 1869); *Saugus*, N.Atl.Sqdn. (Apr 1869-May 1870); w.o. (Jun-Sep 1870); USNA (Sep 1870-Jul 1872); *Yantic*, and flgs., *Hartford*, Asia.Sta. (Aug 1872-Oct 1875); w.o. (Oct 1875-Feb 1876); Naval Observatory, Washington, DC (Mar 1876-May 1879); exec.off., *Wachusett*, S.Atl.Sta. (May 1879-Jan 1882); exec.off., training ship, *Jamestown* (Jan-Jun 1882); w.o. (Jun-Sep 1882); Hydrographic Office, Washington, DC (Sep 1882-May 1885); torp. instruction, Newport, RI (Jun-Sep 1885); NWC (Sep 1885); w.o. (Sep-Oct 1885); exec.off., flgs., *Tennessee*, N.Atl. Sqdn. (Oct 1885-Jan 1886); w.o. (Feb 1886-Jan 1888); cdr, *Alliance*, S.Atl.Sta. (Apr 1888-Aug 1889); insp. of ord., Navy Yard, League Island, PA (Jan 1890-Jan 1891); w.o. (Jan-Mar 1891); ord. instruction, Navy Yard, Washington, DC (Mar-Jul 1891); cdr, *Enterprise*, N.Atl.Sta. (Jul-Oct 1891); w.o. (Oct 1891-Mar 1892); cdr of monitors, Richmond, VA (Mar 1892-Jun 1895); cdr, *Bennington*, Pac.Sta. (Jul 1895-Jan 1897); l.o.a. (Jan-Feb 1897); ord. instruction, Navy Yard, Washington, DC (Mar-Apr 1897); insp. of ord., Newport News, VA (Apr 1897-May 1899); cdr, *Charleston*, Asia.Sta. (Jul-Nov 1899); cdr, *Monterey*, Asia.Sta. (Dec 1899-Jul 1901); home, w.o., and bd. duties (Jul-Dec 1901); cdr, rec. ship, *Wabash*, Boston (Dec 1901-Oct 1904); home and w.o. (Oct 1904-Jan 1905); retired (11 Jan 1905).

JOHN ELLIOTT PILLSBURY Born in Lowell, MA, on 15 Dec 1846, son of John Gilman and Elizabeth Wimble (Smith) Pillsbury. Served as a page in the House of Representatives at age fourteen. Married Florence Greenwood Atchinson on 26 Aug 1873. One daughter. Died in Washington, DC, on 30 Dec 1919. Buried in Arlington National Cemetery.

Ranks Midn (22 Sep 1862); Ens (18 Dec 1868); Mstr (21 Mar 1870); Lt (1 Jan 1872); LCdr (1 Jul 1892); Cdr (10 Aug 1898); Capt (21 Nov 1902); RAdm (4 Jul 1908); placed on Ret.Lst. (15 Dec 1908).

Career Summary Received appointment at large (22 Sep 1862); USNA (Sep 1862-Jun 1867); found deficient and turned back (Feb 1863); *Minnesota*, and *Saginaw*, spec. duty (Jul 1867-Apr 1869); w.o. (May-Jun 1869); Navy Yard, Boston (Jun 1869-Jan 1870); flgs., *Colorado*, and *Benicia*, Asia.Sta. (Feb 1870-Sep 1872); Navy Yard, Boston (Oct 1872)-Sep 1873); torp. duty, Newport, RI (Sep 1873-Apr 1874); *Swatara*, spec.serv. (May

JOHN ELLIOTT PILLSBURY
1846-1919

1874-Jun 1875); cst.surv. duty (Jun 1875-Feb 1877); sick lv. (Feb-Oct 1877); Hydrographic Office, Washington, DC (Oct 1877-May 1879); *Kearsarge*, N.Atl.Sta. (May 1879-Jun 1882); w.o. (Jun-Jul 1882); cst.surv. duty (Jul 1882-Jan 1891); *Newark*, Philadelphia, and N.Atl.Sqdn. (Jan 1891-Jul 1893); home and l.o.a. (Jul-Oct 1893); Navy Yard, Boston (Oct 1893-Oct 1895); NWC (Oct 1895-Jan 1897); cdr, *Vesuvius*, N.Atl.Flt. (Jan 1897-Sep 1898); equip.off., Navy Yard, Boston (Sep 1898-Sep 1901); general insp., then cdr, *Prairie*, spec.serv. and training ship (Apr 1901-Oct 1902); member, Gen Bd. and other bd. duties, Washington, DC (Oct 1902-Feb 1904); asst. to chief, Bur. of Nav., Washington, DC (Nov 1903-Mar 1905); l.o.a. (Jul-Sep 1904); chief of staff, Atl.Flt., *Maine* (Mar 1905-Apr 1907), then *Connecticut* (Apr-Jun 1907); Bur. of Nav., Washington, DC (Jun-Sep 1907); member, Gen Bd. and Army-Navy Joint Bd., Washington, DC (Sep 1907-Jan 1908); chief, Bur. of Nav., Washington, DC (Jan 1908-Jun 1909); placed on Ret.Lst. (15 Dec 1908).

Career Highlights Spent vast majority of his career with surv. duties and particularly with the investigations of currents in the Gulf Stream, using instruments of measure of his own design and invention. After retirement, served as pres. of National Geographic Society.

References

Writings: a) "Charts and Chart Making," U.S. Naval Institute *Proceedings* 29 (1884): 187-202. b) *The Gulf Stream: Methods of the Investigation and Results of the Research* (Washington, DC: 1891, 1894). c) "Wilkes' and D'Urville's Discoveries in Wilkes Land," U.S. Naval Institute *Proceedings* 134 (Jun 1910): 465-68.

CHARLES FREMONT POND Born in Brooklyn, CT, on 26 Oct 1856, son of Enoch and Sarah Ann (Utley) Pond. On 10 Aug 1880, married Emma McHenry. Three children. Retired to Berkeley, CA, where he died on 4 Aug 1929.

Ranks Cadet Midn (13 Jun 1872); Midn (20 Jun 1876); Ens (22 Jul 1878); Ltjg (2 Oct 1885); Lt (19 May 1891); LCdr (13 Jul 1899); Cdr (31 Mar 1905); Capt (12 Nov 1908); RAdm (13 Feb 1914); retired (30 Dec 1918).

Career Summary Received appointment from CT (13 Jun 1872); USNA (Jun 1872-Jun 1876); summer cruise (Jun-Aug 1876); w.o. (Aug-Oct 1876); *Pensacola*, Pac.Sta. (Oct 1876-Aug 1877); *Lackawanna*, Pac.Sta. (Aug-Dec 1877); *Tuscarora*, Navy Yard, Mare Island, CA (Dec 1877-Feb 1878); schoolship, *Jamestown* (Feb-Oct 1878); w.o. (Oct 1878-Mar 1879); USNA (Mar-Apr 1879); w.o. (Apr-May 1879); cst.surv. duty (May 1879-Feb 1883); w.o. (Feb-Jul 1883); Hydrographic Office, Washington, DC (Jul 1883-Feb 1884); branch hydrographic office, San Francisco (Feb-Mar 1884); *Hartford*, Pac.Sqdn. (Apr-Sep 1884); *Wachusett*, Pac.Sqdn. (Sep 1884-Aug 1885); Navy Yard, Mare Island, CA (Aug 1885-Mar 1886); cst.surv. duty (Mar-Jul 1886); Navy Yard, Mare Island, CA (Jul 1886-Sep 1887); *Ranger*, spec. surv. duty (Sep 1887-Sep 1890); w.o. (Sep-Nov 1890); Navy

CHARLES FREMONT POND
1856-1929

Yard, Mare Island, CA (Dec 1890-Apr 1894); *Alert,* Pac.Sqdn. (Apr 1894-Apr 1897); home and l.o.a. (Apr-Jul 1897); asst. insp. of ord., Navy Yard, NY (Jul 1897-Apr 1898); *Lebanon,* Navy Yard, Boston (Apr-May 1898); *Panther,* N.Atl.Flt. (May-Oct 1898); exec.off., *Arethusa,* Navy Yard, Mare Island, CA (Oct 1898); cdr, *Iroquois,* Navy Yard, Mare Island, CA (Oct 1898-Dec 1901); temp. duty, comdt., Naval Sta., Honolulu, Territory of HI (Nov 1900-Jan 1902); home and w.o. (Jan-Feb 1902); Training Sta., San Francisco (Apr 1902-Mar 1904); cdr, *Supply,* Guam (Apr 1904-Jun 1905); home and w.o. (Jun-Sep 1905); insp. of ord., Mare Island, CA (Oct 1905-Apr 1907); temp. duty, cdr, supply ship, *Lawton,* Asia.Sta. (Dec 1905-Mar 1906); cdr, *Buffalo,* Pac.Sta. (Apr 1907-Jun 1908); insp., 13th L.h. Dist., Portland, OR (Jun 1908-Jun 1909); cdr, *Pennsylvania,* Pac.Sta. (Jul 1909-Mar 1912); cdr, *Oregon* and *St. Louis,* Pac. Reserve Sqdn., Puget Sound, WA (Jul 1911-Mar 1912); comdt., 12th Naval Dist., San Francisco (Mar 1912-Apr 1915); cdr, Pac. Reserve Flt., *South Dakota* (Apr-Oct 1915); cdr, Auxiliary Div., Atl.Flt., *Vestal* (Dec 1915-Jul 1916); cdr., Cruiser Force, Atl.Flt., *Memphis* (Jul-Nov 1916), *Hancock* (Nov 1916), *Olympia* (Nov 1916); Naval Hosp., Washington, DC (Nov-Dec 1916); home and w.o. (Dec 1916-Jan 1917); l.o.a. (Jan-Jun 1917); on furlough (Jun 1917-Dec 1918); placed on Ret.Lst. (30 Dec 1918).

References

Personal Papers: 4 cartons (1876-1929) in BL.

Writings: "Naval Discipline," U.S. Naval Institute *Proceedings* 144 (Dec 1912): 1369-77.

WILLIAM PARKER POTTER
1850-1917

WILLIAM PARKER POTTER Born in Whitehall, NY, on 10 May 1850. Married with one daughter. Died at his home in Whitehall on 21 Jun 1917. Buried in Arlington National Cemetery.

Ranks Midn (26 Sep 1865); Ens (12 Jul 1870); Mstr (12 Jul 1871); Lt (9 Aug 1874); LCdr (12 Jun 1896); Cdr (9 Sep 1899); Capt (13 Sep 1904); RAdm (30 Oct 1908); placed on Ret.Lst. (10 May 1912).

Career Summary Received appointment from NY (26 Sep 1865); USNA (Sep 1865-Jun 1869); *Sabine,* spec. cruise (Jun-Dec 1869); flgs., *Franklin,* Eur.Sta. (Dec 1869-Nov 1871); w.o. (Nov 1871-Feb 1872); prac. ship, *Constellation* (Feb-Jun 1872); w.o. (Jun-Jul 1872); l.o.a. (Jul-Oct 1872); flgs., *Hartford,* Asia.Sta. (Oct 1872-Aug 1873); *Lackawanna,* Asia.Sta. (Aug 1873-Apr 1874); *Iroquois,* Asia.Sta. (Apr 1874-Jul 1874); w.o. and l.o.a. (Jul-Nov 1874); USNA (Nov 1874-Aug 1878); flag sec., N.Atl. Sta., *Powhatan* and *Marion* (Aug 1878-Dec 1879): flgs., *Tennessee,* N.Atl.Sta. (Dec 1879-Sep 1881); USNA (Sep 1881-Jun 1884); flgs., *Lancaster,* Eur. and S.Atl.Stas. (Jul 1884-Jun 1887); home and w.o. (Jun-Sep 1887); USNA (Sep 1887-Jun 1891); flgs., *Philadelphia,* N.Atl.Sta. (Jun 1891-Sep 1892); flgs., *Baltimore,* Spec.Serv.Sqdn. (Sep 1892-Mar 1893); flag lt, *Philadelphia,* Naval Review Flt. (Mar-May 1893); flag sec., *Chicago,* Eur.Sqdn. (Jun 1893-Sep 1894); l.o.a. (Oct 1894-Jan 1895); USNA (Jan 1895-

Sep 1897); exec.off., flgs., *New York*, N.Atl.Sta. (Sep 1897-Oct 1899); home and w.o. (Oct 1899); insp. of ord., Navy Yard, League Island, PA (Nov 1899-Oct 1901); cdr, *Ranger*, spec. duty, and Pac.Sta. (Nov 1901-Jun 1903); home and w.o. (Jun-Jul 1903); spec. temp. duty, Navy Dept., Washington, DC (Jul 1903-Mar 1905); asst., Bur. of Nav., Washington, DC (Mar 1905-May 1907); cdr, *Vermont*, 1st Div., "Great White Flt." (Jun 1907-Sep 1908); cdr, 2nd Div., "Great White Flt.," *Georgia* (Sep-Nov 1908); cdr, 4th Div., "Great White Flt.," *Wisconsin* (Nov 1908-Jun 1909); chief, Bur. of Nav., Washington, DC (Jul-Dec 1909); aide for personnel, Navy Dept., Washington, DC (Dec 1909-Jan 1912); l.o.a. (Jan-May 1912); placed on Ret.List (10 May 1912).

Career Highlights Member of the *Maine* court of inquiry looking into that ship's explosion in Feb 1898. Was the exec.off. on the *New York* during Spanish-American War, participating in the Battle of Santiago on 3 Jul 1898, being advanced five numbers for conspicuous conduct.

ROBERT POTTS Born in Dublin, Ireland, on 8 May 1835, son of Robert and Mary (Thompson) Potts. Educated in public schools of NY City. Married Fannie Griffith on 25 Jan 1876. Resided in Baltimore. Died in the Naval Hosp. in Washington, DC, on 24 Jun 1913.

Ranks 3rd Asst.Engr. (17 Feb 1860); 2nd Asst.Engr. (27 Jun 1862); 1st Asst.Engr. (1 Mar 1864); Chief Engr. (22 Jan 1873); Chief Engr. with rel. rank of Cdr (16 Feb 1892); Chief Engr. with rel. rank of Capt (27 Jun 1896); placed on Ret.Lst. (8 May 1897); Chief Engr. with rank of RAdm on Ret.Lst. (29 Jun 1906).

Career Summary Received appointment from PA (17 Feb 1860); w.o. (Feb-Apr 1860); *Niagara*, Pac. and S.Atl.Blk.Sqdns. (Apr 1860-Jun 1862); asst. to chief engr., NY (Jun-Oct 1862); w.o. (Oct-Nov 1862); *Dacotah*, Navy Yard, NY (Nov 1862); *Montauk*, S.Atl.Blk.Sqdn. (Nov 1862-Jul 1863); w.o. (Aug-Sep 1863); *Vicksburg*, Navy Yard, NY (Oct 1863); *Wachusett*, Navy Yard, Philadelphia (Oct-Nov 1863); *Kansas*, Navy Yard, Philadelphia, and N.Atl.Blk.Sqdn. (Nov 1863-May 1865); w.o. (May-Jun 1865); *Chicopee*, N.Atl.Sta. (Jun 1865-Dec 1866); w.o. (Dec 1866-Feb 1867); spec. duty, *Richmond*, Navy Yard, Boston (Feb-May 1867); *Guerriere*, S.Atl.Sta. (May 1867-Jul 1869); w.o. (Jul-Sep 1869); Navy Yard, NY (Sep 1869-Dec 1870); *Nipsic*, W.Indies, and Central America (Dec 1870-Nov 1872); w.o. (Nov 1872-Jul 1873); *Alaska*, Eur.Sta. (Aug 1873-Oct 1875); home and w.o. (Oct 1875-Jan 1876); insp. of coal, and on spec. duty, Philadelphia (Feb 1876-Jun 1878); Navy Yard, League Island, PA (Jul 1878-Feb 1879); w.o. (Feb-Jul 1879); *Michigan*, on Great Lakes (Jul 1879-May 1882); *Adams*, N.Pac.Sta. (Jun 1882-Sep 1884); w.o. (Sep 1884-Aug 1885); insp. of machinery, William Cramp and Sons Iron Works, Philadelphia (Aug 1885-Aug 1890); w.o. (Aug 1890-Jan 1891); *Baltimore*, S.Pac.Sta. (Feb 1891-Aug 1893); l.o.a. (Aug-Sep 1893); insp. of boiler tubes, New Castle, DE, and elsewhere (Sep 1893-Aug 1895); Navy Yard, Boston (Aug 1895-May 1897); placed on Ret.Lst. (8 May 1897).

References
Personal Papers: 1 vol. (1859-1901) in Philadelphia Maritime Museum, Philadelphia.

EBENEZER SCUDDER PRIME Born in NY City on 16 Jan 1847, son of Edward Youngs and Emma (Cotrel) Prime. Early education in Sandusky, OH. Married Eva Prime on 21 Nov 1883. Resided in Huntington, NY, where he died on 27 Apr 1912. Buried in Huntington.

Ranks Midn (21 Sep 1863); Ens (19 Apr 1869); Mstr (12 Jul 1870); Lt (5 Jun 1874); LCdr (29 Dec 1895); Cdr (3 Mar 1899); Capt (24 Aug 1904); retired (25 Jun 1905); RAdm on Ret.Lst. (13 Apr 1911) to rank from 25 Jun 1905.

Career Summary Received appointment from OH (21 Sep 1863); USNA (Sep 1863-Jun 1868); found deficient and turned back (Jun 1865); w.o. (Jun-Sep 1868); *Mohican*, Pac.Sqdn. (Oct 1868-Sep 1869); home and w.o. (Sep-Nov 1869); *Frolic*, Navy Yard, NY (Nov 1869-Feb 1870); *Swatara*, N.Atl.Sta. (Feb 1870-Jan 1872); w.o. (Jan-Apr 1872); rec. ship, *Vermont*, NY (Apr-Nov 1872); *Kansas*, surv. duty (Nov 1872-Sep 1873); *Yantic*, Asia.Sta. (Oct 1873-Sep 1875); home and w.o. (Sep 1875-Jan 1876); rec. ship, *Colorado*, NY (Jan-Apr 1876); *Lackawanna*, N.Pac.Sta. (Apr 1876-Jan 1878); rec. ship, *Independence*, Mare Island, CA (Jan-Mar 1878); cst.surv. duty (Mar 1878-Feb 1879); w.o. (Feb-Apr 1879); training ship, *Minnesota* (Apr 1879-Jul 1880); Navy Yard, Norfolk, VA (Jul-Sep 1880); *Yantic*, N.Atl.Sta. (Sep 1880-Oct 1883); w.o. (Oct-Nov 1883); Navy Yard, NY (Nov 1883-Apr 1884); torp. instruction, Newport, RI (Apr-Aug 1884); Navy Yard, NY (Aug 1884-Sep 1886); *Lancaster*, and *Alliance*, S.Atl. and Eur.Stas. (Sep 1886-Apr 1889); *Quinnebaug*, Eur.Sta. (Apr-Jun 1889); w.o. (Jun-Sep 1889); training ship, *New Hampshire* (Sep 1889-Oct 1890); training ship, *Richmond* (Oct 1890-Jun 1891); Navy Yard, NY (Jun 1891-May 1893); exec.off., *Concord*, spec. cruise (May-Aug 1893); Naval Hosp., NY (Aug-Sep 1893); en route to Asia.Sta. (Sep-Dec 1893); exec.off., *Concord*, Asia.Sta. (Jan 1894-May 1896); home and l.o.a. (May-Nov 1896); insp. of ord., Bethlehem Steel Company, S.Bethlehem, PA (Nov 1896-Jan 1897); inspector of steel, Harrisburg, PA (Jan-Sep 1897); Navy Yard, Pensacola, FL (Oct 1897-May 1898); cdr, *Niagara*, N.Atl.Flt. (May-Oct 1898); equip.off., Navy Yard, League Island, PA (Oct 1898-Jul 1900); home and w.o. (Jul-Aug 1900); NWC (Aug-Sep 1900); w.o. (Sep-Oct 1900); cdr, *Brutus*, Asia.Sta. (Nov 1900-Jan 1901); cdr, *Petrel*, Asia.Sta. (Apr 1901); cdr, *Wilmington*, Asia.Sta. (Apr 1901-Dec 1902); cdr, Naval Sta., Olongapo, P.I. (Dec 1902-Jan 1903); home and w.o. (Jan-Apr 1903); capt.yd., Navy Yard, Port Royal, SC (May 1903-Sep 1905); comdt., Navy Yard, and Sixth Naval Dist., Charleston, SC (May-Sep 1905); retired (25 Jun 1905).

FRANKLIN COGSWELL PRINDLE Born in Sandgate, VT, on 8 Jul 1841, son of Hawley and Olive (Andrew) Prindle.

FRANKLIN COGSWELL PRINDLE
1841-1923

Received early education in public schools and then at the Rensselaer Polytechnic Institute in Troy, NY. Married three times. First wife was Gertrude A. Sticke, whom he married on 19 May 1864. Second wife was Sarah A. Cranston, whom he married on 25 Sep 1878, and his third wife was Mrs. Fidelia E. (White) Mead, whom he married on 8 Apr 1896. In addition to duties in the navy, he served as engr. and off. to several companies, including the American Dredging Company of Philadelphia, the Carolina Oil and Cresote Company of Wilmington, NC, and the Aztec Oil Company of Bakersfield, CA. His home was Washington, DC, where he died on 7 Mar 1923. Buried in Arlington National Cemetery.

Ranks 3rd Asst.Engr. (3 Aug 1861); 2nd Asst.Engr. (21 Apr 1863); resigned (11 Sep 1865); appointed Civil Engr. (17 Apr 1869); resigned (31 Dec 1875); reappointed Civil Engr. (22 Jul 1879); Civil Engr. with rel. rank of LCdr (16 Feb 1882); Civil Engr. with rel. rank of Cdr (1 Sep 1898); Civil Engr. with rel. rank of Capt (5 Jan 1901); retired as Civil Engr. with rank of RAdm (27 Feb 1901).

Career Summary Received appointment from PA (3 Aug 1861); *Ottawa*, S.Atl.Blk.Sqdn. (Sep 1861-May 1864); l.o.a. (May 1864); spec. duty, Novelty Iron Works, NY (May 1864-May 1865); spec. duty, NY (May-Sep 1865); resigned (11 Sep 1865); appointed (17 Apr 1869); Navy Yard, Philadelphia (Apr 1869-Apr 1872); Navy Yard, League Island, PA (Apr 1872-Aug 1875); l.o.a. (Aug-Dec 1875); resigned (31 Dec 1875); reappointed (22 Jul 1879); Navy Yard, NY (Jul 1879-Apr 1885); w.o. (Apr-May 1885); l.o.a. (May 1885-Apr 1887); spec. duty, NY (Apr-May 1887); w.o. (May-Jun 1887); spec. duty, Bur. of Yards and Docks, Washington, DC (Jun-Jul 1887); w.o. (Jul 1887-Jan 1888); spec. duty, Wilmington, NC (Jan-Feb 1888); w.o. (Feb-Apr 1888); spec. duty, Wilmington, NC (Apr-Sep 1888); Naval Asylum, Philadelphia (Sep-Oct 1888); spec. duty, Norfolk, VA (Oct-Nov 1888); l.o.a. (Nov 1888-Apr 1890); Navy Yard, Portsmouth, NH (Jun-Dec 1890); Navy Yard, Boston (Dec 1890-Dec 1893); Navy Yard, Portsmouth, NH (Dec 1893-Aug 1894); Naval Sta., Puget Sound, Bremerton, WA (Aug-Dec 1894); Navy Yard, NY (Dec 1894-Mar 1895); Navy Yard, Norfolk, VA (Mar-Apr 1895); temp. duty, Navy Yard, NY (Apr 1895-Oct 1897); sick lv. (Oct-Dec 1897); Navy Yard, NY (Dec 1897-Feb 1898); sick lv. (Feb-May 1898); Navy Yard, Mare Island, CA (May-Nov 1898); Training Sta., Yerba Buena Island, San Francisco Bay (Nov 1898-Jul 1900); Naval Sta., Honolulu, Territory of HI (Jul 1900-Jan 1901); home and w.o. (Jan-Feb 1901); retired (27 Feb 1901).

ARTHUR JOHN PRITCHARD Born in East New Market, MD, on 12 Feb 1836, son of Nicholas B. and Elizabeth A. Pritchard. Educated in public schools. Married Sarah E. Harrington on 19 Oct 1871. Resided in Baltimore, where he died on 5 Sept 1916. Buried at Madison, MD.

Ranks Asst.Paymstr. (7 Oct 1861); Paymstr. (9 Nov 1864); Pay Insp. (24 Dec 1883); Pay Dir. (10 Apr 1895); placed on

ARTHUR JOHN PRITCHARD
1836-1916

placed on Ret.Lst. (12 Feb 1898); Pay Dir. with rank of RAdm on Ret.Lst. (29 Jun 1906).

Career Summary Received appointment from MD (7 Oct 1861); w.o. (Oct-Nov 1861); *Itasca*, W.Gulf Blk.Sqdn. (Dec 1861-Feb 1863); sick lv. (Feb-Jul 1863); *Itasca*, W.Gulf Blk.Sqdn. (Jul-Oct 1863); s.a. and w.o. (Oct-Dec 1863); *Wyalusing*, N.Atl. Blk.Sqdn. (Dec 1863-Jun 1865); s.a. and w.o. (Jun-Aug 1865); *Ticonderoga*, Eur.Sqdn. (Aug 1865-Apr 1869); s.a. and w.o. (Apr-Oct 1869); *Benicia*, Asia.Sqdn. (Nov 1869-Apr 1871); sick lv. (Apr 1871-Sep 1872); flgs., *Saranac*, N.Pac.Sqdn. (Oct 1872-Jan 1874); flt.paymstr., N.Pac.Sqdn., *Saranac* (Jul 1873-Jan 1874); s.a. and w.o. (Jan-Nov 1874); *Powhatan*, Eur.Sqdn. (Jan 1875-Jul 1877); s.a. and w.o. (Jul 1877-Jan 1878); training ship, *Minnesota*, NY (Jan 1878-Feb 1881); s.a. and w.o. (Feb-Dec 1881); Pay Office, Baltimore (Jan 1882-Jan 1885); s.a. and w.o. (Jan-Mar 1885); flgs., *Pensacola*, Eur.Sqdn. (Mar 1885-Mar 1888); s.a. and w.o. (Mar-Oct 1888); member, naval exam. bd. (Oct 1888-Mar 1894); in charge, Pay Office, Baltimore (Apr 1889-Apr 1893); in charge, Pay Office, Norfolk, VA (Apr 1893-Mar 1896); s.a. and w.o. (Mar-May 1896); in charge, Pay Office, Baltimore (Jun 1896-Feb 1898); placed on Ret.Lst. (12 Feb 1898); spec. duty, Pay Office, Baltimore (Mar 1902-Mar 1905).

EDWIN PUTNAM Born in Bath, ME, on 28 Sep 1840, son of Israel and Sarah Emory (Frost) Putnam. Married Annie M. Salter in Dec 1870. Resided in Portsmouth, NH, where he died on 31 Dec 1925 and where he was buried.

Ranks Asst.Paymstr. (20 Sep 1862); Paymstr. (4 May 1866); Pay Insp. (19 Nov 1891); Pay Dir. (7 May 1899); placed on Ret.Lst. as Pay Dir. with rank of RAdm (28 Sep 1902).

Career Summary Received appointment from ME (20 Sep 1862); w.o. (Sep-Oct 1862); *Nahant*, N.Atl.Blk.Sqdn. (Oct 1862-Oct 1863); s.a. and w.o. (Oct-Dec 1863); *Portsmouth*, W.Gulf Blk.Sqdn. (Jan 1864-Sep 1865); s.a. and w.o. (Sep 1865-Jan 1866); *Mackinaw*, N.Atl.Sqdn. (Jan 1866-Apr 1867); s.a. and w.o. (Apr-Jul 1867); in charge of stores, St. Paul da Loanda, Africa (Aug 1867-Apr 1869); paymstr., Navy Yard, Portsmouth, NH (May 1869-Jul 1872); s.a. and w.o. (Jul-Sep 1872); *Benicia*, N.Pac.Sta. (Oct 1872-Feb 1875); s.a. and w.o. (Feb-Jun 1875); Navy Yard, Portsmouth, NH (Jun 1875-Jul 1878); s.a. and w.o. (Jul 1878-Aug 1880); *Galena*, Pac.Sta. (Sep 1880-Sep 1883); s.a. and w.o. (Sep 1883-Aug 1884); Navy Yard, Portsmouth, NH (Aug 1884-Sep 1887); s.a. and w.o. (Sep 1887-Nov 1888); *Atlanta*, Sqdn. of Evol. (Nov 1888-Oct 1891); s.a. and l.o.a. (Oct 1891-Jun 1892); Navy Yard, Boston (Jun 1892-Apr 1895); general storekeeper, Navy Yard, Washington, DC (Apr 1895-Apr 1898); in charge, Pay Office, Baltimore (Mar-May 1898); general storekeeper, Navy Yard, Norfolk, VA (May 1898-May 1899); general storekeeper, Navy Yard, NY (Jun 1899-Jul 1903); placed on Ret.Lst. (28 Sep 1902).

CHARLES WHITESIDE RAE Born in Hartford, CT, on 30

Jun 1847, son of Rev. Luzern and Martha (Whiteside) Rae. Received his preparatory education at the Champlain Academy in NY. In 1866, received C.E. degree from Rensselaer Polytechnic Institute of Troy, NY. Received D.Sc. degree from the Univ. of PA in 1906. Married Rebecca Gilman Dodge on 9 Jan 1890. Resided in Washington, DC, where he died on 13 May 1907. Buried in the USNA Cemetery, Annapolis.

Ranks Act. 3rd Asst.Engr. (10 Oct 1866); 3rd Asst.Engr. (2 Jun 1868); 2nd Asst.Engr. (2 Jun 1869); PAsst.Engr. (28 Dec 1875); Chief Engr. (21 Feb 1893); Chief Engr. with rel. rank of LCdr (11 Aug 1898); Chief Engr. with rel. rank of Cdr (10 Feb 1899); Cdr (3 Mar 1899); Capt (4 Jan 1903); Engr.-in-Chief, and Chief, Bur. of Steam Engineering with rank of RAdm (9 Aug 1903); died (13 May 1907).

Career Summary Received appointment from NY (10 Oct 1866); USNA (Oct 1866-Jun 1867); Navy Yard, NY (Jun-Sep 1867); l.o.a. (Sep-Oct 1867); USNA (Oct 1867-Jul 1868); flgs., *Contoocook* [renamed *Albany*], N.Atl.Sqdn. (Jul 1868-Sep 1869); Navy Yard, Washington, DC (Oct 1869-Sep 1870); spec. duty, Tehuantepec Surv.Expd. (Sep 1870-Aug 1871); w.o. (Aug-Sep 1871); flgs., *Wabash*, Eur.Sta. (Sep 1871-Jan 1874); USNA (Jan 1874-Jun 1875); *Alert*, Chester, PA (Jun-Sep 1875); USNA (Sep 1875-Jun 1878); *Pensacola*, and *Wachusett*, Pac.Sqdn. (Jul 1878-Jun 1881); spec. duty, Bur. of Steam Engineering, Washington, DC (Jun 1881-Jun 1884); *Powhatan*, N.Atl.Sqdn. (Jun-Jul 1884); flgs., *Lancaster*, Eur., then S.Atl.Sqdns. (Jul 1884-Nov 1887); w.o. (Nov 1887-Apr 1888); bd. duty (Apr-May 1888); Bur. of Nav., Washington, DC (Jun 1888-Oct 1890); l.o.a. (Nov 1890-Nov 1891); temp. duty, Bur. of Steam Engineering, Washington, DC (Nov 1891); *Atlanta*, Sqdn. of Evol. (Nov 1891-Mar 1893); w.o. (Mar-May 1893); l.o.a. (May-Sep 1893); USNA (Sep 1893-Jun 1897); *Iowa*, N.Atl.Flt. (Jun 1897-Mar 1899); Training Sta., Yerba Buena Island, CA (Mar 1899-Feb 1900); insp. of machinery, Bur. of Steam Engineering, Washington, DC (Feb-May 1900); member, naval exam. bd., Washington, DC (May 1900-Aug 1903); chief engr., and chief, Bur. of Steam Engineering, Washington, DC (Aug 1903-May 1907); died (13 May 1907).

CHARLES WHITESIDE RAE
1847-1907

STEPHEN RAND Born in Norwich, VT, on 11 May 1844, son of Stephen and Rebecca (Turner) Rand. Attended Dartmouth College, leaving after two years to enlist in the army. Graduated with his class in 1863 because of meritorious service in the war. Married Susan L. F. Watson on 21 Aug 1871. Retired to Washington, DC, dying there on 12 Jul 1915. Buried in Arlington National Cemetery.

Ranks Volunteer, Berdan's U.S. Sharpshooters (15 Aug 1861); discharged (5 Apr 1863); Act.3rd Asst.Engr. (17 Dec 1864); discharged (8 Aug 1869); Asst.Paymstr. (12 Aug 1869); PAsst. Paymstr. (30 Apr 1874); Paymstr. (31 Jul 1884); Paymstr. with rel. rank of LCdr (18 Jun 1892); Pay Insp. (1 Sep 1899); Pay Dir. (1 Jul 1902); transferred to Ret.Lst. (11 May 1906); Pay Dir. with rank of RAdm on Ret.Lst. (13 Apr 1911) to rank from 11 May

STEPHEN RAND
1844-1915

1906.

Career Summary Volunteer, Berdan's U.S. Sharpshooters (Aug 1861-Apr 1863); honorably discharged (5 Apr 1863); received appointment from NH as Act. 3rd Asst.Engr. (17 Dec 1864); *Merrimac*, E.Gulf Blk.Sqdn. (Dec 1864-Apr 1865); *Tioga*, Navy Yard, Portsmouth, NH, and spec.serv., Gulf of Mexico (Apr 1865-Apr 1866); *Glasgow*, spec.serv. (Apr 1866-Nov 1867); w.o. (Nov-Dec 1867); *Kearsarge*, S.Pac.Sqdn. (Dec 1867-Mar 1869); home and l.o.a. (Mar-Aug 1869); honorably discharged (8 Aug 1869); received appointment from NH as asst.paymstr. (12 Aug 1869); w.o. (Aug-Oct 1869); Navy Yard, Portsmouth, NH (Oct 1869-Aug 1870); *Mayflower*, Tehuantepec and Nicaraguan Surv.Expds. (Aug 1870-Aug 1871); paymstr., Tehuantepec and Nicaraguan Surv.Expds. (Aug 1871-Jan 1872); w.o. (Jan-May 1872); spec. duty, New Orleans (May 1872-Mar 1873); w.o. (Mar-Oct 1873); *Kearsarge*, Asia.Sqdn. (Nov 1873-Jan 1876); s.a. and w.o. (Jan-Aug 1876); *Canonicus*, N.Atl.Sqdn. (Aug 1876-Jun 1877); s.a. and w.o. (Jun 1877-Jan 1878); in charge, *Montauk*, *Wyandotte*, and *Adams*, League Island, PA (Jan-Aug 1878); s.a. and w.o. (Aug-Sep 1878); *Quinnebaug*, Eur.Sta. (Sep 1878-Jun 1881); s.a. and w.o. (Jun-Oct 1881); Bur. of Provisions and Clothing, Washington, DC (Oct 1881-Sep 1882); Torp.Sta., Newport, RI (Sep 1882-Feb 1885); s.a. and w.o. (Feb-Apr 1885); in charge, accounts and stores of naval and marine force, Aspinwall, Panama (Apr-May 1885); s.a. and w.o. (May-Sep 1885); spec. duty, Annapolis (Oct 1885-May 1887); *Mohican*, Pac.Sqdn. (Jun 1887-Dec 1890); s.a. and w.o. (Dec 1890-Mar 1891); spec. duty, Navy Dept., Washington, DC (Mar 1891-Jan 1893); paymstr., Navy Yard, Washington, DC (Jan 1893-Jul 1895); s.a. and w.o. (Jul-Aug 1895); *Texas*, N.Atl.Sqdn. (Aug 1895-Jan 1896); *Columbia*, N.Atl.Sqdn. (Mar 1896-May 1897); s.a. and w.o. (May-Jul 1897); in charge, Pay Office, Washington, DC (Jul 1897-Nov 1901); s.a. and w.o. (Nov 1901-Feb 1902); Navy Dept., Washington, DC, and en route to Asia.Sta. (Feb-Jul 1902); *Culgoa*, Asia.Sta. (Jul-Oct 1902); sick lv. (Oct 1902-Feb 1903); in charge, Pay Office, Manila, P.I. (Apr 1903-May 1904); s.a. and w.o. (May-Oct 1904); gen storekeeper, Navy Yard, Washington, DC (Oct 1904-May 1906); transferred to Ret.Lst. (11 May 1906).

GEORGE BRINKERHOFF RANSOM Born in Chazy, NY, on 28 Jun 1851, son of Harry Sawyer and Martha (Bosworth) Ransom. Graduated in 1869 from the Normal and Training School in Oswego, NY. Received a B.C.E from the Univ. of WI in 1891, and LL.B. from the Suffolk Law School in Boston in 1917. Married Sarah Upham on 15 Sep 1880. One son. Married Ruth Barber on 4 Sep 1917. Resided in Plattsburg, NY, where he died on 25 Feb 1924. Buried in Riverside Cemetery in Plattsburg.

Ranks Cadet Engr. (1 Oct 1871); Asst.Engr. (26 Feb 1875); PAsst.Engr. (4 Jul 1880); PAsst.Engr. with rel. rank of Lt (5 May 1892); Chief Engr. (9 May 1895); LCdr (3 Mar 1899); Cdr (10 Aug 1903); Capt (8 Nov 1907); RAdm (14 Sep 1911); placed on

GEORGE BRINKERHOFF
RANSOM
1851-1924

Ret.Lst. (28 Jun 1913).

Career Summary Received appointment from NY (1 Oct 1871); USNA (Oct 1871-Jun 1874); turned back (8 Jun 1872); *Wachusett*, N.Atl.Sta. (Jun-Dec 1874); w.o. (Dec 1874-Jan 1875); *Worcester*, N.Atl.Sta. (Jan-Dec 1875); w.o. (Dec 1875-Feb 1876); *Mahopac*, Port Royal, SC (Feb-Jul 1876); *Essex*, S.Atl.Sta. (Aug 1876-Oct 1879); w.o. (Oct 1879-Jan 1880); spec. duty, Delaware Iron Works, Chester, PA (Jan-Sep 1880); inst. of steam engineering, USNA (Sep 1880-Aug 1883); *Pinta*, Alaskan waters (Sep 1883-Jan 1884); sick lv. (Jan-Jul 1884); training ship, *Passaic*, USNA (Jul-Aug 1884); *Vandalia*, N.Atl.Sqdn. (Aug-Oct 1884); Navy Yard, Portsmouth, NH (Oct 1884-Mar 1885); *Omaha*, Asia. Sta. (Mar 1885-Mar 1888); *Pensacola*, Navy Yard, Norfolk, VA (Mar-May 1888); w.o. (May-Aug 1888); spec. duty, inst. of steam engineering, Univ. of WI, Madison (Sep 1888-Sep 1891); *Pinta*, spec.serv. (Sep 1891-Oct 1893); spec. duty, Union Iron Works, San Francisco (Oct 1893-Feb 1894); l.o.a. (Feb-Apr 1894); Navy Yard, NY (Apr 1894-Feb 1895); Navy Yard, Portsmouth, NH (Feb-Jul 1895); rec. ship, *Minnesota*, NY (Jul-Oct 1895); w.o. (Oct-Nov 1895); insp. of machinery, Elizabethport, NJ (Nov 1895-Jan 1897); *Boston*, Asia.Sqdn. (Mar 1897-Feb 1898); *Concord*, Asia.Sqdn. (Feb-Dec 1898); *Boston*, Asia.Sqdn. (Dec 1898-May 1899); *Baltimore*, Asia.Sqdn. (May 1899-Apr 1900); Navy Yard, Mare Island, CA (Apr-May 1900); home and w.o. (May-Jun 1900); Navy Yard, Portsmouth, NH (Jun 1900-Aug 1904); chief engr., Navy Yard, Mare Island, CA (Aug 1904-Jun 1906); insp. of engineering material, Sterling Consolidated Boiler Company, Barberton, OH (Jul-Dec 1906); insp. of machinery, Newport News Shipbuilding and Drydock Company, Newport News, VA (Dec 1906-Aug 1908); insp. of engineering material, MA and CT Dists., Boston (Aug 1908-Sep 1912); gen insp. of machinery, Atl.cst., Philadelphia (Sep 1912-Jun 1913); placed on Ret.Lst. (28 Jun 1913).

Career Highlights Served as chief engr. on the *Concord* at the Battle of Manila Bay in 1898, being advanced three numbers for "eminent and conspicuous conduct." Was first engineering officer to attain the rank of RAdm on active duty since amalgamation of the Engineering Corps with the line officers.

JOHN BAYARD REDFIELD Born in Sackett's Harbor, NY, on 13 Apr 1842. Married Martha Abercrombie. Two sons. Died on 19 Apr 1907 in NY City. Buried in Lockport, NY.

Ranks Paymstr's Clerk (11 Feb 1864); Act.Asst.Paymstr. (16 Jan 1865); discharged (23 Nov 1865); Asst.Paymstr. (21 Feb 1867); PAsst.Paymstr (11 Jun 1868); Paymstr. (8 Mar 1879); Pay Insp. (5 May 1899); Pay Dir. (10 Apr 1902); transferred to Ret.Lst. with rank of RAdm (13 Apr 1904).

Career Summary Paymaster's Clerk (16 Feb 1864); *Circassian*, E. and W.Gulf Blk.Sqdns. (Feb 1864-Jan 1865); received appointment from MI as act.asst.paymstr. (16 Jan 1865); Naval Sta., Mound City, IL (Feb-Oct 1865); l.o.a. (Oct-Nov 1865); discharged (23 Nov 1865); received appointment from MI (21 Feb

1867); w.o. (Feb-May 1867); prac. ship, *Dale* (May-Dec 1867); s.a. and w.o. (Dec 1867-Jun 1869); *Mohican*, Pac.Sqdn. (Jun 1869-Jun 1872); s.a. and w.o. (Jun 1872-Feb 1873); *Monocacy*, Asia.Sqdn. (Jun 1873-Feb 1875); s.a. and w.o. (Feb-Nov 1875); cst.surv. duty (Nov 1875-Nov 1878); s.a. and w.o. (Nov 1878-Jun 1879); l.o.a. (Jul 1879-Aug 1880); w.o. (Aug-Oct 1880); rec. ship, *Franklin*, Norfolk, VA (Nov 1880-Jul 1883); s.a. and w.o. (Jul 1883); Navy Yard, Mare Island, CA (Aug 1883-Feb 1886); s.a. and w.o. (Feb-Apr 1886); *Monocacy*, Asia.Sta. (May 1886-Oct 1889); s.a. and w.o. (Oct 1889-Jan 1890); rec. ship, *Independence*, Mare Island, CA (Feb 1890-Apr 1893); s.a. and w.o. (Apr 1893-Mar 1894); *Atlanta*, N.Atl.Sta. (Apr 1894-Sep 1895); s.a. and w.o. (Sep-Oct 1895); *Minneapolis*, Eur.Sta. (Oct 1895-Apr 1897); s.a. and w.o. (Apr-Jun 1897); sick lv. (Jun-Sep 1897); rec. ship, *Richmond*, and Reserve Flt., Navy Yard, League Island, PA (Sep 1897-Jul 1899); gen storekeeper, Navy Yard, Norfolk, VA (Aug 1899-Sep 1900); flgs., *Chicago*, S.Atl.Sta. (Oct 1900-Feb 1902); s.a. and w.o. (Feb-Jun 1902); s.a. for Naval Home, Philadelphia (Jun-Jul 1902); *Michigan*, on Great Lakes (Jul 1902-Apr 1904); transferred to Ret.Lst. (13 Apr 1904).

ALLEN VISSCHER REED
1838-1914

ALLEN VISSCHER REED Born in Oak Hill, Greene County, NY, on 12 Jul 1838, son of James Warren and Adaline (Allen) Reed. Educated in public and private schools. Married Jane Augusta Valentine on 28 Mar 1871. Four daughters. Resided in Washington, DC, where he died on 14 Jan 1914. Buried in Arlington National Cemetery.

Ranks Act.Midn (26 Sep 1854); Midn (11 Jun 1858); Passed Midn (19 Jan 1861); Mstr (23 Feb 1861); Lt (18 Apr 1861); LCdr (3 Mar 1865); Cdr (1 Apr 1872); Capt (28 Jul 1884); Commo (28 Feb 1896); retired (11 Jun 1896); RAdm on Ret.Lst. (29 Jun 1906) to rank from 11 Jun 1896.

Career Summary Received appointment from NY (26 Sep 1854); USNA (Sep 1854-Jun 1858); *Macedonian*, Med.Sqdn. (Jul 1858-May 1860); sick lv. and l.o.a. (May 1860-Jan 1861); *Pawnee*, Navy Yard, Washington, DC (Feb-Mar 1861); *Water Witch*, Gulf Blk.Sqdn. (Mar-Sep 1861); flgs., *Colorado*, W.Gulf Blk.Sqdn. (Sep-Dec 1861); watch off., then exec.off., *Potomac*, W.Gulf Blk.Sqdn. (Dec 1861-Aug 1863); exec.off., *Lackawanna*, W.Gulf Blk.Sqdn. (Aug-Nov 1863); w.o. (Nov 1863-Jan 1864); exec.off., *Tuscarora*, N.Atl.Blk.Sqdn. (Feb-May 1864); exec.off., then cdr, *Pawtuxet*, Navy Yard, Portsmouth, NH (Jun 1864-Aug 1865); w.o. (Aug-Sep 1865); exec.off., *Miantonomoh*, N.Atl.Sqdn. (Sep 1865-Apr 1866); w.o. (Apr-Jun 1866); asst. to exec.off., Navy Yard, Norfolk, VA (Jul-Sep 1866); exec.off., *Resaca*, Pac.Sta. (Sep 1866-Feb 1868); *Saranac*, spec.serv. (Feb 1868-Jul 1869); w.o. (Jul-Sep 1869); exec.off., rec. ship, *Vermont*, NY (Sep 1869-May 1870); equip. duty, Navy Yard, NY (May-Sep 1870); ord., then nav. duty, Navy Yard, NY (Sep 1870-May 1872); w.o. (May-Jul 1872); cdr, *Kansas*, Nicaraguan Surv.Expd., and N.Atl. Sta. (Aug 1872-Jun 1874); w.o. (Jul-Oct 1874); Hydrographic Office, Washington, DC (Nov 1874-Sep 1875); asst. hydrogra-

pher, Hydrographic Office, Washington, DC (Sep 1875-Aug
1880); w.o. (Aug 1880-Apr 1882); instruction, Torp.Sta.,
Newport, RI (May-Aug 1882); w.o. (Aug-Dec 1882); cdr,
Alliance, N.Atl.Sta. (Dec 1882-Jul 1884); w.o. (Jul-Nov 1884);
cdr, training ship, *Minnesota* (Nov 1884-Jan 1886); w.o. (Jan
1886-Nov 1888); cdr, *Richmond,* S.Atl.Sta. (Nov 1888-Oct 1890);
l.o.a. (Oct-Dec 1890); cdr, Navy Yard, Pensacola, FL (Dec
1890-Dec 1893); l.o.a. (Dec 1893-Jun 1894); w.o. and bd. duties
(Jun-Nov 1894); cdr, Navy Yard, Portsmouth, NH (Nov 1894-
Jun 1896); retired (11 Jun 1896).

WILLIAM HERON REEDER Born in Muscatine, IA, on 24
Aug 1848, son of Dr. George and A. L. (Olds) Reeder. Married
Ellinor Wells on 29 Nov 1873. One daughter. Resided in NY
City. Died in Paris on 24 Jan 1911. Buried in USNA Cemetery,
Annapolis.

WILLIAM HERON REEDER
1848-1911

Ranks Midn (20 Sep 1862); Ens (18 Dec 1868); Mstr (21 Mar
1870); Lt (31 Jan 1872); LCdr (4 Dec 1892); Cdr (10 Aug
1898); Capt (2 Dec 1902); retired with rank of RAdm (30 Jun
1907).

Career Summary Received appointment from IA (20 Sep
1862); USNA (Sep 1862-Jun 1867); found deficient and turned
back (Feb 1864); w.o. (Jun-Sep 1867); flgs., *Piscataqua,* then
Unadilla, then flgs., *Delaware,* Asia.Sqdn. (Oct 1867-Dec 1870);
home and w.o. (Dec 1870-Mar 1871); signal duty, Washington,
DC (Apr-Jun 1871); w.o. (Jun-Sep 1871); flgs., *Wabash,* and
Shenandoah, Eur.Sqdn. (Oct 1871-Feb 1874); w.o. (Feb-Apr
1874); Navy Yard, Boston (Apr-Oct 1874); Navy Yard, Philadelphia (Oct 1874-Jun 1877); *Powhatan,* N.Atl.Sta. (Jun-Aug 1877);
Hartford, Navy Yard, NY (Sep 1877); *Powhatan,* N.Atl.Sta. (Sep
1877-Jul 1880); w.o. (Jul-Aug 1880); l.o.a. (Sep-Nov 1880); spec.
duty, Navy Dept., Washington, DC (Nov 1880-Dec 1881); Navy
Yard, Portsmouth, NH (Dec 1881-Apr 1883); Torp.Sta., New-
port, RI (Apr-Aug 1883); Navy Yard, Portsmouth, NH (Aug
1883); cdr, *Despatch,* spec.serv. (Aug 1883-Feb 1885); Bur. of
Nav., Washington, DC (Feb-Apr 1885); *Tennessee,* Navy Yard,
NY (Apr-May 1885); spec. duty, Navy Dept., Washington, DC
(May 1885-Jun 1886); *Galena,* N.Atl.Sqdn. (Jul 1886-Jul 1889);
exec.off., rec. ship, *Dale,* Washington, DC (Jul-Oct 1889); Bur. of
Equipment and Recruiting, Washington, DC (Oct 1889-Jul 1890);
USNA (Jul 1890-Jun 1893); exec.off., *Charleston,* Pac.Sta. (Jun
1893-Jul 1894); temp. duty, Dept. of the Pac., San Francisco
(Jul-Aug 1894); exec.off., *Charleston,* Asia.Sta. (Aug 1894-Jul
1896); Navy Yard, Washington, DC (Aug 1896-Apr 1897); cdr,
training ship, *St. Mary's,* NY (Apr 1897-Apr 1898); in charge, 4th
Dist. Cst. Defense System, Philadelphia (Apr-Aug 1898); cdr,
Marcellus, N.Atl.Flt. (Aug-Sep 1898); home and w.o. (Sep-Oct
1898); cdr, training ship, *St. Mary's* (Nov 1898-Nov 1901); cdr,
training ship, *Hartford* (Nov 1901-Nov 1903); home and w.o.
(Nov 1903-May 1904); NWC (May-Sep 1904); cdr, *Alabama,* N.
Atl.Sta. (Oct 1904-Dec 1905); home and w.o. (Dec 1905-Jan
1906); l.o.a. (Jan-Aug 1906); capt.yd., Navy Yard, NY (Sep

1906-Mar 1907); cdr, rec. ship, *Hancock*, NY (Mar-Jun 1907); retired (30 Jun 1907).

CORWIN POTTENGER REES
1848-1924

CORWIN POTTENGER REES Born on 4 Sep 1848 in Reily, OH, son of Thomas and Elizabeth S. (Griffin) Rees. Married Louise Merrill on 28 Oct 1886. Resided in Erie, PA. Died there on 12 Sep 1924. Buried in the Erie Cemetery.

Ranks Musician, 15th Army Corps (27 Feb 1864); honorably discharged (15 Aug 1865); Midn (30 Jul 1866); Ens (13 Jul 1871); Mstr (21 May 1874); Lt (11 Oct 1880); LCdr (3 Mar 1889); Cdr (12 May 1901); Capt (30 Sep 1905); RAdm (25 Oct 1909); placed on Ret.Lst. (4 Sep 1910).

Career Summary Musician, Co. B. 54th OH Volunteer Infantry, 2nd Brigade, 2nd Div., 15th Army Corps (Feb 1864-Aug 1865); honorably discharged (15 Aug 1865); received appointment from OH (30 Jul 1866); USNA (Jul 1866-Jun 1870); w.o. (Jun-Jul 1870); *Guerriere*, spec.serv. and Eur.Sta. (Aug 1870-Mar 1872); w.o. (Mar-Dec 1872); *Portsmouth*, spec.surv. duty (Dec 1872-Jul 1874); *Saranac*, N.Pac.Sqdn. (Jul 1874-Jun 1875); *Benicia*, N.Pac.Sqdn. (Aug-Nov 1875); *Lackawanna*, Pac.Sqdn. (Nov 1875-Feb 1877); home and w.o. (Feb-Aug 1877); nav. off., *Guard*, spec.serv. (Sep 1877-Nov 1878); w.o. (Nov 1878-Jan 1879); inst., dept. of drawing, USNA (Jan 1879-Aug 1881); w.o. (Aug-Oct 1881); *Essex*, Pac. and Asia.Stas. (Nov 1881-Jan 1885); w.o. (Jan-Mar 1885); training ship, *New Hampshire* (Apr 1885); *Alert*, Greely Relief Expd. (Apr 1885); w.o. (Apr-May 1885); *Michigan*, on Great Lakes (May 1885-Apr 1888); Torp.Sta., Newport, RI (May-Aug 1888); NWC (Aug-Nov 1888); *Kearsarge*, spec.serv. (Nov 1888-Jan 1889); *Tallapoosa*, S.Atl.Sqdn. (Jan 1889-Jan 1892); l.o.a. (Jan-May 1892); exec.off., *Michigan*, on Great Lakes (May 1892-May 1895); home and w.o. (May-Jun 1895); exec.off., *Monocacy*, Asia.Sta. (Aug 1895-Apr 1896); exec.off., *Olympia*, Asia.Sta. (Apr-Oct 1896); exec.off., *Monocacy*, Asia.Sta. (Oct 1896-Mar 1898); exec.off., flgs., *Olympia*, Asia.Sqdn. (Apr-Dec 1898); home and w.o. (Dec 1898-Mar 1899); Torp.Sta., Newport, RI (Mar 1899-Aug 1901); cdr, training ship, *Monongahela* (Aug 1901-Sep 1903); home and l.o.a. (Sep-Oct 1903); NWC (Oct 1903); insp., 1st L.h. Dist., Portland, ME (Oct 1903-Dec 1905); gen court-martial duty, USNA (Dec 1905-Feb 1906); capt.yd., Navy Yard, Portsmouth, NH (Feb 1906-Apr 1908); comdt., Naval Sta., Honolulu, Territory of HI (Apr 1908-Dec 1910); placed on Ret.Lst. (4 Sep 1910).

Career Highlights Served as exec.off. on the *Olympia* during Battle of Manila Bay and the surrender of Manila, for which he was advanced five numbers for eminent and conspicuous conduct in battle.

GEORGE COOK REITER
1845-1930

GEORGE COOK REITER Born in Mt. Pleasant, PA, on 6 Jul 1845, son of Dr. W. C. and Eliza Reynolds Reiter. Early education in Pittsburgh, PA. Married with one son. Resided in Canton, OH, where he died on 9 May 1930. Buried in Canton.

Ranks Act.Midn (20 Sep 1861); title changed to Midn (16 Jul

1862); Ens (1 Dec 1866); Mstr (12 Mar 1868); Lt (26 Mar 1869); LCdr (23 Nov 1880); Cdr (31 Jul 1890); Capt (3 Mar 1899); RAdm (31 Mar 1905); placed on Ret.Lst. (6 Jul 1907).

Career Summary Received appointment from PA (20 Sep 1861); USNA (Sep 1861-Oct 1865); w.o. (Oct-Nov 1865); schoolship, *Sabine* (Nov 1865-Apr 1866); *Lackawanna*, N.Pac. Sqdn. (May 1866-Aug 1868); home and w.o. (Aug 1868-Jan 1869); *Kenosha* [renamed *Plymouth*], Eur.Sqdn. (Jan 1869-Mar 1872); l.o.a. and w.o. (Mar-Oct 1872); rec. ship, *New Hampshire*, Norfolk, VA (Oct 1872-Mar 1873); *Narragansett*, spec.surv. duty, Pac. Ocean (Mar 1873-Jul 1875); w.o. (Jul-Nov 1875); *Lehigh*, N.Atl.Sta. (Nov 1875-Apr 1876); w.o. (Apr-Jul 1876); Hydrographic Office, Washington, DC (Aug-Dec 1876); equip. duty, Norfolk, VA (Jan-May 1877); w.o. and l.o.a. (May-Dec 1877); exec.off., *Tuscarora*, Pac.Sta. (Dec 1877-Sep 1878); sick lv. (Sep-Dec 1878); w.o. (Dec 1878-May 1879); torpedo instruction, Newport, RI (Jun-Sep 1879); insp., 13th L.h. Dist., Portland, OR (Oct 1879-Sep 1882); s.a. and w.o. (Sep 1882-Jan 1883); training ship, *Minnesota* (Jan-Mar 1883); exec.off., *Nipsic*, S.Atl.Sta. (Mar 1883-Jun 1886); w.o. (Jun-Jul 1886); torp. instruction, Newport, RI (Jul-Nov 1886); l.o.a. (Nov 1886-Jun 1887); nav.off., Navy Yard, Norfolk, VA (Jun 1887-Mar 1889); sick lv. (Mar-Oct 1889); cdr, *Ranger*, N.Pac.Sta. (Oct 1889-Nov 1890); w.o. (Nov 1890-Apr 1891); cdr, *Thetis*, Pac.Sta. (May 1891-May 1893); l.o.a. (May-Jun 1893); asst., then insp., 4th L.h. Dist., Philadelphia (Jul 1893-Jun 1896); cdr, *Detroit*, Asia.Sta. (Aug 1896-Jul 1897); Naval Home, Philadelphia (Jul-Sep 1897); insp., 13th L.h. Dist., Portland, OR (Dec 1897-Apr 1898); cdr, *Panther*, unassigned (Apr-Oct 1898); insp., 13th L.h. Dist., Portland, OR (Oct 1898-Jun 1899); w.o. (Jul-Aug 1899); NWC (Aug-Oct 1899); cdr, flgs., *Philadelphia*, Pac.Sta. (Nov 1899-Feb 1900); gen insp., *Wisconsin*, San Francisco (Feb 1900-Feb 1901); cdr, *Wisconsin*, Pac.Sta. (Feb 1901-Dec 1902); home and w.o. (Dec 1902-Feb 1903); Naval Rec.Sta., NY (Feb-Aug 1903); member, L.h. Bd., Washington, DC (Aug 1903-Apr 1905); cdr, P.I.Sqdn., Asia.Flt., *Rainbow* (Jun 1905-Jan 1906); member, L.h. Bd., Washington, DC (Feb 1906-Dec 1907); placed on Ret.Lst. (6 Jul 1907).

ALFRED REYNOLDS Born on 7 Sep 1853 in Hampton, VA, son of MGen Joseph J., USA, and Mary E. (Bainbridge) Reynolds. Married Louise S. Norton on 28 Apr 1880. Married Sarah Josephine LeCand on 4 Oct 1921. Made his home in Gulfport, MS. Died in the Naval Hospital in Washington, DC, on 9 Sep 1936. Buried in Arlington National Cemetery.

Ranks Midn (22 Sep 1869); title changed to Cadet Midn (15 Jul 1870); Midn (31 May 1873); Ens (16 Jul 1874); Mstr (1 Jan 1881); title changed to Ltjg (3 Mar 1883); Lt (9 Nov 1886); LCdr (3 Mar 1899); Cdr (2 Dec 1902); Capt (1 Jul 1907); RAdm (13 Jul 1911); placed on Ret.Lst. (7 Sep 1915).

Career Summary Received appointment from IN (22 Sep 1869); USNA (Sep 1869-May 1873); w.o. (May-Jul 1873); *Narragansett*, Pac.Sta. (Sep 1873-Jul 1875); home and w.o. (Jul-

ALFRED REYNOLDS
1853-1936

Sep 1875); USNA (Oct-Nov 1875); l.o.a. (Nov-Dec 1875); *Saugus*, Key West, FL (Dec 1875-Jul 1876); w.o. (Jul 1876-Mar 1877); *Ranger*, Asia.Sta. (Mar 1877-Feb 1880); w.o. (Feb-Mar 1880); ord. duty, Navy Yard, NY (Apr 1880-Aug 1881); temp. duty, training ship, *New Hampshire* (May-Jun 1881); *Enterprise*, spec.serv. (Aug 1881-Nov 1882); *Alliance*, N.Atl.Sta. (Nov 1882-Mar 1885); w.o. (Mar-Apr 1885); ord. instruction, Navy Yard, Washington, DC (Apr 1885-Feb 1888); *Swatara*, S.Atl.Sta. (Feb 1888-Jan 1891); w.o. (Jan-Feb 1891); ord. duty, Navy Yard, Washington, DC (Mar 1891-Sep 1893); l.o.a. (Sep-Oct 1893); torp. instruction, Newport, RI (Oct 1893-Apr 1894); w.o. (Apr-May 1894); Office of Naval Intelligence, Navy Dept., Washington, DC (May-Oct 1894); *San Francisco*, Navy Yard, NY (Oct 1894-Oct 1897); home and l.o.a. (Oct-Dec 1897); Bur. of Equip. and Recruiting, Washington, DC (Dec 1897-Jun 1898); cdr, *Massasoit*, N.Atl.Flt. (Jun-Jul 1898); Bur. of Equip. and Recruiting, Washington, DC (Aug 1898-Jan 1899); rec. ship, *Franklin*, Norfolk, VA (Jan-Oct 1899); exec.off., *Nashville*, Asia.Sta. (Nov 1899-Oct 1900); cdr, *Yosemite*, Asia.Sta. (Nov-Dec 1900); cdr, *Elcano*, Asia.Sta. (Dec 1900-May 1901); exec.off., flgs., *Kentucky*, Asia.Sta. (May 1901-Jul 1902); home and w.o. (Jul-Nov 1902); ord.off., Navy Yard, League Island, PA (Dec 1902-May 1905); cdr, *Nevada*, Cst.Sqdn. (May 1905-May 1907); NWC (Jun-Oct 1907); cdr, rec. ship, *Franklin*, Norfolk, VA (Nov 1907-May 1908); cdr., *Montana*, Asia.Flt. (May 1908-Nov 1909); cdr, rec. ship, *Franklin*, Norfolk, VA (Nov 1909-Sep 1911); gov., Naval Home, Philadelphia (Sep 1911-Mar 1912); cdr, Pac. Reserve Flt., *Pennsylvania* [renamed *Pittsburgh*], *Colorado*, and *West Virginia* (Mar-Dec 1912); member, then pres., naval exam. and ret. bds., Washington, DC (Dec 1912-Sep 1915); placed on Ret.Lst. (7 Sep 1915); cdr, Naval Reservation and Training Sta., Gulfport, MS (Jul 1917-Dec 1919).

PRESLEY MARION RIXEY Born in Culpeper County, VA, on 14 Jul 1852, son of Presley Morehead and Mary F. (Jones) Rixey. Received his primary education in Culpeper and Warrenton counties, VA, before attending the Univ. of VA from which he received an M.D. degree in 1873. Attended Jefferson Medical College in Philadelphia from 1873-74. On 25 Apr 1877, married Earlena I. English, daughter of RAdm Earl English, USN. Resided in Rosslyn, VA, where he died on 17 Jun 1928. Buried in Arlington National Cemetery.

Ranks Asst.Surg. (28 Jan 1874); PAsst.Surg. (18 Apr 1877); Surg. (27 Nov 1888); Medl.Insp. (24 Aug 1900); Surg.Gen with rank of RAdm (5 Feb 1902); Medl.Dir. (7 May 1907); retired as Medl.Dir. with rank of RAdm (4 Feb 1910).

Career Summary Received appointment from VA (28 Jan 1874); *Sabine*, Eur.Sta. (Feb-Jul 1874); *Congress*, Eur.Sta. and Centennial Exposition, Philadelphia (Aug 1874-Jul 1876); Naval Hosp., Philadelphia (Aug 1876-Apr 1877); w.o. (Apr-Aug 1877); Navy Yard, Norfolk, VA (Aug 1877-Feb 1879); *Tallapoosa*, spec. serv. (Feb 1879-Feb 1882); spec. duty, Washington, DC (Feb

PRESLEY MARION RIXEY
1852-1928

1882-Sep 1884); flgs., *Lancaster*, Eur. and S.Atl.Stas. (Sep 1884-Nov 1887); spec. duty, Naval Dispensary, Washington, DC (Nov 1887-Jan 1893); *Dolphin*, spec.serv. (Feb 1893-Dec 1895); w.o. (Dec 1895-Mar 1896); spec. duty, Naval Dispensary, Washington, DC (Apr 1896-Jul 1898); hosp. ship, *Solace*, N.Atl. Flt. (Jul-Sep 1898); Bur. of Medicine and Surgery, Washington, DC (Sep 1898-Feb 1902); surg.gen, and chief, Bur. of Medicine and Surgery, Washington, DC (Feb 1902-Feb 1910); retired (4 Feb 1910); spec. duty, Bur. of Medicine and Surgery, Washington, DC (Apr 1917-Nov 1918); member, Council of National Defense (Apr 1917-Nov 1918); insp.gen, medl. activities, USN (Apr 1917-Nov 1918).

Career Highlights Served as presidents William McKinley's and Theodore Roosevelt's official physician. In addition, was the official physician to the White House from 1898 to May 1909. Received the Order of Naval Merit from King Alphonso XIII of Spain for the assistance he gave to the crew of the *Santa Maria* after that vessel suffered an explosion in NY Harbor in 1893.

References
Additional Sources: William C. Braisted and William H. Bell, *The Life Story of Presley Marion Rixey*. (Strasburg, VA: 1930).

EDWARD DUNHAM ROBIE Born in Burlington, VT, on 11 Sep 1831, son of Jacob Carter and Louisa Willes (Dunham) Robie. Educated in private schools and at the Binghamton Academy in NY. Married Helen Adams on 3 Jun 1858. Resided in Washington, DC where he died on 7 Jun 1911. Buried in Arlington National Cemetery.

Ranks 3rd Asst.Engr. (16 Feb 1852); 2nd Asst.Engr. (27 Jun 1855); 1st Asst.Engr. (21 Jul 1858); Chief Engr. (30 Jul 1861); placed on Ret.Lst. with rel. rank of Commo (11 Sep 1893); Chief Engr. with rank of RAdm on Ret.Lst. (29 May 1906).

Career Summary Received appointment from NY (16 Feb 1852); flgs., *Mississippi*, E.Ind.Sqdn. and Expd. (Mar 1852-Apr 1855); *Michigan*, on Great Lakes (Sep 1855-Mar 1856); *Susque-hanna*, Eur.Sqdn. and spec. duty, W.Indies (Mar 1856-Apr 1858); w.o. (Apr-Sep 1858); *Niagara*, spec.serv. to Monrovia, Liberia (Sep-Dec 1858); w.o. (Dec 1858-Mar 1859); flgs., *Lancaster*, Pac.Sqdn. (Apr 1859-Jul 1861); senior engr., *Saranac*, Pac.Sqdn. (Jul-Sep 1861); chief engr., *Mohican*, S.Atl.Blk.Sqdn. (Oct 1861-Jul 1862); l.o.a. (Jul-Aug 1862); spec. duty, *Dictator*, NY (Aug 1862-Jan 1863); spec. duty, NY (Jan 1863-Aug 1864); chief engr., *Dictator*, N.Atl.Blk.Sqdn. (Aug 1864-Sep 1865); spec. duty (Sep-Nov 1865); w.o. (Nov-Dec 1865); member, engr.exam.bd., Philadelphia (Dec 1865-Oct 1866); *Ossipee*, Pac.Sta. (Oct 1866-Aug 1867); flt.engr., N.Pac.Sta., *Pensacola* (Aug 1867-Feb 1869); return and w.o. (Feb-Mar 1869); senior engr. member, bd. to examine vessels at navy yards, Atl.cst. (Mar-Aug 1869); insp. of machinery afloat, Navy Yard, Boston (Aug 1869-Oct 1871); flt.engr., Eur.Sta., *Wabash* (Oct 1871-Apr 1874); chief engr., Steam Engineering Dept., Navy Yard, Norfolk, VA (Apr 1874-May 1877); w.o. (May-Aug 1877); spec. duty, Pittsburgh, PA, and

EDWARD DUNHAM ROBIE
1831-1911

Cold Spring, NY (Aug 1877-Jun 1879); flt.engr., Pac.Sta., *Pensacola* (Jul 1879-Jun 1881); return and w.o. (Jun-Jul 1881); chief engr., dept. of steam engineering, Navy Yard, Boston (Jul 1881-Jan 1884); in charge, dept. of steam engineering, Navy Yard, NY (Jan 1884-Jan 1887); sick lv. and w.o. (Jan-Sep 1887); chief engr., dept. of steam engineering, Navy Yard, Norfolk, VA (Oct 1887-Oct 1891); spec. inspection duty (Oct 1891-Feb 1892); Bur. of Steam Engineering, Washington, DC (Feb 1892-Sep 1893); placed on Ret.Lst. (11 Sep 1893); employed in selecting vessels for Auxiliary Naval Force (May-Aug 1898).

Career Highlights His first duty was on the *Mississippi*, Commo Matthew C. Perry's flgs. in the famous circumnavigation of the globe and the opening of Japan to western trade.

LEWIS WOOD ROBINSON
1840-1903

LEWIS WOOD ROBINSON Born in Camden, NJ, on 7 Mar 1840, son of William and Anna (Wood) Robinson. Graduated from the Polytechnic College of PA in 1861 after a course in civil engineering. Received the Master of Mechanical Engineering in 1864. Married Mary De'A. Rupp on 5 Sep 1865. Five children. Resided in Philadelphia where he died on 16 Feb 1903.

Ranks 3rd Asst.Engr. (21 Sep 1861); 2nd Asst.Engr. with rel. rank of Mstr (29 Jul 1863); 1st Asst.Engr. with rel. rank of Lt (11 Oct 1866); title changed to PAsst.Engr. (24 Feb 1874); Chief Engr. with rel. rank of LCdr (19 Aug 1883); Chief Engr. with rel. rank of Cdr (21 Mar 1895); Chief Engr. with rel. rank of Capt (6 Aug 1898); Capt (3 Mar 1899); placed on Ret.Lst. as Chief Engr. with rank of RAdm (21 Sep 1901).

Career Summary Received appointment from NJ (21 Sep 1861); w.o. (Sep-Oct 1861); *Kennebec*, W.Gulf Blk.Sqdn. (Oct 1861-Jul 1864); chief engr., *Kennebec*, W.Gulf Blk.Sqdn. (Jul 1864-Jun 1865); w.o. (Jun-Nov 1865); *Shamokin*, S.Atl.Sta. (Nov 1865-Dec 1868); w.o. (Dec 1868-Apr 1869); Navy Yard, Philadelphia (Apr 1869-Dec 1870); *Nipsic*, Philadelphia (Dec 1870); w.o. (Dec 1870-Jan 1871); *Ticonderoga*, S.Atl.Sta. (Jan 1871-Feb 1874); w.o. (Feb-Jun 1874); *Tennessee*, Navy Yard, Philadelphia (Jun-Aug 1874); w.o. (Aug-Oct 1874); Navy Yard, Philadelphia (Oct 1874-Jul 1875); gen supt., Bur. of Machinery, Centennial Exhibition, Philadelphia (Aug 1875-Jan 1877); senior inst., dept. of steam engineering, USNA (Jan 1877-Jun 1880); w.o. (Jun-Aug 1880); flgs., *Minnesota*, training flt. (Aug 1880-Jul 1882); flgs., *Tennessee*, Home and N.Atl.Stas. (Jul-Oct 1882); w.o. (Oct 1882-Apr 1883); *Tennessee*, N.Atl.Sta. (Apr-Aug 1883); w.o. (Aug-Dec 1883); spec. duty, Navy Yard, League Island, PA (Dec 1883-Jan 1884); *Ossipee*, Asia.Sta. (Jan 1884-Mar 1887); w.o. (Mar-Apr 1887); member, naval exam. bd., Philadelphia (Apr 1887-Sep 1891); chief, dept. of machinery, World's Columbian Exposition, Chicago (Sep 1891-Mar 1894); chief engr., *Atlanta*, N.Atl.Sqdn. (Apr-Oct 1894); flgs., *Newark*, S.Atl.Sqdn. (Nov 1894-Mar 1895); flt.engr., S.Atl.Sqdn., *Newark* (Mar 1895-Aug 1896); *Indiana*, N.Atl.Sqdn. (Aug 1896-Apr 1897); home and l.o.a. (Apr-May 1897); chief engr., Navy Yard, League Island, PA (May 1897-Dec 1898); home and w.o. (Dec 1898-Jan 1899); Naval

Rndv., Chicago, and insp. of engineering material, Milwaukee, WI, St. Paul, MN, and Washington Heights, IL (Feb 1899-Feb 1900); insp. of machinery, torp. boats, Morris Heights, NY (Feb 1900-Sep 1901); placed on Ret.Lst. (21 Sep 1901).

CHARLES HENRY ROCKWELL Born on 29 Apr 1840 in Chatham, MA, son of Rev. Charles and Mary (Howes) Rockwell. Educated in Sharon, PA, and in Philadelphia. Married Esther H. Gould on 7 Apr 1861. Married a second time to Marianna C. Butler. Resided in Chatham, MA. Died on 1 Jul 1908.

Ranks Act.Mstr (5 Jul 1862); Act.Lt (16 Dec 1863); Act.LCdr (27 Mar 1865); honorably discharged (8 Dec 1865); Act.Mstr (19 Nov 1866); Mstr (12 Mar 1868); Lt (18 Dec 1868); LCdr (26 Feb 1878); Cdr (31 Oct 1888); Capt (3 Mar 1899); placed on Ret.Lst. as RAdm (29 Apr 1902).

Career Summary Received appointment from MA (5 Jul 1862); Navy Yard, NY (Jul 1862); *Penguin*, E.Gulf Blk.Sqdn. (Jul 1862-May 1863); *Wanderer*, spec.serv. (May-Jul 1863); cdr, *Two Sisters*, E.Gulf Blk.Sqdn. (Jul-Dec 1863); cdr, *Gem of the Sea*, E.Gulf Blk.Sqdn. (Dec 1863-Nov 1864); cdr, *Hendrick Hudson*, E.Gulf Blk.Sqdn. (Nov 1864-Aug 1865); temp. duty, naval aide to BGen John Newton, USA (Feb-Aug 1865); l.o.a. (Aug-Dec 1865); discharged (8 Dec 1865); received appointment from MA (19 Nov 1866); *Osceola*, W.Indies (Nov 1866-Sep 1867); w.o. (Sep-Oct 1867); *Guerriere*, S.Atl.Sqdn. (Nov 1867-Jul 1869); w.o. (Jul-Dec 1869); rec. ship, *Vandalia*, Portsmouth, NH (Jan-Feb 1870); cdr, *Palos*, Asia.Sqdn. (Feb 1870-Oct 1872); *Alaska*, N.Pac.Sqdn. (Oct 1872-Feb 1873); w.o. (Feb-Mar 1873); Navy Yard, Portsmouth, NH (Mar 1873-Sep 1874); *Plymouth*, N.Atl. Sqdn. (Oct 1874-Feb 1875); flgs., *Colorado*, N.Atl.Sta. (Feb-Apr 1875); insp., 14th L.h. Dist., Cincinnati, OH (Jun 1875-Feb 1876); s.a. and w.o. (Feb-Mar 1876); l.o.a. (Mar-May 1876); exec.off., *Adams*, N.Atl.Sta. (May 1876-Mar 1877); l.o.a. and w.o. (Mar 1877-Apr 1879); exec.off., *Jamestown*, N.Pac.Sta. (May 1879-Sep 1881); w.o. (Sep-Nov 1881); Navy Yard, Boston (Nov 1881-Oct 1882); w.o. (Oct-Nov 1882); rec. ship, *Franklin*, Norfolk, VA (Nov 1882-Dec 1883); w.o. (Dec 1883-Sep 1884); spec.serv., Isthmus of Panama (Oct 1884-May 1885); Torp.School and NWC, Newport, RI (Jun-Sep 1885); w.o. (Sep 1885-Apr 1886); training ship, *Minnesota*, NY (Apr 1886-Oct 1888); w.o. (Oct 1888-Feb 1889); cdr, *Yantic*, spec.serv., W.Indies (Feb 1889-Aug 1891); l.o.a. (Aug-Oct 1891); cdr, rec. ship, *St. Louis*, League Island, PA (Oct 1891-Jun 1894); cdr, rec. ship, *Richmond*, Philadelphia (Jun-Jul 1894); comdt., Naval Sta., Port Royal, SC (Jul 1894-Jun 1899); w.o. (Jun-Aug 1899); temp.cdr, Navy Yard, Norfolk, VA (Aug-Oct 1899); cdr, *Chicago*, spec.serv., and S.Atl. Sqdn. (Oct 1899-May 1901); w.o. (May-Jul 1901); capt.yd., Navy Yard, Mare Island, CA (Aug 1901-Apr 1902); placed on Ret.Lst. (29 Apr 1902).

JOHN AUGUSTUS RODGERS Born in Havre de Grace, MD, on 26 Jul 1848, son of Robert Smith and Sarah (Perry)

CHARLES HENRY ROCKWELL
1840-1908

JOHN AUGUSTUS RODGERS
1848-1933

Rodgers. His paternal grandfather was Commo John Rodgers, USN (1772-1838), and his uncle was RAdm John Rodgers, USN (1812-82). His mother was the daughter of Commo Matthew C. Perry. His elder brother was RAdm Frederick Rodgers, USN (1842-1917) [*q.v.*]. Married Elizabeth Blanche Chambers on 30 Mar 1880. Three sons, including Cdr John Rodgers, USN (1881-1926), a pioneer naval aviator. Died at his home near Havre de Grace, MD, on 3 Mar 1933.

Ranks Midn (30 Jul 1863); Ens (19 Apr 1869); Mstr (12 Jul 1870); Lt (2 Feb 1874); LCdr (1 Mar 1895); Cdr (3 Mar 1899); Capt (29 Dec 1903); RAdm (7 Sep 1908); placed on Ret.Lst. (26 Jul 1910).

Career Summary Received appointment by virtue of being the son of an officer (30 Jul 1863); USNA (Jul 1863-Jun 1868); found deficient and put back (Feb 1865); w.o. (Jun-Sep 1868); *Pensacola*, N.Pac.Sqdn. (Oct 1868-Sep 1869); w.o. (Sep-Oct 1869); *Supply*, Eur.Sta. (Nov 1869-Jul 1870); *Nipsic*, Darien Expd. (Jul 1870-Nov 1871); torp.serv., Newport, RI (Jan-Aug 1872); w.o. (Aug-Sep 1872); *Hartford*, Asia.Sta. (Oct 1872-Oct 1875); w.o. (Oct 1875-Feb 1876); *Juniata*, Baltimore, and Navy Yard, Norfolk, VA (Feb-Sep 1876); training ship, *Monongahela* (Sep 1876-Jan 1877); w.o. (Jan-Feb 1877); flgs., *Trenton*, and *Constellation*, Eur.Sta. (Feb 1877-Jan 1880); w.o. (Jan-Apr 1880); ord. instruction and duty, Navy Yard, Washington, DC (Apr 1880-Jan 1883); Midvale Steel Works, Nicetown, PA (Jan 1883-Jan 1884); *Ossipee*, Asia.Sta. (Jan 1884-Mar 1887); insp. of steel for new vessels (Mar-Aug 1887); member, steel bd., Washington, DC (Sep 1887-Jun 1890); *Pensacola*, S.Atl.Sta. (Jul 1890-Feb 1891); Naval Hospital, NY (Feb-Apr 1891); sick lv. (Apr 1891-Sep 1892); NWC (Sep-Oct 1892); *Miantonomoh*, N.Atl.Sta. (Nov 1892-Nov 1894); l.o.a. (Nov 1894-Mar 1895); insp. of steel, Bethlehem Steel Works, S.Bethlehem, PA (Mar 1895-Jan 1897); exec.off., *Indiana*, N.Atl.Flt. (Feb 1897-Apr 1899); insp., 6th L.h. Dist., Charleston, SC (Apr 1899-Feb 1902); cdr, *Marietta*, N.Atl.Sqdn. (Feb-Sep 1902); cdr, *Albany*, Eur. and Asia.Sqdns. (Oct 1902-Jan 1904); home and w.o. (Jan-Apr 1904); pres., naval wireless telegraph bd., and other temp. duties, Washington, DC (Apr-Nov 1904); *Illinois*, N.Atl.Flt. (Nov 1904-Jun 1906); asst., then insp., 3rd L.h. Dist., Tompkinsville, NY (Jun 1906-Jul 1908); comdt., Navy Yard, Puget Sound, WA (Jul 1908-Jul 1910); placed on Ret.Lst. (26 Jul 1910); comdt., naval units, Harvard Univ., Massachusetts Institute of Technology, Boston Univ., and Tufts Univ. (Oct 1918-Jan 1919).

Career Highlights Member of the famous navy family of Rodgers, served as exec.off. on the *Indiana* which participated in the Battle of Santiago. Was advanced five places for his conduct in the action.

References
Personal Papers: a) Rodgers Family, 15,500 items (1788-1944) in NHF,LC. b) Rodgers Family, 11,150 items (1740-1957) in LC. b) 1872-77 in MD Historical Society, Baltimore.

RAYMOND PERRY RODGERS Born in Washington, DC, on 20 Dec 1849, son of RAdm Christopher Raymond Perry, USN (1819-92) and Julia (Slidell) Rodgers. A grandson of Commo George Washington Rodgers, USN (1787-1832) and of Ann Maria Perry, sister of Oliver Hazard and Matthew C. Perry, his younger brother was RAdm Thomas Slidell Rodgers USN (1858-1931) [*q.v.*], and his cousins were RAdm Frederick Rodgers USN, and RAdm John Rodgers, USN. Married Gertrude Stuyvesant. One daughter. Died in Monte Carlo, Monaco, on 28 Dec 1925. Buried in USNA Cemetery, Annapolis.

Ranks Midn (25 Jul 1864); Ens (19 Apr 1869); Mstr (12 Jul 1870); Lt (10 Oct 1872); LCdr (4 Jul 1893); Cdr (3 Mar 1899); Capt (21 Mar 1903); RAdm (4 Jul 1908); placed on Ret.Lst. (20 Dec 1911).

Career Summary Received appointment by virtue of being the son of an officer (25 Jul 1864); USNA (Jul 1864-Jun 1868); w.o. (Jun-Sep 1868); flgs., *Guerriere*, S.Atl. and Eur.Stas. (Sep 1868-Aug 1869); *Juniata*, and *Plymouth*, Eur.Sta. (Aug 1869-Jun 1873); w.o. (Jun-Aug 1873); USNA (Sep 1873-Sep 1876); flgs., *Pensacola*, Pac.Sta. (Nov 1876-May 1879); USNA (Jun 1879-Jul 1882); *Tennessee*, N.Atl.Sta. (Jul 1882-Nov 1884); Bur. of Nav., Washington, DC (Nov 1884-Apr 1885); chief intelligence off., Navy Dept., Washington, DC (Apr 1885-Jul 1889); *Chicago*, Sqdn. of Evol. (Jul 1889-Jul 1892); spec. duties (Jul-Aug 1892); naval attaché, Paris, St. Petersburg, Russia, and Madrid (Oct 1892-Apr 1897); duty with, then exec.off., *Iowa*, N.Atl.Flt. (May 1897-Apr 1899); Office of Naval Intelligence, Navy Dept., Washington, DC (Apr-Jul 1899); cdr, *Nashville*, N.Atl. and Asia.Stas. (Jul 1899-Jul 1900); home and w.o. (Jul-Oct 1900); on staff, Adm George Dewey, and member, Gen Bd., Washington, DC (Oct 1900-Apr 1901); equip.off., Navy Yard, NY (May 1901-Apr 1904); cdr, *Kearsarge*, and chief of staff, N.Atl.Flt. (Apr 1904-Apr 1906); chief intelligence off., Navy Dept., Washington, DC (Apr 1906-May 1909); duty at, then pres., NWC, and comdt., Naval Sta., Newport, RI (May 1909-Nov 1911); Gen Bd., Washington, DC (Nov 1911); l.o.a. (Nov-Dec 1911); placed on Ret.Lst. (20 Dec 1911).

Career Highlights Served twice as chief intelligence off. of the navy. Was naval attaché to France, Russia, and Spain. Served on the *Iowa* during the war with Spain, participating in the actions at Santiago and off San Juan for which he was advanced five numbers for his actions. Commanded the *Kearsarge* in the P.I. following the war with Spain and off China during the Boxer Rebellion.

References
Personal Papers: a) Rodgers Family, 15,000 items (1788-1944) in NHF,LC. b) Rodgers Family, 11,150 Items (1740-1957) in LC. c) 2 items (1876-79) in WPL.

THOMAS SLIDELL RODGERS Born in Morristown, NJ, on 18 Aug 1858, son of RAdm Christopher Raymond Perry, USN (1819-92) and Julie (Slidell) Rodgers. A grandson of Commo

RAYMOND PERRY RODGERS
1849-1925

THOMAS SLIDELL RODGERS
1858-1931

George Washington Rodgers, USN (1787-1832) and of Ann Maria Perry, sister of Oliver Hazard and Matthew C. Perry. His older brother was RAdm Raymond Perry Rodgers USN (1849-1925) [q.v.], and his cousins were RAdm Frederick Rodgers USN, and RAdm John Rodgers USN. Remained unmarried. Died in NY City on 28 Feb 1931. Buried in Arlington National Cemetery.

Ranks Cadet Midn (24 Sep 1874); Midn (4 Jun 1880); Ens (1 Dec 1881); Ltjg (23 Mar 1889); Lt (1 Oct 1893); LCdr (22 Nov 1900); Cdr (1 Jul 1905); Capt (15 Sep 1909); RAdm (13 Jun 1916); placed on Ret.Lst. (19 Jul 1919).

Career Summary Received appointment by virtue of being the son of an officer (24 Sep 1874); USNA (Sep 1874-Jun 1878); w.o. (Jun-Sep 1878); *Quinnebaug*, Navy Yard, Philadelphia (Sep-Oct 1878); *Trenton*, Eur.Sta. (Oct 1878-Mar 1880); home and w.o. (Mar-May 1880); USNA (May-Jun 1880); *Galena*, Eur.Sta. (Jun 1880); *Lancaster*, Eur.Sta. (Jun 1880-Sep 1884); w.o. (Sep 1884); ord. instruction, Navy Yard, Washington, DC (Sep 1884-Mar 1885); duty with U.S. Senate, Washington, DC (Mar-Aug 1885); Bur. of Ord., Washington, DC (Aug 1885-May 1886); *Juniata*, Navy Yard, NY, and Pac.Sta. (May 1886-Apr 1889); Ord.Dept., Navy Yard, Washington, DC (Apr 1889-Jun 1892); *Chicago*, N.Atl.Sta. (Jun 1892-Jan 1894); *Bennington*, Eur. and Pac.Sqdns. (Jan-Nov 1894); *Ranger*, Pac.Sta. (Nov 1894-May 1895); l.o.a. (May-Aug 1895); ord. duty, Navy Yard, Washington, DC (Aug 1895-May 1897); flag lt, *Brooklyn*, spec.serv. (May-Jul 1897); flag lt, Pac.Sta., *Philadelphia* (Aug-Oct 1897); on staff, Pac.Sta., *Bennington* (Oct-Nov 1897), then *Baltimore* (Nov 1897-Mar 1898); *Bennington*, Pac.Sta. (Mar-May 1898); *Monterey*, Asia.Sta. (May 1898-Apr 1899); *Wheeling*, Asia.Sta. (Apr 1899-Mar 1900); *Scindia*, Pac.Sqdn. (Apr 1900); *Bennington*, Pac.Sqdn. (Apr-May 1900); *Dixie*, spec.serv. (May-Aug 1900); Bur. of Ord., Washington, DC (Aug 1900-Jan 1901); member, then recorder, bd. of inspection and surv. (Jan 1901-Aug 1902); exec.off., *Maine*, Navy Yard, Philadelphia (Aug 1902-May 1903); rec. ship, *Lancaster*, Philadelphia (May 1903-Jul 1905); asst.insp., 3rd L.h. Dist., Tompkinsville, NY (Sep 1905); asst., then insp., 10th L.h. Dist., Buffalo, NY (Sep 1905-Sep 1906); asst.comdt., 4th Naval Dist., League Island, PA (Oct-Dec 1906); cdr, *Dubuque*, spec.serv. (Dec 1906-Jul 1908); equip.off., then act.capt.yd., Navy Yard, Philadelphia (Jul 1908-Oct 1909); cdr, *New Hampshire*, Atl.Flt. (Oct 1909-Nov 1911); supervisor, NY Harbor (Nov 1911-Jan 1912); dir., naval intelligence, Navy Dept., Washington, DC (Jan 1912-Dec 1913); cdr, *New York*, Asia.Flt. (Dec 1913-Oct 1915); w.o. (Oct-Nov 1915); NWC (Dec 1915-Jun 1916); cdr., 7th Div., Battleship Force, Atl.Flt., *Florida* (Jun 1916-Mar 1917), and *Arkansas* (Mar-Nov 1917); cdr, 5th Div., Battleship Force, Atl.Flt., *Connecticut* (Nov 1917-Feb 1918); cdr, 3rd Sqdn., Div. Six, Atl.Flt. (Feb 1918-Feb 1919); pres., naval exam. and ret. bds., Washington, DC (Feb-Jul 1919); placed on Ret.Lst. (19 Jul 1919).

Career Highlights Served as dir. of naval intelligence. During World War I, commanded a battleship div. of Atl.Flt. Awarded

the Distinguished Service Medal.
References
Personal Papers: a) Rodgers Papers, 15,500 items (1788-1944)
in NHF,LC. b) Rodgers Papers, 11,150 items (1740-1957) in LC.

WILLIAM LEDYARD RODGERS
1860-1944

WILLIAM LEDYARD RODGERS Born in Washington, DC,
on 4 Feb 1860, son of RAdm John, USN (1812-82), and Ann E.
(Hodge) Rodgers. His grandfather was Commo John Rodgers,
USN (1772-1838), and his cousins were RAdm Frederick Rodgers,
USN (1842-1917), and RAdm John Augustus Rodgers, USN
(1848-1933) as well as other Rodgers from another branch of the
family. Received his early education in Benicia, CA. Remained
unmarried. Died at the Naval Hosp. in Bethesda, MD, on 7 May
1944. Buried in Oakhill Cemetery.

Ranks Cadet Midn (11 Jun 1874); Midn (4 Jun 1880); Ens (1
Apr 1882); Ltjg (4 May 1889); Lt (4 Feb 1894); LCdr (19 Feb
1901); Cdr (27 Dec 1905); Capt (4 Dec 1909); RAdm (29 Aug
1916); VAdm (28 Jun 1919); placed on Ret.Lst. with rank of
RAdm (4 Feb 1924); VAdm on Ret.Lst. (21 Jun 1930).

Career Summary Received appointment from CA (11 Jun
1874); USNA (Jun 1874-Jun 1878); w.o. (Jun-Sep 1878);
Pensacola, Pac.Sqdn. (Oct 1878-Mar 1880); w.o. (Mar-May
1880); USNA (May-Jun 1880); w.o. (Jun-Aug 1880); Naval
Observatory, Washington, DC (Aug 1880-Jun 1881); *Quinnebaug*,
Eur.Sta. (Jun 1881-Aug 1884); spec. duty, Navy Dept., Washing-
ton, DC (Sep 1884-May 1886); torp. instruction, Newport, RI
(May-Sep 1886); Office of Naval Intelligence, Navy Dept.,
Washington, DC (Sep 1886-Oct 1887); *Yantic*, S.Atl.Sta. (Oct
1887-Jun 1888); l.o.a. (Jun 1888-Dec 1889); *Atlanta*, Eur.Sqdn.
(Dec 1889-Dec 1892); ord. duty, Navy Yard, Washington, DC
(Dec 1892-Sep 1895); training ship, *Alliance* (Oct 1895-May
1897); Columbia Iron Works, Baltimore (May-Jun 1897); duty
with, then cdr, *T. B. Foote*, Torp.Flot. (Jul 1897-Oct 1898); Navy
Yard, Washington, DC (Nov 1898-Apr 1900); temp. duty,
Kentucky, Navy Yard, NY (May-Aug 1900); nav., then exec.off.,
training ship, *Indiana* (Aug-Nov 1900); training ship, *Lancaster*
(Dec 1900-Apr 1902); exec.off., training ship, *Topeka* (Apr
1902-Apr 1903); NWC (May 1903-Feb 1905); spec. duty, Ft.
Leavenworth, KS (Feb-May 1905); exec.off., *Wisconsin*, Asia.Sta.
(Apr 1905-Apr 1906); additional duty, Naval Sta., Cavite, P.I.
(Feb-Apr 1906); cdr, *Wilmington*, Asia.Sta. (Apr 1906-Jul 1907);
home and w.o. (Jul-Sep 1907); duty connected with NWC (Sep
1907-Dec 1909); cdr, *Georgia*, Atl.Flt. (Dec 1909-Nov 1911);
pres., NWC (Nov 1911-Dec 1913); cdr, *Delaware*, Atl.Flt. (Dec
1913-Jun 1915); member, Gen Bd., Washington, DC (Jun
1915-Aug 1916); cdr, training ship, *Vestal*, Atl.Flt. (Aug 1916-
Oct 1918); cd, Asia.Flt., *Brooklyn* (Oct 1918-Feb 1920); member,
Gen Bd. and chairman, exec.committee, Navy Dept., Washington,
DC (Feb 1920-Feb 1924); placed on Ret.Lst. (4 Feb 1924);
member, advice council, Conference on the Limitation of
Armaments, Washington, DC (1921); technical advisor, Commission of Jurists on Laws of War, The Hague, Netherlands (1923).

Career Highlights Served as pres. of the NWC, and as pres. of the Naval Institute. Sat twice on the navy's Gen Bd. Wrote several works, including articles for the Naval Institute's *Proceedings.* Recipient of the Navy Cross.

References

Personal Papers: a) Rodgers Family Papers, 15,500 items (1788-1944) in NHF,LC. b) Rodgers Family Papers, 11,150 items (1740-1957) in LC.

Writings: a) "Notes on the Naval Brigade," U.S. Naval Institute *Proceedings* 44 (1888): 57-96. b) "What Changes in Organization and Drill Are Necessary to Sail and Fight Most Effectively Our War Ships of the Latest Type?" U.S. Naval Institute *Proceedings* 38 (1886): 361-89. c) "An Examination of the Testimony Taken by the Joint Committee of the Senate and House of Representatives in Regard to the Reorganization of the Navy," U.S. Naval Institute *Proceedings* 72 (1894): 747-62. d) "A Study of Attacks upon Fortified Harbors," U.S. Naval Institute *Proceedings* 111 (Sep 1904): 533-66; 112 (Dec 1904): 709-44; 113 (Mar 1905): 97-119. e) "The Field of Work to be Filled by a Naval War College," U.S. Naval Institute *Proceedings* 138 (Jun 1911): 353-77. f) "The Relations of the War College to the Navy Department," U.S. Naval Institute *Proceedings* 143 (Sep 1912): 835-50. g) "The Naval War College Course," U.S. Naval Institute *Proceedings* 144 (Dec 1912): 1235-40. h) "Military Preparedness Necessary to the Economic and Social Welfare of the United States," U.S. Naval Institute *Proceedings* 272 (Oct 1925): 1845-57. i) "Discussion of Limitation of Armament," U.S. Naval Institute *Proceedings* 287 (Jan 1927): 43-49. j) "American Naval Policy and the Tri Power Conference at Geneva, 1927," U.S. Naval Institute *Proceedings* 305 (Jul 1928): 572-78. k) "The Navy as an Aid in Carrying Our Diplomatic Policies," U.S. Naval Institute *Proceedings* 312 (Feb 1929): 99-104. l) *Greek and Roman Naval Warfare: A Study of Strategy, Tactics and Ship Design from Salamis to Actium* (Annapolis: 1937, 1964). m) *Naval Warfare under Oars, Fourth to Sixth Centuries: A Study of Strategy, Tactics and Ship Design* (Annapolis: 1939, 1967). n) "Possible Peace Terms--Present War," U.S. Naval Institute *Proceedings* 450 (Aug 1940): 1088-94.

HUGH RODMAN Born in Frankfort, KY, on 6 Jan 1859, son of Hugh and Susan Ann (Barbour) Rodman. A first cousin and brother-in-law to RAdm William Henry Hudson Southerland, USN [*q.v.*], married Elizabeth Ruffin Sayer on 3 Jul 1889. Resided in Washington, DC, dying on 7 Jun 1940 at the Naval Hosp. there.

Ranks Cadet Midn (18 Sep 1875); Midn (22 Jun 1882); Ensjg (3 Mar 1883); Ens (26 Jun 1884); Ltjg (1 Oct 1893); Lt (13 Jul 1897); LCdr (3 Mar 1903); Cdr (1 Jul 1907); Capt (4 Mar 1911); RAdm (23 May 1917); Adm (1 Jul 1919); placed on Ret.Lst. as RAdm (6 Jan 1923); Adm on Ret.Lst. (21 Jun 1930).

Career Summary Received appointment from KY (18 Sep 1875); USNA (Sep 1875-Jun 1880); w.o. (Jun-Sep 1880); *Yantic,*

HUGH RODMAN
1859-1940

spec.serv. (Sep 1880-Mar 1882); w.o. (Mar-May 1882); USNA (May-Oct 1882); *Wachusett,* Pac.Sta. (Nov 1882-Jun 1884); *Hartford,* Pac.Sta. (Jun 1884-Aug 1885); home and l.o.a. (Aug-Nov 1885); Hydrographic Office, Washington, DC (Nov 1885-Jun 1886); *Essex,* Asia.Sta. (Jul 1886-Jan 1887); *Monocacy,* Asia.Sta. (Jan 1887-Jun 1888); *Palos,* Asia.Sta. (Jun-Nov 1888); *Omaha,* Asia.Sta. (Nov 1888-Jan 1889); *Essex,* Asia.Sta. (Jan-May 1889); Hydrographic Office, Washington, DC (Jul 1889-Oct 1890); Naval Observatory, Washington, DC (Oct 1890-Mar 1891); cst.surv. duty (Apr 1891-Nov 1895); Cst.Surv. Office, Washington, DC (Dec 1895-Apr 1897); *Raleigh,* spec.serv. and Asia.Sta. (Apr 1897-Jun 1899); l.o.a. (Jun-Jul 1899); Fish Commission steamer, *Albatross* (Jul 1899-Dec 1901); cdr, *Iroquois,* Territory of HI (Dec 1901-Mar 1904); exec.off., *New Orleans,* Asia.Sta. (Apr-Dec 1904); *Cincinnati,* Asia.Sta. (Dec 1904-Mar 1905); *Wisconsin,* Asia.Sta. (Mar-Apr 1905); cdr, *Elcano,* Yangtze Patrol, Asia.Sta. (Apr 1905-Feb 1907); staff member, Asia.Sta., *West Virginia* (Feb-Mar 1907); home and w.o. (Mar-May 1907); NWC (Jun-Sep 1907); asst., then insp., 6th L.h. Dist., Charleston, SC (Sep 1907-Dec 1908); Naval Sta., Cavite, P.I. (Jan-Jun 1909); cdr, *Cleveland,* Asia.Sta. (Jun 1909-Aug 1910); home and w.o. (Aug-Sep 1910); inspection off., Navy Yard, Mare Island, CA (Sep 1910-May 1911); capt.yd., Navy Yard, Mare Island, CA (May-Dec 1911); cdr, *Connecticut,* Atl.Flt. (Jan-Oct 1912); *Delaware,* Naval Review and Atl.Flts. (Oct 1912-Dec 1913); temp. duty, Navy Dept., Washington, DC (Dec 1913); home and w.o. (Dec 1913); duty at Isthmian Canal, Panama (Jan-Mar 1914); supt. of transportation, Panama Canal, and dir., Panama Railroad Company (Mar 1914-Sep 1915); home and w.o. (Sep-Oct 1915); cdr, *New York,* Asia.Flt. and Pac. Reserve Flt. (Oct 1915-Oct 1916); member, Gen Bd., and other bd. duties, Navy Dept., Washington, DC (Oct 1916-Apr 1917); cdr, 3rd Div., Atl.Flt., *Rhode Island* (Apr-Aug 1917); cdr, 1st Sqdn., 2nd Div., Battleship Force, Atl.Flt. (Aug-Sep 1917); cdr, 3rd Div., Battleship Force One, Atl.Flt. (Sep-Nov 1917); cdr, 5th Div., Battleship Force Two, Atl.Flt., *Connecticut* (Nov 1917); cdr, Battleship Division Nine, Atl.Flt., *New York* (Nov 1917-Feb 1919); cdr, 6th Battle Sqdn. (Feb-Jul 1919); cdr., Pac.Flt., *New Mexico* (Jul 1919-Jun 1921); cdr, 5th Naval Dist., Hampton Roads, VA (Jun 1921-Jan 1923); placed on Ret.Lst. (6 Jan 1923).

Career Highlights During Spanish-American War, served on the *Raleigh* in the Battle of Manila Bay. Served on and command-ed several of the navy's newest ships between 1898 and 1917. Was on Gen Bd. prior to America's entry into World War I. Commanded several divisions of Atl.Flt. during the war. Received Distinguished Service Medal, as well as other U.S. medals and eight foreign decorations, including Knight Commander of Order of the Bath (Britain), the Order of the Rising Sun (Japan), the Grand Cordon of Leopold II (Belgium), Commander of the Legion of Honor (France), El Sol (Peru), and the El Merite (Chile).

References

Writings: a) "The Sacred Calabash," U.S. Naval Institute

Proceedings 294 (Aug 1927): 867-72. b) *Yarns of a Kentucky Admiral* (Indianapolis: 1928). c) "The Christmas Ship," U.S. Naval Institute *Proceedings* 341 (Jul 1931): 888.

CHARLES RAFAEL ROELKER Born in Osnabruck, Hanover, Germany, on 23 Sep 1841. Married to Parthenia P. Roelker. Six children. Died in Washington, DC, on 28 Sep 1910. Buried in Arlington National Cemetery.

Ranks 3rd Asst.Engr. (8 Dec 1862); 2nd Asst.Engr. (8 Apr 1864); 1st Asst.Engr. (1 Jan 1868); title changed to PAsst.Engr. (23 Jul 1873); Chief Engr. (10 Nov 1890); Chief Engr. with rel. rank of Cdr (28 May 1897); Cdr (3 Mar 1899); Capt (5 Mar 1902); placed on Ret.Lst. with rank of RAdm (23 Sep 1903).

Career Summary Received appointment from NY (8 Dec 1862); w.o. (Dec 1862-Jul 1863); *Sonoma,* and *Nipsic,* N. and S.Atl.Blk.Sqdns. (Jul 1863-May 1865); Bur. of Steam Engineering, Washington, DC (Jun 1865-May 1869); w.o. (May-Nov 1869); Bur. of Steam Engineering, Washington, DC (Nov 1869-Jul 1871); *Tallapoosa,* spec.serv. (Jul 1871-Jan 1872); temp. duty, *Frolic,* N.Atl.Sta. (Jan-Jun 1872); *Fortune,* and *Triana,* spec.serv. (Jun 1872-Jun 1873); *Shenandoah,* Eur.Sta. (Jul 1873-Mar 1874); *Congress,* Eur.Sta. (Apr 1874-Jan 1876); Bur. of Steam Engineering, Washington, DC (Jan 1876-Sep 1882); l.o.a. (Sep-Dec 1882); duty, naval advisory bd., Washington, DC (Dec 1882-Oct 1887); Fish Commission steamer, *Albatross* (Oct 1887-Jan 1891); home and l.o.a. (Jan-Jul 1891); spec. duty, *Raleigh* and other engineering duties, Norfolk, VA (Jul 1891-Mar 1897); l.o.a. (Mar-Apr 1897); member, bd. of inspection and surv. (Apr 1897-Jun 1898); *Newark,* N.Atl.Flt. (Jun-Nov 1898); member, bd. of inspection and surv. (Nov 1898-Sep 1903); duty, Fish and Fisheries Commission, Washington, DC (Jun 1899-Apr 1907); placed on Ret.Lst. (23 Sep 1903); additional spec. bd. duty, Dept. of Commerce and Labor, Washington, DC (Dec 1904-Apr 1907).

References

Writings: a) "The Boiler Power of Naval Vessels," U.S. Naval Institute *Proceedings* 8 (1879): 275-92. b) "Economy of Compound Direct-Acting Pumping Engines," U.S. Naval Institute *Proceedings* 41 (1887): 211-19.

CHARLES CUSTIS ROGERS Born in Smyth County, VA, on 11 May 1856, son of Charles G. and Mary W. (Campbell) Rogers. Married Alice Ashmore Walker on 3 Jan 1888. One son and one daughter. Made his home in Winchester, VA. Died on 4 Dec 1917 in Washington, DC, and was buried in Winchester.

Ranks Cadet Midn (8 Jun 1872); Midn (20 Jun 1876); Ens (26 Apr 1878); Ltjg (2 Jun 1885); Lt (27 Jan 1891); LCdr (1 Jul 1899); Cdr (21 Feb 1905); Capt (25 Oct 1908); RAdm (13 Feb 1914); retired (27 Apr 1914). ·

Career Summary Received appointment from TN (8 Jun 1872); USNA (Jun 1872-Jun 1876); w.o. (Jun-Oct 1876); *Plymouth,* N.Atl.Sta. (Oct 1876-Aug 1877); *Monongahela,* Asia.Sta. (Aug 1877-Feb 1879); w.o. (Feb-Mar 1879); USNA

CHARLES CUSTIS ROGERS
1856-1917

(Mar-Apr 1879); w.o. (Apr-Jul 1879); *Vandalia*, N.Atl.Sta. (Jul 1879-May 1882); w.o. (May-Sep 1882); spec. duty, Bur. of Nav., Washington, DC (Sep 1882-Oct 1883); l.o.a. (Oct 1883-Oct 1884); spec. duty, The Fogg School, Nashville, TN (Oct 1884-Jun 1886); *Essex*, Asia.Sta. (Jul 1886); *Swatara*, spec.serv. (Jul-Oct 1886); *Yantic*, spec.serv. (Oct 1886); *Galena*, spec.serv. (Oct 1886-Aug 1888); *Ossipee*, N.Atl.Sta. (Aug-Nov 1888); *Pensacola*, Eur.Sta. (Nov 1888-Feb 1889); *Yantic*, N.Atl.Sta. (Feb-Jun 1889); w.o. (Jun-Jul 1889); l.o.a. (Jul-Sep 1889); Office of Naval Intelligence, Navy Dept., Washington, DC (Sep 1889-Apr 1892); l.o.a. (Apr 1892-Jul 1893); *Detroit*, S.Atl.Sta. (Jul 1893-Aug 1896); l.o.a. (Aug-Sep 1896); USNA (Sep 1896-Apr 1898); exec.off., *Resolute*, N.Atl.Flt. (Apr-Nov 1898); *Detroit*, Asia.Sta. (Nov 1898-Jul 1899); *New York*, spec.serv. (Jul 1899-Nov 1900); *Massachusetts*, N.Atl.Sqdn. (Nov 1900-May 1901); home and w.o. (May-Jul 1901); Navy Yard, Norfolk, VA (Jul-Nov 1901); Office of Naval War Records, Navy Dept., Washington, DC (Nov 1901-Jan 1902); Bur. of Equip., Washington, DC (Jan 1902-May 1904); comdt., Naval Sta., and cdr, *Amphitrite*, *Vixen*, and *Monongahela*, Guantanamo Bay, Cuba (May 1904-Sep 1906); home and w.o. (Sep-Oct 1906); hydrographer, Bur. of Equipment and Recruiting, Washington, DC (Oct 1906-May 1908); cdr, *Milwaukee*, Navy Yard, Puget Sound, WA (Jun 1908-May 1909); cdr, *Washington*, Puget Sound, WA (May 1909-Jul 1910); w.o. (Jul-Sep 1910); Navy Yard, Norfolk, VA (Sep 1910-Jul 1911); comdt., Navy Yard, and 1st Naval Dist., Portsmouth, NH (Aug 1911-May 1914); retired (27 Apr 1914).

EUSTACE BARRON ROGERS Born in San Francisco on 29 May 1855, son of Robert Clay and Eliza Hamilton (Ritchie) Rogers. Educated at Lehigh Univ. in PA, and at the Univ. of CA. Married Anna N. Alexander on 17 Jan 1882. She died in 1908, and he married Marguerite Bosch of Belgium on 22 May 1913. Resided in Washington, DC. Died on 5 Mar 1929 at the League Island Naval Hosp. in Philadelphia. Buried in Arlington National Cemetery.

Ranks Asst.Paymstr. (3 Mar 1879); PAsst.Paymstr. (2 Nov 1884); PAsst.Paymstr. with rel. rank of Lt (5 May 1892); Paymstr. (24 May 1894); Paymstr. with rel. rank of LCdr (8 Dec 1899); Pay Insp. (21 Sep 1902); Pay Dir. (13 Mar 1905); Paymstr.Gen with rank of RAdm (1 Nov 1906); transferred to Ret.Lst. as Pay Dir. with rank of RAdm (30 Jun 1906).

Career Summary Received appointment from CA (3 Mar 1879); w.o. (Mar-Apr 1879); Bur. of Provisions and Clothing, Washington, DC (Apr-Dec 1879); *Tennessee*, N.Atl.Sta. (Dec 1879-Dec 1881); w.o. (Dec 1881-Apr 1882); insp. of provisions and clothing, Navy Yard, Boston (Apr-Oct 1882); w.o. (Oct 1882-May 1883); prac. ship, *Dale*, USNA (May-Sep 1883); s.a. and w.o. (Sep 1883-May 1884); prac. ship, *Dale*, USNA (May-Sep 1884); s.a. and w.o. (Sep 1884-Jan 1885); in charge of accounts, Naval Hosp., Yokohama, Japan (Feb 1885-Feb 1888); home, s.a. and w.o. (Feb-May 1888); asst.gen storekeeper, Navy Yard,

Boston (Jun-Oct 1888); *Kearsarge,* spec.serv. (Nov 1888-Oct 1891); s.a. and l.o.a. (Oct-Nov 1891); Bur. of Provisions and Clothing [renamed Supplies and Accounts], Washington, DC (Nov 1891-Jun 1894); *Cincinnati,* N.Atl.Sta. (Jun 1894-Jul 1895); in charge, Naval Clothing Factory, Navy Yard, NY (Jul 1895-Feb 1897); *Minneapolis,* Eur.Sta. (Apr-Jul 1897); Navy Yard, NY (Aug-Oct 1897); *Newport,* Navy Yard, Boston (Oct-Nov 1897); s.a. and w.o. (Nov 1897); *Monterey,* Pac.Sta. (Nov 1897-May 1899); *Oregon,* Asia.Sta. (May 1899-Apr 1900); *Baltimore,* Asia.Sta. (Apr-Sep 1900); s.a. and w.o. (Sep 1900); in charge, Naval Clothing Factory, Navy Yard, NY (Oct-Dec 1900); home and sick lv. (Dec 1900-Feb 1901); in charge, Naval Clothing Factory, Navy Yard, NY (Feb 1901-Apr 1904); spec. duty, Cavite, P.I. (May-Jun 1904); flt.paymstr., Asia.Flt., *Wisconsin* (Jul 1904-Apr 1905); home and w.o. (Apr-Jun 1905); member, naval exam. bd., Washington, DC (Jun-Jul 1905); gen storekeeper, Navy Yard, Boston (Aug 1905-Oct 1906); paymstr.gen, and chief, Bur. of Supplies and Accounts, Washington, DC (Nov 1906-Jun 1910); transferred to Ret.Lst. (30 Jun 1910); supply off., 13th Naval Dist., Puget Sound, Bremerton, WA (Apr-Aug 1917); Pac.cst. representative, Emergency Flt. Corporation (Aug 1917-Jan 1918); gen insp., Supply Corps, Pac.cst., San Francisco (Jan 1917-Jan 1918).

References
Writings: a) "The Egyptian Campaign: The Bombardment of Alexandria," U.S. Naval Institute *Proceedings* 22 (1882): 523-40. b) "Naval Intelligence," U.S. Naval Institute *Proceedings* 27 (1883): 659-92.

FRANK BRAMWELL ROSE Born in Tuckerton, NJ, on 5 Apr 1836, son of Francis Bodine and Sarah (Early) Rose. Educated at Central High School in Philadelphia. Married Mary Anna King on 2 Apr 1851. Five children. Ordained a Baptist minister in 1862. Resided in Swarthmore, PA, where he died on 23 Mar 1910. Buried in West Laurel Cemetery, Philadelphia.

Ranks Chaplain, 14th NJ Infantry Volunteers (1 Sep 1862); mustered out (18 Jun 1865); Chaplain (Baptist), USN (3 Feb 1870); Chaplain with rel. rank of Capt (8 Mar 1896); transferred to Ret.Lst. with rel. rank of Capt (5 Apr 1898); RAdm on Ret.Lst. (29 Jun 1906).

Career Summary Appointed chaplain, 14th NJ Infantry Volunteers (1 Sep 1862); chaplain, U.S.A. (Sep 1862-Jun 1865); mustered out (18 Jun 1865); received appointment from NJ as chaplain (Baptist), USN (3 Feb 1870); w.o. (Feb 1870-Mar 1872); flgs., *Lancaster,* S.Atl.Sqdn. (Apr 1872-Jan 1874); sick lv. (Jan-Apr 1874); Navy Yard, Philadelphia (May 1874-Dec 1875); rec. ship, *Potomac,* Philadelphia (Dec 1875-Dec 1876); training ship, *Constitution* (Dec 1876-May 1877); w.o. (May-Jul 1877); flgs., *Pensacola,* Pac.Sta. (Aug 1877-Oct 1878); w.o. (Oct 1878-Jun 1880); training ship, *Constitution* (Jun 1880-Dec 1881); w.o. (Dec 1881-Jan 1883); training ship, *Jamestown* (Jan 1883-Oct 1885); Naval Asylum, Philadelphia (Nov 1885-Sep 1888);

rec. ship, *New Hampshire*, Newport, RI (Sep 1888-Oct 1890); training ship, *Richmond*, Newport, RI (Oct 1890-Apr 1891); *Monongahela*, Training Sqdn. (Apr 1891-Dec 1893); w.o. (Dec 1893-Oct 1894); rec. ship, *Richmond*, Philadelphia (Nov-Dec 1894); Naval Home, Philadelphia (Dec 1894-Apr 1898); transferred to Ret.Lst. (5 Apr 1898); *Constitution*, Navy Yard, Boston (May-Oct 1898).

ALBERT ROSS Born in Clarion, PA, on 3 Jan 1846, son of Dr. James and Mary A. (Wilson) Ross. Received his early education in Clarion. Married Alice Brewer in Mar 1870. One son and one daughter. Married again on 7 Jun 1915 to Henrietta Frances Bartlett, widow of Commo Charles Ward Bartlett, USN. Retired to Cocoanut Grove, FL, where he died on 23 Jan 1926. Buried in Annapolis.

Ranks Midn (23 Jul 1863); Ens (18 Dec 1868); Mstr (21 Mar 1870); Lt (21 Mar 1871); placed on Ret.Lst. (21 Dec 1871); restored to Active List (1 Jul 1875); LCdr (5 Dec 1890); Cdr (28 Aug 1897); Capt (11 Apr 1902); RAdm (13 Oct 1907); placed on Ret.Lst. (3 Jan 1908).

Career Summary Received appointment from PA (23 Jul 1863); USNA (Jul 1863-Jun 1867); *Minnesota*, and *Powhatan*, spec.serv. and Pac.Sqdn. (Jul 1867-Dec 1869); w.o. (Dec 1869-Mar 1870); signal duty, Washington, DC (Mar-Jun 1870); sick lv. (Jun-Nov 1870); experimental duty, Navy Yard, Washington, DC (Nov 1870-Dec 1871); placed on Ret.Lst. (21 Dec 1871); w.o. (Dec 1871-Aug 1872); Naval Observatory, Washington, DC (Aug 1872-May 1874); *Wachusett*, and *Ossipee*, N.Atl.Sta. (May 1874-May 1875); w.o. (May-Jun 1875); restored to Active List (1 Jul 1875); flgs., *Worcester*, N.Atl.Sta. (Jul 1875-Jan 1876); spec. duty, Annapolis (Jan-Aug 1876); w.o. (Aug 1876-Mar 1877); *Passaic*, N.Atl.Sta. (Mar-Jul 1877); cdr, *Wyandotte*, Navy Yard, Washington, DC (Jul 1877-Jan 1879); *Portsmouth*, apprentice training serv. (Jan 1879-Mar 1882); Navy Yard, Washington, DC (Mar 1882-Apr 1883); Torp.Sta., Newport, RI (Apr-Aug 1883); *Miantonomoh*, Navy Yard, NY (Sep 1883); Navy Yard, NY (Sep 1883); USNA (Sep 1883-Aug 1886); w.o. (Aug-Dec 1886); *Alert*, Pac.Sta. (Jan 1887-Aug 1888); sick lv. (Aug 1888-Apr 1889); torp. instruction, Newport, RI (May-Jul 1889); *Pensacola*, N.Atl.Sta. (Aug-Sep 1889); sick lv. (Sep 1889-May 1890); training ship, *Jamestown* (May 1890-Sep 1892); exec.off., *Constellation*, Navy Yard, NY (Sep 1892); l.o.a. (Sep-Dec 1892); USNA (Dec 1892-Jan 1898); cdr, *Alliance*, Spec.Serv.Sqdn. (Jan 1898-Dec 1899); asst., then insp., 5th L.h. Dist., Baltimore (Dec 1899-May 1902); cdr, training ship, *Buffalo* (May 1902-Dec 1903); home and w.o. (Dec 1903-Jan 1904); insp., naval colliers (Jan 1904-May 1905); additional duty, comdt., Training Sta., Great Lakes, IL (Nov 1904-Nov 1911); member, L.h. Bd., Washington, DC (Apr 1905-Nov 1907); placed on Ret.Lst. (3 Jan 1908); various temp. duties (May 1917-Nov 1919).

References

Writings: a) "Aids in the Practical Work of Navigation," U.S.

ALBERT ROSS
1846-1926

Naval Institute *Proceedings* 18 (1881): 461-71. b) "Deck Chart-Board," U.S. Naval Institute *Proceedings* 27 (1883): 759-66.

HARRY HARWOOD ROUSSEAU
1870-1930

HARRY HARWOOD ROUSSEAU Born in Troy, NY, on 19 Apr 1870, son of William White and Jeannette (Parker) Rousseau. Received Civil Engineering degree from Rensselaer Polytechnic Institute in 1891. Served as a draftsman and engineer for private corporations to 1898. Married Gladys Fargo Squiers in 1908. Two sons. Died on 24 Jul 1930 while on board the SS *Cristobal* en route to Panama.

Ranks Civil Engineer with rank of Lt (29 Sep 1898); Chief, Bur. of Yards and Docks with rank of RAdm (5 Jan 1907); Civil Engineer with rank of LCdr (18 Oct 1909); Civil Engineer with rank of RAdm (4 Mar 1915); died (24 Jul 1930).

Career Summary Received appointment from PA (29 Sep 1898); w.o. (Sep-Oct 1898); Navy Yard, NY (Oct-Dec 1898); Naval Sta., New London, CT (Dec 1898-Jun 1899); Bur. of Yards and Docks, Washington, DC (Jun 1899-Jan 1903); engr. for public improvements, Navy Yard, Mare Island, CA (Feb 1903-Dec 1906); Navy Yard, Puget Sound, WA (Dec 1906); Bur. of Yards and Docks, Washington, DC (Jan 1907); chief, Bur. of Yards and Docks, Washington, DC (Jan-Mar 1907); member, Isthmian Canal Commission (Mar 1907-Apr 1914); engr. for terminal construction, Panama Canal (Apr 1914-Jul 1916); home and w.o. (Jul-Aug 1916); member, commission to establish additional navy yards, Bur. of Yards and Docks, Washington, DC (Sep 1916-Mar 1920); manager, shipyard plants div., Emergency Flt. Corporation (1917-1919); dir., Panama Railroad Company (1918-1920); vice-chairman, U.S. Shipping Bd., Port Facilities Commission (1918-1920); dir., Naval Petroleum Reserves (1927-July 1930); chief coordinator, Bur. of Budget of Federal Service (1928-July 1930).

Career Highlights Was greatly involved in the construction and early management of the Panama Canal. Served as coordinator of ships and shipyards during World War I, subsequently receiving the Navy Cross.

References
Writings: a) "Noted on Navy Yard Development," U.S. Naval Institute *Proceedings* 101 (Mar 1902): 55-72. b) "The Terminal Facilities of the Panama Canal," U.S. Naval Institute *Proceedings* 166 (Nov-Dec 1916): 1825-53.

ALEXANDER WILSON RUSSELL
1824-1908

ALEXANDER WILSON RUSSELL Born in MD on 4 Feb 1824. Married to Julia C. Russell. Five children. Resided in Philadelphia where he died on 26 Nov 1908. Buried in Woodland Cemetery in Philadelphia.

Ranks Captain's Clerk (1842); Paymstr. (28 Feb 1861); Pay Insp. (3 Mar 1871); Pay Dir. (23 Feb 1877); placed on Ret.Lst. (4 Feb 1886); Pay Dir. with rank of RAdm on Ret.Lst. (29 Jun 1906).

Career Summary Appointed Captain's Clerk (1842); Captain's Clerk, *Saratoga*, Afr.cst. (1842-1844); Company C (Texas

Rangers), Mounted Rifle Regiment (1846-1848); clerk, Committee of Naval Affairs, U.S. Senate, Washington, DC (1858-1861); received appointment from Washington, DC as paymstr., USN (28 Feb 1861); *Pocahontas*, Potomac River and Chesapeake Bay (Apr-May 1861); *Savannah*, N. and S.Atl.Blk.Sqdns. (May 1861-Feb 1862); s.a. (Feb 1862); *Colorado*, W.Gulf Blk.Sqdn. (Mar-Jun 1862); s.a. and w.o. (Jun-Jul 1862); *New Ironsides*, spec.serv. and S.Atl.Blk.Sqdn. (Jul 1862-Feb 1864); w.o. (Feb-Mar 1864); rec. ship, *North Carolina*, NY (May 1864-Sep 1865); s.a. and w.o. (Sep 1865-Feb 1866); *Chattanooga*, spec.serv. (Feb-Sep 1866); *Sacramento*, spec.serv. (Sep 1866-Dec 1867); s.a. and w.o. (Dec 1867-Mar 1868); bd. duties, Washington, DC (Mar 1868); w.o. (Mar-Jun 1868); insp. of provisions and clothing, Navy Yard, Washington, DC (Jun 1868-Sep 1870); paymstr., Navy Yard, Philadelphia (Oct 1870-Oct 1873); insp. of provisions and clothing, Navy Yard, Philadelphia (Oct 1873-Jan 1874); purchasing paymstr., Pay Office, Philadelphia (Jan 1874-Mar 1877); purchasing paymstr., Pay Office, Baltimore (Mar 1877-Jan 1882); s.a. and w.o. (Jan-Mar 1882); member, naval exam. bd. (Mar-Apr 1882); w.o. (Apr-May 1882); purchasing pay agent, Pay Office, Philadelphia (May 1882-Feb 1886); placed on Ret.Lst. (4 Feb 1886).

Career Highlights While a captain's clerk on the *Saratoga*, served in the operations under Commo Matthew C. Perry against the Barbery States in Dec 1843. Was with the Texas Rangers during the war with Mexico. With the Civil War, saw action against the forts on the Lower Mississippi. While on the *New Ironsides*, received recognition for commanding the powder and shell division during actions against Charleston, SC, in 1863.

JAMES HOBAN SANDS Born on 12 Jul 1845 in Washington, DC, son of RAdm Benjamin F., USN (1812-1883), and Henrietta Maria (French) Sands. Married Mary Elizabeth Meade on 28 Oct 1869. Six children. Died in Washington, DC, on 27 Oct 1911. Buried in Arlington National Cemetery.

Ranks Act.Midn (25 Nov 1859); title changed to Midn (16 Jul 1862); Ens (28 May 1863); Mstr (10 Nov 1865); Lt (10 Nov 1866); LCdr (12 Mar 1868); Cdr (23 Nov 1880); Capt (7 Sep 1894); RAdm (11 Apr 1902); placed on Ret.Lst. (12 Jul 1907).

Career Summary Received appointment from MD (25 Nov 1859); USNA (Nov 1859-May 1863); turned back (Jun 1860); *Tuscarora*, N.Atl.Blk.Sqdn. (Jun 1863-May 1864); *Juniata*, Navy Yard, Philadelphia (Jun-Aug 1864); sick lv. (Aug-Nov 1864); *Shenandoah*, N.Atl.Blk.Sqdn. (Nov 1864-Apr 1865); w.o. (Apr-Jul 1865); flgs., *Hartford*, Asia.Sqdn. (Jul 1865-Aug 1868); w.o. (Aug-Sep 1868); Naval Observatory, Washington, DC (Sep-Dec 1868); *Richmond*, Eur.Sqdn. (Jan-Jun 1869); w.o. (Jun-Jul 1869); Naval Observatory, Washington, DC (Jul 1869-Feb 1870); ord. duty, Navy Yard, Washington, DC (Feb-Nov 1870); flgs., *California*, Pac.Sqdn. (Dec 1870-Jul 1873); w.o. (Jul-Sep 1873); Hydrographic Office, Washington, DC (Oct 1873-Apr 1875); training ship, *Minnesota*, NY (Apr 1875-Dec 1876); Navy Yard,

JAMES HOBAN SANDS
1845-1911

NY (Jan 1877-Jun 1879); l.o.a. and w.o. (Jun 1879-Dec 1880); spec. duty, Washington, DC (Dec 1880-Mar 1882); cdr, *Iroquois*, Pac.Sta. (Apr 1882-Jun 1884); w.o. (Jun-Jul 1884); nav.off., Navy Yard, Washington, DC (Jul 1884-Sep 1886); l.o.a. (Sep 1886-Feb 1891); cdr, training ship, *Monongahela* (Mar 1891-Nov 1892); ord. instruction, Navy Yard, Washington, DC (Nov 1892-Apr 1893); equip.off., Navy Yard, Boston (May 1893-May 1895); capt.yd., Navy Yard, Portsmouth, NH (May-Sep 1895); cdr, *Columbia*, N. Atl.Sqdn., then in ordinary, Navy Yard, Philadelphia (Sep 1895-Aug 1898); additional duty, cdr, *Minnesota*, MA Naval Militia (Jul 1897-Mar 1898); gov., Naval Home, Philadelphia (Aug 1898-Sep 1901); various bd. duties (Sep 1901-Jun 1902); comdt., Navy Yard, League Island, PA (Jun 1902-May 1903); cdr, Cst.Sqdn., N.Atl.Flt., *Texas* (May 1903-Mar 1905); bd. duties (Apr-Jun 1905); supt., USNA (Jul 1905-Jul 1907); placed on Ret.Lst. (12 Jul 1907).

Career Highlights During last stages of Civil War, was in both attacks against Fort Fisher, NC, receiving two recommendations for advancement in grade for gallantry.

References

Personal Papers: in possession of Mr. John H. Sands, Sunnyside, Wawa, PA 19063.

JOHN SCHOULER
1846-1917

JOHN SCHOULER Born in Lowell, MA, on 30 Nov 1846, son of William and Frances (Warren) Schouler. Married Hope Day on 31 Aug 1881. Resided in Catskill, NY. Died in Annapolis on 25 Dec 1917. Buried in the USNA Cemetery.

Ranks Act.Midn (25 Sep 1861); title changed to Midn (16 Jul 1862); Ens (1 Nov 1866); Mstr (1 Dec 1866); Lt (12 Mar 1868); LCdr (3 Jun 1869); Cdr (8 Jun 1885); Capt (5 Jun 1898); retired (21 Nov 1899); RAdm on Ret.Lst. (13 Apr 1911) to rank from 21 Nov 1899.

Career Summary Received appointment from MA (25 Sep 1861); USNA (Sep 1861-Nov 1864); l.o.a. (Nov 1864-Feb 1865); Navy Yard, NY (Feb-May 1865); flgs., *Colorado*, and *Frolic*, Eur.Sta. (May 1865-Sep 1868); w.o. (Sep-Dec 1868); *Portsmouth*, S.Atl.Sta. (Jan 1869-Aug 1870); w.o. (Sep 1870-Mar 1871); ord. duty, Navy Yard, Boston (Mar-Aug 1871); exec.off., *Terror*, N. Atl.Sta. (Aug 1871-Oct 1872); w.o. (Oct-Nov 1872); Hydrographic Office, Washington, DC (Dec 1872-Jun 1873); USNA (Jun 1873-Jun 1876); w.o. (Jun-Sep 1876); exec.off., *Essex*, N.Atl. and S.Atl.Stas. (Oct 1876-Jan 1879); sick lv. (Jan 1879-Jun 1880); USNA (Jun 1880-Jun 1884); exec.off., *Lancaster*, Eur.Sta. (Jul 1884-Jul 1885); USNA (Sep 1885-Jul 1888); l.o.a. (Jul 1888-Jul 1889); cdr, training ship, *Portsmouth* (Jul 1889-Jun 1891); l.o.a. (Jul-Aug 1891); spec. duty, Bur. of Nav., Washington, DC (Aug 1891-Sep 1892); l.o.a. (Sep 1892-May 1893); member, naval exam. and ret. bds. (May 1893-Jun 1895); chief of staff, N.Atl.Sta., *Cincinnati*, then *New York* (Jun 1895-May 1897); spec. duty, Bur. of Nav. and bd. duties, Washington, DC (May 1897-Apr 1899); sick lv. (Apr-Nov 1899); retired (21 Nov 1899).

SEATON SCHROEDER Born in Washington, DC, on 17 Aug 1849, son of Francis and Caroline (Seaton) Schroeder. Married Maria C. B. Wainwright on 16 Jan 1879. One son. Resided in Washington, DC, where he died on 19 Oct 1922.

Ranks Midn (27 Sep 1864); Ens (19 Apr 1869); Mstr (12 Jul 1870); Lt (29 Oct 1872); LCdr (27 Sep 1893); Cdr (3 Mar 1899); Capt (10 Aug 1903); RAdm (11 Jul 1908); placed on Ret.Lst. (17 Aug 1911).

Career Summary Received appointment from SC (27 Sep 1864); USNA (Sep 1864-Jun 1868); w.o. (Jun-Sep 1868); *Saginaw,* and *Pensacola,* Pac.Sqdn. (Oct 1868-Sep 1869); home and w.o. (Sep-Oct 1869); *Benicia,* Asia.Sqdn. (Nov 1869-Sep 1872); l.o.a. (Sep 1872-Jan 1873); *Canandaigua,* N.Atl.Sta. (Jan-Nov 1873); *Pinta,* and *Mayflower,* N.Atl.Sta. (Nov 1873-Apr 1874); *Swatara,* spec.serv., Pac. Ocean (May 1874-Jun 1875); Hydrographic Office, Washington, DC (Jun 1875); l.o.a. (Jun-Sep 1875); Hydrographic Office, Washington, DC (Sep 1875-Aug 1876); w.o. (Aug-Sep 1876); *Gettysburg,* spec.serv., Med. Sea (Sep 1876-Sep 1878); home and w.o. (Sep-Dec 1878); Hydrographic Office, Washington, DC (Dec 1878-Aug 1879); l.o.a. (Aug 1879-Aug 1880); Hydrographic Office, Washington, DC (Aug 1880-Nov 1881); *Despatch,* spec.serv. (Nov 1881-Jul 1882); Bur. of Nav., Washington, DC (Jul-Nov 1882); Fish Commission steamer, *Albatross* (Nov 1882-Dec 1885); spec. duty, Bur. of Nav., Washington, DC (Jan 1886-Apr 1888); torp. instruction, Newport, RI (May-Aug 1888); NWC (Aug-Oct 1888); *Richmond,* in ordinary (Oct-Nov 1888); spec. duty, *Vesuvius,* N.Atl.Sta. (Nov 1888-Jun 1890); cdr, *Vesuvius,* N.Atl.Sta. (Jun 1890-Jun 1893); l.o.a. (Jun-Sep 1983); torp. instruction, Newport, RI (Sep 1893); ord.off., Navy Yard, Washington, DC (Oct 1893-Jan 1894); w.o. (Jan-Mar 1894); bd. of inspection and surv. (Apr 1894-Dec 1896); exec.off., *Massachusetts,* N.Atl.Flt. (Dec 1896-Apr 1899); Navy Yard, Washington, DC (Apr 1899-May 1900); naval gov., Guam (Jul 1900-Feb 1903); cdr, *Yosemite,* Guam (Jul-Oct 1903); cdr, sta. ship, *Brutus,* Guam (Jan-Mar 1901); home and w.o. (Feb-Mar 1903); duty, Gen Bd., Navy Dept., Washington, DC (Mar-Apr 1903); chief intelligence off., Washington, DC (May 1903-Apr 1906); general insp., then cdr, *Virginia,* Atl.Flt. (Nov 1905-May 1908); cdr, 4th Div., 2nd Sqdn., Atl.Flt., *Wisconsin* (May-Nov 1908); cdr, 3rd Div., Atl.Flt., *Louisiana* (Nov 1908-Mar 1909); cdr, Atl.Flt., *Connecticut* (Mar 1909-Jun 1911); temp. duty, Gen Bd., Washington, DC, and NWC (Jun-Aug 1911); placed on Ret.Lst. (17 Aug 1911); spec. duty, Navy Dept., Washington, DC (Dec 1911-May 1914); Hydrographic Office, Washington, DC (Oct 1917-Mar 1919).

Career Highlights Served under Commo John Rodgers on 1871 expd. against Korean forts, participating in a landing party and in several of the actions. Was advanced three numbers for conspicuous behavior while exec.off. of the *Massachusetts* during the war with Spain. Commanded a div. of the "Great White Flt."

References

Writings: a) *Coasts of the Mediterranean Sea* (Washington, DC:

SEATON SCHROEDER
1849-1922

1875-83). b) "A U-Bow Section and a Long Buttock Line," U.S. Naval Institute *Proceedings* 21 (1882): 387-400. c) with Lt William Henry Hudson Southerland, USN, *Azimuth Tables* (Washington, DC: 1882). d) *The Fall of Maximillian's Empire as Seen from a United States Gun-boat* (NY: 1887). e) *A Half Century of Naval Service* (NY: 1922).

WALTER KEELER SCOFIELD
1839-1910

WALTER KEELER SCOFIELD Born in Stamford, CT, on 28 Apr 1839, son of Alfred and Maria Scofield. Received M.D. from the College of Physicians and Surgeons at Columbia Univ. in 1868. Married Mary Candee on 14 Jan 1876. Three children. Resided in Stamford, CT, where he died on 5 Aug 1910. Buried in Woodlawn Cemetery.

Ranks Asst.Surg. (12 Jul 1861); PAsst.Surg. (22 Jun 1864); Surg. (7 Apr 1866); Medl.Insp. (21 Nov 1883); Medl.Dir. (8 Feb 1890); placed on Ret.Lst. as Medl.Dir. with rank of RAdm (28 Apr 1901).

Career Summary Received appointment from CT (30 Jul 1861); rec. ship, *North Carolina*, NY (Aug-Nov 1861); *Sagamore*, E.Gulf Blk.Sqdn. (Nov 1861-Aug 1863); return and w.o. (Aug-Sep 1863); Naval Hosp., NY (Sep-Oct 1863); *Union*, E.Gulf Blk.Sqdn. (Oct 1863-Apr 1864); w.o. (Apr-Jun 1864); Naval Hosp., Norfolk, VA (Jun 1864-Mar 1865); *Bienville*, and *Grand Gulf*, W.Gulf Blk.Sqdn. (Mar-Nov 1865); w.o. (Nov 1865); Naval Hosp., Norfolk, VA (Nov 1865-May 1866); *Augusta*, Eur.Sqdn. (May 1866-Jul 1867); w.o. (Jul 1867-May 1868); bd. duty, Boston (May-Oct 1868); w.o. (Oct-Nov 1868); Naval Rndv., Boston (Nov 1868-Jan 1869); w.o. (Jan-Mar 1869); Naval Rndv., Boston (Mar-Jun 1869); *Saratoga*, N.Atl.Sqdn. (Jun-Jul 1869); w.o. (Jul-Sep 1869); rec. ship, *New Hampshire*, Norfolk, VA (Sep-Nov 1869); *Terror*, spec.serv. (Dec 1869-Dec 1870); w.o. (Dec 1870-Feb 1871); spec. duty, NY (Feb-Apr 1871); Naval Hosp., Chelsea, MA (Apr-Sep 1871); Naval Hosp., NY (Sep-Dec 1871); rec. ship, *Vermont*, NY (Dec 1871-Apr 1872); *Lackawanna*, Asia.Sta. (Apr 1872-Mar 1875); w.o. (Mar-Sep 1875); rec. ship, *Ohio*, Boston (Sep-Oct 1875); rec. ship, *Wabash*, Boston (Oct 1875-Oct 1878); w.o. (Oct 1878-Apr 1880); flt.surg., Pac.Sta., *Pensacola* (May 1880-Dec 1882); Navy Yard, Mare Island, CA (Dec 1882-Apr 1886); w.o. (Apr 1886-Jul 1887); *Lancaster*, Eur.Sta. (Aug 1887-Sep 1889); w.o. (Sep-Dec 1889); spec. duty, NY (Jan 1890-Apr 1892); l.o.a. (Apr 1892-Apr 1893); w.o. (Apr 1893-Oct 1894); pres., medl.exam.bd., League Island, PA (Oct 1894-Apr 1901); additional duty, recruiting office, Philadelphia (Oct 1899-Apr 1901); placed on Ret.Lst. (28 Apr 1901).

URIEL SEBREE
1848-1922

URIEL SEBREE Born in Fayette, MO, on 20 Feb 1848, son of John P. and Louisa (Daly) Sebree. Early education was in public schools in Fayette. Married Annie Bridgman on 16 Jun 1886. Resided in Coronado, CA, where he died on 6 Aug 1922.

Ranks Midn (23 Jul 1863); Ens (18 Dec 1868); Mstr (21 Mar 1870); Lt (21 Mar 1871); LCdr (26 Mar 1889); Cdr (24 Feb 1897); Capt (9 Oct 1901); RAdm (8 Jul 1907); placed on

Ret.Lst. (20 Feb 1910).

Career Summary Received appointment from MO (23 Jul 1863); USNA (Jul 1863-Jun 1867); training ship, *Minnesota,* then *Canandaigua,* Eur.Sqdn. (Jul 1867-Feb 1869); w.o. (Feb-Apr 1869); rec. ship, *Vermont,* NY (Apr-Jun 1869); *Saranac,* Pac.Sqdn. (Jul 1869-Nov 1872); w.o. (Nov 1872-Jan 1873); l.o.a. (Jan-Jun 1873); *Tigress,* Arctic Relief Expd. (Jun-Nov 1873); w.o. (Nov-Dec 1873); *Minnesota,* Navy Yard, NY (Dec 1873); *Dictator,* N.Atl.Sta. (Dec 1873-Mar 1874); flgs., *Franklin,* Eur.Sta. (Mar 1874-Jan 1877); w.o. (Jan-May 1877); torp. duty, Newport, RI (Jun-Sep 1877); l.o.a. (Sep 1877-Jan 1878); Hydrographic Office, Washington, DC (Jan-Mar 1878); cst.surv. duty (Mar 1878-Oct 1881); *Brooklyn,* S.Atl.Sta. (Nov 1881-Sep 1882); w.o. (Sep-Nov 1882); USNA (Nov 1882-May 1883); prac. ship, *Dale* (May-Jun 1883); cdr, *Pinta,* Alaskan waters (Jun-Nov 1883); w.o. (Nov 1883-Jan 1884); *Powhatan,* N.Atl.Sqdn. (Jan-Mar 1884); exec.off., *Thetis,* Greely Relief Expd. (Mar-Aug 1884); w.o. (Aug-Sep 1884); USNA (Sep 1884-Sep 1885); asst., then insp., 13th L.h. Dist., Portland, OR (Oct 1885-Aug 1889); s.a. and w.o. (Aug-Sep 1889); exec.off., *Baltimore,* Philadelphia, then N.Atl. and S.Pac. Sqdns. (Sep 1889-Mar 1892); l.o.a. (Mar-Aug 1892); asst.insp., 3rd L.h. Dist., Tompkinsville, NY (Sep 1892-Jul 1893); USNA (Jul 1893-Jul 1896); cdr, *Thetis,* Pac.Sqdn. (Aug 1896-Jul 1897); duty with, then cdr, *Wheeling,* Bering Sea (Jul 1897-Nov 1898); insp., 12th L.h. Dist., San Francisco (Nov 1898-Oct 1901); cdr, sta. ship, *Abarenda,* Apia, Samoa (Nov 1901-Feb 1902); cdr, Naval Sta., Tutuila, Samoa, and gov. of Samoa (Nov 1901-Feb 1903); cdr, *Wheeling,* sta. ship, Apia, Samoa (Jun 1902-Feb 1903); cdr, *Wisconsin,* Asia.Sta. (Feb 1903-Jan 1904); chief of staff, Cruiser Sqdn., *Wisconsin* (Sep 1903-Jan 1904); home and w.o. (Feb-Mar 1904); member, bd. of examiners (Apr-May 1904); NWC (Jun-Sep 1904); member, bd. of inspection and surv. (Sep-Nov 1904); sec., L.h. Bd., Washington, DC (Nov 1904-Sep 1907); cdr, Spec.Serv.Sqdn., *Tennessee* (Oct 1907-Jan 1908); cdr, 2nd Div., Pac.Flt., *Tennessee* (Jan 1908-May 1909); cdr, 1st Sqdn., and cdr., Pac.Flt., *Tennessee* (May 1909-Feb 1910); placed on Ret.Lst. (20 Feb 1910).

Career Highlights Served on two relief expds. to the Arctic, including the Greely Expd. in 1884.

References

Writings: "Cleaning the Bottom of Steel Ships by Divers when Docking Is Impracticable," U.S. Naval Institute *Proceedings* 69 (1894): 133-47.

EDWIN MALCOLM SHEPARD Born in Oswego, NY, on 16 Sep 1843, son of Elisha H. and A. K. (Gray) Shepard. Married Alice Stevens on 9 Dec 1868. Resided in Washington, DC. Died in Jaffrey, NH, on 17 Aug 1904. Buried in Arlington National Cemetery.

Ranks Act.Midn (25 Nov 1859); title changed to Midn (16 Jul 1862); Ens (25 Nov 1862); Lt (22 Feb 1864); LCdr (25 Jul 1866); Cdr (9 May 1878); Capt (15 May 1893); RAdm (3 Mar

EDWIN MALCOLM SHEPARD
1843-1904

1901); retired (13 Jun 1902).

Career Summary Received appointment from NY (25 Nov 1859); USNA (Nov 1859-May 1861); *Vincennes, Mississippi,* and *Essex,* W.Gulf Blk.Sqdn. and MS Flot. (Jun 1861-Aug 1863); l.o.a. (Aug-Oct 1863); *Wachusett,* spec.serv. (Oct 1863-Nov 1864); w.o. (Nov 1864-Jan 1865); *St. Louis,* S.Atl.Blk.Sqdn. (Jan-Jun 1865); rec. ship, *Vanderbilt,* Portsmouth, NH (Jun-Sep 1865); w.o. (Sep-Oct 1865); *Tacony,* Atl.Sqdn. (Oct 1865-Nov 1866); *Osceola,* Atl.Sqdn. (Nov 1866-Jun 1867); w.o. (Jun-Sep 1867); apprentice ship, *Saratoga* (Oct 1867-Jul 1869); w.o. (Jul-Oct 1869); *Michigan,* on Great Lakes (Oct 1869-Nov 1870); *California,* spec.serv. (Dec 1870-Aug 1871); sick lv. (Aug 1871-Jan 1872); torp.serv., Newport, RI (Jan-Jul 1872); w.o. (Jul-Sep 1872); flgs., *Hartford,* Asia.Sqdn. (Oct 1872-Oct 1875); w.o. (Oct-Dec 1875); ord. duty, Bellevue, WA (Dec 1875-May 1876); Navy Yard, Portsmouth, NH (Jun 1876-Sep 1878); USNA (Sep 1878-Dec 1881); cdr, *Enterprise,* N.Atl.Sta. (Jan-Dec 1882); cdr, schoolship, *St. Mary's* (Dec 1882-Jan 1887); Naval Asylum, Philadelphia (Feb 1887-May 1889); cdr, *Kearsarge,* spec.serv., W.Indies (May-Sep 1889); w.o. (Sep 1889-Jan 1890); cdr, *Mohican,* Pac.Sta. (Feb 1890-Apr 1891); insp., 14th L.h. Dist., Cincinnati, OH (Aug 1891-May 1893); equip.off., Navy Yard, NY (May-Jul 1893); cdr, training ship, *Minnesota,* NY, and bd. duties (Jul 1893-Nov 1894); under arrest (31 Mar 1894); released and restored to duty (7 Apr 1894); cdr, *San Francisco,* Eur.Sta. (Nov 1894-Apr 1897); cdr, *Cincinnati,* Eur.Sqdn. (Apr-Jul 1897); l.o.a. (Jul-Sep 1897); cdr, rec. ship, *Richmond,* Philadelphia (Sep 1897-Apr 1898); insp., 3rd L.h. Dist., Tompkinsville, NY (Apr 1898-May 1901); NWC (Jun-Sep 1901); comdt., Naval Sta., Port Royal, SC (Sep 1901-Apr 1902); bd. duties (Apr-Jun 1902); retired (13 Jun 1902).

Career Highlights Served on the *Vincennes* in 1862, seeing action on the Lower MS River passes. Participated in the final siege of Vicksburg in the summer of 1863, commanding a naval battery on shore. Was with the *Wachusett,* which captured the Confederate privateer *Florida* on 7 Oct 1864.

EDWARD SHIPPEN Born in Mercer County, NJ, on 18 Jun 1826, son of Richard and Anna Elizabeth (Farmer) Shippen. Early education at Bordentown, NJ, and at Bolmer's School in Westchester, PA. Received A.B. degree from Princeton Univ. in 1845, and A.M. in 1848 again from Princeton. Received M.D. from the Univ. of PA in 1848. Married with two children. Resided in Chestnut Hill, Philadelphia, where he died on 16 Jun 1911. Buried at Burlington, NJ.

Ranks Asst.Surg. (7 Aug 1849); PAsst.Surg. (21 Apr 1855); Surg. (26 Apr 1861); Medl.Insp. (3 Mar 1871); Medl.Dir. (17 Mar 1876); placed on Ret.Lst. (18 Jun 1888); Medl.Dir. with rank of RAdm on Ret.Lst. (29 Jun 1906).

Career Summary Received appointment from PA (7 Aug 1849); w.o. (Aug-Dec 1849); *Marion,* E.Ind.Sqdn. (Dec 1849-Jun 1852); l.o.a. and w.o. (Jun-Oct 1852); rec. ship, *Ohio,* Boston

EDWARD SHIPPEN
1826-1911

(Oct 1852-Jun 1853); *Fulton*, Fishing Banks Sqdn. (Jul-Oct 1853); w.o. (Oct 1853-Apr 1854); cst.surv. duty (Apr-Nov 1854); w.o. (Nov 1854-Mar 1855); *Dolphin*, Afr.Sqdn. (Apr 1855-Jul 1857); l.o.a. (Jul-Aug 1857); Naval Rndv., Philadelphia (Jul-Dec 1857); Naval Asylum, Philadelphia (Dec 1857-Dec 1858); *Caledonia*, Paraguay Expd. (Dec 1858-May 1859); w.o. (May-Jun 1859); flgs., *Congress*, Braz. and N.Atl.Blk.Sqdns. (Jun 1859-Mar 1862); recorder, medl.exam.bd., Philadelphia (Mar-May 1862); w.o. (May-Jun 1862); rec. ship, *North Carolina*, NY (Jun 1862-Aug 1864); *New Ironsides*, N.Atl.Blk.Sqdn. (Aug 1864-Mar 1865); w.o. (Mar-Oct 1865); *Shenandoah* (Oct-Nov 1865); *Canandaigua*, Eur.Sqdn. (Nov 1865-May 1868); w.o. (May-Oct 1868); member, naval ret. bd., Philadelphia (Oct-Dec 1868); surg., USNA (Jan 1869-Sep 1871); flt.surg., Eur.Sta., *Wabash* (Sep 1871-Jan 1873); return and sick lv. (Jan-Mar 1873); Navy Yard, Philadelphia (Apr 1873-Jul 1874); Naval Hosp., Philadelphia (Jul 1874-Jul 1877); spec. duty, attending officers, Philadelphia (Jul 1877-Mar 1880); pres., medl.exam.bd., Philadelphia (Feb-Jul 1880); spec. duty, attending officers, Philadelphia (Jul 1880-Feb 1881); pres., bd. of examiners (Mar-Jul 1881); spec. duty, attending officers, Philadelphia (Jul 1881-Feb 1882); pres., medl.exam.bd. (Mar-Sep 1882); w.o. (Sep 1882-Mar 1883); Naval Hosp., Philadelphia (Mar 1883-Oct 1886); spec. duty, Philadelphia (Oct 1886-Jun 1888); placed on Ret.Lst. (18 Jun 1888).

Career Highlights During the Civil War, was on the *Congress*, which fell victim to the Confederate ironclad *Virginia* (formerly *Merrimack*) in Newport News, VA, in Mar 1862, being injured in the action. Was present during both actions at Fort Fisher, NC. A recipient of numerous awards, he was also a prolific writer on numerous topics.

References

Personal Papers: 300 items (1849-75) in Historical Society of PA, Philadelphia.

Writings: a) *Thirty Years at Sea. The Story of a Sailor's Life* (Philadelphia: 1879; reprint, 1979). b) *A Christmas at Sea* (Philadelphia: 1882, 1892). c) *Some Account of the Origin of the Naval Asylum at Philadelphia* (Philadelphia: 1883). d) *Naval Battles, Ancient and Modern* (Philadelphia, 1883). e) with Major William H. Powell, *Officers of the Army and Navy Who Served in the Civil War* (Philadelphia, 1892). f) *Naval Battles of the World and Our New Navy* (Philadelphia: 1894, 1905). g) *Memoir of Henry Bouquet, 1719-1765* (Philadelphia: 1900). h) *Battles and Heroes of the American Navy* (Philadelphia: c.1902). i) *Naval Battles of America* (Philadelphia: 1905).

CHARLES DWIGHT SIGSBEE Born in Albany, NY, on 16 Jan 1845, son of Nicholas and Agnes (Orr) Sigsbee. Married Eliza Rogers Lockwood in November 1870. His wife was the daughter of Gen H. H. Lockwood who served for many years as prof. of math. at the USNA. One son and three daughters, one of whom married RAdm S. E. W. Kittelle, USN (1867-1950). A grandson was RAdm Charles J. Moore, USN (1889-1974). Died on 19 Jul

CHARLES DWIGHT SIGSBEE
1845-1923

1923 at his home in NY City. Buried in Arlington National Cemetery.

Ranks Act.Midn (27 Sep 1859); title changed to Midn (16 Jul 1862); Act.Ens (1 Oct 1863); designation "Act." discontinued (21 Dec 1865); Mstr (10 May 1866); Lt (21 Feb 1867); LCdr (12 Mar 1868); Cdr (11 May 1882); Capt (21 Mar 1897); RAdm (10 Aug 1903); placed on Ret.Lst. (16 Jan 1907).

Career Summary Received appointment from NY (27 Sep 1859); USNA (Sep 1859-Oct 1863); found deficient and turned back (Jun 1860); *Monongahela,* and *Brooklyn,* W.Gulf Blk.Sqdn. (Oct 1863-Jan 1865); w.o. (Jan-Feb 1865); *Wyoming,* and *Ashuelot,* Asia.Sqdn. (Feb 1865-Sep 1869); USNA (Sep 1869-Aug 1871); Hydrographic Office, Washington, DC (Aug-Nov 1871); flgs., *Severn,* N.Atl.Sta. (Nov-Dec 1871); cdr, flgs., *Worcester,* and *Canandaigua,* N.Atl.Sta. (Dec 1871-Nov 1873); Hydrographic Office, Washington, DC (Nov 1873-Jun 1874); cst.surv. duty (Jun 1874-Oct 1878); Hydrographic Office, Washington, DC (Oct 1878-Aug 1882); USNA (Sep 1882-Sep 1885); member, ord.bd. (Sep-Oct 1885); cdr, *Kearsarge,* Eur.Sta. (Oct 1885-Nov 1886); w.o. (Nov 1886-Jan 1887); bd. duties (Jan-Sep 1887); USNA (Sep 1887-Jun 1891); cdr, training ship, *Portsmouth* (Jun 1891-May 1893); chief, Hydrographic Office, Washington, DC (May 1893-Apr 1897); cdr, *Maine,* N.Atl.Sta. (Apr 1897-Mar 1898); home and w.o. (Mar 1898); aide to sec. of navy, Washington, DC (Mar-Apr 1898); cdr, *St. Paul,* N.Atl.Flt. (Apr-Sep 1898); cdr, *Texas,* N.Atl.Flt. (Sep 1898-Jan 1900); chief intelligence off., Navy Dept., Washington, DC (Feb 1900-Apr 1903); comdt., Navy Yard, League Island, PA (May 1903-Feb 1904); cdr, S.Atl.Sqdn., *Newark* (Feb 1904-Apr 1905); cdr, 2nd Div., N.Atl. Flt., *Brooklyn* (Apr 1905-May 1906); spec. bd. duty (May 1906-Jan 1907); placed on Ret.Lst. (16 Jan 1907).

Career Highlights During the Civil War, participated in the Battle of Mobile Bay on 5 Aug 1864 and saw action at both attacks on Fort Fisher, NC. Commanded the *Maine,* which exploded in Havana Harbor on 15 Feb 1898, thereby setting off the chain of events that resulted in the Spanish-American War. Was advanced three numbers in rank owing to his heroism during the "*Maine* Incident" and for his performance during the war. Commanded a spec.sqdn. in Jun and Jul 1905 that returned the remains of John Paul Jones from France to the USNA where they were interred. As one of the navy's chief hydrographers, he introduced numerous inventions and new methods for deep sea exploration.

References

Personal Papers: a) 17 boxes (1845-1923) in NY State Library, Albany, NY. b) 12 letters (1898-1906) in Newport Historical Society, Newport, RI.

Writings: a) *Deep Sea Soundings and Dredging . . . used on Board the Coast and Geodetic Survey Steamer, "Blake"* (Washington, DC: 1880). b) "Graphical Method for Navigation," U.S. Naval Institute *Proceedings* 33 (1885): 241-63. c) *The "Maine": An Account of her Destruction in Havana Harbor* (NY: 1899). d)

"Progressive Naval Seamanship," U.S. Naval Institute *Proceedings* 48 (1889): 95-129. e) "Another Graphic Solution in Coast Navigation," U.S. Naval Institute *Proceedings* 104 (Dec 1902): 923-24.

WILLIAM SOWDEN SIMS Born in Port Hope, Ontario, Canada, on 15 Oct 1858, son of Alfred William and Adelaide (Sowden) Sims. His family returned to the U.S., settling in Orbisonia, PA. Married Anne Hitchcock, daughter of former sec. of the interior, Ethan Allen Hitchcock, on 21 Nov 1905. Died in Boston on 28 Sep 1936.

Ranks Cadet Midn (24 Jun 1876); Midn (22 Jun 1882); Ensjg (3 Mar 1883); Ens (26 Jun 1884); Ltjg (9 May 1893); Lt (1 Jan 1897); LCdr (21 Nov 1902); Cdr (1 Jul 1907); Capt (4 Mar 1911); RAdm (29 Aug 1916); temp. VAdm (22 May 1917); temp. Adm (4 Dec 1918); RAdm (31 Mar 1919); placed on Ret.Lst. with rank of RAdm (15 Oct 1922); Adm on Ret.Lst. (21 Jun 1930).

Career Summary Received appointment from PA (24 Jun 1876); USNA (Jun 1876-Jun 1880); w.o. (Jun-Aug 1880); *Tennessee*, N.Atl.Sta. (Aug 1880-May 1882); USNA (May-Jun 1882); w.o. (Jun-Jul 1882); rec. ship, *Colorado*, NY (Jul 1882-Jan 1883); *Swatara*, N.Atl.Sta. (Jan 1883-Oct 1886); *Yantic*, N.Atl. Sta. (Oct 1886-Nov 1888); l.o.a., language study, Paris (Nov 1888-Dec 1889); nautical schoolship, *Saratoga*, Philadelphia (Jan 1890-Mar 1893); w.o. (Mar-Jun 1893); *Philadelphia*, Pac.Sta. (Jun 1893-Aug 1894); *Charleston*, Asia.Sta. (Aug 1894-Jul 1896); spec. duty, Norfolk, VA (Jul 1896); l.o.a. (Jul-Oct 1896); rec. ship, *Richmond*, Philadelphia (Nov 1896-Feb 1897); naval attaché, U.S. Embassies, Paris, St. Petersburg, Russia, and Madrid (Mar 1897-Jun 1900); temp. duty, Paris Exposition Commission, Paris (Jun-Oct 1900); *Kentucky*, Asia.Sqdn. (Nov 1900-Apr 1901); *Monterey*, Asia.Sqdn. (Apr-Oct 1901); aide on staff of cdr, Asia. Sqdn., *Brooklyn* (Oct 1901-Feb 1902); flt. intelligence off. and insp. of target prac., Asia.Sqdn., *New York* (Feb-Oct 1902); insp. of target prac., Bur. of Nav., Washington, DC (Nov 1902-Feb 1909); additional duty, naval aide to pres., Washington, DC (Nov 1907-Feb 1909); cdr, *Minnesota*, Atl.Flt. (Mar 1909-Apr 1911); home and w.o. (Apr-May 1911); NWC (May 1911-Jun 1913); cdr, Torp. (Destroyer) Flot., Atl.Flt., *Dixie* (Jun 1913-Feb 1914), then *Birmingham* (Feb-Aug 1914); *Dixie*, Atl.Flt. (Aug 1914-Nov 1915); insp., then cdr, *Nevada*, Quincy, MA, and Atl.Flt. (Nov 1915-Dec 1916); home and w.o. (Dec 1916-Jan 1917); pres., NWC, and comdt., Naval Dist., Newport, RI (Feb-Mar 1917); spec. duty to Great Britain (Mar-Apr 1917); cdr, American Naval Operations, Eur. waters, *Wadsworth* (Apr-May 1917); cdr, U.S. Destroyers Operating from British Bases, *Melville*, then cdr, Naval Forces, Eur. waters (May 1917-Mar 1919); additional duty, naval attaché, London (Dec 1917-Mar 1919); pres., NWC (Apr 1919-Oct 1922); additional duty, member, naval exam. bd., Newport, RI (Apr 1921-Oct 1922); placed on Ret.Lst. (15 Oct 1922); temp. duty as member, aircraft bd., Bur. of Nav., Washing-

WILLIAM SOWDEN SIMS
1858-1936

ton, DC (15 Oct 1925).

Career Highlights One of the great reformers and innovators in the USN, made great advances in the areas of naval gunfire. In 1913, while commanding the Atl.Torp.Flot., developing a tactical doctrine for the new naval destroyers. In early 1917, his tenure as pres. of the NWC was cut short by America's entry into World War I, Sims being en route to London for discussions with the British admiralty. As cdr of U.S. forces in Eur. waters, he created the convoy system, which greatly assisted the Allied cause. Received the Distinguished Service Medal in 1919 (which he declined) and several foreign decorations, including the Grand Cross Order of St. Michael and St. George from Britain, the Grand Officer Legion Honor from France, and one each from Japan, Belgium, and Italy. Also received several honorary degrees, including an LL.D. from Yale, Harvard, Tufts, and Juniata Universities in 1919, from the Univ. of PA, Columbia, and Williams in 1921, the D.Sc. from Stevens in 1921, the LL.D. from Union, McGill, and Queen's (Canada) in 1922, and from the Univ. of CA and Wesleyan in 1923. His book, written with Burton J. Hendrick, *The Victory at Sea* (1920) won the Pulitzer Prize for history.

References

Personal Papers: a) 43,000 items (1856-1951) in NHF,LC. b) 1 item (1891) in NHF,WNY.

Writings: a) "Training Ranges and Long-Range Firing," U.S. Naval Institute *Proceedings* 111 (Sep 1904): 511-31. b) "The Inherent Tactical Qualities of All-Big-Gun, One-Caliber Battleships of High Speed, Large Displacement and Gunpower," U.S. Naval Institute *Proceedings* 120 (Dec 1906): 1337-66. c) "What Should Be the Relations Between the Battle Fleet and the Reserve Fleet," U.S. Naval Institute *Proceedings* 151 (May-Jun 1914): 727-39. d) "Naval War College Principles and Methods Applied Afloat," U.S. Naval Institute *Proceedings* 156 (Mar-Apr 1915): 383-403. e) contributor, *The Great War* (Philadelphia: c.1915-21). f) "Cheer Up!! There is No War College," U.S. Naval Institute *Proceedings* 163 (May-Jun 1916): 857-60. g) "Military Character," U.S. Naval Institute *Proceedings* 169 (Mar 1917): 437-62. h) "The United States Naval War College," U.S. Naval Institute *Proceedings* 199 (Sep 1919): 1485-93. i) (with Burton J. Hendrick), *The Victory at Sea* (Garden City, NY: 1920; reprint, Annapolis: 1984). j) "The Practical Naval Officer," U.S. Naval Institute *Proceedings* 218 (Apr 1921): 525-46. k) "Naval War College," U.S. Naval Institute *Proceedings* 219 (May 1921): 705-21. l) "Military Conservatism," U.S. Naval Institute *Proceedings* 229 (Mar 1922): 347-63. m) "Naval Morale after War," U.S. Naval Institute *Proceedings* 235 (Sep 1922): 1461-71. n) "Promotion by Selection," U.S. Naval Institute *Proceedings* 376 (Jun 1934): 769-73. o) "Service Opinion upon Promotion by Selection," U.S. Naval Institute *Proceedings* 388 (Jun 1935): 791-806. p) Benyaurd B. Wygant, "Admiral Sims as I Knew Him," U.S. Naval Institute *Proceedings* 584 (Oct 1951): 1089-91; 589 (Mar 1952): 319-21; 596 (Oct 1952): 1141-43.

Other Sources: a) Elting E. Morison, *Admiral Sims and the Modern Navy* (Boston: 1942). b) Edward B. Parsons, "Admiral Sims' Mission to Europe in 1917-19 and Some Aspects of United States Naval and Foreign Wartime Policy" (Ph.D. diss., State Univ. of NY at Buffalo, 1971).

FREDERIC SINGER Born in Karlsruhe, Baden, Germany, on 3 May 1847, son of Joseph and Frederica (Winterweber) Singer. Emigrating to the U.S. in 1848, he and his family settled in OH. Remained unmarried, dying in New Orleans on 4 Jan 1923. Buried in Arlington National Cemetery.

FREDERIC SINGER
1847-1923

Ranks Midn (27 Jul 1863); Ens (19 Apr 1869); Mstr (12 Jul 1870); Lt (21 May 1874); LCdr (1 Sep 1895); Cdr (3 Mar 1899); Capt (4 Feb 1904); retired (26 Jun 1906); RAdm on Ret.Lst. (13 Apr 1911) to rank from 26 Jun 1906.

Career Summary Received appointment from OH (27 Jul 1863); USNA (Jul 1863-Jun 1868); found deficient and turned back (Jun 1865); w.o. (Jun-Sep 1868); *Nipsic*, N.Atl.Sta. (Oct 1868-Dec 1869); *Terror*, N.Atl.Sta. (Dec 1869-Dec 1870); home and w.o. (Dec 1870-Mar 1871); signal and ord. duty, Washington, DC (Mar 1871-Mar 1872); *Michigan*, on Great Lakes (Mar-Oct 1872); *Benicia*, N.Pac.Sta. (Oct 1872-Jul 1875); sick lv. (Jul 1875-May 1876); l.o.a. (May-Dec 1876); *Canonicus*, N.Atl.Sta. (Dec 1876-Oct 1878); w.o. (Oct-Nov 1878); *Richmond*, and *Ashuelot*, Asia.Sta. (Nov 1878-Sep 1881); home and w.o. (Sep 1881-Feb 1882); rec. ship, *Independence*, Mare Island, CA (Feb 1882-Apr 1883); torp. instruction, Newport, RI (Apr-Aug 1883); rec. ship, *Colorado*, NY (Aug 1883-Jun 1884); *Powhatan*, Eur.Sta. (Jun-Jul 1884); *Quinnebaug*, Eur.Sta. (Jul 1884-Jul 1887); home and w.o. (Aug-Oct 1887); Office of Naval Intelligence, Navy Dept., Washington, DC (Nov 1887-Sep 1890); *Ranger*, Pac.Sta. (Sep 1890-Aug 1891); exec.off., *Pensacola*, Pac.Sta. (Aug 1891-Feb 1892); return and w.o. (Feb-Jul 1892); Office of Naval Intelligence, Navy Dept., Washington, DC (Jul 1892-Jul 1893); chief intelligence off., and member, bd. of construction, Navy Dept., Washington, DC (Jul 1893-Apr 1896); exec.off., *Terror*, N.Atl.Sta. (Apr 1896-Apr 1897); exec.off., *Raleigh*, Eur. and Asia.Stas. (Apr 1897-Jul 1898); cdr, *Manila*, Asia.Sta. (Jul 1898-Jun 1899); home and l.o.a. (Jun-Oct 1899); ord. instruction, Navy Yard, Washington, DC (Oct 1899); insp., 7th L.h. Dist., Pensacola, FL (Oct 1899-May 1902); cdr, *Solace*, spec.serv. (May 1902-Apr 1904); comdt., Naval Sta., New Orleans (May 1904-Jun 1909); retired (26 Jun 1906).

Career Highlights While on the *Raleigh*, saw action at Manila Bay during the war with Spain, being recommended for promotion for his eminent and conspicuous conduct in the action.

JOHN ADDISON BAXTER SMITH Born in Baltimore on 21 Mar 1843, son of John A. and Sophia F. Smith. Educated at the Dickenson Seminary in PA, served an apprenticeship at a Baltimore machine shop, and then took an engineering course in Baltimore before entering the navy in 1863. Married Ella E. Smith after his retirement. Resided in Atlantic City, NJ. Died on 9 Mar 1918 in New Orleans.

Ranks 3rd Asst.Engr. (21 Apr 1863); 2nd Asst.Engr. (28 Sep 1864); 1st Asst.Engr. (11 Jan 1873); title changed to PAsst.Engr. (24 Feb 1874); Chief Engr. (16 Feb 1892); Chief Engr. with rel. rank of Cdr (16 Feb 1898); Cdr (3 Mar 1899); Capt (8 Jun 1902); placed on Ret.Lst. with rank of RAdm (21 Mar 1905).

Career Summary Received appointment from MD (21 Apr 1863); w.o. (Apr-Jul 1863); *Housatonic*, S.Atl.Blk.Sqdn. (Jul 1863-Feb 1864); *Canandaigua*, S.Atl.Blk.Sqdn. (Feb 1864); *Wabash*, S.Atl.Blk.Sqdn. (Feb-May 1864); *Paul Jones*, S.Atl.Blk. Sqdn., and Navy Yard, Boston (Aug-Sep 1864); w.o. (Sep-Oct 1864); *Mohongo*, Navy Yard, NY, and Pac.Sqdn. (Oct 1864-Aug 1867); home and w.o. (Aug-Oct 1867); spec. duty, *Contoocook*, Navy Yard, Portsmouth, NH (Oct 1867-Jan 1868); spec. duty, *Severn*, Navy Yard, NY (Jan-Mar 1868); duty connected with *Ammonoosuc*, Navy Yard, Boston (Mar 1868); w.o. (Mar-May 1868); *Pushmataha*, Navy Yard, Philadelphia (May-Jun 1868); w.o. (Jun-Jul 1868); training ship, *Saco* (Aug-Dec 1868); w.o. (Dec 1868-Mar 1869); *Seminole*, Navy Yard, Boston (Apr 1869-Feb 1870); w.o. (Feb-Sep 1870); chief engr., *Mayflower*, Tehuantepec and Nicaraguan Surv.Expds. (Sep 1870-May 1871); w.o. (May 1871-Jan 1872); Navy Yard, League Island, PA (Jan 1872-May 1873); w.o. (May-Jul 1873); *Saugus*, Key West, FL (Aug 1873-Nov 1874); home and l.o.a. (Nov 1874-Nov 1875); *Huron*, Navy Yard, Philadelphia (Nov-Dec 1875); flgs., *Hartford*, N.Atl.Sqdn. (Dec 1875-Aug 1877); w.o. (Aug-Dec 1877); *Wyandotte*, Navy Yard, Washington, DC (Dec 1877-May 1880); *Tallapoosa*, spec. serv. (May 1880-Jun 1883); w.o. (Jun-Sep 1883); in charge of stores, and chief engr., rec. ship, *Franklin*, Norfolk, VA (Sep 1883-Feb 1886); w.o. (Feb-Apr 1886); rec. ship, *Franklin*, Norfolk, VA (Apr-May 1886); *Atlanta*, on trials, and N.Atl.Sta. (Jun 1886-Nov 1888); w.o. (Nov-Dec 1888); naval advisory bd., Washington, DC (Dec 1888-Mar 1889); inspection duty, *Philadelphia*, William Cramp and Sons Iron Works, Philadelphia (Mar-Dec 1889); insp., Cruiser No. 9, Baltimore (Dec 1889-Jun 1894); additional duty, Columbia Iron Works, Baltimore (Jun 1893-Jun 1894); *Montgomery*, N.Atl.Sqdn. (Jun 1894-Sep 1895); *Texas*, N.Atl.Sqdn. (Sep 1895-Feb 1896); head, dept. of steam engineering, Navy Yard, Norfolk, VA (Feb 1896-Jun 1899); head, dept. of steam engineering, Navy Yard, NY (Jun 1899-Mar 1905); placed on Ret.Lst. (21 Mar 1905); general insp. of machinery, Bur. of Steam Engineering, NY (Mar 1905-Aug 1908).

Career Highlights Served as chief engr. of the *Mayflower* on the expd. surveying the Isthmus of Tehuantepec in 1870-71. Was instrumental in reorganizing the steam engineering depts. at both the Norfolk and NY Navy Yards. As general insp. of Bur. of Steam Engineering, was instrumental in the modernization of the "New Navy" around the turn of the present century.

WILLIAM STROTHER SMITH
1857-1927

WILLIAM STROTHER SMITH Born in Richmond, VA, on 15 Sep 1857, son of Samuel Brown and Margaret (Strother)

Smith. Married Irma Frances St. Clair-Abrams on 2 Dec 1891. One daughter. Resided in Jacksonville, FL. Died in Newport, RI on 6 Sep 1927.

Ranks Cadet Engr. (15 Sep 1875); Asst.Engr. (10 Jun 1882); PAsst.Engr. (27 Jun 1893); PAsst.Engr. with rel. rank of Lt (14 Mar 1897); Lt (3 Mar 1899); LCdr (4 Jan 1903); Cdr (1 Jul 1907); Capt (4 Mar 1911); Act.RAdm. (15 Oct 1917); RAdm (20 Mar 1918); placed on Ret.Lst. (15 Sep 1921).

Career Summary Received appointment from VA (15 Sep 1875); USNA (Sep 1875-Jun 1880); w.o. (Jun-Aug 1880); training ship, *Minnesota* (Aug 1880-Jan 1881); *Pensacola*, Pac.Sqdn. (Feb 1881-Jan 1883); w.o. (Jan-Jul 1883); *Kearsarge*, spec.serv. (Jul 1883-Dec 1886); l.o.a. (Dec 1886-May 1887); *Galena*, spec.serv., and N.Atl.Sta. (May 1887-Jun 1890); w.o. (Jun-Sep 1890); Navy Yard, Norfolk, VA (Sep 1890-May 1893); flgs., *San Francisco*, N.Atl.Sqdn. (May-Aug 1893); *Newark*, spec.serv., and S.Atl.Sqdn. (Aug 1893-May 1896); home and l.o.a. (May-Jul 1896); insp. of machinery, Newport News, VA (Jul 1896-Mar 1898); *Columbia*, N.Atl.Flt. (Mar-Sep 1898); *Yankee*, Navy Yard, League Island, PA (Sep 1898); home and w.o. (Sep 1898); bd. duty (Oct 1898); insp. duty, Bur. of Steam Engineering, Washington, DC (Oct 1898-Feb 1900); *Dolphin*, spec.serv. (Feb-Oct 1900); *Solace*, spec.serv. (Oct-Dec 1900); *Concord*, Asia.Sta. (Dec 1900-Feb 1902); *Wheeling*, Pac.Sqdn. (Feb-May 1902); *Abarenda*, spec.serv. (May-Sep 1902); home and w.o. (Sep 1902); *Raleigh*, spec.serv. (Sep 1902-Feb 1903); asst. insp. of machinery, Newport News, VA (Mar 1903-Jul 1904); *West Virginia*, Newport News, VA (Jul 1904-Aug 1906); Bur. of Steam Engineering, Washington, DC (Aug 1906-Jul 1909); member, bd. of inspection and surv. (Jul 1909-Nov 1912); engineering off., Navy Yard, Philadelphia (Dec 1912-Dec 1915); spec. duty, Navy Dept., Washington, DC (Dec 1915-Sep 1921); placed on Ret.Lst. (15 Sep 1921).

ALBERT SIDNEY SNOW Born in Rockland, ME, on 18 Nov 1845, son of Ephraim L. Snow. Married Frances Maria Keating on 13 Mar 1873. Three children. Resided in Brookline, MA, where he died on 14 Jul 1932.

Ranks Act.Midn (30 Nov 1861); title changed to Midn (16 Jul 1862); Ens (1 Dec 1866); Mstr (12 Mar 1868); Lt (26 Mar 1869); LCdr (11 Jul 1880); Cdr (28 Feb 1890); Capt (3 Mar 1899); RAdm (21 Feb 1905); placed on Ret.Lst. (18 Nov 1907).

Career Summary Received appointment from ME (30 Nov 1861); USNA (Nov 1861-Oct 1865); l.o.a. and w.o. (Oct 1865-Mar 1866); *Chattanooga*, Navy Yard, Philadelphia, and on trials (Mar-Aug 1866); *Pensacola*, N.Pac.Sqdn. (Sep 1866-Apr 1868); *Resaca*, N.Pac.Sqdn. (Apr 1868-Aug 1869); w.o. (Aug-Nov 1869); *Alaska*, Asia.Sqdn. (Dec 1869-Feb 1873); l.o.a. (Mar-Sep 1873); Torp.Sta., Newport, RI (Sep-Nov 1873); *Brooklyn*, Newport, RI (Dec 1873); torp. duty, Newport, RI (Dec 1873-Mar 1874); *Congress*, Eur.Sta. (Mar 1874-Jul 1876); w.o. (Jul 1876-May 1877); rec. ship, *Wabash*, Navy Yard, Boston (May

ALBERT SIDNEY SNOW
1845-1932

1877-Jan 1879); exec.off., training ship, *Portsmouth* (Jan 1879-Dec 1881); w.o. (Dec 1881-May 1882); Navy Yard, Boston (May 1882-May 1883); w.o. (May-Jul 1883); cst.surv. duty (Jul 1883-Apr 1887); w.o. (Apr-Aug 1887); spec. duty, Newport, RI (Sep 1887); NWC (Sep-Dec 1887); member, bd. of inspection and surv. (Jan 1888-Apr 1890); cdr, training ship, *Essex* (Apr 1890-May 1892); w.o. and l.o.a. (May 1892-May 1893); USNA (May 1893-Nov 1894); w.o. (Nov 1894-Jan 1895); asst., then insp., 3rd L.h. Dist., Tompkinsville, NY (Jan 1895-Feb 1898); insp. of ord., Navy Yard, Portsmouth, NH (Feb-Apr 1898); cdr, *Badger*, N.Atl.Sqdn. (Apr-Oct 1898); comdt., Naval Sta., San Juan, Puerto Rico (Nov 1898-Nov 1899); cdr, *New York*, and chief of staff, N.Atl.Sta. (Dec 1899-Nov 1900); Navy Yard, NY (Nov 1900-Mar 1901); cdr, rec. ship, *Vermont*, NY (Mar-Aug 1901); cdr, rec. ship, *Columbia*, NY (Aug 1901-Sep 1903); cdr, rec. ship, *Hancock*, NY (Sep 1903-Feb 1904); capt.yd., Navy Yard, Boston (Feb 1904-Feb 1905); comdt., Navy Yard, Boston (Feb 1905-Nov 1907); placed on Ret.Lst. (18 Nov 1907); various bd. duties, Navy Yard, Boston (Jul 1918-Jul 1919).

THOMAS SNOWDEN
1857-1930

THOMAS SNOWDEN Born in Peekskill, NY, on 12 Aug 1857, son of Dr. Thomas and Catherine Clinton (Wood) Snowden. Married twice: to Adelaide Van Ness Smith on 2 Jun 1881; then to Helen Koerper on 14 Jan 1911. One son. Resided in Washington, DC, where he died on 27 Jan 1930. Buried in Arlington National Cemetery.

Ranks Cadet Midn (25 Jun 1875); Midn (10 Jun 1881); Ensjg (3 Mar 1883); Ens (26 Jun 1884); Ltjg (10 Jan 1892); Lt (11 Mar 1896); LCdr (5 Mar 1902); Cdr (8 Feb 1907); Capt (7 Nov 1910); RAdm (1 Jul 1917); placed on Ret.Lst. (12 Aug 1921).

Career Summary Received appointment from NY (25 Jun 1875); USNA (Jun 1875-Jun 1879); w.o. (Jun-Jul 1879); *Vandalia*, N.Atl.Sta. (Jul 1879-Apr 1881); w.o. (Apr-May 1881); USNA (May-Jun 1881); l.o.a. (Jun-Sep 1881); *Standish* (Sep-Nov 1881); *Brooklyn*, Asia.Sta. (Nov 1881-Oct 1884); Hydrographic Office, Washington, DC (Nov 1884-Mar 1887); *Ossipee*, N.Atl. Sta. (Mar 1887-Nov 1889); Naval Observatory, Washington, DC (Nov 1889-Apr 1892); *Ranger*, Pac.Sta. (Apr 1892-Oct 1894); *Monterey*, Pac.Sta. (Nov 1894-Apr 1895); USNA (Apr 1895-May 1896); training ship, *Monongahela* (May-Nov 1896); USNA (Sep 1896-May 1897); NWC (Jun-Jul 1897); *Dolphin*, spec.serv. (Jul-Nov 1897); training ship, *Constellation* (Nov-Dec 1897); Navy Yard, Washington, DC (Dec 1897-Mar 1898); *Dolphin*, Atl.Flt., and spec.serv. (Mar 1898-Apr 1901); Office of Naval Intelligence, Navy Dept., Washington, DC (Apr 1901-Apr 1902); nav.off., *Illinois*, Eur. and N.Atl.Stas. (Apr 1902-Jul 1905); home and w.o. (Jul-Aug 1905); Office of Naval Intelligence, Navy Dept., Washington, DC (Aug 1905-Jul 1906); compass office, Bur. of Equip. and Recruiting, Washington, DC (Aug 1906-Mar 1908); cdr, presidential yacht, *Mayflower* (Mar 1908-Feb 1910); member, bd. of inspection and surv., Washington, DC (Feb 1910-Nov 1911); cdr, *South Carolina*, Naval Review and N.Atl.Flts. (Nov

1911-Nov 1913); NWC (Nov 1913-Dec 1914); comdt., Navy
Yard, and cdr, Naval Sta., Portsmouth, NH (Jan-Aug 1915); cdr,
Wyoming, Atl.Flt. (Aug 1915-Jun 1916); hydrographer, Navy
Dept., Washington, DC (Jun 1916-Oct 1917); cdr, 1st Div.,
Battleship Force, Atl.Flt., *Alabama* (Oct-Nov 1917); cdr, 3rd
Div., Battleship Force One, Atl.Flt., *Virginia* (Nov 1917-Feb
1918), *Rhode Island* (Nov-Dec 1917), and *Virginia* (Dec 1917-Feb
1918); cdr, Sqdn. One and Div. Two, Battleship Force, Atl.Flt.,
Ohio (Feb 1918-Jan 1919); temp. duty, Office of Naval Opera-
tions, Washington, DC (Jan-Feb 1919); military gov., Santo
Domingo, and U.S. military representative, Haiti (Feb 1919-Jun
1921); Gen Bd., Navy Dept., Washington, DC (Jun-Aug 1921);
placed on Ret.Lst. (12 Aug 1921).

WILLIAM HENRY HUDSON SOUTHERLAND Born in
NY City on 10 Jul 1852, son of William and Phoebe E. Southerland. A first cousin and brother-in-law of navy RAdm Hugh
Rodman [*q.v*], married Mary Rodman on 1 Aug 1877. Two
daughters. Resided in Washington, DC, where he died on 30 Jan
1933. Buried in Arlington National Cemetery.

Ranks Naval Apprentice (14 Jun 1867); Midn (29 Jul 1868);
title changed to Cadet Midn (15 Jul 1870); Midn (1 Jun 1872);
Ens (15 Jul 1873); Mstr (21 Nov 1877); title changed to Ltjg (3
Mar 1883); Lt (9 Feb 1884); LCdr (3 Mar 1899); Cdr (5 Mar
1902); Capt (22 Jan 1906); RAdm (4 May 1910); placed on
Ret.Lst. (10 Jul 1914).

Career Summary Naval apprentice (14 Jun 1867); *Portsmouth*,
spec.serv. (Jun 1867-Jul 1868); received appointment from NY as
Midn (29 Jul 1868); USNA (Jul 1868-Jul 1872); *Tuscarora*,
Pac.Sta. (Jul 1872-Nov 1873); *Kearsarge*, and *Tuscarora*, Asia.
and Pac.Stas. (Nov 1873-Aug 1875); home and w.o. (Aug-Sep
1875); USNA (Sep 1875-Aug 1877); l.o.a. and w.o. (Sep 1877-
Mar 1878); *Plymouth*, N.Atl.Sta. (Mar 1878-May 1879); *Kearsarge*, N.Atl.Sta. (May 1879-Apr 1881); w.o. (Apr-Jul 1881);
Hydrographic Office, Washington, DC (Jul 1881-Oct 1883); in
charge, branch hydrographic office, Philadelphia (Oct 1883-Sep
1884); *Dolphin*, spec.serv. (Oct 1884-Jul 1885); rec. ship, *Wabash*,
Boston (Jul-Oct 1885); *Brooklyn*, N.Atl.Sta. (Oct 1885-Jun
1887); *Monocacy*, Asia.Sta. (Jun-Oct 1887); flag lt, *Brooklyn*,
N.Atl.Sta. (Oct 1887-May 1889); Bur. of Nav., Washington, DC
(Jul 1889-Jun 1895); *Cincinnati*, spec.serv. (Jun-Oct 1895);
exec.off., *Dolphin*, Spec.Serv.Sqdn. (Oct 1895-Nov 1897); Navy
Yard, Washington, DC (Nov 1897); compass office, Bur. of Equip.
and Recruiting, Washington, DC (Nov 1897-Mar 1898); exec.off.,
Dolphin, Navy Yard, NY (Mar 1898); *Eagle*, Wilmington, DE, and
Navy Yard, NY (Mar-Apr 1898); cdr, *Eagle*, N.Atl.Flt. (Apr-Oct
1898); office of asst. sec. of navy, Navy Dept., Washington, DC
(Oct 1898-Jun 1899); cdr, *Dolphin*, spec.serv. (Jun 1900-Nov
1901); hydrographer, Bur. of Equip. and Recruiting, Washington,
DC (Nov 1901-Jan 1904); cdr, *Cleveland*, Spec.Serv.Sqdn. (Jan
1904-Dec 1905); cdr, training ship, *Yankee* (Dec 1905-Aug 1906);
cdr, *Dixie*, spec.serv. (Aug-Nov 1906); home and w.o. (Nov

**WILLIAM HENRY HUDSON
SOUTHERLAND**
1852-1933

1906-Feb 1907); Navy Dept., Washington, DC (Feb-Apr 1907); senior member, bd. of inspection and surv. (Apr-Nov 1907); cdr, *New Jersey,* "Great White Flt." (Nov 1907-May 1909); home and w.o. (May-Sep 1909); member, court-martial bd., Portsmouth, NH (Sep-Oct 1909); member, naval exam. and ret. bds. (Oct 1909-Feb 1910); pres., bd. of inspection of shore stas. (Feb 1910-Mar 1911); cdr, 2nd Div., Pac.Flt., *West Virginia* (Mar 1911-Mar 1912); cdr, Pac.Flt., *California* (Mar 1912-Apr 1913); additional duty, cdr, Nicaragua Expeditionary Force (Aug-Oct 1912); member, Gen Bd., and other bd. duties, Washington, DC (Mar 1913-Jul 1914); placed on Ret.Lst. (10 Jul 1914).

References

Personal Papers: a) diary kept on the *Tuscarora* (1874-75) in Fondren Lib., Rice Institute, Houston.

Writings: a) with Cdr Seaton Schroeder, USN, *Azimuth Tables* (Washington, DC: 1882). b) *The North Atlantic Cyclone of August 1883,* Nautical Monograph No. 4 (Washington, DC: 1883). c) *Armor Question in 1891* (Washington, DC: 1891).

CHARLES STILLMAN SPERRY   Born on 3 Sep 1847 in Brooklyn, NY, son of Corydon Stillman and Catherine Elizabeth (Leavenworth) Sperry. Primary education was in public schools in Waterbury, CT. Received LL.D. from Yale Univ. in 1909. Married Edith Marcy on 11 Jan 1877. She was the granddaughter of NY Gov. William L. Marcy. One daughter and one son. Residing in Waterbury, CT, died in Washington, DC, on 1 Feb 1911. Buried in Arlington National Cemetery.

Ranks   Midn (26 Sep 1862); appointment revoked (6 Jul 1865); restored to position (21 Jul 1865); Ens (12 Mar 1868); Mstr (26 Mar 1869); Lt (21 Mar 1870); LCdr (1 Mar 1885); Cdr (22 Jun 1894); Capt (1 Jul 1900); RAdm (26 May 1906); placed on Ret.Lst. (3 Sep 1909).

Career Summary   Received appointment from CT (26 Sep 1862); USNA (Sep 1862-Jun 1866); condemned by medl. survey and appointment revoked (6 Jul 1865); restored to position (21 Jul 1865); l.o.a. and w.o. (Jun-Sep 1866); *Sacramento,* spec.serv. (Sep 1866-Nov 1867); w.o. (Nov-Dec 1867); ord. duty, Navy Yard, Boston (Jan 1868); *Kearsarge,* Pac.Sqdn. (Jan 1868-Feb 1871); *Supply,* spec.serv. (Feb-Jul 1871); l.o.a. and w.o. (Jul-Dec 1871); flgs., *Worcester,* N.Atl.Sqdn. (Dec 1871-Aug 1874); USNA (Aug 1874-Aug 1878); w.o. (Aug-Sep 1878); *Richmond,* Asia.Sta. (Oct 1878-Sep 1881); USNA (Oct 1881-Jun 1884); *Powhatan,* N. Atl.Sqdn. (Jun-Jul 1884); exec.off., *Quinnebaug,* Eur.Sta. (Jul 1884-Sep 1887); USNA (Oct 1887-Jul 1891); exec.off., *Chicago,* Sqdn. of Evol. and S.Atl.Sta. (Jul 1891-May 1893); Bur. of Ord., Washington, DC (May 1893-Jul 1895); Navy Yard, NY (Jul 1895-Nov 1898); cdr, *Yorktown,* Asia.Sqdn. (Nov 1898-Jun 1900); return home (Jun-Aug 1900); Bur. of Equip. and Recruiting, Washington, DC (Aug-Dec 1900); member, naval exam. bd., Washington, DC (Dec 1900); cdr, *New Orleans,* Asia.Sta. (Feb 1901-Jan 1904); additional duty, cdr, S.Sqdn., Asia.Sta., *New Orleans* (Dec 1903-Feb 1904); cdr, *Rainbow,* Asia.Sta. (Jan-Feb

CHARLES STILLMAN SPERRY
1847-1911

1904); home and l.o.a. (Feb-Mar 1904); spec. temp. duty, Gen Bd., Washington, DC (May 1904); NWC (Jun 1904-May 1906); additional duty as pres., NWC (Nov 1904-May 1906); delegate, international conference to revise rules for treatment of sick and wounded, Geneva (Jun-Aug 1906); spec. duty, NWC (Sep 1906-May 1907); delegate, 2nd Hague Conference on Prize Law, The Hague, Netherlands (Jun-Nov 1907); cdr, 4th Div., 2nd Sqdn., "Great White Flt.," *Alabama* (Nov 1907-May 1908); cdr, "Great White Flt.," *Connecticut* (May 1908-Mar 1909); senior member, bd. to revise navy regulations, Washington, DC (Mar 1909-Apr 1910); placed on Ret.Lst. (3 Sep 1909); NWC (May-Dec 1910); spec. duty, State Dept., Washington, DC (Jan-Feb 1911).

Career Highlights During Spanish-American War, commanded the *Yorktown*, participating in the action against insurgents on the Island of Luzon. Was pres. of the NWC. Two diplomatic missions to Europe. Commanded a battleship div. of the "Great White Flt." until the overall cdr, RAdm Robley D. Evans became ill in May 1909, when Sperry assumed command of the "Great White Flt.," completing the cruise around the globe.

References

Personal Papers: a) 2300 items (1862-1912) in LC. b) 2 items (1899) in NHF,LC.

Writings: a) "To Determine by the Aid of Azimuth Tables the Effect upon the Longitude of a Change in the Latitude Used in Working a Time Sight," U.S. Naval Institute *Proceedings* 14 (1880): 392-94.

ARTHUR BAYARD SPEYERS Born in NY City on 15 Aug 1846, son of James and Fanny (Pigot) Speyers. Remained unmarried. Resided in NY City. Died on 19 Nov 1918 in Montreal. Buried in the USNA Cemetery.

Ranks Midn (24 Jul 1863); Ens (19 Apr 1869); Mstr (12 Jul 1870); Lt (23 May 1874); LCdr (28 Dec 1895); Cdr (3 Mar 1899); Capt (6 Aug 1904); retired (11 Jan 1905); RAdm on Ret.Lst. (13 Apr 1911) to rank from 11 Jan 1905.

Career Summary Received appointment from NY (24 Jul 1863); USNA (Jun 1863-Jun 1868); found deficient and turned back (Jun 1866); w.o. (Jun-Oct 1868); *Guard*, N.Atl.Sqdn. (Oct 1868-Oct 1869); w.o. (Oct-Nov 1869); Navy Yard, NY (Nov-Dec 1869); *Benicia*, Asia.Sta. (Dec 1869-Sep 1872); sick lv. (Sep 1872-Jan 1873); rec. ship, *Vermont*, NY (Jan-Mar 1873); *Juniata*, spec.serv. (Mar 1873); sick lv. (Mar-Nov 1873); rec. ship, *Vermont*, NY (Nov 1873); *Kansas*, N.Atl.Sta. (Nov 1873-Feb 1874); sick lv. (Feb-Aug 1874); *Richmond*, S.Pac.Sta. (Sep 1874-Sep 1877); w.o. (Sep-Oct 1877); l.o.a. (Oct 1877-Feb 1878); USNA (Feb 1878-Sep 1880); w.o. (Sep 1880-Apr 1881); training ship, *Saratoga* (Apr 1881-Jul 1884); w.o. (Jul-Oct 1884); Navy Yard, NY (Oct 1884-May 1885); torp. instruction, Newport, RI (Jun-Sep 1885); NWC (Sep 1885); Navy Yard, NY (Sep 1885-Jun 1887); exec.off., *Chicago*, spec.serv. (Jun-Aug 1887); *Galena*, N.Atl.Sta. (Aug 1887-Jul 1890); l.o.a. (Jul-Oct 1890);

ARTHUR BAYARD SPEYERS
1846-1918

training ship, *Minnesota* (Oct 1890-Jul 1893); exec.off., *Yorktown*, Pac.Sta. (Jul 1893-Apr 1894); in hosp., Seattle (Apr-May 1894); Naval Hosp., Mare Island, CA (May-Jul 1894); home and w.o. (Jul-Oct 1894); exec.off., rec. ship, *Richmond,* Philadelphia (Oct 1894-Apr 1895); exec.off., *Bennington,* Pac.Sqdn. (May 1895-Dec 1896); exec.off., *Monterey,* Pac.Sqdn. (Dec 1896-Jul 1897); w.o. (Jul-Aug 1897); Navy Yard, NY (Aug 1897-May 1898); cdr, *Kingston,* N.Atl.Flt. (May-Dec 1898); Navy Yard, NY (Dec 1898-May 1901); Naval Sta., Cavite, P.I. (Jun-Aug 1901); cdr, *Monadnock,* Asia.Sta. (Sep-Nov 1901); cdr, *Glacier,* Asia.Sta. (Nov 1901-Aug 1903); w.o. (Aug-Sep 1903); Navy Yard, NY (Sep 1903-Jan 1905); retired (11 Jan 1905).

SIDNEY AUGUSTUS STAUNTON Born in Ellicottville, NY, on 7 Jun 1850, son of Joseph Marshall and Mary Elizabeth (Wilber) Staunton. Married Emily Duncan Biddle on 23 Sep 1886. Resided in Washington, DC, dying at the Naval Hosp. there on 11 Jan 1939.

Ranks Midn (20 Sep 1867); title changed to Cadet Midn (15 Jul 1870); Midn (6 Jun 1871); Ens (14 Jul 1872); Mstr (4 Feb 1875); Lt (15 Nov 1881); LCdr (3 Mar 1899); Cdr (9 Oct 1901); Capt (12 Jun 1906); RAdm (20 Feb 1910); placed on Ret.Lst. (7 Jun 1912).

Career Summary Received appointment from WV (20 Sep 1867); USNA (Sep 1867-Jun 1871); w.o. (Jun-Aug 1871); *Iroquois,* N.Atl.Sta. (Aug-Dec 1871); *Congress,* and *Plymouth,* Eur.Sta. (Dec 1871-Jun 1873); w.o. (Jun-Dec 1873); *Franklin,* and *Wabash,* N.Atl. and Eur.Stas. (Dec 1873-Apr 1874); w.o. (Apr-Jul 1874); rec. ship, *Sabine,* Portsmouth, NH (Aug-Sep 1874); Hydrographic Office, Washington, DC (Oct-Dec 1874); *Powhatan,* Home Sqdn. (Jan 1875); *Franklin, Marion,* and *Trenton,* Eur.Sta. (Jan 1875-Oct 1877); home and w.o. (Oct-Nov 1877); USNA (Dec 1877-Dec 1879); *Swatara,* Asia.Sta. (Dec 1879-Dec 1882); home and w.o. (Dec 1882-Feb 1883); ord. instruction, Navy Yard, Washington, DC (Mar-Apr 1883); l.o.a. (May-Oct 1883); Office of Naval Intelligence, Navy Dept., Washington, DC (Oct 1883-Mar 1885); flag lt, *Pensacola,* Eur.Sta. (Apr 1885-Aug 1887); return and w.o. (Aug-Sep 1887); Office of Naval Intelligence, Washington, DC, and sec., American Delegation, International Maritime Conference (Oct 1887-Sep 1889); flag lt, *Chicago,* Sqdn. of Evol. (Oct 1889-May 1893); l.o.a. (May-Aug 1893); torp. instruction, Newport, RI (Aug-Sep 1893); ord. instr., Navy Yard, Washington, DC (Oct 1893-Jan 1894); member, bd. of inspection and surv., Navy Yard, Washington, DC (Jan-Mar 1894); flag lt, *Philadelphia,* Pac.Sqdn. (Apr-Aug 1894); w.o. (Aug-Nov 1894); recorder, bd. of inspection and surv. (Nov 1894-Jun 1897); staff member, *Iowa,* N.Atl.Sqdn. (Jun 1897-Apr 1898); asst. chief of staff, *New York,* N.Atl.Flt. (Apr 1898-Jul 1899); member, Isthmian Canal Commission (Jul 1899-May 1901); cdr, *Yankton,* N.Atl.Sta. (Jun-Oct 1901); home and w.o. (Oct-Nov 1891); cdr, *Rainbow,* Asia.Sta. (Dec 1901-Jan 1903); cdr, *Helena,* Asia.Sta. (Jan-Sep 1903); home and w.o. (Sep-Dec

SIDNEY AUGUSTUS STAUNTON
1850-1939

1903); duty, Gen Bd., Washington, DC (Dec 1903-Feb 1904); NWC (Feb 1904-Jul 1906); cdr, *Colorado*, Asia.Sta. (Jul 1906-Feb 1908); member, Gen Bd., Washington, DC (Mar 1908-Apr 1909); cdr, Spec.Serv.Sqdn., and naval representative to Argentina, *Montana* (Apr-May 1910), then *Tennessee* (May-Jul 1910); cdr, 5th Div., Atl.Flt., *Tennessee* (Jul 1910-Aug 1911); member, Gen Bd., Washington, DC (Aug 1911-Jun 1912); placed on Ret.Lst. (7 Jun 1912); Bur. of Ord., and member, spec. bd. on naval ord., Washington, DC (Oct 1918-Jun 1919).

Career Highlights Graduated first in his class in 1871. Served on RAdm William T. Sampson's staff during the war with Spain. Sat on Gen Bd. and commanded a battleship div. of the Atl.Flt.

References

Writings: "Naval Reserves and the Recruiting and Training of Men," U.S. Naval Institute *Proceedings* 48 (1889): 1-20.

THOMAS HOLDUP STEVENS Born in Honolulu, Sandwich Island, on 12 Jul 1848, son of RAdm Thomas Holdup, USN (1819-96), and Anna Maria (Christie) Stevens and grandson of Capt Thomas Holdup Stevens, USN (1795-1841). Was the third generation of this name to achieve flag rank in the USN Married twice, his second wife was Cara de la Montaigne Hall, daughter of NY mayor Oakey Hall, whom he married on 29 Apr 1903. Died in Washington, DC, on 3 Oct 1914. Buried in Arlington National Cemetery.

Ranks Midn (1 Oct 1863); Ens (19 Apr 1869); Mstr (12 Jul 1870); Lt (6 Jan 1874); LCdr (2 Feb 1896); Cdr (29 Mar 1899); Capt (30 Sep 1904); retired (11 Feb 1905); RAdm on Ret.Lst. (13 Apr 1911) to date from 11 Feb 1905.

Career Summary Received appointment by virtue of being the son of an officer (1 Oct 1863); USNA (Oct 1863-Jun 1868); found deficient and turned back (Jan 1866); w.o. (Jun-Sep 1868); *Resaca*, and *Mohican*, N.Pac.Sqdn. (Oct 1868-Sep 1869); w.o. (Sep-Nov 1869); *Michigan*, on Great Lakes (Nov 1869-Feb 1870); *Colorado*, Pac.Sqdn. (Feb-Mar 1870); w.o. (Mar-May 1870); *St. Mary's*, *Ossipee*, *Cyane*, and flgs., *Pensacola*, Pac.Sta. (May 1870-May 1873); w.o. (May-Aug 1873); Navy Yard, Norfolk, VA (Aug-Nov 1873); despatch boat, *Mayflower* (Nov 1873-Mar 1874); *Wyoming*, N.Atl.Sta. (Mar-Apr 1874); flgs., *Franklin*, Eur.Sta. (Apr 1874-Sep 1876); *Marion*, Eur.Sta. (Sep 1876-Mar 1877); home and w.o. (Mar-Jun 1877); Torp.Sta., Newport, RI (Jul-Sep 1877); w.o. (Sep 1877-Jan 1878); exec.off., rec. ship, *Passaic*, Washington, DC (Jan-Jun 1878); Torp.Sta., Newport, RI (Jun-Sep 1878); flgs., *Richmond*, Asia.Sta. (Oct 1878-Oct 1880); flt. signal off., Pac.Sta., *Richmond* (Oct 1880-Jun 1881); *Pensacola*, Pac.Sta. (Jun-Aug 1881); w.o. (Aug-Dec 1881); War Records Office, Navy Dept., Washington, DC (Dec 1881-Oct 1882); w.o. (Oct 1882-Aug 1883); *Miantonomoh*, Navy Yard, NY (Sep 1883); *Galena*, S.Atl.Sta. (Sep-Nov 1883); l.o.a. and w.o. (Nov 1883-Feb 1885); *Marion*, Asia.Sta. (Feb-Sep 1885); *Palos*, Asia.Sta. (Sep 1885-Nov 1887); home and w.o. (Nov 1887-Aug 1888); rec. ship, *Vermont*, NY (Aug 1888-Nov 1890); l.o.a. and w.o. (Nov

THOMAS HOLDUP STEVENS
1848-1914

1890-Mar 1891); training ship, *Monongahela* (Mar-May 1891); w.o. (May-Nov 1891); *Mohican*, Pac.Sta. (Nov 1891-Mar 1892); *Ranger*, Pac.Sta. (Apr 1892-May 1893); home and l.o.a. (May 1893-Jan 1894); ord. instruction, Navy Yard, Washington, DC (Jan-Apr 1894); exec.off., *Yorktown*, Pac. and Asia.Stas. (May 1894-Jul 1895); w.o. and under suspension (Jul 1895-May 1896); exec.off., *Cincinnati*, N.Atl. and Eur.Stas. (May 1896-Aug 1897); home and l.o.a. (Aug 1897); Navy Yard, Norfolk, VA (Sep 1897-Jun 1898); exec.off., flgs., *Philadelphia*, Pac.Sta. (Jul 1898-Feb 1899); Naval Hosp., Mare Island, CA (Feb-Mar 1899); home and w.o. (Mar-Jun 1899); temp. duty, NWC (Jun-Oct 1899); Navy Yard, Norfolk, VA (Nov 1899-Apr 1900); cdr, *Manila*, Asia.Sta. (Jul 1900-Jan 1902); Naval Hosp., Mare Island, CA (Jan-Feb 1902); Navy Yard, Mare Island, CA (Feb-Aug 1902); Navy Yard, Puget Sound, WA (Aug 1902-May 1903); NWC (Jun-Sep 1903); l.o.a. and w.o. (Sep-Dec 1903); capt.yd., Navy Yard, Pensacola, FL (Dec 1903-Feb 1905); retired (11 Feb 1905).

Career Highlights While attached to the *Mohican*, participated in the observation of the sun's total eclipse off Siberia in Aug 1869. Shortly thereafter, while on the *Cyane* of the Pac.Sqdn., participated in the surveying of the Isthmus of Tehuantepec for a trans-Isthmian canal. In May 1873, while on the *Pensacola*, he commanded a company of Bluejackets during the occupation of Panama in order to protect American lives and interests during the rebellion then.

References

Personal Papers: Stevens Family Papers, 35 items (1810-1952) in NHF,LC.

WILLIAM HENRY STEWART Born in Andover, MA, on 11 Jul 1831, son of John and Dorcas (Baxter) Stewart. Married twice. His first wife was Roline Mayo, whom he married on 11 Jul 1860. Married his second wife, Azuba E. Tolles, on 20 Jan 1885. Resided in De Land, FL, where he died on 31 Mar 1913 and where he was buried.

Ranks Chaplain [Baptist] (10 Mar 1863); placed on Ret.Lst. (11 Jul 1893); Chaplain with rank of RAdm on Ret.Lst. (29 Jun 1906).

Career Summary Received appointment from MA (10 Mar 1863); w.o. (Mar-Jun 1863); Naval Sta., Cairo, IL (Jun 1863-Nov 1865); w.o. (Nov 1865-Oct 1866); USNA (Oct 1866-Sep 1867); *Powhatan*, S.Pac.Sqdn. (Oct 1867-Dec 1869); w.o. (Dec 1869-Mar 1870); Naval Sta., Mound City, IL (Apr-Sep 1870); rec. ship, *Ohio*, Boston (Oct 1870-Apr 1874); w.o. (Apr 1874-Mar 1877); rec. ship, *Wabash*, Boston (Mar-Oct 1877); Navy Yard, Portsmouth, NH (Nov 1877-Oct 1882); w.o. (Oct 1882-Jan 1887); *Richmond*, N.Atl.Sta. (Jan 1887-Sep 1888); w.o. (Sep 1888-Jul 1893); placed on Ret.Lst. (11 Jul 1893).

YATES STIRLING Born in Baltimore on 6 May 1843, son of Archibald and Elizabeth Ann (Walsh) Stirling. Married Ellen Salisbury Haley on 29 Aug 1867. Seven children, including

YATES STIRLING
1843-1929

RAdm Yates Stirling, USN (1872-1948). Resided in Baltimore where he died on 5 Mar 1929. Buried in USNA Cemetery, Annapolis.

Ranks Act.Midn (27 Sep 1860); title changed to Midn (16 Jul 1862); Ens (28 May 1863); Mstr (10 Nov 1865); Lt (10 Nov 1866); LCdr (12 Mar 1868); Cdr (26 Nov 1880); Capt (16 Sep 1894); RAdm (8 Jun 1902); placed on Ret.Lst. (6 May 1905).

Career Summary Received appointment from MD (27 Sep 1860); USNA (Sep 1860-May 1863); *Shenandoah*, N.Atl.Blk. Sqdn. (Jun 1863-Apr 1864); l.o.a. (Apr-Jun 1864); *Shenandoah*, N.Atl.Blk.Sqdn. (Jun 1864-Apr 1865); w.o. (Apr-May 1865); *Mohongo*, Pac.Sqdn. (May 1865-Aug 1867); w.o. (Sep 1867-Jan 1868); *Wampanoag*, spec.serv., and flgs., N.Atl.Sta. (Jan-Mar 1868); flgs., *Contoocook* [renamed *Albany*], N.Atl.Sqdn. (Mar 1868-Sep 1869); Hydrographic Office, Washington, DC (Feb 1870-Jan 1871); w.o. (Jan-May 1871); rec. ship, *Independence*, Mare Island, CA (Jun 1871-Dec 1872); sick lv. (Dec 1872-Oct 1873); exec.off., *Canandaigua*, N.Atl.Sta. (Nov 1873-Jan 1874); sick lv. (Feb 1874-Aug 1875); exec.off., rec. ship, *New Hampshire*, Norfolk, VA (Aug 1875-Jan 1876); exec.off., rec. ship, *Worcester*, Norfolk, VA (Jan-Sep 1876); w.o. (Sep 1876-May 1877); torp. duty, Newport, RI (Jun-Sep 1877); w.o. (Sep 1877-Jan 1878); ord. instruction, Navy Yard, Washington, DC (Jan-Jul 1878); w.o. (Jul-Aug 1878); exec.off., *Lackawanna*, Pac.Sqdn. (Sep 1878-Jan 1881); w.o. (Feb 1881-Jan 1882); ord. duty, Navy Yard, Washington, DC (Feb 1882-Apr 1884); cdr, *Iroquois*, Pac.Sta. (May 1884-Sep 1886); w.o. (Oct 1886-Jan 1887); cdr, rec. ship, *Dale*, Washington, DC (Jan 1887-Jan 1890); w.o. (Jan-Mar 1890); cdr, *Dolphin*, N.Atl.Sta., and Sqdn. of Evol. (Mar 1890-May 1891); l.o.a. and w.o. (May 1891-Feb 1892); bd. duties (Feb-Nov 1892); insp., 5th L.h. Dist., Baltimore (Dec 1892-Oct 1894); s.a. and w.o. (Oct-Nov 1894); bd. duties (Nov 1894-Apr 1895); cdr, *Newark*, S.Atl.Sqdn. (May 1895-Mar 1896); cdr, *Lancaster*, S.Atl.Sta. (Mar 1896-Jun 1897); cdr, S.Atl.Sta., *Lancaster* (Jul-Dec 1897); home and l.o.a. (Dec 1897-Mar 1898); bd. duties (Mar 1898-Jul 1900); additional duties, insp., 5th L.h. Dist., Baltimore (Dec 1899-Jan 1900); sick lv. (Jul-Nov 1900); comdt., Naval Sta., San Juan, Puerto Rico (Nov 1900-Aug 1902); comdt., Navy Yard, Puget Sound, WA (Aug 1902-Apr 1903); cdr, Philippine Sqdn., Asia.Flt., *Rainbow* (Jun-Dec 1903); temp. cdr, Asia.Sta., *Wisconsin* (Dec 1903-Apr 1904); cdr, Cruiser Sqdn., Asia.Flt., *New Orleans* (Apr-Jul 1904); cdr, Asia.Flt., *Wisconsin* (Jul 1904-Mar 1905); home and w.o. (Mar-May 1905); placed on Ret.Lst. (6 May 1905).

EDWARD RHODES STITT Born in Charlotte, NC, on 22 Jul 1867, son of William Edward and Mary (Rhodes) Stitt. Received A.B. from the Univ. of SC in 1885 and M.D. from the Univ. of PA in 1889. Studied tropical medicine at the Univ. of London in 1905. Subsequently received other degrees: the LL.D. from the Univ. of SC in 1917, and from the Univ. of MI in 1921; the Sc.D. from Jefferson Medl. College, Philadelphia, in 1920; the

EDWARD RHODES STITT
1867-1948

Ph.M. from the Philadelphia College of Pharmacy and Science in 1921, and the Sc.D. from the Univ. of PA in 1924. Married three times. His first wife was Emma Woodruff Scott, whom he married on 19 Jul 1892. One son and two daughters. Married again on 22 Jun 1935 to Laura Armistead Carter. His third wife was Helen Bennett Newton, whom he married on 3 May 1937. Resided in Washington, DC. Died on 13 Nov 1948 at the Naval Hosp. in Bethesda, MD, and was buried in Arlington National Cemetery.

Ranks Asst.Surg. with rel. rank of Ens (23 Mar 1889); PAsst.Surg. (23 Mar 1892); Surg. (7 Jun 1900); Medl.Insp. (11 Jun 1911); Medl.Dir. with rank of RAdm (15 Oct 1917); Surg.Gen (30 Nov 1920); reappointed Surg.Gen (30 Nov 1924); placed on Ret.Lst. (1 Aug 1931).

Career Summary Received appointment from SC (23 Mar 1889); w.o. (Mar-Apr 1889); Bur. of Medicine and Surgery, Washington, DC (Apr-Jun 1889); rec. ship, *New Hampshire*, Newport, RI (Jun 1889-Jan 1890); *Baltimore*, N.Atl. and S.Pac. Sqdns. (Jan 1890-Jan 1892); l.o.a. (Jan-Mar 1892); Naval Hosp., Philadelphia (Mar-Jun 1892); Bur. of Medicine and Surgery, Washington, DC (Jun-Sep 1892); rec. ship, *Franklin*, Norfolk, VA (Oct-Dec 1892); Naval Hosp., Norfolk, VA (Dec 1892-May 1893); flgs., *Chicago*, Eur.Sta. (Jun 1893-Apr 1895); spec. duty, Nicaraguan Surv.Expd. (Apr-Aug 1895); *New York*, Navy Yard, NY (Aug-Dec 1895); cst.surv. duty (Dec 1895-Jun 1896); rec. ship, *Vermont*, NY (Jun-Aug 1896); home and w.o. (Aug 1896); Bur. of Medicine and Surgery, Washington, DC (Sep 1896-Sep 1899); training ship, *Hartford* (Sep 1899-Jul 1902); temp. duty, NY (Aug 1902); inst. of bacteriology and pathology, Naval Museum of Hygiene and Medl. School, Washington, DC (Aug 1902-Jun 1905); London School of Tropical Medicine, London, England (Jun-Aug 1905); Naval Hosp., Canacao, P.I. (Sep 1905-Jul 1906); investigation of tropical diseases, P.I., Mariana Islands, Yokohama, Japan, and Honolulu, Territory of HI (Jul-Oct 1906); Naval Medl. School, Washington, DC (Oct 1906-Jul 1909); medl. off. in command, U.S. Naval Hosp., Canacao, P.I. (Aug 1909-Sep 1911); medl.insp., Bur. of Medicine and Surgery, Washington, DC (Sep-Oct 1911); Naval Medl. School, Washington, DC (Oct 1911-Sep 1916); cdr, Naval Medl. School, Washington, DC (Sep 1916-Nov 1920); surg.gen and chief, Bur. of Medicine and Surgery, Washington, DC (Nov 1920-Nov 1928); insp. of medl. dept. activities, Pac.cst., San Francisco (Nov 1928-Aug 1931); placed on Ret.Lst. (1 Aug 1931).

Career Highlights An expert in tropical medicine, owing to his experiences during the war with Spain. Held the chair in medl. zoology, Univ. of the Philippines, from 1909 to 1911, and he was prof. of tropical medicine, Georgetown Univ. and at George Washington Univ., Washington, DC, and lecturer at the Jefferson Medical College in Philadelphia. Helped to develop the new Naval Medical School in Washington, DC, to become an outstanding institution in tropical medicine. Received the Navy Cross for his duties during World War I. Held two consecutive terms as surg.gen and chief of the Bur. of Medicine and Surgery from 1920 to 1928. His publications became standard for medical studies.

References

Personal Papers: miscellaneous papers in LC.

Writings: a) *Practical Bacteriology* (multiple editions, 1909-). b) *The Diagnostics and Treatment of Tropical Diseases* (multiple editions, 1914-). c) *The Navy as a Special Field for Medical Work* (Washington, DC: 1923). d) *Contributions of the Medical Corps, United States Navy, to American Medicine* (Washington, DC: 1926). e) "The Medical Department of the Navy," U.S. Naval Institute *Proceedings* 284 (Oct 1926): 1951-60. f) "Activities of the Medical Corps, United States Navy," U.S. Naval Institute *Proceedings* 308 (Oct 1928): 887-90.

CHARLES HERBERT STOCKTON Born in Philadelphia on 13 Oct 1845, son of Rev. William R. and Emma T. (Gross) Stockton. Early education was at the Germantown Academy and at the Freeland Academy in Collegeville, PA. Received LL.D. degree from George Washington Univ. in 1909. Married twice: to Cornelia Carter on 23 Jun 1875; and to Pauline Lentilhon King on 23 Nov 1880. One son and two daughters. His home was in Washington, DC, where he died on 31 May 1924. Buried in Arlington National Cemetery.

CHARLES HERBERT STOCKTON
1845-1924

Ranks Act.Midn (14 Nov 1861); title changed to Midn (16 Jul 1862); Ens (1 Dec 1866); Mstr (12 Mar 1868); Lt (26 Mar 1869); LCdr (15 Nov 1881); Cdr (3 Apr 1892); Capt (8 Jul 1899); RAdm (7 Jan 1906); placed on Ret.Lst. (13 Oct 1907).

Career Summary Received appointment from PA (14 Nov 1861); USNA (Nov 1861-Oct 1865); *Dacotah*, N.Pac.Sqdn. (Oct 1865-Jan 1866); sick lv. (Jan-Feb 1866); training ship, *Sabine* (Feb 1866); *Chattanooga*, N.Pac.Sqdn. (Feb-Aug 1866); *Mohican*, and *Ossipee*, N.Pac.Sqdn. (Aug 1866-Jul 1869); w.o. (Aug-Oct 1869); Navy Yard, Philadelphia (Oct 1869-Jan 1870); flgs., *Congress*, S.Atl.Sta., and *Brooklyn*, spec. cruise, Europe (Feb 1870-Jul 1873); l.o.a. (Jul-Oct 1873); Navy Yard, Philadelphia (Oct-Dec 1873); *Dictator*, Navy Yard, NY (Dec 1873); torp. instruction, Newport, RI (Dec 1873); Navy Yard, Philadelphia (Dec 1873-Apr 1874); *Swatara*, special cruise (May 1874-Jun 1875); l.o.a. (Jun-Sep 1875); Hydrographic Office, Washington, DC (Sep 1875-Aug 1876); *Plymouth*, N.Atl.Sta. (Aug 1876-May 1879); w.o. (May-Jul 1879); Navy Yard, NY (Jul 1879-May 1880); torp. instruction, Newport, RI (May-Oct 1880); Navy Yard, Washington, DC (Oct 1880-Apr 1882); exec.off., *Iroquois*, Pac.Sqdn. (Apr 1882-May 1885); home and w.o. (May-Aug 1885); duties, Bur. of Yards and Docks, Washington, DC (Sep 1885-Apr 1889); cdr, *Thetis*, N.Pac. Sqdn. (Apr 1889-May 1891); NWC (May 1891-Oct 1894); spec. duty, preparing lectures on international law (Oct-Dec 1894); lecturer, international law, NWC (Dec 1894-Jul 1895); cdr, *Yorktown*, Asia.Sta. (Sep 1895-Dec 1897); NWC (Dec 1897-May 1898); pres., NWC (May 1898-Oct 1900); spec. duty in connection with NWC (Oct 1900-Jan 1901); cdr, *Kentucky*, Asia.Sta. (Mar 1901-Mar 1903); chief of staff, Asia.Sta., *Kentucky* (Oct

1902-Mar 1903); naval attaché, American Embassy, London (May 1903-Dec 1905); home and w.o. (Dec 1905-Jan 1906); pres., bd. of inspection and surv. (Jan-May 1906); pres., naval exam. and ret. bds., Washington, DC (May 1906-May 1907); cdr, Spec.Serv.Sqdn., *Tennessee* (Jun-Aug 1907); pres., bd. of examiners, Washington, DC (Aug-Oct 1907); placed on Ret.Lst. (13 Oct 1907); delegate, International Prize Court, London (Aug 1908-Mar 1909).

Career Highlights Long connection with the study of international law and the NWC at which he lectured and served as pres.. He prepared, by order of the navy sec. in 1900, the laws and usages of war at sea. Owing to his legal training and his international stature, served after retirement as first American delegate to the London Naval Conference in 1908 and 1909. Also served as pres. of George Washington Univ. in Washington, DC, from 1910 to 1918.

References
Personal Papers: a) journals, etc., in NWC, Naval Historical Collection, Newport, RI.
Writings: a) "The Naval Asylum and Service Pensions for Enlisted Men," U.S. Naval Institute *Proceedings* 37 (1886): 53-67. b) *Origins, History, Laws, and Regulations of the United States Naval Asylum, Philadelphia* (Washington, DC: 1886). c) "Simpson's Timber Dry-Dock," U.S. Naval Institute *Proceedings* 41 (1887): 221-25. d) *The Arctic Cruise of the USS "Thetis"* (Washington, DC: c.1890). e) *The Laws and Usage of the Sea* (Washington, DC: 1901). f) *United States Naval War Code* (Washington, DC: 1901). h) *A Manual of International Law for the Use of Naval Officers* (Annapolis, 1911, 1921). i) "Panama Canal Tolls," U.S. Naval Institute *Proceedings* 142 (Jun 1912): 493-98. f) editor, "International Law Manual."

DANIEL DELEHANTY VINCENT STUART Born in Albany, NY, on 15 Sep 1847, son of John and Mary (Delehanty) Stuart. A student at the Albany Academy from 1861 to 1862 before serving briefly in the volunteer navy. Married Alicia A. Smith on 26 Sep 1883. Two sons. Resided in Washington, DC, where he died on 13 Apr 1932.

Ranks Midn (24 Sep 1863); Ens (12 Jul 1870); Mstr (11 Feb 1873); Lt (9 Sep 1876); LCdr (27 Apr 1898); Cdr (11 Feb 1901); Capt (1 Jul 1905); RAdm (3 Sep 1909); placed on Ret.Lst. (15 Sep 1909).

Career Summary Received appointment from NY (24 Sep 1863); USNA (Sep 1863-Jun 1869); found deficient and turned back (Feb 1865, and Oct 1866); training ship, *Sabine* (Jun 1869-Jul 1870); w.o. (Jul-Nov 1870); USNA (Nov-Dec 1870); *California*, and *Pensacola*, Pac.Sqdn. (Dec 1870-Sep 1873); home and w.o. (Sep-Oct 1873); l.o.a. (Oct-Nov 1873); despatch vessel, *Mayflower* (Nov 1873-May 1874); w.o. (May-Jul 1874); *Roanoke*, N.Atl.Sta. (Jul 1874-Jan 1875); *Ashuelot*, and *Kearsarge*, Asia.Sta. (Feb 1875-Jan 1878); w.o. (Jan-Oct 1878); rec. ship, *Colorado*, NY (Oct 1878-Aug 1880); *Galena*, Eur.Sta. (Aug 1880-Sep

1883); w.o. (Sep-Dec 1883); Navy Yard, NY (Dec 1883-Apr 1884); torp. instruction, Newport, RI (Apr-Aug 1884); Navy Yard, NY (Aug 1884-Jun 1885); cst.surv. duty (Jul 1885-Jul 1887); w.o. (Jul-Aug 1887); spec. duty, Philadelphia (Aug-Oct 1887); *Enterprise*, Eur.Sta. (Oct 1887-Jan 1888); w.o. (Jan-May 1888); *Pensacola*, spec.serv. (May 1888-Jun 1889); training ship, *Portsmouth* (Jul 1889-Nov 1890); USNA (Nov 1890-Oct 1893); w.o. (Oct 1893-Jan 1894); temp. duty, rec. ship, *Vermont*, NY (Jan-May 1894); schoolship, *St. Mary's* (May 1894-Apr 1895); *Newark*, S.Atl.Sqdn. (May 1895-Mar 1896); *Yantic*, N.Atl.Sqdn. (Mar 1896-Jul 1897); *New York*, N.Atl.Sqdn. (Jul-Dec 1897); home and l.o.a. (Dec 1897-Feb 1898); Navy Yard, Washington, DC (Jan-May 1898); Navy Yard, Boston (May 1898); exec.off., *Lancaster*, Key West, FL (May-Jun 1898); cdr, *Mangrove*, N.Atl. Flt. (Jun 1898); exec.off., *Puritan*, N.Atl.Flt. (Jun-Aug 1898); exec.off., *Lancaster*, Navy Yard, Portsmouth, NH (Aug-Oct 1898); Navy Yard, NY (Oct 1898-Jan 1899); exec.off., rec. ship, *Vermont*, NY (Jan 1899-Mar 1901); Naval Sta., Cavite, P.I. (May 1901-Jan 1902); cdr, *Isla de Luzon*, Asia.Sta. (Feb-Mar 1902); Naval Sta., Cavite, P.I. (Mar-Jul 1902); cdr, *Don Juan de Austria*, Asia.Sta. (Jul 1902-Apr 1903); cdr, *Yorktown*, Navy Yard, Mare Island, CA (Apr-Jun 1903); home and w.o. (Jun-Aug 1903); in charge, Naval Recruiting Sta., NY (Sep 1903-Jul 1907); additional duty, supervisor of harbor, NY (Apr-Jul 1907); Navy Yard, Norfolk, VA (Jul 1907-Aug 1909); home and w.o. (Aug-Sep 1909); placed on Ret.Lst. (15 Sep 1909).

WILLIAM SWIFT Born in Windham, CT, on 17 Mar 1848, son of William and Harriet Gray (Byrne) Swift. On 18 Sep 1872, married Grace Virginia Ranson, daughter of Commo George M. Ranson, USN. Seven children. Died in Newport, RI, on 30 May 1919. Buried at his home in Richfield Springs, NY.

Ranks Midn (25 Sep 1863); Ens (18 Dec 1868); Mstr (21 Mar 1870); Lt (21 Mar 1871); LCdr (24 Oct 1889); Cdr (6 Apr 1897); Capt (9 Feb 1902); RAdm (3 Jan 1908); placed on Ret.Lst. (17 Mar 1910).

Career Summary Received appointment from CT (25 Sep 1863); USNA (Sep 1863-Jun 1867); flgs., *Susquehanna*, N.Atl. Sqdn. (Jul-Oct 1867); sick lv. (Oct 1867-Jan 1868); *Kearsarge*, Pac.Sta. (Jan 1868-Oct 1870); w.o. (Oct 1870-Mar 1871); signal duty, Washington, DC (Apr-Jun 1871); w.o. (Jun-Aug 1871); *Iroquois*, N.Atl.Sta. (Aug 1871-Jan 1872); *Canandaigua*, N.Atl. Sta. (Jan-Oct 1872); w.o. (Oct-Dec 1872); *Supply*, spec.serv. (Jan-Nov 1873); *Colorado*, N.Atl.Sqdn. (Dec 1873-Jan 1875); w.o. (Jan-Aug 1875); rec. ship, *Colorado*, NY (Aug 1875-Mar 1876); Navy Yard, NY (Mar 1876-Jun 1877); torp.serv., Newport, RI (Jul-Sep 1877); *Plymouth*, N.Atl.Sta. (Oct 1877-May 1879); *Kearsarge*, N.Atl.Sta. (May 1879-Aug 1880); Navy Yard, Boston (Aug 1880-Jul 1881); Naval Sta., New London, CT (Aug 1881-Sep 1883); duty with, then exec.off., *Alert*, Asia.Sta. (Oct 1883-Sep 1886); w.o. (Sep-Oct 1886); ord. duty, Navy Yard, Washington, DC (Nov 1886-Aug 1890); on furlough (Aug

WILLIAM SWIFT
1848-1919

1890-Feb 1891); w.o. (Feb 1891-Feb 1893); on furlough (Feb-Dec 1893); w.o. (Dec 1893-May 1894); Torp.Sta., Newport, RI (Jun-Aug 1894); exec.off., *New York*, N.Atl.Sta. (Sep 1894-Oct 1895); duty with, then exec.off., *Indiana*, N.Atl.Sta. (Oct 1895-Feb 1897); Bur. of Ord., Washington, DC (Mar-Jul 1897); ord.off., Navy Yard, NY (Jul 1897-May 1900); cdr, training ship, *Prairie* (May 1900-Feb 1901); cdr, *Concord*, Asia.Sta. (Apr-May 1901); cdr, *Yorktown*, Asia.Sta. (Jun-Aug 1901); temp.gov., Guam (Aug-Nov 1901); cdr, *Yorktown*, Asia.Sta. (Nov 1901-Apr 1902); member, Gen Bd. and member, Army-Navy Joint Bd., Washington, DC (May 1902-Apr 1907); suspended (May-Oct 1907); w.o. (Oct-Nov 1907); comdt., Navy Yard, and Naval Sta., Boston (Nov 1907-Dec 1909); aide for material, Navy Dept., Washington, DC (Dec 1909-Nov 1910); placed on Ret.Lst. (17 Mar 1910).

WILLIAM THOMAS SWINBURNE Born in Newport, RI, on 24 Aug 1847, son of Daniel Thomas and Harriet (Knowles) Swinburne. Married Katherine Elsie Vincent on 27 Nov 1875. She died in 1904, and he married Mrs. Sophie Cook Poe on 7 Sep 1905. At least one daughter, who married RAdm Luke McNamee, USN (1871-1952). Died in Coronado, CA, on 3 Mar 1928. Buried at sea.

Ranks Midn (29 Sep 1862); Ens (12 Mar 1868); Mstr (26 Mar 1869); Lt (21 Mar 1870); LCdr (6 Mar 1887); Cdr (28 Dec 1895); Capt (3 Mar 1901); RAdm (22 Jul 1906); placed on Ret.Lst. (24 Aug 1909).

Career Summary Received appointment from RI (29 Sep 1862); USNA (Sep 1862-Jun 1866); l.o.a. and w.o. (Jun-Oct 1866); *Saco*, W.Ind.Sqdn. (Oct 1866-Oct 1867); w.o. (Oct-Dec 1867); *Kearsarge*, S.Pac.Sqdn. (Jan 1868-Oct 1870); w.o. (Nov 1870-Feb 1871); *Michigan*, on Great Lakes (Feb 1871-Mar 1872); *Portsmouth*, spec.serv. (Apr 1872); flgs., *Lancaster*, S.Atl.Sta. (Apr 1872-Sep 1874); return and w.o. (Sep 1874-May 1875); Torp. Sta., Newport, RI (Jun-Oct 1875); rec. ship, *Colorado*, NY (Oct-Nov 1875); flgs., *Hartford*, N.Atl.Sta. (Nov 1875-Jun 1877); l.o.a. and w.o. (Jun 1877-May 1879); cst.surv. duty (May 1879-May 1883); w.o. (May-Aug 1883); *Trenton*, Asia.Sta. (Sep 1883-Sep 1886); USNA (Oct 1886-Aug 1890); exec.off., *Boston*, Pac.Sta. (Aug 1890-Apr 1893); l.o.a. (Apr-Aug 1893); head, seamanship dept., USNA (Aug 1893-Jul 1897); cdr, *Helena*, N. Atl.Flt. (Jul 1897-Aug 1899); home and w.o. (Aug-Oct 1899); equip., then ord.off., Navy Yard, Portsmouth, NH (Oct 1899-Nov 1901); court-martial duty, Navy Yard, Portsmouth, NH (Nov 1901-May 1902); NWC (Jun-Oct 1902); cdr, flgs., *Texas*, Cst. Sqdn. (Oct 1902-Oct 1904); member, Gen Bd., Washington, DC (Oct 1904-Jul 1906); cdr, Pac.Sqdn., *Chicago* (Aug-Dec 1906), then *Charleston* (Dec 1906-Feb 1907); title changed to cdr, 2nd Sqdn., Pac.Flt., *Charleston* (Feb 1907-Jul 1908); cdr, Pac.Flt., *West Virginia* (Aug 1908-Apr 1909); w.o. (Apr-May 1909); temp. duty, Navy Dept., Washington, DC (May-Jun 1909); NWC (Jun-Oct 1909); placed on Ret.Lst. (24 Aug 1909); general court-

WILLIAM THOMAS SWINBURNE
1847-1928

martial duty, 3rd Naval Dist., NY (Oct 1918-Sep 1919).

Career Highlights While exec.off. on the *Boston*, commanded a battalion of marines and Bluejackets that landed in Honolulu, Territory of HI, from Jan to Apr 1893 during the settlers' revolt against Queen Liliukalani. As commander of the *Helena* during the war with Spain, captured the Spanish steamer *Miguel Jovar*, saw action at the engagement of Tunas on 1 and 2 Jul, and was at the destruction of the gunboats at Manzanilla on 18 Jul. In Feb 1899 and with the Asia.Flt., was senior off. in command of vessels used against insurgents in Manila Bay in Jun 1899.

FREDERICK MARTIN SYMONDS Born in Watertown, NY, on 16 May 1846, son of Charles F. and Louise Symonds. Married Annie C. Parker in 1871. Resided in Galesville, WI, where he died on 14 Mar 1926.

Ranks Midn (26 Sep 1862); Ens (18 Dec 1868); Mstr (21 Mar 1870); Lt (21 Mar 1871); LCdr (31 Jul 1890); Cdr (19 Jun 1897); Capt (16 Mar 1902); retired (1 Dec 1902); RAdm on Ret.Lst. (13 Apr 1911) to rank from 1 Dec 1902.

Career Summary Received appointment from NY (26 Sep 1862); USNA (Sep 1862-Jun 1867); found deficient and put back (Jun 1863); w.o. (Jun-Sep 1867); *Piscataqua*, and *Delaware*, Asia.Sta. (Oct 1867-Nov 1870); home and w.o. (Nov 1870-May 1871); torp. duty, Newport, RI (Jun 1871-Jan 1872); l.o.a. (Jan-May 1872); *Tuscarora*, surv. duty, Pac. Ocean (May 1872-Jun 1875); home and w.o. (Jul-Sep 1875); training ship, *Minnesota* (Oct 1875-Dec 1878); l.o.a. (Dec 1878-Apr 1879); *Jamestown*, Pac.Sqdn. (May 1879-Sep 1881); w.o. (Sep 1881-Mar 1882); training ship, *New Hampshire* (Apr 1882-Apr 1885); w.o. (Apr-May 1885); *Mohican*, Pac.Sta. (Jun 1885-Aug 1888); w.o. (Aug-Sep 1888); l.o.a. (Oct 1888-Sep 1889); rec. ship, *Wabash*, Boston (Sep-Oct 1889); *Michigan*, on Great Lakes (Oct 1889-Nov 1892); w.o. (Nov-Dec 1892); l.o.a. (Dec 1892-Apr 1894); ord. instruction, Navy Yard, Washington, DC (Apr-May 1894); insp. of ord., Navy Yard, Mare Island, CA (Jun 1894-Sep 1896); cdr, *Pinta*, Pac.Sqdn. (Oct 1896-Aug 1897); *Marietta*, San Francisco (Aug-Sep 1897); cdr, *Marietta*, Pac.Sta., spec.serv., and N.Atl.Flt. (Sep 1897-Jun 1899); asst., then insp., 9th L.h. Dist., Chicago (Jul 1899-Apr 1902); home and w.o. (Apr-May 1902); NWC (Jun-Dec 1902); retired (1 Dec 1902); duty connected with steamboat inspections (Oct 1904-Jun 1905).

BENJAMIN TAPPAN Born in New Orleans on 12 Apr 1856, son of Benjamin S. and Jane (Nichols) Tappan. Early education in Helena, AR. Married Mrs. Alice (Green) Tyssowski on 26 Oct 1918. Died at the Naval Hosp. in Washington, DC, on 18 Dec 1919. Buried in Arlington National Cemetery.

Ranks Cadet Midn (22 Sep 1871); Midn (21 Jun 1876); Ens (5 Feb 1879); Ltjg (20 Jan 1886); Lt (2 Aug 1891); LCdr (1 Jul 1899); Cdr (31 Mar 1905); Capt (30 Oct 1908); placed on Ret.Lst. with rank of RAdm (26 Apr 1916).

Career Summary Received appointment from AR (22 Sep

BENJAMIN TAPPAN
1856-1919

1871); USNA (Sep 1871-Jun 1876); w.o. (Jun-Aug 1876);
Tennessee, Asia.Sta. (Sep 1876-Jul 1878); w.o. (Jul 1878-Mar
1879); USNA (Mar-Apr 1879); w.o. (Apr-Jul 1879); temp. duty,
rec. ship, *Franklin*, Norfolk, VA (Jul-Sep 1879); *Constellation*,
spec.serv., Europe (Oct 1879); *Trenton*, Eur.Sta. (Oct 1879-Oct
1881); w.o. (Oct 1881-Feb 1882); apprentice ship, *New Hampshire* (Feb 1882-Aug 1884); apprentice ship, *Saratoga* (Aug
1884-Dec 1887); l.o.a. (Dec 1887-Mar 1888); Office of Naval
Intelligence, Bur. of Nav., Washington, DC (Mar 1888-Jan 1891);
Newark, N.Atl.Sqdn. (Feb 1891-Jul 1893); *Miantonomoh*, N.Atl.
Sta. (Jul 1893-Nov 1894); l.o.a. (Nov 1894-Feb 1895); equip.
duty, Navy Yard, NY (Feb 1895-Nov 1896); *Amphitrite*, N.Atl.
Sta. (Nov 1896-Apr 1897); *Raleigh*, Asia.Flt. (Apr 1897-Jul
1898); cdr, *Callao*, Asia.Sta. (Jul 1898-Dec 1899); home and w.o.
(Dec 1899-Mar 1900); temp. duty, Navy Yard, Washington, DC
(Mar 1900); in charge, branch hydrographic office, Baltimore
(Mar 1900-Jan 1901); flag lt, Pac.Sta., *Iowa* (Jan 1901-Dec
1902), then *New York* (Dec 1902-Jan 1903); home and w.o. (Jan-
Apr 1903); NWC (Apr-Sep 1903); cdr, *Petrel*, Pac.Sta. (Oct
1903-Apr 1904); Naval Hosp., NY (May-Jul 1904); l.o.a. (Jul-
Aug 1904); Navy Yard, NY (Aug-Sep 1904); aide to comdt.,
Navy Yard, NY (Aug 1904-Jan 1906); cdr, *Newport*, Atl.Flt.
(Jan-Nov 1906); cdr, *Tacoma*, Atl.Flt. (Nov 1906-Dec 1907);
insp., 7th L.h. Dist., Pensacola, FL (Dec 1907-Jul 1908); member,
bd. of inspection and surv., Washington, DC (Jul 1908-Jun 1909);
cdr, *Kearsarge*, and *Kentucky*, Navy Yard, Philadelphia (Jun-Sep
1909); cdr, *Indiana*, Philadelphia (Sep-Dec 1909); capt.yd., Navy
Yard, Mare Island, CA (Dec 1909-Jan 1911); spec. temp. duty,
Bur. of Nav., Washington, DC (Jan-Feb 1911); supervisor, Naval
Auxiliaries, Navy Yard, NY (Feb 1911-Mar 1913); comdt., Naval
Station, Olongapo and Cavite, P.I. (Apr 1913-Nov 1915); home
and w.o. (Nov 1915-May 1916); placed on Ret.Lst. (26 Apr
1916); supervisor of harbor, NY (Apr 1917); comdt., Naval Sta.,
Olongapo, P.I. (Apr 1917-Oct 1918); comdt., 8th Naval Dist.,
New Orleans (Oct 1918-Oct 1919).

Career Highlights Participated in the Battle of Manila Bay,
being advanced five numbers in rank for eminent and conspicuous
conduct. As cdr of the naval sta. at Cavite and Olongapo, he
participated in the actions against the insurrectionists. Returned
to active duty during World War I, commanding at Philadelphia
and New Orleans and receiving the Navy Cross for his services.

EDWARD DAVID TAUSSIG Born in St. Louis on 20 Nov
1847, son of Charles and Anna (Abeles) Taussig. Married Ellen
Knelfer on 9 Nov 1873. Five sons, including VAdm Joseph
Knelfer Taussig, USN (1877-1947). Resided in Jamestown, RI,
dying in Newport, RI, on 29 Jan 1921. Buried in USNA Cemetery, Annapolis.

Ranks Midn (23 Jul 1863); Ens (18 Dec 1868); Mstr (21 Mar
1870); Lt (1 Jan 1872); LCdr (19 Jun 1892); Cdr (10 Aug 1898);
Capt (7 Nov 1902); RAdm (15 May 1908); placed on Ret.Lst.
(20 Nov 1909).

EDWARD DAVID TAUSSIG
1847-1921

Career Summary Received appointment from MO (23 Jul 1863); USNA (Jul 1863-Jun 1867); *Minnesota*, spec. cruise (Jul-Dec 1867); *Wateree, Powhatan, Onward,* and *Resaca*, S.Pac.Sta. (Jan 1868-Apr 1870); home and w.o. (Apr-Sep 1870); *Narragansett*, Pac.Sta. (Oct 1870-Sep 1873); w.o. (Sep 1873-Jun 1874); Torp.Sta., Newport, RI (Jun-Oct 1874); Hydrographic Office, Washington, DC (Oct-Dec 1874); Panama Surv.Expd. (Jan-Apr 1875); spec. duty, Bur. of Nav., Washington, DC (May-Oct 1875); cdr, rec. ship, *Relief*, Washington, DC (Sep 1875); temp. duty, Navy Yard, Washington, DC (Oct 1875-Apr 1876); *Juniata*, Baltimore, and Navy Yard, Norfolk, VA (Apr-Sep 1876); training ship, *Monongahela* (Sep 1876-Feb 1877); flgs., *Trenton*, and *Constellation*, spec.serv., Eur.Sta. (Feb 1877-Jan 1880); w.o. (Jan-Jun 1880); USNA (Jun 1880-Apr 1883); cst. surv. duty (May 1883-Aug 1886); training ship, *Jamestown* (Sep 1886-Dec 1887); Bur. of Nav., Washington, DC (Dec 1887-Dec 1890); spec. duty, Navy Dept., Washington, DC (Dec 1890-Apr 1894); exec.off., *Atlanta*, N.Atl.Sqdn. (Apr 1894-Sep 1895); exec.off., rec. ship, *Richmond*, Philadelphia (Oct 1895-Feb 1896); temp. duty, rec. ship, *Independence*, Mare Island, CA (Feb 1896); exec.off., *Monadnock*, Pac.Sqdn. (Feb-Sep 1896); Hydrographic Office, Washington, DC (Sep-Dec 1896); hydrographic insp., U.S. Cst. and Geodetic Survey, Washington, DC (Dec 1896-Aug 1897); cst.surv. duty (Aug 1897-May 1898); Navy Yard, Norfolk, VA (Jun-Jul 1898); cdr, *Bennington*, Asia.Sta. (Aug 1898-Aug 1899); home and w.o. (Aug-Oct 1899); insp., 13th L.h. Dist., Portland, OR (Oct 1899-Apr 1900); cdr, *Yorktown*, Asia.Sta. (Jun 1900-Jun 1901); home and w.o. (Jun-Oct 1901); Navy Yard, Washington, DC (Nov 1901-Jan 1902); ord.off., Navy Yard, Boston (Jan-May 1902); cdr, training ship, *Enterprise* (May-Oct 1902); home and w.o. (Oct-Dec 1902); capt.yd., Navy Yard, Pensacola, FL (Jan-Oct 1903); cdr, rec. ship, *Independence*, Mare Island, CA (Oct 1903-Oct 1904); cdr, *Massachusetts*, spec.serv. (Nov 1904-Jan 1906); cdr, training ship, *Indiana* (Jan-Dec 1906); home and w.o. (Dec 1906-Feb 1907); capt.yd., Navy Yard, NY (Mar-May 1907); general court-martial duty, Navy Yard, League Island, PA (May-Dec 1907); comdt., Navy Yard and 5th Naval Dist., Norfolk, VA (Dec 1907-Nov 1909); placed on Ret.Lst. (20 Nov 1909); comdt., Naval Unit, Columbia Univ., and at various Ivy League universities (Sep-Dec 1918).

Career Highlights While with the S.Pac.Sta., was recommended for the services he rendered during the 13 Aug 1868 earthquake at Arica, Chile. During the war with Spain, commanded the *Bennington* and took possession of Wake Island from the Spanish. Commanded Guam from 1 Feb 1899.

References
Personal Papers: a) 33 items (1867-1900) in NHF,LC.
Writings: "Old Glory on Wake Island," U.S. Naval Institute *Proceedings* 388 (Jun 1935): 807-8.

DAVID WATSON TAYLOR Born in Louisa County, VA, on 4 Mar 1864, son of Henry and Mary Minor (Watson) Taylor.

DAVID WATSON TAYLOR
1864-1940

After an early education at home, attended Randolph-Macon College from 1877 to his graduation in 1881, then receiving an appointment to USNA. Was subsequently awarded the honorary D.Eng. from Stevens Institute in Hoboken, NJ, in 1907, a D.Sc. from George Washington Univ. in 1915, and an LL.D. from Randolph-Macon in 1922 and from the Univ. of Glasgow in 1924. On 26 Oct 1892, married Imogene Maury Morris. Three daughters and a son. Eventually resided in Waldrop, VA. Died in the Naval Hosp. in Washington, DC, on 28 Jul 1940.

Ranks Cadet Engr. (1 Oct 1881); Asst. Naval Const. (14 Aug 1886); Naval Const. (5 Dec 1891); Cdr (3 Mar 1899); Capt (4 Mar 1901); Chief Const., and Chief, Bur. of Construction and Repair with rank of RAdm (13 Dec 1914); RAdm (29 Aug 1916); transferred to Ret.Lst. (16 Jan 1923).

Career Summary Received appointment from VA (1 Oct 1881); USNA (Oct 1881-Jun 1885); *Pensacola,* Eur.Sta. (Jun-Oct 1885); student of naval construction and marine engineering, Royal Naval College, Greenwich, England (Oct 1885-Aug 1888); w.o. (Aug-Oct 1888); William Cramp and Sons Iron Works, Philadelphia (Oct 1888-Dec 1889); spec. duty, Navy Dept., Washington, DC (Dec 1889-Jan 1890); Bur. of Construction and Repair, Washington, DC (May 1890-Jan 1891); William Cramp and Sons Iron Works, Philadelphia (Jan 1891-Oct 1892); chief const., Navy Yard, Mare Island, CA (Oct 1892-May 1894); Bur. of Construction and Repair, Washington, DC (May 1894-Dec 1914); dir., U.S Navy's Experimental Ship Model Basin, Navy Yard, Washington, DC (1899-Dec 1914); chief const., and chief, Bur. of Construction and Repair, Washington, DC (Dec 1914-Jul 1922); transferred to Ret.Lst. (16 Jan 1923).

Career Highlights One of the most intelligent and influential figures in naval and marine science, graduated from USNA top of his class, recording the highest marks yet achieved. In 1885, sent to study on an advanced course of naval construction and marine engineering at Britain's Royal Naval College, from which he graduated again top of his class and with the highest record achieved there. Became the sheetanchor for the design of modern warships. Primarily through his efforts in designing some of navy's new ships of the 1880s and 1890s, he realized the lack of proper scientific experimentation in ship design and construction. Subsequently spent many years advocating the development of an experimental program to provide the much needed scientific data to design and construct better vessels. Was through his efforts that the navy developed a testing basin for ship models in 1899 at Carderock, MD, with Taylor remaining in charge of it until 1914. It was renamed the David W. Taylor Model Basin in 1937. Served two consecutive terms as naval const. and chief of the Bur. of Construction and Repair, overseeing the design and construction of nearly 900 vessels for the navy, plus many for foreign nations. Was also first recipient of a medal created in his honor in 1936 for notable achievements in the field of naval architecture and marine engineering. Sat on numerous committees dealing with naval construction as well as related subjects, such as naval aeronautics. While chief const., and until the Bur. of Aeronautics was created in Sep 1921, was in charge of the design and construction of aircraft and for submarine vessels, sitting on many boards and committees dealing with such subjects. Served as pres. of the Society of Naval Architects and Marine Engineers from 1925 to 1927. Awarded the Distinguished Service Medal and well as France's Commander of the Legion of Honor.

References

Personal Papers: a) David W. Taylor Naval Ship Research and Development Center: 1) Carderock Laboratory, Bethesda, MD. 2) Annapolis Laboratory, Annapolis.

Writings: a) "On a Method for Calculating the Stability of Ships," U.S. Naval Institute *Proceedings* 58 (1891): 157-229. b) *Resistance of Ships and Screw Propulsion* (NY: 1893; reprint, 1907). c) "Our New Battleships and Armored Cruisers," U.S. Naval Institute *Proceedings* 96 (Dec 1900): 593-98. d) "The Present Status of the Protected Cruiser Type," U.S. Naval Institute *Proceedings* 109 (Mar 1904): 145-49. e) "A Handicap on United States Battleships," U.S. Naval Institute *Proceedings* 111 (Sep 1904): 501-9. f) "Methods of Estimating the Coal Endurance of a Naval Vessel," U.S. Naval Institute *Proceedings* 112 (Dec 1904): 811-22. g) "Comments on 'The Size of Battleships as a Function of the Speed,'" U.S. Naval Institute *Proceedings* 121 (Mar 1907): 133-36. h) "A New Method for Determining the Final Diameter of a Ship," U.S. Naval Institute *Proceedings* 134 (Jun 1910): 501-6. i) *The Speed and Power of Ships*, 2 vols. (NY: 1910, 1933, 1943). j) "Some Reflections upon Commissioned Naval Personnel Problems," U.S. Naval Institute *Proceedings* 261 (Nov 1924): 1771-85.

HENRY CLAY TAYLOR Born in Washington, DC, on 4 Mar 1845, son of Frank and Virginia (Neville) Taylor. Married Mary Virginia McGuire in 1869. Six children. Brother-in-law to RAdm Robley D. Evans, USN [*q.v.*]. Died in Ontario, Canada, on 26 Jul 1904. Buried in Arlington National Cemetery.

Ranks Act.Midn (20 Sep 1860); title changed to Midn (16 Jul 1862); Ens (28 May 1863); Mstr (10 Nov 1865); Lt (10 Nov 1866); LCdr (12 Mar 1868); Cdr (16 Dec 1879); Capt (16 Apr 1894); RAdm (11 Feb 1901); died (26 Jul 1904).

Career Summary Received appointment from OH (20 Sep 1860); USNA (Sep 1860-May 1863); *Shenandoah*, N.Atl.Blk. Sqdn. (Jun 1863-Apr 1864); *Iroquois*, spec.serv. (Apr 1864-Oct 1865); w.o. (Oct 1865-Jan 1866); *Rhode Island*, N.Atl.Sqdn. (Jan 1866-Jan 1867); flgs., *Susquehanna*, N.Atl.Sqdn. (Jan 1867-Jan 1868); w.o. (Jan-Oct 1868); storeship, *Guard*, Eur.Sqdn. (Oct 1868-Oct 1869); inst. of math., USNA (Nov 1869-Sep 1872); w.o. (Sep-Oct 1872); exec.off., flgs., *Saranac*, Pac.Sqdn. (Oct 1872-Mar 1874); cst.surv. duty (Mar 1874-Apr 1877); w.o. (Apr-Oct 1877); Hydrographic Office, Washington, DC (Nov 1877-Sep 1878); equip.off., Navy Yard, Washington, DC (Oct 1878-Dec 1880); cdr, training ship, *Saratoga* (Dec 1880-Jan 1884); aide to mayor, NY City (Jan-Dec 1884); spec. duty, harbor management,

HENRY CLAY TAYLOR
1845-1904

NY (Jan-Apr 1885); member, bd. of inspection and surv. (Apr 1885-Dec 1887); l.o.a. and w.o. (Dec 1887-Dec 1889); cdr, *Alliance,* Asia.Sta. (Jan 1890-May 1891); spec. duty, Navy Yard, Mare Island, CA (Jul-Aug 1891); l.o.a. and w.o. (Sep 1891-Nov 1892); spec. diplomatic duty in Spain (Dec 1892-Jun 1893); l.o.a. (Jun-Aug 1893); member, court of inquiry, Norfolk, VA (Aug 1893); w.o. (Aug-Nov 1893); pres., NWC, and head, torp. school, Newport, RI (Nov 1893-Dec 1896); cdr, *Indiana,* N.Atl.Sqdn. (Jan 1897-Oct 1899); home and w.o. (Oct-Nov 1899); temp. duty, NWC (Nov 1899-Mar 1900); senior member, bd. on coaling stas. (Nov 1899-Mar 1900); cdr, rec. ship, *Vermont,* NY (Mar 1900-Mar 1901); member, Gen Bd., Washington, DC (Mar 1900-Apr 1902); chief, Bur. of Nav., Washington, DC (Apr 1902-Jul 1904); temp. duty, chief of staff for Adm George Dewey, *Mayflower* (Nov 1902, Feb-Mar 1904); died (26 Jul 1904).

Career Highlights Commanded the *Indiana* during the war with Spain, being involved in the bombardment of San Juan, Puerto Rico, in May, commanding the convoy that transported the army from Tampa, FL, to Santiago in Jun, and participating in the destruction of the Spanish fleet at Santiago on 3 Jul 1898. Was subsequently advanced five numbers in rank for conspicuous conduct in battle. Twice served as chief of staff for Adm George Dewey. Best known as a naval philosopher and administrative reformer, overseeing the creation of the navy's Gen Bd. in order to advise the secretary of the navy, and contributing much on naval tactics and other subjects.

References

Personal Papers: 300 items (1862-1904) in NHF,LC.

Writings: a) "The Use of One Angle in Curved Channels," U.S. Naval Institute *Proceedings* 37 (1886): 105-10. b) "Battle Tactics: The Value of Concentration," U.S. Naval Institute *Proceedings* 37 (1886): 141-73. c) (with William Walton and Asa Bird Gardiner), *The Army and Navy of the United States from the Period of the Revolution to the Present,* 2 vols. (Philadelphia: 1889-95). d) "Naval War College," U.S. Naval Institute *Proceedings* 77 (1896): 199-208. e) "Memorandum on General Staff for the U.S. Navy," U.S. Naval Institute *Proceedings* 95 (Sep 1900): 441-48. f) "The Fleet," U.S. Naval Institute *Proceedings* (Dec 1903): 799-807.

JOHN YEATMAN TAYLOR Born in East Nottingham, PA, on 21 Jan 1829, son of Job and Susanna (Yeatman) Taylor. Received M.D. degree from the Jefferson Medical College in Philadelphia in 1852. Married Sabella Barr Bryson, daughter of RAdm Andrew Bryson, USN (1822-92), on 6 Feb 1878. One son and one daughter. Resided in Washington, DC. Died by his own hand on 16 Nov 1911.

Ranks Asst.Surg. (26 Sep 1853); PAsst.Surg. (26 Sep 1858); Surg. (1 Aug 1861); Medl.Insp. (29 Jun 1872); Medl.Dir. (20 Apr 1879); placed on Ret.Lst. (21 Jan 1891); Medl.Dir. with rank of RAdm on Ret.Lst. (29 Jun 1906).

Career Summary Received appointment from DE (26 Sep

JOHN YEATMAN TAYLOR
1829-1911

1853); w.o. (Sep-Dec 1853); *Decatur*, Pac.Sqdn. (Jan 1854-Mar 1857); temp. duty, 4th U.S. Infantry, Washington Territory Volunteers (1855-56); l.o.a. (Mar-Dec 1857); Naval Rndv., Philadelphia (Dec 1857-Mar 1858); w.o. (Mar-Jun 1858); *Preble* and *Dolphin*, Braz.Sqdn. (Jun 1858-Dec 1860); l.o.a. (Dec 1860-Feb 1861); recorder, bd. of examiners (Feb-Jun 1861); Naval Hosp., NY (Jun-Aug 1861); member, bd. of examiners (Aug 1861-Jan 1862); *Oneida*, W.Gulf Blk.Sqdn. (Jan 1862-Aug 1864); temp. duty, Naval Rndv., Philadelphia (Sep-Oct 1864); *Tuscarora*, S.Atl.Blk.Sqdn. (Oct 1864-Jun 1865); w.o. (Jun-Jul 1865); l.o.a. and w.o. (Jul-Dec 1865); recorder, medl.exam.bd., Washington, DC (Dec 1865-Feb 1866); w.o. (Feb-Mar 1866); member, bd. of examiners, NY (Mar-May 1866); w.o. (May-Oct 1866); Naval Hosp., NY (Oct 1866-Jan 1869); *Kenosha* [renamed *Plymouth*], Eur.Sta. (Jan 1869-May 1872); return and w.o. (May-Jul 1872); temp. duty, Navy Yard, Philadelphia (Jul-Aug 1872); w.o. (Aug-Nov 1872); member, naval exam. and ret. bds., Washington, DC (Nov 1872-Jan 1877); w.o. (Jan-Jul 1877); flt.surg., N.Atl.Sta., *Powhatan* (Jul 1877-Apr 1879); in charge, Naval Hosp., Washington, DC (May 1879-Jun 1883); in charge, Naval Hosp., Norfolk, VA (Jun 1883-Sep 1886); in charge, Naval Hosp., NY (Oct 1886-Oct 1888); member, then pres., naval exam. bd. and naval medl. bds. (Oct 1888-Jun 1891); placed on Ret.Lst. (21 Jan 1891).

CHARLES MITCHELL THOMAS Born in Philadelphia on 1 Oct 1846, son of Joseph T. and Belinda J. Thomas. On 3 Nov 1874, married Ruth Simpson, daughter of RAdm Edward Simpson, USN (1824-88). Died in Delmonte, Monterey County, CA, on 3 Jul 1908. Buried in the Berkeley Memorial Chapel Cemetery in Middletown, RI.

Ranks Act.Midn (28 Nov 1861); title changed to Midn (16 Jul 1862); Ens (1 Dec 1866); Mstr (12 Mar 1868); Lt (26 Mar 1869); LCdr (1 Apr 1880); Cdr (28 Feb 1890); Capt (3 Mar 1899); RAdm (12 Jan 1905); died (3 Jul 1908).

Career Summary Received appointment from PA (28 Nov 1861); USNA (Nov 1861-Sep 1865); w.o. (Sep-Oct 1865); *Dacotah*, fitting out (Oct 1865); *Shenandoah*, Asia.Sta. (Oct 1865-May 1869); home and w.o. (May 1869); Navy Yard, League Island, PA (Jun-Sep 1869); *Frolic*, Navy Yard, NY (Sep-Oct 1869); *Supply*, Eur.Sta. (Nov 1869-Jul 1870); *Guerriere*, Eur.Sta. (Aug 1870-Sep 1871); suspended (Sep 1871-Mar 1872); rec. ship, *Potomac*, Philadelphia (Mar-Oct 1872); *Terror*, Key West, FL (Oct 1872-Jun 1873); w.o. (Jun-Aug 1873); torp. duty, Newport, RI (Sep-Nov 1873); *Terror*, Navy Yard, League Island, PA (Dec 1873); torp. duty, Newport, RI (Dec 1873-Apr 1874); *Ajax*, N.Atl.Sqdn. (May-Jun 1874); *Dictator*, Key West, FL (Jun 1874-Apr 1875); w.o. (Apr-Jun 1875); Navy Yard, Philadelphia (Jun-Nov 1875); spec. duty, Centennial Exposition, Philadelphia (Nov 1875-Mar 1877); exec.off., rec. ship, *St. Louis*, League Island, PA (Mar 1877-Jan 1878); training ship, *Constitution* (Jan 1878-Jul 1880); w.o. (Jul-Sep 1880); USNA (Sep 1880-Jun

CHARLES MITCHELL THOMAS
1846-1908

1884); exec.off., flgs., *Hartford*, Pac.Sta. (Jun 1884-Jan 1887); cst.surv. duty (Jan 1887-Mar 1891); Bur. of Nav., Washington, DC (Mar 1891-Jul 1893); cdr, *Bennington*, Eur. and Pac.Stas. (Jul 1893-Jul 1895); home and l.o.a. (Jul-Oct 1895); Naval Home, Philadelphia (Oct 1895-May 1897); NWC, and torp. school, Newport, RI (Jun-Aug 1897); USNA (Sep 1897-May 1898); cdr, *Monongahela*, USNA (May 1898); USNA (May-Aug 1898); insp., 5th L.h. Dist., Baltimore (Aug 1898-Apr 1899); home and w.o. (Apr-May 1899); cdr, training ship, *Lancaster* (May-Dec 1899); spec. duty, Navy Dept., Washington, DC (Dec 1899); cdr, *Baltimore*, Asia.Sta. (Feb-Apr 1900); cdr, *Brooklyn*, Asia.Sta. (Apr 1900-Apr 1901); cdr, *Oregon*, Navy Yard, Puget Sound, WA (Apr 1901-Feb 1902); home and w.o. (Feb-Mar 1902); cdr, rec. ship, *Franklin*, Norfolk, VA (Mar 1902-Jul 1904); comdt., Training Sta., and cdr, 2nd Naval Dist., Newport, RI (Jul 1904-Jan 1907); cdr, 2nd Div., 1st Sqdn., Atl.Flt., *Virginia* (Jan-Aug 1907); cdr, 2nd Sqdn., Atl.Flt., *Minnesota* (Aug 1907-May 1908); cdr., Atl.Flt., *Connecticut* (May 1908); home to convalesce and w.o. (May-Jul 1908); died (3 Jul 1908).

References
Personal Papers: a) 80 items (1907-8) in NHF,LC. b) 2 ft. (1876-1900) in NHF,WNY.

Writings: a) *et. al.*, "Instructions for Infantry and Artillery, United States Navy," U.S. Naval Institute *Proceedings* 60 (1891): 569-751. b) *Drill Regulations for Infantry, Artillery, and Arm and Away Boats, U.S. Navy* (Washington, DC: 1898).

CHAUNCEY THOMAS
1850-1919

CHAUNCEY THOMAS Born in Barryville, NY, on 27 Apr 1850, son of Chauncey and Margaret (Bross) Thomas. Married Carrie Ella Flagg on 12 Sep 1876. Resided in Pacific Grove, CA, where he died on 9 May 1919.

Ranks Midn (25 Sep 1867); title changed to Cadet Midn (15 Jul 1870); Midn (6 Jun 1871); Ens (14 Jul 1872); Mstr (14 Apr 1875); Lt (10 Mar 1882); LCdr (3 Mar 1899); Cdr (26 Oct 1901); Capt (1 Jul 1906); RAdm (11 Mar 1910); placed on Ret.Lst. (27 Apr 1912).

Career Summary Received appointment from PA (25 Sep 1867); USNA (Sep 1867-Jun 1871); w.o. (Jun-Sep 1871); *Wabash*, Eur.Sta. (Oct 1871-Jun 1873); storeship, *Supply*, spec.serv. (Jul-Nov 1873); *Colorado*, and *Wabash*, N.Atl.Sta. (Dec 1873-Apr 1874); w.o. (Apr-Jul 1874); *Colorado*, N.Atl.Sta. (Jul-Sep 1874); *Canandaigua*, N.Atl.Sta. (Sep 1874); flgs., *Worcester*, N.Atl.Sta. (Sep 1874-Mar 1875); flgs., *Colorado*, N.Atl.Sta. (Mar-May 1875); flgs., *Worcester*, N.Atl.Sta. (May-Jun 1875); *Plymouth*, spec. duty (Jun 1875-Feb 1876); on staff, flgs., *Hartford*, N.Atl.Sta. (Feb 1876-Jul 1877); flgs., *Powhatan*, N.Atl.Sta. (Jul 1877-Jun 1878); w.o. (Jun-Jul 1878); Nautical Almanac Office, Washington, DC (Jul 1878-Jul 1881); w.o. (Jul-Sep 1881); *Adams*, Pac.Sta. (Sep 1881-Sep 1884); w.o. (Sep-Nov 1884); Nautical Almanac Office, Washington, DC (Nov 1884); asst.supt., Nautical Almanac Office, Washington, DC (Nov 1884-Mar 1886); spec. duty, aide to Adm David Dixon

Porter, USN, Washington, DC (Mar 1886-Mar 1891); training
ship, *Monongahela* (Mar 1891-Jul 1893); *Bennington*, Eur.Sta. (Jul
1893-Jan 1894); flgs., *Chicago*, Eur.Sta. (Jan-Feb 1894); home and
w.o. (Feb-Mar 1894); Hydrographic Office, Washington, DC (Apr
1894-Aug 1896); l.o.a. (Aug-Dec 1896); exec.off., *Oregon*,
Pac.Sta. (Dec 1896-Dec 1897); exec.off., *Wheeling*, Asia.Sqdn.
(Dec 1897-Nov 1898); exec.off., *Yorktown*, Asia.Sta. (Nov
1898-May 1899); *Oregon*, Asia.Sta. (May-Jul 1899); cdr, *Monadnock*, Asia.Sta. (Jul-Aug 1899); asst. chief of staff, Asia.Sta.,
Baltimore (Aug-Dec 1899); spec. duty, Shanghai, China, then
home and w.o. (Dec 1899-Feb 1900); Navy Yard, Washington,
DC (Feb-Apr 1900); Hydrographic Office, Washington, DC (Apr
1900-Oct 1901); cdr, Fish Commission steamer, *Albatross* (Oct
1901-Feb 1903); cdr, *Bennington*, Pac.Sqdn. (Feb-Dec 1903);
home and w.o. (Dec 1903-Feb 1904); Navy Yard, League Island,
PA (Feb 1904-Aug 1905); asst., then insp., 4th L.h. Dist.,
Philadelphia (Sep 1905-Sep 1906); s.a. and w.o. (Sep 1906-Jan
1907); cdr, *Maryland*, Asia.Sta. (Mar 1907-Jun 1908); insp., 3rd
L.h. Dist., Tompkinsville, NY (Jul 1908-Jan 1910); pres., bd. of
inspection and surv. (Feb-Oct 1910); cdr, 2nd Div., Pac.Flt.,
California (Nov 1910-Jan 1911); cdr, Pac.Flt., *California* (Jan
1911-Mar 1912); home and l.o.a. (Mar-Apr 1912); placed on
Ret.Lst. (27 Apr 1912); Training Sta., San Francisco (Apr 1917-
Jul 1918); duty with, then comdt., Training Unit, Univ. of WA,
Seattle, WA (Jul-Dec 1918).

THEODORE STRONG THOMPSON Born in Northampton,
MA, on 23 Apr 1842, son of Reverend August C. and Sarah
Elizabeth (Strong) Thompson. Graduated from Williams College
in 1862. Served nine months as a volunteer in the 45th MA
Regiment of Volunteers before entering the navy. His home was
Brookline, MA. Died in Plattsburg, NY, on 27 Jul 1915.

Ranks Act.Asst.Paymstr. (9 Oct 1863); honorably discharged
(23 Aug 1865); Asst.Paymstr. (23 Jul 1866); PAsst.Paymstr. (1
Feb 1868); Paymstr. (25 Jan 1878); Pay Insp. (10 Jul 1898); Pay
Dir. (21 Sep 1901); transferred to Ret.Lst. with rank of RAdm
(26 Dec 1903).

Career Summary Received appointment from MA (9 Oct
1863); *Rachel Seaman*, W.Gulf Blk.Sqdn. (Oct 1863-Jun 1865);
l.o.a. (Jun-Aug 1865); honorably discharged (23 Aug 1865);
re-entered as asst.paymstr. (23 Jul 1866); w.o. (Jul-Aug 1866);
Tahoma, W.Ind. and Gulf Sqdns. (Aug 1866-Aug 1867); s.a. and
w.o. (Aug 1867-Dec 1868); *Narragansett*, W.Ind.Sqdn. (Jan-Jul
1869); s.a. and w.o. (Jul 1869-Mar 1870); in charge of stores, Key
West, FL (Apr 1870-May 1871); s.a. (May 1871); cst.surv. duty
(May 1871-Jun 1872); s.a. and w.o. (Jun 1872-Jan 1873); *Juniata*,
spec. duty and Eur.Sta. (Jan 1873-Sep 1876); training ship,
Monongahela (Sep-Dec 1876); s.a. and w.o. (Dec 1876-Dec 1877);
rec. ship, *New Hampshire*, Port Royal, SC (Jan 1878-Nov 1879);
s.a. and w.o. (Nov 1879-Mar 1880); Navy Yard, NY (Mar
1880-Mar 1883); s.a. and w.o. (Mar 1883-May 1884); prac. ship,
Constellation (May-Sep 1884); s.a. and w.o. (Sep-Dec 1884);

Swatara, N.Atl.Sta. (Dec 1884-Oct 1886); s.a. and w.o. (Oct 1886-Feb 1887); spec. duty, Navy Yard, Washington, DC (Feb-Apr 1887); rec. ship, *St. Louis*, League Island, PA (Apr 1887-Jun 1890); s.a. and w.o. (Jun 1890-Feb 1891); *Newark*, spec.serv. (Feb 1891-Jun 1893); s.a. and w.o. (Jun-Jul 1893); Navy Yard, Boston (Jul 1893-May 1896); s.a. (May 1896); *Massachusetts*, N.Atl.Sqdn. and Flt. (Jun 1896-Oct 1898); s.a. and w.o. (Oct 1898-Mar 1899); in charge, Pay Office, San Francisco (Mar 1899-Feb 1902); s.a. and w.o. (Feb-Apr 1902); purchasing pay off., Navy Yard, Portsmouth, NH (Apr 1902-Jun 1903); purchasing pay off., Navy Yard, Boston (Jul 1903-Jun 1904); transferred to Ret.Lst. (26 Dec 1903).

JAMES WILLIAM THOMSON Born in Wilmington, DE, on 10 Nov 1836, son of James William and Sarah (Peters) Thomson. Married Laura N. Troth on 7 Oct 1862. Resided in Moorestown, NJ, where he died on 17 Mar 1914. Buried at Woodlands Cemetery, Philadelphia.

Ranks 3rd Asst.Engr. (26 Jun 1856); 1st Asst.Engr. (2 Aug 1859); Chief Engr. (2 Feb 1862); Chief Engr. with rel. rank of Capt (2 Mar 1892); transferred to Ret.Lst. (26 Jun 1896); Chief Engr. with rank of RAdm on Ret.Lst. (29 Jun 1906).

Career Summary Received appointment from NJ (26 Jun 1856); w.o. (Jun 1856-Mar 1857); *Wabash*, Home Sqdn. (Mar 1857-Feb 1858); l.o.a. (Feb-Apr 1858); *Wabash*, Med.Sqdn. (Apr 1858-Dec 1859); exam. and w.o. (Dec 1859-Feb 1860); *Dacotah*, E.Ind. and Atl.Blk.Sqdns. (Feb 1860-Dec 1861); exam. and w.o. (Dec 1861-Feb 1862); *Galena*, James River Flot. (Feb-Jul 1862); exam. and w.o. (Jul-Sep 1862); *Monongahela*, Navy Yard, Philadelphia (Sep-Dec 1862); *Shenandoah*, N.Atl.Blk.Sqdn. (Dec 1862-Jul 1864); sick lv. (Jul-Sep 1864); spec. duty, Naval Rndv., NY (Sep-Nov 1864); member, bd. of examiners, Philadelphia (Nov 1864-Feb 1869); w.o. (Feb-Mar 1869); l.o.a. (Mar-Sep 1869); *Albany*, N.Atl.Sta. (Sep 1869-Jan 1870); w.o. (Jan 1870); flgs., *Congress*, S.Atl.Sta. (Feb-Sep 1870); spec. duty, Navy Dept., Washington, DC (Sep 1870-Apr 1871); Navy Yard, Philadelphia (Apr 1871-Nov 1872); *Richmond*, spec.serv. (Nov 1872-Aug 1873); *Omaha*, S.Pac.Sta. (Aug 1873-Mar 1875); sick lv. (Mar-Oct 1875); member, bd. of examiners, USNA (Oct-Nov 1875); member, bd. of inspection (Nov 1875-Aug 1876); w.o. (Aug-Oct 1876); special duty with Centennial Exposition, Philadelphia (Oct 1876-Mar 1877); member, bd. of inspection (Mar 1877-May 1878); *Alaska*, Pac.Sta. (May 1878-Apr 1881); w.o. (Apr-May 1881); member, bd. of examiners, Philadelphia (May 1881); member, bd. of inspection, Philadelphia (May 1881-Mar 1885); spec. duty, bd. of examiners, Philadelphia (Apr-May 1885); w.o. (May-Jul 1885); temp. duty, Wilmington, DE (Jul 1885-Feb 1888); *Pensacola*, spec.serv. (Mar 1888-Sep 1890); l.o.a. (Sep-Dec 1890); insp. of machinery, William Cramp and Sons Iron Works, Philadelphia (Dec 1890-Feb 1896); insp. of machinery, Newport News Shipbuilding and Drydock Company, Newport News, VA (Feb-Jun 1896); transferred to Ret.Lst. (26 Jun 1896); insp., Bur.

of Steam Engineering, Thurlow, PA (May-Aug 1898).

WILLIAM JUDAH THOMSON Born in Washington, DC, on 27 Apr 1841, son of William and Mary (Delano) Thomson. Educated in the Baltimore schools, married Maud Spurgeon on 25 Apr 1898. Resided in Seattle where he died on 12 Aug 1909. Buried in Calvary Cemetery, Seattle.

Ranks Act.Asst.Paymstr. (29 Mar 1865); Asst.Paymstr. (23 Jul 1866); PAsst.Paymstr. (20 Mar 1868); Paymstr. (16 Feb 1878); Pay Insp. (9 Apr 1899); Pay Dir. (29 Mar 1902); transferred to Ret.Lst. with rank of RAdm (10 Jan 1903).

Career Summary Received appointment from MD (29 Mar 1865); w.o. (Mar-Apr 1865); *Squando*, N.Atl.Sqdn. (Apr 1865-Sep 1866); *Yantic*, N.Atl.Sqdn. (Sep-Nov 1866); s.a. and w.o. (Nov-Dec 1866); *Unadilla*, Asia.Sqdn. (Dec 1866-Nov 1869); s.a. and w.o. (Nov 1869-Nov 1870); *Pawnee*, N.Atl.Sta. (Dec 1870-Sep 1872); s.a. and w.o. (Sep 1872); Navy Yard, Pensacola, FL (Oct 1872-Jan 1875); s.a. and w.o. (Jan-Apr 1875); Bur. of Provisions and Clothing, Washington, DC (Apr-Dec 1875); *Kearsarge*, Asia.Sta. (Jan 1876-Jan 1878); s.a. and w.o. (Jan-May 1878); court-martial duty (May-Oct 1878); *Ticonderoga*, spec.serv. (Nov 1878-Dec 1880); s.a. and w.o. (Dec 1880); cst.surv. duty (Mar 1881-Jan 1884); s.a. and w.o. (Jan-Jul 1884); *Lackawanna*, Pac.Sta. (Aug 1884-Apr 1885); s.a. and w.o. (Apr-May 1885); *Mohican*, Pac.Sta. (May 1885-May 1887); s.a. and w.o. (May-Jul 1887); spec. duty, Smithsonian Institution, Washington, DC (Jul 1887-Feb 1888); Navy Yard, League Island, PA (Feb-Dec 1888); s.a. and w.o. (Dec 1888-Feb 1889); rec. ship, *Dale*, Washington, DC (Apr 1889-Feb 1892); s.a. and w.o. (Feb-May 1892); l.o.a. (May-Sep 1892); Naval Sta., Port Royal, SC (Sep 1892-Feb 1893); *Monterey*, Pac.Sta. (Feb 1893-Feb 1895); flt.paymstr., Pac.Sta., *Philadelphia* (Feb 1895-Oct 1897); *Philadelphia*, Navy Yard, Mare Island, CA (Oct-Nov 1897); *Monterey*, Pac.Sqdn. (Nov 1897); *Philadelphia*, Navy Yard, Mare Island, CA (Nov-Dec 1897); s.a. and w.o. (Dec 1897-Feb 1898); cst.surv. office, Washington, DC (Mar-May 1898); *Illinois*, Newport News, VA (May-Sep 1898); Naval Hosp., NY (Sep 1898); pay off., cst.surv. vessels (Sep 1898-May 1899); flt.paymstr., Asia.Flt., *Baltimore* (Aug-Dec 1899), then *Brooklyn* (Dec 1899-Apr 1900); Naval Hosp., Yokohama, Japan, home and sick lv. (Apr-Sep 1900); general storekeeper, purchasing paymstr., and pay off., Naval Sta., Puget Sound, WA (Sep 1900-Mar 1901); Naval Hosp., Mare Island, CA, home, and l.o.a. (Apr-Jul 1901); Pay Office, Seattle, WA (Aug 1901-Jan 1904); transferred to Ret.Lst. (10 Jan 1903); spec.temp. duty, Navy Yard, Puget Sound, WA (Oct 1904-Jan 1905).

References

Writings: *Te Pito te Henua: or, Easter Island* (Washington, DC: 1891).

BENJAMIN FRANKLIN TILLEY Born in Bristol, RI, on 29 Mar 1848, son of Benjamin Rogers and Susan W. (Easterbrookes)

BENJAMIN FRANKLIN TILLEY
1848-1907

Tilley. Early education in Bristol public schools. Married Emily Edelin Williamson on 6 Jun 1878. Died on 18 Mar 1907 at the League Island Navy Yard. Buried in Annapolis.

Ranks Midn (23 Sep 1863); Ens (18 Dec 1868); Mstr (21 Mar 1870); Lt (21 Mar 1871); LCdr (4 Sep 1887); Cdr (4 Sep 1896); Capt (2 Sep 1901); RAdm (24 Feb 1907); died (18 Mar 1907).

Career Summary Received appointment from RI (23 Sep 1863); USNA (Sep 1863-Jun 1867); *Franklin,* and *Frolic,* Eur.Sta. (Jun 1867-May 1869); *Lancaster,* and *Portsmouth,* S.Atl.Sta. (Jun 1869-Aug 1872); w.o. (Aug-Nov 1872); temp. duty, Washington, DC (Nov 1872-Jan 1873); Hydrographic Office, Washington, DC (Jan-Aug 1873); *Pensacola,* Pac.Sta. (Sep 1873-Oct 1874); sick lv. (Oct 1874-Mar 1875); rec. ship, *New Hampshire,* Norfolk, VA (Mar-Nov 1875); *Hartford,* Navy Yard, NY (Nov 1875-Jul 1877); flgs., *Powhatan,* N.Atl.Sta. (Jul 1877-Jun 1878); l.o.a. (Jun 1878-Jun 1879); USNA (Jun 1879-Apr 1882); *Tennessee,* N.Atl.Sqdn. (May 1882-Aug 1885); USNA (Sep 1885-Sep 1889); w.o. (Sep-Oct 1889); bd. duties (Oct-Dec 1889); ord. instruction, Navy Yard, Washington, DC (Dec 1889-Apr 1890); flgs., *San Francisco,* S.Pac.Sqdn. (Apr 1890-Jul 1893); USNA (Jul 1893-Jul 1895); l.o.a. (Jul-Sep 1895); USNA (Sep 1895-Jun 1897); NWC (Jun-Oct 1897); cdr, *Newport,* N.Atl.Flt. (Oct 1897-Sep 1898); home and w.o. (Sep-Oct 1898); Navy Yard, Norfolk, VA (Oct 1898-Jan 1899); home and w.o. (Jan-Feb 1899); Navy Yard, Norfolk, VA (Feb-Mar 1899); cdr, sta. ship, *Abarenda,* Apia, Samoa (Mar 1899-Oct 1901); additional duty, cdr, Naval Sta., Tutuila, Samoa (Feb 1900-Oct 1901); home and w.o. (Oct-Dec 1901); Navy Yard, Mare Island, CA (Feb-Apr 1902); capt.yd., Navy Yard, Mare Island, CA (Apr 1902-Jan 1905); cdr, *Iowa,* N.Atl.Sqdn. (Jan 1905-Dec 1906); home and w.o. (Dec 1906-Feb 1907); comdt., Navy Yard, League Island, PA (Feb-Mar 1907); died (18 Mar 1907).

CHAPMAN COLEMAN TODD Born in Frankfort, KY, on 5 Apr 1848, son of Harry Innes and Jane (Davidson) Todd. Married Eliza James in Oct 1872. Resided in Washington, DC, where he died on 28 Apr 1929. Buried in Frankfort, KY.

Ranks Act.Midn (9 Oct 1861); title changed to Midn (16 Jul 1862); Ens (12 Apr 1868); Mstr (26 Mar 1869); Lt (21 Mar 1870); LCdr (9 Nov 1886); Cdr (21 May 1895); Capt (11 Feb 1901); placed on Ret.Lst. as RAdm (31 Oct 1902).

Career Summary Received appointment from KY (9 Oct 1861); USNA (Oct 1861-Jun 1866); found deficient and put back (Jun 1863); l.o.a. and w.o. (Jun-Sep 1866); *Resaca,* and *Dacotah,* N.Pac.Sqdn. (Sep 1866-Sep 1869); w.o. (Oct 1869-Jan 1870); Navy Yard, Philadelphia (Jan-Jul 1870); w.o. (Jul-Aug 1870); *Saginaw,* N.Pac.Sqdn. (Sep 1869-Dec 1870); home and sick lv. (Dec 1870-Jul 1871); flgs., *Severn,* N.Atl.Sta. (Jul-Dec 1871); flgs., *Worcester,* N.Atl.Sta. (Dec 1871-Aug 1872); w.o. (Aug-Sep 1872); ord. duty, Navy Yard, Washington, DC (Nov 1872-Jun 1873); spec. duty, Bur. of Ord., Washington, DC (Jun-Jul 1873); *Wyoming,* N.Atl.Sta. (Aug 1873-Apr 1874); w.o. (Apr-Jun 1874);

CHAPMAN COLEMAN TODD
1848-1929

Hydrographic Office, Washington, DC (Jul-Sep 1874); flgs., *Pensacola*, N.Pac.Sta. (Oct 1874-Nov 1876); under suspension (Nov 1876-Jan 1878); rec. ship, *Franklin*, Norfolk, VA (Feb-Aug 1878); *Lackawanna*, Pac.Sta. (Sep 1878-Apr 1879); under suspension (Apr 1879-Dec 1880); w.o. (Dec 1880-Jun 1881); exec.off., *Wyoming*, Naval Sta., Port Royal, SC (Jun 1881-Oct 1882); w.o. (Oct 1882-Mar 1883); *Nipsic*, Eur.Sta. (Mar-May 1883); exec.off., *Kearsarge*, Eur.Sta. (May 1883-Oct 1885); return and w.o. (Oct-Dec 1885); ord. duty, Navy Yard, Washington, DC (Jan-May 1886); asst. to comdt. of midshipmen, USNA (May 1886-Jul 1889); *Charleston*, San Francisco (Jul-Nov 1889); exec.off., flgs., *Charleston*, Pac.Sta. (Nov 1889-Aug 1891); exec.off., *Pensacola*, Navy Yard, Mare Island, CA (Aug 1891); l.o.a. (Aug-Oct 1891); rec. ship, *Minnesota*, NY (Nov 1891-Jan 1893); Navy Yard, NY (Jan 1893); insp. of ord., Navy Yard, Norfolk, VA (Jan 1893-May 1896); NWC (Jun-Oct 1896); ord. instruction, Navy Yard, Washington, DC (Nov 1896-Feb 1897); Navy Yard, Norfolk, VA (Mar-Apr 1897); cdr, *Wilmington*, S.Atl.Sta. (May 1897-Aug 1899); ord. instruction, Navy Yard, Washington, DC (Sep-Dec 1899); chief hydrographer, Hydrographic Office, Washington, DC (Dec 1899-Nov 1901); cdr, flgs., *Brooklyn*, Asia.Sta. (Dec 1901-Sep 1902); home and w.o. (Sep-Oct 1902); placed on Ret.Lst. (31 Oct 1902).

References

Writings: a) *Report on the Voyage of the USS "Wilmington" in the Amazon River* (Washington, DC: 1899). b) a chapter in *With Sampson Through the War* (NY: 1899).

CHARLES JACKSON TRAIN Born in Framingham, MA, on 14 May 1845, son of Charles Russell and Martha (Jackson) Train. His father served as attorney general of MA and later congressman from MA. Educated at Phillips Exeter Academy. Married Grace Tomlinson on 1 Jun 1871. Two daughters and one son, Capt Charles Russell Train, USN. Died on 4 Aug 1906 while on duty in Chefoo, China. Buried in the USNA Cemetery in Annapolis.

Ranks Act.Midn (28 Nov 1861); title changed to Midn (16 Jul 1862); Ens (1 Nov 1866); Mstr (1 Dec 1866); Lt (12 Mar 1868); LCdr (30 Jun 1869); Cdr (17 Jan 1886); Capt (22 Nov 1898); RAdm (13 Sep 1904); died (4 Aug 1906).

Career Summary Received appointment from MA (28 Nov 1861); USNA (Nov 1861-Nov 1864); l.o.a. (Nov 1864-Feb 1865); Navy Yard, NY (Feb-Apr 1865); flgs., *Colorado*, and *Frolic*, Eur.Sqdn. (Apr 1865-Oct 1868); w.o. (Nov-Dec 1868); Naval Observatory, Washington, DC (Dec 1868-Apr 1869); *Sabine*, spec. cruise (May 1869-Jul 1870); w.o. (Jul-Aug 1870); USNA (Aug 1870-Jul 1873); w.o. (Jul-Aug 1873); spec. duty, Naval Observatory, Washington, DC (Aug 1873-May 1874); *Swatara*, Transit of Venus Observation Expd. (May 1874-Apr 1875); spec. duty, Washington, DC (Apr-Oct 1875); exec.off., *Tuscarora*, N.Pac.Sta. (Nov 1875-Aug 1876); w.o. (Aug-Sep 1876); Navy Yard, Mare Island, CA (Sep 1876-Mar 1877); exec.off., *Lacka-*

CHARLES JACKSON TRAIN
1845-1906

wanna, N.Pac.Sta. (Mar 1877-Jan 1878); w.o. (Jan-Feb 1878); USNA (Mar 1878-Jan 1881); w.o. (Jan-Oct 1881); *Powhatan*, spec.serv. (Oct 1881-Nov 1884); Bur. of Equip. and Recruiting, Washington, DC (Nov 1884-Aug 1886); cdr, training ship, *Jamestown* (Sep 1886-Aug 1888); cdr, training ship, *Constellation* (Sep 1888-May 1889); Bur. of Equip. and Recruiting, Washington, DC (May-Oct 1889); asst., then insp., 5th L.h. Dist., Baltimore (Oct 1889-Dec 1892); s.a. (Jan-Feb 1893); general insp., then cdr, *Machias*, Bath, ME, and N.Atl.Sta. (Mar 1893-Mar 1894); ord. instructor, Navy Yard, Washington, DC (Mar-May 1894); torp. instruction, Newport, RI (Jun-Oct 1894); naval member, Atlanta Expd. (Oct 1894-Jun 1896); insp., 4th L.h. Dist., Philadelphia (Jun 1896-Apr 1898); cdr, *Prairie*, N.Atl.Flt. (Apr-Oct 1898); cdr, *Puritan*, N.Atl.Flt. (Oct 1898-Mar 1899); bd. duties (Apr-Jun 1899); cdr, *Massachusetts*, N.Atl.Sqdn. (Jun 1899-May 1901); bd. duties (May 1901-Sep 1904); cdr, Philippine Sqdn., Asia.Flt., *Rainbow* (Oct 1904-Mar 1905); cdr, Asia.Flt. (Mar 1905-Aug 1906); died (4 Aug 1906).

References

Additional Sources: Mrs. Susan (Train) Hand, *John Trayne and Some of His Descendants, especially Charles Jackson Train, USN* (NY: 1933).

NATHANIEL REILLY USHER Born in Vincennes, IN, on 7 Apr 1855, son of Nathaniel and Pamela (Woolverton) Usher. Married Anne Usher on 29 Jul 1891. Resided in Potsdam, NY, where he died on 8 Jan 1931. Buried in Arlington National Cemetery.

Ranks Cadet Midn (22 Sep 1871); Ens (18 Jul 1876); Mstr (4 Feb 1880); title changed to Ltjg (3 Mar 1883); Lt (31 Oct 1883); LCdr (3 Mar 1899); Cdr (4 Feb 1904); Capt (23 Apr 1908); RAdm (14 Sep 1911); placed on Ret.Lst. (7 Apr 1919).

Career Summary Received appointment from IN (22 Sep 1871); USNA (Sep 1871-Jun 1875); flgs., *Tennessee*, Asia.Sta. (Jun 1875-Aug 1877); *Kearsarge*, Asia.Sta. (Aug 1877-Jan 1878); USNA (Jan 1878); w.o. (Jan-Mar 1878); spec. duty with naval delegation, Paris Exposition, *Constellation* (Mar-Jul 1878); rec. ship, *Independence*, Mare Island, CA (Sep 1878-May 1879); *Jamestown*, N.Pac.Sta. (May 1879-Sep 1881); w.o. (Sep 1881-Jan 1882); gunnery training ship, *Minnesota* (Jan-Mar 1882); *Alarm*, spec.serv. (Mar-Aug 1882); rec. ship, *Passaic*, Washington, DC (Aug-Dec 1882); w.o. (Dec 1882-Jan 1883); training ship, *Saratoga* (Jan 1883-Feb 1884); *Bear*, Greely Relief Expd. (Feb-Nov 1884); w.o. (Nov-Dec 1884); Bur. of Equip. and Recruiting, Washington, DC (Dec 1884-Apr 1885); *Alert*, Greely Relief Expd. (Apr 1885); Bur. of Equip. and Recruiting, Washington, DC (Apr 1885-Jan 1886); *Juniata*, spec. cruise (Jan 1886-Feb 1889); w.o. (Feb-Apr 1889); l.o.a. (Apr 1889-Feb 1890); rec. ship, *Vermont*, NY (Feb 1890-Apr 1892); *Dolphin*, spec.serv. (Apr 1892-Mar 1894); general insp., torp. boat #2, *Ericsson*, Iowa Iron Works, Dubuque, IA (Apr 1894-Mar 1897); cdr, *Ericsson*, on trials, and N.Atl.Flt. (Mar 1897-Sep 1898); exec.off., *Prairie*, Fore River,

NATHANIEL REILLY USHER
1855-1931

MA (Sep-Oct 1898); insp., 7th L.h. Dist., Pensacola, FL (Oct 1898-Oct 1899); *Kearsarge*, N.Atl.Sta. (Nov 1899-Apr 1901); *Illinois*, spec.serv., Eur. and N.Atl.Stas. (Apr 1901-Mar 1903); temp. duty, Bur. of Nav., Washington, D.C. (Mar-Nov 1903); member, Gen Bd., Washington, DC (Nov 1903-Feb 1904); Bur. of Nav., Washington, DC (Feb 1904-Aug 1906); cdr, *St. Louis*, Pac.Flt. (Aug 1906-Mar 1908); home and w.o. (Apr-May 1908); asst., Bur. of Nav., Washington, DC (May 1908-Dec 1909); duty with, then cdr, *Michigan*, Atl.Flt. (Dec 1909-Oct 1911); spec. duty, Navy Dept., Washington, DC (Oct 1911); home and w.o. (Oct-Nov 1911); pres., naval exam. and ret. bds., Washington, DC (Nov 1911-Jan 1912); cdr, 4th Div., Atl.Flt., *Minnesota*, then *Missouri* (Jan-Aug 1912); cdr, 2nd Div., Atl.Flt., *Louisiana*, then *Vermont* (Aug 1912-Jan 1913); cdr, 3rd Div., Atl.Flt., *Nebraska*, *Virginia*, then *Rhode Island* (Jan-Oct 1913); home and w.o. (Oct-Nov 1913); comdt., Navy Yard and Sta., Norfolk, VA (Dec 1913-Sep 1914); comdt., Navy Yard, NY (Sep 1914-Feb 1918); comdt., 3rd Naval Dist., NY (Feb 1918-Apr 1919); placed on Ret.Lst. (7 Apr 1919).

Career Highlights Served on Greely Relief Expd. in 1884. As cdr of the *Ericsson* when war with Spain broke out, credited with taking the first Spanish prize of the war. Participated in the Battle of Santiago and distinguished himself by rescuing Spanish sailors from the burning *Vizcaya*. As comdt. of the NY Navy Yard during World War I, oversaw the efficient embarkation of 80 percent of U.S. troops and a great deal of the supplies and provisions sent to Europe. Subsequently received the Navy Cross.

References
Personal Papers: 77 items (1871-84) in IN Historical Society Lib., Indianapolis.

SAMUEL WILLIAMS VERY Born in Liverpool, England, on 23 Apr 1846, son of Samuel (Jr.) and Sarah Williams (Mckey) Very. Educated in private and public schools. Married Martha Bourne Simonds on 14 Jun 1883. One son. Resided in Newton Centre, MA, where he died on 3 Jan 1919.

Ranks Yeoman (28 Aug 1862); discharged (1 Dec 1862); Midn (23 Feb 1863); Ens (12 Mar 1868); Mstr (26 Mar 1869); Lt (21 Mar 1870); LCdr (4 Mar 1886); Cdr (5 Mar 1895); Capt (19 Feb 1901); RAdm (22 Jul 1906); placed on Ret.Lst. (23 Apr 1908).

Career Summary Received appointment as Yeoman (28 Aug 1862); temp.serv., *Gemsbok*, S.Atl.Blk.Sqdn. (Aug-Dec 1862); discharged (1 Dec 1862); received appointment from MA (23 Feb 1863); USNA (Feb 1863-Jun 1866); l.o.a. and w.o. (Jun-Sep 1866); *Resaca, Mohican,* and *Onward,* Pac.Sta. (Sep 1866-Feb 1871); w.o. (Mar-May 1871); Torp.Sta., Newport, RI (Jun 1871-Mar 1872); *Lancaster,* S.Atl.Sta. (Apr 1872-Aug 1873); *Wasp,* S. Atl.Sta. (Aug 1873-Aug 1874); w.o. and l.o.a. (Sep-Nov 1874); Navy Yard, Boston (Nov 1874-Apr 1875); Hydrographic Office, Washington, DC (Apr-May 1875); *Richmond,* S.Pac. and S.Atl. Stas. (Jun 1875-Sep 1877); USNA (Oct 1877-Aug 1880); l.o.a. (Jul-Nov 1880); temp. duty, Hydrographic Office, Washington,

DC (Nov 1880-Apr 1881); cst.surv. duty (Apr 1881-Jul 1882); in charge, Transit of Venus Observation Expd., cst.surv. (Jul 1882-Jun 1883); *Tennessee*, N.Atl.Sta. (Jun 1883-May 1886); Torp.Sta., Newport, RI (May-Dec 1886); w.o. (Dec 1886-Jan 1887); insp. of new cruisers (Jan-Mar 1887); w.o. (Mar-Aug 1887); NWC (Aug-Oct 1887); USNA (Oct 1887-Jul 1890); spec. duty, *Newark* (Jul 1890-Feb 1891); *Newark*, N.Atl.Sta. (Feb-Jun 1891); sick lv. and w.o. (Jun-Oct 1891); *Mohican*, Pac.Sta. (Nov 1891-Apr 1893); exec.off., *Boston*, Pac.Sta. (Apr-Nov 1893); l.o.a. (Nov 1893-Jan 1894); ord. duty, Navy Yard, Washington, DC (Jan-Feb 1894); insp. of ord., Navy Yard, League Island, PA (Feb 1894-Aug 1895); insp. of ord., William Cramp and Sons Iron Works, Philadelphia (Aug 1895-Jul 1896); Navy Yard, Boston (Jul 1896-Apr 1898); cdr, *Saturn*, N.Atl.Flt. (Apr-Jun 1898); cdr, *Cassius*, N.Atl.Flt. (Jun-Dec 1898); home and w.o. (Dec 1898-Jan 1899); *Castine*, Asia.Sta. (Jan 1899-Jun 1900); Navy Yard, Mare Island, CA (Jul 1900); home and w.o. (Jul-Sep 1900); Navy Yard, Boston (Sep 1900-May 1901); NWC (Jun-Sep 1901); Navy Yard, Boston (Sep 1901-Oct 1903); cdr, *San Francisco*, Med. and Pac.Stas. (Nov 1903-Dec 1904); home and w.o. (Dec 1904-Aug 1905); comdt., Naval Sta., Port Royal, SC, and 6th Naval Dist., Charleston, SC (Sep-Nov 1905); bd. duties, Navy Yard, Boston (Nov 1905-Jul 1906); comdt., Naval Sta., Honolulu, Territory of HI (Jul 1906-Apr 1908); placed on Ret.Lst. (23 Apr 1908).

Career Highlights Serving with the cst.surv. in the 1880s, participating in magnetic observations on Hudson Bay and off Labrador and was in charge of the transit of Venus Expd. to Patagonia.

CHARLES EDWARD VREELAND
1852-1916

CHARLES EDWARD VREELAND Born in Newark, NJ, on 10 Mar 1852. His wife was Kathrina Tolson Vreeland. Died in Atlantic City, NJ, on 27 Sep 1916. Buried in Arlington National Cemetery.

Ranks Midn (27 Jul 1866); Ens (13 Jul 1871); Mstr (2 Apr 1874); Lt (25 Mar 1880); LCdr (3 Mar 1899); Cdr (15 Aug 1901); Capt (13 Apr 1906); RAdm (27 Dec 1909); placed on Ret.Lst. (10 Mar 1914).

Career Summary Received appointment as apprentice navy boy (27 Jul 1866); USNA (Jul 1866-Jun 1870); w.o. (Jun-Jul 1870); *California*, Navy Yard, Portsmouth, NH (Sep 1870); flgs., *Severn*, N.Atl.Sta. (Sep-Oct 1870); *Congress*, and *Brooklyn*, S.Atl. and Eur.Stas. (Oct 1870-Jul 1873); w.o. (Jul-Nov 1873); *Powhatan*, N.Atl.Sta. (Nov 1873-Feb 1876); *Alert*, and *Ashuelot*, Asia.Sta. (Feb 1876-Dec 1877); home and w.o. (Dec 1877-May 1878); l.o.a. (May-Oct 1878); *Ticonderoga*, spec.serv. (Nov 1878-Sep 1881); w.o. (Sep-Nov 1881); Nautical Almanac Office, Washington, DC (Nov 1881-Dec 1883); *Hartford*, Pac.Sta. (Mar 1884-Jan 1887); w.o. (Jan-Mar 1887); Bur. of Nav., Washington, DC (May 1887-Apr 1889); torp. instruction, Newport, RI (May-Jul 1889); Office of Naval Intelligence, Washington, DC (Oct 1889); cst.surv. duty (Oct 1889-Apr 1893); l.o.a. (Apr-May 1893); naval attaché, Rome, Vienna, and Berlin (Jun 1893-Aug

1896); spec. duty, Europe (Aug 1896-Jan 1897); *Massachusetts*, spec. serv., and N.Atl.Sqdn. (Jan-Jul 1897); exec.off., *Helena*, N.Atl.Flt. (Jul 1897-Aug 1898); *Dolphin*, Navy Yard, Norfolk, VA (Aug-Nov 1898); *Concord*, Asia.Sta. (Dec 1898-May 1899); *Monterey*, Asia.Sta. (May-Jun 1899); *Baltimore*, spec.serv. (Jun-Dec 1899); *Solace*, spec.serv. (Dec 1899-Feb 1900); Navy Yard, Mare Island, CA (Mar 1900); home and w.o. (Mar-Apr 1900); member, bd. of inspection and surv. (Apr 1900-Aug 1902); duty with, then cdr, training ship, *Arkansas* (Aug 1902-Oct 1904); member, bd. on changes to navy yards, and other bd. duties (Nov 1904-May 1905); spec. duty, asst. sec. of navy's office, Navy Dept., Washington, DC (Mar 1905-Apr 1907); cdr, *Kansas*, on trials, and "Great White Flt." (Apr 1907-Apr 1909); home and w.o. (Apr 1909); chief intelligence off., Navy Dept., Washington, DC (May-Dec 1909); cdr, 4th Div., Atl.Flt., *Virginia* (Dec 1909-Jul 1910); cdr, 2nd Div., Atl.Flt., *Louisiana* (Jul 1910-Apr 1911); home and w.o. (Apr 1911); bd. duties, Washington, DC (May-Dec 1911); Navy Dept. representative, coronation of King George V, London (May-Jul 1911); aide for operations, Navy Dept., Washington, DC (Dec 1911-Feb 1913); bd. duties (Dec 1911-Mar 1914); placed on Ret.Lst. (10 Mar 1914).

ALBION VARETTE WADHAMS Born at Wadhams Mills, Essex County, NY, on 8 Jun 1847, son of William Luman and Emeline Lorette (Cole) Wadhams. Married Caroline E. Henderson on 28 Feb 1870. Two sons and a daughter. Resided in Wadhams, NY. Died in Nice, France, on 14 Jan 1927.

Ranks Midn (26 Sep 1864); Ens (19 Apr 1869); Mstr (12 Jul 1870); Lt (25 Mar 1873); LCdr (21 Jul 1894); Cdr (3 Mar 1899); Capt (27 Dec 1903); retired with rank of Commo (30 Jun 1907); RAdm on Ret.Lst. (11 May 1925) to rank from 30 Jun 1907.

Career Summary Received appointment from NY (26 Sep 1864); USNA (Sep 1864-Jun 1868); w.o. (Jun-Sep 1868); *Albany*, S.Pac.Sqdn. (Oct 1868-Aug 1869); w.o. (Aug-Oct 1869); ord. duty, Navy Yard, NY (Nov 1869); *Alaska*, Asia.Sta. (Dec 1869-Feb 1873); w.o. (Feb-Aug 1873); torp. duty, Newport, RI (Sep 1873-May 1874); *Powhatan*, N.Atl.Sta. (May 1874-May 1875); *Alert*, Chester, PA (May-Aug 1875); USNA (Aug 1875-Mar 1878); cst.surv. duty (Apr 1878-Dec 1879); experimental battery, Annapolis (Dec 1879-Mar 1880); *Nipsic*, Eur.Sta. (Mar 1880-Mar 1883); w.o. (Mar-Apr 1883); temp. duty, cst.surv. (Apr 1883-Jan 1884); ord. duty, Navy Yard, Washington, DC (Feb 1884-Jun 1886); *Essex*, Asia.Sta. (Jul 1886-Jun 1887); *Brooklyn*, Asia.Sta. (Jun-Dec 1887); *Monocacy*, Asia.Sta. (Dec 1887); *Marion*, Pac. Sta. (Dec 1887-Feb 1889); *Monocacy*, Asia.Sta. (Feb-May 1889); w.o. (May-Jun 1889); asst.insp., 2nd L.h. Dist., Boston (Jun 1889-Oct 1890); member, bd. of inspection of vessels, Boston (Oct 1890-Jun 1891); insp. of steel, Boston (Jun 1891-Jul 1892); w.o. (Jul-Aug 1892); l.o.a. (Sep 1892-Sep 1893); torp. instruction, Newport, RI (Sep-Nov 1893); exec.off., *Mohican*, Pac.Sta. (Nov 1893-Sep 1895); exec.off., *Marion*, Pac.Sta. (Sep 1895); *Boston*, Navy Yard, Mare Island, CA (Sep-Nov 1895); exec.off., *Monterey*,

ALBION VARETTE WADHAMS
1847-1927

Pac.Sta. (Nov 1895-Nov 1896); home and l.o.a. (Nov-Dec 1896); asst., then insp., 8th L.h. Dist., New Orleans (Jan 1897-Sep 1899); additional duty, in charge, 7th Dist. Cst. Defense System (Apr-Aug 1898); cdr, training ship, *Monongahela* (Oct 1899-Dec 1900); Naval Hosp., NY (Nov 1900-Jan 1901); sick lv. (Jan-Feb 1901); duty with insp. of merchant ships, NY (Feb-May 1901); Navy Yard, NY (May-Sep 1901); cdr, nautical schoolship, *St. Mary's* (Nov 1901-Dec 1902); NWC (Dec 1902-Feb 1903); in charge, Naval Rec. Sta. and branch hydrographic office, Chicago (Feb-Nov 1903); cdr, training ship, *Prairie* (Nov 1903-Mar 1905); capt.yd., Navy Yard, Norfolk, VA (Apr 1905-Jul 1907); placed on Ret.Lst. (30 Jun 1907); Navy Dept. representative at HQ, American Red Cross, Washington, DC (Dec 1917-Oct 1919); temp. duties (Dec 1917-Aug 1921); cdr, Naval Prison, Portsmouth, NH (Mar 1920-Jul 1921).

References

Writings: "The Egyptian Campaign: The Transports," U.S. Naval Institute *Proceedings* 22 (1882): 615-19.

GEORGE HENRY WADLEIGH Born in Dover, NH, on 28 Sep 1842, son of George H. and Sarah (Gilman) Wadleigh. Married Clara Robinson on 12 Oct 1869. Two sons and two daughters. Resided in Dover, NH. Died in Lexington, MA, on 11 Jul 1927. Buried in Pine Hill Cemetery, Dover.

Ranks Act.Midn (27 Sep 1860); title changed to Midn (16 Jul 1862); Ens (28 May 1863); Mstr (10 Nov 1865); Lt (10 Nov 1866); LCdr (12 Mar 1868); Cdr (13 Mar 1880); Capt (10 Jul 1894); RAdm (9 Feb 1902); retired (7 Jun 1902).

Career Summary Received appointment from NH (27 Sep 1860); USNA (Sep 1860-May 1863); *Lackawanna*, W.Gulf Blk. Sqdn. (Jun 1863-Mar 1865); *Richmond*, W.Gulf Blk.Sqdn. (Mar-Jul 1865); w.o. (Jul-Aug 1865); *Ticonderoga*, Eur.Sta. (Aug 1865-Apr 1869); w.o. and l.o.a. (Apr-Sep 1869); USNA (Sep 1869-Jun 1870); w.o. (Jun-Oct 1870); torp. duty, Newport, RI (Nov 1870-Mar 1871); exec.off., *Shawmut*, N.Atl.Sta. (Mar 1871-Oct 1873); w.o. (Oct-Nov 1873); exec.off., *Canonicus*, Navy Yard, Boston (Dec 1873-Jan 1874); rec. ship, *Ohio*, Boston (Jan-Aug 1874); ord. duty, Navy Yard, Boston (Aug-Oct 1874); exec.off., nautical schoolship, *St. Mary's* (Oct 1874-Sep 1876); w.o. (Sep-Oct 1876); exec.off., flgs., *Pensacola*, Pac.Sta. (Nov 1876-Oct 1878); nav. dept., Navy Yard, Portsmouth, NH (Nov 1878-Jun 1881); cdr, *Alliance*, spec. duty, *Jeanette* Search Expd. (Jun-Dec 1881); exec.off., *Alliance*, N.Atl.Sta. (Dec 1881-Dec 1882); w.o. (Dec 1882-May 1883); nav.off., Navy Yard, Portsmouth, NH (May-Aug 1883); asst., then insp., 2nd L.h. Dist., Boston (Aug 1883-Sep 1886); s.a. and w.o. (Aug 1886-Sep 1887); nav.off., Navy Yard, Boston (Oct 1887-Nov 1889); cdr, *Michigan*, on Great Lakes (Nov 1889-Dec 1891); l.o.a. (Dec 1891-Feb 1892); insp. of ord., Navy Yard, Boston (Feb 1892-Jul 1894); cdr, rec. ship, *Richmond*, Philadelphia (Jul-Dec 1894); cdr, *Minneapolis*, N.Atl. and Eur.Stas. (Dec 1894-May 1897); l.o.a. (May-Jul 1897); insp., Navy Yard, Boston (Jul-Oct 1897); capt.yd., Navy Yard,

GEORGE HENRY WADLEIGH
1842-1927

Boston (Oct 1897-Jun 1898); cdr, flgs., *Philadelphia*, Pac.Sqdn.
(Jun-Oct 1898); home and w.o. (Oct-Nov 1898); cdr, rec. ship,
Wabash, Boston (Dec 1898-Dec 1901); bd. duties (Dec 1901-Jan
1902); comdt., Navy Yard, League Island, PA (Feb-May 1902);
pres., bd. of inspection and surv. (May-Jun 1902); retired (7 Jun
1902).

Career Highlights During the Civil War, saw action at the
Battle of Mobile Bay in Aug 1864. While on the *Shawmut* in the
early 1870s, cruised the Orinoco River to Bolivar, forcing the
return from insurgents there of two captured American vessels.
Served on the *Jeanette* Search Expd. in 1881.

RICHARD WAINWRIGHT Born in Washington, DC, on 17
Dec 1849, son of Cdr Richard, USN (1817-62), and Sallie
Franklin (Bache) Wainwright. His father commanded RAdm
David G. Farragut's flgs. at New Orleans in 1862. Well connected
with the military; relatives included RAdm Thomas H. Patterson,
USN, Gen Edward D. Townsend, Adjutant General of the Army
during the Civil War, and Alexander Dallas Bache, supt. of the
cst.surv. from 1843 to 1867. Brothers-in-law included RAdm
Seaton Schroeder, USN [*q.v.*], and Gen William W. Wother-
spoon, USA, Chief of Staff in 1914. A cousin was RAdm William
H. Emory, USN, and a nephew was Adm Alex S. Wotherspoon,
USN. Received LL.B. degree in 1884 from Columbian Univ. (now
George Washington Univ.), and LL.D. in 1900 from the same
institution. Married Evelyn Wotherspoon on 11 Sep 1873. One
son and one daughter. Resided in Washington, DC, where he died
on 6 Mar 1926. Buried in Arlington National Cemetery.

RICHARD WAINWRIGHT
1849-1926

Ranks Midn (28 Sep 1864); Ens (19 Apr 1865); Mstr (12 Jul
1870); Lt (25 Sep 1873); LCdr (16 Sep 1894); Cdr (3 Mar 1899);
Capt (10 Aug 1903); RAdm (11 Jul 1908); placed on Ret.Lst.
(17 Dec 1911).

Career Summary Received appointment by virtue of being the
son of an officer (28 Sep 1864); USNA (Sep 1864-Jun 1868);
w.o. (Jun-Sep 1868); *Jamestown*, N.Pac.Sqdn. (Dec 1868-Aug
1869); w.o. (Aug-Oct 1869); Hydrographic Office, Washington,
DC (Oct 1869-Apr 1870); flgs., *Colorado*, Asia.Sta. (Apr 1870-
Mar 1873); w.o. (Mar-Apr 1873); Hydrographic Office, Washington, DC (Apr 1873-Jan 1874); temp. duty, Bur. of Equip. and
Recruiting, Washington, DC (Nov 1873-Jan 1874); Navy Yard,
Washington, DC (Jan 1874); Hydrographic Office, Washington,
DC (Jan-Aug 1874); l.o.a. (Aug-Sep 1874); Naval Observatory,
Washington, DC (Sep 1874); cst.surv. duty (Sep 1874-Jul 1877);
flag lt, Asia.Sta., *Monocacy*, then *Richmond* (Sep 1877-Sep 1880);
home and w.o. (Sep-Nov 1880); spec. duty, Bur. of Nav., Wash-
ington, DC (Nov 1880-Jul 1884); *Tennessee*, N.Atl.Sta. (Jul
1884-Jun 1886); *Galena*, N.Atl.Sta. (Jun 1886-Aug 1887); w.o.
(Aug-Oct 1887); duty with steel bd. (Oct 1887-Apr 1888); w.o.
(Apr-Aug 1888); USNA (Sep 1888-Sep 1890); *Alert*, spec.serv.
(Oct 1890-Oct 1893); Hydrographic Office, Washington, DC
(Oct 1893-Apr 1896); chief intelligence off., Navy Dept.,
Washington, DC (Apr 1896-Nov 1897); member, bd. of person-

nel, Washington, DC (May-Nov 1897); exec.off., *Maine*, N.Atl. Sqdn. (Dec 1897-Feb 1898); spec. duty (Feb-Apr 1898); judge advocate gen's office, Washington, DC (Apr 1898); cdr, *Gloucester*, N.Atl.Flt. (May-Oct 1898); cdr of ships, USNA, *Santee* (Nov 1898-Mar 1900); supt., USNA (Mar 1900-Nov 1902); cdr, *Newark*, S.Atl.Sqdn. (Nov 1902-Oct 1904); temp.cdr, S.Atl.Sta., *Newark* (Jan-Oct 1904); member, Gen Bd., Navy Dept., Washington, DC (Oct 1904-Jun 1907); member, Army-Navy Joint Bd., Washington, DC (Mar 1905-Jun 1907); cdr, *Louisiana*, "Great White Flt." (Jul 1907-May 1908); cdr, 2nd Div., 1st Sqdn., Atl.Flt., *Georgia* (May 1908-Mar 1909); cdr, 3rd Div., Atl.Flt., *Georgia* (Mar-Dec 1909); aide for operations to sec. of navy, Washington, DC (Dec 1909-Dec 1911); member, Army-Navy Joint Bd., Washington, DC (Dec 1909-Dec 1911); placed on Ret.Lst. (17 Dec 1911); member, Gen Bd., Navy Dept., Washington, DC (Dec 1911-May 1912); temp. member, Army-Navy Joint Bd., Washington, DC (Feb-May 1912).

Career Highlights Served as exec.off. on board the *Maine* when she blew up in Havana Harbor on 15 Feb 1898. Subsequently directed the preliminary investigation of the wreckage. Participated in the action at Santiago on 3 Jul 1898 and in the capture of Guanica, being advanced ten numbers for his conduct in his actions. Supt. of the USNA, and aide to the secretary of the navy, he commanded a division in the "Great White Flt.," then served as aide for operations to the sec., the highest naval position at that time.

References

Personal Papers: a) Wainwright Family, 18 items (1842-1941) in NHF,LC. b) 3 items (1880-1900) in NHF,WNY.

Writings: a) "Our Merchant Marine: The Causes of Its Decline and the Means to be Taken for Its Revival," U.S. Naval Institute *Proceedings* 19 (1882): 121-49. b) "Naval Coasts Signals," U.S. Naval Institute *Proceedings* 48 (1889): 61-74. c) "Fleet Tactics," U.S. Naval Institute *Proceedings* 52 (1890): 65-90. d) "Tactical Problems in Naval Warfare," U.S. Naval Institute *Proceedings* 74 (1895): 217-80. e) "Search Curves--Some Applications and Limitations," U.S. Naval Institute *Proceedings* 84 (1897): 663-78. f) "Our Naval Power," U.S. Naval Institute *Proceedings* 85 (1898): 39-87. g) "The Battle of the Sea of Japan," U.S. Naval Institute *Proceedings* 116 (Dec 1905): 779-805. h) "A Further Argument for the Big Ships," U.S. Naval Institute *Proceedings* 119 (Sep 1906): 1057-63. i) edited with Robert M. Thompson, *The Confidential Correspondence of Gustavus Vasa Fox, Assistant Secretary of the Navy*, 2 vols. (NY: 1918-19). j) "The General Board: A Sketch," U.S. Naval Institute *Proceedings* 228 (Feb 1922): 189-210. k) "Laws and Customs of War at Sea as Affected by the World War," U.S. Naval Institute *Proceedings* 224 (Jun 1923): 897-914. l) "The Dacia Dilemma," U.S. Naval Institute *Proceedings* 270 (Aug 1925): 1452-54.

Additional Sources: Damon E. Cummings, *Admiral Richard Wainwright and the United States Fleet* (Washington, DC: 1962).

ASA WALKER Born in Portsmouth, NH, on 13 Nov 1845, son of Asa T. and Louisa (Morrell) Walker. Married Belle W. Grant on 11 Jun 1890. One son. Died in Annapolis on 7 Mar 1916. Buried in the USNA Cemetery.

Ranks Midn (21 Nov 1862); Ens (12 Mar 1868); Mstr (26 Mar 1869); Lt (21 Mar 1870); LCdr (12 Dec 1884); Cdr (11 Apr 1894); Capt (9 Sep 1899); RAdm (7 Jan 1906); placed on Ret.Lst. (13 Nov 1907).

Career Summary Received appointment from NH (21 Nov 1862); USNA (Nov 1862-Jun 1866); l.o.a. and w.o. (Jun-Sep 1866); *Sacramento*, spec.serv. (Sep 1866-Nov 1867); l.o.a. and w.o. (Nov-Dec 1867); ord. duty, Navy Yard, Portsmouth, NH (Jan-Jul 1868); *Lackawanna, Saranac*, and *Jamestown*, Pac.Sta. (Jul 1868-Mar 1871); w.o. (Apr-May 1871); torp. instruction, Newport, RI (Jun 1871-Jan 1872); w.o. (Jan-Feb 1872); *Powhatan*, spec. duty (Feb 1872-Jul 1873); USNA (Jul 1873-Jun 1876); w.o. (Jun-Sep 1876); *Essex*, S.Atl.Sta. (Oct 1876-Oct 1879); USNA (Nov 1879-Aug 1883); *Trenton*, and *Monocacy*, Asia.Sta. (Sep 1883-Sep 1886); w.o. (Sep-Oct 1886); USNA (Oct 1886-Aug 1890); w.o. (Aug 1890-Oct 1891); exec.off., *Miantonomoh*, spec.serv. (Oct 1891-Jan 1893); member, *Bancroft* trial bd., Elizabethport, NJ (Jan-Mar 1893); cdr, training ship, *Bancroft*, USNA (Mar-Jul 1893); USNA (Jul 1893-May 1897); cdr, *Concord*, Pac. and Asia.Stas. (May 1897-May 1899); home and w.o. (May-Aug 1899); NWC (Aug 1899-Oct 1900); member, naval exam. bd. (Oct 1900-Dec 1901); cdr, *San Francisco*, Eur. and N.Atl.Sqdns. (Jan 1902-Nov 1903); home and w.o. (Nov 1903-Jan 1904); member, Gen Bd., Navy Dept., Washington, DC (Jan-Oct 1904); cdr, rec. ship, *Wabash*, Boston (Oct 1904-Jan 1906); supt., Naval Observatory, Washington, DC (Feb 1906-Nov 1907); placed on Ret.Lst. (13 Nov 1907).

Career Highlights With the war with Spain, he was in command of the USS *Concord* with the Asiatic Fleet and thus participated in the Battle of Manila Bay for which he was advanced nine numbers in rank.

References

Writings: a) *Navigation Prepared for Use as a Text-Book at the U.S. Naval Academy* (Baltimore: 1888). b) "Combined Maritime Operations," U.S. Naval Institute *Proceedings* 93 (Mar 1990): 143-55. c) "Notes on Cuban Ports," U.S. Naval Institute *Proceedings* 94 (Jun 1900): 333-40. d) "With Reference to the Size of Fighting Ships," U.S. Naval Institute *Proceedings* 95 (Sep 1900): 515-22.

ASA WALKER
1845-1916

AARON WARD Born in Philadelphia on 10 Oct 1851, son of army Gen Benjamin, and Emily (Ward) Burnett Ward. Educated in Cannstatt, Germany, and at the Lycée Bonaparte in Paris before returning to the United States. Married Annie Cairns Willis on 20 Apr 1876. Two daughters, one of whom married Chief Const. Washington L. Capps, USN [*q.v.*]. Resided in Roslyn, Long Island, NY, where he died on 5 Jul 1918. Buried in Brooklyn's Greenwood Cemetery.

AARON WARD
1851-1918

Ranks Midn (26 Sep 1867); title changed to Cadet Midn (15
Jul 1870); Midn (6 Jun 1871); Ens (4 Jul 1872); Mstr (8 Feb
1875); Lt (25 Nov 1881); LCdr (3 Mar 1899); Cdr (28 Sep
1901); Capt (6 Jun 1906); RAdm (9 Jan 1910); placed on
Ret.Lst. (10 Oct 1913).

Career Summary Received appointment from PA (26 Sep
1867); USNA (Sep 1867-Jun 1871); w.o. (Jun-Aug 1871);
California, Pac.Sta. (Aug 1871-Jul 1873); home and w.o. (Jul-Oct
1873); temp. duty, Hydrographic Office, Washington, DC (Oct-
Nov 1873); *Brooklyn*, W.Indies (Dec 1873-Feb 1874); sick lv.
(Feb-Sep 1874); Hydrographic Office, Washington, DC (Oct-Dec
1874); w.o. (Dec 1874-Jan 1875); *Franklin*, Eur.Sta. (Jan 1875-
Jun 1876); l.o.a. (Jun-Sep 1876); USNA (Sep 1876-Jun 1879);
l.o.a. (Jun-Oct 1879); training ship, *Constitution* (Oct 1879-Aug
1881); training ship, *New Hampshire* (Aug 1881-Apr 1882);
training ship, *Portsmouth* (Apr-Dec 1882); training ship, *Saratoga*
(Dec 1882-Feb 1883); flgs., *New Hampshire*, Apprentice Training
Sqdn. (Feb-May 1883); Navy Yard, NY (May 1883-Apr 1884);
torp. instruction, Newport, RI (Apr-Aug 1884); spec. duty,
Torp.Sta., Newport, RI (Aug 1884-May 1885); *Hartford*, Pac.Sta.
(Jun 1885-Nov 1886); *Iroquois*, Pac.Sta. (Nov-Dec 1886);
Monongahela, Pac.Sta. (Dec 1886-May 1889); home and l.o.a.
(May-Dec 1889); naval attaché, Paris, Berlin, and St. Petersburg,
Russia (Mar 1889-Nov 1892); return and w.o. (Nov 1892-Jul
1893); *New York*, N. and S.Atl.Stas. (Aug 1893-Jan 1894); *San
Francisco*, Med.Sta. (Jan 1894-Aug 1896); l.o.a. (Aug-Nov 1896);
Navy Yard, NY (Nov 1896-Mar 1898); duty with, then cdr,
Wasp, N.Atl.Flt. (Mar-Sep 1898); home and w.o. (Sep 1898); cdr,
then exec.off., *Panther*, N.Atl.Flt. (Oct 1898-Oct 1899); *Dixie*,
League Island, PA (Oct 1899); home and w.o. (Oct-Nov 1899);
asst. chief of staff, Asia.Sta., *Brooklyn* (Dec 1899-Apr 1900);
additional duty, temp.cdr, *Zafiro*, Asia.Sta. (Mar-Apr 1900); senior
aide to cdr, Asia.Sta., *Baltimore* (Apr-Sep 1900); home and w.o.
(Sep-Oct 1900); ord. duty, Navy Yard, NY (Oct 1900-Jan 1902);
Asia.Sta. (Feb-Mar 1902); Naval Sta., Cavite, P.I. (Mar 1902);
cdr, *Yorktown*, Asia.Sta. (Apr 1902-Apr 1903); cdr, *Don Juan de
Austria*, Asia.Sta. (Apr-Oct 1903); home and w.o. (Oct-Dec
1903); court-martial duty, Navy Yard, NY (Dec 1903-Jan 1905);
l.o.a. (Jan-Feb 1905); equip.off., Navy Yard, NY (Feb 1905-Aug
1906); aide to cdr, 4th Div., Atl.Flt., *West Virginia* (Aug-Sep
1906); chief of staff, Asia.Flt., *West Virginia* (Oct 1906-Mar
1907); cdr, *Pennsylvania* (Mar 1907-Mar 1908); home and w.o.
(Mar-Apr 1908); member, court of inquiry, Navy Yard, NY (Apr-
May 1908); supervisor, NY Harbor (May 1908-Nov 1909); bd.
duties, Navy Yard, Washington, DC (Nov-Dec 1909); aide to
secretary of navy, and head, inspection dept., Navy Dept.,
Washington, DC (Dec 1909-Apr 1911); cdr, 3rd Div., Atl.Flt.,
Minnesota (Apr 1911-Jan 1912); temp. duty, cdr, Atl.Flt.,
Minnesota (Nov-Dec 1911); cdr, 1st Div., Atl.Flt., *Florida*
(Jan-Aug 1912); supervisor, NY Harbor (Aug 1912-Oct 1913);
placed on Ret.Lst. (10 Oct 1913).

JAMES HORATIO WATMOUGH Born in Whitemarsh, PA, on 30 July 1822, son of John Godard and Ellen (Coxe) Watmough. Educated at the Univ. of PA. Married twice: to Emmeline Sheaff on 19 Oct 1848, and to Annie Bowie Harris on 15 Jul 1907. Died on 18 Jan 1917 at his home in Washington, DC. Buried in Arlington National Cemetery.

Ranks Paymstr. (12 Dec 1844); Pay Dir. (3 Mar 1871); transferred to Ret.Lst. (30 Jul 1884); Pay Dir. with rank of RAdm on Ret.Lst. (29 Jun 1906).

Career Summary Received appointment from PA (12 Dec 1844); *Portsmouth*, Pac.Sqdn. (Dec 1844-May 1848); s.a. and w.o. (May 1848-Oct 1849); *Perry*, Afr.Sqdn. (Oct 1849-Dec 1851); s.a. and w.o. (Dec 1851-Dec 1852); *Constitution*, Afr.Sqdn. (Dec 1852-Jun 1855); s.a. and w.o. (Jun 1855-Dec 1857); *Michigan*, on Great Lakes (Dec 1857-Mar 1859); *Saratoga*, W.Ind.Sqdn. (Apr 1859-Jul 1860); s.a. and w.o. (Jul-Oct 1860); Navy Yard, Philadelphia (Nov 1860-Oct 1863); *Niagara*, spec.serv. (Oct 1863-May 1864); s.a. and w.o. (May-Jun 1864); flt.paymstr., S.Atl.Blk.Sqdn., *Canandaigua* (Jul 1864-Jun 1865); s.a. and w.o. (Jun 1865-Feb 1866); member, court-martial bd., Philadelphia (Feb-Apr 1866); member, bd. of examiners (Apr-Jul 1866); Navy Yard, NY (Aug 1866-Jan 1869); s.a. and w.o. (Jan 1869); insp. of provisions, Navy Yard, NY (Jan-Oct 1869); s.a. and w.o. (Oct 1869-Oct 1871); l.o.a. (Oct 1871-Mar 1873); general insp. of provisions and clothing, Washington, DC (Mar-Jul 1873); paymstr.gen and act. chief, Bur. of Provisions and Clothing, Washington, DC (Jul 1873-Dec 1876); general insp. of provisions and clothing, Washington, DC (Dec 1876-Mar 1877); chief, Bur. of Provisions and Clothing, Washington, DC (Feb-Nov 1877); w.o. (Nov 1877-Jul 1878); l.o.a. (Jul 1878-May 1881); pres., bd. of naval examiners (May-Nov 1881); w.o. (Nov 1881-Apr 1882); general insp. of provisions and clothing, Washington, DC (Apr-Oct 1882); w.o. (Oct 1882-Jul 1884); transferred to Ret.Lst. (30 Jul 1884).

References

Personal Papers: 1 letterbook and 6 items (1844-55) in BL.

JAMES HORATIO WATMOUGH
1822-1917

EUGENE WINSLOW WATSON Born in Northampton, MA, on 17 Feb 1843, son of Adolphus Eugene and Elisa Hovey (Mellen) Watson. Educated in Philadelphia; married Virginia Cruse on 14 Apr 1869. Three children. Died at his home in Washington, DC, on 11 Dec 1914. Buried in Arlington National Cemetery.

Ranks Master's Mate (2 May 1859); Act.Ens (18 Sep 1863); Ens (12 Mar 1868); Mstr (18 Dec 1868); Lt (21 Mar 1870); LCdr (16 Nov 1883); Cdr (27 Apr 1893); Capt (22 Nov 1899); placed on Ret.Lst. (2 Jun 1902); RAdm on Ret.Lst. (13 Apr 1911) to rank from 2 Jun 1902.

Career Summary Appointed Master's Mate (2 May 1859); flgs., *Lancaster*, Pac.Sqdn. (May 1859-Oct 1861); *Rhode Island*, Gulf Blk. and W.Ind.Sqdns. (Nov 1861-Sep 1863); Navy Yard, Boston (Sep-Oct 1863); supply ship, *Circassian*, E. and W.Gulf Blk.Sqdns. (Oct-Dec 1863); *Flag*, S.Atl.Blk.Sqdn. (Jan 1864-Mar

EUGENE WINSLOW WATSON
1843-1914

1865); *Frolic*, Eur.Sqdn. (Mar 1865-May 1867); *Guard*, Eur.Sta. (Jun 1867-Oct 1868); Navy Yard, League Island, PA (Oct-Dec 1868); *Pequot*, Navy Yard, NY (Jan-Feb 1869); rec. ship, *Vermont*, NY (Feb-Mar 1869); *Seminole*, Navy Yard, Boston (Apr 1869-Feb 1870); w.o. (Feb-Apr 1870); *Frolic*, spec.serv. (Apr-Nov 1870); ord. duty, Navy Yard, Norfolk, VA (Dec 1870-Jan 1872); *Canonicus*, and *Saugus*, N.Atl.Sta. (Feb 1872-Dec 1873); w.o. (Dec 1873-Jan 1874); Navy Yard, Norfolk, VA (Jan 1874-Sep 1875); *Ossipee*, N.Atl.Sta. (Sep 1875-Jul 1877); Navy Yard, Norfolk, VA (Jul 1877-Aug 1880); rec. ship, *Franklin*, Norfolk, VA (Aug 1880-Oct 1882); *Brooklyn*, S.Atl.Sta. (Nov 1882-Oct 1884); w.o. (Oct-Nov 1884); Navy Yard, Norfolk, VA (Nov 1884-Oct 1886); ord. instruction, Washington, DC (Oct 1886-May 1887); torp. instruction, Newport, RI (Jun-Sep 1887); l.o.a. (Sep 1887-Feb 1888); exec.off., *Swatara*, Asia.Sta. (Feb 1888-Feb 1891); l.o.a. (Feb-Oct 1891); exec.off., training ship, *Richmond* (Nov 1891-Apr 1893); insp. of ord., Navy Yard, Portsmouth, NH (Apr 1893-Nov 1894); cdr, *Ranger*, Pac.Sta. (Dec 1894-Dec 1895); cdr, *Adams*, Pac.Sta. (Dec 1895-Dec 1896); ord.off., Navy Yard, Portsmouth, NH (Dec 1896-Jan 1897); home and l.o.a. (Jan-Feb 1897); ord. instruction, Navy Yard, Washington, DC (Feb-Mar 1897); comdt., Naval Sta., New London, CT (Mar 1897-Apr 1898); cdr, *Southery*, Navy Yard, Boston (Apr-May 1898); cdr, *Scindia*, N.Atl.Flt. and spec.serv. (May 1898-Feb 1899); home and w.o. (Feb-Apr 1899); Navy Yard, Washington, DC (Apr-Nov 1899); capt.yd., Navy Yard, Norfolk, VA (Nov 1899-Jun 1902); placed on Ret.Lst. (2 Jun 1902).

References

Writings: a) chapter to John L. Worden's *The "Monitor" and the "Merrimac"* (NY: 1912).

HARRIE WEBSTER Born in Farmington, ME, on 12 Feb 1843, son of Nathan and Ellen Kilshaw (Whittier) Webster. Educated in public schools and at the Farmington Academy, married Mary Simpson Hein on 20 Nov 1870. One daughter. Died on 23 Apr 1921 in Richmond, VA. Buried in Arlington National Cemetery.

Ranks Act. 3rd Asst.Engr. (8 Feb 1862); 3rd Asst.Engr. (20 May 1864); placed on Ret.Lst. (29 Dec 1865); restored to Active List (26 Jan 1866); 2nd Asst.Engr. (1 Jan 1868); PAsst.Engr. (29 Oct 1879); Chief Engr. (7 Oct 1892); Cdr (3 Mar 1899); Capt (4 Jan 1903); retired with rank of RAdm (9 Feb 1903).

Career Summary Received appointment from DC (8 Feb 1862); *Monticello*, James River Flot. (Feb-Aug 1862); Naval Hosp., NY (Aug-Sep 1862); *Ossipee*, N.Atl.Blk.Sqdn. (Oct-Dec 1862); *Genesee*, N.Atl. and W.Gulf Blk.Sqdns. (Dec 1862-Jul 1864); *Manhattan*, W.Gulf Blk.Sqdn. (Jul-Nov 1864); *Winnipec*, Navy Yard, Boston (Nov 1864-Sep 1865); sick lv. (Sep-Dec 1865); placed on Ret.Lst. (29 Dec 1865); restored to Active List (26 Jan 1866); w.o. (Jan-Apr 1866); *Shamrock*, Eur.Sta. (April 1866-July 1868); waiting orders (Jul-Sep 1868); *Nipsic*, Isthmian Canal Surv.Expd. (Oct 1868-Jul 1869); w.o. (Jul-Oct 1869);

Miantonomoh, spec.serv. and N.Atl.Sqdn. (Oct 1869-Jul 1870); w.o. (Jul-Sep 1870); l.o.a. (Sep-Dec 1870); Navy Yard, Washington, DC (Dec 1870-Feb 1872); *Powhatan,* N.Atl.Sta. (Feb 1872-Aug 1874); w.o. (Aug 1874-Jan 1875); Navy Yard, Washington, DC (Jan 1875-Sep 1876); Bur. of Steam Engineering, Washington, DC (Sep 1876-Mar 1882); *Iroquois,* Pac.Sta. (Apr 1882-Jul 1885); home and w.o. (Jul 1885-Mar 1886); *Puritan,* Navy Yard, League Island, PA (Apr-Aug 1886); Bur. of Nav., Washington, DC (Aug 1886-Apr 1887); temp. duty, *Atlanta,* on trials (Apr-Jun 1887); *Chicago,* Chester, PA (Jun-Dec 1887); w.o. (Dec 1887-May 1888); Navy Yard, Mare Island, CA (May 1888-Jan 1889); *Mohican,* Pac.Sta. (Jan 1889); *Vandalia,* Pac.Sta. (Jan-Mar 1889); Navy Yard, Mare Island, CA (May-Sep 1889); chief engr., sta. ship, *Nipsic,* Apia, Samoa (Oct 1889-Oct 1890); l.o.a. (Oct-Dec 1890); *Newark,* spec.serv. (Dec 1890-Dec 1891); Bur. of Steam Engineering, Washington, DC (Dec 1891-Jul 1894); *Bennington,* Pac.Sta. (Aug-Oct 1894); *Yorktown,* Asia.Sta. (Oct 1894-Dec 1897); Bur. of Steam Engineering, Washington, DC (Dec 1897-Jan 1900); insp. of machinery and ord., W. R. Trigg Company Works, Richmond, VA (Jan 1900-Jan 1903); insp. of machinery, Bath Iron Works, Bath, ME (Jan-Feb 1903); retired (9 Feb 1903).

References
Personal Papers: 50 items (1889-1913) in NHF,LC.

CLIFFORD HARDY WEST Born in Brooklyn, NY, on 10 Nov 1846, son of Edward Augustus and Ann (Pierce) West. Remained unmarried. Resided in Brooklyn, NY. Died in Washington, DC, on 2 Nov 1911. Buried in Brooklyn's Greenwood Cemetery.

Ranks Midn (21 Sep 1863); Ens (18 Dec 1868); Mstr (21 Mar 1870); Lt (21 Mar 1871); LCdr (31 Mar 1888); Cdr (11 Oct 1896); Capt (26 Sep 1901); retired (17 Jun 1902); RAdm on Ret.Lst. (13 Apr 1911) to rank from 17 Jun 1902.

Career Summary Received appointment from NY (21 Sep 1863); USNA (Sep 1863-Jun 1867); *Minnesota, Franklin, Kenosha* [renamed *Plymouth*], Eur.Sta. (Jul 1867-Apr 1870); signal duty, Washington, DC (May-Jul 1870); Signal Office, Washington, DC (Jul 1870-Oct 1871); *Wyoming,* W.Ind.Sta. (Oct 1871-Aug 1873); sick lv. (Aug-Oct 1873); ord. duty, Navy Yard, NY (Oct 1873-Jul 1875); *Frolic,* S.Atl.Sta. (Aug 1875-Oct 1877); w.o. (Oct-Nov 1877); ord. duty, Navy Yard, NY (Nov 1877-Nov 1879); *Alliance,* N.Atl.Sta. (Jan 1880-Jun 1881); exec.off., *Alliance,* the *Jeanette* Search Expd., and N.Atl.Sta. (Jun 1881-Jun 1883); ord. duty, Navy Yard, NY (Jun-Jul 1883); asst.insp., 3rd L.h. Dist., Tompkinsville, NY (Jul 1883-Sep 1885); cdr, L.h. steamer, *Madrono* (Sep 1885-Jan 1886); asst.insp., 3rd L.h. Dist., Tompkinsville, NY (Jan-Oct 1886); on staff, Asia.Sta., *Brooklyn, Marion,* and *Omaha* (Nov 1886-Jan 1890); ord. duty, Navy Yard, NY (May-Nov 1890); asst., 3rd L.h. Dist., Tompkinsville, NY (Nov 1890-Aug 1892); cdr, L.h. tender, *Columbine* (Aug 1892-May 1893); asst.insp., 3rd L.h. Dist., Tompkinsville, NY (Jun

CLIFFORD HARDY WEST
1846-1911

1893-Jul 1895); w.o. (Jul-Aug 1895); sick lv. (Aug 1895-Jun 1896); NWC (Jun-Oct 1896); aide to RAdm Montgomery Sicard, Navy Yard, NY (Oct 1896-May 1897); chief of staff, N.Atl.Sta., *New York* (May 1897-Apr 1898); insp., *Princeton*, Navy Yard, Philadelphia (Apr-May 1898); cdr, *Princeton*, N.Atl.Flt. (May 1898-Jan 1899); cdr, *Princeton*, Asia.Sta. (Jan-Aug 1899); home and w.o. (Aug-Oct 1899); aide to RAdm John W. Philip and RAdm Albert Smith Barker, Navy Yard, NY (Oct 1899-Jun 1900); retired (17 Jun 1902).

WILLIAM HENRY WHITING
1843-1925

WILLIAM HENRY WHITING   Born in NY City on 8 Jul 1843, son of William Henry and Mary Jane (Christian) Whiting. Survived by his widow and a daughter, died at his home in Berkeley, CA, on 26 Jul 1925.

Ranks   Act.Midn (21 Sep 1860); title changed to Midn (16 Jul 1862); Act.Ens (1 Oct 1863); designation "Act." discontinued (21 Dec 1865); Mstr (10 May 1866); Lt (21 Feb 1867); LCdr (12 Mar 1868); Cdr (12 Jul 1882); Capt (19 Jun 1897); RAdm (11 Oct 1903); placed on Ret.Lst. (8 Jul 1905).

Career Summary   Received appointment from WI (21 Sep 1860); USNA (Sep 1860-Sep 1863); flgs., *Hartford*, W.Gulf Blk.Sqdn. (Oct 1863-Dec 1864); l.o.a. and w.o. (Dec 1864-Mar 1865); *Kearsarge, Frolic,* and *Ticonderoga,* Eur.Sqdn. (Mar 1865-Apr 1869); w.o. and l.o.a. (Apr-Nov 1869); *Swatara,* N.Atl.Sta. (Nov 1869-Dec 1871); l.o.a. (Dec 1871-Aug 1872); *Benicia,* N.Pac.Sta. (Aug 1872-Dec 1874); spec. duty, court of king of HI (Dec 1874-Feb 1875); *Benicia,* N.Pac.Sta. (Feb-Aug 1875); l.o.a. (Aug-Dec 1875); Navy Yard, NY (Dec 1875-May 1876); torp. instruction, Newport, RI (Jun-Sept 1876); l.o.a. (Sep 1876-Jan 1878); exec.off., *Constitution,* spec.serv. (Jan 1878-Jul 1879); w.o. (Jul-Nov 1879); l.o.a. (Nov 1879-Jan 1881); Navy Yard, NY (Jan 1881-Jan 1884); cdr, training ship, *Saratoga* (Jan 1884-Jun 1886); w.o. (Jun-Aug 1886); Navy Yard, NY (Aug 1886-Oct 1889); cdr, *Kearsarge,* N.Atl.Sta. (Oct-Nov 1889); l.o.a. (Nov 1889-Feb 1890); Navy Yard, NY (Feb 1890-Oct 1892); cdr, *Alliance,* Pac. Sta. (Oct 1892-Oct 1893); l.o.a. (Oct 1893-Jan 1894); comdt., Navy Yard, Pensacola, FL (Jan 1894-Jul 1896); comdt., Naval Sta., Puget Sound, WA (Aug 1896-Jun 1897); cdr, *Monadnock,* Pac.Sta. (Jun 1897-Dec 1898); cdr, *Charleston,* Asia.Sta. (Dec 1898-May 1899); cdr, *Boston,* Asia.Sta. (May-Jul 1899); home, l.o.a., and w.o. (Jul 1899-Feb 1900); capt.yd., Navy Yard, Mare Island, CA (Feb-Mar 1900); cdr, rec. ship, *Independence,* Mare Island, CA (Mar 1900-Jul 1902); comdt., Naval Sta., Honolulu, Territory of HI (Aug 1902-Jun 1903); Training Sta., San Francisco (Jun 1903-Jul 1905); placed on Ret.Lst. (8 Jul 1905).

Career Highlights   Attached to RAdm David G. Farragut's flgs., the *Hartford*, from late 1863, participating in the Battle of Mobile Bay. Received an honorable mention from Farragut for burning a Confederate blockade runner underneath the fire of Fort Morgan. Also hauled down the Confederate flag at Fort Gaines and replaced it with the Union flag on 8 Aug 1864. Commanded the *Monadnock* during the war with Spain, sailing her from San Francisco to Manila under adverse conditions for which he and his crew were commended by the sec. of the navy.

References

Personal papers: 500 items (1731-1952) in NHF,LC.

GEORGE FRANCIS FAXON WILDE Born in Braintree, MA, on 23 Feb 1845, son of William Read and Mary Elizabeth (Thayer) Wilde. Married Emogene B. Howard on 13 Dec 1868. Resided in North Easton, MA, where he died on 3 Dec 1911 and where he was buried.

**GEORGE FRANCIS FAXON
WILDE
1845-1911**

Ranks Act.Midn (30 Nov 1861); title changed to Midn (16 Jul 1862); Ens (1 Nov 1866); Mstr (1 Dec 1866); Lt (12 Mar 1868); LCdr (26 Jun 1869); Cdr (2 Oct 1885); Capt (10 Aug 1898); RAdm (6 Aug 1904); retired (20 Feb 1905).

Career Summary Received appointment from MA (30 Nov 1861); USNA (Nov 1861-Nov 1864); l.o.a. (Nov 1864-Feb 1865); rec. ship, *Vermont*, NY (Feb-Mar 1865); *Susquehanna*, and *Nipsic*, S.Atl.Sqdn. (Mar 1865-Oct 1867); w.o. (Oct-Dec 1867); *Kearsarge*, Navy Yard, Boston (Jan 1868); w.o. (Jan-Mar 1868); flgs., *Contoocook* [renamed *Albany*], N.Atl.Sqdn. (Mar 1868-Jan 1870); w.o. (Jan-Feb 1870); ord. duty, Navy Yard, Boston (Feb-Dec 1870); *Tennessee*, spec.serv. (Jan-Apr 1871); w.o. (Apr-Sep 1871); flgs., *Wabash*, and *Plymouth*, Eur.Sta. (Oct 1871-Jun 1873); w.o. (Jun-Sep 1873); ord. duty, Navy Yard, Boston (Sep 1873-Jan 1874); exec.off., *Canonicus*, N.Atl.Sta. (Jan-Dec 1874); w.o. (Dec 1874-May 1875); Torp.Sta., Newport, RI (Jun-Oct 1875); Navy Yard, Boston (Oct 1875-Jan 1879); exec.off., *Vandalia*, N.Atl.Sta. (Jan 1879-Nov 1881); w.o. (Nov 1881-Jan 1882); Navy Yard, Boston (Jan 1882-Nov 1883); asst., then insp., 7th L.h. Dist., Pensacola, FL (Nov 1883-Oct 1885); s.a. and w.o. (Oct 1885-Nov 1886); cdr, *Dolphin*, N.Atl.Sta. (Nov 1886-Oct 1888); insp., 2nd L.h. Dist., Boston (Nov 1888-Nov 1893); s.a. and w.o. (Nov 1893-May 1894); torp. instruction, Newport, RI (Jun-Aug 1894); sec., L.h. Bd., Washington, DC (Aug 1894-Mar 1898); cdr, *Katahdin*, N.Atl.Patrol Sqdn. (Mar-Sep 1898); cdr, *Boston*, Asia.Flt. (Nov 1898-May 1899); cdr, *Oregon*, Asia.Sqdn. (May 1899-Jan 1901); home and w.o. (Jan-Apr 1901); Navy Yard, Boston (May 1901); NWC (Jun-Sep 1901); capt.yd., Navy Yard, Portsmouth, NH (Sep 1901-May 1903); NWC (Jun 1903); capt.yd., Navy Yard, Boston (Jun 1903-Feb 1904); comdt., Navy Yard, League Island, PA (Feb-May 1904); comdt., Navy Yard, Boston (May 1904-Feb 1905); retired (20 Feb 1905).

Career Summary Commanded the *Dolphin* in the 1880s, the first U.S. steel vessel to circumnavigate the globe. As cdr of the *Boston*, was the first to land the marines in China where they then marched overland in 1899 to Peking to guard the U.S. legation. As cdr of the *Oregon* in the P.I., took several towns from the insurrectionists before handing them over to the army, receiving thanks from the Spanish government in rescuing nearly 160 Spanish officers and their families.

FRANK WILDES Born in Boston on 17 Jun 1843, son of

**FRANK WILDES
1843-1903**

Solomon Lovell and Sophia (Rice) Wildes. Married Lucy A. Smith on 1 Jan 1872. Died on 7 Feb 1903 on board the steamer SS *China* off San Francisco.

Ranks Act.Midn (21 Sep 1860); title changed to Midn (16 Jul 1862); Ens (28 May 1863); Mstr (10 Nov 1866); Lt (10 Nov 1866); LCdr (12 Mar 1868); Cdr (1 Apr 1880); Capt (31 Jul 1894); RAdm (9 Oct 1901); died (7 Feb 1903).

Career Summary Received appointment from MA (21 Sep 1860); USNA (Sep 1860-May 1863); *Lackawanna*, and *Chickasaw*, W.Gulf Blk.Sqdn. (Jun 1863-Jul 1865); w.o. (Jul-Sep 1865); *Monadnock*, and *Vanderbilt*, Pac.Sqdn. (Oct 1865-Feb 1867); *Suwanee*, Pac.Sta. (Feb 1867-Jul 1868); *Pensacola*, Pac.Sta. (Jul-Sep 1868); w.o. (Oct-Dec 1868); rec. ship, *Ohio*, Boston (Dec 1868-Jan 1869); flgs., *Franklin*, Eur.Sta. (Jan 1869-Nov 1871); w.o. (Nov 1871-Jan 1872); Navy Yard, Boston (Jan 1872-Aug 1873); exec.off., *Wyoming*, N.Atl.Sta. (Aug 1873-Apr 1874); exec.off., *Wachusett*, N.Atl.Sta. (Apr-Dec 1874); w.o. (Dec 1874-May 1875); torp. school, Newport, RI (Jun-Oct 1875); w.o. (Oct 1875-May 1876); exec.off., *Dictator*, Port Royal, SC (May 1876-Jun 1877); w.o. (Jun-Dec 1877); spec. ord. duty, West Point Foundry, Cold Spring, NY (Jan 1878-Apr 1881); w.o. (Apr 1881-Nov 1882); cdr, *Yantic*, N.Atl.Sta. (Nov 1882-Sep 1885); Navy Yard, Portsmouth, NH (Oct 1885-Nov 1888); w.o. (Nov 1888-Mar 1889); insp., 1st L.h. Dist., Portland, ME (Mar 1889-Sep 1892); cdr, *Yorktown*, spec.serv. (Oct 1892-Jul 1893); l.o.a. and w.o. (Jul-Aug 1893); equip.off., Navy Yard, Norfolk, VA (Oct 1893-Nov 1894); w.o. (Nov 1894-Jan 1895); cdr, rec. ship, *Independence*, Mare Island, CA (Feb-Nov 1895); cdr, *Boston*, Asia.Sta. (Nov 1895-Nov 1898); home and w.o. (Nov 1898-Feb 1899); Navy Yard, NY (Feb-Apr 1899); capt.yd., Navy Yard, NY (Apr 1899-Oct 1901); comdt., Navy Yard, Pensacola, FL (Dec 1901-Jan 1902); cdr., Junior Sqdn., Asia.Sta., *Kentucky*, then *Rainbow* (Mar 1902-Jan 1903); w.o. (Jan-Feb 1903); died (7 Feb 1903).

Career Summary Fresh from the USNA, joined the *Lackawanna*, thus participating in the Battle of Mobile Bay in Aug 1864. During the Spanish-American War, took part in the Battle of Manila on 1 May 1898 as cdr of the *Boston*. Was present for the surrender of the City of Manila. He then took the *Boston* to China in order to put the guards at Peking and Tientsin. Was promoted five numbers in rank for eminent and conspicuous conduct in battle.

CLARENCE STEWART WILLIAMS Born in Springfield, OH, on 7 Oct 1863, son of Orson Bennett and Pamela (Floyd) Williams. Married Anna Marie Miller on 6 Jun 1888. One son. Resided in Charlottesville, VA, where he died on 24 Oct 1951. Buried in Arlington National Cemetery.

Ranks Naval Cadet (25 Sep 1880); Ens (1 Jul 1886); Ltjg (10 May 1895); Lt (27 May 1898); LCdr (4 Feb 1904); Cdr (1 Jul 1908); Capt (1 Jul 1911); temp. RAdm (15 Oct 1917); RAdm (16 Dec 1918); temp. VAdm (1 Jul 1919); placed on Ret.Lst.

CLARENCE STEWART WILLIAMS
1863-1951

with rank of RAdm (7 Oct 1927); VAdm on Ret.Lst. (21 Jun 1930); Adm on Ret.Lst. (16 Jun 1942).

Career Summary Received appointment from OH (25 Sep 1880); USNA (Sep 1880-Jun 1884); *Hartford,* Pac.Sta. (Jul 1884-Feb 1886); home and to exam. (Feb-Jun 1886); w.o. (Jun-Jul 1886); cst.surv. duty (Jul-Oct 1886); sick lv. (Oct 1886-Apr 1887); *Ossipee,* N.Atl.Sta. (Apr 1887-Nov 1889); USNA (Nov 1889-Jun 1893); *Charleston,* spec.serv. and Asia.Sta. (Jun 1893-Jul 1896); home and l.o.a. (Jul-Aug 1896); USNA (Aug 1896-Mar 1898); *Gwin,* Bristol, RI (Mar-Apr 1898); cdr, *Gwin,* N.Atl.Flt. and USNA (Apr 1898-Feb 1899); *Marblehead,* Pac.Sqdn. (Feb 1899-Apr 1900); *Iroquois,* Marine Hosp.Serv. (May-Aug 1900); *Iowa,* Pac.Sqdn. (Aug 1900-Jun 1901); torp. instruction, Newport, RI (Jun-Aug 1901); USNA (Sep 1901-Jun 1903); *Solace,* spec. serv. (Jun-Aug 1903); exec.off., *Monterey,* Asia.Sta. (Aug 1903-Mar 1904); Naval Hosps., Yokohama, Japan, and Mare Island, CA (Mar-Apr 1904); sick lv. (Apr-Nov 1904); compass office, Bur. of Equip. and Recruiting, Washington, DC (Nov-Dec 1904); training ship, *Prairie* (Dec 1904-Jun 1905); *Massachusetts,* N.Atl.Sqdn. (Jun-Aug 1905); *Iowa,* N.Atl.Sqdn. (Aug 1905-Oct 1907); duty, Gen Bd., Navy Dept., Washington, DC (Oct 1907-Mar 1910); cdr, *Albany,* Pac. and Asia.Flts. (Apr 1910-Aug 1911); home and w.o. (Aug-Sep 1911); Navy Yard, Washington, DC (Oct 1911); member, bd. of inspection and surv., Washington, DC (Oct 1911-Dec 1912); cdr, *Rhode Island,* Atl.Flt. (Dec 1912-Jan 1915); NWC (Jan 1915-Nov 1916); chief of staff, Battleship Force, Atl.Flt., *Wyoming* (Dec 1916-Aug 1917); chief of staff, Battleship Force 2, *Arkansas* (Aug 1917-Aug 1918); cdr, Div. 8, Battleship Force 2, Atl.Flt., *New Mexico* (Aug 1918-Feb 1919); cdr, Div. 1, Pac.Flt., *Chicago,* on detached duty to S.Atl. (Feb-May 1919); chief of staff, NWC (May-Jul 1919); cdr, Sqdn. 1, and Div. 1, Pac.Flt., *Rhode Island* (Jul-Oct 1919); cdr, Battleship Sqdn. 1, and Div. 1, Pac.Flt., *Vermont* (Oct 1919-Jun 1920); cdr, Sqdn. 4, Div. 8, Pac.Flt., then cdr, Battleship Force, Pac.Flt., *New York* (Jun 1920-Jun 1921); dir. of war plans, Office of Naval Operations, Navy Dept., and member, Army-Navy Joint Bd., Washington, DC (Jul 1921-Oct 1922); pres., NWC (Oct 1922-Sep 1925); cdr, Asia.Flt., *Pittsburgh* (Sep 1925-Oct 1927); placed on Ret.Lst. (7 Oct 1927).

Career Highlights One of the senior ranking officers during World War I, and pres. of the NWC, received the Distinguished Service Medal, the Spanish Campaign Medal, Cuban Pacification Medal, the Mexican Campaign Medal, the Victory Medal, and the Yangtze Service Medal.

THOM WILLIAMSON Born on 5 Aug 1833 in Edenton, NC, son of William Price and Penelope Benbury (McDonald) Williamson. His father was the navy's chief engr. from 1842 to 1861 before becoming chief engr. for the Confederate navy and being responsible for raising the USS *Merrimack* and converting her into the CSS *Virginia.* Educated at the Norfolk (VA) Military Academy and at St. Mary's College in Baltimore to 1850. Married

Julia Price on 2 Dec 1861. Six children. Residing in Annapolis, he died in Baltimore on 17 Mar 1918. Buried in USNA Cemetery, Annapolis.

Ranks 3rd Asst.Engr. (21 May 1853); 2nd Asst.Engr. (27 Jun 1855); 1st Asst.Engr. (21 Jul 1858); Chief Engr. (5 Aug 1861); Chief Engr. with rel. rank of Capt (30 Jan 1889); placed on Ret.Lst. (5 Aug 1895); Chief Engr. with rank of RAdm on Ret.Lst. (29 Jun 1906).

Career Summary Received appointment from VA (21 May 1853); *Saranac*, Med.Sqdn. (May 1853-Jun 1856); l.o.a. and w.o. (Jun-Dec 1856); spec. duty, *Powhatan*, Norfolk, VA (Dec 1856-Jun 1857); cst.surv. duty (Jun-Jul 1857); flgs., *Wabash*, Home Sqdn. (Aug 1857-Mar 1858); *Despatch*, spec.serv. (Mar 1858-Apr 1859); *Lancaster*, Pac.Sqdn. (Apr 1859-Aug 1861); w.o. (Aug-Oct 1861); spec. duty, Mystic, CT (Oct 1861-Feb 1863); member, bd. of examiners (Feb-Oct 1863); flgs., *Hartford*, W.Gulf Blk.Sqdn. (Oct 1863-Dec 1864); l.o.a. (Dec 1864-Jan 1865); spec. duty, NY (Jan 1865-Mar 1867); *Richmond*, spec.serv. (Mar-Sep 1867); head, dept. of steam engineering, USNA (Oct 1867-Aug 1869); flt. engr., N.Atl.Sqdn., *Severn* (Aug 1869-May 1871); l.o.a. and w.o. (May-Aug 1871); Navy Yard, Portsmouth, NH (Sep 1871-Mar 1874); w.o. (Mar-Apr 1874); flt.engr., S.Atl.Sta., *Lancaster* (Apr 1874-Aug 1875), then *Brooklyn* (Aug 1875-Feb 1876); member, bd. of examiners (Feb-Apr 1876); in charge of stores, engineering dept., Navy Yard, Portsmouth, NH (May 1876-Jul 1879); flt. engr., N.Atl.Sta., *Powhatan* (Jul-Dec 1879), then *Tennessee* (Dec 1879-Sep 1881); Navy Yard, Norfolk, VA (Sep 1881-Nov 1884); flt.engr., Pac.Sta., *Hartford* (Jan 1885-Jan 1887); w.o. (Jan-Jul 1887); supt., State, War, and Navy Building, Washington, DC (Aug 1887-Aug 1895); transferred to Ret.Lst. (5 Aug 1895); member, bd. for Naval Observatory, Washington, DC (Jun 1898-Jan 1899); spec. duty, Navy Yard and Navy Dept., Washington, DC (Oct 1901-Jun 1912).

Career Highlights Offered but declined a commission from the Confederacy in 1861 to which his father had sided. Became senior engineering officer under RAdm David Farragut's sqdn. in the action at Mobile Bay.

References
Personal Papers: 1 ft (1853-1912) in Old Dominion Univ. Archives, Norfolk, VA.

ALBERT BOWER WILLITS Born in Philadelphia on 7 Mar 1851, son of Alphonso Albert and Eliza Jane (Street) Willits. Married Anna Bain White on 28 Sep 1876. Three daughters. His home was in Philadelphia, dying at the Naval Hosp. there on 7 Jan 1926.

Ranks Cadet Engr. (1 Oct 1872); Asst.Engr. (26 Feb 1875); PAsst.Engr. (12 Oct 1881); Chief Engr. (28 Mar 1896); LCdr (3 Mar 1899); Cdr (11 Oct 1903); Capt (28 Jan 1908); RAdm (14 Sep 1911); placed on Ret.Lst. (7 Mar 1913).

Career Summary Received appointment from PA (1 Oct 1872); USNA (Oct 1872-May 1874); *Brooklyn*, S.Atl.Sqdn. (Jun

1874-May 1875); home and w.o. (May-Nov 1875); *Montauk*, Navy Yard, Philadelphia (Nov 1875-Jul 1876); spec. duty with ironclads, Navy Yard, League Island, PA (Jul 1876-Apr 1877); w.o. (Apr 1877-Mar 1878); *Adams*, Pac.Sta. (Mar 1878-Jul 1879); l.o.a. (Jul-Dec 1879); w.o. (Dec 1879-Feb 1880); *Powhatan*, spec. duty (Feb 1880-Jan 1883); w.o. (Jan-Mar 1883); Navy Yard, Norfolk, VA (Mar 1883-May 1885); *Hartford*, Pac. Sta. (Jun 1885-Jan 1887); Navy Yard, Mare Island, CA (Jan-Apr 1887); l.o.a. (Apr-Jun 1887); rec. ship, *Franklin*, Norfolk, VA (Jun 1887-Feb 1888); *Pensacola*, N.Atl.Sta. (Mar 1888-Jul 1889); *Yorktown*, Eur.Sta. (Jul 1889-Jun 1890); *Boston*, S.Atl.Sqdn. (Jun 1890-Jan 1891); l.o.a. (Jan-Apr 1891); asst. insp. of machinery, William Cramp and Sons Iron Works, Philadelphia (Apr 1891-Dec 1894); *Minneapolis*, N.Atl.Sta. and spec. duty (Dec 1894-Oct 1896); *Marblehead*, N.Atl.Sta. (Oct 1896-Oct 1897); insp. of steel, Thurlow, PA (Oct 1897-May 1898); asst. to chief, Bur. of Steam Engineering, Washington, DC (May 1898-Feb 1901); flt. engr., Pac.Sta., *Iowa* (Mar 1901-Jan 1903), then *Newark* (Jan-Oct 1903); home and w.o. (Oct-Nov 1901); l.o.a. (Nov-Dec 1903); asst. head, dept. of steam engineering, Navy Yard, Norfolk, VA (Jan-Mar 1904); insp. of machinery, Philadelphia (Mar-Dec 1904); head, dept. of steam engineering, Navy Yard, Norfolk, VA (Dec 1904-Apr 1908); insp. of machinery, Camden, NJ (Apr 1908-Apr 1911); spec.temp. duty, Navy Dept., Washington, DC (Apr-Dec 1911); dir. of navy yards, Navy Dept., Washington, DC (Dec 1911-Dec 1912); spec. duty, Navy Dept., Washington, DC (Dec 1912-Feb 1913); placed on Ret.Lst. (7 Mar 1913); insp. of machinery, Bayonne, NJ (Jul 1917-Jun 1919).

References

Writings: a) "Gas *vs.* Steam for Marine Motive Power," U.S. Naval Institute *Proceedings* 128 (Dec 1908): 1099-1127. b) "Some Notes on Parsons Turbine Construction," U.S. Naval Institute *Proceedings* 131 (Sep 1909): 730-47. c) "Notes on Inspection Duty at Shipbuilding Works," U.S. Naval Institute *Proceedings* 144 (Dec 1912): 1275-1300. d) "The Safety and Welfare of the Workman," U.S. Naval Institute *Proceedings* 153 (Sep-Oct 1914): 1351-63.

GEORGE SIDNEY WILLITS Born in Philadelphia on 21 Feb 1853, son of George Sidney and Elizabeth (Githens) Willits. Attended Rutgers College in New Brunswick, NJ, prior to his appointment. Married Sylvia B. Gaston on 3 Aug 1876. Five children. Resided in Philadelphia. Died in Woodbury, NJ, on 3 May 1917.

Ranks Cadet Engr. (1 Oct 1873); Asst.Engr. (1 Jul 1877); PAsst.Engr. (1 Jul 1885); resigned (10 Jan 1890); resignation revoked (23 Aug 1890); PAsst.Engr. with rel. rank of Ltjg (1 Oct 1893); Chief Engr. (4 Jul 1896); rank changed to LCdr (3 Mar 1899); Cdr (13 Sep 1904); Capt (1 Jul 1908); RAdm (26 Mar 1913); placed on Ret.Lst. (21 Feb 1915).

Career Summary Received appointment from PA (1 Oct 1873); USNA (Oct 1873-Jun 1875); w.o. (Jun-Nov 1875); *Hartford*, Navy Yard, NY (Nov-Dec 1875); *Vandalia*, Eur.Sqdn.

GEORGE SIDNEY WILLITS
1853-1917

(Dec 1875-Aug 1876); w.o. (Aug-Oct 1876); *Huron,* Naval Sta., Port Royal, SC (Oct 1876-Mar 1877); Navy Yard, NY (Mar-Jul 1877); Navy Yard, Boston (Jul 1877-Apr 1878); *Enterprise,* spec.serv. (Apr 1878-May 1880); w.o. (May-Jun 1880); despatch ship, *Tallapoosa* (Jun 1880-May 1881); temp. duty, *Speedwell,* Navy Yard, Washington, DC (May-Jul 1881); w.o. (Jul-Dec 1881); spec. duty, Franklin Institute, Philadelphia (Dec 1881-Nov 1884); w.o. (Nov-Dec 1884); *Marion,* Asia.Sta. (Jan 1885-Apr 1886); *Monocacy,* Asia.Sta. (Apr 1886); *Trenton,* Asia.Sta. (Apr-Sep 1886); l.o.a. (Sep-Oct 1886); w.o. (Oct 1886-May 1887); *Boston,* spec.serv. (May 1887-Sep 1889); spec. duty, Pratt Institute, Brooklyn, NY (Sep 1889-Jan 1890); resigned (10 Jan 1890); resignation revoked (23 Aug 1890); w.o. (Aug-Sep 1890); USNA (Sep 1890-Jan 1891); William Cramp and Sons Iron Works, Philadelphia (Jan-Apr 1891); *Marion,* Pac.Sta. (Apr-May 1891); l.o.a. (May-Sep 1891); *Boston,* Pac.Sta. (Sep 1891-Nov 1893); rec. ship, *Independence,* Mare Island, CA (Nov 1893-Jan 1894); *Monterey,* Pac.Sta. (Jan-Aug 1894); l.o.a. (Aug-Nov 1894); American Steel Casting Company, Thurlow, PA (Nov 1894-Oct 1897); *Marblehead,* N.Atl.Sta., and spec.serv. (Oct 1897-Apr 1900); *Solace,* spec.serv. (Apr-Sep 1900); insp. duty, Bur. of Steam Engineering, Harrisburg, PA, Dist. (Oct 1900-Jun 1901); insp. of machinery, Midvale Steel Works, Nicetown, PA (Jul 1901-Apr 1903); *Baltimore,* N.Atl.Flt. (Apr 1903-Mar 1904); flt.engr., N.Atl.Flt., *Kearsarge* (Mar-Sep 1904); home and w.o. (Sep-Dec 1904); insp. of machinery, Philadelphia (Dec 1904-Nov 1905); insp. of machinery, NY Shipbuilding Company, Camden, NJ (Nov 1905-Apr 1905); insp. of boiler works, Ossining, NY, and insp. of machinery, Bayonne, NJ (May-Sep 1908); head, dept. of steam engineering, Navy Yard, Puget Sound, WA (Sep 1908-Oct 1909); insp. of engine material, Midvale Steel Works, Nicetown, PA, and Central PA and Western NY Dists. (Nov 1909-Feb 1915); placed on Ret.Lst. (21 Feb 1915); insp. of engineering material, Chester, PA, Dist. (Apr 1917).

FLETCHER ALOYSIUS WILSON   Born in Nottingham, England, on 7 Feb 1836. Remaining a bachelor, he died on 8 Sep 1907 in Asmeres, France.

Ranks   3rd Asst.Engr. (26 Aug 1859); 2nd Asst.Engr. (21 Oct 1861); 1st Asst.Engr. (1 Oct 1863); Chief Engr. (5 Mar 1871); Chief Engr. with rel. rank of Cdr (10 Nov 1890); Chief Engr. with rel. rank of Capt (5 Jun 1896); placed on Ret.Lst. (7 Feb 1898); Chief Engr. with rank of RAdm on Ret.Lst. (29 Jun 1906).

Career Summary   Received appointment from NY (26 Aug 1859); w.o. (Aug-Sep 1859); *Saranac,* Pac.Sqdn. (Oct 1859-Oct 1861); flgs., *Hartford,* W.Gulf Blk.Sqdn. (Oct 1861-Dec 1864); l.o.a. (Dec 1864-Jan 1865); *Wyoming,* spec.serv. (Jan-May 1865); w.o. (May-Jun 1865); *Hartford,* Asia.Sqdn. (Jun 1865-Aug 1868); w.o. (Aug-Oct 1868); *Neshaminy,* Navy Yard, NY (Oct-Nov 1868); w.o. (Nov-Dec 1868); *Richmond,* Eur.Sqdn. (Jan 1869-Nov 1871); w.o. (Nov-Dec 1871); exam. and w.o. (Jan-May 1872); *Michigan,* on Great Lakes (Jun 1872-May 1874); member, bd. of

FLETCHER ALOYSIUS WILSON
1836-1907

examiners (Jun-Jul 1874); w.o. (Jul-Oct 1874); member, bd. of examiners (Oct 1874); *Baltimore*, spec.serv. (Oct 1874-Apr 1875); *Tennessee*, spec.serv. (Apr-Jun 1875); *Swatara*, N.Atl.Sta. (Jun 1875-Aug 1877); w.o. (Aug 1877-Jul 1878); in charge, engineering stores, Navy Yard, Boston (Jul 1878-Sep 1881); *Vandalia*, N.Atl.Sta. (Sep 1881-Oct 1884); w.o. (Oct-Nov 1884); spec. duty, Waltham, MA (Nov-Dec 1884); w.o. (Dec 1884-Feb 1885); temp. duty, Navy Yard, Boston (Feb-Apr 1885); w.o. (Apr-May 1885); spec. duty, Buffalo, NY (Jun-Oct 1885); w.o. (Oct 1885-Dec 1887); insp. of machinery, new cruisers, San Francisco (Dec 1887-Oct 1890); *San Francisco*, Spec.Serv.Sqdn. (Nov 1890-Mar 1891); *Charleston*, Pac. and Asia.Sqdns. (Mar 1891-Sep 1892); *San Francisco*, spec.serv. (Sep 1892-Oct 1893); l.o.a. (Oct-Dec 1893); member, experimental bd., Navy Yard, NY (Jan-Apr 1894); insp. of machinery, Union Iron Works, San Francisco (May 1894-Jan 1898); home and w.o. (Jan-Feb 1898); placed on Ret.Lst. (7 Feb 1898).

HENRY BRAID WILSON Born in Camden, NJ, on 23 Feb 1861, son of Henry B. and Mary A. Wilson. Married to Ada Chapman Wilson. One daughter and one son. Resided in NY City where he died on 30 Jan 1954. Buried in Arlington National Cemetery.

Ranks Cadet Midn (11 Sep 1876); Ensjg (1 Jul 1883); Ens (26 Jun 1884); Ltjg (2 Feb 1894); Lt (16 Sep 1897); LCdr (3 Mar 1903); Cdr (12 Jul 1907); Capt (4 Mar 1911); RAdm (1 Jul 1917); temp. VAdm (25 Sep 1918); temp. Adm (30 Jun 1919); placed on Ret.Lst. with rank of RAdm (23 Feb 1925); Adm on Ret.Lst. (21 Jun 1930).

Career Summary Received appointment from NJ (11 Sep 1876); USNA (Sep 1876-Jun 1881); w.o. (Jun-Jul 1881); flgs., *Tennessee*, N.Atl.Sqdn. (Jul 1881-May 1883); USNA (May-Jun 1883); w.o. (Jun-Jul 1883); training ship, *Saratoga* (Jul 1883-Nov 1887); branch hydrographic office, Philadelphia (Nov 1887-Sep 1889); flgs., *New Hampshire*, Apprentice Training Sqdn., Newport, RI (Sep 1889); temp. duty, Bur. of Nav., Washington, DC (Sep 1889-Sep 1890); cst.surv. duty (Sep 1890-Jul 1891); Fish Commission steamer, *Albatross* (Jul 1891-Oct 1893); l.o.a. (Oct 1893-Mar 1894); NWC, and Torp.Sta., Newport, RI (Mar 1894-May 1896); *Michigan*, on Great Lakes (May-Aug 1896); *Bancroft*, Eur.Sqdn. and N.Atl.Flt. (Sep 1896-Sep 1898); *Indiana*, N.Atl.Flt. (Oct 1898-Sep 1899); home and w.o. (Sep 1899); equip. duty, William Cramp and Sons Iron Works, Philadelphia (Oct 1899-Apr 1901); temp. duty, *Solace*, spec.serv. (Apr-May 1901); exec. off., *Don Juan de Austria*, Asia.Sta. (May 1901-Jul 1902); navigator, then exec.off., flgs., *Kentucky*, Asia.Sta. (Jul 1902-Jun 1904); in charge, enlisted personnel section, Bur. of Nav., Washington, DC (Jun 1904-Apr 1908); cdr, *Chester*, training serv., and flt. review (Apr 1908-Dec 1909); member, bd. of inspection and surv., Washington, DC (Dec 1909); Bur. of Nav., Washington, DC (Dec 1909-May 1910); asst.chief, Bur. of Nav., Washington, DC (May 1910-Nov 1911); cdr, *North Dakota*, Atl.

HENRY BRAID WILSON
1861-1954

Flt. (Nov 1911-Nov 1913); pres., bd. of inspection and surv., Washington, DC (Nov 1913-May 1916); cdr, flgs., *Pennsylvania*, Atl.Flt. (Jun 1916-Mar 1917); cdr, Patrol Force, Atl.Flt., *Olympia* (Apr-Jun 1917), then *Raleigh* (Jun 1917), then *Columbia* (Jun-Aug 1917), then *Birmingham* (Aug-Oct 1917); spec. duty, London and Paris (Oct-Nov 1917); cdr, U.S. Naval Forces, Brest, France (Nov 1917-Jan 1918); cdr., U.S. Naval Forces, France, *Prometheus* (Jan 1918-Jan 1919); cdr., Sqdn. 4, Div. 8, Atl.Flt., *New Mexico* (Feb-Jun 1919); cdr., Atl.Flt., *Pennsylvania* (Jun 1919-Jun 1921); supt., USNA (Jul 1921-Feb 1925); placed on Ret.Lst. (23 Feb 1925).

Career Highlights One of the naval leaders during the First World War; commanded the Atl. Patrol Force in 1917, which escorted troop and supply ships and convoys to Europe. Thereafter he commanded naval forces on the French cst. and then throughout France. As supt. of the USNA, helped to transform the academy from a training school to a university authorized to award a bachelor of science degree.

References
Writings: a) *An Account of the Operations of the American Navy in France during the War with Germany* (n.p., 1919?). b) *Monuments* (s.l., s.n., 1921?).

WILLIAM AUGUSTUS WINDSOR Born in VA on 13 Feb 1842, son of Griffith and Eliza (Fouchee) Windsor. Educated in grammar and high schools in Baltimore, then studied engineering in the private school of Richard C. Potts in Baltimore and with the Baltimore and Ohio Railroad Company. Married Rachel Josephine Noble on 11 Jun 1874. Died at his home in NY City on 30 Aug 1907.

Ranks 3rd Asst.Engr. (16 Sep 1862); 2nd Asst.Engr. (1 Mar 1864); 1st Asst.Engr. (1 25 Jul 1866); title changed to PAsst. Engr. (24 Feb 1874); Chief Engr. with rel. rank of LCdr (17 Jun 1889); Chief Engr. with rel. rank of Cdr (26 Feb 1897); Cdr (3 Mar 1899); Capt (27 Dec 1901); placed on Ret.Lst. with rank of RAdm (16 Sep 1902).

WILLIAM AUGUSTUS WINDSOR
1842-1907

Career Summary Received appointment from MD (16 Sep 1862); w.o. (Sep-Oct 1862); *Miami*, W.Gulf and N.Atl.Blk.Sqdns. (Oct 1862-Sep 1863); sick lv. (Sep 1863-Jan 1864); spec. duty, Navy Yard, NY (Jan-May 1864); *Nyack*, and *Rhode Island*, N.Atl. Sta. (May 1864-Jan 1867); Navy Yard, League Island, PA (Jan-May 1867); *Franklin*, and *Ticonderoga*, Eur.Sqdn. (Jun 1867-Apr 1869); w.o. (Apr-Jun 1869); *Dictator*, N.Atl.Sta. (Jul 1869-Aug 1870); w.o. (Aug 1870); l.o.a. and w.o. (Aug 1870-Oct 1872); *Hartford*, Asia.Sta. (Nov 1872-Oct 1873); home and sick lv. (Oct 1873-Jul 1874); *Tennessee*, spec.serv. (Jul 1874); *Intrepid*, and *Alarm*, spec.serv. (Jul 1874-Jul 1876); w.o. (Jul-Nov 1876); *Ranger*, Navy Yard, Norfolk, VA (Nov 1876-Mar 1877); w.o. (Mar-Jul 1877); training ship, *Lehigh* (Jul-Aug 1877); w.o. (Aug-Oct 1877); ironclad duty, James River (Oct 1877-Mar 1878); *Plymouth*, N.Atl.Sta. (Mar 1878-May 1879); *Kearsarge*, N.Atl.Sta. (May 1879-Jun 1880); USNA (Jun 1880-Aug 1883);

Tennessee, N.Atl.Sta. (Sep 1883-Sep 1886); w.o. (Sep 1886-Mar 1887); Navy Yard, NY (Apr 1887-Nov 1889); *Dolphin*, spec.serv., N.Atl.Sta. (Nov 1889-Nov 1891); insp. of machinery, Iowa Iron Works, Dubuque, IA (Dec 1891-Jul 1894); *Minneapolis*, N.Atl. Sqdn. (Jul 1894-Mar 1896); flt.engr., Eur.Sqdn., *San Francisco* (Mar 1896-Mar 1897); *Cincinnati*, Eur.Sqdn. (Mar-Apr 1897); *Minneapolis*, Eur.Sqdn. (Apr 1897-Jan 1898); head, dept. of engineering, Navy Yard, NY (Jan 1898-Jun 1899); insp. of machinery, Crescent Ship Yard, Elizabeth, NJ (Jun 1899-Nov 1900); insp. of machinery, Babcock and Wilson Company, Bayonne, NJ (Nov 1900-Jul 1903); placed on Ret.Lst. (16 Sep 1902).

CAMERON MACRAE WINSLOW Born in Washington, DC, on 29 Jul 1854, son of navy Cdr Francis and Mary S. (Nelson) Winslow. A cousin was RAdm John A. Winslow, USN. Married Theodora Havemeyer on 18 Sep 1899. Seven children. Died on 2 Jan 1932 in Boston.

Ranks Cadet Midn (29 Sep 1870); Ens (18 Jul 1876); Mstr (21 Dec 1881); Ltjg (3 Mar 1883); Lt (1 Jul 1888); LCdr (3 Mar 1899); Cdr (11 Oct 1903); Capt (28 Jan 1908); RAdm (14 Sep 1911); temp. Adm (13 Sep 1915); placed on Ret.Lst. with rank of RAdm (29 Jul 1916).

Career Summary Received appointment at large (29 Sep 1870); USNA (Sep 1870-Jun 1875); *Tennessee*, Asia.Sta. (Jun 1875-Aug 1877); *Kearsarge*, Asia.Sta. (Aug 1877-Jan 1878); USNA (Jan 1878); training ship, *Constitution* (Feb 1878-Aug 1879); w.o. (Aug-Nov 1879); *Tennessee*, N.Atl.Sta. (Dec 1879-Jun 1881); w.o. (Jun-Aug 1881); cst.surv. duty (Aug 1881-Jul 1884); *Despatch*, spec.serv. (Jul 1884-Mar 1885); *Pensacola*, Eur.Sta. (Mar-Oct 1885); *Kearsarge*, Eur.Sta. (Oct 1885-Nov 1886); *Galena*, N.Atl.Sta. (Nov 1886-May 1887); torp. instruction, Newport, RI (Jun-Sep 1887); NWC (Sep-Dec 1887); Torp. Sta., Newport, RI (Dec 1887-Dec 1889); spec. duty, Torp. Boat #1, *Cushing*, Sqdn. of Evol. (Dec 1889-Nov 1891); w.o. (Nov 1891-Jan 1892); cdr, *Cushing*, Newport, RI (Jan-Dec 1892); w.o. (Dec 1892-Mar 1893); *Alliance*, Pac. and S.Atl.Stas. (Apr 1893-Jul 1894); l.o.a. (Jul 1894-Jan 1895); equip. duty, Navy Yard, NY (Jan 1895-Oct 1896); *Terror*, N.Atl.Sta. (Oct 1896-Aug 1897); *Nashville*, N.Atl.Flt. (Aug 1897-Sep 1898); *Indiana*, N.Atl.Flt. (Oct 1898-Jul 1899); staff member, N.Atl.Flt., *New York* (Jul-Oct 1899); home and w.o. (Oct-Dec 1899); court-martial duty, Navy Yard, NY (Dec 1899-Feb 1900); in charge, branch hydrographic office, NY (Feb 1900-Apr 1901); flag lt, N.Atl.Flt., *Kearsarge* (Apr 1901-Feb 1902); Bur. of Nav., Washington, DC (Mar 1902-Jul 1905); cdr, *Mayflower*, and naval aide, Pres. Roosevelt (Jul-Dec 1905); cdr, *Charleston*, spec. duty and Pac.Sta. (Dec 1905-Jun 1907); home and w.o. (Jun 1907); asst. chief, Bur. of Nav., Washington, DC (Jul 1907-May 1908); cdr, *New Hampshire*, N.Atl.Sta. (Mar 1908-Nov 1909); supervisor, NY Harbor (Nov 1909-Nov 1911); NWC (Nov-Dec 1911); cdr, 2nd Div., Atl.Flt., *Louisiana* (Dec 1911-Aug 1912); cdr, 3rd Div., Atl.Flt.,

CAMERON MACRAE WINSLOW
1854-1932

New Jersey, then *Virginia* (Aug 1912-Jan 1913); cdr, 1st Div., Atl.Flt., *Utah*, then *Florida* (Jan-Dec 1913); home and w.o. (Dec 1913-Jan 1914); temp. duty, Washington, DC, and NWC (Jan-Apr 1914); cdr, Spec.Serv.Sqdn., *New York* (Apr-Sep 1914); NWC (Sep 1914-Aug 1915); cdr, Pac.Flt., *San Diego* (Sep 1915-Jul 1916); placed on Ret.Lst. (29 Jul 1916); insp. of naval dists., Atl.cst., *Aloha* (Sep 1917-Oct 1919).

Career Highlights During the Spanish-American War while on the gunboat *Nashville*, led a boat expd. off Cienfuegos, Cuba, an action in which he was wounded and for which he was advanced five numbers in rank for this "extraordinary heroism." Served on the staffs of RAdm William T. Sampson and RAdm Francis J. Higginson, before becoming an aide to President Roosevelt. Commanded the Spec.Serv.Sqdn. during the Vera Cruz crisis. Came out of retirement during World War I to serve as inspector of naval districts on the Atl.cst., subsequently receiving the Navy Cross.

References
Personal Papers: a) NYHS. b) 20 items (1882-1911) in NWC, Naval Historical Collection, Newport, RI.

GEORGE FREDERICK WINSLOW
1842-1928

GEORGE FREDERICK WINSLOW Born in New Bedford, MA, on 8 May 1842, son of Giles and Elizabeth (Wilcox) Winslow. Received M.D. from Harvard Univ. in Mar 1864. On 14 Jan 1875, married Virginia Shearman. Three children. Died on 3 Sep 1928 at his home in New Bedford, MA.

Ranks Act.Asst.Surg. (26 Jul 1862); PAsst.Surg. (14 Jun 1867); Surg. (2 Apr 1875); Medl.Insp. (21 Aug 1893); Medl.Dir. (23 Jan 1898); retired with rank of RAdm (19 Jan 1903).

Career Summary Received appointment from MA (26 Jul 1862); *Morse*, N.Atl.Blk.Sqdn. (Aug 1862-Jan 1864); w.o. (Jan-Feb 1864); *Osceola*, N.Atl.Blk.Sqdn. (Feb 1864-Aug 1865); w.o. (Aug-Sep 1865); training ship, *Sabine* (Sep 1865-Jun 1867); w.o. (Jun-Jul 1867); *Wateree*, *Nyack*, and *Powhatan*, S.Pac.Sqdn. (Sep 1867-Dec 1869); w.o. (Dec 1869-Apr 1870); Navy Yard, Boston (Apr 1870-Jan 1871); Naval Hosp., Chelsea, MA (Jan-Apr 1871); *Saratoga*, spec.serv. (May-Sep 1871); flgs., *Wabash*, Eur.Sta. (Oct 1871-Apr 1874); w.o. (Apr-May 1874); l.o.a. (May-Aug 1874); w.o. (Aug-Nov 1874); rec. ship, *Sabine*, Portsmouth, NH (Nov 1874-Nov 1875); w.o. (Nov 1875-Apr 1876); Torp.Sta., Newport, RI (Apr 1876-Apr 1879); w.o. (Apr-May 1879); *Wachusett*, spec.serv. (May-Sep 1879); w.o. (Sep-Dec 1879); *Vandalia*, N.Atl.Sta. (Dec 1879-Jun 1882); Navy Yard, Boston (Jun 1882-Aug 1885); w.o. (Aug 1885-Mar 1886); *Atlanta*, N.Atl.Sta. (Jun 1886-Nov 1888); w.o. (Nov 1888-Sep 1889); Marine Rndv., Boston (Oct 1889-Aug 1891); Navy Yard, Norfolk, VA (Aug 1891-Jul 1892); w.o. (Jul 1892-Feb 1893); *Monterey*, Pac.Sta. (Feb-Sep 1893); flt.surg., Pac.Sqdn., *Philadelphia* (Sep 1893-Feb 1896); home and l.o.a. (Feb-Apr 1896); Naval Sta., New London, CT (May 1896-Apr 1898); member, medl.exam.bd., Washington, DC (May-Sep 1898); Navy Yard, Boston (Sep 1898-Apr 1901); home and w.o. (Apr-Sep 1901);

Naval Recruiting Rndv., Boston (Oct 1901-Nov 1902); w.o. (Nov 1902-Jan 1903); retired (19 Jan 1903).

Career Highlights While with the S.Pac.Sqdn., received thanks from Peru for his assistance for the relief and surgical help to people of Arica, Peru, after the earthquake there of 13 Sep 1868. Received thanks from the British Government for assisting ship-wrecked sailors in the Straits of Magellan who suffered during the winter of 1869.

HERBERT WINSLOW Born in Roxbury, MA, on 22 Sep 1848, son of navy RAdm John Ancrum and Catherine Amelia (Winslow) Winslow. Married Elizabeth Maynard on 6 Jun 1876. One son. Died in Florence, Italy, on 24 Sep 1914.

Ranks Midn (21 Jul 1865); Ens (12 Jul 1870); Mstr (1 Apr 1872); Lt (3 May 1875); LCdr (6 Apr 1897); Cdr (27 Mar 1900); Capt (22 Apr 1905); RAdm (27 May 1909); placed on Ret.Lst. (22 Sep 1910).

Career Summary Received appointment by virtue of being the son of an officer (21 Jul 1865); USNA (Jul 1865-Jun 1869); *Sabine*, and *Richmond*, Eur.Sta. (Jun 1869-Nov 1871); w.o. (Nov 1871-Feb 1872); in charge, contingent of men to Panama, and *Ossipee*, Pac.Sta. (Feb-Nov 1872); w.o. (Nov 1872-Feb 1873); *Narragansett*, N.Pac.Sta. (Feb 1873-Jul 1874); *Saranac*, N.Pac. Sqdn. (Jul 1874-Jul 1875); *Benicia*, Pac.Sqdn. (Jul-Nov 1875); *Lackawanna*, Pac.Sqdn. (Nov 1875-May 1876); home and w.o. (May-Sep 1876); Hydrographic Office, Washington, DC (Oct 1876-Aug 1877); training ship, *Portsmouth* (Sep 1877-Feb 1879); *Marion*, Eur.Sta. (Feb-Nov 1879); *Powhatan*, N.Atl.Sta. (Nov 1879-Oct 1880); w.o. (Oct-Dec 1880); equip. duty, Navy Yard, Portsmouth, NH (Dec 1880-Oct 1882); w.o. (Oct-Dec 1882); training ship, *Portsmouth* (Dec 1882-Oct 1885); w.o. (Oct 1885-Jan 1886); equip. duty, Navy Yard, Washington, DC (Jan 1886-Feb 1887); ord. duty, Navy Yard, Washington, DC (Feb 1887-Apr 1889); *Adams*, Pac.Sta. (Apr 1889-Jul 1890); l.o.a. (Jul-Aug 1890); *Richmond*, Hampton Roads, VA (Sep-Oct 1890); training ship, *Portsmouth* (Oct 1890-Jun 1892); l.o.a. (Jun-Sep 1892); ord. duty, Navy Yard, Washington, DC (Sep 1892-May 1895); NWC (Jun-Oct 1895); *Monocacy*, Asia.Sta. (Nov 1895-Oct 1896); *Yorktown*, Asia.Sta. (Oct 1896-Dec 1897); home and l.o.a. (Dec 1897-Feb 1898); exec.off., training ship, *Constellation*, Newport, RI (Feb-Apr 1898); training ship, *St. Louis* (Apr 1898); cdr, *Fern*, N.Atl.Flt. (Apr-Sep 1898); cdr, *Marcellus*, N.Atl.Flt. (Sep 1898-Feb 1899); exec.off., training ship, *Constellation* (Feb-Sep 1899); cdr, training ship, *Monongahela* (Sep-Oct 1899); exec.off., training ship, *Constellation* (Oct 1899-Apr 1900); cdr, *Solace*, spec.serv. (Apr 1900-May 1902); home and w.o. (May 1902); NWC (Jun-Aug 1902); asst., then insp., 11th L.h. Dist., Detroit (Aug 1902-May 1905); NWC (Jun 1905); general insp., *Charleston*, Newport News, VA (Jun-Oct 1905); cdr, *Charleston*, spec.serv. (Oct-Dec 1905); cdr, *Kearsarge*, N.Atl.Flt. (Dec 1905-Nov 1907); home and w.o. (Nov 1907-Jan 1908); in charge, Naval Recruiting Sta. and New England Dist., Boston (Jan

HERBERT WINSLOW
1848-1914

1908-May 1909); home, w.o., and l.o.a. (May-Jul 1909); Navy Yard, Boston (Jul 1909-Sep 1910); placed on Ret.Lst. (22 Sep 1910).

Career Highlights Participated in the Battle of Santiago on 3 Jul 1898 during the war with Spain. Commanded the *Solace* during the Boxer Rebellion, landing the first detachment of Marines at Taku, China.

**ALBERT GUSTAVUS
WINTERHALTER
1856-1920**

ALBERT GUSTAVUS WINTERHALTER Born in Detroit on 5 Oct 1856. Graduated from Detroit High School in 1873. Married, resided in Washington, DC, dying at the Naval Hosp. there on 5 Jun 1920.

Ranks Cadet Midn (24 Sep 1873); Midn (18 Jun 1879); Ens (11 Jul 1880); Ltjg (14 Dec 1886); Lt (30 Jun 1892); LCdr (18 Jan 1900); Cdr (1 Jul 1905); Capt (1 Jul 1909); RAdm (5 May 1915); Act. Adm (9 Jul 1915); died (5 Jun 1920).

Career Summary Received appointment from MI (24 Sep 1873); USNA (Sep 1873-Jun 1877); w.o. (Jun-Sep 1877); *Swatara*, N.Atl.Sta. (Sep 1877-Oct 1878); *Powhatan*, N.Atl.Sta. (Oct 1878-Apr 1879); USNA (Jun-Jul 1879); l.o.a. (Jul 1879-May 1881); USNA (May-Jun 1881); training ship, *Constitution* (Jun-Dec 1881); training ship, *Jamestown* (Feb 1882-Nov 1884); w.o. (Nov-Dec 1884); Naval Observatory, Washington, DC (Dec 1884-Apr 1889); delegate, International Astrophotographic Congress, Paris (Apr 1887); spec. duty, visiting principal European observatories (Mar-Sep 1887); torp. instruction, Newport, RI (Apr-Jul 1889); Naval Observatory, Washington, DC (Jul-Nov 1889); *Yorktown*, Sqdn. of Evol. (Nov 1889-Oct 1892); home and l.o.a. (Oct 1892-Jan 1893); Bur. of Equip. and Recruiting, Washington, DC (Jan-Mar 1893); in charge, Naval Observatory Exhibit, World's Fair, Chicago (Apr-Nov 1893); Naval Observatory, Washington, DC (Nov-Dec 1893); Bur. of Equip. and Recruiting, Washington, DC (Dec 1893-Jul 1895); member, bd. of control and management, World's Fair, Chicago (Apr 1894-Jun 1895); *Bennington*, Pac.Sta. (Aug 1895-May 1896); *Philadelphia*, Pac.Sta. (May 1896-Oct 1897); *Baltimore*, Pac.Sta. (Oct 1897-Mar 1898); *Bennington*, Pac.Sta. (Mar-Jun 1898); flag lt, Pac.Sta., *Brooklyn*, then *Philadelphia* (Jun-Oct 1898); home and w.o. (Oct 1898); Navy Yard, League Island, PA (Oct 1898-Jan 1900); temp. duty, rec. ship, *Vermont*, NY (Jan 1900): temp. duty, training ship, *Prairie* (Jan-Feb 1900); *Albany*, on trials, and Asia.Sta. (Feb 1900-Mar 1901); exec.off., *Bennington*, Asia.Sta. (Mar-Jun 1901); *Helena*, Asia.Sta. (Jun 1901-Dec 1902); cdr, *Elcano*, Asia.Sta. (Dec 1902-May 1903); home and l.o.a. (May-Nov 1903); equip. and ord.off., Navy Yard, Portsmouth, NH (Nov 1903-Aug 1905); general insp., then cdr, *Paducah*, W.Ind.Sqdn., N.Atl.Flt. (Aug 1905-Aug 1907); home and w.o. (Aug-Sep 1907); Naval Observatory Washington, DC (Sep 1907-May 1908); hydrographer, Navy Dept., Washington, DC (May 1908-Dec 1909); cdr, flgs., *Louisiana*, Div. 2, Atl.Flt. (Jan 1910-Nov 1911); member, Gen Bd., Washington, DC (Nov 1911-Jul 1912); temp. duty, office of sec. of navy, Navy Dept., Washington, DC (Jul 1912); aide for material, Navy Dept., Washington, DC (Jul 1912-May 1915); cdr, Asia.Flt., *Brooklyn* (Jul 1915-Apr 1917); member, Gen Bd., Washington, DC (May 1917-Jun 1920); additional duty, member, bd. of selection, Washington, DC (Jul 1918-Jun 1920); died (5 Jun 1920).

Career Highlights Arranged the naval share in the transfer of Hawaiian sovereignty to the U.S. on 12 Aug 1898. Made adm on the occasion of the accession of the Emperor of Japan from Nov to Dec 1915. Awarded the Distinguished Service Medal.

WILLIAM CLINTON WISE Born in Lewisburg, [W]VA, on 8 Nov 1842, son of James and Virginia F. (Caldwell) Wise. Married Nellie Humphreys on 18 May 1875. Two children. Received an honorary M.A. from Yale Univ. in 1899. Died at Fort Kamehameha, Honolulu, Territory of HI, on 22 Nov 1923.

Ranks Act.Midn (29 Sep 1860); title changed to Midn (16 Jul 1862); Act.Ens (1 Oct 1863); designation "Act." discontinued (21 Dec 1865); Mstr (10 May 1866); Lt (21 Feb 1867); LCdr (12 Mar 1868); Cdr (24 Feb 1881); Capt (11 Nov 1894); RAdm (14 Jun 1902); placed on Ret.Lst. (8 Nov 1904).

Career Summary Received appointment from KY (29 Sep 1860: USNA (Sep 1860-Oct 1863); *New Ironsides*, S.Atl.Blk. Sqdn. (Oct 1863-Sep 1864); *Minnesota*, N.Atl.Blk.Sqdn. (Sep 1864-Jun 1865); *Winooski*, Navy Yard, NY (Jun 1865); w.o. (Jun-Jul 1865); *Hartford*, and *Wachusett*, Asia.Sqdn. (Jul 1865-Aug 1868); w.o. (Aug 1868-Apr 1869); *Saugus*, spec.serv., W.Indies (Apr-May 1869); prac. ship, *Dale* (May-Sep 1869); *Miantonomoh*, spec.serv. and N.Atl.Sta. (Sep 1869-Jul 1870); *Brooklyn*, and *Wabash*, Eur.Sta. (Aug 1870-Jul 1873); w.o. (Jul-Nov 1873); exec.off., *Ajax*, W.Ind.Sta. (Dec 1873-Jul 1874); exec.off., rec. ship, *Vermont*, NY (Jul 1874-Apr 1875); exec.off., flgs., *Tennessee*, then cdr, *Palos*, Asia.Sta. (Apr 1875-Jul 1878); home and w.o. (Jul-Oct 1878); insp. of ord., Navy Yard, Norfolk, VA (Nov 1878-Dec 1881); w.o. (Dec 1881-Apr 1882); torp. duty, Newport, RI (May-Aug 1882); w.o. (Aug-Dec 1882); cdr, training ship, *Portsmouth* (Dec 1882-Oct 1884); insp. of ord., Navy Yard, Portsmouth, NH (Oct 1884-Oct 1887); w.o. (Oct 1887-Jun 1888); cdr, *Juniata*, Pac.Sqdn. (Jul 1888-Feb 1889); w.o. (Feb-Mar 1889); equip.off., Navy Yard, Norfolk, VA (Apr 1889-Sep 1890); insp. of ord., Navy Yard, Portsmouth, NH (Oct 1890); asst., then insp., 15th L.h. Dist., St. Louis (Nov 1890-Jun 1894); s.a. and w.o. (Jun-Sep 1894); ord. instruction, Navy Yard, Washington, DC (Sep 1894-Feb 1895); bd. duties (Feb-Apr 1895); cdr, *Amphitrite*, N.Atl.Sqdn. (Apr 1895-Mar 1897); cdr, *Texas*, N.Atl.Sqdn. (Mar-Oct 1897); capt.yd., Navy Yard, Norfolk, VA (Nov 1897-Apr 1898); cdr, *Yale*, N.Atl.Sqdn. (May-Sep 1898); cdr, rec. ship, *Franklin*, Norfolk, VA (Sep 1898-Mar 1902); member, Gen Bd., Navy Dept., Washington, DC (Mar-Sep 1902); cdr, Naval Defense Dist., Gulf of Mexico, and comdt., Navy Yard, Pensacola, FL (Oct 1902-Jun 1903); cdr, Atl. Training Sqdn., *Minneapolis* (Jul 1903-Oct 1904); home and w.o. (Oct-Nov 1904); placed on Ret.Lst. (8 Nov 1904).

WILLIAM CLINTON WISE
1842-1923

SPENCER SHEPARD WOOD
1861-1940

SPENCER SHEPARD WOOD Born in Brooklyn, NY, on 7 Aug 1861, son of John Wardell and Mary Garrison (Shepard) Wood. Raised in NY City and in Flushing, NY, attending school at the Flushing Institute. Married Mary Margaretta Fryer on 12 Jun 1895. Two daughters, Margaretta and Anne Elizabeth. After retiring, served as treas. and sec. of Navy Relief Society. Resided in Washington, DC. Died on 30 Jul 1940 in NY City. Buried in Arlington National Cemetery.

Ranks Cadet Midn (28 Jun 1878); Ens (1 Jul 1884); Ltjg (11 Apr 1894); Lt (16 Sep 1897); LCdr (18 Jul 1903); Cdr (13 Oct 1907); Capt (4 Mar 1911); temp. RAdm (15 Oct 1917); retired as RAdm (28 Nov 1918).

Career Summary Received appointment from NY as Cadet Midn (28 Jun 1878); USNA (Jun 1878-Jun 1882); *Vandalia*, then *Tennessee*, N.Atl.Sqdn. (Jun 1882-Apr 1884); aid on staff of RAdm George H. Cooper (1883-1884); USNA (May-Jun 1884); w.o. (Jun-Jul 1884); Experimental Battery, Annapolis (Jul 1884-Apr 1885); *Iroquois*, Pac.Sta. (May 1885-Mar 1888); cst.surv. steamer *Patterson*, Alaskan cst. (Mar-Oct 1888); spec. temp. duty for Bur. of Nav. making astronomical observations in Central America (Nov 1888-Sep 1889); *Monocacy*, Asia.Sqdn. (Oct-Nov 1889); *Omaha*, Asia.Sqdn. (Nov 1889-Oct 1890); exec.off. and navigator, *Palos*, Asia.Sqdn. (Oct 1890-Apr 1891); flag lt. to Cdr in Chief, RAdm George E. Belknap, Asiatic Sta., *Monocacy* (Apr-Sep 1891); *Charleston*, flgs., Asia.Sta. (Sep-Nov 1891); *Marion*, Asia.Sta. (Nov 1891-Feb 1892); return and l.o.a. (Feb-May 1892); spec. duty, Navy Dept., then aide to Sec. of Navy, H.A. Herbert, Washington, DC (May 1892-Mar 1893); l.o.a. (Sep-Oct 1892); spec. duty, Bur. of Nav., Washington, DC (Mar 1893-Mar 1894); flag sec., RAdm John G. Walker, Pac.Sta., *Philadelphia*, (Apr-Aug 1894); home and w.o. (Aug-Sep 1894); flag sec. to RAdm R.W. Meade, N.Atl.Sta., *New York* (Sep 1894-May 1895); rec. ship, *Vermont*, NY (May-Oct 1895); Asst. Inspector of Torpedo Boats Nos. 6 and 7 (*Porter* and *Du Pont*), Bristol, RI (Oct 1895-Aug 1897); torpedo boat, *Du Pont*, Bristol, RI (Aug-Sep 1897); cdr., *Detroit*, Newport, RI and Torp.Flot. (Sep 1897-Nov 1898); *Massachusetts*, Navy Yard, NY, and N.Atl. Sqdn. (Nov 1898-Oct 1899); *Brooklyn*, en route to Manila, then Asia. Flt. (Oct 1899-Feb 1900); flag sec. to RAdm John C. Watson, Asia.Flt, *Baltimore* (Feb-May 1900); *Baltimore*, Asia.Flt. (May-Sep 1900); asst. inspector, 3rd L.h. Dist., Tompkinsville, NY (Sep 1900-Jan 1902); *San Francisco*, Eur. Sta. (Jan-Aug 1902); watch and div. officer, *Chicago*, flgs., Eur.Sta. (Aug 1902-Oct 1903); navigator, *Columbia*, Atl.Training Sqdn. (Oct 1903-Oct 1904); aide to Adm of Navy, George Dewey, and duty in connection with Gen Bd., Navy Dept., Washington, DC (Oct 1904-Feb 1908); exec. off., *Idaho*, shakedown cruise, and spec.serv. (Mar 1908-Feb 1909); cdr, *New York*, Armoured Cruiser Sqdn., then in reserve (Mar 1909-Mar 1910); sec., Gen Bd., Washington, DC (Mar 1910-Feb 1912); cdr, *Nebraska*, Atl.Flt. (Feb-Nov 1912); *Illinois*, Navy Yard, Boston (Nov-Dec 1912); *Nebraska*, Atl.Flt. (Dec 1912-Jan 1914); NWC, Newport, RI (Jan-Dec 1914);

member, Gen Bd., Washington, DC (Dec 1914-Jan 1917); cdr,
Oklahoma, Atl.Flt. (Jan 1917-Feb 1918); comdt., 1st Naval Dist.,
Boston (Feb 1918-Apr 1919); cdr, Cruiser Div. 1, Pac.Flt.,
Chicago (Apr-Oct 1919); cdr, Train, Pacific Fleet, *Minneapolis*
(Oct 1919-Oct 1920); pres., Naval Exam. and Ret. Bd. (Oct
1920-Dec 1921); placed on Ret.Lst. (28 Nov 1921).

Career Highlights   Graduated second in class from USNA;
served several tours as flag sec. to fleet cdrs. Sent by Pres. Grover
Cleveland to examine conditions of Terrirtory of HI before
republic's recognition by U.S. While commanding torpedo boat *Du
Pont,* joined fleet blockading Cuba after outbreak of war with
Spain, and was used in dispatching messages. Subsequently
received Sampson and Philippine Campaign medals as well as
Navy Cross. While aide to Adm Dewey, he had duty in connec-
tion with Naval Review at Hampton Roads, VA in 1905. During
the same period, was instrumental in forming Navy Relief Society.
Chief Yeoman Daisy M. Pratt Erd wrote song "Rear Admiral
Wood One Step" in honor of RAdm Wood.

References
Personal Papers: (1882-1940) in Early Records Collection,
Operational Archives, Naval Historical Center,
Washington Navy Yard, Washington, DC 20374.

WALTER FITZHUGH WORTHINGTON   Born in Baltimore
on 8 Mar 1855, son of Nicholas Brice and Sophia Kerr (Muse)
Worthington. Received A.B. degree from the MD Agricultural
College in 1873. Married Grace Winifred Macmillen on 3 Aug
1885. One daughter. Resided in Pasadena, CA, where he died on
1 Aug 1937.

Ranks   Cadet Engr. (1 Oct 1873); Asst.Engr. (1 Jul 1877);
PAsst.Engr. (19 Jul 1885); PAsst.Engr. with rel. rank of Ltjg (1
Oct 1893); Chief Engr. (14 Oct 1896); rank changed to LCdr (3
Mar 1899); Cdr (30 Sep 1904); Capt (1 Jul 1908); RAdm (26
Mar 1913); placed on Ret.Lst. (8 Mar 1919).

Career Summary   Received appointment from MD (1 Oct
1873); USNA (Oct 1873-Jul 1875); w.o. (Jun-Sep 1875); *Alert*,
N.Atl. and Asia.Stas. (Sep 1875-Sep 1878); return and w.o. (Sep
1878-Jan 1879); spec. duty, experimental bd., NY (Jan-Jul 1879);
spec. duty, adjunct prof., Lafayette College, PA (Aug 1879-Aug
1881); *Lancaster*, Eur.Sta. (Aug 1881-Jun 1884); *Powhatan*, N.
Atl.Sta. (Jun-Aug 1884); w.o. (Aug-Oct 1884); Morgan Iron
Works, NY (Oct 1884-May 1885); l.o.a. (May-Sep 1885); USNA
(Sep 1885-Nov 1888); *Atlanta*, spec.serv. (Nov 1888-Sep 1891);
Bur. of Steam Engineering, Washington, DC (Sep 1891-Jul 1892);
USNA (Jul 1892-Sep 1894); *Vesuvius*, N.Atl.Sta. (Oct-Nov
1894); *Castine*, S.Atl.Sta. (Nov 1894-Dec 1896); *Montgomery*,
N.Atl.Sta. (Dec 1896-Sep 1897); prof., Clemson Agricultural
College, Ft. Hill, SC (Sep 1897-Apr 1898); *Yankee*, N.Atl.Flt.
(Apr 1898); *Sterling*, N.Atl.Flt. (Apr-May 1898); *Lancaster*, Key
West, FL (May-Jun 1898); *Terror*, Navy Yard, Norfolk, VA (Jun-
Oct 1898); inspection duty, Bur. of Steam Engineering, Pitts-
burgh, PA (Oct 1898-Sep 1899); Bur. of Steam Engineering,

**WALTER FITZHUGH
WORTHINGTON
1855-1937**

Washington, DC (Sep 1899-Mar 1901); flt.engr., S.Atl.Sta., *Chicago* (Apr 1901-May 1902), then *Illinois* (May 1902-Oct 1903); flt.engr., N.Atl.Flt., *Kearsarge* (Oct 1903-Mar 1904); l.o.a. (Mar-Jun 1904); Bur. of Steam Engineering, Washington, DC (Jun 1904); experimental sta., USNA (Jul 1904-Sep 1910); insp. of engineering materials, Carlton Steel Works, Pittsburgh, PA, Dist. (Oct 1910-Mar 1913); insp. of engineering materials, Brooklyn, NY, Dist. (Mar 1913-Mar 1919); placed on Ret.Lst. (8 Mar 1919).

References
Writings: "Coal Consumption on Warships," U.S. Naval Institute *Proceedings* 110 (Jun 1904): 373-87.

LUCIEN YOUNG
1852-1912

LUCIEN YOUNG Born in Lexington, KY, on 31 Mar 1852, son of Richard Bosworth and Jane Ellen (O'Neil) Young. Married Belle Parker on 18 Jun 1895. Died in NY City on 2 Oct 1912. Buried at Arlington National Cemetery.

Ranks Midn (21 Jun 1869); title changed to Cadet Midn (15 Jul 1870); Midn (31 May 1873); Ens (16 Jul 1874); Mstr (24 Nov 1877); Ltjg (3 Mar 1883); Lt (1 May 1884); LCdr (3 Mar 1899); Cdr (5 Mar 1902); Capt (1 Jul 1906); RAdm (17 Mar 1910); died (2 Oct 1912).

Career Summary Received appointment from KY (21 Jun 1869); USNA (Jun 1869-May 1873); w.o. (May-Jun 1873); *Alaska*, and *Hartford*, Pac. and Asia.Sqdns. (Aug 1873-Oct 1875); USNA (Oct-Nov 1875); *Powhatan*, N.Atl.Sta. (Dec 1875-Feb 1876); *Huron*, Naval Sta., Port Royal, SC, and spec.serv. (Mar 1876-Nov 1877); home and w.o. (Nov 1877-Mar 1878); training ship, *Portsmouth* (Mar 1878-Apr 1880); Bur. of Equip. and Recruiting, Washington, DC (Apr 1880-Jul 1882); *Montauk*, Navy Yard, League Island, PA (Jul-Dec 1882); *Kearsarge*, N.Atl.Sta. (Dec 1882-May 1883); training ship, *Minnesota* (Jun-Oct 1883); spec. duty to Panama, then *Onward*, Pac.Sta. (Nov 1883-Oct 1884); *Shenandoah*, Pac.Sta. (Oct 1884-Oct 1886); w.o. (Oct-Dec 1886); l.o.a. (Dec 1886-Jun 1887); torp. instruction, Newport, RI (Jun-Sep 1887); NWC (Sep-Dec 1887); Bur. of Nav., and aide to sec. of navy, Washington, DC (Dec 1887-Oct 1889); Library and War Records Office, Washington, DC (Oct 1889-Jan 1891); *Boston*, N.Atl. and Pac.Sqdns. (Feb 1891-Oct 1893); home and l.o.a. (Oct-Dec 1893); Library and War Records Office, Washington, DC (Dec 1893-Jul 1896); *Detroit*, Asia.Sta. (Aug 1896-Jan 1897); *Boston*, Asia.Sta. (Jan-Sep 1897); *Yorktown*, Asia.Sta. (Sep-Nov 1897); exec.off., *Alert*, Pac.Sta. (Nov 1897-Feb 1898); Naval Hosp., Mare Island, CA (Feb-Mar 1898); sick lv. (Mar-Jun 1898); cdr, *Hist*, N.Atl.Flt. (Jun 1898-Feb 1899); *Resolute*, N.Atl.Flt. (Feb-Apr 1899); comdt., Naval Sta., Havana, Cuba (Apr-Aug 1899); capt. of port, Havana, Cuba (Aug 1899-Dec 1901); additional duty, comdt., Naval Sta., Havana, Cuba (Mar 1900-Dec 1901); home and w.o. (Dec 1901-Jan 1902); ord. instruction, Navy Yard, Washington, DC (Jan-Mar 1902); asst., then insp., 9th L.h. Dist., Chicago (Mar 1902-Mar 1904); cdr, *Montgomery*, N.Atl.Sqdn. (Mar-Sep 1904); home and w.o. (Sep-

Oct 1904); cdr, *Bennington*, Pac.Sqdn. (Nov 1904-Oct 1905); Navy Yard, Mare Island, CA (Oct 1905-Sep 1907); capt.yd., Navy Yard, Mare Island, CA (Sep 1907-Dec 1909); home and w.o. (Dec 1909-Feb 1910); comdt., Navy Yard, Pensacola, FL (Feb 1910-Oct 1911); comdt., Naval Sta., Key West, FL (Oct 1911-Oct 1912); died (2 Oct 1912).

Career Highlights Was commended for "gallant conduct and extraordinary heroism" for saving the life of a sailor fallen overboard from the *Alaska* on 23 Jul 1873. Also commended for the same thing during the loss of the *Huron* on 24 Nov 1877 off Nag's Head, NC. Subsequently, Pres. Rutherford B. Hays successfully requested the Senate to promote him from ensign to master. While with the *Boston*, he participated in protecting American interests during the Hawaiian Revolution in 1893. Was advanced in Feb 1901 three numbers for eminent and conspicuous conduct in battle as cdr of the *Hist* at Manzanillo during the war with Spain.

References

Writings: a) *Catalogue of Works by American Naval Authors* (Washington, DC: 1882). b) *Simple Elements of Navigation* (NY: 1890, 1894, 1898). c) *The "Boston" at Hawaii* (Washington, DC: 1898). d) *The Real Hawaii* (NY: 1899, 1902, 1906).

Additional Sources: Broeck Newton Oder, "The USS *Bennington*: Policy or Personnel" (M.A. thesis, Univ. of San Diego, 1975).

ABRAHAM VANHOY ZANE Born in Philadelphia on 14 Aug 1850, son of Abraham V. and Mary R. (McNeir) Zane. Married Grace Helen Southgate on 21 Jun 1883. Four children. Resided in Washington, DC, dying there on 2 Jan 1919.

Ranks Cadet Engr. (1 Oct 1871); Asst.Engr. (26 Feb 1875); PAsst.Engr. (27 Aug 1881); PAsst.Engr. with rel. rank of Lt (5 May 1892); Chief Engr. (11 Sep 1895); LCdr (3 Mar 1899); Cdr (11 Sep 1903); Capt (6 Dec 1907); RAdm (14 Sep 1911); placed on Ret.Lst. (14 Aug 1912).

Career Summary Received appointment from PA (1 Oct 1871); USNA (Oct 1871-Jun 1874); turned back (8 Jun 1872); *Wachusett*, spec.serv. (Jun-Dec 1874); w.o. (Dec 1874-Jan 1875); *Worcester*, N.Atl.Sta. (Jan-Jul 1875); w.o. (Jul-Nov 1875); *Catskill*, N.Atl.Sta. (Nov 1875-Jul 1876); w.o. (Jul 1876-Apr 1877); temp. duty, *Dictator*, N.Atl.Sta. (Apr-May 1877); w.o. (May-Jul 1877); *Speedwell*, Navy Yard, Portsmouth, NH (Jul-Oct 1877); w.o. (Oct-Nov 1877); spec. duty, Chester, PA (Nov 1877-Feb 1878); *Wyoming*, Eur.Sta. (Feb-Sep 1878); USNA (Sep 1878-Aug 1880); despatch vessel, *Tallapoosa* (Sep 1880-Apr 1881); *Mary and Helen* [renamed *Rodgers*], spec.serv., *Jeanette* Search Expd. (Apr 1881-Jul 1882); w.o. (Jul-Sep 1882); Bur. of Steam Engineering, Washington, DC (Sep 1882-Feb 1885); Northern Alaska Expd. (Feb 1885-Oct 1886); w.o. (Oct 1886-Jan 1887); l.o.a. (Jan-Jun 1887); w.o. (Jun-Oct 1887); spec. duty, *Terror*, Philadelphia (Oct 1887-Jan 1888); w.o. (Jan-Feb 1888); *Pensacola*, Navy Yard, Norfolk, VA (Mar-May 1888); *Omaha*, Asia.Sta. (May 1888-Jun 1889); *Monocacy*, Asia.Sta. (Jun-Jul 1889); *Omaha*, Asia.Sta. (Jul

1889-Jun 1891); l.o.a. (Jun-Jul 1891); Naval Observatory, Washington, DC (Jul 1891-May 1894); *Monocacy*, Asia.Sta. (Jul 1894-Mar 1896); *Machias*, Asia.Sta. (Mar 1896-Jul 1897); home and w.o. (Jul-Sep 1897); temp. duty, Navy Yard, Washington, DC (Sep-Dec 1897); Civil Service Commission, Washington, DC (Dec 1897-Jul 1898); rec. ship, *Vermont*, NY (Jul-Sep 1898); *Buffalo*, Navy Yard, NY (Sep 1898); Civil Service Commission, Washington, DC (Oct 1898-Jan 1899); insp. of machinery, Midvale Steel Works, Nicetown, PA (Jan-Jun 1899); member, engineering inspection bds. (Jun 1899-Oct 1900); in charge, engineering dept., *Alabama*, N.Atl.Flt. (Oct 1900-Feb 1901); flt.engr., N.Atl.Flt., *Kearsarge* (Feb 1901-Apr 1902), then *Olympia* (Apr-Jul 1902), then *Kearsarge* (Jul 1902-Aug 1903); insp. of machinery, William Cramp and Sons Iron Works, Philadelphia (Aug 1903-Aug 1908); head, dept. of steam engineering, Navy Yard, Portsmouth, NH (Aug 1908-Apr 1911); general insp. of machinery, Atl.cst., Philadelphia (May 1911); pres., bd. of inspection for shore stas., Navy Dept., Washington, DC (Jun 1911-Aug 1912); placed on Ret.Lst. (14 Aug 1912); spec. duty, Bur. of Steam Engineering, Washington, DC (Apr 1917-Jan 1919).

Note on Sources

One of the most frustrating aspects of seeking biographical information is the diverse, varied, and frequently unreliable or conflicting nature of the material. In some cases, there might exist an extremely accurate and complete career record, although only in manuscript form. The careers and personal information for many others, unfortunately, have never been compiled. Discovering one man's entire military career or, for example, pinpointing just if and when he was stationed on a particular vessel or at some navy yard requires many tedious and often disappointing hours of research at various inconveniently located repositories. The following is intended both as an explanation of this volume's sources and as a guide for those pursuing further research into the biographies of those in the navy.

MANUSCRIPT SOURCES AND REPOSITORIES

There are, naturally, many collections of manuscripts on naval history scattered all over the country. Many of these provide very valuable information of a biographical nature. By far the best catalogue of these collections is *U.S. Naval History Sources in the United States*, compiled and edited by Dean C. Allard, Martha L. Crawley, and Mary W. Edmison (Washington, D.C.: Department of the Navy, Naval History Division, 1979). This very convenient, thorough, and essential guide lists and in many cases describes collections on a state-by-state basis. It is well indexed and should be one of the first sources consulted to find records and manuscripts, biographical in nature or not, on naval history.

The National Archives of the United States in Washington, D.C., is the central depository for official records and documents of a historical nature or value. While there are numerous guides for the manuscripts in the National Archives, the *Guide to the National Archives of the United States* (Washington, D.C.: Government Printing Office, 1974) is the best. The *Catalogue of National Archives Microfilm Publications* (Washington, D.C.: Government Printing Office, 1974) is also very useful. The Archives groups information into various categories. Some of the more valuable records groups for naval biographical material are: Record Group 19 (records of the Bureau of Ships); Record Group 24 (records of the Bureau of Personnel); Record Group 45 (naval records collection of the Office of Naval Records and Library); Record Group 80 (general records of the Department of the Navy); and Record Group 405 (records of the U.S. Naval Academy). Besides these and other valuable collections in the central repository, the National Archives also operates the National Personnel Records Center in St. Louis, MO. While containing much, the National Archives normally takes considerable time to respond to requests for information.

The Manuscript Division of the Library of Congress in Washington, D.C., has many collections on naval subjects and personnel. For information on what the library holds, see *The National Union Catalogue of Manuscript Collections* (Washington, D.C.: Library of Congress, 1959-) as well as Philip M. Hamer, ed., *A Guide to Archives and Manuscripts in the United States* (New Haven: Yale University Press, 1961). The library's annual accessions are reported in the *Quarterly Journal of the Library of Congress*. In addition, Richard B. Bickel compiled *Manuscripts on Microfilm: A Checklist of the Holdings in the Manuscript Division* (Washington, D.C.: Library of Congress, 1975).

Besides its own collections, the Library of Congress also houses part of the very rich and extremely valuable collections owned by the Naval Historical Foundation, a nonprofit, private organization that preserves material on naval and maritime subjects. Those collections held by the Library of Congress are described in *Naval Historical Foundation Manuscript Collection: A Catalogue* (Washington, D.C.: Library of Congress, 1974). Those sources not deposited in the Library of Congress are located in the same building as the Naval Historical Center at the Washington Navy Yard.

The Naval Historical Center is a very convenient central repository of many sources and manuscript collections, both official and private. There are several different departments within the Naval Historical Center. Of great importance is the Operational Archives branch. This branch contains the Early Records Collections, which house the historical reference (Z) files, including biographical material (ZB). Other important branches of the Naval Historical Center are the Ships' History Branch and the Still Photo Library. Located in the same building is the Navy Department Library, which owns many publications difficult to find elsewhere. The center and library are extremely pleasant places to work, and the staffs are most professional, cordial, and helpful.

Another extremely important storehouse of manuscripts and information on naval history and naval personnel is the U.S. Naval Academy in Annapolis, MD. The Academy's Nimitz Library, like the Navy Department Library, contains many rare and difficult-to-find monographs and journals. The Nimitz Library also has Special Collections and Archives departments. Private collections of papers as well as some of the more essential printed primary sources are housed here and overseen by extremely helpful and professional staff members. Similarly, the Naval Academy Museum possesses manuscripts, photographs, and memorabilia that are most useful to the researcher.

Also in Annapolis is the U.S. Naval Institute. While located on the grounds of the Naval Academy, the Institute is separate and owns both a naval library and an extremely valuable photographic collection.

The United States Naval War College in Newport, RI, also owns much valuable information, including manuscript collections, information and documents on the college itself, as well as naval documents of a more general nature from the nineteenth and twentieth centuries.

While the above material is intended to describe most of the sources used for the information found in this volume, it does not cover all. Manuscript collections as well as secondary sources from which specific biographical information was extracted are found under the bibliographical sections for those particular admirals.

Printed Primary and Secondary Sources

One of the most useful sources of career information is the *Abstract of Service Records, 1798–1893*. These are microfilmed manuscripts from the Record Group 24 (records of the Bureau of Personnel) in the National Archives. While not particularly easy to use and containing numerous discrepancies, especially up to the Civil War, they provide good career summaries. The *Register of Commissioned and Warrant Officers of the United States Navy, Including Officers of the Marine Corps* (Washington, D.C.: Department of the Navy, 1814-) gives the names, dates of commission, ranks, and present stations for all officers of the sea services and has appeared annually since 1814, with some variations. Sadly, some volumes are more complete than others, and normally the month when an officer saw a change of duty is not given. Beginning in July 1908, the *Register* became the *Navy and Marine Corps List and Directory*. The information within each volume since 1908 becomes far more detailed and reliable. A source of obituaries and social news is the *United States Army-Navy Journal*, which began its weekly publications on 29 August 1863.

Another source is Lewis Randolph Hamersly's *The Records of Living Officers of the U.S. Navy and Marine Corps*, 7 editions (Philadelphia: L. R. Hamersly and Co., 1870–1902), which is considered the standard work for career information on naval officers to the early twentieth century. Hamersly acquired his information from the official records of the Bureau of Personnel, but the editions are far from complete, leaving large gaps within the careers and normally not including the squadron or fleet with which a man served while on board a particular ship. Other works produced by Hamersly are: *A Naval Encyclopedia, Comprising a Dictionary of Nautical Words and Phrases; Biographical Notices, and Records of Naval Officers. . . .* (Philadelphia: L. R. Hamersly and Co., 1884; Rpr. 1971); *Biographical Sketches of Distinguished Officers of the Army and Navy* (New York: L. R. Hamersly and Co., 1905); and *List of Officers of the Navy of the United States and of the Marine Corps from 1775 to 1900*, edited by Edward W. Callahan (New York: L. R. Hamersly and Co., 1901, Rpr. 1969).

Along the same lines are Thomas Holdup Stevens Hamersly's *General Register of the United States Navy and Marine Corps for One Hundred Years, 1782–1882* (Washington, D.C.: 1882), and his *Complete General Navy Register of the United States, from 1776 to 1887, Containing the Names of all the Officers of the Navy, Volunteer and Regular* (New York: L. R. Hamersly, 1888).

There are more recent works dealing with the careers of those in the military. A work that deals only with select individuals is Roger J. Spiller, ed., with Joseph G. Dawson and T. Harry Williams, *Dictionary of American Military Biography*, 3 vols. (Westport, CT: Greenwood Press, 1984). See also *Webster's American Military Biographies* (Springfield, IL: G. & C. Merriam Co., 1978). The most recent work that includes almost every major military figure is *Who Was Who in American History—The Military* (Chicago: Marquis Who's Who, Inc., 1975). While including many individuals, this work contains only short and abbreviated, albeit reliable, information. Finally, there is Karl Schuon's *U.S. Navy Biographical Dictionary* (New York: Franklin Watts, 1964), which is very selective in choosing officers for inclusion.

For personal information on officers, there are standard biographical dictionaries. Among these are: *Dictionary of American Biography*, eds. Allen Johnson and Dumas Malone, 20 vols. (New York: Charles Scribner's Sons, 1928–1936); *Appleton's Cyclopaedia of American Biography*, eds. James Grant Weston and John Fiske, 10 vols. (New York: Appleton, 1887–1924); and *The National Cyclopaedia of American Biography*, multivolume (New York: James T. White & Company, 1898–). Lastly, an extremely useful, indeed essential, work that associates officers and the location of ships on which they served is James L. Mooney, ed., *Dictionary of American Naval Fighting Ships*, 8 vols. (Washington, D.C.: Government Printing Office, 1959–81).

The **Naval Institute Press** is the book-publishing arm of the U.S. Naval Institute, a private, nonprofit professional society for members of the sea services and civilians who share an interest in naval and maritime affairs. Established in 1873 at the U.S. Naval Academy in Annapolis, Maryland, where its offices remain today, the Naval Institute has more than 100,000 members worldwide.

Members of the Naval Institute receive the influential monthly magazine *Proceedings* and discounts on fine nautical prints, ship and aircraft photos, and subscriptions to the quarterly *Naval History* magazine. They also have access to the transcripts of the Institute's Oral History Program and get discounted admission to any of the Institute-sponsored seminars regularly offered around the country.

The Naval Institute's book-publishing program, begun in 1898 with basic guides to naval practices, has broadened its scope in recent years to include books of more general interest. Now the Naval Institute Press publishes more than forty new titles each year, ranging from how-to books on boating and navigation to battle histories, biographies, ship and aircraft guides, and novels. Institute members receive discounts on the Press's more than 375 books.

Full-time students are eligible for special half-price membership rates. Life memberships are also available.

For a free catalog describing the Naval Institute Press books currently available, and for further information about U.S. Naval Institute membership, please write to:

Membership & Communications Department
U.S. Naval Institute
118 Maryland Avenue
Annapolis, Maryland 21402-5035

Or call, toll-free, (800) 233-USNI. In Maryland, call (301) 224-3378.